Comparative Modernization

Perspectives on Modernization
Cyril E. Black, General Editor

Comparative Modernization

A Reader

Edited, with an Introduction by
Cyril E. Black

THE FREE PRESS
A Division of Macmillan Publishing Co., Inc.
NEW YORK

Collier Macmillan Publishers
LONDON

The Free Press
A Division of Macmillan Publishing Co., Inc.
866 Third Avenue, New York, N.Y. 10022

Collier Macmillan Canada, Ltd.

Library of Congress Catalog Card Number: 75–16647

Printed in the United States of America

printing number

1 2 3 4 5 6 7 8 9 10

Library of Congress Cataloging in Publication Data
Main entry under title:

Comparative modernization.

(Perspectives on modernization)
Includes index.
CONTENTS: O'Connell, J. The concept of modernization.--Huntington, S. P. The change to change.--Tipps, D. C. Modernization theory and the comparative study of societies. [etc.]
     1. Social history--Addresses, essays, lectures.
2. Economic history--Addresses, essays, lectures.
I. Black, Cyril Edwin
HN13.C64   301.24   75-16647
ISBN 0-02-903530-9

Contents

111795

Introduction

Modernization

A number of conceptions have dominated the interpretation of human development since the Enlightenment, when an essentially theological view of history gave way to a more critical mode of thinking. The idea of progress was an early result of this change in the eighteenth century, but its proponents tended to overestimate the power of reason in human affairs, and hence to deprecate all earlier periods of history. A new appreciation of the past accompanied the formation of national states in the early nineteenth century, and this trend resulted in the study and publication of vast resources of literary and political documents that served to bolster the traditional heritage of the national states that arose from the ashes of the dynastic empires. This essentially romantic approach tended to set one national tradition against another, however, and failed to provide a basis for a general interpretation of world history.

At the same time, efforts to provide a unity to world history were made by philosophers who sought to interpret human development as the working out of abstract concepts. Hegel's view of history as the realization of the principle of freedom, through a dialectical process in which restraints on freedom were overcome in a series of phases, exerted a wide influence on subsequent thinkers. Marx used this dialectical method in his interpretation of history, which looked toward the universal victory of the proletariat after a long struggle between exploited and exploiters in the course of which systems of slavery, feudalism, and capitalism succeeded one another. This view forms the basis of the Marxist-Leninist interpretation of history, which is dominant in one form or another in the U.S.S.R. and in other Communist countries today.

Underlying all contemporary historical writing is a common tradition of the study and criticism of historical sources on the basis of foundations laid in the nineteenth century. These critical principles have been significantly refined as a result of the application of methods borrowed from the other behavioral and social sciences. Anthropology has contributed a deeper understanding of the use of oral and archeological sources, and of the value of holistic frames of reference that take into account the entire culture and world view of a society. Economics has contributed not only a much more accurate view than was hitherto possible of the relationship of agricultural and industrial pursuits to other aspects of society, but a sophisticated measurement of the dimensions and structure of growth. Political scientists have analyzed the organization of power and of policy-making institutions, and have elaborated an appreciation of the nature of political participation that is useful in the study of societies. Philosophers, psychologists, and natural scientists have

1

studied the relation of the biological nature of human beings to their social life, the development of an understanding of the natural and human environment, and the ways in which this understanding affects behavior. Sociologists and social psychologists, for their part, have made great progress in analyzing the social structures that form the basis for all human action, and the ways in which the wide variety of structures created by the different peoples of the world perform the functions essential to social cohesion and development.

All of these trends have contributed to the view of history that is taught in the American educational system, but the general interpretation within which historical material is presented has been limited to a rather ethnocentric perspective based essentially on the assumed dominance of the way of life developed by West European and English-speaking peoples. This view, which may be referred to briefly as Western or Westernizing, tends to predominate in both higher and secondary education in the United States.

A typical college freshman survey course in "Western Civilization," for instance, will start by tracing the roots of European culture from Mesopotamia through Egypt, Greece, and Rome. The story then moves on to the interaction of the Roman and numerous barbarian institutions that formed what is traditionally known as the European "Middle Ages," and a rather sophisticated description has been developed of the complex of institutions known as "feudalism." The relatively static character of this group of societies is terminated first by the Crusades and later and more decisively by the Renaissance and Reformation, which form the background of the modern and contemporary eras.

In such a conception, the history of other societies is normally introduced as they come under Western influence. Thus, Russia becomes a part of "Western Civilization" at the beginning of the eighteenth century with the reign of Peter the Great, Turkey with the beginning of the reform movement in 1839, and Japan with the Meiji Restoration in 1868. The Asian and African societies do not form part of such a course until the twentieth century, when they gain independence and are described as adopting Western political institutions. Various alternative interpretations of "Western Civilization" tend to conform to the same general outlook. Whether the West is seen as a source of freedom and democracy, or as the leading center of industrialization, or even as an evil force of capitalist domination, it is still considered, from the Western standpoint, as decisively displacing the traditional cultures of other parts of the world.

The essence of this Western interpretation of history is that in the course of the modern era, the West European and English-speaking peoples have developed the political, economic, and social institutions that are the best adapted to the modern way of life, and that are of universal validity. The strength of this argument lies in the fact that it was in Western Europe that the rapid growth of knowledge characteristic of the modern era got its start, and that the societies of Western Europe and their offshoots in the new world (the United States, Canada, Australia, and New Zealand) have in general been the most successful in making use of this knowledge for human betterment. The comparatively high standards achieved by these societies in health, education, and welfare are widely recognized, and as a group they represent the models by which other societies are measured. They are in this sense the most "modern" societies, and it is not surprising that they should regard their institutions as appropriate for other societies to follow.

The interpretation of history associated with this Westernizing view, which is still the dominant one in American scholarship, is particularly concerned with the freedom of the individual from undue restraints on the part of the state, with the development of a representative political system, with institutions providing for the accumulation and investment of capital with a minimum of regulation by the state, and in general with the promotion of as much freedom for the individual as is consistent with changing standards of public order and equity. This emphasis on the freedom of the individual is reflected in the Latin root of the term "liberal" and lies at the heart of this conviction.

Realities in the West European and English-speaking countries have of course not always matched the ideals held up by the liberal doctrine. In general, however, the average man enjoys greater freedom for development and self-expression in these societies than elsewhere, and in times of crisis, when threatened by the real menace of Hitlerism or a perceived threat of Stalinism, the peoples of these societies have sought with courage and determination to defend their legacy of freedom. Relative to the potentialities of modern knowledge this freedom is often remarkably limited, but relative to the state of affairs in other parts of the world it is very real indeed.

To question the universal applicability of the doctrinaire liberalism characteristic of the Western tradition is not to question the achievements of the West European and English-speaking countries in enhancing human welfare within their societies and in comparison with other societies. The issue in question is not the extent of these achievements, but the conclusions that have been drawn from them in the interpretation of world history. Those favoring the Westernizing approach are inclined to maintain that the *institutions* as well as the *levels of achievement* of the West European and English-speaking societies—the *way* in which things are done as well as *what* is done—are of universal validity. It would follow from this opinion that not only the political institutions but also the social, economic, and religious institutions of the West should be adopted by other societies if they wish to match the West.

An extreme instance of the Westernizing view is reflected in a debate among Chinese intellectuals in the nineteenth century as to whether China could have railroads without Christianity—inasmuch as the countries that had developed railroads were all Christian. The answer, as we now know, is that railroads can be built and operated without Christianity (or democracy), but not without certain other characteristics that are essential to modern industry: knowledge of science and technology, the ability to mobilize extensive resources for specific ends, and habits of work markedly different from those that normally prevail in agrarian societies. There are certain characteristics that must be present if a society is to take advantage of the advancement of knowledge for human welfare, but these characteristics do not necessarily embrace all of the institutional means employed by Western societies.

Criticism of the Westernizing approach to history has focused on this distinction between the characteristics of modern societies that are truly universal and those that are simply contemporary versions of the different institutional heritages of individual advanced societies. This criticism has emanated both from within Western societies and from other societies that have come under Western influence. In these other societies the question has been asked whether they must abandon their cultural heritage in order to gain the advantages of modern knowledge, or whether they can adapt their institutional heritage to the requirements of modernization.

The initial impact of the advanced Western societies has been so profound that other societies have frequently been inclined to borrow their institutions wholesale, and to abandon their own. More often than not, such borrowings have not been successful, and thoughtful observers have come to the conclusion that the adaptation of native traditional institutions to new functions is more effective in the long run than the borrowing of Western institutions in a more or less unaltered form.

The concept of "modernization" embraces a considerable range of interpretations of human development, but these views share certain common assumptions that give the term a distinctive meaning and at the same time distinguish it from other conceptions. Four assumptions in particular deserve mention regarding the concept of modernization: the importance attributed to the capacities relevant to modernization developed by a society before the modern era; the role of the advancement of knowledge, as reflected mainly in the scientific and technological revolution, as the primary source of change that distinguishes the modern era from earlier eras; the capacity of a society in political, economic, and social terms to take advantage of the possibilities for development offered by the advancement of knowledge; and the utility of various policies that the political leaders of a society may follow in seeking both to convert its heritage of values and institutions to modern requirements and to borrow selectively from more modern societies.

These assumptions will be more fully discussed in the next two sections of this Introduction, but it should be noted here that most interpretations of the process of modernization stress the differences in the institutional heritage of the Western and other societies, and assume that the latter are likely to retain many distinctive characteristics long after they have undergone modernizing transformations. It would follow from this view that not just Western institutions but those of other societies as well can be adapted in varying degrees to the requirements of modernity. The problem of the later developing societies is not to discard their institutions in favor of those borrowed from the West, but rather to evaluate their institutional heritage and decide to what extent it can be converted to the requirements of the modern era.

The diverse societies of the world should be studied for their own interest, and not simply in terms of their relationship to Western influence. To say this is not to say that Western influence is not a significant force, but rather that it is secondary to the conversion that the native institutional heritage of these societies must undergo.

One important contribution of the concept of modernization to the interpretation of human development—as compared with its interpretation in terms of liberalism, Marxism, or Marxism-Leninism—is that modernization places more emphasis on the behavioral and social sciences and less on Western or other models; it is more concerned with process than with goals.

Along with the common assumptions that set the interpretation of social change in terms of modernization somewhat apart from other views, there is also considerable disagreement among those advocating this interpretation. Perhaps the most common approach is that which regards economic growth as the principal source of change and relates everything else to it. One problem with this approach is that it does not explain what causes economic growth. It also devotes inadequate attention to the differing heritages of values and institutions, and is inclined to see all societies as converging as they modernize. Another approach takes economic growth for granted, and focuses primarily on political and social change. Research on certain aspects of change written from this standpoint may advance our knowledge of special topics, but usually it fails to take into account the larger context of change. More ambitious but also more hazardous are the approaches that seek to encompass the entire process of the impact of the scientific and technological revolution on all aspects of human activity. Such holistic interpretations, typical of anthropologists, seek a very broad approach to societies and are especially concerned with the interrelationships of the various aspects of social change. To the extent that such relationships can be quantified, it is possible to visualize the activities of societies and peoples in terms of a single "system."

The differences separating the concept of modernization from the liberal and socialist approaches have been noted, yet these differences deal with the same subject matter and therefore inevitably have much in common. Studies of specific topics by scholars writing from the point of view of liberalism, socialism, or modernization may differ very little. The important differences have to do with the trends and patterns of which such topics form a part.

Comparative Modernization

Narrowly defined aspects of societal development can often best be studied in terms of the experience of individual countries, but the broader question of the commonalities and variations among societies in the course of modernization can only be examined comparatively. The comparative study of modernization seeks to contribute to an understanding of how the advancement of knowledge—the scientific and technological revolution—affects societal development. Such an understanding naturally has implications for the inherent opportunities and dangers that public policy should take into account.

An analysis of this kind may sound like a large order, but any study of the process of change in the modern era must be set in a framework that is both global and multidisciplinary. The comparative study of modernization starts with the observation that unprecedented changes have taken place in the modern era in the advancement of knowledge, political development, economic growth, social mobilization, and psychological adaptation. It seeks to understand these changes, to evaluate the results of different policies of change in the various societies of the world, to study the capacities and obstacles brought to the process of change by the differing institutional heritages. It is an approach that seeks to reduce ethnocentric bias through the application of the comparative method, and does not assume that any of the patterns of policy currently predominant in the advanced societies are necessarily applicable to other societies or are themselves immune to drastic change.

As regards the advancement of knowledge, for example, the comparative study of modernization is concerned with the world views of premodern and modernizing leaders; the modes and structures of intellectual controversy; the share of a society's resources that is devoted to basic and applied research; the proportion of the population that is engaged in primary, secondary, and higher education; and the extent and nature of its communications network. In the case of the less developed societies, crucial considerations include their capacity for borrowing from the more advanced societies, their employment of foreign specialists, and their interest in sending students abroad for specialized training. All these concerns are to some degree measurable, and all change over time.

In the political realm, the comparative study of modernization focuses on the relations between the central structures of coordination and control and the individuals and groups that make up a society. Size and specialization is one indication of the level of development of a state bureaucracy; this level may also be measured by how much money the central bureaucracy spends in relation to the regional and local bureaucracies. A political system may be gauged too by the effectiveness of its performance, that is, by its capacity to maintain order, to endure without violent change, and to command the loyalty of citizens. The participation of individuals in governmental decision-making may be judged both in terms of a society's formal institutions, such as elected local, regional, and national representative bodies, and in terms of its informal institutions, such as political parties and special interest groups—and the means by which political, economic, ethnic, and other social interest groups influence political decision-making. Societies may also be compared with regard to their prevailing political ideologies, especially as they relate to the role of the public and private sectors.

In the economic realm, both the changing structure of economic activity and rate of growth may be compared. It is customary to think of economic activity as divided into three main sectors: agriculture, industry, and the services. It is also customary to consider each of these sectors in relation to the proportion of the labor force they employ, the proportion of investments they absorb, their contribution to the gross national product, and their rates of growth. Growth is usually calculated in terms of gross national product. Though such estimates are not very accurate, they reflect adequately the main distinctions among societies at different stages of development. The relationship of a society's economy to that of other societies may also be assessed by the rate of growth of foreign trade, the composition of the foreign trade in terms of raw materials and manufactured goods, and the ratio of foreign trade to gross national product.

In many ways the most visible aspect of change as it affects human welfare is what may be called social mobilization—those changes that transform a society from many small and relatively isolated communities to one that is tightly knit by bonds of education, communications, transportation, urbanization, and common interests. The improvement of health from the advancement of knowledge leads to an abrupt increase in births over deaths, resulting in a population explosion that does not regain stability for several generations. This factor alone is a barrier to human welfare, as production must rise not only absolutely but also relative to population growth if people are to benefit. The relationship of strata within a society is also drastically altered. A modern society of managers, specialists of many kinds, industrial workers, office workers, and farmers with technical skills must be created out of a population that is normally four-fifths peasants, and such a transformation influences the life of every individual. In some degree the sense of community and mutual self-help characteristic of premodern villages is created at a national level in the urban way of life, in the common education and socialization of children in national school systems, and in the expanding communication system of newspapers, radio, television, and rapid transportation. Yet even in the most advanced societies human relationships remain less personal and cohesive than in agricultural communities, and individuals have a sense of isolation that is difficult to measure and evaluate. Further, with the drastic changes in stratification in the course of economic growth, the distribution of income tends to lag. Though the income of all strata of a population grows markedly in the long run, distribution of income has thus far remained decidedly unequal even in the most advanced societies.

The personality of an individual results from the interaction of biological characteristics with social environment—the immediate family, the community, and the larger society with which the individual comes into contact. Personalities vary as these biological attributes and environments differ, and the general process of change in the modern era has substantially transformed the environment within which individual personalities are formed. To attempt an understanding of personality adaptation, what needs to be measured, or at least evaluated, is the ability of an individual to empathize with others beyond his immediate circle of acquaintances; the individual's acceptance of both the desirability of change and the recognition of a need for delayed gratification in the interest of future benefits; and the capacity of the individual to judge peers according to their performance rather than their status. As compared with individuals in earlier times, a modern personality may be described as more open, more tolerant of ambiguity, and more concerned with controlling the environment—and by the same token perhaps less self-assured and stable. The psychological aspect of modernization has not been the subject of extensive research, but it has been demonstrated that modern characteristics can be measured and compared.

Modernization as a Process

Most writing on modernization deals with specific political, economic, and social problems in individual societies and limited periods of time, but it is also important to visualize how these problems interrelate within and among societies. The modern era may be seen as having its roots in the Renaissance in the twelfth century and more immediately in the scientific revolution in the seventeenth. Knowledge of the human environment has expanded rapidly since that time and seems likely to continue into the indefinite future. This growth of knowledge has had a multiple impact on all aspects of human activity, taking effect in myriad small actions that together have caused sweeping transformations in the way people live. All efforts to divide this process into periods are by definition artificial, but they are no less necessary if one is to make the subject manageable.

For our purposes here, the simplest possible periodization of the modernization process is: preconditions, transformation, advanced modernization, and international integration. Periodizations of this process vary, depending on an author's purpose and point of view, but all descriptions of it rely on a common body of data. The characteristics that may be attributed to these periods are summarized in the introductions to the separate parts of this book, and are further elaborated in the selected readings.

The readings have been chosen, from the many hundreds or thousands available, as examples of the type of work being done on the study of political development, economic growth, and social mobilization in a comparative context. They are designed as an introduction to the subject seeking to stimulate further interest, rather than as a systematic coverage of all aspects and points of view. Despite the large literature in this field, there are not all that many selections appropriate for a volume such as this one. Many are either too long or too short, too general or too specific, too bland or too idiosyncratic. A wide spectrum of viewpoints is represented, and it will be noted that many are explicitly or implicitly critical of the way the comparative study of modernization is developing. It should be kept in mind that the interpretation of societal transformation in terms of the concept of modernization has evolved only in the past decade or two, and is still characterized more by questions than by answers. This is a limitation and also a challenge.

PART 1

MODERNIZATION: THE CONCEPT AND ITS CRITICS

The background on the concept of modernization provided in the Introduction is supplemented by the first two readings in this section. The first discusses modernization rather abstractly as a concept, and the second reviews the main trends in the development of the concept.

Because this selection of readings assumes the validity of modernization as an approach to the study of societal transformation, critics of the concept do not receive much space in the volume as a whole. It is therefore appropriate to devote attention to their views at this point. Generally speaking, there are two main lines of criticism: that the concept is vague and unsystematic; and that it is biased in favor of stability and order for the benefit of an affluent minority at the expense of the freedom and welfare of the majority of citizens.

The contention that the concept is vague and imprecise is that of critics who seek a theory, such as those in the natural sciences, which not only explains relevant relationships in a series of falsifiable statements, but also predicts that one event will lead to another. Some believe that Marxism and Marxism-Leninism are scientific in this sense. They ask if students of modernization can tell them whether capitalism is more "modern" than "socialism"; what form of social institutions will follow capitalism in the West in future years or centuries; what patterns of institutions and values are universally most appropriate to a given level of science and technology.

Most students of modernization are not, at least at this stage in the development of the concept, concerned with formulating theories in this sense. Their interest is rather in replacing what they regard as simplistic political and economic interpretations of societal transformation with one that takes into better account the complexity and interrelatedness of human affairs, and that employs the variety of methodologies offered by the behavioral and social sciences. Any effort to encompass the totality of human experience is bound to be inadequate, but less inadequate than those seeking to explain everything in terms of a few simple causes. The criticism that the concept lacks rigor should thus be evaluated on the basis of the extent to which rigor is possible in this field, and other concepts or theories which are considered to be more scientifically valid.

The criticism that the concept of modernization is in some sense a conservative ideology derives from a variety of considerations. In its essence, the issue can perhaps best be stated as a conflict between *development* and *distribution*. Development, whether economic, political, or social, involves rates of savings and patterns of investment that are difficult to achieve without tight organization and central coordination. The U.S.S.R. and Japan, in many respects at opposite ends of the socialism-capitalism dichotomy, are both characterized by high rates of savings and centralized management of resources and skills. Most studies of modernization draw attention to the greater capacity for development of those countries with a heritage of effective central government (notably Japan and the Soviet Union, but also the Western nations) in contrast with most other countries which did not even exist as autonomous polities before the nineteenth century.

More often than not, political control and coordination are seen as prerequisites if societies wish to mobilize resources for development. Policies in support of rapid development involve postponement (or at least delays) of gratification for all but the privileged few. Research which assumes that modernization is a desirable process bringing long-term benefits to the members of a society is thus viewed by critics as favoring elites, bureaucrats, bankers, and concentrations of political power at the expense of the great majority of the population that does the work and pays the taxes. The latter are considered exploited in the sense that they are called upon to postpone gratification while the privileged few reap immediate rewards. Evidence in support of this view is presented in the introduction to Part III in the estimates that show that the distribution of income between the highest and lowest fifths of a population has changed little in the course of transformation.

Distribution—the allocation of resources to incomes and welfare rather than to investment—is generally seen as an alternative to rapid growth. Especially in the 1970's, when development seems to be heading toward a crisis of resources, a case can be made for a change in priorities from growth to welfare. A typical populist view would see both the U.S. and the U.S.S.R. as dominated by governments pursuing policies leading to growth, war, and pollution at the expense of the freedom and welfare of the mass of their citizens. The alternative policy is the Maoist approach that regards distribution of wealth and equality of incomes as the highest priority. Some would argue that though China may have adopted such a policy out of necessity, due to its large population in proportion to food and other resources, the advanced countries may also have to turn from development to distribution as their voracity pushes them to the limits of available resources. Similarly on a global basis, an argument can be made for urging the rich countries to share their wealth with the poor rather than press their own further development at the expense of the poor nations. Development and distribution are often discussed as alternatives, but there is in fact an infinite variety of mixes between investment for production and distribution for welfare. Since the Second World War the Western countries have allocated substantially more of their production to distribution for consumption than either Japan or the Soviet Union.

Another view sees writings on modernization as designed to set forth a program for the global expansion of Western capitalism as a means of protecting its interests from the threat of socialist revolutions. Emphasis on political control and coordination is conceived as favoring Western support of dictatorial regimes that can be counted on to control social unrest while concentrating on the development of heavy industry and transportation at the expense of the consumer. Because the concept of modernization is not a rigid doctrine but embraces a variety of opinions, advocates of intervention in Vietnam, for example, can be found among those who would include themselves under its banner. Proponents of intervention in Indochina have seen it as a means of preventing a chain reaction of revolutions (perhaps led by the U.S.S.R. or China or both) that might eventually encompass the United States.

The more narrowly Marxist-Leninist critique includes most of these arguments, but focuses more particularly on discrediting interpretations that point out the common effects of industrialization on all societies and the tendency toward a similarity of values and institutions as levels of development converge. Most writing on modernization in the West stresses the interaction of levels of development with cultural heritages. This is incompatible with the Marxist emphasis on successive stages of development in a struggle between exploiters and exploited, leading ultimately to a society based on the principle of "from each according to his ability, to each according to his need." In the Marxist-Leninist view, the Soviet Union and other Communist-led countries accepted as orthodox by the Communist Party of the U.S.S.R., represent a more advanced social formation than the countries they designate as "bourgeois" or "capitalist." Most writers on modernization, by contrast, would be inclined to see the socialist societies as less developed than the most advanced Western societies, insofar as explicit political, economic, and social indicators are concerned, though more developed than many other societies, including some that are nonsocialist and Western.

In general response to this second line of criticism, and to some extent to the first as well, let it be noted that writing on modernization includes a profusion of viewpoints, not all of which employ the concept explicitly. As a group, those employing the concept of modernization differ from the liberals who emphasize the predominance of political institutions, and also from the various Marxists and Marxist-Leninists. But there are also many variants among those who form the concept. There is a small minority that sees "modernization" as an alternative to "communism"; but most would regard societies of the Soviet type as following one of the possible alternative current policies of modernization. There are also those within the group who are as narrowly wedded to the universal validity of the "free" institutions as the Marxist-Leninists are to the "planned." Most within the group, however, are more inclined to the view that societies are currently seeking to adapt their values and institutions to the opportunities for development offered by the scientific and technological revolution, and that in so adapting they are promulgating a wide variety of policies—policies that derive in part from the cultural heritage of the society; in part from ideology, including foreign influence; and in part from the pragmatic experience of adapting and borrowing from year to year.

Critics of the concept of modernization also often fail to take account of the fact that advanced societies have been given as much attention as the developing. There is a large literature on highly modernized societies, sometimes under the rubric of "post-industrial," and also on the logical sequence to the integration of national states into larger units. Though some see international organizations, and especially multinational corporations, as instruments of the strong against the weak, others see them as forerunners of worldwide integration in much the same way as nationwide institutions came to predominate over regional and local institutions in the process of nation-building.

Above all, it must be kept in mind that such generalizations, uniformities, or "laws" as may be derived from the comparative study of modernizing societies are still in an early stage of formulation. Many have rushed in with sweeping hypotheses and "theories." Fewer have put their minds to the comparative study of specific societies, and to the development of relevant political, economic, and social indicators.

The Concept of Modernization

James O'Connell

In the course of discussing the concept of modernization in this thoughtful essay, O'Connell stresses the universal character of modernization as distinct from both its particular Western political forms and the narrowly economic approach that frequently dominates analyses of this subject. The three central aspects of modernization that O'Connell emphasizes are common to the universal process, though they take various institutional forms in societies with differing heritages.

The term that is used in the social sciences to designate the process through which a traditional or pretechnological society passes as it is transformed into a society characterized by machine technology, rational and secular attitudes, and highly differentiated social structures is *modernization*.[1] It is not a pretty term, and it is open to some ambiguities. Not the least of these is the suggestion of a linear development that leads directly to the present time—as if every age were not modern for its contemporaries. However, the term is the one in our possession and is more convenient to use than any others. This paper is meant as a search for its precise meaning. In other words, the paper is trying to disengage those general aspects of change that are involved in, and are a precondition for, the passing of traditional society and the coming of the type

"The Concept of Modernization" by James O'Connell is reprinted with permission of Duke University Press from the *South Atlantic Quarterly*, LXIV (Autumn 1965), 549–564.

Father O'Connell heads the Department of Government at Ahmadu Bello University, Nigeria. He is joint editor, with L. Gray Cowan and David G. Scanlon, of *Education and Nation-Building in Africa* (1965).

In his first footnote to the article, O'Connell declares: "I should like to express my gratitude to my colleagues, Professor M. S. Baratz and Dr. R. J. Gavin, of the University of Ibadan, and to Dr. J. A. Ballard, of the University of Ife, for their valuable comments on an earlier draft of this paper."

[1] Two recent books, L. W. Pye (ed.), *Communications and Political Development* (Princeton, 1963) and J. LaPalombara (ed.), *Bureaucracy and Political Development* (Princeton, 1963), contain some excellent discussions of modernization by various contributors. Pye's and LaPalombara's own discussions of the theme are extremely thoughtful. Valuable also is *Studies on Modernization of Japan* in Asian Cultural Studies, III (October, 1962).

of society that exists in the so-called advanced and economically prosperous countries of the contemporary world.[2]

Though it is easy to form a general understanding of the changes that occur in the transition from tradition to modernity, there is much to gain in our search by listing in a more detailed fashion various kinds of change that mark the process. In that way more adequate data are available to be interpreted. Here are some of the changes that could be remarked during the course of transition in Western and Japanese societies (examples of societies that successfully modernized) and that are to be seen occurring in contemporary developing countries: Age-old agricultural implements and methods give way before tractors and fertilizers; health improves through more varied food and better medical care; distances are shortened by the speed of machines; larger political units become viable from the improved systems of communications; printing and other technical media of linguistic and visual communication supplement a reliance on oral communication; an interdependence comes into being between communities that previously were separated from and independent of one another; population shifts from the countryside to the towns, and urbanization takes place rapidly; money is used more commonly as a medium of exchange and replaces unwieldy barter systems; self-sustaining economic growth begins to occur; an endeavor is made to institutionalize the control of economic growth through planning agencies; a taste for consumer goods becomes more diversified; formal schooling replaces tribal initiation; by and large, ascriptive or inherited status tends to give way before achieved status, or those with ascriptive status seek to complement it with achieved status; occupations become more skilled and specialized; salaried employment in industry and elsewhere starts to spread, and more impersonal labor relations dominate; civil services, established according to rational and universalist norms, replace the slow-going personal administration of royal courts and village elders; sharper distinctions arise between work and leisure.

Not all these phenomena—and others that have been omitted—take place together; and they do not usually take place at the same pace in any single society or interconnected group of societies. Because these phenomena are manifold and take place unevenly, one of the serious problems that faces a modernizing society is the extent and temporal sequence and length of tolerable variation. Rapidly changing societies face problems that arise from the weakening of accepted social sanctions, family disorganization, excessive individualism in the modernizing sectors, and a sense of uncertainty about

---

[2] See the title of D. Lerner's book, *The Passing of Traditional Society: Modernizing the Middle East* (Glencoe, Ill., 1958). Briefly one might say that traditional society is characterized by the dominance of oral tradition and kinship bonds, the use of magic (in a wide sense), and the lack of developed tools. R. N. Bellah writes: "Primitive societies are characterized by the dominance of oral tradition. They are traditional societies *par excellence*. The tendency in primitive society is for religion, or magic as Weber preferred to call it at this level, to permeate all aspects of life. Every moral norm, every obligation of behavior, tends to have some sacred sanction. Also, the society is organized fundamentally by kinship and practically only by kinship. The organization of primitive society then focuses on two poles: one kinship, the other ritual, both of which tend to be very pervasive" ("Values and Social Change in Modern Japan," *Studies on Modernization of Japan*, p. 15).

social and cultural identity—all of which impose considerable mental strain on the members of a society.[3]

In trying to understand modernization an obvious temptation is to take all these data and to interpret them in economic terms. In fact, the terms *modern* and *traditional* as applied to two societies tend to conjure up a contrast of a society that is highly industrialized and one that has not yet moved far from subsistence agriculture. Yet modernization is much more than industrialization.[4] Two remarks will suffice here. For one thing, economic growth itself can proceed through technical change (broadly construed) in services and agriculture as well as in manufacture. For another, highly mechanized industry can exist in a country, especially in areas where the extractive industries dominate, without having any serious impact on attitudes and social structures. To interpret modernization in the wider category of economic growth—the rate of increase of per capita goods and services—is to use an index of change that is highly quantifiable, and thus useful; and it is one that is readily comprehensible in modernizing societies because it is easily translated into issues that touch on the lives of the masses of the people and that political leaders give the highest practical priority to in organizing energies for social change. But this interpretation—though employing a more satisfying criterion than industrialization—is also inadequate. An economy in which self-sustaining growth is occurring involves more than economic achievement. A developed economy is one element in a system of interrelated and interacting components that include among other elements rational attitudes geared to universalist norms, achievement criteria, and the systematic organization of education to prepare subjects for performing highly differentiated functions and employing complex techniques.[5]

But if modernization is not to be equated with industrialization or economic growth, it is also important to avoid identifying it with the development of democratic institutions. There is evidence that some connection exists between the technological exigencies of a modern society and democratic attitudes.[6] Technology fosters efforts to spread mass literacy, facilitates the general availability of knowledge, multiplies communication media between members and classes of a society, and tends to differentiate status according to skills and capacity. Nonetheless, in spite of trends toward a greater egalitarianism it is remarkably clear from recent history that no deterministic link exists between technological advance and the emergence of social attitudes embodying respect for the individual, tolerance for minority rights, and willed restraints on government that go to make up the elusive phenomenon we call democracy.

[3] See P. Bohannan's interesting remarks on "detribalization" in *Social Anthropology* (New York, 1963), pp. 392–97.

[4] For a treatment of modernization that lays greater stress on industrialization and economic growth than does this paper see W. E. Moore, *Social Change* (Englewood Cliffs, N.J., 1963), pp. 89–112.

[5] See S. H. Frankel, "Some Conceptual Aspects of Technical Change," *Social Change and Economic Development* (Paris, 1963), pp. 53–59.

[6] See S. M. Lipset's chapter, "Economic Development and Democracy" in *Political Man* (London, 1960), pp. 45–76.

In any case, through the centralization and control that technology has made possible, a benevolent (or totalitarian) despotism or technocratic dictatorship is in many ways more easily possible now than at any previous moment of history. Russia and China bear witness to this.

Those societies that we venture to call modern have become so through a long historical process. A great scholar like Max Weber spent most of his life working out the nature and details of the process in the West. The West was the first society to become modern.[7] And so there is something to be gained from noticing the ingredients that went into the making of modernity in the West: There was the Greek conviction of an ordered cosmos that was finally removed from a polytheistic arbitrariness and underpinned by the Judeo-Christian concept of the conserving creation of one God; there was the Roman elaboration of a rational legal system that was made less individualistic and was adapted to local conditions in fusing with the customary law of the Franco-Germanic peoples; the Roman Church made available during crucial centuries a literate bureaucracy (clerks) that was largely removed from the bonds of kinship obligation; culture began to be secularized in the Renaissance, and its secularization was consolidated in the Enlightenment; there was that initiative of the human spirit at the ending of the Middle Ages that seemed to urge men on to seek knowledge with greater intensity than ever before in history and to apply the knowledge gained—it was an era that saw explorers setting sail to new lands, scientists pursuing new inventions, and the early capitalists (among others, the Puritans, their predecessors and successors) developing commerce and industry. These ingredients—and many others—went into the modernization of the West.

However, it would be a mistake to think that the accumulation of ingredients in itself makes for modernity. In the last resort being modern is an attitude of mind that gives form to various ingredients. It is also important to remark that there is a spontaneous and utterly individual aspect to the human mind that escapes any effort to conceptualize it completely or to formulate it within the limits of any law, no matter how fully data are gathered or interpreted.[8] Each individual mind or social interaction of minds that goes to make a culture possesses a distinct individuality. That such distinctiveness exists is

[7] Bellah summarizes excellently Weber's contribution to comparative historical sociology in his study of the modernization of Europe. J. M. Echavarria has a good discussion of Weber's model of economic growth in "A Theoretical Model of Development Applicable to Latin America," *Social Aspects of Economic Development in Latin America* (Paris, 1963), pp. 21–49.

[8] It was this aspect of mind that Charles Peirce endeavored to convey through his category of "Firstness" (see his *Collected Papers* [Cambridge, Mass., 1931-1935], Vol. I, pars. 306, 307, 422, 423, 426, and elsewhere). Emphasis on this kind of spontaneity is central in contemporary phenomenological philosophy. M. Merleau-Ponty writes: "Le propre d'une philosophie phénoménologique nous parait donc de s'établir à titre definitif dans l'ordre de la spontanéité enseignante qui est inaccessible au psychologisme et à l'historicisme, non moins qu'aux metaphysiques dogmatiques . . . . Il n'y a finalité qu'au sens où Heidegger la définissait lorsqu'il disait à peu près qu'elle est le tremblement d'une unité exposée à la contingence et qui se recrèe infatigablement. Et c'est à la mème spontanéité nondelibéré inépvisable, que Sartre faisait allusion quand il disait que nous sommes 'condamnés à la liberte.' " ("Sur la Phénoménologie du Language," *Problèmes Actuels de la Phénoménologie* [Tournai, 1952], pp. 108, 109).

important to those cultures that are modernizing now under the impact of the West. We shall look again at this issue later. For the moment a few remarks will suffice that also serve to throw light on our immediate preoccupations. Non-Western cultures have accepted certain forms and techniques that were first developed in the West. But epistemologically the vast majority of these forms are modern rather than Western; they belong to the universalist human spirit rather than to any of its particular manifestations. In the new cultures native ingredients are fusing with those that have come from outside and give modernization a shape and a tempo different from that which it had in the West. But in the new cultures as in the West it is possible to disengage those attitudes that are involved in, and are a precondition for, becoming modern. Modernization is a historical process that ends in those attitudes—though it must be understood that like truth itself modern attitudes are ideal-limits[9] that take their meaning from the extent of achievement that is reached at any particular moment and not from any complete embodiment or fulfilment of modernization. It is time now after these preliminary historical and theoretical considerations to turn to a more detailed examination of what being modern means.

If a short expression were being sought to describe the mental attitude that develops once the modernization process itself has "taken off," the expression "creative rationality" would fit the purpose—two words that are meant to combine the concepts of innovation and order. But it is possible to go beyond the density of a short expression to analyze modernization by discerning in it three basic connected and interactive aspects: (1) A tested conviction of the existence of correlations and causes that maintains a continuing, systematic, and inventive search for knowledge—in other words, an analytico-causal and inventive outlook; (2) The multiplication of tools and techniques that both results from the first aspect and nourishes it; (3) A willingness to accept continuous change on the plane of both an individual and social structure, together with a capacity all the while to preserve individual and social identity.

1. Analytico-causal and inventive outlook: An analytico-causal approach lies at the heart of modernization. There is an order in the world; a relation exists between all things; nothing happens without a cause; and no happening, sacred or profane, can escape the possibility of being questioned, analyzed, and obliged to yield its secrets. Every idea is open, and no state of knowledge is final. Some statements may be absolutely true, but there is no full and absolute truth. This analytico-causal and inventive approach (the scientific spirit) has developed a systematic methodology (the scientific method). Scientific research works through an interwoven pattern of observation, hypothesis, experiment, and verification; it is empirical and predictive. Moreover, such research has been institutionalized through training centers and through the facilities provided by universities and institutes of various kinds. The long-established universities, for example, which had become largely moribund by the eighteenth century, suddenly came to life in a modernizing context once it

[9] On truth as an ideal-limit, see Peirce, Vol. V, pars. 416 and 565; also P. Ricoeur's fascinating essay "L'histoire de la philosophie et l'unité du vrai" in his *Histoire et vérité* (Paris, 1955), pp. 53–73.

was grasped that they offered an organizational structure within which advanced learning could be imparted effectively and pursued creatively in a way that respected scholarly freedom and social utility. The interrelation of the aspects of modernization appears already from the manner in which, in discussing the first aspect, the third, which includes the possession or development of organizational structures, has become involved. In any case, the discussion of the scientific spirit reveals how far removed the analytico-causal attitude is from attitudes that would halt at the invocation of a magical explanation or that would allow the order of the universe to be upset by the arbitrary intervention of a god. It is even further removed from attitudes that accept the dominance of inherited wisdom, guarded by and often reserved to the elders of a people, that characterizes most traditional societies.

2. *Multiplication of tools and techniques:* The most practical outcome of the questions of inquiry and the hypotheses of invention has been the constant devising of new techniques and tools—methods and instruments—that have, in a reciprocal causality with inventiveness, accelerated inquiry and facilitated research. Hence, we have the rapid accumulation of machines and methods that stamps modern technology and that has changed the physical appearance of the earth. The contrast with traditional society is startling, where the same tools remained so long in use that they were hallowed through religious rites.

Contemporary technology is an intricate combination of skills or techniques with the use and rapid development of machines. In other words, we have, for example, a combination of the ability to read, to count, to diagnose medical symptoms, and to work out the interplay of physical forces with printing presses, computers, medicines, and multispan steel bridges. In this connection it is important to stress the key roles that have been played in modernization by printing, auto-propelled vehicular conveyance, and urbanization. What these three factors have in common is that they are communication media. Printing especially made it possible to enlarge the corporate pursuit of scientific knowledge and to facilitate the retention of knowledge already acquired.[10]

The machines and their techniques (especially the mathematical techniques), embodying rational and universal norms, impose on the men who use them a discipline that tends to promote individual and social attitudes that approximate more and more closely to the norms of the machines. For example, industrial workers cannot follow the traditional agricultural workers' relatively unconstrained synchronization with the sun; they must respect the rigidly patterned labor sequence of which the mechanical clock is the symbol. In another sphere, political leaders who wish seriously to promote economic growth find that their decisions must carefully take into account the exigencies of the feasibility-studies worked out by economists and engineers. In a different way a young boy can learn the beginnings of scientific methods as much from mechanical toys as from a lesson in physics—one of the disadvantages that children suffer from in a developing country is that they have

---

[10] Pye says simply: "It was the pressure of communications that brought about the downfall of traditional societies" (p. 3).

to learn formally at school ideas and methods that children in economically advanced countries pick up informally at home and in their environment.

We need, however, to be careful not to exaggerate the importance of the link between modern techniques and machines and the human experience that controls their use and accepts their discipline. No purely quantitative allocation of economic priorities, for example, is possible. Leaders and planners implicitly or explicitly draw up their priorities—and often must do so if only for the sake of political survival—according to the temperaments, set of value judgments, and social systems of their peoples.[11] Similarly, though writers in different countries make use of the novel as an organizational form for presenting "sensibility," the presentation of insights does differ—the writers are in differing ways "significant in terms of the human awareness they promote." [12] One has only to contrast Trollope and Dostoevski within Europe, not to mention the range of sensibility that the Indian and Japanese novels make manifest.

The tools and techniques of modern man have enabled him to approach the world in a new spirit of transforming conquest. For the first time in history man feels that he is not at the mercy of the elements. He realizes that already in many places and soon everywhere even the age-old threat of hunger will have been repelled. And urban man especially lives in a world constructed by himself and bearing his image. Such conquest has posed problems for the religious thinking and practice of modernizing men.[13] In most traditional societies religion was polytheistic. Modern science with its convictions of explanation and its control of tools exorcises the intervention of the gods and desacralizes the world. Also the new communications systems throw open the closed cosmologies to new worlds not provided for in the old myths. So a storm is now only a series of physical events; the god of the storm is dead. But science poses problems even for the monotheistic world religions. For so long their adepts called on God to intervene to help them to cope with the world. Now men can apparently cope by themselves. Hence, Marx could claim that men should hope to set up their paradise in this world. And even within Christian monotheism the German theologians, especially Bultmann, have been hard at work trying to dissociate their religious faith from its connections with nature religions and an imagery derived from the seasons.[14] Some thinkers of the

---

[11] La Palombara comments on the value of Weber's ideal type of bureaucracy and suggests that useful though it is it can be misleading for situations of economic growth (pp. 48–55).

[12] F. R. Leavis, *The Great Tradition* (London, 1948), p. 2.

[13] A well-reasoned appraisal of the present situation is made from a Christian viewpoint by J. Daniélou in his chapter, "Christianity and Technological Civilization," *The Scandal of Truth* (English trans., London, 1962), pp. 115–28; see also H. V. von Balthasar, *Science, Religion and Christianity* (English trans., London, 1958).

[14] This task is older than some contemporary thinkers appear to realize. Writing about Old Testament Judaism, H. Duméry says: "Le judaisme . . . refuse tout naturalisme; il lui substitue, dans le domaine religieux comme dans le domaine politique, un humanisme qui dépasse la nature, qui prend appui sur elle mais pour créer librement ses propres valeurs. Vue sous cet angle, la religion hébraïque n'est pas une mythologie inconsistente parce que 'non maturelle'; elle est un symbolisme cohérente, une reprise orientée de situations humaines, une manière de réaménager l'espace et le temps en fonction d'un but que

scientific era, however, were too hasty in proclaiming that God, as well as the gods, was dead. The gods were swept away because the *functioning* of existent things could be explained without them. Monotheists have not yet lost completely the opportunity to convince their contemporaries that existence itself needs God as its ground; and that without him it is eternally contradictory. So, too, no matter how comfortably man ensconces himself in the world about him, he has to ask questions about his identity and his destiny. Not only does death still mock all man's victories, but his greatest scientific success holds a mushroom menace of nuclear destruction over history itself.

3. *Flexibility of social structures and continuing identity*: To pursue knowledge without ceasing, to remain open to new ideas, and to cope with the adaptations in thinking and living that new inventions bring with them, human minds must have the will and the capacity to accept change. But unless the mind can maintain a continuing identity on an individual and social level, it tends to disintegrate. Hence, if a society is to modernize adequately, it must possess beliefs about itself and its members that are compatible with change and social structures that can modify without breaking. Some societies have historically been unable to acculturate in this way—the American Indians and the Australian bushmen are perhaps two such examples.[15] But in every society in rapid transition individuals and communities are apt to find themselves caught in a mesh of conflicting social criteria as beliefs, forms of production, and time-space relations change. The core of this trouble lies in the inability of the members of a changing social system to predict what other members will do under given conditions. From this inability to know what can be expected follows a breakdown of trust. Nepotism (placing trust in family ties to the detriment of merit criteria), tribalism (improper trust in ethnic ties), and corruption (disregarding of objective claims and seeking security in financial accumulation) almost inevitably mark this kind of transitional period.[16] But most recent history suggests that these defects can be overcome quite quickly in societies that are successfully modernizing.

The machines have either made possible large groupings (for example, Nigeria) or have confirmed existing groupings (for example, Russia—indeed, Russia has also been able to incorporate Central Asian peoples who at most belonged ambiguously to her territory). But size is not the decisive factor in modern social structure. More important are complex structural differentiation, functioning expertise, and systematic goal-formulation—all of which are conditioned by a speed that machines ranging from jet planes to computers have made possible and even necessary. It is methodologically useful to con-

---

l'esprit se fixe lui-même. . . . le judaisme travaille à purger la nature de toute trace d'animisme et . . . a souci de mettre Dieu à l'abri des divers modes de representation. . . . Hegel et Marx en ont eu pleine conscience. Il est dommage que les croyants l'oublient . . ." (*La Foi n'est pas un cri* [Paris, 1959], pp. 51–52).

[15] M. Mead, *The Changing Culture of an Indian Tribe* (New York, 1932), presents a famous case study of social change among the Omaha Indians.

[16] Wraith and Simpkins, *Corruption in Developing Countries* (London, 1963), offer an interesting comparison and some useful detail. It is doubtful, however, whether the authors bring forward the most important data that were available for throwing light on their subject, and their analysis leaves a lot to be desired.

centrate on the role of the wider and more formally structured groups in social change—the role of the bureaucracy, for example. But it is important to notice also that change extends as far as the interior of the family structures. In most traditional societies that were polygynous, the marital system revolved around the economic hegemony of the older men. The new technological order with its wage system and labor mobility has hastened considerably economic achievement by the young—so it has enabled young men earlier to compete for wives, and it has negatively struck a blow against the older order by making it more difficult through its price system for polygynists to obtain for their children the educational training that is the key to achievement in the new order. Similarly, it would be possible to examine the changes in attitudes that result from the kinds of leisure that have become possible through technological devices—motion pictures, television, long-playing records, and holidays abroad. But in relation to the speed and complexity of relations within technological society, it is the bureaucrats (those of the state and those of private organizations) who compose those formally organized groups that are the precondition and the instrument of functional organization.[17] Within such groups there is normally a built-in readiness to adjust to new conditions; a premium is placed on specialized skills; members are admitted and promoted according to achievement and merit; and members are guaranteed reasonable stability of employment. Administration, while remaining in the hands of persons, has to maintain relations with the society within which it functions and serves that are as impersonal as possible and that are impervious to the claims of kin and friendship where these flout objective criteria or regulations.

The key co-ordinating bureaucrats are those in public service. They supervise the general pursuit of welfare and the maintenance of order in the modern state. Though certain final decisions remain in the hands of the political leaders, the civil servants—administrators and technologists—usually suggest, formulate, and execute the decisions of the government. Hegel, who before most Western thinkers grasped the coming importance of the bureaucrats, called them the "universal class" who look after the "maintenance of the state's universal interest, and legality, in this sphere of particular rights, and the work of bringing these rights back to the universal. . . ." [18] To understand how far the contemporary bureaucrats are from the leisurely rulers of traditional societies and their royal courts or from the improvising half-amateurs of earlier Western countries, one has only to consider the economic skill and technical co-ordination required to prepare a single year's governmental budget in an economically advanced country. Moreover, this kind of bureaucratic organization and planning applies techniques that are valid for an economic situation that is worldwide in character—the application of the techniques differs only in emphasis according to whether a society calls itself capitalist or socialist.

We might sum up our analysis of modernization by saying that it is the development of an inquiring and inventive attitude of mind, individual and

---

[17] Important though bureaucracies are as carriers of modernizing values, they are no guarantee in themselves of modernization. See M. Fainsod's remarks in "Bureaucracy and Modernization: The Russian and Soviet Case," in La Palombara, pp. 233–40.

[18] *Philosophy of Right* (English trans., London, 1953), p. 189.

social, that lies behind the use of techniques and machines and inspires new forms of social relations between individuals. Its three aspects assume the existence of and act on one another. Though his concept of modernization differs somewhat from that presented in this paper, the exposition here fits in perfectly with Professor Lerner's proposition that "modernity is an interactive behavioral system. It is a 'style of life' whose components are *interactive* in the sense that the efficient functioning of any one of them requires the efficient functioning of all the others. The components are *behavioral* in the sense that they operate only through the activity of individual human beings. They form a *system* in the sense that significant variation in the activity of one component will be associated with significant variation in the activity of all other components." [19] This contention can be illustrated by simply pointing out that unless individuals in a society are guided by universalist and rational norms, adequate use cannot be made of new techniques, the complicated machines of recent technology break down or work far below capacity, and the complex social organization that technology makes possible is damaged by lack of trust between individuals—the interference of the bonds of kinship with achievement criteria and the distortion of the decision-making process by political arbitrariness. Developing countries that have imported elements of advanced technology and managed them badly furnish a negative but important confirmation of the intricate interweaving—a reciprocal causality that does not suppose any chronological priority—of the attitudes and tools and structures that compose modernity.

After developing the three aspects of modernization, it is worthwhile to point out that the changes taking place at present in many non-Western societies are part of modernization. In spite of the superficial assumption of various Western appearances, they do not mean the Westernization of these societies. They involve no more than the making use of some Western forms and inventions which it is easier to take over at present than to spend precious time in working out anew amidst the many pressing issues that are having to be resolved. This *conclusion of modernization* rather than westernization flows easily from all that has already been said. A French thinker, Paul Ricoeur, has put the essential point pithily and well:

> We must remain mindful that if science is Greek in origin, then European through Galileo, Descartes, Newton, etc., it is not in so far as it is Greek and European but in so far as it is human that it develops its power of gathering together the human race; . . . . When Pascal wrote: "All humanity can be con-

---

[19] "Towards a Communication Theory of modernization," Pye, p. 329. After he has grouped the traits that he considers modern societies show (his views go broadly in the same direction as those of this paper), M. B. Jansen remarks: "A modernized society . . . is one in which these things appear together. When they appear together the role of the city, for instance, is different from the role cities, however large, played in the ancient world. China's imperial bureaucracy, or the Tokugawa administrative structure, were rational but were not accompanied by other elements described here. The totality of function and operation is different. It is not a matter of wealth or poverty; Saudi Arabia is wealthy but premodern; Ireland is poor but modern" ("On Studying the Modernization of Japan," *Studies on Modernization of Japan*, p. 3).

sidered as a single man who learns unceasingly and remembers," his proposition means simply that every man who is put before a proof of a geometrical or experimental character is capable of drawing the same conclusion provided that he has gone through the required learning process. . . . Techniques . . . have no country. Even if it is possible to attribute to a particular nation or culture the invention of alphabetical writing, printing, the steam engine, etc., an invention belongs by right to mankind. Sooner or later it creates an irreversible situation for everyone; its spread can be slowed down but not absolutely impeded. . . . As soon as an invention appears in one part of the globe, it is guaranteed universal diffusion. The technical revolutions add together and because they add together they escape cultural confinement. We can say that, apart from delays in particular parts of the globe, there exists a world technology.[20]

Once the essential spirit of a culture survives the shock of the intellectual, technical, and organizational impact of modernization and has even begun to burst into spontaneous development, there need be no fear of borrowing or imitating. If the latter processes mean that a society adopts ideas and takes over techniques and organizational forms from the West, it is in part no more than convenient and time-saving to take what is ready to hand—the West has had a longer time during which to evolve structures that are compatible with the scientific spirit and its methodology. A superficial appearance of Westernization will mislead no one who looks closely. And where Western forms prove useful, they are rapidly infused with another tempo and accent in other contexts. Indeed, a great deal can be hoped for these days from the way the great cultures of the world have drawn close to one another, have become conscious of one another, and can contrast their achievements. The result is a mutual stimulation and cross-fertilization. Africa, for example, has offered a hint of new rhythms to Western music and a glimpse of an original sensibility of significant proportion to Western art. The West is providing musical forms (the symphony among others) for the elaboration of African folk music into a more sophisticated accomplishment and is teaching a conscious theory of technique to African sculptors. Such fruitful exchanges are the most natural thing in the world. An isolated culture stagnates; the graveyard of history is full of such stunted corpses. Great cultures learn ideas from others, are stimulated by these ideas, and watch with rich wonder what happens when their own ideas are borrowed by others and begin to live with a new life in the other cultures. Cultures can in fact become most consciously themselves and aware of their distinctiveness when they have some measure of comparison. And when two great cultures endeavor to comprehend one another with sympathy and to imitate one another with fidelity, each grows in stature and remains truer to its own genius than before the encounter.

To end this paper, two points may be made. The first is that a transitional society more than a technologically advanced society needs multicultured individuals.[21] It requires men who appreciate the values of prescientific tradition and who yet have the mental and moral caliber to understand and

[20] "Civilisation universelle et cultures nationales," *Esprit* (October, 1961), pp. 440–41.
[21] Bohannan, pp. 394–95, contrasts "multicultural" with "detribalized."

implement the universalist norms of the modern world. It takes much knowledge and great courage to build up those patterns of behavior that make for predictability and so generate solidarity and trust in the new states of the developing world. The second point is that all those whose function it is to play prominent roles in the modern world (grown so small through its communications and so powerful through its available energy) must possess what for want of better name we might call a "planetary consciousness." Such men will have to lead in devising and supporting world institutions, especially political institutions, that rationalize and co-ordinate the efforts of the various human communities that make up the world. Only through intelligent goodwill organized so that it can reach out beyond anachronistic political divisions and narrow selfishness will the benefits of technology be shared as fast as they should with the developing countries. And only through the same intelligent good will can the peoples of the world avoid blowing themselves to pieces with the terrible power they now command and instead join their resources.

The Change to Change: Modernization, Development, and Politics

Samuel P. Huntington

This comprehensive treatment of modernization examines the process of change in a political framework. After a theoretical discussion of the process, the diverse contemporary approaches to political development in terms of system-function, social process, and comparative history are described. The essay concludes with a review of the recent theories of political change that have been generated by the new understanding that the concept of modernization has brought to the subject.

Political Science and Political Change

Change is a problem for social science. Sociologists, for instance, have regularly bemoaned their lack of knowledge concerning social change. In 1951 Talcott Parsons flatly stated, in italics, that *"a general theory of the processes of change in social systems is not possible in the present state of knowledge."* Thirteen years later Don Martindale could see little improvement. Sociology, he argued, could account for structure but not for change: *"its theory of social change,"* said he, also in italics (!), *"is the weakest branch of sociological theory."* Other sociologists have expressed similar views.[1] Yet, as opposed to

"The Change to Change: Modernization, Development, and Politics" is reprinted by permission of the author and publisher, *Comparative Politics*, III (April 1971), 283–322.

Samuel P. Huntington is Professor of Government and Associate Director of the Center for International Affairs at Harvard University. His principal publications on modernization are *Political Order in Changing Societies* (1968) and, as co-editor, *Authoritarian Politics in Modern Society: The Dynamics of Established One-Party Systems* (1970).

Huntington notes at the beginning of his article: ["]This essay was written while I was a Fellow of the Center for Advanced Study in the Behavioral Sciences in Palo Alto. It will subsequently appear in a volume edited by Daniel Bell, *Theories of Social Change*, copyright by The Russell Sage Foundation. I am indebted to Ronald D. Brunner and Raymond F. Hopkins for helpful comments.["]

[1] Talcott Parsons, *The Social System* (Glencoe, 1951), p. 486; Don Martindale, "Introduction," in George K. Zollschan and Walter Hirsch, eds. *Explorations in Social Change* (Boston, 1964), p. xii; Alvin Boskoff, "Functional Analysis as a Source of a Theoretical Repertory and Research Tasks in the Study of Social Change," ibid., p. 213; Robin Williams, *American Society* (New York, 1960), p. 568. By 1969, however, Williams

political scientists, the sociologists are relatively well off. Compared with past neglect of the theory of political change in political science, sociology is rich with works on the theory of social change. These more generalized treatments are supplemented by the extensive literature on group dynamics, planned change, organizational change, and the nature of innovation. Until very recently, in contrast, political theory in general has not attempted to deal directly with the problems of change. "Over the last seventy-five years," David Easton wrote in 1953, "political research has confined itself largely to the study of given conditions to the neglect of political change." [2]

Why did this happen? Several factors would seem to play a role. While the roots of political science go back to Aristotle (whose central concern was "to consider things in the process of their growth"), modern political science is a product of the late nineteenth and early twentieth centuries. It came into being in the stable political systems of Western Europe and North America, where radical change could be viewed as a temporary deviation in, or extraordinary malfunctioning of, the political system. In Parson's terminology, political scientists might study change *in* a system (such as the fluctuations in power of political parties or of Congress and president), but they did not concern themselves with change *of* the system.[3] Political scientists neglected change because they focused their primary attention on states where change did not seem to be much of a problem.

Reinforcing this tendency was the antihistorical temper of the more avant garde movements in political science. Born of history out of law, political science could establish itself as a discipline only by establishing its independence from its parents. Consequently, political scientists deemphasized their ties with history and emphasized the similarities between their discipline and other social sciences. Political science evolved with the aid of periodic infusions of ideas, concepts, and methods from psychology (Harold Lasswell in the 1930s), social psychology (David Truman and the group approach of the late 1940s), sociology (structural-functionalism of the 1950s), and economics (equilibrium, input-output, game theory, in the 1960s). The behavioral stress on survey data, interviewing, and participant-observation reinforced the rejection of history.

Political scientists attempt to explain political phenomena. They view politics as a dependent variable, and they naturally look for the explanations of politics in other social processes and institutions. This tendency was reinforced by the Marxian and Freudian intellectual atmosphere of the 1930s and 1940s. Political scientists were themselves concerned with the social, psychological, and economic roots of political behavior. Consequently, social change, personality change, and economic change were, in their view, more funda-

---

felt a little more optimistic about the prospects for a breakthrough in the sociological study of change. See Robin Williams, *Sociology and Social Change in the United States* (St. Louis, Washington University Social Science Institute, Studies in Comparative International Development, vol. 4, no. 7, 1968–69).

[2] David Easton, *The Political System* (New York, 1953), p. 42.

[3] Talcott Parsons, *The Social System* (Glencoe, 1951), pp. 480 ff.

mental than political change. If one could understand and explain the former, one could easily account for the latter.

Finally, political change tended to be ignored because comparative politics tended to be ignored. With rare exceptions, such as the work of Carl Friedrich and a few others, political scientists did not attempt systematic comparative analyses of similar processes or functions in different political systems or general comparisons of political systems as systems. In book titles and course titles, comparative government meant foreign government. The study of political change is, however, intimately linked to the study of comparative politics. The study of change involves the comparison of similarities and differences through time; comparative politics involves the analysis of similarities and differences through space. In addition, the comparison of two political systems which exist simultaneously but which differ significantly in their major characteristics inevitably raises the questions: Is one system likely to evolve into a pattern similar to that of the other? Are the two systems related to each other in an evolutionary sense? Thus, the analysis of political change is not likely to progress unless the study of comparative politics is also booming.

Not until the mid-1950s did a renaissance in the study of comparative politics get under way. That renaissance began with a concern with modernization and the comparison of modern and traditional political systems. It evolved in the early 1960s into a preoccupation with the concept of political development, approached by way of systems theory, statistical analysis, and comparative history. In the late 1960s, the focus on political development in turn yielded to broader efforts to generate more general theories of political change.

The Context of Modernization

GENERAL THEORY OF MODERNIZATION

The new developments in comparative politics in the 1950s involved extension of the geographical scope of concern from Western Europe and related areas to the non-Western "developing" countries. It was no longer true that political scientists ignored change. Indeed, they seemed almost overwhelmed with the immensity of the changes taking place in the modernizing societies of Asia, Africa, and Latin America. The theory of modernization was embraced by political scientists, and comparative politics was looked at in the context of modernization. The concepts of modernity and tradition bid fair to replace many of the other typologies which had been dear to the hearts of political analysts: democracy, oligarchy, and dictatorship; liberalism and conservatism; totalitarianism and constitutionalism; socialism, communism, and capitalism; nationalism and internationalism. Obviously, these categories were still used. But by the late 1960s, for every discussion among political scientists in which the categories "constitutional" and "totalitarian" were employed, there must have been ten others in which the categories "modern" and "traditional" were used.

These categories were, of course, the latest manifestation of a Great Dichotomy between more primitive and more advanced societies which has been a common feature of Western social thought for the past one hundred years. Their post-World War II incarnation dates from the elaboration by Parsons and Edward Shils of their pattern variables in the early 1950s and the subsequent extension of these from "choices" confronting an "actor" to characteristics of social systems undertaken by Frank Sutton in his 1955 paper on "Social Theory and Comparative Politics." [4] Sutton's summary of modern and traditional societies (or, in his terms, "industrial" and "agricultural" societies) encompasses most of the generally accepted distinguishing characteristics of these two types:

AGRICULTURAL SOCIETY	MODERN INDUSTRIAL SOCIETY
1. Predominance of ascriptive, particularistic, diffuse patterns	1. Predominance of universalistic, specific, and achievement norms
2. Stable local groups and limited spatial mobility	2. High degree of social mobility (in a general—not necessarily "vertical"—sense)
3. Relatively simple and stable "occupational" differentiation	3. Well-developed occupational system, insulated from other social structures
4. A "deferential" stratification system of diffuse impact	4. "Egalitarian" class system based on generalized patterns of occupational achievement
	5. Prevalence of "associations," i.e., functionally specific, nonascriptive structures

The essential difference between modern and traditional society, most theorists of modernization contend, lies in the greater control which modern man has over his natural and social environment. This control, in turn, is based on the expansion of scientific and technological knowledge. To a sociologist such as Marion Levy, for instance, a society is "more or less modernized to the extent that its members use inanimate sources of power and/or use tools to multiply the effects of their efforts." [5] Cyril Black, an historian, argues that modern society results from adaptation of "historically evolved institutions . . . to the rapidly changing functions that reflect the unprecedented increase in man's knowledge, permitting control over his environment, that accompanied the scientific revolution." [6] Among political scientists, Dankwart A. Rustow holds that modernization involves a "rapidly widening control over nature through closer cooperation among men." [7] To virtually all theorists, these differences in the extent of man's control over his environment reflect differ-

[4] Frank X. Sutton, "Social Theory and Comparative Politics," in Harry Eckstein and David Apter, eds. *Comparative Politics: A Reader* (New York, 1963), pp. 67 ff.

[5] Marion Levy, *Modernization and the Structure of Societies* (Princeton, 1966), I:11.

[6] Cyril E. Black, *The Dynamics of Modernization* (New York, 1966), p. 7.

[7] Dankwart A. Rustow, *A World of Nations* (Washington, 1967), p. 3.

ences in his fundamental attitudes toward and expectations from his environment. The contrast between modern man and traditional man is the source of the contrast between modern society and traditional society. Traditional man is passive and acquiescent; he expects continuity in nature and society and does not believe in the capacity of man to change or to control either. Modern man, in contrast, believes in both the possibility and the desirability of change, and has confidence in the ability of man to control change so as to accomplish his purposes.

At the intellectual level, modern society is characterized by the tremendous accumulation of knowledge about man's environment and by the diffusion of this knowledge through society by means of literacy, mass communications, and education. In contrast to traditional society, modern society also involves much better health, longer life expectancy, and higher rates of occupational and geographical mobility. It is predominantly urban rather than rural. Socially, the family and other primary groups having diffuse roles are supplanted or supplemented in modern society by consciously organized secondary associations having more specific functions. Economically, there is a diversification of activity as a few simple occupations give way to many complex ones; the level of occupational skill and the ratio of capital to labor are much higher than in traditional society. Agriculture declines in importance compared to commercial, industrial, and other nonagricultural activities, and commercial agriculture replaces subsistence agriculture. The geographical scope of economic activity is far greater in modern society than in traditional society, and there is a centralization of such activity at the national level, with the emergence of a national market, national sources of capital, and other national economic institutions.

The differences between a modern polity and a traditional one flow from these more general characteristics of modern and traditional societies. Political scientists have attempted various formulations of these differences. Perhaps the most succinct yet complete checklist is that furnished by Robert E. Ward and Rustow.[8] A modern polity, they argue, has the following characteristics which a traditional polity presumably lacks:

1. A highly differentiated and functionally specific system of governmental organization;
2. A high degree of integration within this governmental structure;
3. The prevalence of rational and secular procedures for the making of political decisions;
4. The large volume, wide range, and high efficacy of its political and administrative decisions;
5. A widespread and effective sense of popular identification with the history, territory, and national identity of the state;
6. Widespread popular interest and involvement in the political system, though not necessarily in the decision-making aspects thereof;

[8] Dankwart A. Rustow and Robert E. Ward, "Introduction," in Ward and Rustow, eds. *Political Modernization in Japan and Turkey* (Princeton, 1964), pp. 6–7.

7. The allocation of political roles by achievement rather than ascription; and
8. Judicial and regulatory techniques based upon a predominantly secular and impersonal system of law.

More generally, a modern polity, in contrast to a traditional polity, is characterized by rationalized authority, differentiated structure, mass participation, and a consequent capability to accomplish a broad range of goals.[9]

The bridge across the Great Dichotomy between modern and traditional societies is the Grand Process of Modernization. The broad outlines and characteristics of this process are also generally agreed upon by scholars. Most writers on modernization implicitly or explicitly assign nine characteristics to the modernization process.

1. Modernization is a *revolutionary* process. This follows directly from the contrasts between modern and traditional society. The one differs fundamentally from the other, and the change from tradition to modernity consequently involves a radical and total change in patterns of human life. The shift from tradition to modernity, as Cyril Black says, is comparable to the changes from prehuman to human existence and from primitive to civilized societies. The changes in the eighteenth century, Reinhard Bendix echoes, were "comparable in magnitude only to the transformation of nomadic peoples into settled agriculturalists some 10,000 years earlier." [10]
2. Modernization is a *complex* process. It cannot be easily reduced to a single factor or to a single dimension. It involves changes in virtually all areas of human thought and behavior. At a minimum, its components include: industrialization, urbanization, social mobilization, differentiation, secularization, media expansion, increasing literacy and education, expansion of political participation.
3. Modernization is a *systemic* process. Changes in one factor are related to and affect changes in the other factors. Modernization, as Daniel Lerner has expressed it in an oft-quoted phrase, is "a process with some distinctive *quality* of its own, which would explain why modernity is felt as a *consistent whole* among people who live by its rules." The various elements of modernization have been highly associated together "because, in some historic sense, they *had to* go together." [11]
4. Modernization is a *global* process. Modernization originated in fifteenth and sixteenth century Europe, but it has now become a worldwide phenomenon. This is brought about primarily through the diffusion of modern ideas and techniques from the European center, but also in part through the endogeneous development of non-Western societies. In any

[9] See Samuel P. Huntington, *Political Order in Changing Societies* (New Haven, 1968), pp. 32–37.
[10] Black, *Modernization*, pp. 1–5; Reinhard Bendix, "Tradition and Modernity Reconsidered," *Comparative Studies in Society and History*, IX (April 1967), 292–93.
[11] Daniel Lerner, *The Passing of Traditional Society* (Glencoe, 1958), p. 438.

event, all societies were at one time traditional; all societies are now either modern or in the process of becoming modern.

5. Modernization is a *lengthy* process. The totality of the changes which modernization involves can only be worked out through time. Consequently, while modernization is revolutionary in the extent of the changes it brings about in traditional society, it is evolutionary in the amount of time required to bring about those changes. Western societies required several centuries to modernize. The contemporary modernizing societies will do it in less time. Rates of modernization are, in this sense, accelerating, but the time required to move from tradition to modernity will still be measured in generations.

6. Modernization is a *phased process*. It is possible to distinguish different levels or phases of modernization through which all societies will move. Societies obviously begin in the traditional stage and end in the modern stage. The intervening transitional phase, however, can also be broken down into subphases. Societies consequently can be compared and ranked in terms of the extent to which they have moved down the road from tradition to modernity. While the leadership in the process and the more detailed patterns of modernization will differ from one society to another, all societies will move through essentially the same stages.

7. Modernization is a *homogenizing* process. Many different types of traditional societies exist; indeed, traditional societies, some argue, have little in common except their lack of modernity. Modern societies, on the other hand, share basic similarities. Modernization produces tendencies toward convergence among societies. Modernization involves movement "toward an interdependence among politically organized societies and toward an ultimate integration of societies." The "universal imperatives of modern ideas and institutions" may lead to a stage "at which the various societies are so homogeneous as to be capable of forming a world state. . . ." [12]

8. Modernization is an *irreversible* process. While there may be temporary breakdowns and occasional reversals in elements of the modernizing process, modernization as a whole is an essentially secular trend. A society which has reached certain levels of urbanization, literacy, industrialization in one decade will not decline to substantially lower levels in the next decade. The rates of change will vary significantly from one society to another, but the direction of change will not.

9. Modernization is a *progressive* process. The traumas of modernization are many and profound, but in the long run modernization is not only inevitable, it is also desirable. The costs and the pains of the period of transition, particularly its early phases, are great, but the achievement of a modern social, political, and economic order is worth them. Modernization in the long run enhances human well-being, culturally and materially.

[12] Black, *Dynamics of Modernization*, pp. 155, 174.

MODERNIZATION IN INTELLECTUAL HISTORY

This theory of modernization, as it emerged in the 1950s, contrasted sharply with the theories of historical evolution and social change which prevailed in Western thought during the 1920s and 1930s. The social theory of these decades was overwhelmingly pessimistic in its view of the future of man and society. Two schools of pessimism can be distinguished. One, typified by writers such as Oswald Spengler, Vilfredo Pareto, Pitirim Sorokin, and Arnold Toynbee, focused on the patterns of evolution of particular civilizations or cultures. They attempted to generalize sequences of the origins, growth, maturity, and decline of these great human societies. Theirs were, in essence, cyclical theories of history. The lesson applied to contemporary Western civilization was that it was at, or had passed, its zenith and that it was beginning the process of degeneration. The other strand of pessimism focused more exclusively on Western society. Its proponents tended to argue that Western society had earlier been integrated and conducive to human self-fulfillment. At some point in the past, however, a fundamental change had set in and Western history had begun a downward course. The breakup of human community, the attenuation of religious values, the drift into alienation and anomie, the terrifying emergence of a mass society: these were the products of secularization, industrialization, urbanization, and democratization. The processes which the 1950s viewed benevolently as modernization, the 1930s viewed with alarm as disintegration. Some authors dated the fall from grace with the Reformation; others, with the Renaissance, the industrial revolution, or the French Revolution. At some point, however, Western history went off the track, and a special process started. It began with the rejection of religion and the breakup of community and led consistently and irreversibly down the steep hill to mass politics, world wars, the purge trials, and Dachau. In some versions of this essentially conservative *Weltanschauung*, modern liberalism became only a "soft" version of the fundamental misconceptions which underlay communism and fascism. "In almost every instance," as Reinhold Niebuhr said, "the communist evil is rooted in miscalculations which are shared by modern liberal culture. . . ." "If you will not have God (and He is a jealous God)," agreed T. S. Eliot, "you should pay your respects to Hitler or Stalin." [13]

Other thinkers stressed the decline of religion less and the disintegrative effects of industrialization and democratization more. Some, like Karl Mannheim and Hannah Arendt, warned of the totalitarian tendencies toward mass society.[14] Those who were reluctant to trace the downward turn of the West back to the sixteenth or even the eighteenth century saw World War I as the turning point. At about that time, Lasswell argued, the trend of history was reversed "*from* progress toward a world commonwealth of free men, *toward* a

---

[13] Reinhold Niebuhr, *Christian Realism and Political Problems* (New York, 1953), p. 5; T. S. Eliot, *The Idea of a Christian Society* (New York, 1940), p. 64.

[14] Karl Mannheim, *Man and Society in the Age of Reconstruction* (London, 1940); Hannah Arendt, *The Origins of Totalitarianism* (New York, 1951).

world order in which the garrison-prison state reintroduces caste-bound social systems." In similar vein, Walter Lippmann started in 1938 to develop his argument that 1917 was the truly revolutionary year in which governments began to crack under the strains of war and upheaval and Western society began moving toward paralysis, chaos, and totalitarianism.[15] The secular pessimism of the interwar years reflected the perceived catastrophes and chaos of Western society brought about by the processes of industrialization, urbanization, and the like. The modernizing optimism of the 1950s and 1960s reflected the perceived social, economic, and political successes of Western society brought on by those same processes.

The modernization theory of the 1950s and 1960s thus contrasts starkly with the secular pessimism of the 1920s and 1930s. Its most striking resemblance is, instead, to the evolutionary optimism of a half century earlier. The social theory of the late twentieth century more closely resembles that of the late nineteenth century than it does that of the early twentieth century. Victorian styles of thought, like Victorian styles in furniture, suddenly acquired a new respectability in the late 1950s. The Great Dichotomy of tradition and modernity had itself, of course, received its most influential original formulations in Sir Henry Maine's 1861 distinctions between status and contract, in Ferdinand Tonnies' contrast between *gemeinschaft* and *gesellschaft* in 1887, and in Max Weber's discussion of traditional and rational sources of authority.[16] Similarly, many of the characteristics and consequences which the post-World War II theorists ascribed to the Grand Process of Modernization will be found in the writings of nineteenth-century writers such as Herbert Spencer and Karl Marx. In both cases, human society is seen as moving in response to essentially economic causes through an identifiable sequence of ever more beneficent phases.

The nineteenth-century theories of progress were discredited by world wars, economic collapse, political chaos, and totalitarianism in the first part of the twentieth century. Neither Social Darwinism nor Marxism provided an accurate key to the future. The question remains whether twentieth century theories of progress will be any more successful. Twentieth century social scientists have been as confident of modernization in the Third World as nineteenth century Marxists were of revolution in the First World. The latter were predicting the future by the extension of the past; the former are predicting the future by the transfer of the past. The failure of the one suggests caution as to the possibilities for success of the other.

The optimism of the Social Darwinists and Marxists of the late nineteenth century was rooted in the contemplation of the progress which Western

---

[15] Harold D. Lasswell, "The Universal Peril: Perpetual Crisis and the Garrison-Prison State," in Lyman Bryson, Louis Finkelstein, and R. M. MacIver, eds. *Perspectives on a Troubled Decade: Science, Philosophy, and Religion, 1939–1949* (New York, 1950), p. 323; and Walter Lippmann, *The Public Philosophy* (Boston, 1955), pp. 3–8.

[16] Sir Henry Maine, *Ancient Law: Its Connection with the Early History of Society and Its Relation to Modern Ideas* (London, 1861); Ferdinand Tonnies, *Gemeinschaft und Gesellschaft* (Leipzig, 1887); Max Weber, *Wirtschaft und Gesellschaft*, Part I (Tübingen, 1922).

society was making at that time and consequently looked forward to the future bliss of Spencer's industrial society or Marx's socialist commonwealth. It was an optimism of future progress. The optimism of the twentieth century theorists of modernization, on the other hand, is essentially an optimism of retroactive progress. Satisfaction about the present leads to an optimism about the past and about its relevance to other societies. The modernization theory of the 1950s and 1960s had little or nothing to say about the future of modern societies; the advanced countries of the West, it was assumed, had "arrived"; their past was of interest not for what it would show about their future but for what it showed about the future of those other societies which still struggled through the transition between tradition and modernity. The extraordinary acceptance of modernization theory in both Western and non-Western societies in the 1950s derived in part from the fact that it justified complacency in one and hope in the other. The theory of modernization thus rationalized change abroad and the status quo at home. It left blank the future of modernity. Modernization theory combined an extraordinary faith in the efficacy of modernity's past with no image of the potentialities of modernity's future.[17]

MODERNIZATION REVISIONISM

Modernization theory, like any social theory, thus suffered from a limited perspective deriving from its particular temporal and social origins. In addition, however, there were some logical and inherent weaknesses in the theory itself. In the later 1960s a small-scale corrective reaction set in which tended to pinpoint some of the difficulties of mainstream modernization theory. Among the theorists associated with modernization revisionism were Joseph Gusfield, Milton Singer, Reinhard Bendix, Lloyd and Suzanne Rudolph, S. N. Eisenstadt, and F. C. Heesterman.[18] Perhaps significantly, the empirical work of

[17] The late 1960s saw the emergence of "postmodern" theorizing, the leading scholars of which, however, had not been primarily involved in the analysis of the transition from tradition to modernity. These theories arose out of concern with the impact of technology on modern rather than traditional society. See Daniel Bell, "Notes on the Post-Industrial Society," *The Public Interest*, VI (Winter 1967), 24–35, and VII (Spring 1967), 102–18, and Zbigniew Brzezinski, *Between Two Ages: America's Role in the Technetronic Era* (New York, 1970). Both Brzezinski and Bell would probably assign many of the nine characteristics of modernization mentioned above to the transition from modernity to what follows. Both stand generally in the optimistic stream and in that sense share more with the modernization theorists than they do with the early twentieth century pessimists. More than the modernization theorists, however, both have been criticized by other writers who view with alarm the prospect of a postindustrial or technetronic society. Political scientists have yet to probe very deeply the political implications of this new historical transition.

[18] See Joseph R. Gusfield, "Tradition and Modernity: Misplaced Polarities in the Study of Social Change," *American Journal of Sociology*, LXXII (January 1966), 351–62; Reinhard Bendix, "Tradition and Modernity Reconsidered," *Comparative Studies in Society and History*, IX (April 1967), 293–346; Lloyd and Susanne Rudolph, *The Modernity of Tradition* (Chicago, 1967); S. N. Eisenstadt, "Breakdowns of Modernization," *Economic Development and Cultural Change*, XII (July 1964), 345–67, and "Tradition, Change,

many of these scholars focused on India, the twentieth century's most complex traditional society. The criticisms which these analysts made of the traditional theory of modernization focused on: (a) the meaning and usefulness of the concepts of modernity and tradition; (b) the relationship between modernity and tradition; and (c) the ambiguities in the concept of modernization itself.

In the first place, as many modernization theorists themselves pointed out, modernity and tradition are essentially asymmetrical concepts. The modern ideal is set forth, and then everything which is not modern is labeled traditional. Modernity, as Rustow said, "can be affirmatively defined," while "tradition remains largely a residual concept." [19] Dichotomies which combine "positive" concepts and residual ones, however, are highly dangerous analytically. In point of fact, they are not properly dichotomies at all. They encourage the tendency to assume that the residual concept has all the coherence and precision of the positively defined concept. They obfuscate the diversity which may exist in the residual phenomenon and the fact that the differences between one manifestation of the residual concept and another manifestation of the same concept may be as great as or greater than the differences between either of the residual manifestations and the more precisely defined other pole of the polarity. This is a problem common to many dichotomies; the concept "civil-military relations," for instance, suffers from a similar disability and one which has had a serious impact upon the understanding of the relationship between the military and the multifarious nonmilitary groups in society, whose differences among themselves often exceed their differences from the military.[20] Tradition is likewise simply too heterogeneous to be of much use as an analytical concept. The characteristics which are ascribed to traditional societies are the opposites of those ascribed to modern societies. Given the variety among nonmodern societies, however, obviously the "fit" of any particular society to the traditional ideal type will be haphazard and inexact at best. Pigmy tribes, Tokugawa Japan, medieval Europe, the Hindu village are all traditional. Aside from that label, however, it is difficult to see what else they have in common. Traditional societies are diverse in values and heterogeneous in structures.[21] In addition, the concept of a tradition as essentially changeless came under attack. Traditional societies, it was argued, are not static. "The view that tradition and

and Modernity," Eliezer Kaplan School of Economic and Social Sciences, Hebrew University; J. C. Heesterman, "Tradition in Modern India," *Bijdragen Tot de Taal-, Land- en Volkenkunde*, Deel 119 (1963), 237–53; Milton Singer, ed. *Traditional India: Structure and Change* (Philadelphia, 1959); Rajni Kothari, "Tradition and Modernity Revisited," *Government and Opposition*, III (Summer 1968), 273–93; C. S. Whitaker, Jr., *The Politics of Tradition: Continuity and Change in Northern Nigeria, 1946–1966* (Princeton, 1970).

[19] Rustow, *World of Nations*, p. 12.

[20] See Samuel P. Huntington, "Civilian Control of the Military: A Theoretical Statement," in Heinz Eulau, Samuel J. Eldersveld, and Morris Janowitz, eds. *Political Behavior: A Reader in Theory and Research* (Glencoe, 1956), 380–85 and "Civil-Military Relations," *International Encyclopedia of the Social Sciences* (New York, 1968), II: 487.

[21] See, especially, Singer, ed. *Traditional India*, pp. x–xvii and Heesterman, "Tradition in Modern India," pp. 242–43.

innovation are necessarily in conflict has begun to seem overly abstract and unreal." [22]

The concept of modernity also suffers some ambiguities. These stem from the tendency to identify modernity with virtue. All good things are modern, and modernity consequently becomes a mélange of incompatible virtues. In particular, there is a failure to distinguish between what is modern and what is Western. The one thing which modernization theory has not produced is a model of Western society—meaning late twentieth century Western European and North American society—which could be compared with, or even contrasted with, the model of modern society. Implicitly, the two are assumed to be virtually identical. Modern society has been Western society writ abstractly and polysyllabically. But to a nonmodern, non-Western society, the processes of modernization and Westernization may appear to be very different indeed. This difficulty has been glossed over because the modern, non-Western box in the four-way breakdown of modern-nonmodern and Western-non-Western societies has, at least until the present, been empty. Presumably, however, Japan is either in or about to enter that box, and it is consequently not surprising that a Japanese scholar should take the lead in raising squarely the issue of how much of modernity is Western and how much of Western society is modern.[23] How do two modern societies, one of which is non-Western, resemble each other as compared to two Western societies, one of which is nonmodern? (It should also be noted that non-Western is, like nonmodern, a residual concept: the differences between two non-Western societies may well be greater than the differences between any one non-Western society and a Western society.)

Other questions have developed about the relations between tradition and modernity The simpler theories of modernization implied a zero-sum relation between the two: the rise of modernity in society was accompanied by the fading of tradition. In many ways, however, modernity supplements but does not supplant tradition. Modern practices, beliefs, institutions are simply added to traditional ones. It is false to believe that tradition and modernity "are mutually exclusive." [24] Modern society is not simply modern; it is modern *and* traditional. The attitudes and behavior patterns may in some cases be fused; in others, they may comfortably coexist, one alongside the other, despite the apparent incongruity of it all. In addition, one can go further and argue not only that coexistence is possible but that modernization itself may strengthen tradition. It may give new life to important elements of the preexisting culture, such as religion. "Modern developments," as Heesterman has said, "more often than not go to strengthen tradition and give it a new dimension. To take a well-known example: modern means of mass communications, such as radio

---

[22] Gusfield, "Misplaced Polarities," p. 352.

[23] See Hideo Kishimoto, "Modernization versus Westernization in the East," *Cahiers d'Histoire Mondiale*, VII (1963), 871–74, and also Heesterman, "Tradition in Modern India," 238.

[24] Bendix, "Tradition and Modernity," p. 326, and also Whitaker, *Politics of Tradition*, pp. 3–15.

and film, give an unprecedented spread to traditional culture (broadcasting of Sanskrit mantras or of classical Indian music, films on mythological and devotional themes)." Tribal and other ascriptive "traditional" identities may be invigorated in a way which would never have happened in "traditional" society. Conversely, traditional attitudes and behavior may also help modernization: the extended family may become the entrepreneurial unit responsible for economic growth; the caste may be the group facilitating the operation of political democracy. "Traditional symbols and leadership forms can be vital parts of the value bases supporting modernizing frameworks." [25]

For all the ambiguities involved in the concepts of modernity and tradition, their rough outlines nonetheless appear possessed of comparative conceptual clarity when compared with the fuzziness which goes with the concept of modernization. In general, the writings on modernization were much more successful in delineating the characteristics of modern and traditional societies than they were in depicting the process by which movement occurs from one state to the other. They focused more on the direction of change, from "this" to "that," than on the scope, timing, methods, and rate of change. For this reason, they were more theories of "comparative statics" than they were theories of change.[26] The dichotomic developmental theories, moreover, were often ambiguous as to whether the phases which they posited were actual stages in historical evolution or whether they were Weberian ideal-types. As ideal-types, they were abstract models which could be used to analyze societies at any point in time. As historical concepts, however, the traditional category was presumably losing relevance and the modern category was gaining it. Inevitably, also, the dual character of the concepts undermined the conceptual dichotomy. Obviously all actual societies combine elements of both the traditional and modern ideal-types. Consequently, all actual societies are transitional or mixed. Viewed in terms of static ideal-types, this analysis presented no problems. One could still use the traditional and modern models to identify and relate the traditional and modern characteristics of any particular society. Viewed as a theory of history or change, however, the addition of a transitional category tended to exclude the traditional and modern stages from the historical process. Traditional society (like the state of nature) could only have existed as a hypothetical starting point in the distant past. A truly modern society would only exist if and when traditional remnants disappear in the distant future. Traditionalism and modernity thus cease to be stages in the historical process and become the beginning and ending points of history. But if all real societies are transitional societies, a theory is needed which will explain the forms and processes of change at work in transitional societies. This is just what the dichotomic theory failed to provide.

[25] Gusfield, "Misplaced Polarities," p. 352; Heesterman, "Tradition in Modern India," p. 243; Lloyd I. and Suzanne Hoeber Rudolph, "The Political Role of India's Caste Associations," *Pacific Affairs*, XXXIII (March 1960), 5–22.

[26] See Wilbert Moore, "Social Change and Comparative Studies," *International Social Science Journal*, XV (1963), 523; J. A. Ponsioen, *The Analysis of Social Change Reconsidered* (The Hague, 1962), pp. 23–25.

Beyond this, each of the assumptions which underlay the original, simple image of modernization could also be called into question. Contrary to the view that modernization is revolutionary, it could be argued that the differences between traditional and modern societies are really not that great. Not only do modern societies incorporate many traditional elements, but traditional societies often have many universalistic, achievement oriented, bureaucratic characteristics which are normally thought of as modern.[27] The cultural, psychological, and behavioral continuities existing within a society through both its traditional and modern phases may be significantly greater than the dissimilarities between these phases. Similarly, the claim that modernization is a complex process could be challenged by the argument that modernization involves fundamental changes in only one dimension and that changes in other dimensions are only consequences of changes in that fundamental dimension. This was, of course, Marx's argument.

Contrary to Lerner's view of the systemic qualities of modernization, it can be argued that the various elements of the modernization process are historically discrete and that, while they have their roots in common causes, progress along one dimension has no necessary relationship to progress along another. Such a view is, indeed, implied by rejection of the mutually exclusive nature of modernity and tradition. If these concepts, moreover, are thought of simply as ideal types, and "If we are to avoid mistaking ideal types for accurate descriptions, we must take care to treat the clusters of attributes as *hypothetically*, not as actually correlated." In addition, as Bendix went on to argue, a distinction ought to be maintained between modernization and modernity. "Many attributes of modernization, like widespread literacy or modern medicine, have appeared, or have been adopted, in isolation from other attributes of a modern society. Hence, modernization in some sphere of life *may* occur without resulting in 'modernity.' "[28] By extension, this argument also challenges the assumption that modernization is a global process. Modernization may be simply a peculiarity of Western culture; whatever changes are taking place in African and Asian cultures could be of a fundamentally different character and have very different results from those changes which occurred in Western societies.

The early assumptions about the timing and duration of modernization were also brought under criticism. The latecomers, it could be argued, can modernize rapidly through revolutionary means and by borrowing the experience and technology of the early modernizers. The entire process can thus be telescoped, and the assumption that there is a well-defined progression of phases—preconditions, takeoff, drive to maturity, and the like—through which all societies must move is likely to be invalid. Contrary to the common idea that modernization produces homogenization or convergence, it could be said that it may reinforce the distinctive characteristics of each society and thus broaden the differences between societies rather than narrow them. To the

---

[27] Bendix, "Tradition and Modernity," pp. 313–14; Gusfield, "Misplaced Polarities," pp. 352–53.

[28] Bendix, pp. 315, 329; Eisenstadt, "Tradition, Change, and Modernity," pp. 27–28.

contrary of the idea that modernization is irreversible, it could be argued that it is a cyclical process with major ups and downs over time or that a turning point in the process will eventually be reached where the "upward" secular trend of modernization will be replaced by a sustained "downward" trend of disintegration or primitivization. Finally, contrary to the view that modernization is a progressive process, it may be argued, as earlier twentieth century thinkers asserted, that modernization destroys the more intimate communities in which alone man can realize his full personality; it sacrifices human personal, and spiritual values to achieve mass production and mass society. This type of argument against change was very popular at times in the past. The relative absence of such a traditional, romantic opposition to modernization among theorists in modern societies and politicians in modernizing societies was some evidence of the extent to which the fever of modernization gripped the intellectually and politically conscious world of the 1950s. Nonetheless, by the late 1960s some opposition to and criticism of modernization along these lines were beginning to appear among intellectuals in many developing societies.

The Concept of Political Development

DEFINITIONS OF THE CONCEPT

Sharing the concern of other social scientists with the Great Dichotomy of modernity and tradition and the Grand Process of Modernization, political scientists in the 1960s began to pursue more actively their interests in what was variously called political modernization or political development. Their starting point was the concepts of tradition and modernity; eventually this essentially comparative and static focus gave way to a more dynamic and developmentally oriented set of concerns. This shift can be clearly seen in the work of the Social Science Research Council (SSRC) Committee on Comparative Politics and particularly of Gabriel Almond, its chairman and intellectual leader during the 1950s and early 1960s.

The volume which undoubtedly played the major role in first focusing the attention of political scientists on developmental problems was *The Politics of the Developing Areas*, edited by Almond and James S. Coleman and published in 1960 under the sponsorship of the Comparative Politics Committee and the Princeton Center for International Studies. The bulk of the book consisted of descriptions and analyses in terms of a common format of politics in five developing areas. The principal intellectual impact of the book, however, came from the introduction by Almond and, to a lesser degree, the conclusion by Coleman. This impact was very largely the result of their application to the politics of non-Western countries of a general concept of the political system. Almond used this framework to distinguish between "developed" and "under-developed" or "developing" political systems. Developed political systems are characteristic of modern societies and underdeveloped ones of traditional societies. Almond's concepts of "traditionality" and of "modernity" or, as he seemed to prefer, "rationality," are described in Parsonian terms derived from the central stream of sociological analysis. Almond's distinctive contribution in this respect, however, was the insistence that all political systems are culturally mixed, combining elements of modernity and tradition. "All political systems —the developed Western ones as well as the less-developed non-Western ones —are transitional systems. . . ." He was appropriately critical of some socio-logical theorists for promoting "an unfortunate theoretical polarization" in not recognizing this "dualistic" quality of political systems.[29]

The *Politics of the Developing Areas* is a work in comparative politics, not one in political development. This volume presents a behavioral and systems approach for the analysis of comparative politics; it does not present a concept or theory of political development. The phrase "political development" is, indeed, notably absent from its vocabulary. It is concerned with the analysis of the political systems of societies which are presumed to be developing (or modernizing) and the comparison of those systems with the political systems presumed to exist in modern societies. Its key categories are system, role, cul-ture, structure, function, socialization. With the possible exception of socializa-tion, no one of these refers to a dynamic process. They are categories essential to the comparative analysis of political systems; they are not oriented to the change and development of political systems. Almond posited a number of functions which must be performed in any political system and then compared systems in terms of the structures which perform those functions. "What we have done," he said, "is to separate political function from political structure." Almond also argued that, "We need dualistic models *rather than* monistic ones, and developmental *as well as* equilibrium models if we are to understand differences precisely and grapple effectively with the processes of political change."[30] In this book, Almond and his associates presented the elements of a dualistic model of the political system, but they did not attempt to present a "developmental model" which would contribute to the understanding of "the processes of political change."

For Almond that task came six years later with another major theoretical work coauthored with C. Bingham Powell, Jr. Unlike the earlier volume, this book was concerned with political dynamics and focused explicitly on political development as a subject and as a concept. Almond recognized the limitations of his earlier work in relation to the problems of political change. That earlier framework, he said, "was suitable mainly for the analysis of political systems in a given cross section of time. It did not permit us to explore developmental patterns, to explain how political systems change and why they change."[31] The earlier set of political functions (now called "conversion functions") was now

[29] Gabriel Almond, "Introduction: A Functional Approach to Comparative Politics," in Almond and James S. Coleman, eds., *The Politics of the Developing Areas* (Princeton, 1960), pp. 23–24.

[30] Ibid., p. 25.

[31] Gabriel A. Almond and G. Bingham Powell, Jr., *Comparative Politics: A Developmental Approach* (Boston, 1966), p. 13.

supplemented by categories which described more fully the demands and supports which operate on the "input" side of the political system and by categories which described the "output" capabilities of the political system in relation to its environments (extractive, regulative, distributive, symbolic, and responsive).

Political development, Almond and Powell argued, is the response of the political system to changes in its societal or international environments and, in particular, the response of the system to the challenges of state building, nation building, participation, and distribution. Political development itself was thought of primarily in terms of political modernization. The three criteria of political development were held to be: structural differentiation, subsystem autonomy, and cultural secularization. Almond thus came face to face with the problem which was gripping many other political scientists at that time: What is political development?

The answers to this question were more numerous than the answerers. Almost every scholar or group of scholars concerned with the politics of the developing areas had to come up with at least one formulation. Even to attempt to itemize them all here would be a tiresome and not particularly useful task. Fortunately, however, in 1965 Lucian W. Pye compiled a fairly comprehensive listing of ten meanings which had been attributed to the concept of political development:

1. The political prerequisite of economic development;
2. The politics typical of industrial societies;
3. Political modernization;
4. The operation of a nation-state;
5. Administrative and legal development;
6. Mass mobilization and participation;
7. The building of democracy;
8. Stability and orderly change;
9. Mobilization and power;
10. One aspect of a multidimensional process of social change.

In a noble effort at synthesis, Pye attempted to summarize the most prevalent common themes on political development as involving movement toward: increasing *equality* among individuals in relation to the political system; increasing *capacity* of the political system in relation to its environments; and increasing *differentiation* of institutions and structures within the political system. These three dimensions, he argued, are to be found "lying at the heart of the development process." [32] In a similar vein, another effort to generalize about definitions of political development found four oft-recurring concepts: rationalization, national integration, democratization, and mobilization or participation.[33]

---

[32] Lucian W. Pye, *Aspects of Political Development* (Boston, 1966), pp. 31–48.
[33] Samuel P. Huntington, "Political Development and Political Decay," *World Politics*, XVII (April 1965), 387–88.

This "quest for political development," in John Montgomery's phrase,[34] necessarily led political scientists to grapple with three more general issues. First, what was the relationship between political development and political modernization? The tendency was to think of political development as virtually identical with political modernization. Political development was one element of the modernization syndrome. Political scientists might disagree as to what types of change constituted political development, but whatever they did choose was almost invariably thought of as a part of the more general process of modernization. The principal dissent from this point of view came in 1965 from Samuel P. Huntington, who argued that it was highly desirable to distinguish between political development and modernization. The identification of the two, he said, limited too drastically the applicability of the concept of political development "in both time and space." It became restricted to a particular phase of historical evolution, and hence it was impossible to talk about the "political development" of the Greek city-state or of the Roman Empire. In addition, political development as political modernization made the former a rather confusing complex concept, tended to reduce its empirical relevance, and made it difficult if not impossible to conceive of its reversibility, i.e., to talk about political decay.[35]

A second issue which political scientists had to deal with in their definitional efforts was whether political development was a unitary or a complex concept. Since so many people had so many ideas as to what constituted political development, the prevalent tendency was to think of it as a complex concept. This tendency was explained or, perhaps, rationalized by Pye on the grounds that the "multi-function character of politics . . . means that no single scale can be used for measuring the degree of political development." [36] Hence, most scholars used several dimensions: Pye himself, as indicated above, suggested three; Almond also had three; Ward and Rustow, eight; Emerson, five; Eisenstadt, four.[37] This all seems very reasonable, since political development clearly would appear to be a complex process. Yet, obviously also, this approach can lead to difficulties. What are the relationships among the component elements of political development? Thus, although Pye argued that equality, capacity, and differentiation constitute the development syndrome, he also had to admit that these do not "necessarily fit easily together." On the contrary, "historically the tendency has usually been that there are acute tensions between the demands for equality, the requirements for capacity, and the processes of greater differentiation." In a similar vein, Almond argued that "there is a tendency" for role differentiation, subsystem autonomy, and secularization "to

[34] John D. Montgomery, "The Quest for Political Development," *Comparative Politics*, I (January 1969), 285–95.

[35] Huntington, "Political Development and Political Decay," pp. 389–93.

[36] Lucian W. Pye, "Introduction," in Pye, ed. *Communications and Political Development* (Princeton, 1963), p. 16.

[37] See Pye, *Aspects*, pp. 45–48; *Almond and Powell, Comparative Politics*, pp. 299 ff.; Ward and Rustow, *Japan and Turkey*, pp. 6–7; Rupert Emerson, *Political Modernization: The Single-Party System* (Denver, 1963), pp. 7–8; S. N. Eisenstadt, "Bureaucracy and Political Development," in Joseph LaPalombara, ed. *Bureaucracy and Political Development* (Princeton, 1963), p. 99.

vary together," but that the relation between each pair of these three variables "is not a necessary and invariant one." [38] Almond, indeed, presented a two-way matrix with secularization and differentiation on one axis and subsystem autonomy on the other. He found some type of political system to occupy each of the nine boxes in his matrix. The question thus necessarily arises: What does political development mean if it can mean everything? On the other hand, if political development is defined as a unitary concept, the tendency is either to define it narrowly—as Huntington, for instance, did in identifying it exclusively with institutionalization—and thus to rob it of many of the connotations and the richness usually associated with it, or to define it very generally, as for instance Alfred Diamant did, which in effect masks a complex concept under a unitary label. [39]

A third problem in the definitional quest concerned the extent to which political development was a descriptive concept or a teleological one. If it was the former, it presumably referred either to a single process or to a group of processes which could be defined, in terms of their inherent characteristics, as processes. If it was a teleological concept, on the other hand, it was conceived as movement toward a particular goal. It was defined not in terms of its content but in terms of its direction. As in the more general case of modernization, the goals of political development were, of course, valued positively. The definition of political development in terms of goals would not have created difficulties if there were clearcut criteria and reasonably accurate indices (e.g., the political equivalent of per capita Gross National Product) to measure progress toward those goals. In the absence of these, however, there was a strong tendency to assume that, because both scholarly analyst and, presumably, the political actors he was analyzing, wanted political development, it was therefore occurring. The result was that "Almost anything that happens in the 'developing' countries—coups, ethnic struggles, revolutionary wars—becomes part of the process of development, however contradictory or retrogressive this may appear on the surface." [40]

These definitional problems raised very real questions about the usefulness of political development as a concept. Referring to Pye's list of ten definitions, Rustow argued that this "is obviously at least nine too many." [41] In truth, however, one should go one step further. If there are ten definitions of political development, there are ten too many, and the concept is, in all likelihood, superfluous and dysfunctional. In the social sciences, concepts are useful if they perform an aggregating function, that is, if they provide an umbrella for a number of subconcepts which do share something in common. Modernization is, in this sense, an umbrella concept. Or, concepts are useful because they

[38] Pye, *Aspects*, p. 47; Almond and Powell, *Comparative Politics*, p. 306. For an intriguing analysis of some of these problems, see Fred W. Riggs, "The Dialectics of Developmental Conflict," *Comparative Political Studies*, I (July 1968), 197 ff.

[39] Alfred Diamant, "The Nature of Political Development," in Jason L. Finkle and Richard W. Gable, eds. *Political Development and Social Change* (New York, 1966), p. 92.

[40] Huntington, "Political Development and Political Decay," p. 390.

[41] Dankwart A. Rustow, "Change as the Theme of Political Science" (Paper delivered at International Political Science Association Round Table, Torino, September 1969), pp. 1–2.

perform a distinguishing function, that is, because they help to separate out two or more forms of something which would otherwise be thought of as undifferentiated. In this sense, manifest functions and latent functions are distinguishing concepts.

Political development in general is of dubious usefulness in either of these ways. To the extent that political development is thought of as an umbrella concept encompassing a multiplicity of different processes, as in the Almond and Pye cases discussed earlier, these processes often turn out to have little in common except the label which is attached to them. No one has yet been able to say of the various elements subsumed under the label political development what Lerner, at a different level, was able to say about the broader processes subsumed under the label modernization: that they went together because "in some historical sense, they *had* to go together." Instead, it is clear that the elements included in most complex definitions of political development do not have to go together and, in fact, often do not. In addition, if political development involves differentiation, subsystem autonomy, and secularization, as Almond suggests, do not the really interesting and important questions concern the relations among these three, as Almond himself implies in his conclusion? The use of the term political development may thus foster a misleading sense of coherence and compatibility among other processes and obscure crucial questions from discussion. To the extent, on the other hand, that political development is identified with a single, specific process, e.g., political institutionalization, its redundancy is all the more obvious. What is to be gained analytically by calling something which has a good name by a second name? As either an aggregating concept or a distinguishing concept, in short, political development is superfluous.

The principal function that political development has in fact performed for political scientists is neither to aggregate nor to distinguish, but rather to legitimate. It has served as a way for political scientists to say, in effect: "Hey, here are some things I consider valuable and desirable goals and important subjects to study." Such would indeed appear to be the principal function for the discipline served by the debates over the meaning of political development. This aspect of the use of the concept has perhaps been particularly marked in the arguments over the relation of democratization to political development and the perennial uneasiness faced by political scientists when they consider the issue: Is the Soviet Union politically developed? The concept of political development thus serves in effect as a signal of scholarly preferences rather than as a tool for analytical purposes.[42]

[42] Some people may say that people in glass houses should not throw stones on the grounds that I did, after all, argue that political development should be defined as political institutionalization in my 1965 article on "Political Development and Political Decay." My answer would be: true enough. But I do not mind performing a useful function by throwing stones and thus encouraging others to move out of their glass houses, once I have moved out of mine. In my 1968 book, *Political Order in Changing Societies*, which otherwise builds extensively on the 1965 article, the concept of political development was quietly dropped. I focus instead on what I conceive to be the critical relationship between political participation and political institutionalization without worrying about the issue of which should be labeled "political development."

The popularity of the concept of political development among political scientists stems perhaps from the feeling that they should have a political equivalent to economic development. In this respect, political science finds itself in a familiar ambiguous methodological position between its two neighboring disciplines. In terms of the scope of its subject matter, political science is narrower than sociology but broader than economics. In terms of the agreement within the discipline on goals, political scientists have more shared values than sociologists, but fewer than economists. Sociology is comprehensive in scope; economics is focused in its goals; political science is not quite one or the other. The eclecticism and diffuseness of sociological theory are excused by the extent of its subject. The narrowness and parochialism of economics are excused by the precision and elegance of its theory.

In this situation, it is quite natural for political scientists to borrow concepts from sociologists and to imitate concepts of economists. The sociological concept of modernization is, quite properly, extended and applied to political analysis. The concept of political development is created in the image of economic development. In terms of choosing its models, one might generalize, a discipline will usually tend to copy the more structured and "scientific" of its neighboring disciplines. This leads to difficulties comparable to those normally associated with the phrase "misplaced concreteness." Economists, it will be said, do differ over what they mean by economic development and how one measures it. These differences, however, shrink to insignificance in comparison with the difficulties which political scientists have with the term political development. If, on the other hand, political scientists had modeled themselves on the sociologists and talked about political change in imitation of social change rather than political development in imitation of economic development, they might have avoided many of the definitional and teleological problems in which they found themselves.

APPROACHES TO POLITICAL DEVELOPMENT

Many of the things that are often labeled studies in political development are not such in any strict sense. The study of political development is not the study of politics in societies at some given level of development. If this were the case, there would be few if any studies of politics which were not studies in political development, since those polities which are usually assumed to be developed are also presumably still developing. Yet not infrequently studies in the politics of less developed societies are treated as if they were studies in political development. Tunisia, it is said, is a developing society; therefore, its polity is developing polity; therefore, a study in Tunisian politics is a study in political development. The fallacy here is to look at the subject of the study rather than at the concepts with which that subject is studied. Depending on the concepts which were used and hence the questions which were asked, for instance, a study of John F. Kennedy's presidency might be a study in the uses of power, the institutionalization of an office, legislative-executive relations, consensus-building, the psychology of leadership, the role of intellectuals in politics. Or it could, conceivably, be a study in political development or political change. Exactly the same possibilities would exist for a study of Habib Bourguiba's presidency. There is nothing in the latter which makes it inherently more "developmental" than the former. Precisely the same is true for the innumerable studies of the role of the military, bureaucracy, and political parties in developing societies. More likely than not, these are simply studies of particular institutions in particular types of societies rather than studies in change or development. Depending upon the conceptual framework with which these subjects were approached, they could just as easily be studies in civil-military relations, organizational behavior, and political behavior, as studies in political development. They are the latter only if the categories employed are formulated in terms of change.

It could, of course, be argued that change is so pervasive that it is virtually synonymous with politics itself and that hence it cannot be studied as a separate subject. The rejoinder is that, to be sure, politics is change, but politics is also ideas, values, institutions, groups, power structures, conflict, communication, influence, interaction, law, and organization. Politics can be studied, and has been studied, in terms of each of these concepts. Each sheds a different light on the subject, illuminates different areas, suggests different relationships and generalizations. Why not also analyze politics in terms of change or development?

In fact during the 1950s and 1960s a variety of scholars did just that. Many different approaches were employed. Without making any claim to inclusiveness or to systematic rigor, it is perhaps useful to focus on three of these approaches: system-function, social process, and comparative history.

System-function

In the analysis of political development, a close relation existed between systems theory, in the strict sense, and structural-functional theory. It is, indeed, impossible to apply a functional approach without employing some concept of the political system. The varieties of theory encompassed in this general category are reflected in the names: Talcott Parsons, Marion Levy, David Easton, Gabriel Almond, David Apter, Leonard Binder, Fred Riggs. The principal contribution of these scholars has been to develop a set of concepts and categories, central to which are those of "system" and "function," for the analysis and comparison of types of political systems. Among their other key concepts are: structure, legitimacy, input and output, feedback, environment, equilibrium. These concepts and the theories associated with them provide an overall model of the political system and the basis for distinguishing types of political systems in terms of the structures which perform the functions which must be performed in all political systems.

The advantages of the system-function approach clearly rest in the generality of the concepts which it deploys on the plains of analysis. One problem of the approach for the study of political change is the defect of this great virtue. It is primarily a conceptual framework. This framework does not necessarily in and of itself generate testable hypotheses or what are often referred to as "middle level generalizations." Scholars using the framework may come up with such hypotheses or generalizations, but it is an open question whether the conceptual framework is not more of a hindrance than a help in this respect. The approach itself provides little incentive for scholars to dig into empirical data. Indeed, the tendency is in just the opposite direction. The theory becomes an end in itself. It is striking how few facts there are not only in general works, such as Levy's two volumes, but even in case studies attempting to apply the system-function approach to a specific society, such as Binder's study of Iran.[43]

A more fundamental problem is that this approach does not inherently focus on the problem of change. It is possible to employ the concept of "system" in a dynamic context, focusing on lags, leads, and feedback. In actuality, however, much of the theorizing on political development which started from a systems approach did not primarily employ these dynamic elements in that approach. The stress was on the elaboration of models of different types of political systems, not different types of change from one system to another. In his two-volume opus, *Modernization and the Structure of Societies*, Levy, for instance, is overwhelmingly concerned with the second element in his two-component title. The bulk of his work is devoted to discussing the characteristics of societies in general and then distinguishing between those of "relatively modernized societies" and of "relatively nonmodernized societies." The question of modernization and its political components gets short shrift in the first and last chapters of this 800-page work. As we noted earlier, Almond himself saw somewhat comparable limitations in the framework which he used in *The Politics of Developing Areas*. The much more elaborate and change-oriented scheme which he and Powell present in *Comparative Politics: A Developmental Approach* does not entirely escape from this difficulty. Among those works in the system-function tradition directly concerned with political development, David Apter's *The Politics of Modernization* has probably been most successful in bringing to the fore dynamic concerns with the rate, forms, and sources of change. Yet to the extent that he has done this, it has in large part flowed from his independent concerns with normative questions and ideologies, which are derived from sources other than the system-function framework which he also employs. The structural-functional approach, as Kalman Silvert has pointed out, was initially employed by social scientists interested in studying either very primitive societies (the anthropologists) or very complex societies (Parsons). It is an approach peculiarly limited in what it can contribute to the understanding of societies undergoing fundamental change. It is, moreover, rather ironic that political scientists should have seized upon this approach in order to study political change at the

---

[43] See Levy, *Modernization and the Structure of Societies*, and Leonard Binder, *Iran: Political Development in a Changing Society* (Berkeley and Los Angeles, 1962).

same time that the approach was coming under serious criticism within sociology because of its insensitivity to, and limited usefulness in, the study of change.

As has often been pointed out, a related difficulty in attempting to deal with change in this intellectual context is the extent to which the concept "equilibrium" also tends to be implicitly or explicitly linked to the system-function approach. The equilibrium concept presupposes the existence of a system composed of two or more functionally related variables. Changes in one variable produce changes in others. The concept, as Easton has pointed out, is closely linked with the ideas of multiple causation and pluralism. In addition, however, equilibrium also means that the variables in the system tend to maintain "a particular pattern of interaction." [44] In its pure form the theory conceives of equilibrium as a state of rest. In all forms it presupposes tendencies toward the restoration of an original condition or a theoretically defined condition of equilibrium.

Equilibrium theory has obvious limitations as a framework for exploring political change. As one sociologist observed, the theory "does not attend to intrinsic sources of change, does not predict changes that have persistent directionality (but only those that restore balance if that is disturbed), and thus does not readily handle past changes that clearly affect the current state of the system." [45] In effect, change is viewed as an extraneous abnormality. It is held to be the result of strain or tension, which gives rise to compensating movements that tend to reduce the strain or tension and thus restore the original state. Change is "unnatural"; stability or rest is "natural." Some thinkers have attempted to reconcile equilibrium and change through the concept of moving equilibrium. By itself, however, this concept is inadequate to account for change. If the equilibrium remains the same but is itself moving as a whole, the concept does not explain the cause or direction of its movement. If the equilibrium is itself changing, then moving equilibrium really means multiple equilibria, and again some theory is necessary to explain the succession of one equilibrium by another.

Social Process

The social-process approach to political development starts not with concepts of the social system and the political system but rather with a focus on social processes—such as industrialization, urbanization, commercialization, literacy expansion, occupational mobility—which are presumed to be part of modernization and to have implications for political change. The emphasis is on the process, not the system. The approach is more behaviorally and empirically oriented than the system-function approach, and it typically leads to the accumulation of substantial amounts of data, often quantitative in nature (surveys or aggregate ecological data), about these social processes

[44] Easton, *Political System*, pp. 266–67, 272 ff.; Harold Lasswell and Abraham Kaplan, *Power and Society* (New Haven, 1950), p. xiv.

[45] Moore, "Social Change and Comparative Studies," pp. 524–25.

which it then tries to relate to political changes. While the scholar working with the system-function approach typically attempts to impute functions, the scholar employing the social-process approach attempts to correlate processes. He may attempt to move beyond correlation to causation and to shed light on the latter through various techniques of causal or path analysis.

The scholars most prominently associated with this type of approach to political development and related questions in the 1950s and 1960s included Daniel Lerner, Karl Deutsch, Raymond Tanter, Hayward Alker, Phillips Cutright, and Michael Hudson. The two most important early works, which stimulated much of what followed, were Lerner's *The Passing of Traditional Society* (1958) and Deutsch's 1961 article, "Social Mobilization and Political Development." [46] The system-function scholar begins with a concept of the political system, then differentiates different types or models of political systems, and finally attempts to spell out the consequences and implications of these distinctions. His approach typically is concerned with linking a pattern of action to the system as a whole, i.e., identifying its function within the system, while the social-process scholar is concerned with relating one pattern of action to another pattern of action.

The great virtue of the social-process approach is its effort to establish relationships between variables and particularly between changes in one set of variables and changes in another. In this respect, it does focus directly on change. Its limitations in dealing with change are threefold. First, more often than not, the variables which have been used concern levels of development rather than rates of development. Since it is empirically oriented, the variables employed are shaped by the availability of data. Data on levels of literacy in different societies at the same time (i.e., now) are easier to come by than data on levels of literacy in the same society over time. The latter, however, are necessary for longitudinal analysis and the use of rates of change in literacy. While cross-sectional analyses may be useful and appropriate in studying some types of relationships, they are also frequently inferior to longitudinal analyses in studying other types of relationships. The difficulty of getting data on the changes in variables over time in most modernizing societies in Asia, Africa, and even Latin America has consequently led many social-process analysts back to the study of Western European and North American societies. Here is a clear case where knowledge of political change or political development is advanced by studying developed rather than developing societies. A related difficulty is the extent to which the social-process approach has been applied primarily to the comparison of national societies, which are often units too large and complex to be useful for comparative generalization for many purposes.

A second problem in the social-process approach concerns the links between

---

[46] Karl W. Deutsch, "Social Mobilization and Political Development," *American Political Science Review*, LV (September 1961), 493–514. For a suggestive effort to relate Almond, Huntington, and SSRC Comparative Politics Committee theories of political development to the available quantitative data, see Raymond F. Hopkins, "Aggregate Data and the Study of Political Development," *Journal of Politics*, XXXI (February 1969), 71–94.

the usually social, economic, and demographic independent variable and the political dependent ones. The problem here is the general methodological one of the causal relationship between an economic or social change (which is in some sense "objective") to political changes which are normally the result of conscious human effort and will. If the problem is, for instance, to explain voting participation in elections or the frequency of coups, how meaningful is it to correlate these phenomena with rates of economic growth, fluctuations in price levels, or literacy levels? The relation between the "macro" socioeconomic changes and "macro" political changes has to be mediated through "micro" changes in the attitudes, values, and behavior of individuals. The explanation of the latter is the weak link in the causal chain which is assumed to exist in most social-process analysis. To date, the most prevalent and effective means of dealing with this problem has been the various forms of the "relative deprivation" and "frustration-aggression" hypotheses utilized to relate socioeconomic changes to political instability.[47] Finally, at the dependent end of the causal chain, social process analysts often have trouble in defining political variables, identifying indices for measuring those variables, and securing the data required for the index.

One more general criticism which can be raised about the social-process approach concerns the extent to which it makes politics dependent upon economic and social forces. That the latter are a major influence on politics is obvious, and this influence is perhaps particularly important in societies at middle levels of social-economic modernization. In its pure form, which, to be fair, most of its practitioners rarely use, the social-process approach would leave little room for social structure and even less for political culture, political institutions, and political leadership. One of the great problems of the social-process approach to political change has been to overcome this initial deficiency and to find ways for assigning independent roles to cultural, institutional, and leadership factors.

Comparative History

A third approach to political development is somewhat more diverse and eclectic than the two just considered. Its practitioners share enough in common, however, to be loosely grouped together. They start neither with a theoretical model nor with a focus on the relationship between two or more variables, but rather with a comparison of the evolution of two or more societies. What "the system" is to the system-functions man and "process" is to the social-process man, "society" is to the comparative-history man. He is, however, interested not just in the history of one society but rather in the comparison of two or more societies. The system-functions man conceptualizes;

---

[47] Ibid.; James C. Davies, "Toward a Theory of Revolution," *American Sociological Review*, XXVII (February 1962), 5 ff.; Ivo K. and Rosalind L. Feierabend, "Aggressive Behaviors within Polities, 1948–1962: A Cross-National Study," *Journal of Conflict Resolution*, X (September 1966), 253–54; Ted Gurr, *Why Men Rebel* (Princeton, 1970).

the social-process man correlates; the comparative history man, naturally, compares. Among social scientists concerned with political development who would fit primarily into this school are Cyril Black, S. N. Eisenstadt, Dankwart Rustow, Seymour Martin Lipset, Barrington Moore, Jr., Reinhard Bendix, and, in some measure, Lucian W. Pye and the members of the SSRC Committee on Comparative Politics.

The work of these people tends to be highly empirical but not highly quantitative. They are, indeed, concerned with precisely those factors with which the social-process analysts have difficulty: institutions, culture, and leadership. Their approach is to categorize patterns of political development either by general stages or phases through which all societies must pass or by distinctive channels through which different societies may pass, or by some combination of these "vertical" and "horizontal" types of categories. Moore, for instance, distinguishes three patterns of modernization, under bourgeois (England, United States), aristocratic (Germany, Japan), and peasant (Russia, China) auspices. While he admits there may conceivably be a fourth way (India?), he is very dubious that this possibility will materialize. Consequently, every modernizing society will presumably have to find its way to modernity by way of liberal capitalism, reactionary fascism, or revolutionary communism. Cyril Black, on the other hand, starts by identifying four phases of modernization through which all societies pass: the initial challenge to modernity; the consolidation of modernizing leadership; economic and social transformation from a rural, agrarian to an urban, industrial society; and the integration of society, involving the fundamental reordering of social structure. He then specifies five criteria for distinguishing among societies in terms of how they have evolved through these phases and proceeds to classify all contemporary societies into "seven patterns of political modernization" on the basis of these criteria. He thus combines vertical and horizontal categories into a truly all-encompassing scheme of comparative history, and he very appropriately subtitles his book, "A Study in Comparative History." [48]

In a slightly different vein, Dankwart Rustow and the SSRC Committee on Comparative Politics have attempted to identify the types of problems which confront modernizing societies and to compare the evolution of these societies in terms of the sequences with which they have dealt with these problems. Rustow argues that there are three key requirements of political modernization: "identity is essential to the nation, authority to the state, equality to modernity; the three together form the political basis of the modern nation-state." [49] The critical differences among societies concern the extent to which they had to deal with these problems simultaneously or sequentially,

---

[48] Barrington Moore, Jr., *Social Origins of Dictatorship and Democracy* (Boston, 1966); Cyril E. Black, *The Dynamics of Modernization: A Study in Comparative History* (New York, 1966).

[49] Rustow, *World of Nations*, p. 36. For a thoughtful discussion of sequences in political development, see Eric A. Nordlinger, "Political Development: Time Sequences and Rates of Change," *World Politics*, XX (April 1968), 494–520.

and, if the latter, the order in which these problems were dealt with. On the basis of comparative analysis, Rustow suggests that the identity-authority-equality sequence leads to the most successful and least traumatic moderniza-tion. In a somewhat similar spirit and parallel endeavor, the SSRC Committee identified five crises which societies would have to deal with in the process of political modernization: identity, legitimacy, penetration, participation, and distribution. A rough equivalence presumably exists between these two efforts as well as that of Almond:

ALMOND—CHALLENGES	RUSTOW—REQUIREMENTS	CCP—CRISES
nation-building	identity	identity
state-building	authority	legitimacy, penetration
participation, distribution	equality	participation, distribution

Interestingly, the SSRC Committee originally had a sixth crisis, integration, which concerned the "problems of relating popular politics to governmental performance. . . ." [50] This, however, turned out to be a rather nebulous and slippery crisis to handle; eventually it was dropped from the scheme.

The great virtue of the comparative-history approach is that it starts by looking at the actual evolutions of societies, attempts to classify those evolu-tions into patterns, and then attempts to generate hypotheses about what factors are responsible for the differences in patterns. It starts, in short, with the "real" stuff of history, at the opposite end of the methodological scale from the system-function approach with its abstract model of the system. Nor does it, like the social-process approach, assume that certain variables, such as urbanization and instability, can be lifted out and generalized about indepen-dently of their context. This approach thus clearly lacks generality. In effect, it comes back to a focus on the historically discrete phenomenon of moderniza-tion, and it deals with particular phases in the evolution of particular societies. Like most "developmental" analyses, its concepts are "less generalized than those of equilibrium analysis." [51] In comparison to the system-function man with his conceptual complexity and the social-process man with his high-powered quantitative analyses, the comparative-history fellow often seems like a rather pedestrian, traditional plodder, whose findings lack theoretical and scientific precision. On the other hand, he is, unlike his competitors, usually able to communicate those findings to readers who will not read jargon and cannot read numbers.

Each of these three approaches has obviously contributed much to the study of political development. At the same time each has the defect of its

[50] See Pye, *Aspects*, pp. 62–67.
[51] Lasswell and Kaplan, *Power and Society*, p. xv.

virtues. From the viewpoint of a theory of political change, the system-function approach is weak in change, the social-process approach is weak in politics, and the comparative history approach is weak in theory. By building upon and combining the strengths of all three approaches, however, it may be possible to overcome the deficiencies of each.

Theories of Political Change

The study of modernization and political development thus generated concern for the formulation of more general theories of political change. In the late 1960s the analysis of political change became in itself a direct focus of political science work, quite apart from any relations it might have had with the social-economic-cultural processes of modernization or the teleological preoccupations which underlay much of the work on political development. In the course of a decade the work of political scientists moved from a generalized focus on the political system to the comparative analysis of modern and traditional political systems, to a more concrete concern with the discrete historical process of modernization, to an elaboration of related concepts of political development, and then back to a higher level of abstraction oriented toward general theories of political change. The transition from the static theory to dynamic theory, in short, was made by way of the historical phenomenon of modernization.

These new theories of political change were distinguishable from earlier approaches because of several characteristics. First, the theoretical frameworks could be utilized for the study of political changes in societies at any level of development. Second, these frameworks were either unrelated to the process of modernization or, at best, indirectly related to that process. Third, the variables and relationships which were central to the theories were primarily political in character. Fourth, the frameworks were sufficiently flexible to encompass sources of change and patterns of change in both the domestic and the international environments of the political system. Fifth, in general the theories were relatively more complex than earlier theories of political modernization and political development: they encompassed more variables and looked at the more extensive relationships among those variables.

One transitional approach was presented by Huntington in his 1968 volume on *Political Order in Changing Societies*. In this volume, the central focus of political change is held to be the relationship between political participation and political institutionalization. The relationship between these determines the stability of the political system. The fundamental source of expansion of political participation is the nonpolitical socioeconomic processes identified with modernization. The impact of modernization on political stability is mediated through the interaction between social mobilization and economic development, social frustration and nonpolitical mobility opportunities, and political participation and political institutionalization. Huntington expresses these relationships in a series of equations:[52]

1. $$\frac{\text{Social mobilization}}{\text{Economic development}} = \text{Social frustration}$$

2. $$\frac{\text{Social frustration}}{\text{Mobility opportunities}} = \text{Political participation}$$

3. $$\frac{\text{Political participation}}{\text{Political institutionalization}} = \text{Political instability}$$

Starting with a central concern of the social-process approach to modernization, i.e., the relationship between socioeconomic changes (urbanization, industrialization), on the one hand, and the political participation, political instability, and violence, on the other, this approach thus attempts to introduce into the analysis elements of social (mobility opportunities) and political (political institutionalization) structure.

Huntington is concerned with the relationship between political participation and political institutionalization. The source of the former is ultimately in the processes of modernization. What about the sources of the latter? Here he is less explicit. Implicitly, however, he suggests that there are two principal sources. One is the political structure of the traditional society. Some traditional political systems are more highly institutionalized than others (i.e., more adaptable, complex, coherent, and autonomous); these presumably will be better able to survive modernization and accommodate broadened patterns of participation. In addition, Huntington suggests that at particular phases in the process of modernization certain types of political leadership (aristocratic, military, revolutionary) and certain types of conflict may also produce institutionalization.

The relationship between political institutionalization and political participation, however, is clearly one that can be abstracted from a concern with modernization. The latter may be one major historical source of changes in participation, but it need not be the only one. The problem of balancing participation and institutionalization, moreover, is one which occurs in societies at all levels of development. The disruptions involving Negroes and students in the United States during the late 1960s could be profitably analyzed from this framework. In central cities and in universities, existing structures were challenged to provide new channels through which these groups, in the cliché of the times, could "participate in the decisions which affect them."

This theoretical approach, originally focused on the relationship between two political variables, could be extended to include more or different ones. One of the striking characteristics of much of the work on political development was the predominance of concern with the *direction* of change over the concern with the *objects* of change. This, of course, reflected the origins of political development research in the study of the transition from traditional to

[52] Huntington, *Political Order*, p. 55.

modern society. The first step in analyzing political change, however, is simply, as William Mitchell put it, to identify "the objects that are susceptible to changes." [53] It is to identify what are or may be the components of a political system and then to establish what, if any, relations exist in the changes among them. Such an approach focuses on *componential change*.

A political system can be thought of as an aggregate of components, all changing, some at rapid rates, some at slower ones. The questions to be investigated then become: What types of change in one component tend to be related to similar changes or the absence of change in other components? What are the consequences of different combinations of componential changes for the system as a whole? The study of political change can be said to involve: (1) focusing on what seem to be the major components of the political system; (2) determining the rate, scope, and direction of change in these components; and (3) analyzing the relations between changes in one component and changes in other components. The political system can be defined in a variety of ways and conceived of as having various components, as, for instance, the following five:

a. culture, that is, the values, attitudes, orientations, myths, and beliefs relevant to politics and dominant in the society;
b. structure, that is, the formal organizations through which the society makes authoritative decisions, such as political parties, legislatures, executives, and bureaucracies;
c. groups, that is, the social and economic formations, formal and informal, which participate in politics and make demands on the political structures;
d. leadership, that is, the individuals in political institutions and groups who exercise more influence than others on the allocation of values;
e. policies, that is, the patterns of governmental activity which are consciously designed to affect the distribution of benefits and penalties within the society.

The study of political change can fruitfully start with the analysis of changes in these five components and the relations between change in one component and change in another. How is change in the dominant values in a system related to change in its structures? What is the relation between mobilization of new groups into politics and institutional evolution? How is turnover in leadership related to changes in policy? The starting assumption would be that, in any political system, all five components are always changing, but that the rate, scope, and direction of change in the components vary greatly within a system and between systems. In some instances, the rate of change of a component may approach zero. The absence of change is simply one extreme rate of change, a rate rarely if ever approximated in practice. Each component, moreover, is itself an aggregate of various elements. The political culture, for instance, may include many subcultures; the political structures

[53] William C. Mitchell, *The American Polity* (New York, 1962), pp. 369–70.

may represent a variety of institutions and procedures. Political change may be analyzed both in terms of changes among components and in terms of changes among the elements of each component.

Components and elements are the objects of change. But it is still necessary to indicate what types of changes in these are significant to the study of *political* change. One type of change which is obviously relevant is change in the power of a component or element. Indeed, some might argue that changes in power are the only changes with which political analysis should be concerned. But to focus on power alone is to take the meaning out of politics. Political analysis is concerned with the power of ideologies, institutions, groups, leaders, and policies. But it is also concerned with the content of these components and with the interrelation between changes in content and changes in power. "Power" here may have the usual meaning assigned to it in political analysis.[54] The "content," on the other hand, has to be defined somewhat differently for each component. The content of a political culture is the substance of the ideas, values, attitudes, and expectations dominant in the society. The content of the political institutions of the society, on the other hand, consists of the patterns of interaction which characterize them and the interests and values associated with them. The content of political groups refers to their interests and purposes and the substance of the claims which they make on the political system. The content of the leadership refers to the social-economic-psychological characteristics of the leaders and the goals which they attempt to realize. And the content of policies, of course, involves the substance of the policies, their prescriptions of benefits and penalties.

The analysis of political change may in the first instance be directed to simple changes in the power of components and elements of the political system. More important, however, is the relation between changes in the power of individual components and elements and changes in their content. If political analysis were limited to changes in power, it could never come to grips with their causes and consequences. The recurring problems of politics involve the trade offs of power and content. To what extent do changes in the power of a political ideology (measured by the number of people who adhere to it and the intensity of their adherence) involve changes in the substance of the ideology? Under what circumstances do rapid changes in the power of political leaders require changes in their purposes and goals (the "moderating" effects of power) and under what circumstances may the power of leaders be enhanced without significant changes in their purposes? History suggests, for instance, that professional military officers can acquire political power in liberal, socialist, or totalitarian societies only at the expense of abandoning or

<hr>

[54] Major contributions to the analysis of power by contemporary social scientists include: Lasswell and Kaplan, *Power and Society*, pp. 74 ff.; Herbert Simon, "Notes on the Observation and Measurement of Political Power," *Journal of Politics*, XV (November 1953), 500–16; James G. March, "An Introduction to the Theory and Measurement of Influence," *American Political Science Review*, XLIX (June 1955), 431–51; Robert A. Dahl, "The Concept of Power," *Behavioral Science*, II (July 1957), 201–15; Carl J. Friedrich, *Man and His Government* (New York, 1963), pp. 159–79; Talcott Parsons, "On the Concept of Influence," *Public Opinion Quarterly*, XXVI (Spring 1963).

modifying the conservative military values.[55] In most systems, the enhancement of the power of an ideology, institution, group, leader, or policy is bought at the price of some modification of its content. But this is by no means an invariable rule, and a variety of propositions will be necessary to specify the trade offs between power and content for different components in different situations. One important distinction among political systems may indeed be the prices which must be paid in content for significant increases in the power of elements. Presumably the more highly institutionalized a political system is, the higher the price it exacts for power.

Political change may thus be analyzed at three levels. The rate, scope, and direction of change in one component may be compared with the rate, scope, and direction of change in other components. Such comparisons can shed light on the patterns of stability and instability in a political system and on the extent to which change in one component depends upon or is related to change or the absence of change in other components. The culture and institutions of a political system, for instance, may be thought of as more fundamental to the system than its groups, leaders, and policies. Consequently, stability might be defined as a particular set of relationships in which all components are changing gradually, but with the rates of change in culture and institutions slower than those in other components. Political stagnation, in turn, could be defined as a situation in which there is little or no change in the political culture and institutions but rapid changes in leadership and policies. Political instability may be a situation in which culture and institutions change more rapidly than leaders and policies, while political revolution involves simultaneous rapid change in all five components of the system.

As a second level of analysis, changes in the power and content of one element of one component of the system may be compared with changes in the power and content of other elements of the same component. This would involve, for instance, analysis of the rise and fall of ideologies and beliefs, of institutions and groups, and leaders and policies, and the changes in the content of these elements associated with their changing power relationships. Finally, at the most specific level of analysis, attention might be focused upon the relation between changes in power and changes in content for any one element, in an effort to identify the equations defining the price of power in terms of purposes, interests, and values.

A relatively simple set of assumptions and categories like this could be a starting point either for the comparative analysis of the more general problems of change found in many societies or for the analysis in depth of the change patterns of one particular society. It could furnish a way of bringing together the contributions which studies of attitudes, institutions, participation, groups, elites, and policies could make to the understanding of political change.

A somewhat different approach, suggested separately by both Gabriel Almond and Dankwart Rustow, focused on *crisis change* and also provided a

---

[55] See Samuel P. Huntington, *The Soldier and the State* (Cambridge, 1957), pp. 80–97 and *passim*.

general framework for analyzing political dynamics. Earlier theories of comparative politics and development, Almond argued, could be classified in terms of two dimensions.[56] To what extent did they involve an equilibrium or developmental models? To what extent were they predicated upon determinacy or choice? Reviewing many of the writers on these problems, Almond came up with the following classification:

Approaches to Comparative Politics

	Equilibrium	Developmental
Determinacy	I Parsons Easton	III Deutsch Moore Lipset
Choice	II Downs Dahl Riker	IV Harsanyi Leiserson

He then went on to argue that each of these approaches has its appropriate place in the analysis of political change. Change from one state to another can be thought of as going through five phases. In the first phase, an antecedent equilibrium can be assumed to exist, and for the analysis of this phase Type I and Type II theories are most appropriate. Change can be assumed to begin with the impact on the equilibrium of exogenous variables from the nonpolitical domestic environment or from the international environment of the political system. These Phase 2 developments produce changes in the structure of political demand and in the distribution of political resources, and can be most appropriately analyzed by Type III theories. In the next phase, political factors—the changing structure of political demand and distribution of political resources—become the independent variables. Political leadership manipulates these variables so as to produce new political coalitions and policy outcomes. For this purpose, Type IV "coalition theory and leadership skill and personality theory" are most useful. In the next or fourth phase, these policy outcomes and political coalitions produce cultural and structural changes. The relations in this phase require analysis by all four types of theories. Finally, a new "consequent equilibrium" emerges in Phase 5, which again can be studied in terms of Type I and Type II theories.

In formulating this theoretical framework, Almond once again played a leading and a representative role in changing thinking on comparative politics. Unlike his earlier formulations, this framework was precisely designed to deal with the problem of change and it was also clearly independent of any particular historical context. It was not tied in with modernization. It was instead a general framework for the analysis of political change which could be applied

---

[56] Gabriel A. Almond, "Determinacy-Choice, Stability-Change: Some Thoughts on a Contemporary Polemic in Political Theory," (Center for Advanced Study in the Behavioral Sciences, Stanford University, August 1969).

to a primitive stateless tribe, a classical Greek city-state, or to a modern nation-state. It encompassed both political and nonpolitical variables and recognized that each could play both dependent and independent roles. Perhaps most significantly, it effectively incorporated leadership and choice into a model of political change. All in all, it neatly synthesized several conflicting approaches to development and change in such a way as to capitalize on the particular strengths of each. The model was especially relevant to the analysis of intense changes of limited duration. Hence, it is not surprising that Almond and his associates applied it to the study of clearly delimitable historical crises, such as the Reform Act of 1832, the creation of the Third Republic, the Meiji Restoration, the Bolshevik Revolution, and the Cárdenas reforms of the 1930s.[57]

In a parallel endeavor, Rustow came up with a somewhat similar model.[58] Political change, he suggested, is the product of dissatisfaction with the existing situation. This dissatisfaction produces political action; political action, indeed, is *always* the result of dissatisfaction. This action either succeeds or fails. If it succeeds, the organization, movement, or other group responsible for the success either develops new goals or it withers and dies. If its effort for change fails, either the group responsible for the effort dissolves or it continues to pursue its old objective with decreasing expectation of ever achieving it. In addition, Rustow argues, the forces involved in the creation of a government or the conquest of power by a group or individual are very different from those which sustain the government or keep the individual or group in power over the long haul. A theory of political change has to account for and to systematize these differences. Thus Rustow, like Almond, puts a primary emphasis on the choices which have to be made by political leadership.

A third approach to the analysis of political change was developed by Ronald D. Brunner and Garry D. Brewer.[59] In their study of the political aspects of modernization, they developed a model of a *complex change* involving twenty-two variables and twenty parameters. Ten of the variables and eight of the parameters were disaggregated in terms of rural and urban sectors; three variables and three parameters constituted the demographic subsystem, nine variables and six parameters the economic subsystem, and ten variables and eleven parameters the political subsystem. The relations among these variables and parameters were expressed in twelve equations derived from general theories of modernization and from analysis of the evolution of Turkey and the Philippines from the 1940s to the 1960s. Their model included variables which could be directly influenced by governmental action and others

[57] For an initial application of the Almond model, see Wayne A. Cornelius, Jr., "Crisis, Coalition-Building, and Political Entrepreneurship in the Mexican Revolution: The Politics of Social Reform under Lázaro Cárdenas," (Project on Historical Crises and Political Development, Department of Political Science, Stanford University, July 1969).

[58] Dankwart A. Rustow, "Change as the Theme of Political Science," pp. 6–8. See also his "Communism and Change," in Chalmers Johnson, ed. *Change in Communist Systems* (Stanford, 1970), pp. 343–58, and "Transitions to Democracy: Toward a Dynamic Model," *Comparative Politics*, II (April 1970), 337–63.

[59] Ronald D. Brunner and Garry D. Brewer, *Organized Complexity: Empirical Theories of Political Development* (New York, 1971).

not subject to such influence. Using the model it is possible to calculate the probable effects on support for the governments (measured by the proportion of the population voting for the government party) and on the standard of living (measured by per capita consumption) of governmental policy changes —such as birth control programs producing a 5 percent decrease in the rate of natural increase of population, increases or decreases of 5 percent in urban tax rates, and changes in the relative preference accorded the urban and rural sectors in governmental expenditures. Alternatively, one policy parameter— such as governmental preference for urban and rural sectors—can be intensively analyzed to demonstrate how various degrees of change within it might affect dependent variables such as government support and standard of living.

The Brunner-Brewer approach opened up new horizons in political analysis. Theoretically, it provided a highly simplified but highly precise model of a political system encompassing a significant number of demographic, economic, and political variables, the relations among which could be expressed by equations. Practically, it pointed scientific inquiry in a direction which could ultimately provide policymakers with a means of analyzing the probable consequences of policy choices for outcomes directly relevant to their purposes. In effect, this model building introduced into political science the type of complex analysis of relations among variables which has long prevailed in economics. On the other hand, the Brunner-Brewer approach was limited by its initial theoretical assumptions and the relevance of those assumptions to the actual political systems to which the model was oriented. The twelve-equation model furnished a reasonably good guide to the interaction of the variables and parameters in Turkey and the Philippines during the 1950s and 1960s. Its relevance to the future was based on the assumption that the structure of the model and the magnitude of the parameters did not vary over time. The model provided ways of testing the consequences of major changes in governmental policy or major changes in other variables brought about by other means. It did not provide means for predicting major changes of the system unless or until these changes were reflected in significant changes in some variables in the model. Thus, the model could not predict a military coup bringing to power a radical, nationalist junta of officers. Once such a junta came to power the model might be able to predict some of the consequences of new policies they introduced. Its ability to do this would depend upon the continued existence of the relationships among variables which had existed in the past. The first goals of the revolutionary junta might be to change those relationships. Thus, the usefulness of the Brunner-Brewer approach was limited by the degree of discontinuity in the political system.

These various theories of componential change, crisis change, and complex change all tended, in one way or another, to liberate political analysis from the static assumptions which had limited it in one earlier phase and from the teleological concerns with modernization and development which had preoccupied it in a later phase. They indicated increasing parallelism between the study of political change and the study of social change. Most important, they were the very modest and first steps toward the formulation of general theories of political dynamics, the initial response to Rustow's challenge: "Aside from the refinement of evolutionary models and the more sophisticated use of historical data, is it not time to introduce some notion of change into our very conception of politics itself?" [60]

[60] Dankwart A. Rustow, "Modernization and Comparative Politics: Prospects in Research and Theory," *Comparative Politics*, I (October 1968), 51.

Modernization Theory and the Comparative Study of Societies: A Critical Perspective

Dean C. Tipps

Dean C. Tipps recognizes that writers employing the concept of modernization have exerted an important influence in calling attention to the interconnections among the diverse strands that make up societal transformation. He questions, however, whether it is a scientific concept in the sense that it offers the most adequate set of categories for understanding change in modern times.

While advocates of the concept will be inclined to take issue with a number of the positions advanced in this essay, it provides a valuable critique that both probes some of the weaknesses in writing on this subject and provides a reasoned analysis of a wide range of critics.

Use of the term 'modernization' in its present connotations is of relatively recent origin, becoming an accepted part of the vocabulary of American, if not international, social science only in the decade of the 1960s. Despite its relatively rapid rise to currency, the popularity of the term does not appear to be matched by any widespread consensus concerning its precise meaning. The proliferation of alternative definitions has been such, in fact, that the ratio of those using the term to alternative definitions would appear to approach unity. The popularity of the notion of modernization must be sought not in its clarity and precision as a vehicle of scholarly communication, but rather in its ability to evoke vague and generalized images which serve to summarize all the various transformations of social life attendant upon the rise of industrialization and the nation-state in the late eighteenth and nineteenth centuries. These images have proven so powerful, indeed, that the existence of some phenomenon usefully termed 'modernization' has gone virtually unchallenged. While individuals may differ on how precisely this phenomenon should be conceptualized and a number of critics have addressed themselves to the relative merits of

"Modernization Theory and the Comparative Study of Societies: A Critical Perspective" by Dean C. Tipps is reprinted with permission of Cambridge University Press from *Comparative Studies in Society and History*, XV (March 1973), 199–226.

Tipps is associated with the Department of Sociology at the University of California, Berkeley.

alternative conceptualizations, both critics and advocates alike tend to assume the basic utility of the idea of modernization itself, treating only the manner of its conceptualization as problematic.

In what follows an effort will be made to subject this assumption to a critical examination. 'The function of scientific concepts,' says Kaplan (1964: 52), 'is to mark the categories which will tell us more about our subject matter than any other categorical sets.' The issue posed here is whether or not the notion of modernization is capable of performing this function. What sort of problems beset current versions of the concept? Can these problems best be resolved within the framework of yet another version of the concept or are they such that the entire idea of modernization should be discarded in favor of some alternative approach? And if the latter possibility is to be seriously entertained, are there alternatives to the notion of modernization which do in fact promise to 'tell us more'?

My purpose here is to address the first two of these questions. The discussion is divided into two parts. As a preface to the subsequent analysis, the first section of the paper outlines some of the origins and characteristic features of modernization theory.[1] The core of the argument is presented in the second section. In order to obtain an overview of some of the problems raised by current usage of the concept, previous critiques of various formulations of modernization theory are reviewed, complemented where necessary, and codified, with the resulting codification serving as an analytical tool in the task of assessing the scientific usefulness of the modernization perspective.

I. Preliminary Considerations

THE ORIGINS OF MODERNIZATION THEORY

The proximate origins of modernization theory may be traced to the response of American political elites and intellectuals to the international setting of the post-Second World War era. In particular, the impact of the Cold War and the simultaneous emergence of Third World societies as prominent actors in world politics in the wake of the disintegration of the European colonial empires converged during this period to channel—for the first time, really—substantial intellectual interest and resources beyond the borders of American society, and even of Europe, into the study of the societies of Asia, Africa, and Latin America. During the two decades after the war, American social scientists and their graduate students, with the generous support of governmental and private agencies, turned increasing attention to the problems of economic development, political stability, and social and cultural change in these societies.

---

[1] The term 'modernization theory' is used throughout this paper simply to refer to that body of literature in which the concept of modernization is prominently featured.

A good portion of this attention was devoted to the elaboration of numerous conceptual schemes which in many respects served as surrogates for a tradition of inquiry into the problems of these societies which was almost entirely lacking (see Shils, 1963: 11–12; Schwartz, 1972: 74 ff.; cf. Nisbet, 1969: 240 ff.). Unable to rely for guidance in the design, execution, and interpretation of their research upon a previously accumulated literature, it is hardly surprising that social scientists engaged in this task should turn for assistance to the familiar intellectual traditions of Western thinking about the nature of social change. The influence of such received traditions is particularly evident in the case of modernization theory. Though their terminology may be somewhat novel, the manner in which modernization theorists tend to approach the study of social change in non-Western societies is deeply rooted in the perspective of developmentalism which was already firmly established in the conventional wisdom of Western social science well before the end of the nineteenth century. Indeed, Robert Nisbet (1969) has recently argued that this perspective —which may be traced to the idea that social change may be studied by analogy with the biological growth of individual organisms—has dominated Western thinking about social change from the Pre-Socratics through eighteenth- and nineteenth-century theorists of progress and social evolution to contemporary social science (see also Bock, 1964).

Within this tradition of thought, evolutionary theory and twentieth-century functionalism have been particularly influential in the shaping of modernization theory. Evidence of their influence may be found in many features of modernization theory: the frequent use of dichotomous type constructions and concepts such as 'social differentiation' and 'social system'; an emphasis upon the ability to adapt to gradual, continual change as the normal condition of stability; the attribution of causal priority to immanent sources of change; and the analysis of social change as a directional process. These attributes of modernization theory, it should be noted, are not simply remarkable parallels with earlier theories; many of the leading contributions to modernization theory have come from men such as Lerner, Levy, and Eisenstadt who have been schooled in functionalist theory and the intellectual milieu from which it emerged.[2]

SOME CHARACTERISTIC FEATURES OF MODERNIZATION THEORY

Beyond the very general sorts of attributes listed above, the task of identifying 'characteristic' features of modernization theory is not an easy one. The heterogeneous meanings which have been attached to the concept of modernization embody a wide range of substantive interests, levels of abstraction, and

---

[2] Some of the parallels between modernization and evolutionary theories are discussed in Mazrui (1968). Mazrui tends to overemphasize the impact of Darwinism on social evolutionism (on this point see Bock, 1964: 35–7; and Nisbet, 1969: 161–4). For a discussion of the influence of functionalist theory on contemporary comparative studies emphasizing the political aspects of modernization, see Collins (1968).

degrees of attentiveness to definitional problems. Still, since our purpose is not the piecemeal criticism of one or another version of modernization theory but the evaluation of modernization theory itself as a theoretical orientation or 'idea system,' an effort in this direction is essential to establish some common ground upon which the critique can proceed.

Two methodological similarities may be noted at the outset. The first is the search by modernization theorists for definitional inclusiveness. Modernization is generally taken to be, in the words of one author, 'a multifaceted process involving changes in all areas of human thought and activity' (Huntington, 1968a: 52). Accordingly, the concept tends to be a 'summarizing' rather than a 'discriminating' one, as every effort is made to specify its meaning in terms which are sufficiently general to avoid excluding any of the possible ramifications of this 'multifaceted process.' Attempts at definition are aimed more at telling us what modernization is (or might be) than what it is not (cf. Apter, 1965: 67; Black, 1966: 7; Smelser, 1967: 717–18; and Hall, 1965; a notable exception is Levy, 1966: 9–15, who carefully distinguishes the task of definition from that of description).

The second methodological similarity concerns the question of units of analysis. Though studies of modernization have focused upon many different levels, ranging in scale from the individual through local communities to national and international units, it is the national territorial state which is of critical theoretical significance, even if this does remain largely implicit. It is here at the national level that the various facets of the modernization process are seen to be aggregated. However it may be conceptualized, whether as industrialization, economic growth, rationalization, structural differentiation, political development, social mobilization and/or secularization or some other process, each component of the modernization process is viewed as representing a source of change operative at the national level, although it obviously may be studied at a variety of other levels as well. Even in the case of someone such as Inkeles (1969), who focuses upon individual responses to modernization in search of a cross-cultural personality syndrome of 'modernity,' these responses are aggregated and compared at the level of national units. Thus, theories of modernization are fundamentally theories of the transformation of national states (which are implicitly taken to be coterminous with the boundaries of whole societies).

There are, of course, other similarities which are readily apparent among various conceptualizations of modernization as well. However, as might be suspected from the introductory comments to this paper, the greatest areas of agreement tend to be on those points which are most superficial. Thus, there is general agreement that whatever else it may be, modernization is a type of social change which is both transformational in its impact and progressive in its effects. It is also generally viewed as extensive in scope, as a 'multifaceted process' which not only touches at one time or another virtually every institution of society, but does so in a manner such that transformations of one institutional sphere tend to produce complementary transformations in others (for a forceful statement asserting the systemic character of modernization see Lerner, 1958).

Beyond these generalities, the task of sorting out similarities and differences between alternative approaches becomes somewhat more difficult. Such is the variety of usages that they cannot be easily encompassed within the framework of a single classification. In some contexts, the concept is used primarily as a classificatory device, as when Levy (1966, 1967) distinguishes between 'relatively modernized' and 'relatively nonmodernized' societies on the basis of the extent to which tools and inanimate sources of power are utilized. For others, the concept identifies a peculiar and open-ended type of social change, as when the historian Benjamin Schwartz (1972: 76) draws upon Max Weber to define modernization in terms of the expansion of man's rational control over his physical and social environment (see also Hall, 1965: 21 ff.; and Rustow, 1967). Yet another orientation to the definition of modernization views it not as a type of change but rather as a response to change, as in definitions such as that of Halpern (1966) which stress the capacity of institutions to adapt to or control rapid and continuous change. Distinctions between usages such as these are often tenuous, however, particularly since alternative orientations are often combined within a single definition. Thus, Eisenstadt (1966: 43), for example, argues that modernization is characterized by two features, one a type of change (structural differentiation) and the other a type of response to change (the capacity of institutions to absorb 'continually changing problems and demands'). Much of this definitional variety may be traced to the constant search for more inclusive conceptualizations. Thus, while some associate modernization with industrialization or economic development and others define it more broadly to emphasize man's increasing control over his natural and social environment, still others, not to be outdone, speak of a total transformation of all aspects of human existence, ranging from individual personality to international relations.

There is, however, one distinction which can be made between usages of the term 'modernization' that is of particular importance because it establishes a basis from which the following critique of modernization theory can proceed. Most conceptualizations of modernization fall into one of two categories: they are either 'critical variable' theories, in the sense that they equate modernization with a single type of social change, or they are 'dichotomous' theories in that modernization is defined in such a manner that it will serve to conceptualize the process whereby 'traditional' societies acquire the attributes of 'modernity.' The approaches of Schwartz and Levy, cited above, represent two instances of 'critical variable' theories: for Schwartz, 'modernization' may be taken as a synonym for the process of rationalization, while in the case of Levy it is defined in terms of two technological indicators of industrialization. In fact, in an essay published well over a decade before his more recent works on modernization, Levy (1953) employed this same definition to define not modernization, but rather the term 'industrialization' (cf. Levy, 1966: 9). Another example of a 'critical variable' approach to the conceptualization of modernization comes from Wilbert Moore (1963: 89–112), who is somewhat more straightforward in this respect than Levy. Arguing that for most purposes modernization may be equated with industrialization, he then proceeds to discuss the former in terms of the conditions, concomitants, and consequences of the latter. As these examples illustrate, the distinguishing trait of 'critical variable' theories is that the term 'modernization' may be freely substituted either for or by some other single term. Perhaps it is because of this trait that the 'critical variable' method of conceptualizing modernization has not been widely adopted by modernization theorists.

Most modernization theorists have opted instead for the second method, choosing to set their definitions within the larger conceptual framework provided by the 'dichotomous' approach. Nowhere is the influence of nineteenth-century evolutionary theory more evident than here. Through the device of ideal-typical contrasts between the attributes of tradition and modernity, modernization theorists have done little more than to summarize with the assistance of Parsons' pattern variables and some ethnographic updating, the earlier efforts by men such as Maine, Tönnies, Durkheim, and others in the evolutionary tradition to conceptualize the transformation of societies in terms of a transition between polar types of the status-contract, *Gemeinschaft-Gesellschaft* variety (see Nisbet, 1969: 190–2). Modernization, then becomes a transition, or rather a series of transitions from primitive, subsistence economies to technology-intensive, industrialized economies; from subject to participant political cultures; from closed, ascriptive status systems to open, achievement-oriented systems; from extended to nuclear kinship units; from religious to secular ideologies; and so on (cf. Lerner, 1958: 43–75; Black, 1966: 9–26; Eisenstadt, 1966: 1–19; Smelser, 1967: 718; and Huntington, 1968a: 32–5). Thus conceived, modernization is not simply a process of change, but one which is defined in terms of the goals toward which it is moving.

II. The Critique of Modernization Theory

As noted in the introductory comments to this essay, individual approaches to the study of modernization have not escaped criticism. Unfortunately, however, such criticism has tended to be not only relatively infrequent, but partial in scope, widely scattered, and too often simply ignored. Still, these critiques, taken together, constitute a useful starting point. When systematized and supplemented where necessary, they provide the basis for a more general and thoroughgoing critique of the theoretical orientation embodied by modernization theory.

The task in this section, then, will be twofold: first, to codify the criticisms to which modernization theory is vulnerable and, second, to evaluate the implications of these criticisms for the future of modernization theory. To the extent that the criticisms leveled against modernization theory are valid, a choice must be made between two alternative courses. On the one hand, modernization theory might be reformed. This would require the formulation of yet another version of modernization theory, though hopefully one better able to meet the various objections which have been raised against earlier versions. On the other hand, the idea of modernization may be rejected in its entirety. This second, 'radical' option implies the need for the formulation of an alternative approach more suitable to the analysis of the sorts of problems which modernization theory is intended to address. While previous critiques have been overwhelmingly 'revisionist' in orientation, the purpose of this critique is to consider the future of modernization theory in the light of both of these two alternatives.

CRITICAL VARIABLE APPROACHES

The contrasting strategies of the 'critical variable' and 'dichotomous' approaches to the conceptualization of modernization invite somewhat different criticisms. The 'critical variable' approach will be examined first not only because it is less frequently adopted but also because it may be criticized in relatively brief and straightforward terms. The 'dichotomous' approach, on the other hand, because of the complexity of the issues it raises and because it is more representative of the 'mainstream' of thinking about modernization, will require a lengthier, more involved discussion.

The 'critical variable' approach, though infrequently resorted to, is not without its advantages. It avoids many of the difficulties of the 'dichotomous' approach by conceptualizing modernization as an open-ended rather than a goal-directed process and by defining it in terms which are relatively narrow and concrete, thus giving the concept greater operational clarity. Unfortunately, however, the 'critical variable' approach suffers from deficiencies of its own. When defined in relation to a single variable which is already identified by its own unique term, the term 'modernization' functions not as a theoretical term but simply as a synonym. To equate modernization with industrialization, for example, or with indicators typically associated with industrialization, adds nothing to the utility of the latter concept and renders the former redundant. The only effect of such terminological sleight of hand is to superimpose, and at the cost of a considerable loss in precision, a term ('modernization') heavily laden with conventional meanings on an otherwise relatively unambiguous concept. Once decoded, of course, research conducted under the rubric of 'modernization' thus conceived may be of considerable merit, but the rubric itself, which necessitates such decoding, is superfluous and can only detract from that merit. In short, when 'modernization' is employed as a synonym for some already relatively well-defined variable it performs no useful function and, as a consequence, should be abandoned. Thus, in so far as 'critical variable' theories are concerned, the second, 'radical' option must be exercised concerning the future prospects of modernization theory.

DICHOTOMOUS APPROACHES

Conceptualizations of modernization incorporating some version of the tradition-modernity contrast are less easily dismissed. In order to assess fully the implications of the criticisms which may be directed at theories of this sort, it is helpful to distinguish between three levels of criticism: the first level is ideological, the second empirical, and the third methodological or 'meta-theoretical.'

1. The Ideological Critique. One of the most frequently heard complaints against modernization theories in the dichotomous tradition is that they are the product of an essentially ethnocentric world-view. As modernization theorists began to adapt for their own purposes the dichotomous approach as it was developed by social evolutionists during the late nineteenth century, they did feel constrained to make certain changes. Not only were blatantly ethnocentric terms such as 'civilized' and 'barbarism' clearly unacceptable, but the explicit racism of the biological school of evolutionary theory had to be laid to rest. However, such changes were in many respects merely cosmetic. Though the language was changed and racial theories were discarded, modernization theorists have continued to be motivated by what Mazrui (1968: 82) has termed 'the self-confidence of ethnocentric achievement.' Thus, though the terminology of contemporary modernization theory has been cleaned up some to give a more neutral impression—it speaks of 'modernity' rather than 'civilization,' 'tradition' rather than 'barbarism'—it continues to evaluate the progress of nations, like its nineteenth-century forebears, by their proximity to the institutions and values of Western, and particularly Anglo-American societies.[3] The assumption upon which much of modernization theory is based is that, in the words of one author (Shils, 1965: 10), ' "modern" means being Western without the onus of dependence on the West.' By deriving the attributes of 'modernity' from a generalized image of Western society, and then positing the acquisition of these attributes as the criterion of modernization, modernization theorists have attempted to force the analysis of non-Western societies into what Bendix has termed 'the Procrustes bed of the European experience' (Bendix, 1967: 323; see also pp. 309–12, 316; and Rudolph and Rudolph, 1967: 6–8).

This attempt by modernization theorists to universalize historically specific values and institutions deriving from Western societies may be understood in part at least as a means by which fledgling students of the 'underdeveloped areas' could resolve the cognitive crisis they confronted as they turned their attention during the 1950s and 1960s to the task of attempting to comprehend the course of events in societies whose history, culture, and social organization appeared alien and unfamiliar. The dichotomous approach, as it gradually took shape in the tradition-modernity contrast, was admirably suited to fill this intellectual vacuum.[4] It provided the modernization theorist with a cognitive

[3] Thus, Nisbet (1969: 190–1) writes that 'the Comparative Method, as we find it in the writings of the nineteenth-century social evolutionists, and to a considerable degree at the present time, is hardly more than a shoring-up of the idea of progressive development generally and, more particularly, of the belief that the recent history of the West could be taken as evidence of the direction which mankind as a whole *would* move, flowing from this, *should* move.' See also *ibid.*, pp. 201–8, 284–7.

[4] Earlier theories in the dichotomous tradition fulfilled similar functions. See Bock (1964: 28–9). On this point, it is interesting to note that theories of modernization seem to be least popular among anthropologists, whose discipline has a longer, more intensive exposure to non-Western societies than other social sciences; this point is also supported by the widespread failure of modernization theorists to apply their perspective to the study of their own societies.

map consisting of familiar, stable categories derived from his immediate experience as a citizen of a 'modern' society, according to which data derived from 'relatively nonmodernized' societies could be gathered, sorted, and interpreted. Moreover, this map not only provided a set of categories for ordering the present of these societies, but by depicting modernization as an inexorable process of change in the direction of 'modernity' it provided a glimpse of their future as well, a glimpse made all the more comforting to the West by the assurance it gave that these societies would follow along its own familiar path to modernity.

However, the specific character of this perspective was shaped not only by the cognitive disorientation of modernization theorists as they explored their new subject matter, but also by their ideological commitments and presuppositions. As the dichotomous tradition was taking shape during the initial period of industrialization in Europe in the nineteenth century, the ambivalence of many Western intellectuals toward industrialism was reflected in a nostalgic sense of 'Paradise lost' that pervaded many characterizations of the traditional past, leading to romantic visions of a society in which, though materially poor and uneducated, people led simple, contented lives in harmony with nature and bound by strong affective ties into an intensive and cohesive communal existence (see Bendix, 1967: 294 ff.).

Although this view of tradition has continued to be of some influence, as is illustrated by the persistent tendency to dramatize the supposedly traumatic impact of modernization on the individual as it wrenches him from his idyllic traditional setting,[5] modernization theorists generally speaking have been animated by other considerations. By the mid-twentieth century the ambivalence toward industrialism which in many instances had tempered earlier versions of the tradition-modernity contrast had dissipated. Thus, contemporary versions of the contrast have been influenced less by a nostalgic view of tradition than by the self-confident optimism of modernization theorists to whom 'modernity' represented the very embodiment of virtue and progress, and 'tradition' merely a barrier to its realization. Characterizations of modernity in this vein have tended to be no less selective and romantic than earlier characterizations of tradition (see Lauer, 1971: 884–6). Consider, for example, the following eloquent declaration:

> 'modernity' assumes that local ties and parochial perspectives give way to universal commitments and cosmopolitan attitudes; that the truths of utility, calculation, and science take precedence over those of the emotions, the sacred, and the non-rational; that the individual rather than the group be the primary unit of society and politics; that the associations in which men live and work be based on choice not birth; that mastery rather than fatalism orient their attitude toward the material and human environment; that identity be chosen and achieved, not ascribed and affirmed; that work be separated from family, residence, and community in bureaucratic organizations; that manhood be delayed

---

[5] For recent evidence contradicting this hypothesis, see Inkeles (1969: 223–4), Lauer (1971: 882–5), Singer (1971), and Khare (1971).

while youth prepares for its tasks and responsibilities; that age, even when it is prolonged, surrender much of its authority to youth and men some of theirs to women; that mankind cease to live as races apart by recognizing in society and politics its common humanity; that government cease to be a manifestation of powers beyond man and out of the reach of ordinary men by basing itself on participation, consent, and public accountability (Rudolph and Rudolph, 1967: 3–4).

Combining strains of rationalism, progressivism, and libertarianism, statements such as this sound more like liberal utopias than analytical constructs; nowhere is found that ambivalence toward modern industrial society which characterized the writing of men such as Marx, Weber, and Durkheim (see Nisbet, 1966: 264–312; Hughes, 1958; and Huntington, 1971: 290–3; cf. Nisbet, 1969: 202 ff.).

Both the values and the cognitions embodied in modernization theory have been highly reflexive of the social and historical conditions under which they have been developed. The idea of modernization is primarily an American idea, developed by American social scientists in the period after the Second World War and reaching the height of its popularity in the middle years of the 1960s. Two features of this period stand out: a widespread attitude of complacency toward American society, and the expansion of American political, military, and economic interests throughout the world. American society tended to be viewed as fundamentally consensual, combining an unmatched economic prosperity and political stability within a democratic framework. Such social problems as might exist, moreover, were treated not as endemic but rather as aberrations which could be resolved by normal political processes within existing institutions. After two decades of turmoil, the postwar tranquility of prosperity and stability seemed no mean accomplishment. The future of modern society now seemed assured; only that of the 'developing areas' appeared problematic. Such an atmosphere of complacency and self-satisfaction could only encourage the assumption among social scientists that 'modernity' was indeed an unmixed blessing and that the institutions and values of American society, at least as they existed in their more idealized manifestations, represented an appropriate model to be emulated by other, less fortunate societies.

It is important to remember, however, that these attitudes themselves were occasioned only by a new concern with the role of the United States in the international sphere. While the imperial societies of Western Europe were confronted with reconstruction at home and decolonization abroad, the United States emerged from the Second World War at the height of its industrial and military strength. It also emerged from the war with a peculiar conception of world politics as a struggle between Good and Evil; if Hitler was the embodiment of evil during the War, then Stalin and Mao became its embodiment in the postwar era. Spurred on by this belief, by the encouragement of its European allies, and by its expanding economic interests abroad, the United States assumed leadership of the 'forces of freedom,' involving itself not only in the international but also the domestic affairs of scores of nations in its efforts to save the world from the menace of the Communist conspiracy and to secure a stable world order on terms favorable to its own political and economic interests.[6]

As decolonization proceeded in the face of emerging nationalist and revolutionary movements in the Third World, the acquiescence of Third World societies to these interests became increasingly problematic. As a result, these societies soon began to assume a significant place in the consciousness of American political elites both inside and outside the government as an arena of Cold War conflict. The rapid expansion of research by social scientists on Third World societies was in many respects a by-product of this new concern, as government agencies and private foundations encouraged and facilitated such research in order to expand the flow of information concerning these societies in the United States, and especially in official circles.

That ethnocentric theories of modernization should abound in this context is hardly surprising, especially if it is remembered that similar developmental theories were also popular during earlier expansionist periods in both English and American social history.[7] After all, by virtue of their underlying ethnocentrism, such theories are capable of providing an implicit justification for asymmetrical power relationships between 'modern' and 'traditional' societies since, whatever their other effects, they may be pointed to as advancing the cause of 'modernization' (see Nisbet, 1969: 201–12; and Rudolph and Rudolph, 1967: 9–12). Such an argument was in fact commonly offered to justify European colonialism. In keeping with the times and the liberal political persuasions of many modernization theorists, no explicit effort has been made to use modernization theory in this manner. Still, the idea of modernization has proven congenial to American policy-makers, so much so in fact that 'development' and 'modernization' came to be viewed as long-range solutions to the threats of instability and Communism in the Third World. Certainly, by virtue of its overriding concern with political stability, its often explicit anti-Communism, and its indifference to the entire issue of economic and political imperialism, there is little in the modernization literature that would seriously disturb White House, Pentagon, or State Department policy-makers.

This analysis should not be interpreted as suggesting that all modernization theorists are necessarily apologists of American expansionism. This is, of course,

---

[6] For an interesting discussion of American imperialism see Zevin (1972), who identifies three sources of expansionist-interventionist policies: relatively narrow but well-placed private economic interests, the military bureaucracy, and (ibid.: 358) the 'extension of successful domestic efforts at political, social, and economic reform.

The expanded international presence of the United States after the Second World War is reflected in the high level of military expenditures during this period. In contrast to the three decades after the Civil War and the two decades after the First World War when the percentage of the federal expenditures going to the military fell to less than 30 per cent of the national budget, in the two decades after the Second World War military expenditures averaged well over half of the budget—and this despite the expansion of the government's welfare functions in contrast to the earlier periods (Lieberson, 1971: 574).

[7] Thus, evolutionary theory reached the height of its popularity in England during the Victorian period, while widespread acceptance of Social Darwinism in political and intellectual circles coincided with the growth of imperialist sentiments in the United States at the end of the nineteenth century. See Burrow (1966) and Hofstadter (1955).

far from the case. Nevertheless, regardless of how well-intentioned or critical of American policy abroad a modernization theorist might be, the limited cultural horizons of the theory tend to involve him in a subtle form of 'cultural imperialism,' an imperialism of values which superimposes American or, more broadly, Western cultural choices upon other societies, as in the tendency to subordinate all other considerations (save political stability perhaps) to the technical requirements of economic development. On the other hand, the fact that some modernization theorists have applied their theories under the guise of scientific objectivity in the service of American national interests cannot be ignored. Thus, while condemning the critics of the Vietnam War for 'misplaced moralism' (as contrasted to the 'unwarranted optimism' of the American government), one modernization theorist could apply his theoretical perspective to the War to suggest that the answer to such 'wars of national liberation' is to be found in the forced concentration of populations in urban areas—a solution which clearly involves a number of moral choices of its own, a fact which the author conveniently chooses to ignore.[8]

I have discussed the ideological dimensions of modernization theory at some length because they are frequently touched upon only briefly or simply ignored. Once the relationship between modernization theory, the functions it performs, and the specific setting out of which it developed is understood, it is possible to place the theory in its proper perspective. Far from being a universally applicable schema for the study of the historical development of human societies, the nature of modernization theory reflects a particular phase in the development of a single society, that of the United States. Indeed, as the conditions which gave rise to modernization theory have changed—as, with the quickening pace of political assassination, racial and generational conflict, foreign war, and domestic violence, consensus has given way to conflict and complacency to concern about the future of American society—many of the fundamental values associated with 'modernity' such as those of rationality and progress have come under attack and, interestingly, the flow of new 'theories' of modernization also seems to have ebbed.

Essential as is the ideological critique to an understanding of the nature of modernization theory, however, it constitutes only the introduction to a critical evaluation of the utility of modernization theory. A critique limited to an analysis of the ideological elements which have entered into modernization theory cannot in itself provide an adequate basis for determining whether the notion of modernization merits further consideration or should be rejected in its entirety. There is in principle no reason to assume that the notion of modernization itself is inherently incompatible with a variety of ethnocentrisms or that a revolutionary or socialist version of modernization theory could not be developed. That much of contemporary modernization theory has been Western-centered, reformist, and bourgeois does not preclude the possibility of alternative formulations. Even if one were to suggest that the idea of modernization should be dropped entirely because of the distortions these

---

[8] See Huntington (1968b) and the exchange on this essay between Huntington and Noam Chomsky in Huntington (1970).

commitments introduce, whatever approach is substituted would be no less subject to these or other ideological distortions. The ideological critique of modernization theory is addressed to the motivations, cognitions, and purposes which gave it birth; it does not speak directly to the truth-content of the theory. While selective and distorted cognitions born of partisan commitments may be presumed to result in a disproportionate number of assertions which upon examination turn out to be false, incomplete, or misleading, this can be established in each case only by an appeal to the available evidence. Analysis of the ideological bases of modernization theory can help us to explain and predict its empirical shortcomings, but cannot confirm them. Thus, the ideological critique must be supplemented by other critical perspectives. This brings us to the second level of criticism, the empirical.

2. *The Empirical Critique.* Although this category has the appearance of something of a catch-all, the criticisms subsumed within it do share some important common ground in that each draws attention to some empirical inadequacy of modernization theory, in the form of either an erroneous or misleading empirical assertion that has been incorporated into its conceptual framework or of a critical range of phenomena which it has overlooked. Since the bulk of criticisms which have been directed against modernization theory have been formulated primarily at this level, the main points of the empirical critique are already fairly well developed and can be summarized relatively briefly.

Like other theories in the developmental tradition, theories of modernization have been criticized for viewing the transformation of societies as largely the result of immanent processes of change (e.g., Bendix, 1967: 324–7; Collins, 1968: 57–61; cf. Nisbet, 1969: 170–4, 275–82). Viewed in the context of the above analysis of the origins and ideological components of modernization theory such criticism is not entirely unexpected. By focusing largely upon variables relating to indigenous aspects of social structure and culture, modernization theorists have either underestimated or ignored many important external sources of or influences upon social change. Even modernization theorists such as Lerner, for example, who emphasize the role of the 'Western impact' in modernization tend to look at this 'impact' only in terms of its consequences for the diffusion of particular cultural attributes, ignoring the structural mechanisms of the interactions between societies. The limitations of this perspective are particularly evident when applied to the new states of Asia and Africa, whose emergence did so much to stimulate the development of modernization theory. Any theoretical framework which fails to incorporate such significant variables as the impact of war, conquest, colonial domination, international political and military relationships, or of international trade and the cross-national flow of capital cannot hope to explain either the origins of these societies or the nature of their struggles for political and economic autonomy— struggles, it should be added, which all societies face, though perhaps in varying degrees and contexts at different historical moments.

Other difficulties are raised by the notion of 'traditional society.' As Huntington (1971: 293–4) has recently noted, 'modernity and tradition are essentially asymmetrical concepts. The modern ideal is set forth, and then everything which is not modern is labeled traditional' (see also Rustow, 1967: 11–13). Thus, the notion of 'tradition' was formulated not upon the basis of observation but rather as a hypothetical antithesis to 'modernity.' This fact is reflected in a number of the empirical limitations of the concept. Take, for example, the conventional stereotype that traditional societies are essentially static. From the perspective of the tradition-modernity contrast, history begins with the transition from traditional to modern society. Since this transition is generally assumed to have begun in non-Western areas as a result of contact with European societies, this amounts to an implicit denial of the relevance of the pre-contact experience of these areas to their subsequent development. As knowledge of pre-contact history has increased, however, such a static image of traditional societies has proven untenable. In fact, 'traditional societies' appeared changeless only because they were defined in a manner that allowed no differences between traditions and recognized no significant change save that in the direction of the Western experience.

Since the tradition-modernity contrast focuses only upon the presumed similarities of traditional societies, moreover, it fails to allow for a multiplicity of traditions in a spatial as well as a temporal sense. Thus, social structures of the most diverse sort are thrown together in the same category, sharing little more than the label 'traditional' and the fact that they are not modern industrial societies. By thus ignoring the diversity of traditional societies, the dichotomous approach ignores precisely those differences between societies which contribute to the determination of the specific character of their development, as illustrated so well by Levy's (1953) classic contrast between the alternative courses of economic change in China and Japan (see also Rothman, 1961). Moreover, this diversity may be found within as well as between traditional societies. Clifford Geertz (1963: 155) comments in his essay on the 'integrative revolution' that 'a simple, coherent, broadly defined ethnic structure, such as is found in most industrial societies, is not an undissolved residue of traditionalism but an earmark of modernity.' While Geertz perhaps exaggerates the homogeneity of industrial societies, his basic point is a sound one: many 'traditional' societies are not highly integrated, socially and culturally homogeneous communities, but rather tend to encompass multiple 'traditions.'[9] Even to apply the adjectives 'traditional' and 'modern' to the same noun— 'society'—is misleading since it obscures the transformation of 'traditional' social and political units into national societies maintained by a territorial state. Indeed, the internal diversity of traditions is often compounded in the course of this transformation as a number of such 'traditional' units are consolidated into a single national society (see, e.g., Geertz, 1963; Kuper and Smith, 1969; and Harrison, 1960).

The colonial experiences of the new states pose an additional problem. Since the superimposition by conquest of one 'tradition,' albeit a 'modern'

---

[9] Benjamin Schwartz (1972) has argued recently that this is true of *both* sides of the tradition-modernity dichotomy. See also Lauer (1971: 884–6). For additional evidence on traditional societies see Gusfield (1967), Levine (1968), and Heesterman (1963).

one, upon one or more other 'traditions' produces a hybrid society neither 'traditional' nor 'modern' as these terms are usually employed by modernization theorists, these experiences can be assimilated to the dichotomous tradition-modernity contrast only with great difficulty, either by treating colonialism as an instrument of modernization—an argument, as noted earlier, which often has been asserted in order to legitimize colonial domination—or as a transitional phase between 'tradition' and 'modernity.' Neither solution is adequate. Like 'tradition,' colonialism may be conducive to 'modernization' in some contexts but in others it may constitute a barrier. Neither can the effects of colonial domination be dismissed as 'transitional' since their scope and duration are often just as significant as is that of pre-colonial conditions, particularly in those instances where colonialism endured for a number of generations (see Bendix, 1967: 323; Geertz, 1966).

Another set of criticisms has been directed against the notion that tradition and modernity represent two mutually exclusive, functionally interdependent clusters of attributes. This notion may be broken down into two constituent assertions: first, that the attributes of tradition and modernity are mutually exclusive and, second, that the attributes of each are functionally interdependent. Several critics of the first assertion have pointed to the persistence of many 'traditional' values and institutions in supposedly modern industrial societies and to the importance of these institutions in shaping the development of these societies, while others have argued that in both 'modern' and 'modernizing' societies the dynamics of modernization have consisted not in the substitution of one set of attributes for another, i.e., of 'modernity' for 'tradition,' but rather in their mutual interpenetration and transformation.[10] To assert that tradition and modernity are mutually exclusive is to impose, in the words of two critics, 'an imperialism of categories and historical possibilities' by artificially constructing an 'analytic gap' which denies the possibility of innovation, mutual adaptation, and synthesis (Rudolph and Rudolph, 1967: 6–7, *passim*). Once these possibilities are acknowledged, modernization can no longer be equated simply with the destruction of tradition, for the latter is not a prerequisite of modernization—since in many instances 'traditional' institutions and values may facilitate rather than impede the social changes usually associated with modernization—nor is it in itself a sufficient condition of modernization—since the destruction of 'tradition' as, for example, by colonial domination may lead in directions other than 'modernity.'

This brings us to the second assertion, that concerning the 'systemic' character of tradition and modernity. Generally, critics of the first assertion have also been critical of the second, for once it is conceded that modernity and tradition are not mutually exclusive then the notion that each constitutes a closed, functionally interdependent system of attributes is also open to question. Specifically, three implications of this notion have been attacked. The first is that those particular functional interdependencies observed in the transformation of Western societies will be recapitulated elsewhere, a notion

---

[10] For evidence on these points see Bendix (1967: 316, 324, 326), Eisenstadt (1968: 40–52), Gusfield (1967), Huntington (1971: 295–6), Lauer (1971: 885–6), Whitacker (1967), Rothman (1961), Heesterman (1963), Singer (1971), and Khare (1971).

which strongly implies, moreover, acceptance of the 'convergence' thesis t.... as modernization proceeds societies will become increasingly alike in their essential characteristics. Against these ideas it has been argued that because of differences in their starting points—i.e. in their 'traditional' institutions and values—and in the timing of their transformations, many of the institutional configurations which characterized the modernization of Western societies are unlikely to be duplicated in the subsequent modernization of other societies. At the level of technology, there is no need to recapitulate the stages of techno- logical development in the advanced societies since the latest technologies lie ready for adoption. Moreover, the size of the gap between modern and non- modern societies and the availability of a variety of models of modernity create conditions which, when combined with the unique heritage of each society, make the reproduction of Western institutional patterns in the modernization process most unlikely. To ignore differences such as these in the setting of modernization is to risk an undue generalization of the particularities of the Western experience and to overlook diversity in the search for convergence (see Bendix, 1963 and 1967: 327–35; Huntington, 1971: 298; Lauer, 1971: 884–6; Gerschenkron, 1962: 3–51, 353–64; and Weinberg, 1969).

The last two implications derived from the assertion of the systemic character of modernization are closely related. They hold that (1) the attributes of modernity form a 'package,' thus tending to appear as a cluster rather than in isolation, and, consequently, that (2) modernization in one sphere will necessarily produce compatible ('eurhythmic') changes in other spheres. Critics of these assertions have argued that, on the contrary, the attributes of modernity do not necessarily appear as a 'package.' Rather, its attributes may be 'unbundled' and absorbed selectively. Moreover, as Bendix (1967: 329, 316) has observed, such piecemeal 'modernization' need not lead to 'modernity.' Modern medicine, the transistor radio, and a modern military establishment are all instances of 'modernization' in the sense that each represents a case of the acquisition of a trait or set of traits associated with modernity. However, whether or not such 'modernization' implies eventual acquisition of the entire 'package' of modernity is problematic. Indeed, the introduction of modern medicine may only compound poverty by increasing population pressures, the transistor radio may be employed merely to reinforce traditional values, and a technologically sophisticated military may be placed in the service of the most reactionary of regimes. Thus, such selective modernization may only strengthen traditional institutions and values, and rapid social change in one sphere may serve only to inhibit change in others.[11]

Taken together, the critics of modernization theory have marshalled an impressive array of argument and evidence revealing the inadequacies of modernization theory's view of the nature of tradition and modernity, their dynamics and interrelationships. Moreover, these limitations, which have been argued largely on empirical grounds, tend to confirm the prediction made at

---

[11] This point is made by a number of the authors cited above in note 10. Political scientists have come increasingly to accept the view that 'modernization' is negatively correlated with the creation of stable political institutions. Perhaps the most influential advocate of this position is Huntington (1965; 1968a).

the conclusion of the ideological critique to the effect that the ideological distortions of modernization theory should be reflected in its empirical limitations. Thus, in one way or another, each point in the empirical critique may be related to some manifestation of the fundamental ethnocentrism of modernization theory in its conception of history as a unilinear process of progressive change toward a model of modernity patterned after a rather utopian image of 'Western' society. Indeed, the empirical critique strongly suggests that in its approach to the notion of 'tradition' and 'traditional' societies modernization theory is not only ethnocentric but temperocentric as well.

What implications concerning the future of modernization theory are to be drawn from the cumulative weight of these critiques? Should the appropriate response be sought in some form of 'revisionism' designed to retain the idea of modernization in the context of some new, more empirically grounded framework, or should a 'radical' solution be opted for which would simply reject the notion of modernization in its entirety? Among critics who have challenged modernization theory on empirical grounds, each of these alternatives has its advocates. However, the first, 'revisionist' option has proven by far the most popular, with critics such as Bendix, Eisenstadt, Huntington, and others continuing to see, even if only implicitly in some cases, sufficient utility in the idea of modernization and the tradition-modernity contrast to warrant their continued use upon suitable reformulation. By way of contrast, only Whitacker from among these critics has argued explicitly that the entire notion of modernization should be abandoned.

To those who would opt for the revisionist alternative, the question is simply one of eliminating some of the more glaring deficiencies of present theories. As a result, they argue for approaches to modernization which avoid dubious assumptions concerning the nature of traditional institutions and their contribution to the modernization process, which incorporate 'external stimuli' as significant variables, which view modernization as essentially multilinear, and which emphasize discontinuities as well as functional relationships in modernization (see, e.g. Bendix, 1967; Eisenstadt, 1968). Whitacker, however, is far less sanguine concerning the future prospects of modernization theory. In his view, if modernization is not an all-or-nothing process, i.e., if it does not either displace tradition or fail, then the entire idea should be rejected. Moreover, to argue that tradition and modernity are not mutually exclusive categories, he contends (Whitacker, 1967; 190–2), is 'to nullify the supposed significance of the terms, namely, that they identify distinguishable classes of societies.' Noting that 'there remains a paucity of comparably developed models,' Whitacker (1967: 201–2) suggests that the formulation of relatively limited, empirically grounded generalizations is more useful for the present than attempting to construct alternative models at the same level of abstraction as modernization theory.[12]

12 However, it should be noted that the suggestion that research should concentrate on establishing limited-range empirical generalizations hardly constitutes a very promising alternative to modernization theory. The task of explaining the transformation of macro-level social structures cannot be accomplished simply by summarizing or accumulating the results of micro-level research. Moreover, such generalizations cannot be 'established' between societies in the absence of some larger framework of comparison.

Upon reflection, neither the position of the revisionists nor that of Whitacker can be accepted. The essential difficulty with the revisionist position is that it ignores the fundamental issue because it fails to seriously question the usefulness of the modernization perspective. In this respect, Whitacker's position represents an important advance over that of the revisionists. However, the underlying rationale of his position is open to question. As revisionists such as Bendix, Eisenstadt, and others have demonstrated, the notion of modernization cannot be rejected simply by showing that particular assumptions or hypotheses incorporated into modernization theory are false or misleading. Clearly, the cumulative weight of the ideological and empirical critiques provides strong presumptive evidence that Whitacker's conclusion may be correct, that the usefulness of the modernization theory approach is questionable, to say the least. However, these critiques fail to specify whether its lack of utility is inherent in the notion of modernization itself or, rather, attributable to the inability to discover an appropriate framework for its analysis—a conclusion which would support the revisionist position. So long as this latter possibility may be seriously entertained, definitions, type constructions, and 'theories' of modernization are likely to proliferate endlessly and, like the mythological Hydra, every 'theory' of modernization attacked and destroyed will only raise two in its place.

3. *The Metatheoretical Critique.* The final critique is methodological, or 'metatheoretical' in the sense that it focuses upon the underlying strategy of conceptualization involved in modernization theory and its usefulness. Thus, it focuses directly upon the central issue raised by the choice between the revisionist and radical alternatives. In spite of its importance, however, this level of criticism has been less thoroughly explored than the previous two.

In the definition of any concept or set of concepts there is a perennial tension between the logical requirements of comparability and those of explanation, the first straining in the direction of increasing generality in order to extend the range of the concept's applicability to larger numbers of cases, the latter in the opposite direction of an increasing specificity which enhances its powers of discrimination. As noted earlier, modernization theorists have chosen to resolve this tension in the former direction. In their effort to achieve descriptive inclusiveness, however, they have relied upon conceptualizations of modernization which are both unparsimonious and vague. Rather than specifying the minimum conditions necessary for the appropriate application of the term, modernization theorists have attempted to encompass within a single concept virtually every 'progressive' social change since the seventeenth century. Moreover, to obtain this end, they have defined modernization in terms which are so open-ended that it is almost impossible to identify precisely the range of phenomena to which the concept is intended to apply.

These difficulties become all too evident when one considers the possibility of arriving at something approximating a theory of modernization. When the concept of modernization is defined as referring to the adaptation of institutions 'to the unprecedented increase in man's knowledge permitting control over his environment, that accompanied the scientific revolution' (Black, 1966: 7) or to 'the fact that technical, economic, and ecological changes ramify through the whole social and culture fabric' (Smelser, 1967: 717–18), it becomes very difficult to specify the limits of its applicability and, thus, to identify just what it is that an explanation of modernization would explain. Moreover, when modernization is seen as 'a multifaceted process involving changes in all areas of human thought and activity' (Huntington, 1968a: 32), the very comprehensiveness of the definition serves only to reduce theoretical statements to meaningless tautologies.[13]

There is, moreover, a certain amount of irony in the lengths to which modernization theorists have gone in their search for descriptive inclusiveness since, all the pretension of the theory to the contrary, it has done remarkably little to stimulate or facilitate the actual comparative study of societies. The reason for this is not hard to find; indeed, it has already been touched upon in the previous section of this paper: in their preoccupation with the attributes distinguishing the 'traditional' from the 'modern' modernization theorists have failed to consider the attributes of the noun to which these adjectives are applied, viz., 'society.' As a result, the empirical referents of the term tend to vary according to the side of the dichotomy under consideration. At the 'modern' end the typical referent is, as noted earlier, the national society as defined by the boundaries of the territorial state. On the 'traditional' side, however, the residual nature of the category is reflected in a variety of referents including civilizations, culture areas, empires, kingdoms, and tribes. Since the first requirement of comparative analysis is that the entities being compared be of the same domain or universe of discourse (Kalleberg, 1966: 75–6; Hempel, 1965: 137 ff.), the failure to specify a common set of operational criteria for application of the term 'society' imposes severe limitations upon the utility of the ideas of 'traditional society' and 'modern society' as comparative concepts. As they are currently employed in the literature, not only are comparisons between these two types ruled out but, to the extent the term 'society' in each of these concepts itself lacks a common set of empirical referents, comparisons within each type are precluded as well.

Yet another fundamental metatheoretical defect of modernization theory involves neither problems of definition nor of comparability, but rather the tendency to mistake concept for fact; indeed, the former difficulties are in many respects merely symptoms of the latter. This tendency, of course, is not unique to modernization theory; Nisbet (1969: 240 ff.) argues that it has been characteristic of all developmental theories of change. Nor can it be said that this defect has been recognized only recently. Over three quarters of a century ago Emile Durkheim condemned this very tendency, noting how easy it is for the social scientist to become caught up in the study of his own ideas and images while losing sight of their relation to observable social phenomena. Writing in *The Rules of Sociological Method*, Durkheim (1938: 14–5) discussed this

---

[13] Much the same point has been made by Levy (1966: 10–11). It should also be noted that another important consequence of the revisionist position is that modernization theory has become increasingly conceptual rather than theoretical in its orientation as more 'open,' indeterminate assumptions and hypotheses have been substituted for the more determinate but empirically dubious ones of earlier versions.

tendency to substitute the study of concepts for the study of social phenomena in these characteristic terms:

> Man cannot live in an environment without forming some ideas about it according to which he regulates his behavior. But, because these ideas are nearer to us and more within our mental reach than the realities to which they correspond, we tend naturally to substitute them for the latter and to make them the very subject of our speculations. Instead of observing, describing, and comparing things, we are content to focus our consciousness upon, to analyze, and to combine our ideas. Instead of a science concerned with realities, we produce no more than an ideological analysis.
>
> . . . These ideas or concepts, whatever name one gives them, are not legitimate substitutes for things. Products of everyday experience, their primary function is to put our actions in harmony with our environment; they are created by experience and for it. Now, a representation may successfully fulfil this function while theoretically false. Several centuries have elapsed since Copernicus dissipated the illusions of the senses concerning the movements of heavenly bodies; and yet we still habitually regulate our time according to these illusions. In order to invoke the reaction required by the nature of a certain stimulus, an idea need not express that nature faithfully. . . . In fact, many times [these ideas] are as dangerously incorrect as they are inadequate. By elaborating such ideas in some fashion, one will therefore never arrive at a discovery of the laws of reality. On the contrary, they are like a veil drawn between the thing and ourselves, concealing them from us the more successfully as we think them more transparent.

Durkheim continued on, in fact, to condemn this tendency in an earlier developmental theory, that of Auguste Comte. Comte's mistake, observed Durkheim, was that he 'identified historical development with the idea he had of it,' an idea, he adds, 'which does not differ much from that of the layman.' Specifically, Comte's error according to Durkheim was to assume the existence of a process of continuous, progressive human evolution and to then proceed to investigate the stages of this evolutionary process as if it were already an established social fact. Admitting that it is easy to understand how the superficial impression of a simple, unilinear evolution of mankind might arise, Durkheim (1938: 19–20) nevertheless maintains that for the social scientist 'the existence of this assumed evolution can be established only by an already completed science; it cannot, then, constitute the immediate subject of research, excepting as a conception of the mind and not as a thing.'

One need not subscribe to Durkheim's epistemological position in order to appreciate the value of his remarks here or their salience to the critique of modernization theory. His point, after all, is a rather elementary one. The essence of the social scientist's task is to formulate and investigate problems concerning some aspect of concrete social phenomena. The social scientist who loses sight of the empirical referents of his concepts and ideas, who is no longer concerned with the truth-content of his assertions, has ceased to be a social scientist and, in the end, his ideas and images of society become indistinguishable from those of the ordinary layman. This is not to say, of course, that the social scientist's task is ever completed. As Weber (1949: 104 ff.) noted, the social sciences have been granted 'eternal youth,' as their history 'is and remains a continuous process passing from the attempt to order reality analytically through the construction of concepts—the dissolution of the analytical construct so constructed through the expansion and shift of the scientific horizon—and the reformation anew of concepts on the foundations thus transformed.' Moreover, an essential condition of this dialectical process, Weber emphasizes, is the constant confrontation of such analytical constructs with empirical reality. Thus, though writing from rather different perspectives, both Durkheim and Weber appear particularly sensitive to the dangers inherent in the social scientist taking the empirical referents of his concepts as given rather than problematic.

Unfortunately, modernization theorists have failed to demonstrate the same sensitivity. Though Durkheim directed his critique at Comte, it may be applied with equal force to modernization theory. It is generally assumed among modernization theorists that the concept of modernization 'is useful despite its vagueness because it tends to evoke similar associations in contemporary readers' (Bendix, 1967: 292). However, when the empirical content of these 'similar associations' is subjected to a critical examination, it soon becomes evident that the concept of modernization is one of those 'products of everyday experience' of which Durkheim spoke. In the case of modernization, the 'everyday experience' which provides the basis for the concept and the 'similar associations' it evokes may be found in the consciousness that the social setting of the human species has experienced a number of profound transformations in recent centuries, including the rise of the nation-state and mass political participation, industrialization, urbanization, bureaucratization, the rapid expansion of human knowledge, and the increasing secularization of cultures, and that these various transformations have been unequally distributed among societies. Modernization theorists have attempted to define the concept of modernization in terms of some unique referent or set of referents which might serve to summarize or order the experience of these transformations. Thus, it has been defined in terms of some formal property (e.g. rationalization or structural differentiation) thought to be a common denominator of these transformations, or in terms of the acquisition of some attribute or set of attributes (e.g. those associated with the tradition-modernity contrast) thought to distinguish societies which have experienced these transformations from those which have not, or perhaps in terms of some aspect of these transformations (e.g. industrialization) thought to stand in a critical causal relationship to the others.

However, it is one thing to sense that societies have indeed experienced a number of profound transformations but quite another to attempt to comprehend all of these transformations directly by means of a single scientific concept. Inevitably, vague images of the former result in equally vague definitions of the latter. But this is not the only difficulty; indeed, as conceptualizations of modernization become more precise they seem even more problematic. Perhaps the most precise (and least frequent) formulations are those which focus on a single critical variable. However, as noted in the critique of this approach, when modernization is conceptualized in terms of a single variable such as rationalization or industrialization it functions merely as a synonym for other, already well-defined concepts, thus tending to be not only superfluous, but obfuscating. On the other hand, definitions of modernization as a collective term referring to multiple attributes or processes may be more common, but they fare little better. Many of the points made in the empirical critique are especially damaging to this sort of an approach. Perhaps the most damaging argument comes from those who have challenged the 'systemic' character of modernization by showing that many processes of change associated with modernization may occur in isolation from other such processes, that some of these processes of change may be incompatible with others, and that because of differences in timing and initial setting processes of institutional change associated with modernization in one context need not be recapitulated in others. Given these observations, if modernization is to be conceived as a compound of elements, it is a very strange compound indeed, for it may occur even in the absence of some of its elements and apparently it is unaffected by the substitution of some elements for others.

Thus, the concept of modernization not only lacks a precise cutting-edge because of the vagueness with which it is defined, but many of the assumptions built into it concerning the nature of its empirical referents also turn out, upon examination, to be either false or misleading. The attempt by modernization theorists to aggregate in a single concept disparate processes of social change which rather should have been distinguished has served only to hinder rather than facilitate their empirical analysis. Reified images of some universal evolutionary process connecting the poles of a dichotomy which, by its nature, assumes that 'societies' are most usefully studied in terms of two or three all-embracing categories simply provide inadequate tools for comprehending the diversity of the human experience during several centuries of social transformation.[14]

In the end, however, the most important referents of the concept are normative, not empirical. Stripped of its scientific pretensions, the concept of modernization becomes little more than a classificatory device distinguishing processes of social change deemed 'progressive' from those which are not. Its effect is to substitute vague and superficial images of profound change—images, moreover, heavily laden with ethnocentric assumptions and the conventional wisdom inherited from earlier evolutionary theories—for the

[14] Even a moment's reflection reveals the primitive nature of such formulations. A contemporary chemist would hardly be satisfied if he were forced to employ the fourfold typology of elements of the ancient Greeks in his investigations. Yet many social scientists seem perfectly content with attempts to explain three centuries or more of social change by use of half that number of categories. The implication would seem to be that the social world is less complex and more amenable to conceptual ordering than the physical, but what social scientist would accept such a premise? Rather, a more plausible inference is that the relationship of modernization theory to the future study of the transformations of human society is roughly analogous with that of the Greek classification of elements to the periodic table of contemporary chemistry.

empirical analysis of these dimly perceived transformations. Thus, as documented in the ideological critique, the functions of the concept are primarily ideological and cognitive in precisely the sense in which Durkheim speaks of concepts which serve 'to put our actions in harmony with our environment.' As Durkheim also observes, a concept which is useful in this sense may be nothing more than an illusion, and as such it is all the more dangerous because it is represented as a scientific concept. The concept of modernization, alas, fits this pattern all too well.

For all the attention it has received, the conceptual apparatus of modernization theory has done remarkably little to advance our understanding of the many transformations which have been experienced by human societies.[15] It has encouraged a preoccupation with questions of a descriptive and taxonomic nature while ignoring or obscuring more fundamental issues. Where modernization theory has not been wrong or misleading, it has all too often been irrelevant. It has stimulated few empirical studies explaining the supposed 'modernization' of actual societies, and even less in the way of systematic comparative research. Instead it has perpetuated a hiatus between 'theory' and research, between the work of modernization theorists on the one hand and the practitioners of 'area studies' on the other. Both the number and vagueness of attempts to conceptualize modernization are in fact symptomatic of its lack of utility.[16] Perhaps the greatest single failing of modernization theorists lies in their inattention to the task of defining what it is precisely they wish their theories to explain. While modernization theorists obviously share a general concern with the analysis of variations in the transformations of societies, their 'theories' tend to be vague, diffuse, descriptive, and ultimately non-comparable, because they have failed to establish a fruitful, empirically-grounded problem structure which could lend focus to their work.

At some point in the future, perhaps, some all-encompassing process of social change which might usefully be termed 'modernization' may be discovered. However, the preceding critique suggests that such a point is not near at hand. For the present, the cumulative weight of the ideological, empirical, and metatheoretical critiques leads to the conclusion that the conceptual apparatus of modernization theory does *not*, to repeat Kaplan's dictum, 'tell us more about our subject matter than any other categorical sets.' Thus, the critique of modernization theory clearly supports the 'radical' position. Constant revision will not lend substance to the illusion of modernization; it must be superseded.[17]

---

15 This is not to say, of course, that one cannot find useful insights scattered throughout the modernization literature. The point is rather that such contributions tend not only to be incidental to the modernization perspective rather than dependent upon it, but that they also tend to be obscured and undeveloped because of the inadequacies of that perspective.

16 Kuhn (1962) has noted that the proliferation of versions of a theory is a common sign of paradigmatic crises. By this criterion, modernization theory has been in a state of crisis from its inception. See, for example, Kuhn's (1962: 69–72) discussion of the decline of the theory of phlogiston in eighteenth-century chemistry.

17 This conclusion does not rule out the purely nominal use of the terms 'traditional' or 'modern' to refer to the past or present of a society; however, their contribution in this

III. Concluding Remarks

Kaplan's criterion that our concepts should 'tell us more' obviously is a relative one, implying the availability of alternative conceptualizations. If the argument against modernization theory is to be conclusive, then, it must be shown not only that the conceptual apparatus of modernization theory is inadequate and unworkable, but also that a more viable alternative is available. At present, no such alternative exists, a situation which may be attributed to the failure of modernization theorists and their critics alike to make, or even to consider making, a decisive break with the intellectual traditions of modernization theory.

While the preceding analysis has sought to provide a rationale for such a break, the critique of modernization theory must remain incomplete until such time as a more fruitful approach can be demonstrated. While such an approach must avoid the errors of modernization theory, it cannot abandon its concerns. Although modernization theory has been unable to provide a satisfactory basis for systematic comparative research into the causes and consequences of patterns of variability and convergence in the formation and transformation of national societies, this does not mean that the task itself must be abandoned for the comforts of monographic research or so-called 'middle-range' *ad hoc* theorizing. It does mean, however, that if the sorts of difficulties raised by the ideological, empirical, and methodological critiques of modernization theory are to be avoided, an alternative perspective must be rooted firmly in an empirically-grounded problem structure which clearly specifies both the problems which are to be explained and—most important for comparative research—the contexts within which they are problematic. Rather than attempting simply to describe the various transformations of societies, such a problem structure should identify in more or less operational terms the underlying core structural problems common to all national societies to which these transformations are a response—problems relating to the formation and maintenance of societal boundaries, the organization and performance of political and economic institutions, and the social distribution of power resources. Thus, such an alternative must take seriously the logic of comparative analysis by rigorously defining its units of analysis, classifying them, and comparing the ranges of variation they reveal in relation to a set of common problems. But whatever the ultimate shape which an eventual alternative to modernization theory might take, it will require a fundamental rethinking of how we approach the analysis of long-term, macro-level transformations of societies. The results of almost two decades of modernization theory do not justify a third. The time has come to begin working toward an alternative paradigm.

---

context is a linguistic rather than an analytic one. Nor does it imply that these or related terms should not be employed in the identification of more rigorously defined substantive concepts (as in Weber's discussion of modes of legitimation).

Bibliography

APTER, DAVID E. (1965) *The Politics of Modernization.* Chicago: University of Chicago Press.

BENDIX, REINHARD (1963) 'Concepts and Generalizations in Comparative Sociological Studies.' *American Sociological Review*, 28 (4): 532–9.

——— (1967) 'Tradition and Modernity Reconsidered.' *Comparative Studies in Society and History*, 9 (3), 292–346.

BLACK, C. E. (1966) *The Dynamics of Modernization: A Study in Comparative History.* New York: Harper Torchbooks.

BOCK, KENNETH E. (1964) 'Theories of Progress and Evolution.' Pp. 21–41 in Werner J. Cahnman and Alan Boskoff (eds.), *Sociology and History.* New York: The Free Press.

BURROW, J. W. (1966) *Evolution and Society: A Study in Victorian Social Theory.* London: Cambridge University Press.

COLLINS, RANDALL (1968) 'A Comparative Approach to Political Sociology.' Pp. 42–67 in Reinhard Bendix, et al. (eds.), *State and Society: A Reader in Comparative Political Sociology.* Boston: Little, Brown.

DURKHEIM, EMILE (1938) *The Rules of Sociological Method.* New York: The Free Press.

EISENSTADT, S. N. (1966) *Modernization: Protest and Change.* Englewood Cliffs, N.J.: Prentice-Hall.

——— (1968) 'Reflections on a Theory of Modernization.' Pp. 35–61 in Arnold Rivkin (ed.), *Nations by Design: Institution Building in Africa.* Garden City, N.Y.: Anchor Books.

GEERTZ, CLIFFORD (1963) 'The Integrative Revolution: Primordial Sentiments and Civil Politics in the New States.' Pp. 105–57 in Clifford Geertz (ed.), *Old Societies and New States.* New York: The Free Press.

——— (1966) *Agricultural Involution: The Process of Ecological Change in Indonesia.* Berkeley: University of California Press.

GERSCHENKRON, ALEXANDER (1962) *Economic Backwardness in Historical Perspective.* New York: Frederick A. Praeger.

GUSFIELD, JOSEPH R. (1967) 'Tradition and Modernity: Misplaced Polarities in the Study of Social Change.' *American Journal of Sociology*, 72 (4), 351–62.

HALL, JOHN WHITNEY (1965) 'Changing Conceptions of the Modernization of Japan.' Pp. 7–41 in Marius B. Jansen (ed.), *Changing Japanese Attitudes Toward Modernization.* Princeton, N.J.: Princeton University Press.

HALPERN, MANFRED (1966) 'The Revolution of Modernization in National and International Society.' Pp. 178–214 in Carl J. Friedrich (ed.), *Revolution.* New York: Atherton Press.

HARRISON, SELIG S. (1960) *India: The Most Dangerous Decades.* Princeton, N.J.: Princeton University Press.

HEESTERMAN, J. C. (1963) 'Tradition in Modern India.' *Bijdragen: Tot de Taal-, Land-, en Volkenkunde*, 119, (3), 237–53.

HEMPEL, CARL G. (1965) *Aspects of Scientific Explanation*. New York: The Free Press.

HOFSTADTER, RICHARD (1955) *Social Darwinism in American Thought*. Boston: Beacon Press.

HUGHES, H. STUART (1958) *Consciousness and Society: The Reorientation of European Social Thought*. New York: Random House.

HUNTINGTON, SAMUEL P. (1965) 'Political Development and Political Decay.' *World Politics*, 17 (3), 386–430.

———— (1968a) *Political Order in Changing Societies*. New Haven: Yale University Press.

———— (1968b) 'The Bases of Accommodation.' *Foreign Affairs*, 46 (4) 642–56.

———— (1970) Letter to the Editor, with a Reply by Noam Chomsky. *The New York Review of Books*, 14 (4, February 26), 45–6.

———— (1971) 'The Change to Change: Modernization, Development, and Politics.' *Comparative Politics*, 3 (3): 283–322.

INKELES, ALEX (1969) 'Making Men Modern: On the Causes and Consequences of Individual Change in Six Developing Countries.' *American Journal of Sociology*, 75 (2), 208–55.

KALLEBERG, ARTHUR L. (1966) 'The Logic of Comparison: A Methodological Note on the Study of Political Systems.' *World Politics*, 19 (1) 69–82.

KAPLAN, ABRAHAM (1964) *The Conduct of Inquiry*. San Francisco: Chandler Publishing Co.

KHARE, R. S. (1971) 'Home and Office: Some Trends of Modernization among the Kanya-Kubja Brahmans.' *Comparative Studies in Society and History*, 13 (2), 196–216.

KUHN, THOMAS S. (1962), *The Structure of Scientific Revolutions*. Chicago: University of Chicago Press.

KUPER, LEO, and M. G. SMITH, eds. (1969) *Pluralism in Africa*. Berkeley: The University of California Press.

LAUER, ROBERT H. (1971) 'The Scientific Legitimation of Fallacy: Neutralizing Social Change Theory.' *American Sociological Review*, 36 (5), 881–89.

LERNER, DANIEL (1958) *The Passing of Traditional Society: Modernizing the Middle East*. New York: The Free Press.

LEVINE, DONALD N. (1968) 'The Flexibility of Traditional Culture.' *Journal of Social Issues*, 24 (4) 129–41.

LEVY, MARION J., Jr. (1953) 'Contrasting Factors in the Modernization of China and Japan.' *Economic Development and Cultural Change*, 2 (3), 161–97.

———— (1966) *Modernization and the Structure of Societies*. Princeton, N.J.: Princeton University Press.

———— (1967) 'Social Patterns (Structures) and Problems of Modernization.' Pp. 189–208 in Wilbert E. Moore and Robert M. Cook (eds.), *Readings on Social Change*. Englewood Cliffs, N.J.: Prentice-Hall.

LIEBERSON, STANLEY (1971) 'An Empirical Study of Military-Industrial Linkages.' *American Journal of Sociology*, 76 (4), 562–84.

MAZRUI, ALI A. (1968) 'From Social Darwinism to Current Theories of Modernization.' *World Politics*, 21 (1), 69–83.

MOORE, WILBERT (1963) *Social Change.* Englewood Cliffs, N.J.: Prentice-Hall.

NISBET, ROBERT (1966) *The Sociological Tradition.* New York: Basic Books.

——— (1969) *Social Change and History: Aspects of the Western Theory of Development.* New York: Oxford University Press.

ROTHMAN, STANLEY (1961) 'Modernity and Tradition in Britain.' *Social Research,* 28 (3), 297–320.

RUDOLPH, LLOYD I., and SUSANNE HOEBER RUDOLPH (1967) *The Modernity of Tradition: Political Development in India.* Chicago: University of Chicago Press.

RUSTOW, DANKWART A. (1967) *A World of Nations; Problems of Political Modernization.* Washington, D.C.: The Brookings Institution.

SCHWARTZ, BENJAMIN I. (1972) 'The Limits of "Tradition Versus Modernity" as Categories of Explanation: The Case of the Chinese Intellectuals.' *Daedalus,* 101 (2), 71–88.

SHILS, EDWARD (1963) 'On the Comparative Study of the New States.' Pp. 1–26 in Clifford Geertz (ed.), *Old Societies and New States.* New York: The Free Press.

——— (1965) *Political Development in the New States.* The Hague: Mouton & Co.

SINGER, MILTON (1971) 'Beyond Tradition and Modernity in Madras.' *Comparative Studies in Society and History,* 13 (2), 160–95.

SMELSER, NEIL J. (1967) 'Processes of Social Change.' Pp. 674–728 in N. J. Smelser (ed.), *Sociology,* New York: John Wiley & Sons.

WEBER, MAX (1949) *The Methodology of the Social Sciences.* New York: The Free Press.

WEINBERG, IAN (1969) 'The Problem of the Convergence of Industrial Societies: A Critical Look at the State of a Theory.' *Comparative Studies in Society and History,* 11 (1), 1–15.

WHITACKER, C. S. (1967) 'A Dysrhythmic Process of Political Change.' *World Politics,* 19 (2), 190–217.

ZEVIN, ROBERT (1972) 'An Interpretation of American Imperialism.' *Journal of Economic History,* 32 (1), 316–60.

Need for Revaluation of the Concept

A. R. Desai

Professor Desai is concerned with those aspects of current writing on modernization that apply the term indiscriminately to a wide variety of phenomena, that tend to assume that Western values and institutions have universal validity, and that consider developed societies to have successfully achieved a transition that other societies may or may not have the capacity to complete. He recognizes the potential usefulness of the concept, but suggests that latecomers to modernization are following a different path from that of the early modernizers. The core processes may well have general applicability, but in his view students of the subject should exercise greater discrimination in distinguishing between the Western path which is essentially capitalist and that of the societies where public ownership is the driving force.

In this paper I urge the necessity of a careful and critical reassessment of the concept of modernization of underdeveloped societies for a number of reasons.

1. The term "modernization" is seeking to supersede several other earlier concepts as a comprehensive concept aimed at capturing, describing and evaluating the profound, qualitative and quantitative changes that have been taking place in human society from the sixteenth century onwards. These changes have inaugurated, according to Professor Black and others, a new epoch in the history of mankind. Concepts like Anglicization, Europeanization, westernization, urbanization, evolution, development, progress, etc., are either being replaced by "modernization" or are being fitted into the matrix of this concept.

2. The concept "modernization" seeks to describe the period of transition of human society during which man enters a modern-rational phase of acquiring skills and reaches a new level of mastery over nature to construct his own social environment based on affluence and rationality.

"Need for Revaluation of the Concept" by A. R. Desai is reprinted with permission of the author from *Essays on Modernization of Underdeveloped Societies*, ed. A. R. Desai, 2 vols. (Bombay, 1971), 1:458–474.

Desai is a leading Indian sociologist who has written extensively about rural and urban conditions in his country. This essay forms a chapter in a two-volume international symposium that he edited on the occasion of the fiftieth anniversary of the Department of Sociology of the University of Bombay, of which he is chairman.

e term "modernization of underdeveloped societies" needs to be comprehended because it seeks to define and delineate a gigantic and rapid process of change, involving, directly, two-thirds of humanity, which was inaugurated after World War II in the ex-colonial and semicolonial countries which have formally liberated themselves from the political tutelage of imperialist-capitalist countries of the West.

4. In the literature, both "technical and popular," growing at a prolific rate during last two decades, the concepts "modernization" and "modernity" are used in such an indiscriminate manner that they are losing their edge and sharpness as efficient tools of analysis. These terms, as Nettl and Robertson have very rightly pointed out, exhibit three major deficiencies: (1) confusion and vagueness, (2) prominence of prescriptive statements and ideological preferences in the processes of describing modernization. "The most obvious tendency to note at this point is the suggestion—sometimes implicit, sometimes explicit—that the typical condition of modernity pertains to the social political and economic characteristics of Western democracies." (3) Another ideological bias in close proximity to the second is that "modernity represents a single final state of affairs, namely the 'state of affairs' to be found in a number of Western societies which everyone should try to emulate and which the most successful could reach." The numerous terms emerging out of the term, modernization, such as "split-modernization," "break-down of modernization," "post-modern," etc. are creating peculiar semantic "smoke-screens" to escape the dilemma arising out of this distorted vision, viz. that advanced capitalist western societies are the ideal types or represent a new Utopia.

This value bias and ideological intonation underlying the use of the concept by modern western scholars has created certain dangerous consequences for a correct understanding of the processes of change that are taking place in human societies during recent periods.

1. The use of the concept with this specific pro-western bias, distorts *ab initio* the ability of these scholars to observe and analyze the processes of change that are taking place in societies which are following a non-capitalist path. It also colours the perspective of historical stages through which various countries have modernized themselves and are modernizing themselves. It has also created a faulty vision of the nature of the relationship between the developed and the underdeveloped countries and has tended to provide prescriptions of practical actions, policies and measures which operate as obstacles to the generation of the right type of processes for modernizing these countries. In fact, this ideological bias leads scholars to urge measures which may even bring about the breakdown of modernization, creating profound "crisis situations" in the underdeveloped countries. This realization is dawning upon a number of scholars whose earlier enthusiasm based on crude evolutionism is being replaced by profound pessimism with regard to the development that is taking place in underdeveloped countries. The Gunnar Myrdal *magum opus*, *Asian Drama* epitomizes this trend.

Core Processes Assumed While Using the Concept of Modernization

While indicating the reasons why the concept of modernization requires to be reassessed, one should recognize that compared to other concepts used by western scholars to comprehend the changing social reality, the concept, *modernization,* has proved to be more useful in describing certain core processes of social transformation that have been taking place during the last three hundred years. These core processes are attempted to be presented by many eminent scholars, including Weiner, Apter, Lerner, Black, Inkeles, Bendix, Marion Levy, Smelser, Eisenstadt, Nettl and others.

"Modernization," according to these scholars, is both a process and product. Compared to urbanization, industrialization, westernization or Europeanization, modernization conveys the picture of a more complex process and also implies an equally complex product in the form of a particular type of society. The process called modernization is not restricted to one domain of social reality but envelops all the basic aspects of social life.

We will briefly review the type of processes which are subsumed under the rubric of modernization.

Modernization *in the intellectual sphere* exhibits itself in the new awareness that it is *"possible to seek a rational explanation of physical and social phenomena."* This approach presumes that physical, social and psychological phenomena are law-governed, have regularities, uniformities and causal relationship and could be understood, and therefore could be modified or regulated by human reason. This rational attitude is the core process of modernization.[1]

The first stage in the history of the growth of this attitude was symbolized most dramatically by the *Novum Organum* of Bacon, the influential atheistic materialist world outlook of the Encyclopaedists like Helvetius, Holbach and Diderot and the Statue of Reason in Peril, symbolizing the advent of the modern epoch through the French Revolution. The second stage in the growth of this attitude unfolded itself in three major intellectual currents, viz., positivism and empiricism with its many variants; rationalism starting from Descartes and culminating with Hegel with his profound dialectical idealism and neo-Hegelianism and neo-continentalism; and third from Hegel via Feuerbach to Marx and Engels into dialectical materialism, shaping an ontological and epistemological framework for comprehending the natural and socio-cultural human reality.

The historical development of the growth of the rational approach and the social forces which stimulated this approach and the social forces which hampered its growth is a fascinating feature of modern times.

Other characteristics of modernization which almost logically follow from a rational approach is the development of secularism, in contrast to a sacred

---

[1] C. E. Black [*The Dynamics of Modernization: A Study in Comparative History* (New York: Harper, 1966)], pp. 7, 10.

approach: a this-worldly attitude in contrast to an other-worldly attitude; "Man-Human Species—and its security, development and betterment on this earth as a measure and aim of human endeavours and norms" (humanism); non-acceptance of anything on faith and subjection of everything to critical, rational scrutiny; a change-oriented, forward-looking attitude in contrast to a change-resistant one.

Modernization as a complex process of "system transformation" manifests itself in certain socio-demographic features termed "social mobilization" and "structural changes."

Social mobilization implies "the process in which major clusters of old social, economic and psychological commitments are eroded and broken and people become available for new patterns of socialization and behaviour." [2]

Social-structural changes. Modernization is "high differentiation and specialization with respect to individual activities and institutional structure," "separation of different roles held by the individuals—especially among the occupational and political roles, and between them and the family and kinship roles," "specificity" and not "diffuseness" is implied in the separation of roles and recruitment to the roles is not determined by ascription based on any fixed kinship, territorial, caste or estate basis but "free floating," based on achievement. [3]

Political Changes. Modernization implies four major features:

1. The legitimacy of the sovereign authority of the state is derived not from supernatural sanctions but from secular sanctions inhering in the people and based on accountability to citizens.
2. Continual diffusion of "political power to wider groups of society— ultimately to all adult citizens, and their incorporation into a consensual moral order."
3. "Growing extension of the territorial scope and especially by the intensification of power of the central, legal, administrative and political agencies of the society."
4. Unlike the rulers of traditional societies, the rulers of modern societies, whatever may be their nature—totalitarian, bureaucratic, oligarchic or democratic—"accept the relevance of their subjects as the objects, beneficiaries, and legitimizers of policy." The difference between the modern democratic or semi-democratic forms of government lies in the "extent to which they permit institutional expression in political institutions," "public liberties and in the welfare and cultural policies." [4]

Economic Changes. Modernization manifests itself in the following features: (1) substitution of inanimate power such as steam, electricity or atomic for human and animal power as the basis of production, distribution, transport and communication; (2) separation of economic activities from the traditional setting; (3) "increasing replacement of tools by machine and technology";

---

[2] S. N. Eisenstadt [*Modernization: Protest and Change* (Englewood Cliffs: N.J.: Prentice-Hall, 1966)], pp. 41–42.
[3] *Ibid.*, p. 2.
[4] *Ibid.*, p. 3.

(4) as a corollary to this high level of technology, growth of an extensive sector of secondary (industrial, commercial) and tertiary (service) occupations over-shadowing the primary (extractive) ones in quantitative and qualitative signifi-cance; (5) "growing specialization of economic roles and units of economic activity—production, consumption and marketing"; (6) "a degree of self-sustaining growth in the economy"—at least growth sufficient to increase both production and consumption regularly; and finally, (7) growing industrializa-tion—the key characteristic of economic modernization.[5]

In the ecological field, modernization is characterized by an advancing degree of urbanization.

Modernization manifests itself in the *cultural sphere* in the following ways:

1. Growing differentiation of the major elements of cultural systems, "the spread of literacy and secular education; a more complex, intellectual and institutional system for the cultivation and advancement of specialized roles based on intellectual disciplines." [6]
2. Emergence of a new cultural outlook characterized by emphasis on pro-gress and improvement, on happiness and spontaneous expression of abilities and feelings, on the development of individuality as a value, and efficiency.
3. Emergence of a new personality orientation, traits and characteristics revealed in greater ability to adjust to the broadening societal horizons; some ego-flexibility; widening spheres of interests; growing potential empathy with other people and situations; a growing evaluation of self-advancement and mobility; a growing emphasis on the present as the meaningful temporal dimension of human existence; a growing aware-ness of the dignity of others and an increased disposition to respect them; a growing awareness in the individual that "his world is calculable, that other people and institutions around him can be relied on to fulfil their delegations and responsibilities"; a growing faith in science and technology and a growing awareness that "rewards should be according to contribution and not according to either whim or special properties of person not relating to his contribution."
4. Finally, modernization implies "the ability of society to develop an institutional structure capable of adjusting to continually changing problems and demands." The emergence of such a flexibility constitutes, according to Prof. Eisenstadt, the central issue and challenge of modern-ization.[7]

The processes and characteristic features described above basically cover the "core processes" according to Western scholars.

The shift from use of human and animal power to inanimate power from tool to machine as the basis of production and its implications in terms of

[5] *Ibid.*, p. 4.
[6] *Ibid.*, p. 4.
[7] J. P. Nettl and Roland Robertson [*International Systems and the Modernization of Societies: The Formation of National Goals and Attitudes* (London: Faber, 1968)], pp. 38–41; and C. E. Black, *op. cit.*, p. 19.

growth of wealth, technical diversification, differentiation, and specialization leading to a novel type of division of labour; and industrialization and urbanization are accepted by all scholars as features of modernization. The shift of the sanction behind the state from the supernatural to secular; the extension and increasing diffusion of power to a wider strata of population and the supremacy of law over other regulative systems are also recognized as basic features of modernization. Similarly, a shift in the social structure based on allocation of roles on the principle of ascription to one based on the principle of achievement and merit, thus qualitatively transforming the very basis of role recruitment and therefore of the social structure, is accepted as a trait of modernization. The major shift in the principle of social solidarity from a "mechanical" one, built on a pre-contractual, diffused and particularistic basis, to one of organic solidarity, built on a contractual, specific universalistic basis, is also recognized. Scholars also recognize that the modernization process implies a shift from sacred, other-worldly, change-resistant outlook to a secular, this-worldly, forward-looking change-prone outlook. Similarly scholars implicitly or explicitly acknowledge that rationality, humanism, and feasibility and necessity of improvement in the conditions of life of the human beings in this world and not in the other world constitute the hallmark of the cultural outlook of modernization.

Some Controversies and Conflicts in Approaches

After having described the "core processes" implied in the concept of modernization, we will now examine the differences arising among scholars interpreting the historical origin, the stages of development, the paths of modernization, the agencies of modernization, the content of modernization and its future. These differences arise from certain major conscious or unconscious assumptions accepted by scholars who are attempting to study modernization both as a process and product; as a historical category emerging at certain stage of development of mankind and increasingly enveloping all mankind. They arise also because of the different ontological-epistemological positions taken by scholars in cognizing and interpreting the nature of the changes, the relative significance attached to various factors which have been responsible for change, and also their fundamental characterization of societies on the basis of their individual sociological assumptions. These differences further arise from the fact that scholars differ about the relationships between developed or modernized countries and underdeveloped but modernizing countries. These differences are also responsible for the various reasons given for stresses and strains experienced by modernizing countries and the solutions offered for certain problems connected with the modernization of underdeveloped countries. We will briefly mention these differences and indicate the controversies they create.[8]

---

[8] I would here like to draw attention to Professor Yogendra Singh's effort to classify basic approaches to modernization in the following four categories: Evolutionary-Historical, Evolutionary-Componential, Relationistic-Historical, and Relationistic-Componential.

The massive literature on modernization that has emerged after World War II can be broadly divided into two major currents: (1) a dominant current arising from certain western liberal-bourgeois assumptions (this current has taken to the 'modernization' concept with a gusto) and (2) a current originating with Marxist and socialist scholars, which examines the same processes but not exclusively under the rubric of 'modernization.'

The first current which shares common assumptions may further be divided into two distinct sub-currents: the sub-current of scholarship on modernization which blossomed in the fifties, and another which engaged in the sixties and which is slowly gaining ascendence over the first.

In the fifties, crude evolutionary theories in economics of underdevelopment passing through "take off" to development and "sociological theories of transformation of 'traditional' societies into 'modern ones,' through a 'transitional stage' " emerged.[9] These theories were based on the naive assumption that the western capitalist model of "development" was a fit and ultimate end for the whole world. This view suffered from a simplistic, automatistic view of development. According to this view, the entire epoch of modernization could be divided into two stages. In the first stage, through a peculiar constellation of circumstances, a well-developed westernized society emerges and becomes a model. In the second stage, the modernizing process envelops all countries. Though the underdeveloped countries are developing under a different set of conditions, they are, in the main, evolving the same features as those of modernized societies and are being stimulated to overcome their lag through accelerated development under the aegis of, and inspired by the highly developed, modern, western countries. This approach reminds us of the earlier similar approach in the nineteenth and early twentieth century when it was presumed that capitalist West-European countries which were already highly civilized were aiding and assisting the "barbarian" colonial peoples, and were pursuing a civilizing mission when they subjugated them and brought them under their economic, political and cultural heel. At present, it is presumed that highly modernized, neo-capitalist countries of the west are involved in altruistic activities in aiding, through economic, political, social, educational and cultural assistance, the modernization of traditionally underdeveloped, backward societies, and that this aid will assist these underdeveloped countries to reach a take-off stage quickly and would launch them in the path of harmonious modernization.

The scholarship which is emerging in the sixties and which forms the second sub-current of modernization studies, does not take such a simplistic view of the spread of the modernization process. It attempts to probe deeper and recognizes the profound stresses and strains associated with the problems of modernization. It does not hold that the present, underdeveloped, traditional societies will automatically evolve into modernized societies. It recognizes that there is no inevitability of modernization of underdeveloped countries even with the aid of developed countries. According to this group of scholars, there is also a great danger of the modernization process breaking

---

[9] S. N. Eisenstadt, *op. cit.*, pp. 5, 6; and J. P. Nettl & Roland Robertson, *op cit.* Ch. 1.

down in these countries. In fact, these scholars are seriously perturbed, are even alarmed, at the spectre of a "breakdown of modernization" as is threatened by the changes that are taking place in these countries and their calamitous implications for two-thirds of humanity. Eisenstadt, Apter, Nettl, Robertson, Bendix, Gunnar Myrdal and a large number of other scholars have started probing into the problems of modernization at a more sophisticated level.

These scholars also believe that the entire process of modernization takes place in two phases. The first phase of modernization was limited to Western Europe, the United States and the English-speaking dominions which had an autochthonous development of modernization arising out of inner forces—the traditional societies were reshaped into modern ones *sui juris*. The most important structural and cultural characteristics of this phase of modernization were "the relatively small-scale of the scope of various new organizations, the development of many relatively specific goal-oriented organizations; the development of as yet restricted markets and free-floating resources in the major institutional spheres; and the relative predominance of public—the representations, communal or professional—regulative and allocative arrangements." The chief feature of this phase of modernization was the development of "strong, modern, centralized political framework . . . before the onset of industrialization and the rapid political aspirations to wider groups and strata." [10]

These scholars assume that countries belonging to this phase of modernization, having evolved a strong modern political, democratic framework, permit a peaceful and a relatively gradual eradication of their limitations, and enter a phase of sustained growth of modernization in the form of social mobilization, industrialization and economic growth and consequent impingement of the broader strata into an already existing and established framework. Thus these scholars assume that modernization has acquired a solid central framework in the earlier phase and, therefore, has become flexible and viable enough to absorb further doses of modernization and satisfy the rising aspirations of the masses and groups. It has evolved capacities to produce resources to satisfy rising demands. Thus these countries have already evolved the power of sustained growth for an uninterrupted expansion of the modernization processes. The challenges they face are essentially of a minor nature and such as are not likely to result in a breakdown of modernization.

According to this group of scholars, the rest of the world is composed basically of colonial or semi-colonial countries, which have remained underdeveloped in comparison with modernized societies, and which historically started modernizing themselves only early in the twentieth century and which liberated themselves from foreign rule and took to the path of active modernization only after World War II.

The problems confronted by these "late starters" in modernization differ in several respects from those faced by advanced modernized countries.

1. In the very process of liberating themselves from foreign rule, there was an intense political and social mobilization of the masses. The impinge-

---

[10] S. N. Eisenstadt, *op. cit.*, pp. 52–53.

ment upon central political authorities of the masses has emerged as a new phenomenon. This growing, conscious mass participation called the "mass aspect" is a peculiar feature of these underdeveloped societies which took to active modernization after World War II in contrast to the earlier modernizers.

2. This growing tempo of social mobilization has been "first characterized by the growth of large-scale and multipurpose, specialized, i.e., non-ecological and non-kinship-groups and associations. Second, it is characterized by the continuous extension and inter-penetration of various internal markets in the institutional spheres of society.

3. It is "characterized by the continually growing and spreading urbanization and by the continual spread of mass media of communication." [11]

Thus, in contrast to gradual social mobilization and lower impingement on the broader strata and on the existing and established central political framework in the early modernizers, the tempo of social mobilization and direct and active impingement on the masses at the very establishment of the new centres is extremely swift, sudden and of a qualitatively different scale among late modernizers. Further, this tempo of social mobilization in various institutional spheres is different from its tempo in societies belonging to the first phase. In most of the newly liberated states suffering from extreme economic backwardness, "the process of differentiation and social mobilization was stronger in the political, ecological and educational spheres than in the industrial and economic spheres," owing to their peculiar subject relationship to the imperialist masters.

This unique feature of late modernizers is crucially expressed in the following dilemma: acute awareness of poverty and misery and sub-standard living, a revolution of rising aspirations of the masses, sharper and sharper demands on the central political authorities to secure resources to satisfy these demands and the inability of central authorities to satisfy them owing to their inability to raise resources as a result of their weak economic and industrial bases and the absence of viable institutional and cultural mechanisms.

The crucial issues faced by underdeveloped societies, according to these scholars, are:

1. New expectations and hopes built on the basis of the picture of modernized societies, extensively accentuated and made acute by the spread of modern mass-media of communication. These new expectations and hopes have stimulated an acute desire to change in a situation of inability to augment resources rapidly enough to satisfy it.

2. Mass wants in these traditional societies are rapidly becoming mass demands. The mass of people in these countries have been poor, have lacked resources, and have been denied many elementary necessities for thousands of years. However, in the process of modernization a new awakening has taken place, *viz.*, a realization that these wants can be

[11] *Ibid.*, p. 53.

satisfied, that an improved standard of life is possible, and that there are resources which can be developed to satisfy these wants. This awakening has transformed these wants into active demands by the masses, which are accelerated by the "multiplier effect of mass media" and the demonstration effect of developed modernized societies.

3. This newly awakened demand which articulates more and more aggressively, results, on the one side in the desire to destroy the present framework which does not give enough to the vast bulk of the population and, on the other, in a desperate struggle among those who already have something to modify the social structure in such a way that their share in the growing resources increases at a faster rate than that of the others. This creates an acute need for an appropriate politico-economic framework which can generate resources to meet these persisting and accelerating demands.

The scholars belonging to the second sub-group feel that it is the failure of the modernizing underdeveloped societies to augment supply at a "sufficient rate to balance accelerating demand that generates a new poignancy and a new meaning to poverty and has become a crucial hurdle affecting smooth, gradual, peaceful modernization." This school, like the earlier one, also presumes that highly modernized countries are aiding these underdeveloped countries rapidly to modernize themselves. But unlike the earlier optimistic school, it is not convinced that underdeveloped societies will peacefully and gradually, automatically evolve into modernized societies. They feel that the underdeveloped countries, due to peculiar historical, "inherent situations," in spite of this aid, will not be able to generate resources at a rate which will satisfy the accelerating demands. According to these scholars, these countries, while modernizing, are caught in the coils of a situation where they are losing in a race with the developed societies in modernizing themselves and also, further, may be heading internally towards a stage when the growing assertion of the masses for resources from the central political authority may result in violent upheavals, leading to a development which may generate "involuntionary" trends. The poor, underdeveloped countries, according to these scholars, have populations suffering from an "inability to earn enough to raise their essential consumption (wants) and have something left to invest." This debacle is further accentuated by what are called "explosions" of population, urbanization and literacy that consume all the gains in production as soon as they are made and often more rapidly than they are made.

In fact this school of scholars visualizes, unlike the first school, a gloomy, pessimistic picture of modernization of underdeveloped societies. In fact, they are concerned with the breakdown of modernization in underdeveloped countries.

Whatever may be the differences between these two sub-currents of scholarship on modernization, there is an underlying unity of assumptions which characterize their approach. These assumptions distinguish this current from the Marxist and socialist current of scholarship. I will briefly state these assumptions.

1. For both the sub-currents, the highly developed neo-capitalist societies of the USA and the West European countries are considered as classically modernized societies and are assumed as models (or reference) for indicating specific ingredients of modernization to be followed ultimately by underdeveloped societies. The socio-economic and cultural ingredients of these countries are postulated as ingredients of the ideal-type in modernization.

2. For these scholars, the modernization concept is basically meant to describe the processes and system of transformation that are taking place in societies which have remained within the broad framework of the capitalist mode of production, sometimes described as "free enterprise economies" or "free economies." A variety of terms have now been coined to avoid the stigma attached to the words "capitalist societies." "Open society," "particularly society," "free society," "active society," "achieving society," "secular society," etc. have encouraged to describe these societies, highlighting one or the other process in them. Very few scholars acknowledge that the capitalist mode of production is the common substratum underlying these variously described societies.

Scholars studying the modernization process basically generalize on the basis of their study of capitalist societies, be they highly industrialized neo-capitalist societies of the west or that section of underdeveloped societies which has taken the capitalist path of development after independence. These scholars are also attempting to elaborate universal laws in this limited field of study. The group of societies which have taken the non-capitalist path after the October Revolution in Russia and which comprise at present two-thirds of the world population are either considered as deformations and abnormalities not worthy of examination or analysis, or are very superficially referred to or brushed aside with a few superficial observations. This objective neglect, arising out of a conscious or sub-conscious pro-western bias, and even reluctance to include in their consideration such countries as Mainland China, East European countries, North Korea, North Vietnam, Cuba (and even the USSR by many) which were colonial or semi-colonial underdeveloped countries till recently, like other underdeveloped countries, is significant and deserves to be noted. These countries are also modernizing themselves on a qualitatively different principle of social organization based on public ownership of the means of production and production geared to the objective of the satisfaction of the assessed needs of the people rather than to the profits of the private owners of the means of production, and elaborating a qualitatively distinct principle of social stratification and distribution of wealth. To neglect a scientific analysis of the modernization process of these countries, which are also endeavouring to proceed from an underdeveloped to developed state, and compare their achievements and limitations with those of similar endeavours to modernize on capitalist lines by other groups of underdeveloped countries, is to my mind a grave deficiency depriving scholars of a rich field of investigation of vital significance.

It is high time that scholars frankly recognize that modernization processes are manifesting themselves along two lines. As Peter Worsley rightly pointed out, there is nothing like modernization *per se,* there is either modernization on capitalist lines or on socialist lines, with all their respective implications. Modernization on capitalist lines . . . takes place on the axis of private property in the means of production and the capitalist class as the main driving force of this modernization. Modernization on non-capitalist lines takes place on the axis of public ownership of means of production and where capitalist and land-owning classes are being eliminated as driving forces.

It is my submission that the classification of modernization on the basis of the two paths will help us to distinguish the nature of the core processes going on in various countries. It will also help us to properly appreciate the nature of the stresses and strains that modernizing societies are experiencing. It will also enable us to eliminate the fallacy which usually arises as a result of selecting disparate units for comparison. The economic, political, social, educational, cultural and other aspects, undergoing modernization on one path are not compared with the economic, political, social, educational, cultural and other aspects of society modernizing on a different path: economic and educational aspects are compared with political aspects, etc.

I will clarify my position by discussing how the current confusion concerning the concept of modernization arises from an inability or unwillingness to accept the qualitative distinction implicit in the two paths of development.

Both paths have certain processes in common; for instance, in both there is a process which we have described as 'social mobilization.' Both are attempting to transform social structure from the ones based on ascriptive to achieving roles. Both are evolving structural differentiation on a principle which is also based on specialization of roles based on universalistic and specificity principles. Both are attempting to transform the economy from subsistence-production based on human and animal power to mass production based on inanimate power like steam, electricity and atomic energy. Both are elaborating programmes of industrialization, thereby transforming an economy founded on predominance of the primary sector into one founded on predominance of the secondary and tertiary sectors. Both are launching the process of urbanization, and both are elaborating a large-scale organization to co-ordinate the complex and expanded scale of relationships based on the legal-rational authority system. Both are also transforming the traditional political sub-system by making the sanction behind the sovereignty of the political power this-worldly rather than other-worldly, thereby making it accountable to people. Both are elaborating central institutions which will provide a framework for economic growth, urbanization, industrialization and increasing involvement of larger and larger numbers of people. Both are also attempting to work out the supremacy of law over other regulative systems. Both appreciate the role of knowledge, of science, and recognize the significance of formal education as well as that of mass media of communication as a tremendously important ingredient of the modernization process.

In spite of these similarities, there are sharp differences in the content of and shape of the two paths followed in the modernization process. I will illustrate this by citing a few instances.

1. Modernization on capitalist lines assumes the private entrepreneur, the capitalist, as the main axis of the entire social structure of modernized or modernizing society. Modernization on non-capitalist lines assumes the opposite. It assumes elimination of the capitalist class as a strata and public ownership as the axis of the entire structure of a modernized or modernizing society. Clearly, these two approaches are qualitatively different as principles of social organization.

2. Modernization on capitalist lines assumes profits accruing to the "free-entrepreneur" as the central objective of production. It also assumes mass production based on machine power, but producing for the market and operating through competition among "free entrepreneurs." Modernization on non-capitalist, socialist lines assumes the meeting of the assessed needs of the society as the central objective of production. It also assumes mass production based on machine power, but not producing for an anonymous market but production according to a central plan based on assessed needs.

3. Modernization on capitalist lines elaborates a social stratification wherein the fundamental distinction between classes owning means of production and classes who live by selling their labour-power, skilled or unskilled, persists and is perpetuated. Private ownership of means of production remains a crucial and ingrained feature of stratification shaping distribution of wealth, the consumption pattern, styles of life, and leisure activities. Modernization on non-capitalist, socialist lines is based on elimination of the propertied class which owns the means of production and elaborates a new principle of stratification based on public ownership of the means of production, transforming social groups into various strata of skilled and unskilled categories differing from one another in diversities of skills. This principle of stratification is qualitatively different from the principle of stratification in capitalist societies. This crucial difference is very often forgotten, leading to a tremendous amount of confusion in the proper study of modernization.

4. The fundamental strategy adopted for sustained growth on capitalist lines relies on providing the primary incentives to the capitalist class, giving active assistance to that class and elaborating various socio-economic, and politico-cultural devices to create an adequate climate for this class to strengthen itself and invest for the process of economic growth. The political authority will strive to create or sustain a legal and social framework which is conducive, basically, to the growth of this class. It will elaborate means which will control all those forces which obstruct this mode of economic development and which tend to weaken the entrepreneur class. In contrast, a strategy adopted for sustained growth, on non-capitalist lines relies basically on eliminating the capitalist class, as a category; it is based on social ownership of the means of production which would elaborate strategies of growth on the basis of elaborating various socio-economic and politico-cultural devices which would lead to sustained economic growth. Modernization on non-capitalist lines relies on providing incentives to non-owning, toiling sections of humanity and mobilizes them through various measures which hasten the disappearance of the capitalist class and its social and cultural power-centres. In under-

developed societies these strategies acquire sharp and clear distinctions. The political authority in societies attempting modernization on non-capitalist lines will try to create and stabilize a legal and social framework which will negate the very existence of the capitalist class and will coercively control all the forces which may assist it and the mode of production it owns and controls. Thus political authority in capitalist countries, whatever formal shape it may take, viz., democratic, semi-democratic, authoritarian, totalitarian or dictatorial, in essence becomes the coercive apparatus sustaining a social order based on capitalist property relations and thus becomes the conscious agent of modernization on capitalist lines. The political authority, whatever its form of government, in societies developing on non-capitalist lines becomes in essence the coercive apparatus sustaining the social order based on public ownership of the means of production and, by eliminating the capitalist class, becomes the major agent of modernization on non-capitalist lines.

It is my submission that great confusion prevails among scholars who do not distinguish between the essence of a state and forms of government. The essence of a state is revealed in the type of property structure it tries to buttress and develop. For instance, a government may be monarchic, oligarchic, dictatorial, democratic, federal or unitary in countries following the capitalist path of development. For instance, forms of government in India, Pakistan, Saudi Arabia, Israel, Italy, France, Spain, the USA, Japan, Taiwan or South Korea may be different, but in all of them the essence of the state is the preservation and development of capitalist private property as a mode of production.

5. Modernization on capitalist lines assumes that work, education, medical facilities, and a number of other social amenities are commodities to be purchased, their availability being dependent upon the purchasing power of the citizen and the market conditions in the society. The state may intervene in the market and elaborate a technique whereby some of these facilities are available either free or on the basis of some concessions, irrespective of the purchasing power of the consumers. However, with all the encroachments made on the market by the state, these elements continue, basically to be commodities. Modernization on non-capitalist lines assumes at the very start that education, medical facilities, work and a number of other social amenities are to be supplied by society as a basic right to its citizens. These opposite approaches to such services as education, medical facilities and work lead to different types of structural organization to supply these needs. They also determine the extent and quality of these services provided to the citizens.

I presume the few illustrations mentioned above are enough to establish a *prima facie* basis for urging that a clear distinction between modernization on capitalist and socialist lines is very urgent if we want to avoid confusion in our studies of modernization. This classification also has a relevance if we want to properly assess the types of stresses and strains which underdeveloped societies will experience while modernizing themselves. It will also help us to correctly appraise the relationship between modernized societies and modernizing underdeveloped societies.

Underdeveloped societies attempting to modernize themselves will have different social, economic, political, educational, religious and cultural patterns of development, depending upon whether they take to the capitalist path or the non-capitalist path. It is high time we made a more systematic, more methodical and more objective study of modernization of underdeveloped countries on this typological basis.

The "Third World" has been trying for the last twenty-two years the path of capitalist development to modernize itself. A number of scholars who were optimistic in the fifties about this path of development are slowly becoming sceptical about it and are also forecasting a very gloomy future on the basis of current trends. Gunnar Myrdal's *Asian Drama,* Fanon's *The Wretched of the Earth,* Peter Worsley's *The Third World,* the studies of Horowitz of the results of development of two decades in the Third World, the findings of scholars like Gunda Frank on Latin American "development of underdevelopment" and the studies of sociologists like Eisenstadt reveal that the capitalist path of modernization followed in these countries is leading them to a peculiar involutionary trend, *viz.,* "breakdown of modernization." Professor Wertheim has summed up this crucial dilemma by posing a significant question: "Can underdeveloped countries modernize themselves and break the vicious circle of poverty by depending on the strategy of 'Betting on the Strong'?" [12]

This is a crucial poser of world historic significance.

Will modernization on capitalist lines not lead to further and further explosive situations in underdeveloped countries? Should not scholars clearly distinguish between modernization on capitalist lines and modernization on non-capitalist lines and start a systematic inquiry on that basis? Should they not examine more systematically the impact of modernization on social, economic, political, educational and cultural life in underdeveloped societies if they follow a capitalist or non-capitalist path?

[12] W. F. Wertheim, *East-West Parallels: [Sociological Approaches to Modern Asia* (The Hague: Van Hoeve, 1964)], Ch. 12.

PART **2**

PRECONDITIONS OF MODERNIZATION

Change, evolution, adaptation, or, more generally, innovation is a process characteristic of all human development. Modernization is an aspect of this process, taking place in societies within a particular period of time and in response to a specific incentive: the revolution in science and technology. Change in the modern era is unprecedented in both scope and universality and represents a revolution in human affairs.

Whatever one's view as to when modernization starts, generally or within a given society, one is confronted with the problem of the relationship between the values and institutions of the modern era and of those that preceded it. Early students were impressed with the scope of change inherent in the modernizing process, and were inclined to believe that the old values and institutions were displaced and destroyed by the new. This opinion was particularly strong among those who saw modernization as a "Westernizing" process: parliament may have evolved from earlier English institutions, but in China, Romania, or Nigeria, native institutions would have to be demolished and cleared away before a parliamentary system could be constructed. Clearly, cobblers and wagonmakers must give way to shoe and automobile factories, but the institutions through which societies regulate their affairs are not changed in such a drastic fashion. To draw a rather sharp line between "modern" and "traditional"—although within societies, advocates of modernization have sometimes decried the established premodern institutions in almost moral terms—has not proved to be a fruitful approach toward solving the problem of the relationship between modern and premodern institutions and values.

Recent studies incline to the view that adaptation is as important as borrowing, and that the values and institutions a society brings to the process are indeed among the principal factors influencing its future course of development. This premise has led to renewed interest in societies before the modern era, and a realization of their great dissimilitude. To call all premodern societies "feudal," for example, as is sometimes done by simplistic Marxists, conceals their diversity. Some societies before the modern era have been dynamic, with well-developed bureaucracies, vigorous urban and commercial networks, intensive forms of organization, and a keen sense of the need to relate to their changing natural and human environment. Others have shown little capacity for change over many generations, and have held to values that identify all ideas and institutions other than their own as heretical or barbaric.

But again, in this dichotomy between the "modern" and the "traditional," those inclined to stress the importance of old institutions and values have assumed a stance as untenable as those so impressed by the new. Indeed, some would place so much emphasis on a society's premodern experience as to question whether a society that is not reasonably well developed before the modern era possesses the capacity for modernizing transformation.

This general question of preconditions, or the relation of the premodern forms of a society to its subsequent development, is one of the least studied aspects of the process of modernization. It is therefore helpful as a point of departure to introduce the subject by citing the conception of preconditions proposed by a new study that has given particular attention to this question— *The Modernization of Japan and Russia: A Comparative Study*.[1] The preconditions that this study suggests as being strategic for the subsequent process of modernization, as applied to latecomers rather than to the earlier modernizers, include:

1. Receptivity to radically new foreign influences. Some societies, like Japan and Russia, derived their premodern culture to a significant degree from foreign sources. In the cases of Japan and Russia it was Chinese and Byzantine respectively. This earlier experience with borrowing seems to have made it easier for these two countries to borrow once again when the modern West emerged as both model and threat. Other societies—the Chinese and the Ottoman, for example—had, for a variety of reasons, to overcome serious cultural obstacles before they could bring themselves to evaluate the West in pragmatic terms. The Chinese educated elite thought of China as the center of the world, and considered all foreigners to be barbaric. The Ottoman Turks had expanded their empire as proselytizers for Islam, and regarded Westerners primarily as Christian infidels unworthy of imitation.

2. The capacity to administer and mobilize the resources. This precondition includes the ability of a society both to defend itself militarily against more advanced societies and at the same time to borrow from them without critically weakening its own national identity. Japan and Russia possessed this capacity to a rather remarkable degree, but relatively few among today's developing countries have a similar capacity. India and Nigeria, for example, are finding it much more difficult in the 1960's to administer radical programs of change

[1] By Cyril E. Black; Marius B. Jansen; Herbert S. Levine; Marion J. Levy, Jr.; Henry Rosovsky; Gilbert Rozman; Henry D. Smith, II; and S. Frederick Starr (New York: Free Press, 1975).

and to mediate between domestic adaptation and foreign borrowing than did Japan and Russia a century ago.

3. Economic productivity. Such productivity—principally from agriculture and trade—must be sufficient to provide a surplus for investment in transportation, communications, and industry. The Japanese and Russian governments were able to mobilize a quarter or more of the agricultural production for state purposes, and their relatively high rates of annual investment during the next century owed much more to this premodern capacity than to the introduction of new foreign institutions. Both achieved economic productivity by exploiting the peasants, no doubt; they made the classic choice between development and distribution. A more humane policy in the short run would have been to reduce taxes to the extent possible, and let the peasants consume what they produced. But under such a policy the societies would have remained relatively stagnant. Where peasants themselves become little entrepreneurs, saving for investment in their own land, strong central authorities are still needed to build railroads and telegraph lines, or maintain currencies and conduct foreign relations. Societies vary widely in their capacity for economic growth. And there are exceptional cases of those that do not even have it—societies that may discover vital resources, notably petroleum, that can provide a much larger source of savings for investment than anything available to Japan and Russia a century ago.

4. The ability to urbanize. As premodern societies vary in their capacity for economic growth, so too do they vary in the extent to which a proportion of their population is settled in towns—and is not scattered in relatively isolated self-contained villages—to form part of a network of trade, communications, and government. The degree of urban growth is one of the critical indicators of a premodern society's capacity to mobilize skills and resources. Japan possessed this capacity to a greater degree than Russia before modernization, but both were much closer to the Western premodern norm than to that of most other societies.

5. An emphasis on education and knowledge. In this precondition there are also many differences among premodern societies. Some, again like Japan and Russia, have the beginnings of school systems and traditions of learning that can readily be expanded into a system of universal primary and secondary education, and of libraries and research centers. Some, like China, may have a great respect for knowledge and high standards of training for civil servants, but combine this with an attitude that makes its adaptation to modern purposes very difficult. Others have so few schools and so little in the way of libraries and research that they must rely on borrowing rather than adaptation in the modern era.

The above listing is intended to be suggestive rather than inclusive. It merely points to the type of questions that one should ask about a premodern society in seeking to know how its premodern heritage of values and institutions bears on its prospects for modernization.

The Historical Experience of
Nation-Building in Europe

Joseph R. Strayer

In this brief essay Professor Strayer describes, in the authoritative and simple style that only an experienced scholar can successfully employ, the emergence of the modern state in Western Europe from the amorphous regna *of the early Middle Ages. He notes that this development was motivated initially by the need for elementary administration, justice, and security. As needs changed, the state gradually assumed increasing responsibilities until it came to administer a very substantial proportion of the economic and social activities within its borders.*

The roots of modern European states go back to the barbarian *regna* which arose in the period of the collapse of the Roman Empire and the concomitant migration of peoples. I am using the Latin term for these units because the English word "kingdom" carries too many overtones of an organized state. The barbarian *regnum* was certainly not a state, although it is rather difficult to say just what it was. Though the ruler often took an ethnic title (*rex Anglorum, rex Francorum,* and so on), most of the *regna* were not ethnic units. The usual pattern was a dominant warrior group, drawn from several Germanic peoples, ruling a subject population which was Latin, Celtic, or Slav. To take the most famous example, the Franks were themselves a federation of peoples; they conquered and gradually merged with other Germanic groups, such as the Burgundians and the Alemanni; they ruled Romanized Gauls, Italians, Celtic refugees from Britain, and a certain number of Slavs. It is clear that such a *regnum* could not be a cultural unit any more than it was an ethnic unit— there were always many dialects, frequently many languages, always different customs, and usually different laws for each of the constituent groups. Even

Strayer is a leading American medievalist who has served as professor of history at Princeton University. His numerous publications include *Feudalism* (1965), *On the Medieval Origins of the Modern State* (1970), and *Medieval Statecraft and the Perspective of History* (1971).

geography does not help much, for a *regnum* was only roughly a geographical unit. It might have had a core, but it would be hard to define its boundaries—there were, everywhere, contested districts and loosely attached, more or less autonomous dependencies (e.g., Aquitaine for the Franks, Wales for the Anglo-Saxons).

Thus, a *regnum* had to be defined in terms of its king, or better, its royal family. A *regnum* was made up of the people who recognized a certain family as *their* royal family. This group may have fluctuated in size and the territories which it occupied, but as long as a sizable number of people held a certain man to be their king, a *regnum* existed.

These *regna* were amorphous and, at first, ephemeral. Yet, some of them survived and, merely by surviving, took the first step in nation-building. Very slowly, very gradually, they built up a persisting identity. Certain peoples, occupying certain areas, long constituted and were, therefore, expected to go on constituting, a certain *regnum*. And, because their *regnum* endured for many generations, there began to be a feeling that it was a permanent part of the political landscape and that it should continue.

It is not surprising that the *regnum* had little resemblance to a state, for, in the early Middle Ages, it is doubtful that anyone had a concept of a state. Some memory of the state lingered among the better-educated members of the clergy, but even they were not able to express the idea very clearly. Some kings, taught by the Church and, perhaps, by surviving Roman traditions, tried to preserve some of the governmental apparatus and public authority of a Roman emperor. Their efforts were frustrated. Most members of the ruling class had no idea of an impersonal continuing public power. Loyalty was to individuals or to families, not to the state. And even this personal loyalty was not wholly reliable; it was tested afresh every time there was a request for service or a demand for obedience. Political power more and more entered the domain of private law; it was a personal possession which could be transmitted by marriage or divided among heirs. Being personal, political power was hard to exercise at a distance or through agents. Hence, there was a constant tendency for local representatives of the king to become independent rulers, a tendency aggravated by the low level of economic activity, which made each district almost self-sufficient. All these factors—the emphasis on personal loyalty, the treatment of public power as a private possession, and the tendency to local autonomy—existed long before feudalism became established. In fact, feudalism was simply the recognition of an already existing political situation.

The process of building a state out of these unpromising materials took a long time, especially as it was done almost entirely with internal resources. The Byzantine model had little influence, and the Roman model was not very well known until the revival of legal studies in the twelfth century. By that time, some of the essential steps in state-building had already been accomplished.

The process seems to have been started by purely practical considerations. The mass of the population suffered from petty wars and general insecurity; it wanted more and better government, especially better administration of justice. This popular desire might have had little influence—after all, the people always want peace and seldom get it—but it was backed by the Church, then at the height of its power. Churchmen played important roles in every government and consistently taught that justice was the highest attribute of a king. They gave their prestige and their administrative skill to any effort to improve the administration of justice. Finally, the rulers themselves wanted to preserve and increase their political power and to hand it on unimpaired to their heirs. They found that the best way to do this was by trying to satisfy the popular demand for law and order. By suppressing violence, by forcing powerful men to settle their disputes through the courts, they gained a much greater degree of control over their vassals and subjects than they had ever had before. But to do this, rulers had to develop systems of law and regularly functioning courts. They had to get a monopoly of all the important cases for their courts or develop an effective appellate jurisdiction which could control the courts of their vassals. They had to create a corps of judges and administrators entirely dependent on them, men who could be rotated from district to district and office to office. And, in doing this, they had to create stable and enduring institutions. These institutions, built up in the late eleventh and twelfth centuries, became the nuclei around which states were formed.

While these institutions were developing, a great revival of learning took place. As a part of this revival, the logical, scientific, and political works of Aristotle were translated into Latin and the *Corpus Juris* of Justinian was studied with greater and greater intensity. Universities began to appear, and many university graduates became administrators and judges. A considerable number of teachers of law, philosophy, and theology began to speculate on political subjects. Out of this intellectual ferment, a theory of the state began to develop. It owed much to the revived study of Roman law, but it was not just a copy of Roman doctrines. Twelfth- and thirteenth-century scholars had to pay some attention to the political environment in which they lived, which was very different from that of Roman lawyers of the classical period. Thus, they had to consider problems of interstate relations, of Church-state relations, and of feudal or semifeudal relations—topics which had not been of any great importance in Roman law. Working with this mixture of old and new ingredients, medieval scholars developed a theory of the state which persisted, in its main outlines, well into the seventeenth century; that is, well past the period in which the European state-system became firmly established.

This theory, when it reached its full development at the end of the thirteenth century, contemplated a Europe divided into a number of sovereign states. The word "sovereignty" had not yet been invented, but the fact of sovereignty was there, even if it took a series of phrases to describe it. The idea of external sovereignty was rather easily accepted and there was no great difficulty in defining it. It was obvious that there were a number of political units which were entirely independent of one another, and phrases were soon found which described this independence. Early in the century, Pope Innocent III spoke of a "king who recognizes no superior in temporal affairs." [1] Later (the exact date and author are still in dispute), someone coined the phrase: "*Rex*

---

[1] Robert W. Carlyle and A. J. Carlyle, *A History of Medieval Political Theory in the West* (London: Blackwood, 1928), V, 143–148; Gaines Post, "Two Notes on Nationalism: II. Rex Imperator," *Traditio*, IX (1953), 296–320.

est imperator in regno suo" ("The king who has no superior, the king who is emperor in his own realm, is sovereign as far as any outside power goes.") [2]

The idea of internal sovereignty was more difficult to accept and to state in unambiguous terms. Most scholars of the period used the organic analogy: the state is a body; all members must obey the head; all members must work together for the common welfare, and so on. By the middle of the thirteenth century, some writers were saying that this body politic was a *corpus mysticum* (just as was the Church), which would imply that it should be preserved at all costs.[3] This conclusion was quickly drawn; by 1300, it was almost commonplace to say that the head of the state can demand the lives and goods of all other members of the body politic to preserve the common welfare or establish the common defense.[4] One man even argued that an individual should not hesitate to commit a mortal sin if, by doing so, he could save the state. As this example shows, and, as Gaines Post has pointed out, "reason of state" is no invention of the Renaissance; it exists already in the thirteenth century.[5]

But this theory of internal sovereignty came up against other theories of a permanent and unchanging body of law, of imprescriptible rights and privileges held by local lords and autonomous communities, and of irremovable limitations on the power of central governments. As a result, the theory was usually stated in comparative terms: the king has *superioritas*, he has "greater power." [6] The theory of internal sovereignty also came up against some hard political facts. Although Western rulers, in general, found it fairly easy to make good their claim to external sovereignty, even against the Pope, they did not yet have the authority or the administrative machinery needed to establish fully their claim to internal sovereignty. As a result, there was a long period of floundering, and it was not until the sixteenth century that the more advanced states could really assert sovereignty in all internal affairs. And it was only then that the theory of sovereignty could be purged of some of its ambiguities and stated in clear and definitive terms.

Nevertheless, before this process was complete, another important change had taken place. This was the transfer of basic loyalties from the Church to the secular state, a change which, more than anything else, marks the end of the Middle Ages and the beginning of the modern period. In the period

---

[2] *Ibid.*, pp. 304–307, 320. Cf. E. H. Kantorowicz. *The King's Two Bodies* (Princeton: Princeton University Press, 1957), pp. 51, 97.

[3] *Ibid.*, p. 208, but the reference to Vincent of Beauvais should be *Speculum Doctrinale* VII, 15, and not VII, 8.

[4] Joseph R. Strayer, "Defense of the Realm and Royal Power in France," in *Studi in onore di Gino Luzzatto* (Milan: A. Giuffrè, 1949), I, 289–296; Post, "Ratio Publicae Utilitatis, Ratio Status und 'Staatsräson' (1100–1300)," *Die Welt als Geschichte*, XXI (1961), 8–28, 71–99.

[5] *Ibid.* On p. 96 he cites an anonymous author who says adultery is justified if it leads a woman to betray plans that would destroy the community.

[6] For example, when Philip the Fair was trying to establish his rights over the Gévaudan (held by the bishop of Mende) the argument was over who was *major dominus*, who had *major jurisdictio* or *superioritas*. See A. Maisonobe, *Mémoire relatif au Paréage de 1307* (Mende: Société d'Agriculture, Sciences, et Arts de la Lozère, 1896), pp. 506–507, 517, 531.

between the Gregorian reform (c. 1075) and the middle of the thirteenth century, the Church had set the standards and goals of European society. When its policies were opposed, the Church had had the support of the bulk of the population, and had often been able to coerce lay rulers by urging their subjects to rebel against them. This tactic was increasingly ineffective after 1250. Habits of obedience to secular governments had been established, and a certain attachment to the laws of the country and the person of its ruler had developed. This was not yet patriotism (except in a few rare cases),[7] but it was a feeling that no outside authority should intervene in the internal affairs of an established political community. People were not very eager to give up their lives and property for any cause, but they were more willing to make these sacrifices for the state than for the Church. It was a rather tepid loyalty, but nothing else was hotter. The test came when Boniface VIII (r. 1294–1303) entered into open conflict with the kings of France and England and found that he had almost no support in either country. Even the clergy told him that they would lose all influence if they were suspected of disloyalty to their kings. From that time on, the only loyalty which had much chance of being built up into a powerful, emotional factor was loyalty to the state or to the ruler who embodied the state.

At about this time (c. 1300), differing patterns began to develop out of the general process of state-building. The most important difference was between the *regnum* which became a single state and the *regnum* which splintered and gave birth to many states. England and France are obvious examples of the first type; Germany and Italy, of the second. Almost as important was the difference between the unitary state with no significant provincial liberties and the "mosaic" state in which a king had slowly extended his authority over one province after another and in which, therefore, each province had had time to develop its own peculiar laws and institutions. England was the best example, and one of the few early ones, of the unitary state; France was the model of the "mosaic" state.

Both these differences are important in the next stage—changing the state into a nation. Where a whole *regnum* became a state, nationalism developed early and naturally, with no great strain or exaggerated emotional appeals. In such a state, people were gradually brought into closer and closer association with each other. The ringwall of the state cut them off, to some extent, from the rest of the world; they were forced to work together and to adapt to each other. They had time to gain a clear sense of identity, to smooth out some of their regional differences, and to become attached to their ruler and the institutions through which he ruled. Where the framework of the state was strong enough and persistent enough, it even created a common nationalism out of very different linguistic and cultural groups. Languedoc was very like Catalonia and very unlike north France, yet it finally became thoroughly French.

It is also clear that the unitary state had an advantage over the "mosaic" state. The central government of a unitary state did not have to worry about

[7] Kantorowicz, *op. cit.*, pp. 232–272; Post, "Two Notes on Nationalism . . . ," *op. cit.*

provincial privileges, nor did it have to create a huge, and often unpopular, bureaucracy to coordinate and control diverse and quarrelsome local authorities. Local leaders did not have to be looked on with suspicion as men whose primary loyalty was to their province. Instead, they could be used to explain and adapt the government's program to their communities. They gradually began to think in terms of the national interest, because there were no provincial interests to distract their attention. Common laws and common institutions created a greater sense of identity than there was in countries where a man from one province could not understand the governmental procedures of a neighboring province. Thus, England was clearly a nation-state in the fifteenth century, at a time when a French prince (the duke of Burgundy) could still hope to split off provinces from France and combine them with his holdings in the Low Countries to make a new kingdom. The great surge of French nationalism at the end of the eighteenth century coincided with a successful effort to destroy provincial privileges and create a unitary state.

On the other hand, where several states grew up within a splintered *regnum*, the process of building a nation-state was much more difficult. Many of these states were too small to satisfy any political emotion except the desire for law and order. Even the larger ones found it hard to appeal to the same sentiments that were so easily tapped by the governments of France and England. There was no correspondence between the political framework and the ancient traditions of the people. The historical, cultural, and linguistic group to which people felt they belonged was always larger than the state to which they were supposed to give their allegiance. At the same time, many of the splinter-states developed strong administrative and military systems which could not easily be overthrown. Thus, when, in the nineteenth century, nationalism seemed to ensure both political success and psychological satisfaction, violent efforts were still needed to make the state and the nation coincide. The Germans and Italians could assemble and hold together the fragments of their old *regna* only through repeated wars and only by pitching nationalist appeals at a dangerously high emotional level. The Hapsburg monarchy was in even worse shape, since it was a "mosaic" state largely made up of splinters of several *regna*. No nationalism could be developed for the state as a whole, and there was considerable confusion as to which nationalisms were appropriate for each of its fragments. The European provinces of the Ottoman Empire were in a somewhat similar condition. The resulting instabilities in these two areas were one of the major causes of the European tragedy of the twentieth century.

Historians look for morals as sociologists do for models; perhaps we can find both in this hastily sketched story. Building a nation-state is a slow and complicated affair, and most of the political entities created in the past fifty years are never going to complete this process. Mere imitation will not solve their problems; institutions and beliefs must take root in native soil, or they will wither. The new states that have the best chance of success are those which correspond fairly closely to old political units; those where the experience of living together for many generations within a continuing political framework has given the people some sense of identity; those where the political unit coincides roughly with a distinct cultural area; and those where there are indigenous institutions and habits of political thinking that can be connected to forms borrowed from outside. Poland and Czechoslovakia are such states, and it is interesting to see how their strong personalities assert themselves even under Communist control.

On the other hand, a state whose boundaries bear no relation to an earlier political unit, whose inhabitants are well aware that their state is only a splinter of an ancient political or cultural grouping, and whose institutions have no connection with the mores of the people is a state which will certainly not become a nation and which will probably soon cease to be a state. Jordan is the best example of this type, though many of the new African states may be as bad. Creating a viable system of states in most of the former colonial areas is going to be a painful process. We can only hope that the rest of the world can avoid being drawn into what promises to be an endless round of coups, conquests, revolutions, and wars.

The *Philosophes* in the Light of Present-Day Theories of Modernization

Arthur M. Wilson

The significance of this essay for an understanding of modernization is that it illustrates the extent to which French intellectual leaders in the century before their revolution were preoccupied with many of the same problems as are their counterparts in today's modernizing societies. Wilson shows with particular clarity the goals for society advocated by the philosophes. The inability of the conservative establishment in France to adapt to the pressure for meliorative change led to the Great Revolution in 1789. Similarly, today revolution seems to be endemic in developing societies where there is resistance to change on the part of domestic or colonial authorities.

In the social sciences since World War II there has emerged a whole new range of theoretical studies having to do with the principles and techniques requisite for assisting under-developed countries to improve their disadvantaged position. It all began very simply and naturally: newly independent countries obviously needed technical and economic assistance if they were not to relapse into a condition of concealed but no less real colonialism; and the competitiveness of the cold war made each side willing to invest vast sums of wealth in trying to make the newly emergent nations opt for his side rather than for the other.

Soon it became apparent that the simple proffering of economic and financial aid was not sufficient in itself to bring about the hoped-for improvement. Unless applied in accordance with coherent theoretical principles, the aid might be misdirected or work against the very purposes for which it was being offered. Quite evidently there was a real and urgent need for testing hypotheses and refining conceptualizations. This field of studies has now come to be known as development theory or modernization theory.

"The *Philosophes* in the Light of Present-Day Theories of Modernization" by Arthur M. Wilson is reprinted with the permission of the Voltaire Foundation from *Studies on Voltaire and the Eighteenth Century*, LVIII (1967), 1893–1913, and the author.

Wilson has pursued his interest in eighteenth-century France as a Rhodes scholar and as professor of biography at Dartmouth College. He has also served on the editorial boards of the *Journal of Modern History* and *French Historical Studies*. He is known in particular for his biographical studies of Cardinal Fleury and Diderot.

At first it was supposed, not unnaturally, that the adaptation and application of economic theory alone would be sufficient to guide the modernization of backward economies, and that, therefore, no general social theory would be needed. Thus we have the pioneer book of Ragnor Nurkse, *Problems of capital formation in underdeveloped countries* (1953). But soon the realization spread on all sides that economic development could be achieved only in coordination with fundamental changes in other aspects of a nation's life. This was explicitly recognized by the book that has become the single most famous and influential in this field of studies, Walt W. Rostow's *The Stages of economic growth* (1960). A whole 'group of sociological and psychological changes would now be agreed to be at the heart of the creation of the pre-conditions for take-off' (p. 26).

Thus development theory has had to learn to spread its nets wider and wider, drawing upon the researches and insights not only of economists but also of sociologists, political scientists, anthropologists, social psychologists, and historians. Accordingly development theory has taken on the air of a study inherently interdisciplinary and comparative. This is abundantly to be seen in the writings of Almond and Coleman, of Silvert, of Lucien W. Pye, of David E. Apter, and a host of others.[1]

Carrying economic development successfully to the point of achieving and sustaining industrialization entails massive changes and transformations in many aspects, perhaps in almost all aspects, of a nation's life. These changes, by definition, involve a break with, or at least substantial modification of, past continuities, a process often painful because it challenges the efficacy of traditional forms. The history of modernization is the history of traditionalist societies in the process of radical transformation. So inherent is this challenge, so essential to successful change is the adaptation from the old to the new, that the very name for this branch of social science is itself in the process of change. 'Development theory' is now being replaced by the phrase 'modernization theory.' The name 'development theory' still seems suitable to many economists; but to most other social scientists the phrase 'modernization theory' feels more adequate. It connotes the conflict between traditionalism and change, and it implies that such a conflict is ineluctable.

In our day attention is focused upon the clamorous needs of newly-born nations and upon the necessity of bringing about their modernization within a very short span of time. Yet among the theorists of modernization it is recognized that countries that are now fully industrialized—as, for example, Great Britain, France, and the United States—have all at some time in their history gone through these same stages of change and adaptation, the only difference being that they were accomplished at a much more leisurely rate and therefore over a much greater stretch of time. 'It is evident, indeed,' it has been remarked recently, 'that the main outlines of Westernization have been

[1] See especially Gabriel A. Almond and James S. Coleman, eds., *The Politics of the developing areas* (Princeton 1960); Kalman H. Silvert, ed., *Expectant peoples: nationalism and development* (New York 1963); Lucian W. Pye, *Aspects of political development* (Boston 1966); and David E. Apter, *The Politics of modernization* (Chicago 1965).

followed by many countries. Westernization, understood in its broad sense, is therefore not a single, unique, historical experience but rather a general repetitive series of social events.' [2] 'The developing countries of Asia, Africa and parts of Latin America,' writes a contemporary prophet of modernization, 'may have to accomplish within a few decades a process of political change which in the history of Western Europe and North America took at least as many generations.' [3] And another authority writes: 'It is our great good fortune that we and the culture from which we derive our traditions have had about five hundred years in which to adjust ourselves to this revolution, whereas the majority of mankind has had only decades.' [4]

Theorists of modernization such as Smelser, Lipset, and Black have applied case studies from history in order to illuminate present-day problems and suggest present-day solutions.[5] But just as the historical method can sharpen our understanding of present-day problems of modernization, so, inversely, it may be possible to illuminate further our comprehension of the Enlightenment by flashing back upon the eighteenth century the light beamed by the use of newly discovered analytical tools. If modernization, as we are assured, 'involves the transformation of all systems by which man organizes his society—the political, social, economic, intellectual, religious and psychological systems' (Halpern, p. 179), then perhaps it is possible to identify in the events of a bygone era, say in France of the eighteenth century, phenomena which might hitherto have seemed a little discrete and disjointed, but which are now seen to fit neatly into the pattern, to use Rostow's term, of the preconditions for take-off.

If the history of the Enlightenment be reexamined from this vantage point, the interesting conclusion emerges that the *philosophes* were striving for almost every condition now considered an essential ingredient of successful modernization. The changes that they wanted to see accomplished were exactly the kinds of change that present-day theorists tell us are necessary to transform a traditional society into a modern one; and the freedoms the *philosophes* sought to achieve were precisely the ones leading to that type of open society that modernization theorists tell us is most effective in the *aggiornamento* of nations. This paper does not, of course, contend that the *philosophes* had more than intuitive convictions of what was requisite for melioration. But this paper does contend that there is a striking congruence between the changes consistently sought by the *philosophes* and the conditions that social scientists today tell us must be brought about if modernization is to be accomplished.

2 Summary of remarks by Leonard Reissman, in Kalman H. Silvert, ed., *Discussion at Bellagio* (New York 1964), p. 134.

3 Karl W. Deutsch, 'Social mobilization and political development,' *American political science review* (1961), lv. 498.

4 Manfred Halpern, 'The Revolution of modernization in national and international society,' *Nomos* (New York 1966), viii. 195.

5 Neil J. Smelser, *Social change in the industrial revolution* (Chicago 1959); Seymour M. Lipset, *The First new nation: the United States in historical and comparative perspective* (New York 1963); Cyril E. Black, *The Dynamics of modernization: a study in comparative history* (New York 1966).

Let us compare, in demonstration of this, the goals towards which modern-izing societies strive with the goals that the *philosophes* had in mind. For example, we are told by theorists that modernizing peoples constantly exert pressure towards a condition of greater equality. As Apter points out, 'the achievement of equality is an ever spreading moral objective in the modern world. Few modern societies, even if they institutionalize inequality, regard it as a good thing' (p. 73). Traditionalist societies, on the other hand, such as was the establishment during the *ancien régime*, almost invariably resist any pressure for greater equality.

Now, the latter half of the eighteenth century witnessed in America the declaration, penned by the man who is generally conceded to be a very model of Enlightenment, that 'all men are created equal.' A French document of comparable fame declares that 'Les hommes naissent et demeurent libres et égaux en droits. Les distinctions sociales ne peuvent être fondées que sur l'utilité commune.' [Individuals are born and remain equal as regards rights. Social distinctions may only be justified by their usefulness for the common good.] The remarkable synthesis of eighteenth-century history recently pub-lished by R. R. Palmer establishes that the latter part of the eighteenth century was indeed the age of the democratic revolution.

But in the earlier years of the Enlightenment, when revolution was still far away, expressions of desire for greater equality, coupled with a corresponding distaste for inequality, were common. A generation before the Declaration of Independence the *chevalier* de Jaucourt was writing in his article in the *Encyclopédie* on 'égalité naturelle': 'Cette *égalité* est le principe & le fonde-ment de la liberté. . . . Puisque la nature humaine se trouve la même dans tous les hommes, il est clair que selon le droit naturel, chacun doit estimer & traiter les autres comme autant d'êtres qui lui sont naturellement égaux, c'est-à-dire qui sont hommes aussi bien que lui.' [6] [This *equality* is the principle and the basis of freedom. . . . Since human nature is the same in all individuals, it is clear that in accordance with natural law each one should value and treat others as beings who are naturally equal, that is to say as though each individual were as good as another.] And the same author, in the article 'Primogeniture, droit de,' with a fine regard for natural justice and a splendid uncertainty regarding grammatical antecedents, declared that primogeniture was a 'droit contraire à la nature': 'il détruit *l'égalité* des citoyens qui en fait toute l'opulence' (xiii. 370; my italics). Rousseau made bold to answer the question, 'Quelle est l'origine de l'inégalité parmi les hommes, et si elle est autorisée par la loi naturelle?' Diderot confided to Brosses that this question was 'very fine but impossible to deal with under a monarchy,' clearly implying that the eighteenth-century establishment was so inegalitarian that it would not tolerate a candid appraisal.[7] The weight of *philosophe* opinion was on the side of equality. Even Voltaire, as a result of his experience in Geneva, inclined to-

---

[6] *Encyclopédie*, v. 415. Cf. Eberhard Weis, *Geschichtsschreibung und Staatsauffassung in der französischen Enzyklopädie* (Wiesbaden 1956), pp. 180–182.
[7] Arthur M. Wilson, *Diderot: the testing years* (New York 1957), pp. 224–225.

wards democracy, as *L'A.B.C.* clearly shows.[8] Though it may be true that the *Contrat social* was not widely influential the first twenty years after its publication, it cannot be gainsaid that its teaching is firmly based upon the doctrine of political equality.[9] Greatly influenced by Rousseau's work is Beccaria, preaching egalitarianism and social utility at one and the same time. Finally, Condorcet, in the tenth stage of his *Esquisse d'un tableau historique des progrès de l'esprit humain*, writes eloquently of the decrease in inequality that he descries approaching.

The desire for equality is frequently made manifest by the hatred of inequality. Often one can observe in the attitude of the *philosophes* a sense of alienation because of prevailing conditions of inequality. Here we tread upon familiar ground. Hegel thought that this was the heart of the meaning of Diderot's *Le Neveu de Rameau*.[10] The trigger word that set the *philosophes* off into fireworks of frustration was the word *privilège*. And therefore posterity accepts as the trademark of an epoch the words of Figaro when in his imagination he apostrophizes his noble master: 'Noblesse, fortune, un rang, des places, tout cela rend si fier! Qu'avez-vous fait pour tant de biens? Vous vous êtes donné la peine de naître.' [Nobility, fortune, rank, position, all these make one so proud! What have you done to deserve such assets? You have taken the trouble to be born.] The hatred of privilege, the passionate indictment of unequal treatment, provided the fuel for the *abbé* Sieyès's *Qû'est-ce que le tiers état?* A modern social scientist, aware that modernization is 'associated with the breaking down of norms of government based on privilege,' comes upon a surprisingly familiar word when reading this piece. Describing what he calls the privileged estate, Sieyès is already using, and using frequently, the one word that expresses the ultimate in social stratification and social immobility, the word 'caste.' [11]

Modernization theorists, besides emphasizing that modernizing peoples demand a greater extent of equality, recognize also that such groups desire to experience a greater sense of participation in the civic experience (Silvert, p. 367). This desire is easy to identify in the twentieth century. But what was there, if anything, to correspond to it in the age of the Enlightenment? One must look for such correspondence beneath the surface of things, the reason being that the absolutistic establishment in the eighteenth-century church and state continued to lay emphasis, as it had been doing for centuries, on conformism and passiveness rather than upon active participation. But if one does look beneath the surface, one discovers a great difference between the 'feel' of

[8] Peter Gay, *Voltaire's politics* (Princeton 1959), pp. 220–238; the same, *The Party of humanity* (New York 1964), p. 95.

[9] cf. David Williams, 'The Influence of Rousseau on political opinion, 1760–1795,' *English historical review* (1933), xlviii. 414–430; Joan McDonald, *Rousseau and the French Revolution* (London 1965), pp. 43–50.

[10] Jean Hyppolite, *Genèse et structure de la* Phénoménologie de l'esprit *de Hegel* (Paris [1946]), pp. 387, 398–404. Cf. Gottfried Stiehler, ' "Rameaus Neffe" und die "Phänomenologie des Geistes" von Hegel,' *Wissenschaftliche Zeitschrift der Humboldt-Universitätzu Berlin: Gesellschafts-und sprachwissenschaftliche Reihe* (1964), xiii. 163–167.

[11] Apter, p. 224. Emmanuel Joseph Sieyès, *Qu'est-ce que le tiers-état?* (seconde éd. [Paris] 1789), pp. 6, 9, 9 n., 19, 40 n., 65 n.

France in the time of Louis xiv and the 'feel' of France in the reign of Louis xvi. There is a striking contrast between the diffident manner of Vauban and Boisguillebert and the pamphleteering of Raynal and Mirabeau.

The fact is that what made the *siècle des lumières* so exciting to the *philosophes* was the hope they had of communicating their ideas to ever-widening circles of people. An increased sense of partaking thus came to the persons who tried to do the enlightening, and also to the public, to the persons to whom this enlightenment was transmitted. For the *philosophes* and their ever more numerous followers, enlightenment in itself signified participation. Thus Diderot, castigating an author who was praising the good old days, wrote: 'Maudit soit l'impertinent qui ne voit pas que les sciences et les arts ont fait des progrès incroyables, et que ces progrès ont amené une douceur de caractère ennemie de toute action barbare. Maudit soit l'impertinent qui ne s'aperçoit pas qu'en aucun temps les lumières ne furent aussi populaires, et que cette popularité ne peut nous acheminer qu'à quelque chose d'utile' (A.-T. vi. 373). [A curse on the impertinent ones who do not see that the sciences and the arts have made incredible progress, and that this progress has softened the harsh character of all cruel acts. A curse on the impertinent ones who fail to recognize that never before have the luminaries been so popular, and that this popularity can only lead us to something useful.] This sense of permeation, of participation in enlightenment, is also to be seen in the peroration of Holbach's *Système social* (1773): 'Tout homme qui voudra jetter un coup d'œil attentif sur la plupart des contrées de l'Europe, ne pourra s'empêcher d'y reconnoître les effets les plus sensibles du progrès des lumières. . . . Les nations les plus frivoles commencent à penser; leur attention se fixe sur des objets utiles, les calamités publiques forcent à la fin les hommes à méditer, & à renoncer aux vrais jouets de leur enfance' (iii. 160–161). [All who would cast an attentive eye on most of the countries of Europe would not fail to recognize the most perceptible effects of the progress of the luminaries. . . . The most frivolous of nations are beginning to think; their attention is fixed on useful objects, public misfortunes finally force people to meditate, and to abandon their truly childish beliefs.]

This extended participation in the civic experience can be detected in the *siècle des lumières* by the rise in importance of public opinion. By the decade of the 1780's this was clearly observable. In fact, it is clearly to be seen in the 1760's in the way in which Voltaire mobilized public opinion in the Calas case. Claude de Rulhière, in his reception address to the French Academy on 4 June 1787, remarked that in 1749, because of the publication of a number of important books, a change had begun to occur in French life: 'Ce fut alors que s'éleva parmi nous ce que nous avons nommé *l'empire de l'opinion publique.*' Later in his discourse Rulhière referred to 'le nouveau tribunal de l'opinion publique,' and spoke of there being at the time that he wrote 'une déférence plus attentive à l'opinion publique.' [12] Rulhière was a publicist rather than a belle-lettrist, a man whose career in letters had been concerned with public matters—events in Poland, the putsch of 1762 in Russia, etc.—so that he can fairly be considered to be a man capable of judging the effect of public

[12] Claude Carloman de Rulhière, *Œuvres* (Paris 1819), ii. 26, 35, 45.

opinion with some expertise. In an essay written in 1788 and entitled 'De l'action de l'opinion sur les gouvernements,' he began, 'On n'a jamais tant parlé de l'opinion que depuis quelques années, et c'est une preuve infaillible qu'il est arrivé dans l'état quelque changement qui a donné naissance à cette puissance invisible qu'on a justement nommée la reine du monde' (ii. 203). [There has never been so much talk about opinion as in recent years, and this is an infallible proof that a change has taken place in the conditions which have given birth to that invisible power which has justly been named the queen of the world.]

Modernization theorists are all of them aware of the essential rôle played by the intellectuals in the modernization of a country.[13] Apter believes that the reason they have a special rôle to play is that 'they are most inclined to respect the culture of freedom. . . . The intellectuals are the critical mediators between traditionality and modernity' (pp. 75, 154). Terminology has changed since the eighteenth century, but it seems evident that what we now call 'intellectuals' the eighteenth century called 'gens de lettres.' The assertiveness of dr Johnson in his letter to lord Chesterfield, the independent spirit that Alembert would have liked to display in his Réflexions sur l'état présent de la république des lettres (1760)—he thought better of publishing it—are indicative of a sense of greater independence. And these writings may also be interpreted as showing that the men of letters of the Enlightenment clearly understood that they were playing an important rôle. This rôle (a word dear to twentieth-century sociologists) was the formation of public opinion. Rulhière (ii. 16–20) attributed the change in public opinion to the works of Fontenelle, Voltaire, Montesquieu, Buffon, Rousseau, and to the administrative policies of Malesherbes. And Diderot, who can fairly be regarded as the very paradigm (to use another word dear to twentieth-century social scientists) of the intellectual, said right out in the article 'Encyclopédie' that the object of the work was 'de changer la façon commune de penser' (A.-T. xiv. 463). So engagé were the philosophes, so far removed from the detachment of the ivory tower, that it has had the paradoxical effect of making them seem to posterity less philosophical than they really were.

In pursuit of evidence that there was in the eighteenth century a mood for greater participation in the civic experience, one may point to the greatly increased use of the word 'citizen' in the writings of the philosophes as the century advanced. In contrast to the word 'subject,' the very word 'citizen' connotes partaking and participation. 'Je suis un bon citoyen,' wrote Diderot humanistically in 1748, 'et tout ce qui concerne le bien de la société et la vie de mes semblables est très-intéressant pour moi' (A.-T. ix. 223). [I am a good citizen, and all that concerns the welfare of the society and life of my fellow beings is of great interest to me.] The word citoyen became one of the pleasant and slightly radical words of the eighteenth century. Granted that the article 'Citoyen' in the Encyclopédie was technical and inclined to be unventuresome, nevertheless it did point out the notion of participation inherent in the word:

---

[13] E.g., Edward Shils, 'The Intellectuals in the political development of new states', World politics (1959–1960), xii. 329–368.

a citizen 'doit être homme public.' [14] And in the article 'Bourgeois, citoyen, habitant' Diderot wrote: 'la qualité de citoyen [suppose] une société dont chaque particulier connaît les affaires et aime le bien, et peut se promettre de parvenir aux premières dignités' (A.-T. xiii. 506–507). [Citizenship presupposes a society where each individual is aware of what is going on and supports public welfare, and can hope to attain the highest rank.] The concept that citizenship implies participation in civic affairs was an abiding one in the *Encyclopédie,* so that in the article 'Puissance,' for example, it was stated that when each one occupies himself with only his individual affairs, then 'il n'y aura plus de citoyens' (A.-T. xvi. 468). The important article 'Représentants,' now known to have been written by Holbach, constantly referred to citizens and citizenship, which, very conservatively, he made depend upon the ownership of property.[15] More democratic, indeed all embracing in its inclusion of citizens in civic participation, are Rousseau's ideas in the *Contrat social,* of which Diderot wrote in 1763 that 'imprimé et réimprimé, [il] s'est distribué pour un petit écu sous le vestibule du palais même du souverain.' [16] [printed and reprinted, it is distributed for a few pennies even under the door of the sovereign's palace.] *La volonté générale* is inherently a concept of equal sharing by citizens in what is the ultimate in authority, namely sovereignty itself.

Furthermore, the use of the word 'nation,' signifying at least community if not participation, became more frequent as the century progressed. The word was used by the Encyclopedists, but in a rather muted way.[17] It was especially the physiocrats who couched their arguments in terms of the nation. 'Il faut que toute la Nation,' wrote Le Trosne in 1779, 'qui semble aujourd'hui privée de vie et d'action, qui n'a qu'une sorte d'existence passive, devienne animée et organisée dans toutes ses parties, pour former un véritable corps social.' [18] [It is necessary that the whole nation, which appears today to be deprived of life and of action, which only has a kind of passive existence, should become animated and mobilized, so that it may become a truly social organism.] Thus the physiocratic writings familiarized people with the concept of nationhood, a concept that was rather juridical and without the mythopoeic tendency of a Herder or a Fichte and without the ethnocentric flavour of nineteenth-century nationalism. Nevertheless this physiocratic concept of nationalism, being implicitly secular in character, set up the ideal of a secular state in a way very similar to that postulated by present-day theorists of modernization, who declare that

14 A.-T. xiv. 192. Cf. Jacques Proust, *Diderot et l'Encyclopédie* (Paris 1962), pp. 344, 346, 423, 481.

15 *Encyclopédie,* xiv. 143–146; also A.-T. xvii. 11–22. For attribution, see Herbert Dieckmann, 'L'Encyclopédie et le Fonds Vandeul,' *Revue d'histoire littéraire de la France* (1951), li. 332.

16 Denis Diderot, *Sur la liberté de la presse,* ed. Jacques Proust (Paris [1964]), p. 82.

17 *Encyclopédie,* xi. 36, s.v. 'Nation': 'Mot collectif dont on fait usage pour exprimer une quantité considérable de peuple, qui habite une certaine étendue de pays, renfermée dans de certaines limites, et qui obéit au même gouvernement.'

18 Le Trosne, *De l'administration provinciale et de la réforme de l'impôt* (Basle 1779), i. 534, quoted by Mario Einaudi, *The Physiocratic doctrine of judicial control* (Cambridge [Mass.] 1938), p. 34. For other references by physiocrats to the 'nation,' see pp. 36, 37, 39, 41, 42, 57 *et passim.*

'Nationalism is the acceptance of the state as the impersonal and ultimate arbiter of human affairs' (Silvert, p. 19). The emphasis that came to rest in the eighteenth century upon the concepts of 'citizen' and 'nation' is exemplified by the fact that these words appear on almost every page of the *abbé* Sieyés's *Qu'est-ce que le tiers état?*

The ideal of participation in the civic experience, an ideal that animated the *philosophes* and in general the whole group that Peter Gay calls the 'party of humanity,' may be seen, inside out, in the common detestation of despotism.[19] Even the physiocrats, who wrote favourably of something called 'legal despotism,' meant by that the authority of law, not the whim of an arbitrary ruler (Einaudi, p. 28). 'Despotism' or 'oriental despotism,' following the example set by Montesquieu, became the *philosophe*'s favourite term of denigration. Moreover, where there are despots, subjects become slaves, and to speak of slaves is to speak of something that is the ultimate in non-participation in the civic enterprise.

Thus it can be seen that when present-day theorists emphasize that modernization postulates widespread participation in the civic experience, many analogues can be detected in the age of Enlightenment. But, it might be argued, these are only coincidental and accidental. Is there an example of a *philosophe* who knowingly made a plea for broadening the base of participation in the civic experience? There most certainly is. It is Diderot, making recommendations to Catherine for broader political participation on the part of the Russians, for the development of a larger middle class, for the encouragement of a much more numerous class of skilled artisans, for the 'formation d'un tiers état.' M. Paul Vernière's recent edition of Diderot's *Mémoires pour Catherine II* (1966) allows us to judge how consciously and deliberately these memoirs were intended to affect her policies (pp. iv, ix-xxi, 242). It had been known that Diderot had made such suggestions during his visit to St Petersburg, but it had previously been supposed that they had been merely conversational, rather superficial, perhaps not much more than chit-chat by which to beguile an idle hour. M. Vernière's edition shows that Diderot's recommendations had been carefully researched, were systematic rather than adventitious, were based upon determined efforts to get empirical knowledge of Russian conditions, and constituted a deliberate attempt to show the way by which a numerous but backward people might be modernized. It can well be argued that Diderot here shows himself a conscious advocate of modernization.

Broadly speaking, then, the goals of the *philosophes* were congruent with the goals for modernizing societies formulated by twentieth-century theorists. This suggests—terminology differing between the two centuries—that what a twentieth-century social scientist means when he says 'modernization' a *philosophe* meant when he said *lumières*. Certainly the thrust of the Enlightenment was consistently in the direction of innovation, almost never in the direc-

---

[19] See Richard Koebner, 'Despot and despotism: vicissitudes of a political term,' *Journal of the Warburg and Courtauld institutes* (1951), xiv. 275–302; and Franco Venturi, 'Despotismo orientale,' *Rivista storica italiana* (1960), lxxii. 117–126; translation under the title of 'Oriental despotism,' *Journal of the history of ideas* (1963), xxiv. 133–142.

tion of traditionalism. New art forms in the theatre, as in the *drames* of Diderot, Sedaine, Beaumarchais, and Mercier; a new theory of criminal juris-prudence, as in the ideas of Voltaire and Beccaria; a new aesthetic, discarding the baroque and rococo and exploring the moral values to be found in neo-classicism; a new theory of the novel, as we see analyzed in the recent works by Georges May and Vivienne Mylne—all tended to challenge the ancients in favour of the moderns. When the *philosophes* addressed themselves to the tempting but dangerous subjects of religion and government, when if ever did they express enthusiasm and devotion for traditional forms? Not for the symbol of the crown in the person of Louis xv. The popular outpouring of affection for him when he lay sick at Metz in 1744 did not last. For whom did the *philosophes* express affection? For the modernizing and tough-minded Turgot. But not unanimously for Maupeou, for it was feared that his reforms would make 'despotism' easier in France. Nor for his victims, the *parlements*, for people like Diderot knew very well that the *parlements*, though they posed as being champions of liberty against a 'despotic' king, were motivated much more by *esprit de corps* and vested interest than they were by a disinterested regard for the commonweal. 'Examinons notre corps remontrant sous ces différentes faces,' wrote Diderot for Catherine ii. 'Jouissait-il de la considération publique? Non. Il n'en jouissait pas, parce qu'il ne la méritait pas, et il ne la méritait pas, parce que toutes ses résistances aux volontés du souverain n'étaient que de la mômerie; que l'intérêt de la nation était toujours sacrifié et qu'il ne se battait bravement que pour le sien' (p. 16). [Let us examine our public institutions in their different aspects. Do they enjoy public support? No. They do not enjoy it because they do not deserve it, and they did not deserve it because all their semblances of resistance to the will of the sovereign are no more than mummery; the interests of the nation are always sacrificed and they only fight courageously for their own.] *Philosophe* pressure was always for greater liberty from the trammels of traditional institutions. The symbol and example of this is to be seen in Diderot's *Sur la liberté de la presse* which he wrote for Sartine, the lieutenant general of police. It is, of course, a plea for greater freedom.

But the yearning for greater equality and the desire for greater participation in the affairs of the polity, which are the earmarks of modernizing societies, are more emotions than policies. They need to be made concrete, to be imple-mented. Thus twentieth-century modernization theorists have trained them-selves to identify the crucial areas in the society and in the polity where innova-tion must be introduced, where it must be applied if the process is to gain momentum and be successful at all. I shall mention the most important of these areas, for the purpose of then pointing out that the *philosophes* developed comparable policies in order to serve comparable purposes. Although the specific programmes of twentieth-century modernization theorists and eighteenth-century *philosophes* may in some instances be diametrically opposed, as, for example, in their ways of looking at population growth, it can nevertheless be easily demonstrated that both centuries were deeply con-cerned with the same clusters of political and social problems. Both centuries worried about the same sorts of things.

A twentieth-century modernization theorist, for example, is concerned about whether the economy is making sufficient accumulation of capital to make further development possible. Are adequate savings being amassed and are they then being properly invested in order to maintain the desired rate of economic development? A modern theorist worries about this and keeps his finger upon this particular pulse. But were not these questions of the accumulation and the proper allocation of capital at the heart of the confused eighteenth-century debate about luxury? 'Traditional economies tend to consume virtually all that is produced, leaving little for investment and growth' (Black, p. 18). Some eighteenth-century writers, like Mandeville and Voltaire, justified this, arguing that luxury, of whatever kind, was beneficial because it stimulated employment. But others, like Saint-Lambert in his article on 'Luxe' in the *Encyclopédie*, and like Diderot, argued that there was a beneficial *luxe* and a noxious *luxe*. Thus Diderot was grappling with the concept, though he was not able to articulate it very well, of greater capital savings and greater productivity in the national economy.[20] He worried about that.

Another area of great concern to modernization theorists is that of demography. Twentieth-century theorists worry because there is too much population, unlike the *philosophes*, who worried lest there be too little. But the central preoccupation was the same, namely the proper relationship of the number of the people to the strength and well-being of the national economy.[21] In his day, the conditions of public health being what they were, Diderot feared depopulation: 'Lorsque je repasse en revue la multitude et la variété des causes de la dépopulation, je suis toujours étonné que le nombre des naissances excède d'un dix-neuvième celui des morts' (A.-T. ii. 431). [When I review the large number and variety of the causes of depopulation, I am always surprized that the ratio of births to deaths is ten to nine.] For Diderot also believed that 'La principale source de la puissance d'un Etat est sa population' (A.-T. xvi. 467, *s.v.* 'Puissance').

Still another area of solicitude to latter-day modernization theorists is the whole problem of fiscal theory and taxation policy (*e.g.* Apter, p. 65; Silvert, p. 445). The *siècle des lumières* was deeply concerned with the same subject— witness Voltaire's jokes about farmers-general, Damilaville's article in the *Encyclopédie* on 'Vingtième,' Rousseau's youthful encounter with the peasant who was afraid of the arbitrariness of the tax collector, Diderot's calling for a graduated income tax in his *Mémoires pour Catherine II*.[22] In no matter of necessary change were the *philosophes* in greater agreement than they were on the matter of tax policy. The concluding paragraph of Quesnay's article in the

[20] For Diderot's views on *luxe*, see A.-T. ii. 414–416; A.-T. xi. 89–94: 'Satire contre le luxe, à la manière de Perse'; *Mémoires pour Catherine II*, pp. 145–160. Cf. René Hubert, *Les Sciences sociales dans l'Encyclopédie* (Paris 1923), pp. 306–307; and Anita Fage, 'Les Doctrines de population des Encyclopédistes,' *Population* (1951), vi. 620–622.

[21] See Sir Julian Huxley, 'A factor overlooked by the *philosophes*: the population explosion,' *Studies on Voltaire* (1963), xxv. 861–872; Agnes Raymond, 'Le Problème de la population chez les encyclopédistes,' *Studies on Voltaire* (1963), xxvi. 1379–1388; and Fage, vi. 609–624.

[22] P. 152: 'mais il n'y a rien au monde que je ne fisse pour que sa répartition fût en raison des fortunes.'

Encyclopédie on 'Fermiers,' in which he enumerates all the wonderful and desirable advantages that would result 'si les habitants des campagnes étoient délivrés de l'imposition arbitraire de la taille,' is witness to the emphasis put by the *philosophes* upon this grave problem.

Another subject of serious concern in modernization theory is that of education. 'Education, related as it is to civic training, on the one hand, and functional skills for particular occupations, on the other, is perhaps the most sensitive indicator of the structure of a society in terms of the hierarchy of power and prestige' (Apter, p. 147). But the *philosophes* knew this already, as their great preoccupation with education—from Alembert's article 'Collège' in the *Encyclopédie* to Rousseau's *Emile*, from the anonymous *De l'éducation publique* (1762) to La Chalotais's *Essai d'éducation nationale* and Diderot's *Plan d'une université pour le gouvernement de la Russie*—clearly shows. Moreover, the *philosophes* approved another tenet of twentieth-century modernization theorists: 'the acceptance of the state as the impersonal and ultimate arbiter of human affairs' (Silvert, p. 19). The *philosophes* showed their adherence to this principle by stressing the necessity of secular control in public education and by emphasizing that education is the concern of the nation. Thus the title of La Chalotais's book, *Essai d'éducation nationale*; and thus the emphasis in *De l'éducation publique*, a book to which Diderot anonymously contributed a great deal, and in which it is stated that 'la Direction des Ecoles appartient à la grande Police de l'Etat.' [23]

The importance of technology in modernization programmes is so obvious to a twentieth-century man that it goes without saying. He applies it, he does not argue it. To his eighteenth-century predecessors, however, the point, though equally important, was not so self-evident; and it was one of the purposes, as well as one of the glories, of the *Encyclopédie* to give a complete picture of current technology. Thus, by portraying the utility of producing goods for human use and by portraying the dignity of productive labour, the *Encyclopédie* helped to modernize a traditional society.

Technology, unless it is to degenerate into mere rule of thumb, is nurtured by discoveries in basic science and by the mental attitudes implicit in the methods of scientific inquiry. Again this is obvious to a twentieth-century theorist, so that he uses all the resources of scientific method as a matter of course. For the *philosophes* this was a point that had to be established, thus explaining the Encyclopedists' praise of Bacon, their emphasis on experimental method, and their worship of Newton. As a present-day modernization theorist has perspicaciously remarked, Galileo is 'a kind of folk hero of modernization. His triumph is the triumph of reason, and reason as applied to human affairs is the foundation of modernity.' [24] The Enlightenment insistence upon critical

---

[23] *De l'Education publique*, p. 187. Regarding Diderot's connection with this volume, see Denis Diderot, *Correspondance*, ed. Georges Roth (Paris 1955–   ), iv. 234; Best. 10165 and 10187; *Correspondance littéraire*, v. 259; and J. G. Hamann to F. H. Jacobi, 31 May 1788 (Roland Mortier, 'Le Prince de Ligne, imitateur de Diderot,' *Marche romane* [1955], v. 129 n.).

[24] Apter, p. 43. Cf. Diderot's remark on Galileo (A.-T. ii. 369); and Voltaire on Galileo (Peter Gay, *The Rise of modern paganism* [New York 1966], p. 228).

rather than mythopoeic thought, the equally insistent emphasis in numerous articles in the *Encyclopédie* upon correct and rigorous methodology, as in Alembert's article 'Expérimental' and in innumerable other articles, are excellent illustrations of the fact, so familiar to modernization theorists that they accept it as a truism, that the scientific revolution and modernization go hand in hand (Black, pp. 7, 11, 76–77; Apter, pp. 316–318).

In spite of an approach to their problems on the part of twentieth-century modernization theorists that might sometimes seem to some persons as more than a little cocksure, there is one unsettled issue that greatly perplexes and confuses these theorists. This is the question of whether to acquiesce in or to deplore the tendency of modernizing regimes to become anti-democratic or proto-totalitarian. What should be the attitude towards personalistic regimes such as was that of Nkrumah? Quite consistently, though, the attitude of twentieth-century theorists is to hope for a regime that ultimately will favour pluralism and democracy. Thus Rostow concludes his book by saying, 'Man is a pluralistic being . . . and he has the right to live in a pluralistic society' (p. 167, cf. Silvert, pp. 357, 359). And Apter closes his by saying that 'even though it does not seem likely that most of the modernizing countries can move directly in a democratic direction, important subgroups already exist within these societies that are the long-run carriers of democratic values and that will be important in the future for democratic society' (p. 459; cf. pp. 449, 452, 461, 463).

Now, this is just exactly the problem encountered by the *philosophes* in the form of benevolent despotism. On the whole, as is being demonstrated to the point of unanimity by historians of late, the *philosophes* did not favour enlightened despotism. Yet to do so was a temptation to them because the enlightened despots, as the nineteenth century called them—the phrase had not yet been coined in the age of the *philosophes*—were themselves quite likely to be innovators and anti-traditionalists. Joseph II, for example, got into all the trouble he did precisely because he was anti-traditionalist. It should be accounted of great credit to the *philosophes* that they resisted temptation and instead quite clearly favoured a pluralistic solution to political, religious, and social problems. Thus Voltaire wrote that 'If there were only one religion in England, there would be danger of tyranny; if there were two, they would cut each other's throats; but there are thirty, and they live happily together in peace.' So Diderot wrote, 'Tout gouvernement arbitraire est mauvais; je n'en excepte pas le gouvernement arbitraire d'un maître bon, ferme, juste et éclairé. . . . Le droit d'opposition me semble, dans une société d'hommes, un droit naturel, inaliénable et sacré.' [25] [All arbitrary government is bad; I do not except arbitrary government under good, firm, just, and enlightened leadership. The right of opposition seems to me, in a society of men, to be a right that is natural, inalienable, and sacred.] And Kant, defining *Was ist Aufklärung*, said that 'if only freedom is granted enlightenment is almost sure to follow.'

As one approaches the end of a tentative and exploratory investigation into comparative history, such as this paper has been, one naturally asks, What can

[25] Diderot, *Mémoires pour Catherine II*, p. 117.

this method do for students of the Enlightenment? For one thing, it can perhaps allow us to analyze more precisely the venerable and vexed question as to how revolutionary the *philosophes* really were. The question is vexed because of the emphasis that has been placed on one of two antithetical views. On the one hand the *philosophes* have been represented as being revolutionaries in every respect save that of enjoying the knowledge of the Marxist dialectic; while, on the other, they have been represented as well-intentioned but naif do-gooders who were so non-revolutionary that they did not even know that they were playing with fire. Does not a more realistic view lie between these extremes, as a result of which the *philosophes* appear as modernizers—though lacking models to follow—attempting to transform a traditionalist society as best they knew how? Such a view also offers some sort of resolution to the long-standing controversy, represented by the names of Rocquain and Rostand, as to whether the *philosophes* had great influence or no influence upon the outbreak of the Revolution.

This comparative approach afforded by the use of modernization theory can help to reveal to us the nature and the inner consistency of the intellectual pressures for change in the eighteenth century. It can also reveal more clearly the anatomy of the forces in opposition to change. And in gauging the interplay of these forces for and against change, modernization theory offers to us a hypothesis, which by repeated testing is advancing to the status of an axiom, that a successfully modernizing society creates in its members a capacity for 'anticipatory and reactive self-adjustment' to the necessity for successive change.[26] Thus a successfully modernizing society avoids the discontinuity of utter breakdown and violent revolution. I am prepared to believe that the political thought of the *philosophes*, certainly that of Voltaire as we see it in Peter Gay's *Voltaire's politics*, certainly that of Diderot, certainly that of Rousseau in the *Contrat social*, in *Le Projet de constitution pour la Corse* and *Les Considérations sur le gouvernement de Pologne*, were instinctively oriented towards this process of 'anticipatory self-adjustment' that would help society to accept change. Now, as is well known, there was a conservative reaction in France in the 1780's. Does not the use of the concepts and methods of the twentieth-century theorists of modernization explain to us ever more clearly why the failure of the *philosophes*, so sapiently studied by Furio Diaz in his *Filosofia e politica nel settecento francese*, did indeed make the French Revolution inevitable because the conservative reaction inhibited the possibility of anticipatory self-adjustment to change? If this line of thought is *probant*, it suggests ways in which this comparative method of applying modernization theory to the history of the Enlightenment opens up new perceptions and fruitful new strategies of research.

It is notorious that the Enlightenment believed in progress. The men of the Enlightenment nourished their faith in progress by the realization that man was continuously increasing his capacity to understand and manipulate nature.

---

[26] Silvert, p. 436: 'It is neither illogical nor romantic to presume that the more voluntary the association, the greater the degree of anticipatory and reactive individual self-adjustment one should expect, and thus the better able the society will be to integrate change.'

(Diderot was wont to remark that nature is man's constant enemy.[27]) But the twentieth-century modernization theorists likewise pin their faith on this kind of progress. 'The concept must be spread,' writes Rostow, 'that man need not regard his physical environment as virtually a factor given by nature and providence, but as an ordered world which, if rationally understood, can be manipulated in ways which yield productive change and, in one dimension at least, progress' (p. 19). The Enlightenment faith in progress, however, was not without apprehensions, as Vyverberg's *Historical pessimism in the French Enlightenment* shows. In fact, that faith in progress was a little tremulous. This same faith, coupled with tremulousness, characterizes our century as well. The similarity in hopes and aspirations of the *philosophes* and of the present-day prophets of modernization—even to the metaphors they use—can well be seen in these words of Gabriel Almond: 'The magnitude of the formal and empirical knowledge required . . . staggers the imagination and lames the will. . . . As we learn that a stronger and steadier illumination is possible, our first reaction is to blink and withdraw in pain. And yet (Almond and Coleman, p. 64) . . . we cannot hesitate in the search for a greater illumination.'

---

[27] A.-T. ii. 431; cf. ii. 276; and Gay, *The Rise of modern paganism*, pp. 182–183.

The Influence of Colonial and Traditional Political Systems on the Development of Post-Traditional Social and Political Orders

S. N. Eisenstadt

It is one of the main tenets of the concept of modernization that societies confront the opportunities for change in terms of their heritage of premodern, or traditional, political, economic, and social orders. While Eisenstadt's particular concern here is with Southeast Asian societies, he assesses their problems in terms of those of later modernizing societies generally. Among the variations that characterize these societies are their differing capacities to guide change by means of a central administrative system. Most of them had a weak domestic tradition of central government. In those cases where a stronger government was imposed by a colonial power, its apparatus of personnel and institutions tended to be alienated from the mass of its citizens.

I

The major premise of this paper is that while we witness today throughout the world a breakdown of traditional socio-political orders, this does not necessarily mean that the development system or order will be patterned according to the initial modern model that developed in Europe, that, in fact, there may arise a great variety of post-traditional orders—and that some such types are developing now in South-East Asia.

These different post-traditional social and political orders may also vary greatly with regard to many crucial aspects of social and political organization, their very conception of modernity or post-traditionality, as well as their attitude to change and their ability to centre formation.

"The Influence of Colonial and Traditional Political Systems on the Development of Post-Traditional Social and Political Orders" by S. N. Eisenstadt is reprinted by permission of the author and Oxford University Press from *Modernization in South-East Asia*, ed. H. D. Evers (London, 1973), 3–18.

Eisenstadt is a professor at the Eliezer Kaplan School of Economic and Social Science, Hebrew University, Jerusalem, and is one of the leading students of modernization. His numerous publications include *The Political System of Empires* (1963), *Modernization: Protest and Change* (1966), and *Comparative Perspectives on Social Change* (1968).

In the following, we shall first briefly analyse the difference between traditional and post-traditional social and political orders. Second, we shall point out some of the basic differences between various post-traditional social orders, and last, some conditions giving rise to them, especially those which may be relevant for the analysis of South-East Asian societies. . . .

This analytical approach presented here stems from a reconsideration of some of the assumptions which have guided the initial studies of modernization and development.

II

The study of the conditions under which modern societies emerge, the differences among them and the condition of their stability and continuity, has been of central interest in the development of modern sociology since its beginning in the late eighteenth and early nineteenth centuries, through the classical period of its founding fathers—de Toqueville, L. V. Stein, Marx, Durkheim, Max Weber and others—and has been revived again in the late forties and fifties of this century.

It was but natural that this concern became transformed in sociological thought into confrontation between modern and non-modern, modern and pre-modern society; and given the conception of modern society as a society oriented towards 'progress' or 'change'. This confrontation tended very often to become defined in terms of modern versus traditional society.

This confrontation of modern versus traditional society in the history of modern social analysis initially took the form of depicting both as more or less completely 'closed' dichotomous types. These types were described in various ways, among the most famous of which were Tönnies' distinction between Gemeinschaft and Gesellschaft and Redfield's, more anthropologically oriented, distinction between primitive, folk, and urban societies.

Whatever the methodological and substantive criticism raised against these and similar typologies for decades, they dominated the thinking on this subject for a long period of time and they inspired many researches and investigations. Out of them emerged the picture of traditional and modern societies which prevailed in sociological thought for many years.

In this picture, traditional society was depicted as a static one with but little differentiation of specialization, with a low level of urbanization and of literacy. Modern society, on the other hand, was seen as a society with a very high level of differentiation, literacy and exposure to mass media. In the political realm, traditional society has been depicted as based on a 'traditional' elite ruling by virtue of some Mandate of Heaven, while modern society is based on wide participation of the masses who do not accept any traditional legitimation of the rulers and who hold these rulers accountable in terms of secular values and efficiency. Above all, traditional society has been conceived as bound by the cultural horizons set by its tradition while the modern society is culturally dynamic, oriented to change and innovation.

It is only in the 1940s and 1950s that this view became undermined; and more refined analytical approaches, as well as new *Problemstellungen*, with regard to this whole area, began to develop in the social sciences. True, the conception of modern society in terms of opposition to traditional society and the sharp dichotomization of the two has become even more pronounced with the great upsurge of interest in the breakthrough of non-Western societies into modernity, with the so-called underdeveloped or developing countries, 'New States' and the like, which have emerged since the Second World War. Yet the convergence of this growing interest in underdeveloped societies with the growth of analytical tools in sociology gave rise first of all in the later 1940s and early 1950s, to an analytically more refined and differen- tiated approach, especially in terms of the study of the two major types of such indices—namely the socio-demographic and the 'structural' which have been mentioned and analysed at least partially above. These new approaches were developed under the impact of the concern with the problem of under- developed countries, or New Nations, etc.

Accordingly, instead of concentrating on the distinct characteristics of each of these types of societies, there emerged a growing interest in the *conditions of emergence* of modern societies; instead of taking the emergence of these institutions, of a visible social order, for granted and concentrating on the analytical description of the nature of such an order, the growing concern with the possibility of relatively unsuccessful transition of these societies into modernity gave rise to asking about the *precondition* of such successful 'take-off' into modernity.

Furthermore, given the conception of modern society as a society oriented towards change and having to deal with continuous change, there developed also the search for the conditions of such continued, sustained growth in modern societies.

III

Many researches which took off from the preceding considerations led to or were based on the—usually implicit—assumption that the conditions for sustained growth, for continuous development and modernization in different institutional fields are dependent on, or tantamount to, continuous extension of these various socio-demographic and/or structural indices of modernization. According to this view, the more a society exhibits or develops the basic characteristics of structural specialization and the higher it is on various indices of social mobilization, the less traditional and the more modern it would be, i.e. by implication the better it would be able to develop con- tinuously, to deal continuously with new problems and social forces and to develop a continuously expanding institutional structure.

In the initial stages of these researches, relatively little analytic distinction between these different *Problemstellungen* was made. Thus, initially, in many of the works which dealt with this problem, the preconditions of emergence of modern societies were very often described in the very same terms which denoted their characteristics (e.g. in terms of universalism, achievement orientation, etc.)—thus in a way neglecting the more specific question about the conditions of emergence of modern societies, of the processes through which they emerge—or fail to emerge—successfully from within the pre-modern societies.

These implicit assumptions about the conditions of continuous modernization became shattered through the experience of the late 1950s and the early 1960s when more and more countries which seemed to have 'taken off' into modernization were tending towards 'breakdown'.

The implicit assumption that existed in many of these studies—namely that the less traditional society is more capable of such sustained growth—has been proved incorrect. The various socio-demographic or structural indices of modernization indicate only the extent to which traditional, self-contained societies or communities became weakened, or disintegrated, the extent to which—to paraphrase the title of Dan Lerner's book—Traditional Society is Passing. But they do not in themselves indicate the extent to which a new, viable, modern society, which is capable of continuous growth, may develop or exactly what kind of a society will develop and what its exact institutional contours will be.

Similarly, it became clear that the mere destruction of traditional forms of life does not necessarily assure the development of such a new, viable, modern society, and that very often the disruption of traditional settings— be they family, community, or even sometimes political settings—tends to lead more to disorganization, delinquency and chaos rather than to the setting up of a viable modern order.

There was a continuously growing awareness of basic historical facts that in many countries modernization has been successfully undertaken under the aegis of traditional symbols—and even traditional elites. In such countries as Japan, or even England, many of their traditional symbols—be they the Emperor, the Japanese crown, the symbols of aristocracy in Britain or the traditional symbols of provincial life in Holland—were retained. In many cases, when the initial impetus to modernization was given under the aegis of anti-traditional elites, there soon followed an attempt, even if in a halting way, to revive some of the traditional symbols.

All these considerations have also contributed to the undermining of the assumption about the assurance of continuity of growth after the 'take-off'. In both the economic and the political spheres it became quite obvious that any assurance of such continuity does not exist. The Argentine in the economic sphere, Burma or Indonesia in the political sphere, are among the most pertinent examples of the possibility of breakdown after some initial—or even sometimes relatively advanced—stages of modernization have been reached.

These examples, however, have also shown that the relation between processes of change which tend to undermine or destroy traditional societies and the development of a viable modern society are not simple. The one does not always necessarily lead to the other. The awareness that a great part of contemporary history in general and of contemporary international relations in particular, is in a way the history of breakdowns or of stagnation of political regimes or economic systems—which have seemingly 'taken-off' into modernity but yet have been unable to continue to fly at all or to attain higher attitudes —and this slowly became accepted as fact.

But the more paradoxical of these processes was that such breakdowns or stagnations did not necessarily lead to the total collapse of these new regimes or to their return to some traditional social and political forms. Such politics and societies certainly differ in many ways from the 'older' (Western) modern ones nor do they necessarily develop into the direction of these 'older' societies. Yet, they are by no means any longer simply traditional societies. Moreover, however stagnating or unstable these regimes are, they evince some capability of reorganization and continuity and they develop various internal and external policies which aim at assuring for themselves the conditions of such continuity.

IV

All these developments have given rise to a series of many critiques of the initial assumptions of studies of modernization—especially of the ways in which the difference between traditional and modern societies was formulated. There are several important themes—all focused around the place of tradition in the studies of modernization.

One such theme was the 'rediscovery' of persistence in modern or modernizing societies of strong traditions, in the sense of some binding ways of behaviour rooted to some degree in the past, in modern societies.

Second, and closely connected with the former theme was the emphasis— by many scholars—on how traditional forces or groups, be they castes or tribal units, tend to reorganize in a very effective way, in new modern settings.

Third, and of special importance for our point of view, was the growing recognition that within many of the New States after the initial phases of independence whose politics were yet greatly shaped by modern models of politics, a new phase emerges in which older, traditional models of politics tend to reassert themselves.

V

While, as we shall see later on, all these and similar critical considerations have not necessarily invalidated the distinction between traditional and modern societies and politics, yet they have necessitated the reformulation of this distinction, and have, first of all, shown that while talking about modernity or modernization, we have to distinguish between several aspects of what has been usually designated as 'modernity' or 'modernization.'

They have shown that it is necessary to distinguish, first, between the impingement of forces of modernity and the consequent undermining of the existing traditional settings, second, the 'break-through' to modernity on the structural and cultural levels, and third, the ways in which the new emerging social systems tend to deal with these problems, and their capacity to deal with them.

Let us explicate these distinctions. Given the historical spread of modernity from the seventeenth/eighteenth centuries until today, almost all traditional societies have been, or are being, caught up in the sense that modern forces 'impinge' on them, undermining their existing settings in at least three different ways.

First, they impinge on many of the bases of the various existing traditional institutional spheres—economic, political or community life, or social organization—make various new demands on them, and open new vistas for their members. There obviously exist very great differences among the various modern and modernizing societies with regard to the intensity of this impingement and its specific institutional location.

Second, these forces have a new international system within which difference in strength in modern economic or political terms is a major determinant of relative international standing. Here too, however, great variations exist with regard to the extent of the impingement of these international forces on different traditional societies and of the extent to which they are exposed to it.

These forces of modernity may impinge on different 'traditional' societies by undermining the traditional economic structure and creating more differentiated social and economic frameworks. They may also impinge on many traditional societies in creating the vogue of demand for a growing participation of the citizens in the centre, most clearly manifested in the tendency to establish universal citizenship and suffrage and some semblance of a 'participant' political or social order. These different forces may impinge on various constellations in different historical cases and each of these constellations tends to create different types of breakthrough to modernity and to institutional and cultural problems with which these societies and their new emerging structures have to deal.

But, whatever the details of these differences—some of which we shall analyse in greater detail later on—given the unique setting in which modernity has taken place, its spread has given rise to some common characteristics and problems—even though the response to these may indeed vary greatly.

These common problems are derived from the crucial difference between the symbolical and cultural premises of traditionalism, with their structural and cultural limitations, and those which develop with modernity. The most important of these premises in the political field is the continuing symbolic and cultural differentiation between the centre and the periphery; and the concomitant limitation of the access of members of broader groups to the political centre or centres, and on participation within them.

In traditional regimes these premises were closely connected, first, to the fact that the legitimation of the rulers was couched in basically traditional religious terms, and second, to the lack of distinction of the basic political role of the subject societal roles, such as, for instance, membership in local communities; and although it was often embedded in such groups, the citizens or subjects did not exercise any actual direct or symbolic political rights through a system of voting or franchise.

In the cultural sphere, the basic premise of traditionality, common to all 'traditional' societies, however great the differences between them, has been the acceptance of tradition, of the givenness of some past events, order or figure (whether real or symbolic) as the major focus of their collective identity, as the scope and nature of their social and cultural order, as the ultimate legitimizer of change, and as the delineator of the limits of innovation.

The most important structural derivations of these premises were (a) limitation in terms of reference to some past event of the scope, content and degrees of changes and innovations; (b) limitation of access to positions, the incumbents of which are the legitimate interpreters of the scope and the contents of traditions; and (c) limitations of the right to participate in these centres and in forging the legitimate contents and symbols of the social and cultural orders.

Whatever the extent and scope to which the various traditional forms of life in various spheres of society persist, it is then, insofar as such changes in the connotation of tradition on central levels have taken place, that we witness the break-through—which may be gradual or abrupt—to some sort of modern socio-political or cultural order. And insofar as such changes in the connotation of tradition on central levels have not taken place, whatever the extent of structural changes or possible transformation of tradition in different parts of the society, we still have before us some type of traditional order.

Thus, the break-through to modernity is focused both in the change in the contents of the symbols of the centre, in their secularization and in the growing emphasis on values of human dignity and social equality, as well as in the growing possibility of the participation, even if in an intermittent or partial way, of broader groups in the formulation of its central symbols and institutions.

It is such changes in the connotation of tradition and of their major structural implications that provide the impetus to continuous processes of change and to the perception of change as a positive value in itself, and which create the problem of the absorption of change as the major challenge of modernization.

The preceding analysis brings out perhaps the most central characteristics and the problems of modern post-traditional societies—their basic mass-consensual orientation and their predisposition to continuous change.

The consensual or mass aspect of these societies is rooted in the growing impingement of broader strata on the centre, in their demands to participate in the sacred symbols of society and in their formulation, and in the replacement of the traditional symbols by new ones which stress these participatory and social dimensions.

This tendency to broad, mass-consensuality does not, of course, find its fullest institutionalized expression in all types of modern societies. In many regimes in the first stages of modernization it may be weak or intermittent, while totalitarian regimes naturally tend to suppress its fullest expression. But even totalitarian regimes attempt to legitimize themselves in terms of such values, and it is impossible to understand their policies and their attempts to create symbols of mass consensus without taking into consideration their assumption of the existence of such consensual tendency among its strata and its acknowledgement by the rulers.

VI

The preceding discussion brings out some of the most salient characteristics and problems in modern political orders. First, it brings out the fact that it is the break-through from a traditional socio-political order in the direction of a mass consensual one that contains within itself the specific characteristics of social changes to be found in modernity: the propensity to system-transformation, and the persistence of demands for change, protest and transformation. These demands for change could, of course, develop in different directions: they could be reformatory, demanding the improvement of existing institutions, or they could aim at total transformation of a system.

Thus we see that modernization evinces two closely connected, yet distinct aspects. There is the development of a social structure with great variety of structural differentiation and diversification, of continuously changing structural forms, activities and problems, and propensities to continuous change and to system transformation. But the mere development of these propensities does not in itself assume the development of an institutional structure which is capable of dealing, in a relatively stable way, with these continuous changes and of assuring concomitantly the maintenance of a civil order.

Thus the crucial problem that modernization creates is that of the ability of the emerging social structure to deal with such continuous changes or, in other words, the problem of sustained development—i.e. the ability to develop an institutional structure which is capable of 'absorbing' continuously changing problems and demands. It is this which constitutes the central change and subsequent problem of modernization. This is the challenge of modernity, of post-traditional social orders.

But if the spread of the forces of modernity creates problems, to some degree common to all modern societies, both its concrete manifestations as well as the responses to it, vary greatly.

All these various orientations to growing participation, to social justice, as well as the various structural aspects of change, are related to the common symbolic and structural cores of modernity mentioned above and derived from them; they vary greatly in their concrete expression or manifestation in different historical situations, giving rise to a very great variety of models of modern social and political order.

VII

One of the weaknesses of the first approaches to modernization has been the assumption that not only some of these problems may be common—but also that the natural direction for answers to these problems lies in the same direction that developed in Europe.

Since the first such break-through from a traditional to a modern social order took place in Europe, and it was here that the problem of defining such order in new terms first became fully articulated, the first definition of the parameters of the modern social order has been closely related to the specific characteristics of the symbolic institutional pattern of modern socio-political order that has developed in the West and constituted, in a sense, part of this pattern or universe.

The major form of this socio-political order—in the post-Counter-Reformation period throughout the eighteenth and nineteenth centuries, and later in the U.S., Australia, Canada, etc.—was the nation-state.

The major characteristics of this type of modern socio-political order have been enumerated as: (a) a high degree of congruence between the cultural and the political identities of the territorial population; (b) a high level of symbolic and effective commitments to the centre and a close relation between these centres and the more primordial dimensions of human existence; and (c) a marked emphasis on politically defined collective goals for all members of the national community.

In greater detail this model assumed that all the major components of centre-formation—i.e. first, the institutionalization, both in symbolic and organizational terms, of the quest for some charismatic ordering of social and cultural experiences, and for some participation in such orders; second, the crystallization of the common societal and cultural collective identity based on common attributes or on participation in common symbolic events; third, the crystallization and articulation of collective goals; fourth, the regulation of intrasocietal and intergroup relations; and fifth, the regulation of internal and external, or power-relations—tend to converge around the political centre of the nation-state.

In many ways many of these characteristics of the European nation-state were derived or transmitted from several parts of their pre-modern socio-political traditions; that is from Imperial traditions, and from those of city-states and of feudal societies. They combined the strong activist orientation of the city-state, the broad conception of the political order as actively related to the cosmic or cultural order of many Imperial traditions, and the tradition of Great Religions and the pluralistic elements of the feudal traditions.

In the European (especially Western European) traditions these various orientations were rooted in a social structure characterized by a relatively high degree of commitment of various groups and strata to the cultural and political orders and their centres, as well as by a high degree of autonomy in their access to these orders and their respective centre.

It was out of these orientations that some of the specific assumptions about patterns of participation and protest characteristics of the nation-state developed. The most important of these assumptions was that the political forces, the political elites and the more autonomous social forms—the State on the one hand and 'Society' on the other—continuously struggle over their relative importance in the formation and crystallization of the cultural and political centre of the nation-state and in the regulation of access to it: that the various processes of structural change and dislocation—which the periphery was continuously undergoing as a result of processes of modernization— give rise not only to various concrete problems and demands, but also to a growing quest for participation in the broader social and political order; and that this quest for participation of the periphery in such social, political and cultural orders is mostly manifested in the search for access to these centres.

This pattern of modern political order was not homogeneous or unitary even in Western Europe. But it was relatively homogeneous, at least in its ideal form, in comparison with the pattern of post-traditional political order that has developed in non - (Western) European societies. These orders have crystallized into a pattern which has evinced several important differences from the 'original' European one—even though the original models of modernity presented to them have indeed mostly been influenced by the pattern.

The difference could have been discerned already from the very beginning of the spread of modernization beyond the Empires in Russia or Japan where already new patterns of such orders—which in their turn served as such models with further spread of modernity—have developed.

But these differences can be most clearly seen in the shaping of post-traditional socio-political orders in many of the countries which have not adopted any of these models—especially in the various countries of Latin America, South-East Asia and Africa. In most general terms it can be said that the centres that tended to crystallize in these societies were characterized by what may be called 'modern patrimonialism', i.e. the establishment or continuation of new political and administrative central frameworks which have a tendency to maintain the external contents of traditional or of modern symbols without simultaneously maintaining any strong commitments to them. Such centres tend to display almost exclusive concern for the preservation of the existing weak frameworks of power, thus giving rise to a continuous succession of weak centres.

The major difference between these regimes and seemingly similar regimes that developed frameworks of 'Nation-States' can be seen in many ways— such as in the function of parties, voting and of political participation—all of which tend to develop in all types of modern centres and yet whose significance in the political process greatly differs among them.

Thus, to take just a few illustrations, the function of parties seems to vary greatly among them. The tendency to monolithic—and yet not totalitarian—parties, or to single non-totalitarian party regimes in many new states, indicates that many of these parties may seem more as instruments for the forging out of some new common collective identities for the struggle between different contestants of power representing different interests and/or ideological orientations. Such struggle seems to take place more inside such parties than among them.

Concurrently, bureaucracies may seem here often not only as administrative branches of the centre or as small contending groups or cliques within them, but also custodians of whatever common symbols and such centres as may represent whatever civil order they may be able to maintain. Just because of this they may here compete with the parties for the full representation of the centre—a fact which can perhaps to some degree explain the quick succession of a party regime by a military regime—with each regime maintaining some of the organizational framework and activities of the former.

Similarly, voting and suffrage may, in many of these regimes, be only a manifestation of some broad, not fully articulated, orientation to such centre, and neither of total commitment to the regime as in totalitarian regimes, nor as expression of specific concrete interests or ideologies as in many of the pluralistic-constitutional nation-state regimes.

The special characteristics of these regimes can also be seen in the nature —and especially in the outcome—of crises and breakdowns that may occur within them. The general reasons and symptoms of such crises and breakdowns—the rifts and cleavages between different types of elites, between the central and the parochial symbols, between classes and regions—are to a large extent common to all of them.

The specific crises or problems which these regimes face are first, their effectiveness on the new modern international scene; second, the upsurge of unregulated demands of various broader groups, which are very often fostered by these elites, and the concomitant waste of resources. They are confronted with potentially continuous conflicts within the elite and the new centres. The crises and problems that they may develop out of the great intensity of the conflicts between traditionalistic and more modern elites, the new modern ways in which the claims of many of these groups about the nature of the centre itself and the bases of its legitimation, may minimize the possibilities of establishing new, stable and viable centres of any kind.

Similarly the outcomes seem to differ. In societies with strong centres the tendency is more a 'total', dramatic breakdown of the centre—possibly leading to its reconstitution on a new level.

In the patrimonial centres such instability and oscillation tends very often to continue with mobilization, partial economic development and political activity. They may lead to a continuous succession of such patrimonial centres, together with economic regression and growing political apathy.

But within several types of post-traditional regimes, there are many differences. They tend also to vary greatly among themselves, on such dimensions as the scope of political mobilization, the relative predominance of different institutional settings (bureaucracy, military, political parties), the relations between the political and ethnic-national communities, the conception of social hierarchy and organization of social strata, or the degree of relative stability of their respective regimes and collective political boundaries. . . .

VIII

How can the differences between various types of post-traditional social orders be explained? While, needless to say, there are indeed many factors and conditions which may influence the shaping of these differences, yet it may be worthwhile to point out some conditions which seem to be of special interest, and of great importance.

One such set of conditions is the broad differences in the antecedent traditional political structure and order. As we have seen already above, many differences from the original European pattern can be discerned. For instance, in many of the tribal societies the very existence of a distinct centre or of a status of relatively homogeneous ethnic or national communication could not be taken for granted.

Even in societies, like the Imperial or patrimonial ones, in which there could be no doubt about the existence of a specific centre and State-apparatus, the very inter-relations of the state of the political order with the social order have been envisaged in ways different from those of the Western tradition.

In general, most of these societies did not share the Imperial, city-state and feudal traditions which were specific to the European traditional order. Thus, for instance, in the Imperial Asian societies—as in Russia or Japan—the pluralistic elements were much weaker than in the feudal or city-states. In Russia, for example, there lacked the conception of a relatively autonomous access of the major strata to the political and cultural centres, and the cultural orders were often perceived as subservient to the political one.

Similarly, in Japan, there existed a conception of the close identity between the cosmic and political order and of a very high degree of unconditional commitment of broader strata to the centre which represented this cosmic-political identity.

In many other societies—in South-East Asia, in Africa, and to some degree in Latin America—the forces of (later) modernity impinged on patrimonial systems where the level of commitment to a socio-political order was much smaller and in which also the active, autonomous relation between the political and the cosmic order was much weaker—even if there existed a closer coalescence between the two.

Their political traditions rarely envisaged the same type of split or dichotomy between State and Society as did the European tradition. Instead, it tended to stress the congruent but often passive relations between the cosmic order on the one hand, and the socio-political order on the other. Unlike the Western tradition, the interrelation between the political and the social orders was not envisaged in terms of an antithesis between two entities of power; rather, it was more often stated in terms of the coalescence of different functions within the same group of organization, centred around a common focus in the cosmic order.

IX

Another set of conditions which may greatly influence the shaping of the different contour of post-traditional societies is the structure of the historical process of impingement of modern forces on the various institutions' spheres, i.e. the economic, political, or the sphere of social organization and stratification of the societies.

It may also take place under different degrees of structural differentiation: with broad strata evincing a relatively high level of resistance to change in the new setting, or, conversely, a high level of adaptability to it; with secondary elites and especially with more central elites which may be resistant to change, i.e. 'traditionalistic' in a militant or an erosive way; with elites which are highly adaptable to the new settings, with but a few transformative orientations; or with elites which have transformative capacities, either in a flexible or in a coercive way.

It may take place under different temporal sequences of development in different institutional spheres which may greatly influence both the problems with which these societies were confronted and the responses that they had to develop.

These various structural and temporal differences greatly affect the nature of the concrete problems which arise within these societies, the levels of aspirations and conflicts of various groups as well as some aspects or conditions of the ability of the central elites to deal with these problems, and especially the level of economic, organizational, and educational resources available for the crystallization of new institutional settings.

Each constellation of these processes tends to create the impetus for the break-through to modernity in the socio-political and cultural order and the concomitant impetus to continuous intensive change. But each specific constellation also tends to create different patterns of break-through, different types of institutional and cultural problems with which these societies and their new emerging structures have to deal—as well as the patterns of institutional response to the problem of continuous change—and different degrees and types of ability or lack of ability to deal with the problems and crises specific to each type of modern or modernizing society.

X

Within this context it is important, especially for the study of South-East Asian societies to analyse the specific characteristics of those societies whose major initial experience with modernity was under a colonial regime.

The most important of such common characteristics of these societies was the imposition of an alien centre which is always, to some degree or another, segregated from the other parts of the society, and while it creates various administrative frameworks, it, at the same time, deprives them of legitimate foci of the collective identity.

This situation gave rise, as is well-known, to the development of political mobilization, new elites, and a variety of social and national movements, all of which aimed at the establishment of a new centre which initially was modelled after the European pattern, and which later greatly diverged from it, creating new types of post-traditional regimes.

But these types of regimes differed not only from those which developed within non-European societies like Japan or China which have maintained their independence, they also differed among themselves. Some of these differences also can be attributed to their different experience under colonial rule.

XI

Of these different experiences, of special importance seem to be the initial patterns of establishment of central institutional modern frameworks; the relative tempo of modernization; and processes of, and the extent of, structural flexibility of strategic groups and elites in the society.

The establishment and continuity of flexible political symbols and central political and legal frameworks, of common symbols of political-national identification, of organs of political struggle, legislation and administration is a basic prerequisite for the development of a sense of modern, differentiated political identity and affinity among different groups and strata which are drawn into the context of modern political community.

The non-development of such frameworks may reinforce the isolation of the various modern elites, as manifested by their lack of ability to forge new, cohesive symbols and by the development of policies which were incapable of forging new interlinking mechanisms in the society and creating cohesive symbols and frameworks which are of crucial importance in the development and institutionalization of adequate regulative mechanisms which can deal with new emerging problems.

Of special importance in this context has been the establishment and institutionalization—whether formal or informal—of certain rules of the political game such as systems of election or less formal institutional devices of different types which establish some procedural consensus in the society.

Similarly, such successful institutionalization has been usually greatly dependent on, and related to, the development of a relatively flexible and differentiated legal system which, whatever its social or political underpinnings, could assure some basic legal rights to individuals and some protection against the undermining of long-term commitments and activities, and some minimal rights of the citizens.

All such developments greatly facilitate the development of a more cohesive and flexible modern institutional centre which is capable both of promoting and regulating change and which can be responsive to various needs and demands, without succumbing to them so as to become totally ineffective. Last, of great importance here is the structure of the international setting in which the process of modernization takes place, the distribution of political and economic power among the various societies and strata, and the types and processes of dominance and dependence that tend to develop among them.

It is the interaction among these various variables subsumed under the three broad conditions specified above—the different socio-political directions and traditions of these societies in their premodern settings, the nature of the impingement of modernization on them, and the structure of the situation of change—that can . . . explain the development patterns of post-traditional socio-political orders, and of change of any one society from one pattern to another.

Modernization — and Early Modern China

Knight Biggerstaff

*In this essay, which is the text of his presidential address before the
Association of Asian Studies in 1966, the author applies to China eight criteria
of modernization drafted at a conference of American and Japanese scholars.
A century or more ago most persons acquainted with the two countries
would have predicted that China was much more likely than Japan to "catch
up" with the West. The administrative and technological achievements
of China all pointed to a greater capacity for adaptation in the modern era.
Confining his analysis to the period up to 1919, from which he dates
the positive determination of Chinese leaders to transform their society,
Biggerstaff discusses the strengths and weaknesses of premodern China in the
light of Japan's record.*

Modernization is a word that has been widely and rather loosely used for
some time to characterize the fundamental changes that have been taking
place during the nineteenth and twentieth centuries among non-Western
peoples. It was first used in this sense to describe developments in Japan,
China and Turkey, but with the multiplication of newly independent nations
in Asia and Africa since World War II the term has been applied to them,
also.

The past fifteen years have seen a remarkable increase in the study of this
phenomenon, both in the United States and abroad. The motive in some cases
has been to understand a people or a society better; in others, to identify
common characteristics which might throw more light on human behavior
generally; and in still others, to discover means by which future developments
in a particular country, or in all "developing" countries, might be influenced
—or even pushed in a particular direction.

Because of the diversity of purpose, approach and knowledge among those
using the term, there is today some confusion regarding the meaning of
"modernization." A broad definition calls it a process by which a society

"Modernization—and Early Modern China" by Knight Biggerstaff is reprinted with permission of the Association for Asian Studies, Inc., from the *Journal of Asian Studies*, XXV
(August 1966), 607–619.

Biggerstaff has been a member of the Department of History at Cornell University during
most of this career, specializing in modern Chinese history. He is the author of *The Earliest
Modern Government Schools in China* (1961) and co-editor of the *Annotated Bibliography
of Selected Chinese Reference Works* (3rd ed., 1971).

146

replaces institutions, ideas and practices that it regards as no longer appropriate. In this sense modernization would have occurred in any part of the world at any time where basic changes were taking place—during the century that began with the Ch'in dynasty in China, for example, or in Western Europe following the Renaissance. However, much of the discussion today relates to the somewhat narrower definition with which I began: the far-reaching changes in non-Western societies that have been stimulated and largely inspired by the activities and examples of Western nations or of already partly modernized nations such as Japan and China which had themselves been thus stimulated and inspired.

Some scholars prefer the term "Westernization" to modernization, feeling that it is a more precisely definable concept and that it need imply no more than the great influence of Western models, which all admit. I myself prefer the more neutral term, feeling that Westernization may suggest the complete replacement of indigenous cultures by Western civilization rather than what is actually taking place—the adaptation by non-Western countries of selected Western ideas and techniques to their own peculiar ways of life. In using the word "Western" I have in mind that there have been two streams of Western influence since the early nineteen twenties, one flowing from Western Europe and the United States, sometimes via Japan—which has contributed a flavor of its own, the other flowing from Russia, increasingly with Chinese additives in recent years.

The Western origin of many of the major innovations in the developing non-Western nations and the fact that these nations must deal with an external world that has been fashioned largely by Western nations to meet Western interests, mean that the new nations now have much in common with one another in spite of the great diversity among them based upon geographical differences and their own distinctive cultural heritages. One of the most interesting questions to be asked about these nations is whether their future development will be more influenced by traditional and indigenous factors or by their common borrowings from the West and from each other. But since the process is still going on not only in the newly independent nations but even in those which began changing during the nineteenth century, it is too early to expect an answer. A major source of confusion in much discussion of modernization is the fact that "modern" is not necessarily a fixed condition or a point in time. What is considered modern today may not still be so regarded next year.

So far, most of the scholarly analysis of modernization has been carried on within the boundaries of particular academic disciplines. This is understandable in view of the increased compartmentalization of scholarship and of the current disinclination of scholars to expose themselves to expert criticism from other disciplines by generalizing beyond their own special competence. There certainly are advantages to the disciplinary approach in the precision and sophistication of analysis it promotes. But there are also disadvantages in the frequency of distortion of the full picture made possible, perhaps even inevitable, by the focusing of attention on and building up of formidable evidence relating to particular aspects of a culture while others of no less importance are ignored or inadequately considered. The disciplines can be led astray even in their own fields by the isolation of certain institutions or activities from others in which they are not specifically interested but which cannot in fact be so isolated without distorting their understanding of the subjects of their own particular concern.

The need for an interdisciplinary approach to the study of modernization is generally admitted, although the tendency is to leave it to somebody else, or to postpone it until the disciplines have assembled and analyzed all the data. Probably the interdisciplinary study of modernization that is easiest to manage is one directed toward a particular culture, where all discussants, regardless of discipline, have some knowledge of and feeling for the whole culture even though each is devoting most of his research effort to those aspects which are the concern of his own particular discipline.

A serious attempt to deal with the broad meaning of modernization was made by the Conference on Modern Japan, a special project operating under the auspices of this Association, at a meeting at Hakone, Japan, in 1960. The results are reported by John Whitney Hall in Chapter One of *Changing Japanese Attitudes Toward Modernization*.[1] There a group of some thirty Japan specialists, most of them from Japanese, American and British Commonwealth universities, representing a variety of disciplines and points of view and well read in the theoretical literature on modernization, struggled with the problem of definition. Particularly beneficial was the participation of some scholars whose approach was Marxist and who helped to exclude from the definitions agreed upon the capitalistic bias which many Asians feel has overinfluenced some Western thinking about this subject.

At the beginning of the Hakone conference lists of detailed characteristics of modernization were assembled under disciplinary headings, but it was recognized that these tended to be "partial in scope ... [and] specific to certain problems peculiar to the disciplines themselves."[2] From that point the conference proceeded to designate a series of eight general characteristics of a modern society which emerged from discussions of the more detailed characteristics that had been arranged by disciplines as well as of some previously published general definitions of modernization. The eight criteria proposed by the Hakone conference are:

1. A comparatively high concentration of population in cities and the increasingly urban-centeredness of the total society.
2. A relatively high degree of use of inanimate energy, the widespread circulation of commodities, and the growth of service facilities.
3. Extensive spatial interaction of members of a society and the widespread participation of such members in economic and political affairs.
4. A widespread breakdown of communal and hereditary social groupings leading to greater individual social mobility and a more widely diversified range of individual performance in society.

[1] Marius B. Jansen, ed. Princeton University Press, 1965.
[2] *Ibid.*, p. 31. These lists are to be found in a long footnote on pp. 20–23 of Professor Hall's chapter.

5. Widespread literacy accompanied by the spread of a secular, and increasingly scientific, orientation of the individual to his environment.
6. An extensive and penetrative network of mass communication.
7. The existence of large-scale social institutions such as government, business, industry, and the increasingly bureaucratic organization of such institutions.
8. Increased unification of large bodies of population under one control (nations) and the growing interaction of such units (international relations).[3]

Although the characteristics of a modern society agreed upon at Hakone are more likely to fit Japan than any other country because those who formulated them were most familiar with the Japanese experience, it seems to me that it might be meaningful to apply them to other modernizing nations. Such a procedure could have two benefits: First, it might enrich other national studies by forcing scholars to break away from such parochialism and preconceptions as may result from devoting themselves entirely to a single culture and to look for developments they had not expected to find there or the importance of which was minimized by neglect. Secondly, this particular model might be tested elsewhere with a view to determining which segments of it may be universally valid.

Although I am not wholly satisfied with the details of the Hakone definition of a modern society—and I imagine that most of those who shared in its formulation would favor some modifications after further study, it has seemed to me worthwhile to apply the Hakone model in a very sketchy and tentative examination of Chinese modernization prior to 1919. I select this somewhat arbitrary date because I believe the May Fourth Movement of 1919 marks a significant shift in Chinese thinking from what had been mostly scattered reactions against the more obvious shortcomings of the traditional culture to a widespread and positive determination to create a "new China."

From my reading of economic studies of modernization (most economists seem to prefer the term "economic development"), I feel that the phrase "a substantial per capita increase in capital" should be added to the second Hakone criterion. Furthermore, I believe that in considering modernization some attention must be given to changes in values, as vague and difficult to define as that term is. I agree with the Indonesian historian Soedjatmoko that we are so preoccupied with political, social and economic data that we tend to ignore the tremendous motivational forces at work in men and societies. Because significant changes in values are involved in nearly all of the eight Hakone criteria, it would probably not be logical to consider this as a separate characteristic of a modern society. However, because it tends to be neglected under those headings, I propose to ask at the end how far

---

[3] *Ibid.*, pp. 19, 27. I have changed Professor Hall's numbering by inserting as number 4 an eighth characteristic added after initial agreement had been reached on a list of seven. At the suggestion of Shūichi Katō this "working summation of the 'modern' elements of a society" came to be called a "syndrome of symptoms," to indicate their interrelationship.

fundamental changes had taken place in the traditional Chinese value system.

I now turn to a very brief application of the eight characteristics of a modern society to developments in China prior to 1919, to see what preliminary conclusions emerge.

"1. A comparatively high concentration of population in cities and the increasingly urban-centeredness of the total society."

Although China has always been an agricultural country, where the vast majority of the inhabitants lived in farm villages, throughout the imperial period there were cities and these were especially numerous and large during the past thousand years. However, the spread of modern transportation and commerce since the middle, and of modern industry since the end, of the nineteenth century has given unusual stimulus to urban growth. While this development, like most other aspects of modernization, occurred first in the foreign-controlled treaty ports, there appears also to have been some growth of strictly Chinese cities prior to 1919. Unfortunately there are few reliable demographic data on China for this period and comparatively little has been done yet to pull together the scattered materials that might throw light on trends toward urbanization. Even the obvious fact that the population of some cities had increased considerably during the eighty years before 1919 does not necessarily prove that there was a much higher proportion of the Chinese people living in cities in that year than there had been eighty or eight hundred years earlier.

Urban-centeredness would seem to be measurable in terms of the extent of the dependence of the agricultural population upon the urban sector of the society. Such dependence was relatively small in traditional China, and it has not been demonstrated that there was a significant increase during the decades before 1919. It has been claimed that farm handicrafts such as cotton-spinning and -weaving were severely undermined early in the twentieth century by competition from cotton yarn and goods imported from abroad or produced by modern factories in the treaty ports and other Chinese cities. Imports of cotton manufactures indeed showed a remarkable increase between 1880 and 1919, and the output of the nearly fifty modern cotton mills established in China during that period must have been considerable. But we do not know how far these manufactures penetrated the countryside, thus increasing rural dependence upon the cities. It was observed that growing numbers of country people obtained work in Shanghai and some other cities during this period, increasing rural dependence upon cities to the extent that a part of the income of these migrants went to support their families at home. But the numbers were small in relation to the total rural population of China.

Another aspect of urban-centeredness is the dependence of the rural population upon cities for ideas, information and direction. Although little pertinent evidence has been assembled, I suspect that with the improvements in a communications there was some increase in such dependence during the period being surveyed.

"2. A relatively high degree of use of inanimate energy, a substantial per capita increase in capital, the widespread circulation of commodities, and the growth of service facilities."

Reduction of Chinese dependence upon animate energy has been hindered down to the present day by an overabundance of human labor and a shortage of capital. Foreigners introduced Shanghai to the stationary steam engine during the eighteen fifties and operated steamships between Chinese sea and river ports from the eighteen sixties. The Chinese government itself sponsored the use of steam-powered machinery when modern arsenals and shipyards were built at Nanking, Shanghai, Foochow and Tientsin during the eighteen sixties; and during the following twenty-five years progressive provincial officials established a steamship line, two short steam railways, two modern mining enterprises and a steel mill. The first electric generator was installed in Shanghai by foreigners in 1882 and the Chinese themselves began installing electric power in 1890, beginning with a plant at Canton.

Although several power-operated cotton spinning and silk reeling factories were established by Chinese during the eighteen nineties, modern light industry was most actively promoted by foreign interests, after the Treaty of Shimonoseki (1895) had given Japan the right to operate factories in the treaty ports and this right had been claimed by the Western powers under the most-favored-nation clauses of their treaties with China. Private foreign and Sino-foreign industry expanded rapidly for a while, principally in Shanghai, most of it producing cotton textiles. There was also a burst of railway construction after the Sino-Japanese War, nearly all of it carried out by foreign concessionaires and financed with foreign loans. Japanese interests developed coal, iron, soy bean oil and other mechanized industries in south Manchuria after Japan's defeat of Russia in 1905.

While there was also some growth of Chinese-owned modern consumer goods industries after 1900, mostly in the foreign concessions and settlements, and inanimate power began to be used even in a few traditional handicraft factories, a more vigorous expansion occurred during World War I while European imports were cut off. It is worth noting that the value of imported machine tools increased from U. S. $36,000 in 1913 to U. S. $620,000 in 1920, and of textile machinery from U. S. $612,000 in 1913 to U. S. $4½ million in 1920. Although it cannot be said that steam, electric and gas energy had by 1919 significantly replaced the man, animal, wind and water power China had so long depended upon, yet a strong start had been made, particularly in the provinces subject to foreign influence.

In pre-modern China capital was invested largely in land, which was relatively secure, in usury, which brought quick and high profits, and in houses, clothing, art treasures and other contributions to a life of prestige and comfort. Even the successful merchant preferred to invest his profits in these things because trade and manufacturing were subject to a number of hazards, including arbitrary exactions by the government and extortion by corrupt officials. The Chinese was a circular flow economy in which there was relatively little capital accumulation.

Most of the capital in the modern enterprises developed prior to 1919 came from abroad. But Chinese compradores working with foreign firms, and some independent Chinese merchants, began developing modern economic enterprises of their own largely within the shelter of the treaty ports, and in fact their profits supplied much of the capital in the "official-supervised and merchant-managed" (kuan-tu shang-pan) companies launched by Li Hung-chang and Chang Chih-tung between 1872 and 1900. But both in "official-supervised and merchant-managed" and in private Chinese companies capital accumulation was difficult because of the demand of Chinese stockholders for high dividends (which were seldom reinvested in productive enterprise), at the expense of depreciation allowances and reinvestment of profits for development or expansion of the business. Even though there was substantial reinvestment of their profits in China by foreign companies, and growing investment by overseas Chinese after 1900, these gains to the Chinese economy were probably neutralized by the enormous payments that the Chinese government had to make on indemnities to foreign governments and on foreign loans. While some modern methods of developing capital had been introduced into China, and while the government at least formally encouraged modern business and industry after 1900, there is no basis for believing that there had been a significant per capita increase in capital by 1919.

The extension of navigation by vessels driven by steam or internal combustion engines along China's coast and many rivers and canals, and the construction of nearly seven thousand miles of railways during the sixty years before 1919 greatly speeded up and expanded the circulation of commodities. Nearly half a billion U. S. dollars worth of goods were imported into China in 1919, and there had been a steady increase in the products of modern factories. While most of these goods were destined for relatively few cities and their environs, we know from scattered observations that some ultimately reached into the countryside; and that modern transportation also increased the movement of traditional products. The faster and cheaper modern transportation also encouraged the cultivation of cash crops and the expansion of cottage handicraft production for shipment to other parts of China or abroad. Thus, by 1919, circulation of commodities had increased, though there remained a great deal of room for further development.

Western merchants took with them to China their own service facilities such as banking, insurance, shipping and marketing, and such business techniques as accounting and rationalized management. The Chinese had long before developed some such services themselves, but on a relatively simple level. Traditional banking agencies handled drafts, promissory notes and bills of exchange, transmitted funds, and managed domestic exchange, but they did not create institutional credit by accepting savings on deposit and lending funds for productive enterprise. Chinese merchants had early developed means of spreading risks on goods in transit, but they had no such elaborate and secure system of marine and other types of insurance as prevailed in Europe. There was an extensive and reasonably efficient system of water transportation covering large parts of China, supplemented by carriage, by carts, beasts and men which was slow, decentralized, and expensive. Management, generally associated with ownership, was conservative; accounting was adequate for small scale enterprises but not very flexible.

In the treaty ports Westerners established banks and operated insurance companies. Their steamships provided dependable and rapid freight and passenger transportation between the various ports, and they aggressively promoted markets for modern manufactures in the interior and organized the collection of an expanding variety of Chinese commodities for export and for sale in other parts of China. The foreigners associated with themselves Chinese compradores who, either as employees or agents, handled much of the Chinese business of foreign companies. These compradores of necessity learned Western management and accounting techniques, which they adapted to the Chinese situation, and ultimately many of them or their descendants became independent businessmen, operating mainly in the modern sector of the Chinese economy.

Traditional Chinese banks proved incapable of meeting the demands of foreign trade, of modern industry or of modern governmental finance, with the result that these were left at first largely to foreign banks. The earliest modern Chinese bank was established in 1896, and by 1919 there were two large semi-government banks and fifty-six modern private banks wholly Chinese owned. But at that time foreign and Sino-foreign banks still dominated the field, just as foreign insurance companies still commanded most of the Chinese business, although a Chinese insurance company had been established as early as 1875 and others had followed. While the China Merchants Steam Navigation Company had been operating since 1873 and there were several smaller Chinese lines, in 1919 British, Japanese and American interests still dominated the steamship business between Chinese coastal and large river ports.

The essentially foreign-manned Maritime Customs Service of the Chinese government, which was created during the third quarter of the nineteenth century, efficiently administered a modern system of tariff collection on imports and exports and also introduced modern harbor controls, pilotage service and aids to navigation. In 1896 the Chinese government established a modern post office to replace the old-fashioned and altogether inadequate postal services of private Chinese merchants. By 1919 China's postal facilities were said to be as efficient and up-to-date as any in the world.

"3. Extensive spatial interaction of members of a society and the widespread participation of such members in economic and political affairs."

There has always been some movement about China: by officials, who were never allowed to serve in their home areas; by candidates for official rank, who went to prefectural, provincial and imperial capitals to take the civil service examinations; by soldiers and corvée laborers moved about by the government; by merchants and transport workers operating outside their native districts; and in times of grave economic or political disorder by dispossessed persons seeking better conditions in the borderlands or overseas. With these exceptions, the Chinese people ordinarily did not venture farther from home than to nearby market towns.

Although it is difficult to measure, the first two decades of the twentieth century saw an increase in geographical mobility as cheaper and more rapid means of transportation became available. The modernizing cities, particularly Shanghai, drew ever-growing numbers of both peasants and the well-to-do from the hinterland; young people poured into the cities or went abroad in pursuit of modern education; increasing internal and external trade required the travel of larger numbers of merchants; and millions of peasants went to Manchuria, Inner Mongolia or to Southeast Asia, some of them for brief sojourns, some to stay permanently. But probably a large majority of the Chinese people, living away from the principal routes of transportation, had little or no more contact with persons from outside their native marketing areas in 1919 than had their ancestors centuries earlier.

Ordinarily none but the educated participated in the national or local political processes of traditional China except as taxpayers, soldiers or laborers on government projects. People of education still monopolized political affairs in 1919, though this group now included a larger proportion of military officers and businessmen than formerly. The early twentieth century had seen the development of political parties and a few elections, but there was very little popular participation in either.

Participation in the traditional economy beyond the simple face to face relations of local marketing areas involved comparatively few people. Significant changes had occurred by 1919 as increasing numbers of people were caught up in the industries, commercial agriculture, service activities and expanding national market of the modern economy. Even so, a large proportion of the population still did not participate in any of these new developments.

"4. A widespread breakdown of communal and hereditary social groupings leading to greater individual social mobility and a more widely diversified range of individual performance in society."

Traditionally Chinese society consisted of four basic classes: (1) scholars, (2) farmers, (3) craftsmen, and (4) merchants, in that order of prestige, with a privileged official class ranking above them all and a tiny minority of "declassed" people below. This hierarchy was actually far from inflexible, wealthy landlords and large merchants having more in common than landlords and small farmers or large merchants and peddlers. There was considerable upward social mobility, as merchants and craftsmen succeeded in acquiring land or education. All four classes were eligible for the civil service examinations which were the principal route to officialdom, but an ordinary farmer could rarely afford to educate a son sufficiently to compete. In fact the gulf between the "have-nots" and the "haves" was wide and difficult to cross. There was also downward mobility, thanks to the inheritance system which divided a family's property among all sons, and to the rules by which the descendants of officials ordinarily did not remain members of that superior class unless they, too, could pass the examinations. While official position has apparently remained the highest aim of most ambitious Chinese down to the present day, such modern professions as medicine, law and engineering, and leadership in modern business and finance, had begun to be recognized as equally prestigious by 1919. Social mobility was also speeded up as new opportunities for self-betterment presented themselves and spatial mobility increased.

Regardless of class, the basic social institution in traditional China was the family, and the duty of the individual to his family outweighed all other obligations. The lineage or clan (*tsu*) was the largest corporate kinship group, although it was not as prevalent in some parts of China as in others. The lineage as well as smaller extended family groups performed various political, economic and ritualistic functions below the level of formal government. Because of the traditional emphasis on filial duty, family elders exercised complete control over their younger relatives; moreover this subordination of younger to older people prevailed throughout the society. However, the movement of young men and women to the cities to take jobs in modern commerce and industry lessened their economic dependence on their families and removed them from the supervision of their elders. At the same time modern education imported Western ideas such as individual freedom, sexual equality and the inevitability of progress, which further weakened the authority of the family. Actually the organized protest of youth against the old kinship system was just beginning in 1919 and very few changes were observable as yet. Other traditional social groups, such as secret societies and the less formal ones that existed around temples and teahouses within the standard marketing community, seem to have remained largely untouched up to that time.

Modernization of the economy, of government, of education, and of other aspects of Chinese life required increased individual specialization. Attempts to induce members of the official class to enter a special school for diplomats in the eighteen sixties foundered on the conviction that a general classical education was all that was required by any official. But this view was beginning to change by 1900, and by 1919 the need for a wide variety of specialized knowledge and skills in government, as well as in other activities, was generally recognized, although China still was far from being able to supply it.

"5. Widespread literacy accompanied by the spread of a secular, and increasingly scientific, orientation of the individual to his environment."

A modern educational system, greatly influenced by the West but modeled upon that of Japan, was inaugurated in 1905, the same year in which the civil service examinations that had been both the end and the determinant of traditional education were abolished. In 1912 the Republican government declared its intention to achieve universal primary education and to promote adult education. But the formidable costs, coupled with the political turmoil of the nineteen tens, prevented much progress toward universal literacy by

1919. Actually, the estimated three to five million students in modern government and private schools in that year may not have been much more numerous than those who had been studying traditional subjects in China a century earlier. Moreover the National Language (*kuo-yü*) Movement, which advocated writing in the colloquial instead of in classical Chinese and general acceptance of which was prerequisite to any feasible program of universal education, had only just been launched and instruction in colloquial Chinese was not to be introduced into the primary school curriculum until 1921. The first serious program of adult education in China—that of James Y. C. Yen —did not begin until 1923.

Some knowledge of modern science began to enter China with the establishment of the earliest modern government schools in the eighteen sixties and of Christian missionary colleges from 1879 onward. Probably even more influential during the later decades of the nineteenth century was the translation into Chinese and wide distribution of hundreds of works on science and technology by the Kiangnan Arsenal and by missionaries, and the publication of many articles on these and other modern subjects in Chinese-language periodicals. By the end of the century more translations were pouring in from Japan, and such famous Chinese translators as Yen Fu and Lin Shu were contributing their own. With the rapid expansion thereafter of modern education, and the despatch of thousands of Chinese students abroad to study, modern knowledge, including at least an elementary knowledge of modern science, spread rapidly among the educated class.

Actually, educated Chinese have for centuries held a largely secular view of their environment, which modern science could do no more than strengthen. On the other hand, the vast mass of illiterate farmers, perhaps in part because of their greater vulnerability to the vicissitudes of nature, have had a less secular view of their environment; and this remained unchanged in 1919.

"6. An extensive and penetrative network of mass communication."

While the principal cities of China have for many centuries been connected by a network of stone-paved roads and natural and artificial waterways, rapid intercommunication has been a development of the last hundred years. As noted earlier, speedy and cheap transportation was provided by steamships as they invaded Chinese waters after the eighteen fifties and by railroads as they reached inland from the eighteen nineties. The telegraph was introduced in 1881 and steadily spread across the country, and modern postal facilities expanded rapidly after the turn of the century.

Before the late nineteenth century, even educated people knew little of what was going on outside their own communities, virtually the only sources of news being peddlers, a few travelers, and occasional letters from friends. The introduction of the newspaper was therefore a major event in Chinese history. Although missionary periodicals appeared sporadically even before the Opium War, Chinese journalism may be said to have begun in Hongkong in 1858 and in Shanghai in 1862, after which it spread gradually to other cities. The earliest Chinese-language newspapers were published by foreigners as separate editions of English-language newspapers or as independent money-making ventures, and by Protestant missionaries, though Chinese publishers began to compete during the eighteen seventies.

Although circulation was small at first, China's defeat by Japan in 1895 and the subsequent growth of interest in reform greatly stimulated the reading of newspapers and magazines. A few used a colloquial style from the turn of the century, but the vast majority were written in the literary Chinese that none but the well educated could read. It was no until after the National Language Movement, launched in Peking University in 1917, had been spread across the country by the May Fourth Movement of 1919 that nearly all magazines and most newspapers began to use colloquial Chinese. Even then, so low was the rate of literacy that although periodicals can be said to have constituted an extensive and penetrative network of communication, they could not yet be regarded as mass media.

"7. The existence of large-scale social institutions such as government, business, industry, and the increasingly bureaucratic organization of such institutions."

The only organized establishment of country-wide extent in pre-modern China was the imperial government, in which provincial, prefectural and district officials, as well as those of the central administration, comprised an integrated bureaucracy under the emperor. Local government was left to local leaders consisting of large landowners, officials in retirement and other educated persons as long as taxes were paid, order was preserved, and established customs were upheld. But this venerable system, like the tradition it supported, proved unable to cope with the modern world. Adjustments made during the closing years of the Ch'ing did not prevent the collapse of that dynasty or of the imperial system itself; and the "republic" which replaced them soon fell apart. By 1919 control of China was dispersed among regional military politicians who were assisted in part by bureaucrats left over from the old regime. Only a beginning in the specialization of officials, generally considered characteristic of modern governments, was apparent in China by that time.

Another political institution of traditional China was the secret society. These were organized among the common people for mutual protection and were frequently united in regional federations. In times of dynastic decline the secret societies led resistance to misgovernment and oppression and they were generally regarded as seditious by the authorities. The T'ung-meng Hui, which led the anti-Ch'ing movement immediately prior to 1912, more closely resembled a secret society than a political party. In 1919 old-fashioned secret societies continued to be more vigorous and influential than the supposedly new-style political parties, which still consisted of little more than a leader and his personal followers.

The economic institutions of pre-modern China were comparatively simple. In cities and towns the various trades were organized into guilds which included both entrepreneurs and craftsmen. Rural trading centered in periodic fairs conducted in the market towns. During early Ch'ing two groups of merchants had been granted monopolies by the government: the producers and distributors of salt, and certain firms trading with foreigners at Canton. As noted earlier, the first modern industries created by the Chinese were organized as "official-supervised and merchant-managed" companies. They operated under the patronage of a high official on funds partly subscribed by private investors and partly borrowed from government agencies, and were managed by a representative of the shareholders who usually held official rank.

In the treaty ports foreign and Sino-foreign firms were organized and operated much as they would have been in the West except for some accommodation to Chinese conditions. Probably most of the Chinese firms located there were family enterprises, as they would have been elsewhere in China, even when there were scores or hundreds of employees. Although Chinese joint-stock enterprises increased in number after 1900, not only in the treaty ports but elsewhere, and Chinese Chambers of Commerce were organized, commencing in 1902 in Shanghai, in 1919 the guild system still prevailed nearly everywhere, the organization of labor unions had barely started, and altogether the modernization of Chinese economic institutions had only begun.

"8. Increased unification of large bodies of population under one control (nations) and the growing interaction of such units (international relations)."

China has been a unified political entity during most of the twenty-two hundred years since Ch'in Shih Huang-ti established the empire. Even during intervals of political disruption there remained cultural unity based on a common written language, shared values, and pride in a rich tradition. But from the end of the nineteenth century growing numbers of Chinese, the first among them Sun Yat-sen, complained that because the Chinese people were insufficiently unified and because family and regional loyalties were stronger than loyalty to China, their country was being discriminated against and exploited by other nations. Consequently what we call nationalism—the militant promotion of national interests as against personal interests or those of other nations—has grown steadily in China during the twentieth century. While there were a few bursts of it earlier, nationalism became a clearly recognizable general manifestation only during the May Fourth Movement in 1919.

The concept of equality among nations did not exist in Chinese thinking until after the Western multistate system forced itself upon China during the nineteenth century. Previously the Chinese had regarded China as the center of the civilized world, with all other political entities inferior to it. The only pattern of international relations they recognized was the tributary system under which all other rulers were expected to acknowledge the suzerainty of the Emperor of China.

In contrast to its earlier posture of superiority, China during the nineteenth century was relegated by the treaties forced upon it by the Western Powers and Japan to an inferior position which it still held in 1919 even though its government was participating in international relations as fully as it was allowed to. Even though still treated as an inferior, however, there is no question but that China was interacting with other nations much more fully than had been the case a century earlier.

Finally, I want to speak briefly about fundamental changes in values, which although not specified in the eight Hakone characteristics of a modern society are implied in most of them.

Although Chinese civilization was far from static, the changes that occurred during the more than two thousand years of the empire generally took place within a universally accepted body of assumptions which was largely Confucian but also included Taoist and Legalist elements and even some absorbed along the way from alien Buddhism. The good society was based upon an ideal state believed to have existed in antiquity in which government was conducted by a virtuous ruler who was responsible to Heaven for the welfare of the people, and by educated officials who were responsible to the emperor and to precedents and rules handed down from the past. Personal conduct was prescribed by the requirements of filial duty and hierarchy within the patriarchal family and by an ancient code of ritual relationships. The traditional values clearly supported the political and social status quo.

Most Chinese advocates of reform during the latter half of the nineteenth century were concerned only with means to check European aggression and would have avoided basic changes at all cost. "Chinese learning as the foundation, Western learning for practical use" (*Chung-hsüeh wei t'i, hsi-hsüeh wei yung*) was their slogan, and what borrowing they did from the West was intended to strengthen traditional values, not to weaken them. When K'ang Yu-wei, worried by the increasingly obvious inability of China to meet the Western challenge, tried in the eighteen nineties to modify the tradition by reinterpreting Confucius as a reformer, he was rejected by nearly all of his more conservative fellow officials.

The subsequent erosion of confidence in established beliefs was hastened by the threat of China's dissolution as a political entity. Abolition of the Confucian civil service examinations in 1905, the transformation of traditional into modern schools, and the collapse both of the Ch'ing dynasty and of the dynastic system during 1911–1912 were lethal blows. Growing ideological confusion marked the first two decades of the twentieth century, even though the vast majority of the Chinese people still continued to carry on in accordance with the old beliefs and standards. Disillusionment with traditional values spread particularly among young intellectuals as they combined observation of the plight of their country with study of Western ideas and ideals. Liang Ch'i-ch'ao before 1911 cried out against the dead hand of the past. During the New Culture Movement launched at Peking University in 1917 Ch'en Tu-hsiu called upon Mr. Science and Mr. Democracy to drive Confucius from the land, and Hu Shih demanded that the classical written language, which he regarded as no longer capable of producing a living literature, be discarded in favor of colloquial Chinese.

By 1919 many Chinese had come to question the validity of traditional ideals for the present and future. This tendency to reject the past, together with an almost frantic search for new values to replace those that were being discarded, spread rapidly after 1919.

There are two conclusions, I believe, that are to be drawn from this necessarily sketchy application of the Hakone characteristics of a modern society to China prior to 1919:

First, we still have too much to learn about that period of Chinese history to be able to speak with real assurance about it. At many points in this survey what is known has been overshadowed by what is not known. The difficulty is not that there is a scarcity of source materials, but that comparatively few of the relevant data have been gathered together and analyzed. Fortunately the large lacunae in our knowledge are now being filled as an increasing number of scholars—Chinese, Japanese, Americans and Europeans —engage in the study of early modern China. Not only are historians at work, but more and more social scientists are committing themselves to historical studies.

My second conclusion is that the development of a modern society in China was both limited and uneven prior to 1919. Probably the most far-reaching changes had taken place in communications and transportation, contributing not only to greater mobility of people and goods, but of ideas as well. There had also been drastic changes in China's international relations, in its governmental system (except at the local level), and in education. Within the educated class, especially among its younger members, many of the traditional values had lost their appeal by 1919. In the coastal and middle Yangtze provinces modern business and industry and related service facilities had developed in the larger cities and inanimate energy was increasingly employed. Moreover there had been some urban growth and probably some increase in urban-centeredness. The new education and new professional and technological opportunities made for somewhat greater social mobility. There were, as yet, however, almost no changes in the old kinship system or in most other traditional social and economic groups. And for a great majority of the Chinese people—the illiterate peasant masses—life was very little different from what it had always been.

By 1919 the way had been prepared for the modernization of China, and in some parts of the country and in certain levels of the society significant steps had been taken along that road. But there still remained a long way to go.

PART 3

SOCIETAL TRANSFORMATION

Only a few of today's 148 sovereign states have undergone the fundamental transformation from premodern to highly modernized societies. Without employing a strict definition of the stages in this transformation, it may safely be estimated that no more than one-fifth of the world's population has achieved a relatively advanced level of modernization, and one measure of this transformation is that this one-fifth accounts for about four-fifths of the world's gross product.

The countries that have undergone transformation still represent a rather limited basis for generalizing about a process that is currently affecting many more peoples with widely differing values and institutions. Analysts must do the best they can with the data at hand, drawing on the common experience of the countries already relatively advanced and discriminating to the extent possible between the modern values and institutions that appear to incorporate significant elements of their divergent heritages and those that seem to be universally valid. Political systems are likely to be in the former category, for example, and levels of education in the latter.

In the course of this process, the world view of a society's leaders and of large numbers of its inhabitants changes from one that sees the relations of human beings to their environments as governed by unknowable forces that cannot be questioned to one that favors the employment of vast resources to uncover the secrets of nature and put them to human use. Today's advanced societies have covered the vast distance in three centuries from forcing Galileo's recantation (1632) of the new science under penalty of death to awarding Einstein the most honorific international prize for his revolutionary discoveries. The continuing revolution in science and technology is the cornerstone of the modern era, and so long as knowledge continues to advance society may be expected to change.

The institutions that have implemented policies of societal transformation, both public and private, have grown with their responsibilities. The budgets of national, regional, and local administrative systems that in earlier times absorbed no more than a fraction of the national wealth now absorb one-third to one-half of the gross national product. In the United States, for example, the size of government expenditures as related to gross national product has grown from 2.5 percent in 1900 to 34 in 1970. Societies may achieve a high level of administrative integration either through public institutions, as in Sweden and the Soviet Union, or with a much larger role played by private institutions, as in Australia, Switzerland, and the United States. The differing roles of public and private institutions in the process of political centralization are as much a product of cultural heritage and of policy as of level of development, and private institutions (banks, enterprises, transportation systems) are no less concerned than public institutions with gaining control and coordination over the society. In many countries it took little more than a century to change from a way of life in which most people lived in isolated communities little touched by government to one in which literally all citizens are registered

T A B L E 1.   Levels of Economic Development

	Low	High
GNP per capita (U.S. 1973 dollars)[1]	200–300	4,000–6,000
Energy consumption (in kilograms of coal equivalents per capita)[2]	10–100	5,000–10,000
Employment of labor force (in percentages)[3]		
Agriculture	85–95	5–10
Industry	5–10	30–40
Services	5–10	40–60
National product by sectors (in percentages)[4]		
Agriculture	40–60	5–10
Industry	10–20	40–60
Services	20–40	40–60
National product by end uses (in percentages)[5]		
Consumption	80–85	55–60
Capital formation	5–10	20–30
Government	5–10	25–30

SOURCES:
1. Herbert Block, *Political Arithmetic of the World Economies* (Beverly Hills: Sage Publications, 1974), 80–85.
2. *World Handbook of Political and Social Indicators*, 2nd ed. (New Haven: Yale University Press, 1972), 326–328.
3. Ibid., 329–337.
4. Ibid., 338–340.
5. *World Handbook of Political and Social Indicators*, 1st ed. (New Haven: Yale University Press, 1964), 56–59, 166–177.

in and responsible to several government offices for purposes of taxation, social security, or military service.

Few aspects of societies have been changed so greatly in the course of modernization as those relating to the structure and growth of economic production. The accompanying table on Levels of Economic Development, based on contemporary figures, conveys a sense of the scope of this transformation.

The figures in Table 1 speak pretty much for themselves and graphically reflect the enormous distance that separates lower and higher levels of development. It should not be assumed, however, that these great differences necessarily represent the distance covered by societies that are now highly modernized. Many of the least developed countries today are much poorer in relevant

TABLE 2. Levels of Social Mobilization

	Low	High
Urbanization (percent in cities of 100,000 or more)[1]	0–10	50–70
Education[2]		
Primary and Secondary (ratio of enrollment to relevant age group)	5–20	90–100
Higher (students per one million inhabitants)	100–1,000	10,000–30,000
Health[3]		
Infant mortality (deaths per 1,000 live births)	150–500	13–25
Food supply (calories per capita per day)	1,500–2,000	3,000–3,500
Physicians (per 1 million population)	10–100	1,000–2,400
Communications[4]		
Mail (domestic letters per capita per year)	1–10	100–350
Telephones (per 1,000 population)	1–10	100–500
Newspapers (circulation per 1,000 population)	1–15	300–500
Radio (receivers per 1,000 population)	10–20	300–1,200
Television (receivers per 1,000 population)	1–50	100–350
Income Distribution (percent of income received by)[5]		
Lowest fifth	8–10	4
Highest fifth	40–50	45
Highest 5 percent	20–30	20

SOURCES:

1. *World Handbook of Political and Social Indicators,* 2nd ed. (New Haven: Yale University Press, 1972), 219–221.
2. Ibid., 225–231.
3. Ibid., 253–262.
4. Ibid., 236–248.
5. Irving R. Kravis, "A World of Unequal Incomes," *Annals of the American Academy of Political and Social Science,* CCCCIX (September 1973), 61–80.

respects than were England or Japan in 1600 or even earlier. Those that have developed furthest are, by and large, those that had the best basis for growth before the modern era.

The differences in social mobilization are no less striking than those in the economic realm, as indicated by the table on Levels of Social Mobilization. Though these selected indicators refer to ranges during the third quarter of the twentieth century, they nevertheless describe the extent of change that may occur within countries during the modern era in the course of only a few generations. As in the economic sphere, the countries that have the greatest degree of social mobilization today were in most respects more developed one or two centuries ago than the least socially developed countries today.

Regrettably, no comparable indicators exist on personality transformation. We can only speculate on the extent to which education, exposure to mass media, the urban-industrial environment, and travel may alter the ways in which individuals relate to one another. There can be no doubt, however, that such alteration does take place.

Yet it would be a mistake to describe societal transformation entirely in terms of human betterment, even though this is the way in which it has been seen by most participants. The costs have also been high. Many values and institutions have been destroyed before they could be adequately replaced; millions of lives have been lost in wars resulting from the political disruption caused by efforts to dismantle old empires and unify peoples in national states; many have had to bear the burdens of economic growth without sharing its benefits; millions have felt a sense of alienation in moving from the close relationships in premodern communities to the impersonality of urban and industrial life. Poverty and unemployment, crime and mental illness have also been part of the price of societal transformation.

The French Experience of Modernization

Bernard E. Brown

This essay, employing the example of France, provides both a critique of current conceptions of modernization and an analysis of an early-modernizing society that has undergone the extensive transformation to advanced industrialization. Significant also is the author's contention that the French experience is more typical than the American or British of the problems that other societies are likely to face, because like these newly developing societies its leaders have not been in agreement over basic institutions.

Few theorists today admit to a belief in the "idea of progress." But, if the literature in comparative politics in the past several years is any guide, virtually all political scientists now believe in the concept of "modernization." Modernization theory is being invoked to compare traditional and modern societies, to analyze the evolution of individual political systems, and to appraise the effectiveness of political institutions in one or several political systems. All of the problems and subjects of political science are now being reexamined in terms of some concept of modernization.

It is generally argued that the enormous development of science and technology since the early nineteenth century has brought about a fundamental transformation of all political systems. Most recent studies present a polar contrast between "traditional" and "modern" societies in terms of four major elements of any social system: the economy, social structure, political institutions, and the values that permeate the whole and justify coercion. The kind of change that involves modernization of each of these elements may be briefly summarized: (1) In traditional *economies* the overwhelming mass of the population is engaged in various forms of subsistence agriculture or husbandry. Modern economies are characterized by the use of science and technology in

"The French Experience of Modernization" by Bernard E. Brown is reprinted from *World Politics*, XXI, No. 3 (April 1969), 366–391. Reprinted by permission of Princeton University Press.

Brown is professor of political science at Brooklyn College of the City University of New York. He is the author of *New Directions in Comparative Politics* (1962), and co-author of *The DeGaulle Republic: Quest for Unity* (rev. ed., 1963).

He comments in a footnote at the beginning of his article: "This article is a slightly revised version of a paper presented at the meeting of the American Political Science Association in Washington, D.C., September, 1968. I am happy to acknowledge invaluable assistance from the Research Center in Comparative Politics at Brooklyn College."

the production of the means of existence. (2) Traditional *social structures* are relatively simple. The family is the dominant social unit, and face-to-face relations (through the tribe, clan, or feudal order) characterize the entire society. Modern social structure is complex, bureaucratized, and highly differentiated. An individual belongs to any number of specialized associations, such as trade unions, business groups, sporting societies, religious organizations, and the like. (3) Traditional *states* resemble large families, while modern states resemble specialized associations. In modern states political functions, like social functions, are assigned to different categories of people. A civil service is created, with a logical structure, hierarchy of command, and power based on knowledge rather than on family connections. (4) Traditional *values* are those of the family, emphasizing personal and filial loyalty. Attempts to view and understand the universe are in terms of mysticism, religion, and unprovable speculation; these constitute useful myths that hold together the social system and bring about acceptance of its structures and rules. Modern values are those of science. Political rule is justified by rational principles, not by invocation of divine right or heredity.

Modernization implies a particular kind of change in at least one of the above factors, bringing about corresponding changes in the other categories. A social system has an internal logic in that its various parts bear a *necessary* relationship to one another. Thus, a society imbued with ancestor-spirit, and in which authoritative decisions are made by witch doctors, is not capable of sustaining a massive industrial economy. Conversely, once an advanced industrial economy comes into being, the habits of thought and of science and the discipline of the machine are incompatible with a feudal social structure. Such assertions are broad; as Thorstein Veblen pointed out in a seminal work rather neglected by students of modernization, changes in the level of technology do not immediately bring about corresponding social changes. New social classes emulate the values and life styles of their "betters," a propensity that introduces a note of dissonance.[1] Correlations among the economic, social, political, and cultural factors are loose, but they exist; if they did not there would be no point in discussing modernization as a process.

One problem is evident from any survey of the literature. In order to sharpen the contrast between the two types, the "traditional" model is made so primitive that it is relevant only to tribal societies and prehistoric Europe. The kind of traditional society that preceded the modern form in Western Europe and North America, for example, was quite complex by any standard, and probably closer to "modernity" than to the ideal type of traditionalism. These extreme typologies also blur the significant differences among traditional societies—the kind of differences so brilliantly illuminated by Alexis de Tocqueville in his works on France, England, and the United States. Ideal types

---

[1] *The Theory of the Leisure Class* (1899). Veblen's essay on the "discipline of the machine," in *The Theory of Business Enterprise* (1904) is an excellent statement of the influence of technology upon social and political values. One major exception to the general view that the above defined factors are correlated in any social system is Wilbert S. Moore, *Social Change* (Englewood Cliffs, N.J. 1963), in which the looseness of social structure is stressed.

based on polar contrasts may be analytically useful as a check-list for observers or as a means of directing attention to the relationships among factors in any social system. The disadvantage is that the typology may take on a life of its own. Instead of seeking to grasp the internal logic of a political system with the aid of typological schemes, the observer may spend all his energy working out the abstract logic of a typology that has no relation to reality.

Whatever the mathematical and logical beauty of typologies, political scientists presumably are interested in the payoff for research. Does modernization theory deepen our understanding of political life? What difference does it make in the organization of research and study? Does it have explanatory power? One way of answering these questions—perhaps the best way, in fact—is to apply modernization theory to an individual political system. In this paper we shall take as a case study the French political system. Surely no argument is needed to demonstrate the importance of France in the development of modern Europe, or the contribution of the French to the industrial and scientific revolutions of the nineteenth century. We shall first examine the specific application of modernization theory to France by three highly imaginative and skilled observers: C. E. Black, Samuel P. Huntington, and Stanley Hoffmann.[2] Taken together, their writings offer a comprehensive view of the French experience of modernization from nation-building through late industrialization. We shall then return to the larger question of the utility and relevance of modernization theory in comparative politics.

Three Views of French Modernization

C. E. Black's *The Dynamics of Modernization* is probably the best single book on the subject yet to appear. Professor Black moves fluently and surely from theory to practice and back again. He identifies four stages of political modernization:

> (1) *the challenge of modernity*—the initial confrontation of a society, within its traditional framework of knowledge, with modern ideas and institutions, and the emergence of advocates of modernity; (2) *the consolidation of modernizing leadership*—the transfer of power from traditional to modernizing leaders in the course of a normally bitter revolutionary struggle often lasting several generations; (3) *economic and social transformation*—the development of economic growth and social change to a point where a society is transformed from a predominantly rural and agrarian way of life to one predominantly urban and industrial; and (4) *the integration of society*—the phase in which economic and social transformation produces a fundamental reorganization of the social structure throughout the society.[3]

[2] C. E. Black, *The Dynamics of Modernization: A Study in Comparative History* (New York 1966); Samuel P. Huntington, "Political Modernization: America vs. Europe," *World Politics* xvii (April 1966), 378–414; and Stanley Hoffmann, "Paradoxes of the French Political Community," in Hoffmann, ed., *In Search of France* (Cambridge, Mass. 1963), 1–117.

[3] Black, 67–68.

Black's typology of political modernization is based on the timing of the consolidation of modern political leadership (whether early or late in relation to other countries), the nature of the challenge of modernity to traditional institutions (whether internal or external), the continuity of territory and population in the modern era, the independent or dependent status of the nation, and the solidity of political institutions when the nation entered the modern era. The first of seven patterns that make up the typology is formed by the experience of Great Britain and France. In both countries the revolution that consolidated political leadership came early as compared to that of other countries (1649–1832 in Britain and 1789–1848 in France), the major challenge of modernity was primarily internal, there was an unusual continuity of both territory and population in the modern era, and the political institutions were fairly stable as the country entered the modern era. Professor Black then cites 1832–1945 as the period of economic and social transformation in Britain, 1848–1945 in France; and since 1945 as the phase of social integration in both countries.

In this analysis the similarities between British and French modernization are emphasized. The major differences between the two nations are thus the earlier rise to power of a modern leadership and the somewhat earlier industrialization in Britain. Black recognizes that the French never achieved the same degree of political concensus as did the British. But he suggests that the basis for orderly development in France was laid by the modern institutional framework established by the Napoleonic Code in 1802. In spite of the apparent political instability, he concludes that "France has nevertheless undergone at the administrative level a relatively gradual and stable transformation under many generations of skilled civil servants trained in the *grandes écoles*." [4]

Professor Black's typology of seven patterns is a stimulating way of comparing and evaluating the general process of political modernization in the world. But its specific application to France raises several questions. Was modern leadership in France first consolidated in 1789? The implication in Black's analysis is that this stage occurred in Britain more than a century earlier. No one would deny the importance of the English Civil War or the French Revolution as decisive turning points in British and French political history, especially as regards the shaping of political institutions and the evolution of consensus. But that Britain and France, so closely related in all things, were a century apart in political modernization is implausible. Britain and France were both presented with the same kind of challenge in the course of the seventeenth century—basically the inability or unwillingness of the country as a whole to sustain the burden of a greatly expanded monarchical apparatus. The French monarchy proved somewhat more flexible and adaptable at the time; it was thus able to weather the storm. In spite of the political turmoil in seventeenth-century Britain, and the success of reformers in France, it would appear that similar developments were taking place in the two societies during the seventeenth and eighteenth centuries. De Tocqueville pointed out, for example, in his classic study, *The Old Regime and the French Revolution*,

4 *Ibid.*, 109.

that the entire political, administrative, and social structure of the nation was being transformed well before the Revolution. In a famous passage, he wrote, "Chance played no part whatever in the outbreak of the Revolution; though it took the world by surprise; it was the inevitable outcome of a long period of gestation, the abrupt and violent conclusion of a process in which six generations had played an intermittent part. Even if it had not taken place, the old social structure would nonetheless have been shattered everywhere sooner or later." [5] Undoubtedly, a new political leadership emerged in 1789. But new social forces came to the fore, and began to participate in the political system, long before that date.

On the other hand, Professor Black may be overstating the similarities between Britain and France when he argues that in both countries there was "a relatively orderly and peaceful adaptation of traditional institutions to modern functions." In one sense this was certainly the case; France today is roughly as "modern" as Britain, and presumably her traditional institutions (at least those dating from the Revolution and the Napoleonic Code) have proved adaptable. But how useful is this approach for an understanding of French development? Modernization there has been, yes; but its pace, the way in which new social groups created by modernization have entered into the political system, and the role played by the State in furthering modernization have all been quite distinctive in France.

The contention that the *grands corps* really run France, despite the political bickering on the surface, is a venerable thesis. Studies of decision-making suggest that in France, as in all complex parliamentary systems, the civil service is itself divided politically. Major interest groups develop special channels of access to the civil service as well as to parliament, thus creating "whirlpools" of influence and power throughout the political system. For example, with regard to the issue of state subsidies to beetgrowers and other producers of alcohol there is a split within the French civil service; the Ministry of Agriculture is generally in favor of subsidies and the Treasury is generally opposed. Alliances are thus formed that include civil servants, interest groups, deputies, and party leaders on both sides of issues. The French civil service has been fortunate in the past in recruiting exceptional talent; but it has not been a unified political force, nor has it been able to resolve the problem of political legitimacy. In this sense, the French experience provides us with a contrast to that of Britain and other nations where there is general agreement on fundamental political values and institutions.[6]

---

[5] Alexis de Tocqueville, *The Old Regime and the French Revolution* (Garden City, N.Y. 1955), 20.

[6] For example, Jean Meynaud describes the governmental universe in France as a system of power centers negotiating and bargaining with one another, *Nouvelles études sur les groupes de pression en France* (Paris 1962), 249–50, 279. Among the case studies that point up the pluralistic nature of decision-making in France: Aline Coutrot, "La loi scolaire de décembre 1959," *Revue française de science politique* (June 1963), 352–88; and Gaston Rimareix and Yves Tavernier, "L'élaboration et le vote de la loi complémentaire à la loi d'orientation agricole," *ibid.*, 389–425. Also B. E. Brown, "France," in J. B. Christoph, ed., *Cases in Comparative Politics* (Boston 1965), 129–206.

Our attention is directed especially to the period preceding the Revolution by Samuel P. Huntington, in his study of political modernization in America and Europe. He argues that modernization involves three things: rationalization of authority (replacement of traditional political authority by a single, secular, national authority), the development of specialized political structures to perform specialized functions, and mass participation in the political system. "On the Continent," comments Huntington, "the rationalization of authority and the differentiation of structures were the dominant trends of the seventeenth century," and he cites Richelieu, Mazarin, Louis XIV, Colbert, and Louvois as "great simplifiers, centralizers, and modernizers." [7] In addition, the seventeenth century saw the growth and rationalization of state bureaucracies and standing armies. Thus, in two important respects, the process of modernization took place on the Continent by 1700. A new political leadership rose to power in 1789; yet the way had been prepared over a long period of time.

It seems strange that divine right and hereditary monarchy should be considered forces for modernization. But Huntington explains that a prime requisite of modernization is the belief that men can act purposefully and effect change. Traditional society is permeated by a belief in unchanging custom and fundamental law. The modernization that began in the sixteenth century on the Continent required a new concept of authority, namely, that there was a sovereign who could make decisions. "One formulation of this idea was the new theory, which developed in Europe in the late sixteenth century, of the divine right of kings. Here, in effect, religious and, in that sense, traditional forms were used for modern purposes." Since mass participation in politics was a later phenomenon, modernization in the seventeenth century meant the rise of the absolute monarchy. "In terms of modernization, the seventeenth century's absolute monarch was the functional equivalent of the twentieth century's monolithic party." [8]

Huntington's analysis of Continental developments is a useful and necessary corrective. Most observers are fascinated by the Revolution, and have neglected the modernizing reforms of the Old Regime. But to consider monarchy the spearhead of modernization is an oversimplification of the situation in France. The absolute monarchy both furthered the trend to modernization and slowed it. It contributed to modernization by breaking the power of the local lords; it slowed modernization by glorifying irrational values, sustaining an archaic social structure, and imposing a terrible financial load upon the people. The modernizers in France before the Revolution also included the social critics, some who demanded parliamentary control of the executive, and some who greeted the American Revolution as the harbinger of a new era in history.

Nor were the advocates of fundamental law all opponents of modernization. It is true that some traditionalists invoked fundamental law to protect the privileges of the corporations. On the other hand, some modernizers tried to secure popular participation in the political system by appealing to funda-

[7] Huntington, 379.
[8] Ibid., 384, 386.

mental law above the will of the monarch. In France as in colonial America, the doctrine of higher law was used for several political purposes, among which was the promulgation of rational principles of legitimacy.

Stanley Hoffmann deals with the later stages of modernization in France in his essay, "Paradoxes of the French Political Community." He begins with the two familiar models of feudal-agrarian society and industrial society, and then places France on the continuum. He suggests that a "Republican synthesis" gradually emerged in the century after the French Revolution and flourished in the period 1878–1914. The basis of the Republican synthesis was a unique mixture of the two models, neither one nor the other, but rather a "halfway house between the old rural society and industrialization." The French economy was both static and modern at the same time. Industrialization took place, but without an industrial revolution. The business class adopted many of the attitudes of the aristocracy that it had replaced, particularly that of emphasizing family continuity and social prominence rather than efficient production. The agricultural sector remained massive and largely traditional in orientation. Slow industrial growth in turn made it difficult to grant concessions to the working class, which was consigned to a "social ghetto." Comments Hoffmann, "For more than a century the political problem of France was to devise a political system adapted to the stalemate society." [9]

The basic solution to this problem under the Third Republic was the combination of a centralized and efficient bureaucracy with a strictly limited state. Politics became a kind of game in which a divided parliament prevented the formation of effective political executives. "But this game, played in isolation from the nation-at-large by a self-perpetuating political class, saw to it that the fundamental equilibrium of society would not be changed by the state." [10] However, the foundations of the Republican synthesis were undermined by the crises of the 1930's. The depression and the rise of Nazi Germany produced tensions in French society that the regime could not overcome. The assailants of the Republic converged and overwhelmed it. Writing in 1962, Hoffmann concluded that "the stalemate society is dead"—though many of the old tensions remained. It was killed by the transformation of French society during and after World War II—by the emergence of fully industrial attitudes, the more active role of the state in planning economic development, a reorientation of the French business class, and structural changes in the working class.

But the use of ideal types as literary devices makes French society appear to be far more static than was the case under the Third and Fourth Republics, and more dynamic than it actually was under the Fifth Republic. For example, there was a period of very rapid and impressive economic growth from 1896 to 1914, with important social and political consequences. The Third Republic created conditions in which the whole infrastructure of the modern economy was perfected—including the railroad network, canals, and modern communications. Its greatest contribution perhaps was to lay the foundation of a universal, free, and secular educational system. This may not be the most

[9] Hoffmann, 12.
[10] *Ibid.*, 16.

desirable way to bring about modernization, but it surely is one way to do so. The balance among social forces and economic sectors was shifting, more or less rapidly, under both the Third and Fourth Republics. French society was, and still is, a mix of traditional and modern elements; but this is hardly unique. All industrial societies are characterized by tension between traditional and modern sectors. Nor is the French political system the only one alleged by critics to be "incoherent." If there is a distinctive French experience of modernization it will be found in the timing of the crises of modernization and in the persistent alienation of large groups at all stages of modernization, up to and including the present.

Modernization theory obviously is not a magic wand that eliminates the need for research or produces universal agreement among observers. But it is a fruitful way of organizing study, and permits significant comparison among political systems. In order to further comparative study of modernization, we offer the following generalizations concerning the French experience.

1. The traditional phase in France that preceded modern society was feudalism. But feudal society in France was relatively advanced compared to, say, tribal societies. Feudalism contained important elements of "modernity." The process of modernization in France, therefore, has been long and complex, dating at least from the eleventh century, and perhaps from as far back as the Roman conquest.

2. In the century before the Revolution, the social structure of France was gradually transformed. A system in which privilege derived from heredity was at least partly replaced by a system based on wealth and individual effort. The Revolution was the culmination of a long period of social change, whose pace then was greatly accelerated.

3. The values justifying feudalism and absolute monarchy lost their popular base under the Old Regime. The trend toward rationalization of political authority, brought to a logical conclusion by the Revolution, was a development of centuries.

4. In spite of continuing political turmoil the economic and social foundations of modernity were laid during the nineteenth century. Far from being a stalemate society, France under both the Third and Fourth Republics took on the characteristics of all modern societies.

We shall now discuss each of these generalizations at length.

1. THE TRADITIONAL SOCIETY

Feudalism was a highly personal political relationship between man and man, between subordinate and superior. As one historian has put it: "It is the possession of rights of government by feudal lords and the performance of most functions of government through feudal lords which clearly distinguishes feudalism from other types of organization." [11] Feudalism was a "model" traditional society in every respect. The mass of the population was engaged in subsistence agriculture or animal husbandry, the primary social unit was the family, the basic values of the society were those of personal loyalty, fealty, and courage, and the state (in so far as it continued to exist) was a larger version of family organization and power. The feudal system reposed on mutual duties and rights of people in a direct personal relationship, with the enjoyment of land rights as the foundation of the structure.

If typological analysis is a checklist of characteristics, the contrast between feudalism and contemporary society in France is virtually total. But historical processes are too complex to be reduced to these terms. When placed in the context of French historical development, it may be seen that feudalism departed from the traditional model in a number of ways. First, feudalism throughout Western Europe was a response to the decay of the highly organized Roman Empire. Until the tenth century, the Roman way of life prevailed in Gaul. Citizens owned land and slaves, subject to restrictions imposed upon them by the state. But the state then disintegrated. No central authority was able to protect the inhabitants of Western Europe from the incessant incursions of Saracens and Scandinavians. Under these new circumstances the Roman notion of a centralized state became obsolete. Defense and security inevitably became local responsibilities. Thus, feudalism was not comparable to primitive tribal societies; it rather should be viewed as a civilized society in decline or decay. The difference is important. Under feudalism the memory of the centralized authority of the past always remained alive. One leading French historian contends that in the Middle Ages in France there were, strictly speaking, no feudal institutions. Only the monarchy was legitimate; the functions of administering justice, raising armies, and levying taxes were generally recognized as attributes of monarchy, conceded to or usurped by feudal powers.[12] When conditions and the technology of warfare changed, it was possible for the Capetian kings to revive the spirit of social and national unity. The reconstruction of authority that has fallen into decay is quite different as a political process from the creation of central authority where none has ever existed.

Most important, the rise of feudalism in the eleventh century coincided with a resurgence of the cities, a development that eventually sapped the feudal system. The period in France that most closely approximates the model traditional economy was the five centuries that preceded feudalism, rather than feudalism itself. It was from the sixth through the eleventh centuries,

---

[11] Joseph R. Strayer, "Feudalism in Western Europe," in Rushton Coulborn, ed., *Feudalism in History* (Princeton 1956), 16. On feudalism in France see also Marc Bloch, *Feudal Society* (Chicago 1961); A. Tilley, ed., *Medieval France* (New York 1964); and for an excellent synthesis, J. Touchard et al., *Histoire des idées politiques* (Paris 1959), 1, 155–63.

[12] See the seminal work by Ferdinand Lot with the collaboration of Robert Fawtier, *Histoire des institutions françaises au moyen âge* (Paris 1957), I, viii; and II, p. 9 for the comment, "the only political regime France had in the Middle Ages was the monarchy." Vol. II is an extraordinarily complete analysis of the rise of the royal power.

apparently, that the Franks became an almost wholly rural people engaged in subsistence agriculture. Artisans during this period abandoned the towns and retired to the countryside. Commerce declined abruptly, the cities were largely deserted, and municipal administration ceased to exist. By the eleventh century the process of urbanization resumed. The renaissance of town life was the result of many factors: a deliberate desire to create the conditions of a peaceful and secure existence within the confines of a commune; technological innovations in transport and manufacturing that made it economically feasible for merchants and artisans to congregate in towns; and a general desire on the part of merchants to terminate their nomadic existence and degrading dependence upon the goodwill of the local lords.

Everywhere, the city people sought to free themselves from the domination of feudal lords. This became easier as the cities prospered and could afford to recruit mercenaries. Nobles then found it necessary, in some cases profitable, to grant special charters to the towns, in effect exempting them from feudal obligations. Many communes were based on a clearly modern rather than traditional theory of governance. They were created by "common oath" on the part of the inhabitants, that is, an agreement among equals rather than between a superior and his subordinates. The "consular cities" enjoyed complete municipal liberty, with citizens electing representative councils invested with large financial and executive powers.

The inhabitants of the *bourgs* (or bourgeois) did not fit into the feudal structure. Merchants and artisans worked on their own, handled money, had no obligations to the lords, and were receptive to new ideas. The bourgeois became likewise a firm support for the royal power, which alone could integrate the resources of large domains and provide adequate security for the towns. The medieval towns were breeding grounds of new values and ideologies that challenged the traditional notions of religion, cultivated skepticism concerning the established order, and glorified the qualities of intelligence, liberty, and work.[13]

There was no steady, ineluctable progression from traditional to modern. The balance among the rival forces shifted frequently—particularly during the period of economic stagnation in the fourteenth century which brought about a decline of the middle class and a corresponding increase in the power and prestige of the clergy and lords. The secular trend, however, was to transform military vassalage into nobility in the service of the crown, and to transfer the idea of contract to the level of people and monarch. In brief, the social structure, economy, political institutions, and cultural values of medieval France by the thirteenth century already contained major elements of "modernity."

---

13 On urbanization in the Middle Ages: Roland Mousnier, *Les XVI et XVII siècles* (Paris 1965), especially chap. 3; H. Van Werveke, "The Rise of Towns," in *The Cambridge Economic History of Europe*, III, edited by M. M. Postan, E. E. Rich, and E. Miller (Cambridge 1963), 3–40; L. Halphen, "Industry and Commerce," in A. Tilley, ed., *Medieval France*, 183–92; and J. Touchard and others, I, 169–79. On the bourgeois support for monarchy, Robert Fawtier, *The Capetian Kings of France* (London 1964), 199–215.

2. THE BREAKUP OF THE TRADITIONAL SOCIETY

The dramatic events of the Revolution have tended to draw the attention of observers away from the rapid pace of social change in the seventeenth and eighteenth centuries. In each of the social orders of the Old Regime—the clergy, aristocracy, and third estate—structural transformations took place that eventually undermined the whole delicate balance of feudal privilege.[14]

As is natural in any pre-industrial society, religious values permeated medieval France. The clergy propagated and popularized the values that sustained the feudal regime, and enjoyed a privileged position as the "first estate." Church revenue from the tithe and other levies amounted to about 13 percent of the gross national income, to which must be added income from vast church-held lands. The church performed a number of vital functions within the society, including the maintenance of a network of welfare and educational institutions.

Yet the clergy's grip on power was shaken. The priestly life was subjected to serious criticism and satire by the intellectuals. That respect so necessary to the maintenance of any priestly class began to evaporate, and concern became general over the waste and irrationality of a system of tithes. Furthermore, the clergy was itself divided sharply into a small group of high-living and wealthy archbishops, and a mass of impoverished priests. When the great explosion took place, a divided priestly class was unable to rally mass support for the old regime.

The position of the nobility likewise was transformed in the century preceding the Revolution. It, too, was affected by the process of modernization. The very composition of the nobility underwent a change. It was not a completely closed caste, since new elements were admitted to noble rank by a variety of methods. The king had the right of conferring nobility upon deserving commoners (usually men of great wealth, civil servants, and military officers). Whatever their origins, the nobles enjoyed extensive feudal privileges, which they sought desperately to maintain against pressures from the peasantry, the rising middle classes, and from the king. After 1750 the power of the aristocracy increased along with that of the middle classes. As Gordon Wright has put it: "The eighteenth century nobility was increasingly inclined to attack and destroy the *status quo*. The revolutionary goal of the discontented nobles was a return to a semi-mythical medieval system, to an unwritten constitution that had allegedly been torn up by the absolutist kings and their bourgeois ministers." [15]

All the rest of the population—some 98 percent—was the third estate. In the course of the eighteenth century the bourgeoisie rose in spectacular fashion within the social structure. Considerable fortunes were made in industry (by

---

[14] For an excellent social and political analysis of this period, see Georges Dupeux, *La société française, 1789–1960* (Paris 1964), 59–102, and Gordon Wright, *France in Modern Times* (Chicago 1960), chaps. 1 and 2.

[15] Gordon Wright, 18.

such entrepreneurs as Decretot, Van Robais, Oberkampf, Réveillon, and Dietrich), in trade (especially by the shipping interests of Havre, Bordeaux, and Marseilles) and in finance. Perhaps 10 percent of the bourgeoisie was enabled, through investments and loans, to live entirely on dividends, without engaging in any kind of work. As the bourgeois acquired wealth, he tended to buy up land and cultivate it, thereby reestablishing a link between the middle class and agriculture. It has been estimated that perhaps 25 to 30 percent of all arable land in France by 1789 was in the hands of the bourgeoisie. Most of the *petite bourgeoisie* were engaged in trade or skilled work, and usually were organized in corporations.

There were stirrings within the peasantry, too. In 1779, serfdom was legally abolished in the last few places where it had survived. The peasants were juridically free, and altogether owned perhaps 40 to 45 percent of the land. However, the individual holdings were small, and relatively few peasants were well off. The number of landless peasants and seasonal workers in rural areas probably was greater than the number of individual landholders.[16]

The implications of these social trends were very great. First, they contradicted the assumption on which the Old Regime was based—that society was a pyramid, with peasants and middle classes at the base, with aristocracy above them and a king above all. Says Cobban: "The division of the nation into *noblesse, noblesse de robe,* clergy, bourgeois and peasants was a simplification which concealed the real complexity of French society. Each class had in fact its own internal divisions, which prevented it from being a coherent unit." Basically, it was impossible for the old feudal political system to survive in this kind of society. The new standards of performance related to wealth, ability, talent, and occupational role; considerations of noble birth were less relevant, and in the long run, if taken seriously would have led to an impairment of the efficiency of the society. As R. R. Palmer has pointed out, "Western Europe in the eighteenth century was already a complicated society, with elaborate mechanisms operating in the fields of government, production, trade, finance, scientific research, church affairs, and education. The allocation of personnel to these enterprises on the basis of birth and social standing could not but hamper, and even pervert (one thinks of the established churches, some of the universities, and many branches of government), the achievement of the purposes for which such institutions were designed. The old feudal days were over. It was no longer enough for a lord to look locally after the needs of his people. The persistence and even the accentuation of an aristocratic outlook derived from earlier and simpler conditions presented problems for European society itself, as well as for the individuals and classes that made it up."[17]

The rise of the bourgeoisie did not have to mean a fight to the death between the middle class and the nobility. Several different solutions were conceivable: The middle class could have disdained aristocratic values altogether, in which case the nobility might have ceased to be a political power; or

[16] Georges Dupeux, 72–73.

[17] Citations are from Alfred Cobban, "The Decline of Divine Right Monarchy in France," *New Cambridge Modern History* (Cambridge 1957), VII, 235, and R. R. Palmer, *The Age of the Democratic Revolution* (Princeton 1959), 68.

the nobility could have opened its ranks to the newcomers and gradually absorbed its leading elements, thereby creating a greatly expanded new ruling class. But time ran out for peaceful solutions. Relations among aristocracy, bourgeoisie, and peasantry became increasingly bitter. The nobility resisted the pretensions of the middle classes and tried to block the development of embryonic capitalism. Eighteenth-century France had all the characteristics of a political system unsettled by the process of modernization.

3. REASON AND REVOLUTION

One of the basic assumptions of modernization theory is that as a society becomes more complex, the values serving to legitimize political authority become more rational. Or, rather than imply any causal relationship, rationalization of authority proceeds along with industrialization and increasing complexity of social structure. This assumption is borne out in a striking manner by the French experience, because of the great divide marked by the Revolution of 1789. The pattern of legitimacy clearly underwent a radical transformation, and took a form of greater rationality. But closer examination makes it apparent that the rationalization of authority was accentuated, not created, by the Revolution. It was part and parcel of the secular trend of modernization in all spheres of French society under the Old Regime.

Huntington has emphasized the modernizing role of the monarchy in breaking up feudal society. Hence, the theory of divine right of kings was more rational, or more modern, than feudalism itself. He comments, "The modernization that began in the sixteenth century on the Continent and in the seventeenth century in England required new concepts of authority, the most significant of which was the simple idea of a sovereignty itself, the idea that there is, in the words of Bodin, a 'supreme power over citizens and subjects, unrestrained by law.' One formulation of this idea was the new theory, which developed in Europe in the late sixteenth century, of the divine right of kings. Here, in effect, religious and, in that sense, traditional forms were used for modern purposes." [18]

Huntington's view is a useful reminder that ideal types make little sense outside historical context. The notion that a ruler receives a mandate from a divine source is characteristic of traditional societies; yet in the Europe of the seventeenth century it was part of the breakthrough to modernity. But even here we must beware of historical oversimplification. Divine right of kings was not a new theory. The Franks, before the conquest, combined hereditary right with election; an Assembly of Warriors elected a king from among members of the Merovingian family, which presumably had divine connections. After the Frankish conquest, the Merovingians tried to free themselves of this dependence upon the assemblies, but were only partially successful. The rise of the Carolingian and Capetian dynasties brought a renewed emphasis upon election, since heredity could not be invoked as the overriding principle of legitimacy in an era of dynastic rivalries. Once their grip on power seemed secure, the

[18] Huntington, 384.

Capetians sought to reestablish the principle of divine right, which gradually became accepted by the thirteenth century—though even in the fourteenth century there were several occasions when an Assembly of Barons played at least a subsidiary role in choosing a king. Divine right and religious consecration was the ancient theory of governance, was weakened under feudalism, and then revived as the centralizing forces in French society triumphed over feudalism. Under Louis XIV an absolute monarchy replaced a weak feudal monarchy; in a sense the monarchy reverted to the pre-feudal principle of divine right.[19]

The thesis that the absolute monarch was the agent of modernization can also be reversed, with perhaps even more validity. H. R. Trevor-Roper has argued cogently that the general European crisis of the seventeenth century had its origins in the rise of absolute monarchy. The Renaissance state, he contends, grew up in the sixteenth century at the expense of the cities. One by one, the great cities fell under the control of assorted princes and kings, whose military and administrative machines were irresistible. Monarchy helped bring about national unity, but once the Renaissance court was created, it became a wholly uneconomic and parasitic agency. The tested principles of commerce and industry were replaced by ostentation and deliberate waste. The burden of monarchy became too great to be borne; the sensible course was to eliminate the whole parasitic crew and return to the productive way of life that had made the medieval cities great. In England the royal power resisted and was swept away; in France the king, perhaps out of luck and apathy, allowed Richelieu to reduce royal expenses and enforce a mercantilist policy. The old regime was given a reprieve. According to Trevor-Roper, "By the seventeenth century the Renaissance courts had grown so great, had consumed so much in 'waste,' and had sent their multiplying suckers so deep in the body of society, that they could only flourish for a limited time, and in a time, too, of expanding general prosperity. When that prosperity failed, the monstrous parasite was bound to falter." [20]

This is not to deny the importance of the monarchy, and especially of the royal administrations, as a channel for innovative practices. But the medieval monarchy cannot be understood through the simple use of ideal types, nor can it be considered the sole agency of modernization. The rise of absolute monarchy in France coincided with the general modernization of French society, but so did the rise of opposition to absolutism.

It is also misleading to contrast divine right of kings with the concept of

---

19 On the principle of election and religious consecration in the feudal period, see Ch. Petit Dutaillis, *The Feudal Monarchy in France and England* (London 1936), 28; Robert Fawtier, *The Capetian Kings of France*, 48–49; and Maurice Duverger, *Les constitutions de la France* (Paris 1950), 11–17.

20 H. R. Trevor-Roper, "The General Crisis of the Seventeenth Century," in T. Aston, ed., *Crisis in Europe, 1560–1660* (New York 1965), 95. See also the dissent by Roland Mousnier, arguing that the monarchy was a progressive force, *ibid.*, 102. The thesis that modernization of French society took place through the crown is also presented by Barrington Moore, Jr., in *Social Origins of Dictatorship and Democracy* (Boston 1967). But note the strong statement by Alfred Cobban on the inherent incapacity of the French monarchy, as early as the reign of Louis XIV, to deal with changing conditions, in "The Decline of Divine Right Monarchy in France," 239.

fundamental law, as if the latter characterized static traditional societies and the former embodied the principle of change. In France the situation was more confused. There were actually two different trends in theorizing about the fundamental laws of the kingdom. One view can properly be called "traditional," in that the fundamental laws were considered the creation of history and of God, beyond the competence even of the king to change. But a second view also developed, according to which fundamental laws were made by the people, and could be modified by the people through the Estates General. This conception, derived from the doctrine of social contract, was clearly more compatible with the process of modernization than were theories of divine right and hereditary monarchy. As Rushton Coulborn put it, the theory of divine right was a "clumsy idea," an "interim notion," and a "slogan, not an argument." And he concludes, "the return to serious thought about the relations between rulers and ruled is marked by the extraordinary doctrine of Original Compact, or Contract." [21]

The social contract is in one sense an extension of the doctrine of "fundamental laws" under the Old Regime. The political struggles of the eighteenth century revolved around the question of whether fundamental laws restrained the powers of the monarch. It was generally accepted under the Old Regime that the monarch could not change the rules concerning succession to the throne, or alienate the public domain, or be anything but a Catholic. An effort was made by a number of Estates General to establish the principle of parliamentary approval of all new taxes as a fundamental law, but the monarchy managed to defeat these efforts. This view of fundamental law led ultimately to the notion that the people originally possessed sovereign powers, and then delegated these powers to their governors.

Once again it is necessary to emphasize the length and complexity of the process of modernization. By the eighteenth century the view was general that man was a creature of unlimited possibilities, that he was basically rational, and that the major purpose of political institutions was to permit him to develop his creative abilities to the fullest. As Gordon Wright has commented: "Enlightenment concepts were far more subversive than its proponents knew; they could scarcely be reconciled with the dominant ideas on which the old regime rested. The institutions of eighteenth-century France were still based on authority and tradition, not on any rational or utilitarian test; the old ideal of an organic society could not be harmonized with the new concept of an atomistic one made up of autonomous individuals." [22]

The ideas of the Enlightenment undermined the positions of both of the main contenders for power in the two decades that preceded the Revolution. The *Parlements* tried, with some success, to check the monarch, basically in the interest of the hereditary aristocracy. The king replied by affirming that full sovereignty resided in his person only. "Public order in its entirety," Louis XV proclaimed in the *séance de la flagellation*, in 1766, "emanates from me, and

[21] Rushton Coulborn, ed., 311–12. On the fundamental laws under the Old Regime and social contract theory, see M. Duverger, 31–37.
[22] Gordon Wright, 31.

the rights and interests of the Nation, which some dare to set up as a body distinct from the Monarch, are necessarily joined with mine, and rest only in my hands." Neither the claims of absolute monarchy nor the proposals to restore aristocratic privilege were consonant with the intellectual mood of the time. By the standards of reason and the Enlightenment, the assertion that all sovereignty reposed in the king was absurd; and the contention that hereditary officeholders of the *Parlements* represented the nation only a little less so. When the showdown came, both protagonists found themselves without popular support.[23]

The new principles of political authority were rational in essence; they were compatible with either constitutional monarchy or a parliamentary republic, but marked an irrevocable break with both absolutism and feudalism. The Tennis Court Oath, the August decrees abolishing feudalism, and the Declaration of the Rights of Man and Citizen signalled the emergence of a wholly new principle of political legitimacy. Contrast, for example, Louis XV's pronouncement at the *séance de la flagellation*, the remonstrance of the *Parlement* of Paris in March, 1776, (glorifying the inequalities of feudalism) with the clear, forceful language of 1789. The Declaration was drawn up, in its own terms, "so that this Declaration, constantly present before all members of the social body, shall recall to them ever their rights and their duties; so that the acts of the legislative and executive Powers, being compared at every instant with the goal of all political institutions, shall be more respected. . . ." And the Constitution of 3 September, 1791, "abolishes universally the institutions that infringe upon liberty and the equality of rights—there is no longer any nobility, nor peerage, nor hereditary distinctions, nor distinctions among orders, nor feudal regime. . . . There is no longer, for any part of the Nation, nor for any individual, any privilege, nor any exception to the common law of all Frenchmen."

The revolutionary principle of political legitimacy was not accepted by conservatives, and the revolutionaries were themselves divided; the result was a long period of constitutional instability. Although France was converted almost overnight into a modern state as regards the official principle of legitimacy, it did not thereby achieve a large popular consensus on its basic institutions. The transformation of French society continued. But the way in which the successive crises of modernization were surmounted was drastically affected by endemic constitutional instability. In turn, the nature of controversy over the regime evolved in response to the pressures of modernization.

4. MODERNIZATION AND CONSENSUS

Science and technology shape the politics of all modern societies. The development of industry necessarily brings about a redistribution of the active

---

[23] On the clash between the king and the Parlements, see Palmer, 86–99, and René Rémond, *La vie politique en France, 1789–1848* (Paris 1965), 31–40. On the Enlightenment, see notably Gordon Wright, 28–39; and the fine synthesis in Jean Touchard and others, II, 383–449.

population within the economy. The percentage of the population engaged in agriculture decreases, those remaining on farms are able greatly to expand production in spite of their reduced numbers, and the percentage of the population engaged in industry, services, and administration increases. New social groups form and make claims upon the political system. In terms of historical sequence, these groups are the capitalists and businessmen in general, the managerial class, and the working class. At a later stage of industrialization the scientists and intellectuals become so numerous and important in the society that they also become a distinct force. In France, as in all other nations that have gone or are going through the process of industrialization, the entry of these social groups into the political system has posed an acute problem.

The first task is to gain an overall view of the extent to which French society has been reshaped. In French census statistics the active population is classified on the basis of participation in three large sectors of the economy: the primary sector (agriculture, forestry, fishing), the secondary (industry, mining, construction, production of energy), and the tertiary (all other activities, including distribution, administration, and personal services). One century ago the agricultural sector was more important than the other two combined; there were slightly more than two farmers for one worker and one person in the tertiary sector. In 1964 the agricultural sector was the least important of the three; the number of persons engaged in farming had been reduced by almost two-thirds, with corresponding increases in the other two sectors. The following table summarizes these trends.[24]

YEARS	1851	1881	1901	1921	1931	1936	1954	1962	1964
Primary sector (%)	53	48	42	43	37	37	28	21	18
Secondary sector (%)	25	27	31	29	33	30	36	38	42
Tertiary sector (%)	22	25	27	28	30	33	36	41	40

One striking feature of contemporary France is the swift pace of social change. In the ten-year period from 1954 to 1964 the number of people engaged in agriculture declined by almost 40 percent, while the number of those in the secondary and tertiary sectors increased by about 15 percent. The political implications of these trends are obvious. The peasantry is now the smallest of the major social groups. Given their minority position, the peasants must make their claims upon the political system mainly through interest groups rather than through political parties seeking to form a political majority. Although the industrial workers have become more numerous, they still do not constitute a majority by themselves. Only through alliance with either the peasantry or elements of the middle classes can they form a majority. Not only are the

[24] Table based on Georges Dupeux, 33 and *Tableaux de l'économie française* (Paris 1966), 48a; and *Atlas historique de la France contemporaine* (Paris 1966), 45.

middle classes—business, proprietary, managerial, and professional groups—important because of the functions they perform, they are also a massive political force, about as numerous as all workers engaged in industrial production.

France now resembles the other industrial nations of the world, with roughly the same kind of balance among the three major sectors of the economy. In 1964 the number of people in the agricultural sector in France amounted to 18 percent of the total—smaller than in Italy (25 percent), or Japan (26 percent) or the Soviet Union (34 percent), but larger than in Germany (12 percent), the United States (8 percent), or Britain (4 percent). The number of people engaged in the tertiary sector in France was about 41 percent of the total, as compared to 58 percent in the United States, 48 percent in Britain, 42 percent in Japan, 38 percent in Germany, 33 percent in Italy, and 32 percent in the Soviet Union.[25]

In all other respects as well, French society is displaying the general characteristics of modernization. The movement of population toward urban centers has been massive, as is normal. In 1846 the number of people living in communes of two thousand inhabitants or more amounted to 24 percent of the population, and those living in communes of five thousand inhabitants or more to about 17 percent; the comparable figures in 1962 were 62 percent and 55 percent. Particularly striking has been the growth of the Paris metropolitan area as an industrial and administrative center. Almost 20 percent of the nation's population now lives and works in the Paris region, as compared to only about 3 percent a century ago.[26]

Although the outlines of French social structure are like those of most other industrialized nations, the manner in which that social structure evolved was quite distinctive. Industrialization in France up to 1815 was slow, and generally a result of the application of English methods in the field of textile manufacture. The way to industrialization had been prepared by the Revolution, which eliminated feudal barriers and created a vast market. But French energies were then directed mainly toward defense of the Republic and the creation of the far-flung Napoleonic empire. The industrial revolution did not begin until about 1815, and even then development was sluggish.

Protected by high tariffs, French businessmen were more interested in financial speculation than in creasing mass industries. Aristocratic values were amazingly resilient in France after the Revolution, when the successful bourgeois sought to adopt the life-style of the class that had been virtually wiped out as an economic force. David S. Landes has emphasized the contrast between the British and French entrepreneurial classes throughout the eighteenth century: "What distinguished the British economy . . . was an exceptional sensitivity and responsiveness to pecuniary opportunity. This was a people fascinated by wealth and commerce." The French business class was handicapped by its greater attentiveness to what was considered gracious living.

[25] All figures are from *Tableaux*, 48a.
[26] Figures on urbanization from Dupeux, 20–21, 23–26.

Landes speaks of the development within the French body social of "psychological and institutional antibodies to the virus of modernization." [27]

French industrialization was delayed, not prevented. Production increased regularly in the period from 1815 to 1848. Coal production and pig iron output went up dramatically, and a start was made in the metallurgical and chemical industries and in the building of railways. In all spheres, economic development followed the English pattern, but at a slower pace and less energetically.

Another phase of economic development began under the Second Empire, when industrial production roughly doubled between 1852 and 1870. The government of Louis Napoleon tried deliberately to create favorable conditions for capitalist development, and succeeded rather well. The banking system was adapted to the needs of an industrializing economy, providing a channel from the public and its savings to the entrepreneurs. This was also a period of adventurous experimentation by French businessmen, who introduced many innovations in the merchandising field (including the department store) and thoroughly modernized the metallurgical and textile industries. In addition, an extensive railway network was constructed. After a slow start, France seemed well on the way to catching up to and surpassing Great Britain. By 1870 France's industrial production exceeded the value of its agricultural production, and its economic growth in the preceding fifty years had been second only to that of Britain.

After the defeat by Prussia in 1870 and the establishment of the Third Republic, there was a period of relatively slow economic growth that lasted until the 1890s. In a sense this was an understandable consequence of losing the war. As J. H. Clapham has remarked, "But the war of 1870, even more the Parisian turmoil of 1871 and the long years of national gloom and self-distrust which followed, chilled the confident ardor without which no nation ever did great work—even in factory building. France was doubting the value of her government and her Republican institutions, and doubting of her own destiny, for the best part of a generation after 1870. Contrast the self-confident, not to say self-satisfied, frame of mind in the England of 1860, in the Germany of 1875, in the United States of always." [28]

There followed, from 1895 to World War I, a period of economic development comparable to that under the Second Empire. From 1870 to 1914 industrial production tripled and real wages went up by some 50 percent. The discovery and exploitation of vast iron ore deposits in Lorraine gave a new impetus to French industrialization. At the same time, a protectionist agricultural policy largely shielded the peasants from the challenge of competition. It was during this period that the contrast between the "two Frances"—one modern and dynamic and the other pre-industrial and static—became signif-

---

[27] Citations from David S. Landes, "Technological Change and Development in Western Europe, 1750–1914," in H. J. Habakkuk and M. Postan, *The Industrial Revolution and After*, IV of *The Cambridge Economic History of Europe*, 298, 463. On early industrialization in France, see J. H. Clapham, *The Economic Development of France and Germany, 1815–1914* (Cambridge 1955); Georges Dupeux, 35–48; and Gordon Wright, 196–209, 343–53.

[28] Clapham, 233.

icantly sharp. From 1924 to 1930 there was a brief period of rapid economic growth, averaging about 4 percent a year, and then the general decline of the depression. After the destruction of World War II, it took several years simply to regain the pre-war level. But beginning in 1950 there began a new era of rapid growth—about 6 percent a year, far larger than in any other period of French history. Between 1949 and 1965, for example, annual production of steel increased from 9 million tons to 20 million; of automobiles from 286,000 to 1.6 million; of agricultural tractors from 17,000 to 90,000; of housing units from 51,000 to 412,000. National revenue in this period more than doubled, and industrial production as a whole almost tripled.[29]

From this brief survey, several points stand out. (1) Rapid economic growth took place from 1815 to 1848 (Restoration and July Monarchy), from 1851 to 1870 (Second Empire), from 1895 to 1914, from 1924 to 1930 (Third Republic), and from 1950 to the present (Fourth and Fifth Republics). There were thus periods of relative stagnation and of vitality under both monarchies and republics. (2) Until recently the size of the nonindustrial and even pre-industrial sector in the French economy was large compared to that of countries like Britain, Germany, and the United States. (3) Since 1950 there has been a réal breakthrough in the attitude of businessmen and intellectuals toward modernization. The pre-industrial mentality glorified individuality and family enterprise ("mon verre est petit, mais je bois dans mon verre," etc.). This has largely given way to an affirmative view of science, technology, and industrial progress. But the political consequences of these developments are still obscure. The Fourth Republic was overthrown after eight years of impressive economic progress. The Fifth Republic has been beset periodically by grave crises, and its constitution has been under challenge by opposition parties from the day of its promulgation. Rapid modernization since 1950 has brought no discernible consensus concerning the basic values and institutions of the political system.

The French experience of modernization calls attention to the importance of the timing of crises, and the manner in which new social groups have entered upon the political scene. The brutal change of the Revolution produced a series of shock waves in public opinion that made it exceedingly difficult to establish solid political institutions. The aristocracy refused to accept the Republic, and the beneficiaries of the Revolution were restive under monarchy. Even after the establishment of a durable compromise in the form of the Third Republic, the rival forces continued to promulgate incompatible views concerning the way in which the Republic ought to be structured. In short, the French by an accident of timing had to confront the staggering problems of industrialization without the benefit of a stable political system. Industrialization took place anyway, and a series of regimes was able to help the process along.

Fitful industrialization created special problems for the leaders of the emergent social groups. In France, as elsewhere, the first great political crisis of modernization involved the relationship between the rising capitalist and

---

29 On late industrialization in France, Gordon Wright, 453–63, 548–67. Also, Charles P. Kindleberger, *Economic Growth in France and Britain* (Cambridge, Mass. 1964). Kindleberger identifies the periods of economic expansion as 1851–68, 1879–82, 1896–1913, 1919–29, and since 1949.

managerial classes on the one hand, and the landed aristocracy on the other. These relations were marked by hostility on the part of the aristocracy and lack of firm purpose on the part of the business elements. Instead of fusing, the two social groups tended to distrust one another, even though the middle class emulated the life-style of their social "betters." The same pattern was repeated in the second great political crisis of modernization—the relationship between the established business class and the increasingly articulate and politically conscious proletariat. Once again there was hostility on the one side and distrust on the other. There was established a tradition, then, of alienation rather than participation, of rejection rather than acceptance.[30]

France is now going through a period of rapid change comparable to that under the Second Empire and Third Republic. One novel aspect of this change is the spectacular rise of the intellectuals, managers, and highly skilled workers as a new kind of professional elite. Will the latest phase of modernization bring about a new spirit in politics, or will the rising social groups perpetuate the tradition of alienation, rejection, and hostility inherited from the earlier confrontations? It has long been the hope of Gaullists that politics would become more pragmatic and less ideological as modernization proceeds. But the Gaullist regime has not been able to provide for meaningful participation in the political system by the major social groups. Instead of being readily and willingly absorbed into the new industrial society, large numbers of university students and intellectuals have repudiated the regime, the educational system, and even the society itself. Modernization in France has always provoked movements of anarchistic and nihilistic protest. Like the Republic itself, modernization has enemies on both the Left and the Right. Whether a modern Republic can survive and advance in a divided society has been, and remains, the chief interest and potential tragedy of French politics.

The democratic or liberal prototype for modernization in Asia, Africa, and Latin America may prove to be France, rather than Britain or the United States. In most developing countries that aspire to parliamentary democracy today, as in France in the past, there is an absence of consensus over the basic institutions of the nation. At the same time there is a determination on the part of the political elites to modernize their nations as quickly as possible. But pre-industrial attitudes permeate the society; the business class is lacking in entrepreneurial vigor; the civil service and military are relatively well organized and are disposed to direct national purposes, and strong Communist and other revolutionary movements signal alienation of workers and intellectuals from the national community. Industrialization is now taking place under conditions of bitter social antagonism and unstable parliamentary institutions in many countries of the "third world." For purposes of comparative analysis the most relevant model among the democratic industrial societies may well be the French experience of modernization.

[30] The entry of major social groups into the political system is dealt with by Gordon Wright, 210–26, 354–65; and in especially suggestive fashion by Georges Dupeux, 104–64, 171–218, 240–78. Shepard B. Clough stresses the importance of the timing of political and social conflict in "Social Structure, Social Values and Economic Growth," E. M. Acomb and M. L. Brown, Jr., eds., *French Society and Culture Since the Old Regime* (New York 1966), 66–84.

Modern Economic Growth:
Findings and Reflections

Simon Kuznets

Simon Kuznets received the Nobel Prize in Economic Science in 1971. This essay is the lecture he delivered in Stockholm when he received this award.

Professor Kuznets is noted for his studies of national income and related concepts. In this essay he summarizes in layman's language a lifetime of distinguished research.

Whatever definition of modernization one may wish to employ, economic growth is bound to be one of its key features. Here Kuznets identifies the principal characteristics common to modern economic growth as they reflect rates of growth, the accompanying structural transformations, and the world-wide influence of the presently developed countries. He also explores the implications of economic growth in changing pre-existing patterns of settlement, relations among social strata, and political institutions; and speculates on the prospects for economic growth in the less developed countries.

I. Definitions

A country's economic growth way be defined as a long-term rise in capacity to supply increasingly diverse economic goods to its population, this growing capacity based on advancing technology and the institutional and ideological adjustments that it demands. All three components of the definition are important. The sustained rise in the supply of goods is the *result* of economic growth, by which it is identified. Some small countries can provide increasing income to their populations because they happen to possess a resource (minerals, location, etc.) exploitable by more developed nations, that yields a large and increasing rent. Despite intriguing analytical

"Modern Economic Growth: Findings and Reflections" by Simon Kuznets is reprinted with the permission of the author and the American Economic Association from *American Economic Review*, LXIII (June 1973), 247–258.

Kuznets has been professor of economics at Johns Hopkins University and at Harvard University. His many publications include *Cyclical Fluctuation* (1926), *National Income and Capital Formation* (1938), and *Modern Economic Growth* (1966).

186

problems that these few fortunate countries raise, we are interested here only in the nations that derive abundance by using advanced contemporary technology—not by selling fortuitous gifts of nature to others. Advancing technology is the *permissive* source of economic growth, but it is only a potential, a necessary condition, in itself not sufficient. If technology is to be employed efficiently and widely, and, indeed, if its own progress is to be stimulated by such use, institutional and ideological adjustments must be made to effect the proper use of innovations generated by the advancing stock of human knowledge. To cite examples from modern economic growth: steam and electric power and the large-scale plants needed to exploit them are not compatible with family enterprise, illiteracy, or slavery—all of which prevailed in earlier times over much of even the developed world, and had to be replaced by more appropriate institutions and social views. Nor is modern technology compatible with the rural mode of life, the large and extended family pattern, and veneration of undisturbed nature.

The source of technological progress, the particular production sectors that it affected most, and the pace at which it and economic growth advanced, differed over centuries and among regions of the world: and so did the institutional and ideological adjustments in their interplay with the technological changes introduced into and diffused through the growing economies. The major breakthroughs in the advance of human knowledge, those that constituted dominant sources of sustained growth over long periods and spread to a substantial part of the world, may be termed epochal innovations. And the changing course of economic history can perhaps be subdivided into economic epochs, each identified by the epochal innovation with the distinctive characteristics of growth that it generated.[1] Without considering the feasibility of identifying and dating such economic epochs, we may proceed on the working assumption that modern economic growth represents such a distinct epoch—growth dating back to the late eighteenth century and limited (except in significant *partial* effects) to economically developed countries. These countries, so classified because they have managed to take adequate advantage of the potential of modern technology, include most of Europe, the overseas offshoots of Western Europe, and Japan—barely one quarter of world population.[2] This paper will focus on modern economic growth, but with obviously needed attention to its worldwide impact.

Limitations of space prevent the presentation of a documented summary of the quantitative characteristics commonly observed in the growth of the presently developed countries, characteristics different from those of economic growth in earlier epochs. However, some of them are listed, because they contribute to our understanding of the distinctive problems of economic life in the world today. While the list is selective and is open to charges of omission, it includes those observed and empirically testable characteristics that

[1] For a discussion of the economic epoch concept, see Kuznets (1966), pp. 1–16.

[2] For a recent classification identifying the non-Communist developed countries, see United Nations *Yearbook*, notes to Table 5, p. 156. These classifications vary from time to time, and differ somewhat from those of other international agencies.

lead back to some basic factors and conditions, which can only be glimpsed and conjectured, and forward to some implications that have so far eluded measurement.

II. The Six Characteristics

Six characteristics of modern economic growth have emerged in the analysis based on conventional measures of national product and its components, population, labor force, and the like. First and most obvious are the high rates of growth of per capita product and of population in the developed countries—both large multiples of the previous rates observable in these countries and of those in the rest of the world, at least until the recent decade or two.[3] Second, the rate of rise in productivity, i.e., of output per unit of all inputs, is high, even when we include among inputs other factors in addition to labor, the major productive factor—and here too the rate is a large multiple of the rate in the past.[4] Third, the rate of structural transformation of the economy is high. Major aspects of structural change include the shift away from agriculture to nonagricultural pursuits and, recently, away from industry to services; a change in the scale of productive units, and a related shift from personal enterprise to impersonal organization of economic firms, with a corresponding change in the occupational status of labor.[5] Shifts in several other aspects of economic structure could be added (in

[3] For the non-Communist developed countries, the rates of growth per year over the period of modern economic growth, were almost 2 percent for product per capita, 1 percent for population, and 3 percent for total product. These rates—which mean roughly a multiplication over a century by five for product per capita, and three for population, and by more than fifteen for total product—were far greater than premodern rates. The latter can only be conjectured, but reasonable estimates for Western Europe over the long period from the early Middle Ages to the mid-nineteenth century suggest that the modern rate of growth is about ten times as high for product per capita (see Kuznets (1971), pp. 10–27. A similar comparison for population, either for Europe or for the area of European settlement (i.e., Europe, the Americas, and Oceania), relating to 1850–1960, as compared with 1000–1850, suggests a multiple of 4 or 5 to 1 (see Kuznets (1966), Tables 2.1 and 2.2, pp. 35 and 38). The implied acceleration in the growth rate of total product is between forty and fifty times.

[4] Using the conventional national economic accounts we find that the rate of increase in productivity is large enough to account (in the statistical sense) for almost the entire growth of product per capita. Even with adjustments to allow for hidden costs and inputs, growth in productivity accounts for over half of the growth in product per capita (see Kuznets (1971), pp. 51–75, particularly Table 9, p. 74; and Table 11, p. 93).

[5] The rapidity of structural shifts in modern times can be easily illustrated by the changes in the distribution of the labor force between agriculture (and related industries) and the nonagricultural production sectors. In the United States, the share of labor force attached to the agricultural sector was still 53.5 percent in 1870 and declined to less than 7 percent in 1960. In an old European country like Belgium, the share of agriculture in the labor force, 51 percent in 1846, dropped to 12.5 percent in 1947 and further to 7.5 percent in 1961 (see Bairoch et al., Tables D-4 and C-4). Considering that it took centuries for the share of the agricultural sector in the labor force to decline to 50 percent in any sizable country (i.e., excluding small "city enclaves"), a drop of 30 to 40 percentage points in the course of a single century is a strikingly fast structural change.

the structure of consumption, in the relative shares of domestic and foreign supplies, etc.). Fourth, the closely related and extremely important structures of society and its ideology have also changed rapidly. Urbanization and secularization come easily to mind as components of what sociologists term the process of modernization. Fifth, the economically developed countries, by means of the increased power of technology, particularly in transport and communication (both peaceful and warlike), have the propensity to reach out to the rest of the world—thus making for one world in the sense in which this was not true in any premodern epoch.[6] Sixth, the spread of modern economic growth, despite its worldwide partial effects, is limited in that the economic performance in countries accounting for three-quarters of world population still falls far short of the minimum levels feasible with the potential of modern technology.[7]

This brief summary of two quantitative characteristics of modern economic growth that relate to aggregate rates, two that relate to structural transformation, and two that relate to international spread, supports our working assumption that modern economic growth marks a distinct economic epoch. If the rates of aggregate growth and the speed of structural transformation in the economic, institutional, and perhaps even in the ideological, framework are so much higher than in the past as to represent a revolutionary acceleration, and if the various regions of the world are for the first time in history so closely interrelated as to be one, some new major growth source, some new epochal innovation, must have generated these radically different patterns. And one may argue that this source is the emergence of modern science as the basis of advancing technology—a breakthrough in the evolution of science that produced a potential for technology far greater than existed previously.

Yet modern growth continues many older trends, if in greatly accelerated form. This continuity is important particularly when we find that, except for Japan and possibly Russia, all presently developed countries were well in advance of the rest of the world before their modern growth and industrialization began, enjoying a comparative advantage produced by premodern trends. It is also important because it emphasizes that distinction among economic epochs is a complicated intellectual choice and that the continuation of past trends and their changing patterns over time are subjects deserving the closest attention. Does the acceleration in growth of product and productivity in many developed countries in the last two decades reflect a major change in the potential provided by science-oriented technology, or a major change in the capacity of societies to catch up with that potential? Is it a way of recouping the loss in standing, relative to such a leader as the

[6] The outward expansion of developed countries, with their European origin, goes back to long before modern economic growth, indeed, back to the Crusades. But the much augmented transportation and communication power of developed countries in the nineteenth century permitted a much greater and more direct political dominance over the colonies, the "opening up" of previously closed areas (such as Japan), and the "partition" of previously undivided areas (such as sub-Saharan Africa).

[7] For further discussion see Section IV below, which deals with the less developed countries.

United States, that was incurred during the depression of the 1930's and World War II? Or, finally, is it merely a reflection of the temporarily favorable climate of the U.S. international policies? Is the expansion into space a continuation of the old trend of reaching out by the developed countries, or is it a precursor of a new economic epoch? These questions are clearly illustrative, but they hint at broader analytical problems suggested by the observation of modern economic growth as a distinct epoch.

The six characteristics noted are interrelated, and the interrelations among them are most significant. With the rather stable ratio of labor force to total population, a high rate of increase in per capita product means a high rate of increase in product per worker; and, with average hours of work declining, it means still higher growth rates in product per man-hour. Even if we allow for the impressive accumulation of capital, in its widest sense, the growth rate of productivity is high, and, indeed, mirrors the great rise in per capita product and in per capita pure consumption. Since the latter reflects the realized effects of advancing technology, rapid changes in production structure are inevitable—given the differential impact of technological innovations on the several production sectors, the differing income elasticity of domestic demand for various consumer goods, and the changing comparative advantage in foreign trade. As already indicated, advancing technology changes the scale of production plants and the character of the economic enterprise units. Consequently, effective participation in the modern economic system by the labor force necessitates rapid changes in its location and structure, in the relations among occupational status groups, and even in the relations between labor force and total population (the last, however, within narrow overall limits). Thus, not only are high aggregate growth rates associated with rapid changes in economic structure, but the latter are also associated with rapid changes in other aspects of society—in family formation, in urbanization, in man's views on his role and the measure of his achievement in society. The dynamic drives of modern economic growth, in the countries that entered the process ahead of others, meant a reaching out geographically; and the sequential spread of the process, facilitated by major changes in transport and communication, meant a continuous expansion to the less developed areas. At the same time, the difficulty of making the institutional and ideological transformations needed to convert the new large potential of modern technology into economic growth in the relatively short period since the late eighteenth century limited the spread of the system. Moreover, obstacles to such transformation were, and still are being, imposed on the less developed regions by the policies of the developed countries.

If the characteristics of modern economic growth are interrelated, in that one induces another in a cause and effect sequence or all are concurrent effects of a common set of underlying factors, another plausible and significant link should be noted. Mass application of technological innovations, which constitutes much of the distinctive substance of modern economic growth, is closely connected with the further progress of science, in its turn the basis for additional advance in technology. While this topic is still to be studied in depth, it seems fairly clear that mass-uses of technical innovations (many based on recent scientific discoveries) provide a positive feedback. Not only do they provide a large economic surplus for basic and applied research with long time leads and heavy capital demands, but, more specifically, they permit the development of new efficient tools for scientific use and supply new data on the behavior of natural processes under the stress of modification in economic production. In other words, many production plants in developed countries can be viewed as laboratories for the exploration of natural processes and as centers of research on new tools, both of which are of immense service to basic and applied research in science and technology. It is no accident that the last two centuries were also periods of enormous acceleration in the contribution to the stock of useful knowledge by basic and applied research —which provided additional stimuli to new technological innovations. Thus, modern economic growth reflects an interrelation that sustains the high rate of advance through the feedback from mass applications to further knowledge. And unless some obstacles intervene, it provides a mechanism for self-sustaining technological advance, to which, given the wide expanse of the universe (relative to mankind on this planet), there are no obvious proximate limits.

III. Some Implications[8]

I turn now to a brief discussion of some social implications, of some effects of modern economic growth on conditions of life of various population groups in the countries affected. Many of these effects are of particular interest, because they are not reflected in the current measures of economic growth; and the increasing realization of this shortcoming of the measures has stimulated lively discussion of the limits and limitations of economic measurement of economic growth.

The effects on conditions of life stem partly from the major role of technological innovations in modern economic growth, and partly from the rapid shifts in the underlying production structure. To begin with the latter, the major effects of which, for example, urbanization, internal migration, shift to employee status and what might be called the merit basis of job choice, have already been noted as characteristics of modern economic growth. Two important groups of effects of this rapid transformation of economic structure deserve explicit reference.

First, the changes in conditions of life suggested by "urbanization" clearly involved a variety of costs and returns that are not now included in economic measurement, and some of which may never be susceptible to measurement.

[8] Many of the points touched upon in this section are discussed in greater detail in Kuznets (1971), particularly in ch. 2, pp. 75–98, which deals with the nonconventional costs of economic growth, and ch. 7, pp. 314–54, which deals with various interrelations between aggregate change and structural shifts in economic and other aspects of social structure.

Internal migration, from the countryside to the cities (within a country, and often international) represented substantial costs in the pulling up of roots and the adjustment to the anonymity and higher costs of urban living. The learning of new skills and the declining value of previously acquired skills was clearly a costly process—to both the individuals and to society. But if such costs were omitted from measurement, as they still are in conventional accounts, so were some returns. Urban life, with its denser population, provided amenities and spiritual goods that were not available in the "dull and brutish" life of the countryside; and the new skills, once learned, were often a more adequate basis for a richer life than the old. This comment on the hidden costs and returns involved in the shift toward urban life may apply to many other costs and returns involved in other shifts imposed by economic growth, for example, in the character of participation in economic activity, in the social values, and in the new pressures on deviant members of society.

The second intriguing aspect of structural change is that it represents shifts in the relative shares in the economy of the specific population groups attached to particular production sectors. Since economic engagement represents a dominant influence in the life of people, the shift in the share of a specific sector, with its distinctive characteristics and even mode of life, affects the population group engaged in it. Economic growth perforce brings about a decline in the relative position of one group after another—of farmers, of small scale producers, of landowners—a change not easily accepted, and, in fact, as history teaches us, often resisted. The continuous disturbance of preexisting *relative* position of the several economic groups is pregnant with conflict—despite the rises in absolute income or product common to all groups. In some cases, these conflicts did break out into overt civil war, the Civil War in the United States being a conspicuous example. Other examples, in the early periods of industrialization among the currently developed countries, or, for that matter, more recently within some less developed countries, are not lacking.

Only if such conflicts are resolved without excessive costs, and certainly without a long-term weakening of the political fabric of the society, is modern economic growth possible. The sovereign state, with authority based on loyalty and on a community of feeling—in short, the modern national state —plays a crucial role in peacefully resolving such growth induced conflicts. But this and other services of the national state may be costly in various ways, of which intensified nationalism is one and other effects are too familiar to mention. The records of many developed countries reveal examples of resolutions of growth conflicts, of payments for overcoming resistance and obstacles to growth, that left burdensome heritages for the following generations (notably in Germany and Japan). Of course, this is not the only economic function of the state; it can also stimulate growth and structural change. And, to mention a closely related service, it can referee, select, or discard legal and institutional innovations that are proposed in the attempt to organize and channel effectively the new production potentialities. This, too, is a matter that may generate conflicts, since different legal and institutional arrangements may have different effects on the several economic groups in society.

In that modern economic growth has to contend with the resolution of incipient conflicts continuously generated by rapid changes in economic and social structure, it may be described as a process of controlled revolution. The succession of technological innovations characteristic of modern economic growth and the social innovations that provide the needed adjustments are major factors affecting economic and social structure. But these innovations have other effects that deserve explicit mention; and while they are discussed below in terms of effects of technological innovations, the conclusions apply *pari passu* to innovations in legal forms, in institutional structure, and even in ideology.

A technological innovation, particularly one based on a recent major invention, represents a venture into the partly unknown, something not fully known until the mass spread of the innovation reveals the full range of direct and related effects. An invention is a major one if it provides the basis for extensive applications and improvements (for example, the stationary steam engine in the form attributable mostly to James Watt). Its cumulative effects, all new, extend over a long period and result in an enormous transformation of economic production and of production relations. But these new effects can hardly be fully anticipated or properly evaluated in advance (and sometimes not even post facto). This is true also of electric power, the internal combustion engine, atomic energy, the application of short rays to communication and computation, the inventions resulting in such new industrial materials as steel, aluminum, and plastics, and so on through a long list that marked modern economic growth. Even when the technological innovation is an adaptation of a known technique by a follower country, the results may not be fully foreseeable, for they represent the combination of something known, the technology, with something new, an institutional and ideological framework with which it has not previously been combined. Needless to say, the element of the uniquely new, of exploration into the unknown, was also prominent in premodern times, since innovations in knowledge and technology are the prerequisites for any significant growth. But the *rate* of succession of such innovations was clearly more rapid in modern economic growth, and provided the base for a higher rate of aggregate growth.

The effects of such ventures into the new and partly unknown are numerous. Those of most interest here are the *surprises*, the unexpected results, which may be positive or negative. An invention or innovation may prove far more productive, and induce a far wider mass application and many more cumulative improvements than were dreamed of by the inventor and the pioneer group of entrepreneurs. Or the mass application of a major invention may produce unexpected diseconomies of a scale that could hardly be foreseen in the early phases of its diffusion. Examples of both positive and negative surprises abound. Many Schumpeterian entrepreneurs failed to grasp, by a wide margin, the full scope and significance of the innovations that they were promoting and that eventually brought them fame and fortune. And most of us can point at the unexpected negative effects of some technological or social invention that first appeared to be an unlimited blessing.

The significant aspect here is that the surprises cannot be viewed as accidents: they are inherent in the process of technological (and social) innovation in that it contains an element of the unknown. Furthermore, the diffusion of a major innovation is a long and complicated sequence that cannot be accurately forecast, with an initial economic effect that may generate responses in other processes. These will, in turn, change the conditions under which the innovation exercises its effect on human welfare, and raise further problems of adjustment. To illustrate: we can today follow easily the sequence from the introduction of the passenger car as a mass means of transportation, to the growth of the suburbs, to the movement of the more affluent from the city centers, to the concentration of lower income recipients and unemployed immigrants in the slums of the inner city core, to the acute urban problems, financial and other, and to the trend toward metropolitan consolidation. But the nature and implications of this sequence were certainly not apparent in the 1920's, when passenger cars began their mass service function in the United States.

Indeed, to push this speculative line further, one can argue that all economic growth brings *some* unexpected results in its wake, positive as well as negative, with the latter taking on greater importance as the mass effects of major innovations are felt and the needs that they are meant to satisfy are met. If the argument is valid, modern economic growth, with the rapid succession of innovations and shortening period of their mass diffusion, must be accompanied by a relatively high incidence of negative effects. Yet one must not forget that premodern economic growth had similar problems, which, with the weaker technology, may have loomed even larger. Even if we disregard the threatening exhaustion of natural resources, a problem that so concerned Classical (and implicitly even Marxian) economics, and consider only early urbanization, one major negative effect was the significant rise in death rates as population moved from the more salubrious countryside to the infection-prone denser conditions of unsanitary cities. Two points are relevant here. First, the negative effects of growth have never been viewed as so far outweighing its positive contribution as to lead to its renunciation— no matter how crude the underlying calculus may have been. Second, one may assume that once an unexpected negative result of growth emerges, the potential of material and social technology is aimed at its reduction or removal. In many cases these negative results were allowed to accumulate and to become serious technological or social problems because it was so difficult to foresee them early enough in the process to take effective preventive or ameliorative action. Even when such action was initiated, there may have been delay in the effective technological or policy solution. Still, one may justifiably argue, in the light of the history of economic growth, in which a succession of such unexpected negative results has been overcome, that any specific problem so generated will be temporary—although we shall never be free of them, no matter what economic development is attained.

IV. The Less Developed Countries

Two major groups of factors appear to have limited the spread of modern economic growth. First, as already suggested, such growth demands a stable, but flexible, political and social framework, capable of accommodating rapid structural change and resolving the conflicts that it generates, while encouraging the growth-promoting groups in society. Such a framework is not easily or rapidly attained, as evidenced by the long struggles toward it even in some of the presently developed countries in the nineteenth and early twentieth centuries. Japan is the only nation outside of those rooted in European civilization that has joined the group of developed countries so far. Emergence of a modern framework for economic growth may be especially difficult if it involves elements peculiar to European civilization for which substitutes are not easily found. Second, the increasingly national cast of organization in developed countries made for policies toward other parts of the world that, while introducing some modern economic and social elements, were, in many areas, clearly inhibiting. These policies ranged from the imposition of colonial status to other limitations on political freedom, and, as a result, political independence and removal of the inferior status of the native members of the community, rather than economic advance, were given top priority.

Whatever the weight of the several factors in explaining the failure of the less developed countries to take advantage of the potential of modern economic growth, a topic that, in its range from imperialist exploitation to backwardness of the native economic and social framework, lends itself to passionate and biased polemic, the factual findings are clear. At present, about two-thirds or more of world population is in the economically less developed group. Even more significant is the concentration of the population at the low end of the product per capita range. In 1965, the last year for which we have worldwide comparable product estimates, the per capita GDP (at market prices) of 1.72 billion out of a world total of 3.27 billion, was less than $120, whereas 0.86 billion in economically developed countries had a per capita product of some $1900. Even with this narrow definition of less developed countries, the intermediate group was less than 0.7 billion, or less than 20 percent of world population.[9] The preponderant population was

[9] The underlying data are from Everett Hagen and Oli Hawrylyshyn. These are primarily from United Nations publications, supplemented by some auxiliary sources (mostly for the Communist countries), and use conventional conversion rates to U.S. dollars in 1965. The estimates for the Communist countries have been adjusted to conform to the international GDP concept. The developed countries include most countries with per capita GDP of $1000 or more and Japan, but exclude those small countries with a high GDP per capita that is due to exceptional natural endowments (for example, Netherlands Antilles, Puerto Rico, Kuwait, and Qatar).

thus divided between the very low and the rather high level of per capita economic performance. Obviously, this aspect of modern economic growth deserves our greatest attention, and the fact that the quantitative data and our knowledge of the institutional structures of the less developed countries are, at the moment, far more limited than our knowledge of the developed areas, is not reason enough for us to ignore it.

Several preliminary findings, or rather plausible impressions, may be noted. First, the group of less developed countries, particularly if we widen it (as we should) to include those with a per capita product somewhat larger than $120 (in 1965 prices), covers an extremely wide range in size, in the relations between population and natural resources, in major inherited institutions, and in the past impact upon them of the developed countries (coming as it did at different times and from different sources). There is a striking contrast, for example, in terms of population size, between the giants like Mainland China and India, on the one hand, and the scores of tiny states in Africa and Latin America; as there is between the timing of direct Western impact on Africa and of that on many countries in Latin America. Furthermore, the remarkable institutions by which the Sinic and East Indian civilizations produced the unified, huge societies that dwarfed in size any that originated in Europe until recently, bore little resemblance to those that structured the American Indian societies or those that fashioned the numerous tribal societies of Africa.

Generalizations about less developed countries must be carefully and critically scrutinized in the light of this wide variety of conditions and institutions. To be sure, their common failure to exploit the potential of modern economic growth means several specific common features: a low per capita product, a large share of agriculture or other extractive industries, a generally small scale of production. But the specific parameters differ widely, and because the obstacles to growth may differ critically in their substance, they may suggest different policy directions.

Second, the growth position of the less developed countries today is significantly different, in many respects, from that of the presently developed countries on the eve of their entry into modern economic growth (with the possible exception of Japan, and one cannot be sure even of that). The less developed areas that account for the largest part of the world population today are at much lower per capita product levels than were the developed countries just before their industrialization; and the latter at that time were economically in advance of the rest of the world, not at the low end of the per capita product range. The very magnitudes, as well as some of the basic conditions, are quite different: no country that entered modern economic growth (except Russia) approached the size of India or China, or even of Pakistan and Indonesia; and no currently developed country had to adjust to the very high rates of natural increase of population that have characterized many less developed countries over the last two or three decades. Particularly before World War I, the older European countries, and to some extent even Japan, relieved some strains of industrialization by substantial emigration of the displaced population to areas with more favorable opportunities— an avenue closed to the populous less developed countries today. Of course, the stock of material and social technology that can be tapped by less developed countries today is enormously larger than that available in the nineteenth and even early twentieth centuries. But it is precisely this combination of greater backwardness and seemingly greater backlog of technology that makes for the significant differences between the growth position of the less developed countries today and that of the developed countries when they were entering the modern economic growth process.

Finally, it may well be that, despite the tremendous accumulation of material and social technology, the stock of innovations most suitable to the needs of the less developed countries is not too abundant. Even if one were to argue that progress in basic science may not be closely tied to the technological needs of the country of origin (and even that may be disputed), unquestionably the applied advances, the inventions and tools, are a response to the specific needs of the country within which they originate. This was certainly true of several major inventions associated with the Industrial Revolution in England, and illustrations abound of necessity as the mother of invention. To the extent that this is true, and that the conditions of production in the developed countries differed greatly from those in the populous less developed countries today, the material technology evolved in the developed countries may not supply the needed innovations. Nor is the social technology that evolved in the developed countries likely to provide models of institutions or arrangements suitable to the diverse institutional and population-size backgrounds of many less developed countries. Thus, modern technology with its emphasis on laborsaving inventions may not be suited to countries with a plethora of labor but a scarcity of other factors, such as land and water; and modern institutions, with their emphasis on personal responsibility and pursuit of economic interest, may not be suited to the more traditional life patterns of the agricultural communities that predominate in many less developed countries. These comments should not be interpreted as denying the value of many transferable parts of modern technology; they are merely intended to stress the possible shortage of material and social tools specifically fitted to the different needs of the less developed countries.

If the observations just made are valid, several implications for the growth problems of the less developed countries follow. I hesitate to formulate them explicitly, since the data and the stock of knowledge on which the observations rest are limited. But at least one implication is sufficiently intriguing, and seems to be illuminating of many recent events in the field, to warrant a brief note. It is that a substantial economic advance in the less developed countries may require modifications in the available stock of material technology, and probably even greater innovations in political and social structure. It will not be a matter of merely borrowing existing tools, material and social; or of directly applying past patterns of growth, merely allowing for the difference in parameters.

The innovational requirements are likely to be particularly great in the social and political structures. The rather violent changes in these structures that occurred in those countries that have forged ahead with highly forced industrialization under Communist auspices, the pioneer entry going back over forty years (beginning with the first Five-Year Plan in the USSR), are conspicuous illustrations of the kind of social invention and innovation that may be involved. And the variants even of Communist organization, let alone those of democracy and of non-Communist authoritarianism, are familiar. It would be an oversimplification to argue that these innovations in the social and political structures were made primarily in response to the strain between economic backwardness and the potential of modern economic growth; or to claim that they were inexorable effects of antecedent history. But to whatever the struggle for political and social organization is a response, once it has been resolved, the results shape significantly the conditions under which economic growth can occur. It seems highly probable that a long period of experimentation and struggle toward a viable political framework compatible with adequate economic growth lies ahead for most less developed countries of today; and this process will become more intensive and acute as the *perceived* gap widens between what has been attained and what is attainable with modern economic growth. While an economist can argue that some aspects of growth must be present because they are indispensable components (i.e., industrialization, large scale of production, etc.), even their parameters are bound to be variable; and many specific characteristics will be so dependent upon the outcome of the social and political innovations that extrapolation from the past is extremely hazardous.

V. Concluding Comments

The aim of the discussion was to sketch the major characteristics of modern economic growth, and to note some of the implications that the empirical study of economic growth of nations suggests. This study goes back to the beginning of our discipline, as indicated by the title of Adam Smith's founding treatise, Wealth of Nations, which could as well have been called the Economic Growth of Nations. But the quantitative base and interest in economic growth have widened greatly in the last three to four decades, and the accumulated results of past study of economic history and of past economic analysis could be combined with the richer stock of quantitative data to advance the empirical study of the process. The sketch above draws upon the results of many and widely varied studies in many countries, most of them economically developed; and the discussion reflects a wide collective effort, however individual some of my interpretations may be.

The most distinctive feature of modern economic growth is the combination of a high rate of aggregate growth with disrupting effects and new "problems." The high rate of growth is sustained by the interplay between mass applications of technological innovations based on additions to the stock of knowledge and further additions to that stock. The disrupting effects are those imposed by the rapid rate of change in economic and social structure. The problems are the unexpected and unforseeable results of the spread of innovations (with emphasis on the new and unknown indicated by that term). Added to this is the range of problems raised by the slow spread of economic growth to the less developed countries, all of which have a long history, separate and relatively isolated from the areas within which modern economic growth originated. Thus, concurrent with the remarkable positive achievements of modern economic growth are unexpected negative results even within the developed countries; while the less developed countries are struggling in the attempt to use the large potential of modern technology in order to assume an adequate role in the one and interdependent world (from which they cannot withdraw even if they wished to do so).

We have stressed the problem aspects of modern economic growth because they indicate the directions of further research in the field. These aspects, the "surprises" and the implicit explanatory "puzzles," are problems not only in the sense of departures from the desirable (that may call for policy amelioration) but also in the sense that our quantitative data and particularly our analytical hypotheses do not provide us with a full view and explanation. As already noted, the conventional measures of national product and its components do not reflect many costs of adjustment in the economic and social structures to the channeling of major technological innovations; and indeed, also omit some positive returns. The earlier theory that underlies these measures defined the productive factors in a relatively narrow way, and left the rise in productivity as an unexplained gap, as a measure of our ignorance. This shortcoming of the theory in confrontation with the new findings, has led to a lively discussion in the field in recent years, and to attempts to expand the national accounting framework to encompass the so far hidden but clearly important costs, for example, in education as capital investment, in the shift to urban life, or in the pollution and other negative results of mass production. These efforts will also uncover some so far un-measured positive returns—in the way of greater health and longevity, greater mobility, more leisure, less income inequality, and the like. The related efforts to include the additions to knowledge in the framework of economic analysis, the greater attention to the uses of time and to the household as the focus of economic decision not only on consumption but also on invest-ment, are steps in the same direction. It seems fairly clear that a number of analytical and measurement problems remain in the theory and in the evaluation of economic growth in the developed countries themselves; and that one may look forward to major changes in some aspects of the analysis, in national economic accounting, and in the stock of empirical findings, which will occupy economists in the developed countries in the years ahead.

For the less developed countries the tasks of economic research are some-what different: the great need is for a wider supply of tested data, which means essentially data that have been scrutinized in the process of use for economic analysis. As already noted, the stock of data and of economic analysis is far poorer for these countries than that for the developed countries —a parallel to the smaller relative supply of material capital. Yet in recent years there has been rapid accumulation of data for many less developed areas, other than those that, like Mainland China, view data as information useful to their enemies (external or internal) and are therefore either not revealed by government or possibly not even collected. The lag has been in the analysis of these data by economists and other social science scholars, because of the scarcity of such scholars who cannot be spared for research within the less developed countries themselves and because of the natural preoccupation of economists in the developed countries with the problems of their own countries. One may hope, but with limited expectations, that the task of refining analysis and measurement in the developed countries will not be pursued to the exclusion or neglect of badly needed studies of the less developed countries, studies that would deal with the quantitative bases and institutional conditions of their performance, in addition to those concentrating on what appear to be their major bottlenecks and the seemingly optimal policy prescriptions.

References

P. BAIROCH et al., *The Working Population and Its Structure, International Historical Statistics*, vol. I, Brussels 1968.

E. E. HAGEN and O. HAWRYLYSHYN, "Analysis of World Income and Growth, 1955–1965," *Econ. Develop. Cult. Change*, Oct. 1969, 18, Part II, 1–96.

S. KUZNETS, *Economic Growth of Nations: Total Output and Production Structure*, Cambridge, Mass. 1971.

———, *Modern Economic Growth: Rate, Structure, and Spread*, New Haven 1966.

United Nations, *Yearbook of National Accounts Statistics, 1969*, vol. II, *International Tables*, New York 1970.

The History of the Human Population

Ansley J. Coale

*There are few more significant concomitants of societal transformation
than the demographic transition—from relatively low population growth due
to high death as well as birth rates, through a period of fast growth
because of reduced mortality without a compensating decline in births, to
the low rates of both birth and death in the developed countries. The
interconnected causes of this transition are not fully understood, but its
consequences are clear enough. The enormous growth of population
in the many countries that are still in the process of transformation threatens
to outrun the capacity of the earth to provide food.*

In designating 1974 World Population Year the United Nations has given
expression to worldwide interest in the rapid rate of population increase and
to apprehension about the consequences of continued rapid growth. Much
less attention is given to the growth of the population in the past, to the
process by which a few thousand wanderers a million years ago became
billions of residents of cities, towns and villages today. An understanding
of this process is essential if one would evaluate the present circumstances
and future prospects of the human population.

Any numerical description of the development of the human population
cannot avoid conjecture, simply because there has never been a census of
all the people in the world. Even today there are national populations that
have not been enumerated, and where censuses have been taken they are
not always reliable. Recent censuses of the U.S., for example, have under-
counted the population by between 2 and 3 percent; some other censuses,
such as the one taken in Nigeria in 1963, are evidently gross overcounts.
Moreover, in many instances the extent of the error cannot be estimated
with any precision.

If the size of the population today is imperfectly known, that of the past

"The History of the Human Population" by Ansley J. Coale is reprinted by permission of
the publisher from *Scientific American*, CCXXXI (September 1974), 40–51.

Coale is professor of economics and director of the Office of Population Research at
Princeton University. He is the co-author of *Population Growth and Economic Development
in Low Income Countries* (1958), *New Estimates of Population and Births in the United
States* (1963), and *Regional Model Life Tables and Stable Populations* (1966).

is even more uncertain. The first series of censuses taken at regular intervals of no more than 10 years was begun by Sweden in 1750; the U.S. has made decennial enumerations since 1790, as have France and England since 1800. The census became common in the more developed countries only in the 19th century, and it has spread slowly to other parts of the world. India's population has been enumerated at decennial intervals since 1871, and a number of Latin American populations have been counted, mostly at irregular intervals, since late in the 19th century. The first comprehensive census of Russia was conducted in 1897, and only four more have been made since then. The population of most of tropical Africa remained uncounted until after World War II. A conspicuous source of uncertainty in the population of the world today is the poorly known size of the population of China, where the most recent enumeration was made in 1953 and was of untested accuracy.

As one considers earlier periods the margin of error increases. The earliest date for which the global population can be calculated with an uncertainty of only, say, 20 percent is the middle of the 18th century. The next-earliest time for which useful data are available is the beginning of the Christian era, when Rome collected information bearing on the number of people in various parts of the empire. At about the same time imperial records provide some data on the population of China, and historians have made a tenuous estimate of the population of India in that period. By employing this information and by making a crude allowance for the number of people in other regions one can estimate the population of the world at the time of Augustus within a factor of two.

For still earlier periods the population must be estimated indirectly from calculations of the number of people who could subsist under the social and technological institutions presumed to prevail at the time. Anthropologists and historians have estimated, for example, that before the introduction of agriculture the world could have supported a hunting-and-gathering culture of between five and 10 million people.

From guesses such as these for the earlier periods and from somewhat more reliable data for more recent times a general outline of the growth of the human population can be constructed. Perhaps the most uncertain figure of all in these calculations is the size of the initial population, when man first appeared about a million years ago. As the human species gradually became distinct from its hominid predecessors there was presumably an original gene pool of some thousands or hundreds of thousands of individuals. The next date at which the population can be estimated is at the initiation of agriculture and the domestication of animals, which is generally believed to have begun about 8000 B.C. The median of several estimates of the ultimate size of the hunting-and-gathering cultures that preceded the introduction of agriculture is eight million. Thus whatever the size of the initial human population, the rate of growth during man's first 990,000 years (about 99 percent of his history) was exceedingly small. Even if one assumed that in the beginning the population was two—Adam and Eve—the annual rate of increase during this first long interval was only about 15 additional persons per million of population.

After the establishment of agriculture the growth of the population accelerated somewhat. The eight million of 8000 B.C. became by A.D. 1 about 300 million (the midpoint of a range of informed guesses of from 200 million to 400 million). This increase represents an annual growth rate of 360 per million, or, as it is usually expressed, .36 per 1,000.

From A.D. 1 to 1750 the population increased by about 500 million to some 800 million (the median of a range estimated by John D. Durand of the University of Pennsylvania). It was at this time that the extraordinary modern acceleration of population growth began. The average annual growth rate from A.D. 1 to 1750 was .56 per 1,000; from 1750 to 1800 it was 4.4 per 1,000, bringing the population at the end of this 50-year interval to about a billion. By 1850 there were 1.3 billion people in the world, and by 1900 there were 1.7 billion, yielding growth rates in the respective 50-year intervals of 5.2 and 5.4 per 1,000. (These totals too are based on estimates made by Durand.)

By 1950, according to the UN, the world population was 2.5 billion, indicating an annual growth rate during the first half of the 20th century of 7.9 per 1,000. From 1950 to 1974 the growth rate more than doubled, to 17.1 per 1,000, producing the present world population of 3.9 billion. The median value of several projections made by the UN in 1973 indicates that by 2000 the population will be 6.4 billion, an increase that implies an annual growth rate during the next 25 years of 19 per 1,000.

It is evident even from this brief description that the history of the population can be readily divided into two periods: a very long era of slow growth and a very brief period of rapid growth. An understanding of the development of the population during these two phases can be derived from a few simple mathematical relations involving the absolute size of the population, the growth rate and the factors that determine the growth rate.

Persistent growth at any proportionate rate produces ever increasing increments of growth, and the total, even at a relatively modest rate of increase, surpasses any designated finite limit in a surprisingly short time. An increasing population doubles in size during an interval equal to 693 divided by the annual rate of increase, expressed in additional persons per 1,000 population. Thus in the period from A.D. 1 to 1750, when the growth rate was .56 per 1,000, the population doubled about every 1,200 years; in the next few decades, when a growth rate of about 20 per 1,000 is anticipated, the population will double in 34.7 years.

The cumulative effect of a small number of doublings is a surprise to common sense. One well-known illustration of this phenomenon is the legend of the king who offered his daughter in marriage to anyone who could supply a grain of wheat for the first square of a chessboard, two grains for the second square and so on. To comply with this request for all 64 squares would require a mountain of grain many times larger than today's worldwide wheat production.

In accordance with the same law of geometric progression, the human population has reached its present size through comparatively few doublings. Even if we again assume that humanity began with a hypothetical Adam and Eve, the population has doubled only 31 times, or an average of about once every 30,000 years. This is another way of saying that the peopling of the world has been accomplished with a very low rate of increase, when that rate is averaged over the entire history of the species. The average annual rate is about .02 additional persons per 1,000. Even when only the more rapid growth of the past 2,000 years is considered, the average rate is modest. Since A.D. 1 the population has doubled no more than four times, or about once every 500 years, which implies an annual rate of 1.4 persons per 1,000.

In the context of these long-term averages the rate of growth today seems all the more extraordinary, yet the source of this exceptional proliferation is in the conventional mathematics of geometric series. The population of the world increases to the extent that births exceed deaths; the growth rate is the difference between the birth rate and the death rate. Another way of stating the relation is that the average rate of increase, over a long period, is dependent on the ratio of the sizes of successive generations. This ratio is approximately equal to the average number of daughters born to women who pass through the span of fertile years multiplied by the proportion of women surviving to the mean age of childbearing. This product specifies the average number of daughters born during the lifetime of a newborn female, after making allowance for those women whose biological fertility is abnormal and for those who die before reaching the age of childbearing. When the product is 1—signifying one daughter per woman, under the prevailing conditions of fertility and mortality—successive generations are the same average size. When the product is 2, the population doubles with each generation, or about every 28 years.

The fertility of a population can also be measured by the number of offspring, both sons and daughters, born per woman during a lifetime of childbearing; this number is called the total fertility rate. Mortality is summarized by the average age at death, or the average duration of life, which is expressed as the expectation of life at birth. In 1973 the total fertility rate of American women was 1.94; the expectation of life at birth was 75 years. Thus women experiencing 1973 birth rates at each age would bear an average of 1.94 children, and women experiencing 1973 death rates at each age would have an average duration of life of 75 years.

When the average life span is short, the proportion of women surviving to the mean age of reproduction is small. In fact, among populations for which there are adequate data there is a close relation between these two numbers, and we can with some confidence estimate the proportion of women surviving to become mothers from the average duration of life. Another predictable characteristic of the human population is the ratio of male births to female births; for any large sample it is always about 1.05 to 1.

Because of these constant relations in the population it is possible to calculate all the combinations of female life expectancy and total fertility that will yield any specified growth rate. Of particular interest are the conditions producing zero population growth, since during most of the past million years the population has approached zero growth. In a static population the average duration of life is the reciprocal of the birth rate. Expressed another way, in a population of constant size the birth rate is the number of births per person-year lived and the average duration of life is the number of person-years lived per birth.

There are many combinations of fertility and mortality that will just maintain a population at fixed size. Consider a static population in which the average duration of female life is 70 years. Given this mortality rate, the proportion of women surviving to the mean age of childbearing is 93.8 percent. Because the size of the population is to remain constant the average number of daughters born per woman must be 1/.938, or 1.066; since there are 1.05 male births for each female birth, the total fertility rate must be 2.05 × 1.066, or 2.19. The birth rate in such a population is 1/70, or 14.3 per 1,000 population.

If the average duration of female life is 20 years, as it probably was at times during the premodern period, then 31.6 percent of the women survive to the mean age of childbearing and those who live to the age of menopause have an average of 6.5 children; the birth rate under these circumstances is 50 per 1,000. (It should be pointed out that there is no inconsistency in the survival of many women to menopause in a population in which the average age at death is 20 years. When the death rate is high, the average age at death is not at all a typical age at death. When the life expectancy in a static population is 20 years, for example, about half the deaths occur before age five, about a fourth occur after age 50, and only about 6.5 percent occur in the 10-year span centered on the mean age at death.)

The importance of these relations is that they express the possible combinations of fertility and mortality that must have characterized the human population during each era of its history. If some other combination of fertility and mortality had been maintained for more than a few generations (as has happened during the past two centuries), the population would have expanded or contracted dramatically.

These combinations also determine the most extreme fertility and mortality rates possible in a static population. One limit is set by the minimum feasible mortality. When the average life expectancy is 75 years, 97.3 percent of all women survive to the mean age of reproduction, and it is necessary for them to have only 2.1 children to maintain the population; this represents a birth rate of 13.3 per 1,000. Any further reduction in mortality might raise the average duration of life to 80 years or more, but it would not significantly change the proportion of women surviving to childbearing age, nor would it much reduce the number of births per woman required to maintain the population. The other limit is imposed by fertility. When the life expectancy falls to 15 years, only 23.9 percent of all women live to have children, and those who do must have an average of 8.6 in order to prevent a decline in population. Although it is certainly biologically possible for a woman to bear more than eight or nine children, no sizable populations have been observed with total fertility much higher than eight births per woman.

Accurate records of human fertility and mortality are even more meager than records of numbers of people. Today fewer than half of the world population live in areas where vital statistics are reliably recorded; in most of Asia, almost all of Africa and much of Latin America, for example, the registration of births and deaths is inadequate. Precise information about fertility and mortality is therefore limited to the recent experience of the more developed countries, beginning in the 18th century in Scandinavia, the 19th century in most of the rest of Europe and the 20th century in Japan and the U.S. Much has been inferred about the present vital rates of underdeveloped countries from the age composition recorded in censuses, from the rate of population increase between censuses and from retrospective information collected in censuses and demographic surveys. For past populations, however, valid data on births and deaths are very rarely available, and they must therefore be derived by analyzing the forces that affect fertility and mortality.

Differences in fertility can be attributed to two factors; the differential exposure of women of childbearing age to the risk of childbirth through cohabitation with a sexual partner, and differences in the rate at which conceptions and live births occur among women who are cohabiting. In many populations the only socially sanctioned cohabitation is that between married couples, and thus the laws and customs governing the formation and dissolution of marriages influence fertility. A conspicuous example is the pattern of late marriage common until a generation ago in many Western European nations. For many years before World War II in Germany, Scandinavia, the Low Countries and Britain the average age of first marriage for women was between 24 and 28, and from 1 to 30 percent remained unmarried at age 50. As a result the proportion of women of reproductive age who by being married were exposed to the risk of childbearing was less than half, and in some cases, such as Ireland, was as low as a third.

A much different nuptial custom that may also reduce fertility is common in areas of Asia and North Africa. Women are married at age 17 or 18, but the average age of the married male population is often eight or nine years greater than that of the married women. The fertility of some of the women is probably reduced by marriage to much older men, often widowers. Marriages are made by arrangement with the bride's parents, in many cases requiring the payment of a bride price, and older men are more likely to have the property or the prestige needed to claim the more desirable young women. Still another social influence on fertility is found in India, where Hinduism forbids the remarriage of widows. Although the prohibition has not always been scrupulously observed, it has doubtless reduced Indian fertility below what it might otherwise have been.

Among cohabiting couples fertility is obviously influenced by whether or not measures are employed to avoid having children. Louis Henry of the

Institut National d'Études Démographiques has defined "natural fertility" as the fertility of couples who do not modify their behavior according to the number of children already born. Natural fertility thus defined is far from uniform: it is affected by custom, health and nutrition. Breast-feeding, for example, prolongs the period of postpartum amenorrhea and thereby postpones the resumption of ovulation following childbirth. In some populations low fertility can be attributed to pathological sterility associated with widespread gonorrheal infection. Finally, fertility may be influenced by diet, as has been suggested by the work of Rose E. Frisch and her colleagues at Harvard University. Age at menarche appears to be determined at least in part by the fat content of the body and is hence related to diet. Furthermore, among women past the age of menarche a sufficient reduction in weight relative to height causes amenorrhea. In populations with meager diets fertility may therefore be depressed. Because of the severe caloric drain of pregnancy and breast-feeding, it is probable that nursing prolongs amenorrhea more effectively in populations where the average body fat is near the threshold needed for a regular reproductive cycle.

The most conspicuous source of differences in fertility among cohabiting couples today is the deliberate control of fertility by contraception and induced abortion. In some modern societies very low fertility rates have been obtained: the total fertility rate has fallen as low as 1.5 (in Czechoslovakia in 1930, in Austria in 1937 and in West Germany in 1973).

The prevalence of birth-control practices is known from the direct evidence of fertility surveys for only a few populations, and for those only during the past two or three decades. (The International Statistical Institute has begun a World Fertility Survey that should illuminate present practices but not those of the past.) Indications that fertility was deliberately controlled in past societies must be inferred from such clues as the cessation of childbearing earlier among women who married early than among those who married late. Evidence of this kind, together with the observation of a large reduction in the fertility of all married women, indicates that birth control was common in the 17th century among such groups as the bourgeoisie of Geneva and the peers of France. Norman Himes, in his *Medical History of Contraception*, has shown that prescriptions for the avoidance of birth, ranging from magical and wholly ineffective procedures to quite practical techniques, have been known in many societies at least since classical Greek times. A doctoral dissertation at Harvard University by Basim Musallam has demonstrated that *coitus interruptus*, a contraceptive method that compares in effectiveness with the condom and the diaphragm, was common enough in the medieval Islamic world to be the subject of explicit provisions in seven prominent schools of law. On the other hand, analysis of parish registers in western Europe from the 17th and 18th centuries and observations in less developed countries today suggest that effective birth-control practices are not common in most rural, premodern societies.

Large fluctuations in fertility, and in mortality as well, are not inconsistent with the long period of near-zero growth that characterizes most of the history of the population. Although the arithmetic of growth leaves no room for a rate of increase very different from zero in the long run, short-term variations were probably frequent and of considerable extent. In actuality the population that from our perspective appears to have been almost static for hundreds of thousands of years may well have experienced brief periods of rapid growth, during which it expanded severalfold, and then suffered catastrophic set-backs. The preagricultural population, for example, must have been vulnerable to changes in climate, such as periods of glaciation, and to the disappearance of species of prey. Once the cultivation of crops had become established the population could have been periodically decimated by epidemics and by the destruction of crops through drought, disease or insect infestation. Moreover, at all times the population has been subject to reduction by man's own violence through individual depredation and organized warfare.

Because earlier populations never expanded to fill the world with numbers comparable to the billions of the 20th century, we must conclude that sustained high fertility was always accompanied by high average mortality. Similarly, sustained low fertility must have been compensated for by low mortality; any societies that persisted in low fertility while mortality remained high must have vanished.

In the conventional outline of human prehistory it is assumed that at each earlier date the average duration of life was shorter, on the principle that early man faced greater hazards than his descendants. It is commonly supposed, for example, that hunters and gatherers had higher mortality than settled agriculturists. The greater population attained by the agriculturists is correctly attributed to an enhanced supply of food, but the appealing inference that reduced mortality was responsible for this acceleration of growth is not necessarily justified.

The advent of agriculture produced only a small increment in the growth rate; if this increment had been caused by a decline in mortality, the change in the average life expectancy would have been hardly noticeable. If in the hunting-and-gathering society the average number of births per woman was 6.5, for example, the average duration of life must have been 20 years. If the fertility of the early cultivators remained the same as that of their predecessors, then the increase in the life span required to produce the observed acceleration of growth is merely .2 year. The increase in life expectancy, from 20 to 20.2 years, would not have been perceptible.

If one assumes that preagricultural man had substantially higher mortality than the early cultivators, it must also be assumed that the hunters and gatherers had much higher fertility. If the earlier culture had an average age at death of 15 instead of 20, for example, then its fertility must have been 8.6 births per woman rather than 6.5. Such a change is not inconceivable; the complete reorganization of life represented by the adoption of agriculture could certainly be expected to influence both fertility and mortality. There is reason to suspect, however, that both vital rates increased rather than decreased.

Both disease and unpredictable famine might have increased the death rate of the first cultivators. Village life, by bringing comparatively large numbers into proximity, may have provided a basis for the transmission of pathogens and may have created reservoirs of endemic disease. Moreover, the greater density of agricultural populations may have led to greater contamination of food, soil and water. Greater density and the more or less total reliance on crops may also have made agriculturists extremely vulnerable to crop failure, whereas the hunting-and-gathering culture may have been more resistant to adversity.

If mortality did increase on the introduction of agriculture, then it is certain that fertility also rose, and by a slightly larger margin. The supposition that both vital rates did increase is supported by observations of the fertility rates of contemporary peoples who maintain themselves by hunting and gathering, such as the Kung tribe of the Kalahari Desert in southwestern Africa. Nancy Howell of the University of Toronto, analyzing observations made by her and by her colleague Richard Borshay Lee, has found that Kung women have long intervals between births and moderate overall fertility. A possible explanation, suggested by the work of Rose Frisch, is that the Kung diet yields a body composition low enough in fat to cause irregular ovulation. Interbirth intervals may be further prolonged by protracted breastfeeding combined with low body weight. If such conditions were common among preagricultural societies, the cultivation of crops could have increased fertility by increasing body weight and possibly by promoting the earlier weaning of infants so that mothers could work in the fields.

Unfortunately these speculations on the demographic events that may have accompanied the Neolithic revolution cannot be adequately tested by direct evidence. Until relatively recent times the only available indicators of mortality rates were tombstone inscriptions and the age-related characteristics of skeletons. Because the sample of deaths obtained in these ways may not be representative, it is not possible to reliably estimate for early periods such statistics as the average duration of life.

The accelerated growth in the world population that began in the 18th century is more readily understood if the areas classified by the UN as "more developed" and "less developed" are considered separately.

A general description, if not a full explanation, of the changing rates of increase in the more developed areas since the 18th century is provided by what demographers call the demographic transition. The changes in fertility and mortality that constitute the demographic transition are in general expected to accompany a nation's progression from a largely rural, agrarian and at least partly illiterate society to a primarily urban, industrial and literate one. Virtually all the populations classified by the UN as more developed have undergone demographic changes of this kind, although the timing and extent of the changes vary considerably.

The demographic experience common to all the more developed countries includes a major reduction in both fertility and mortality at some time during the past 200 years. In the 18th century the average duration of life was no more than 35 years, and in many of the nations that are now counted among the more developed it must have been much less. Today, almost without exception, the average life expectancy in these nations is 70 years or more. Two hundred years ago the number of births per woman ranged from more than 7.5 in some of the now more developed areas, such as the American colonies and probably Russia, to no more than 4.5 in Sweden and probably in England and Wales. In 1973 only Ireland among the more developed countries had a fertility rate that would produce more than three children per woman, and in most of the wealthier nations total fertility was below 2.5. Thus virtually all the more developed nations have, during the past two centuries, doubled the average life expectancy and halved the total fertility rate.

If the decline in fertility and mortality had been simultaneous, the growth in the population of the developed countries since 1750 might have been modest. Indeed, that was the experience of France, where the birth rate as well as the death rate began to decline before the end of the 18th century. As a consequence the increase in the French population was much less than that of most other European nations. The combined population of the developed countries experienced extraordinary growth after 1750, however, a growth that accelerated until early in the 20th century. The reason for the increase in numbers is that the decline in mortality has in almost all cases preceded the decline in fertility, often by many years.

The decline in fertility in the U.S., as in France, began early; it appears to have been under way by the beginning of the 19th century. Because of early marriage, however, fertility in the U.S. had been very high, so that the excess of births over deaths was still quite large. In most of the other more developed countries the birth rate did not begin to fall until late in the 19th century or early in the 20th.

Another universal feature of the transition is a change in the stability of the vital rates. In the premodern era the high birth rate was relatively constant, but the death rate fluctuated from year to year, reflecting the effects of epidemics and variations in the food supply. In those countries that have completed the demographic transition this pattern is reversed: the death rate remains constant but fertility varies considerably.

The causes of the event that began the demographic transition—the decline in mortality in the late 18th century—are a matter of controversy to social and medical historians. According to one school of thought, until the middle of the 19th century medical innovations in England could not account for the reduction of the English death rate; the principal factor proposed instead is an improvement in the average diet. Others argue that protection from smallpox through inoculation with cowpox serum, a procedure introduced late in the 18th century, was sufficient to markedly reduce the death rate. They propose that the further decline in mortality in the early 19th century may have been brought about by improvements in personal hygiene.

A third hypothesis is that before the 18th century fortuitous periods of low mortality were not exceptional, but that they were followed by periods of very severe mortality caused by major epidemics. According to this view, the late 18th century was a normal period of respite, and improved conditions early in the 19th century averted the next cycle of epidemics, which would otherwise have produced a recurrence of high mortality rates.

Whetever the cause of the initial decline in the death rate, there is no doubt that subsequent improvements in sanitation, public health and medicine made possible further reductions during the 19th century; indeed, the process continues today. It is equally clear that the reduction in mortality was dependent on the increased availability of food and other material resources. This rise in living standards was in turn brought about by the extension of cultivation, particularly in the Western Hemisphere, by increased productivity in both agriculture and industry and by the development of efficient trade and transportation.

The decline in the birth rate that eventually followed the decline in the death rate in the more developed countries was, with the exception of late-19th-century Ireland, almost entirely a decline in the fertility of married couples and can be attributed directly to the practice of contraception and abortion. The reduction in fertility was not a result of the invention of new contraceptive techniques, however. Among selected Americans married before 1910, English couples interviewed in the 1930's and couples surveyed in France and several eastern European nations after World War II, the principal method of birth control was *coitus interruptus*, a technique that had always been available. The birth rate declined because the perceived benefits and liabilities of having more children had changed, and perhaps also because the couples' view of the propriety of preventing births had been modified.

Reduced fertility can be considered one of the consequences of the characteristics by which the more developed countries are defined. In an urban, industrial society the family is no longer the main locus of economic activity, nor are children the expected means of support in old age. In an agrarian, preindustrial society, on the other hand, the family is a basic economic unit and sons are a form of social security. Moreover, in the less developed countries the costs of raising and educating a child are minimal; indeed, a child may contribute to the welfare of the family from an early age. In the industrial society child labor is prohibited, education is compulsory and it often extends through adolescence. These conditions conspire to discourage couples in the more developed countries from having large families, whereas in long-established agrarian societies social norms supporting childbearing tend to be perpetuated.

In the less developed countries the estimated rate of population growth was virtually zero until about 200 years ago, when a moderate rate of increase, about four per 1,000, was apparently induced by a reduction in mortality. The cause of this reduced death rate is uncertain. Durand has suggested that the interchange of staple foods between regions that had previously been isolated might have contributed to population growth in Asia and in Europe as well. In particular the introduction of the potato into Europe and of maize and the sweet potato into China have been cited as possible contributing factors.

Since the aggregate population of the less developed countries includes many large areas that have not been reliably enumerated, a description of the historical course of population growth in these countries is subject to much uncertainty. A slight reduction in the average rate of increase in the latter half of the 19th century, for example, can be attributed entirely to an estimated zero rate of growth in China, and that estimate is based on uncertain data. There is no doubt, however, that in the poorer nations rapid growth began in the 1920's, 1930's and 1940's, and that since World War II the population increase has accelerated dramatically.

The enormous recent growth of the populations of the less developed nations can be interpreted in terms of the demographic transition, but some parts of the process have been more rapid and more extreme than they were in the industrial nations; morever, the transition is not yet complete, and its future course cannot be predicted. Mortality has dropped precipitously, but fertility has so far remained unchanged or declined only moderately. In the combined populations of the less developed countries the number of births per woman is about 5.5, and the average duration of life is more than 50 years, yielding an annual growth rate of about 25 per 1,000. Since World War II mortality in the less developed countries has fallen much more quickly than it did in 19th-century Europe, largely because modern technology, and particularly medical technology, can be imported more rapidly today than it could be discovered and developed 100 years ago. Insecticides, antibiotics and public health measures that were unknown during the European demographic transition are now commonplace in the less developed countries.

According to estimates prepared by the UN, the average duration of life in the less developed areas has risen from 32 to 50 years during the past three decades, an increase of 56 percent. During the same period the birth rate is estimated to have declined by no more than 7 to 8 percent. The actual fall in fertility is in fact even less, by about 4 percent, since demographic changes have reduced the proportion of women in the childbearing years. (Although the fertility of the less developed countries as a group remains very high, there are some countries where the birth rate has fallen significantly— by from 25 to 50 percent— and very rapidly. They include Hong Kong, Singapore, Taiwan, South Korea, West Malaysia, Barbados, Chile, Cuba, Jamaica, Trinidad and Tobago, Puerto Rico and Mauritius. According to reports from travelers, there has also been a decline in fertility in China, particularly in the cities.)

The present rapid growth in the world population is a result of a high rate of increase in the less developed areas and a moderate rate in the rest of the world. According to projections prepared by the UN, more than 90 percent of the increase in population to be anticipated by 2000 will be contributed by the less developed nations, even though a large reduction in fertility in these countries is expected in the next 25 years. The future course of the world's population depends largely on demographic trends in these countries.

The events of the demographic transition provide no sure way of calculating when or how quickly fertility will decline in the less developed nations. The experience of the industrial world is not a satisfactory basis for prediction. The history of the Western population during the past 200 years suggests that vital rates normally fall as a concomitant of modernization, but it provides no checklist of advances in literacy, mortality reduction and urbanization that would enable one to estimate when fertility will fall. In the more developed world there are instances of large reductions in fertility in populations that were still rural, mostly illiterate and still subject to moderately high mortality, as in the Garonne valley in southwestern France before 1850. In other instances fertility did not decline until after education was almost universal, the population was mostly urban and agriculture had become the occupation of a small minority, as in England and Wales.

The present rate of world population increase—20 per 1,000—is almost certainly without precedent, and it is hundreds of times greater than the rate that has been the norm for most of man's history. Without doubt this period of growth will be a transitory episode in the history of the population. If the present rate were to be maintained, the population would double approximately every 35 years, it would be multiplied by 1,000 every 350 years and by a million every 700 years. The consequences of sustained growth at this pace are clearly impossible: in less than 700 years there would be one person for every square foot on the surface of the earth; in less than 1,200 years the human population would outweigh the earth; in less than 6,000 years the mass of humanity would form a sphere expanding at the speed of light. Considering more realistic limits for the future, if the present population is not multiplied by a factor greater than 500 and thus does not exceed two trillion, and if it does not fall below the estimated population of preagricultural society, then the rate of increase or decrease during the next 10,000 years must fall as close to zero as it was during the past 10,000 years.

Arithmetic makes a return to a growth rate near zero inevitable before many generations have passed. What is uncertain is not that the future rate of growth will be about zero but how large the future population will be and what combination of fertility and mortality will sustain it. The possibilities range from more than eight children per woman and a life that lasts an average of 15 years, to slightly more than two children per woman and a life span that surpasses 75 years.

Education and Modernization in Japan and England

Marius B. Jansen and Lawrence Stone

This essay was written in the form of a review of several recent works on Japanese and English education: Herbert Passin's Society and Education in Japan *(1965), R. P. Dore's* Education in Tokugawa Japan *(1965), Kenneth Charlton's* Education in Renaissance England *(1965), Joan Simon's* Education and Society in Tudor England *(1966), and Mark H. Curtis's "Education and Apprenticeship,"* Shakespeare Survey, *XVII (1964), 53–72.*

Japan and England offer a fascinating study in similarities and contrasts, although it is the contrasts that come first to mind in thinking of the two countries. It is of particular interest that the marked similarities of the early periods of Tudor England and Tokugawa Japan change into equally marked differences at a later stage. By 1900 the very success of Britain's growth and expansion led to what Stone refers to as "the cult of the amateur and the domination of classical studies" in English higher education. This conservative approach to the training of leaders is one of the important reasons for the difficulties Britain has faced in adapting to twentieth-century realities— in contrast with Japan's emphasis on the natural and social sciences and on engineering in its higher education.

I. Education in Tokugawa Japan

In 1962 the Tokyo Ministry of Education issued a White Paper entitled *Japan's Growth and Education*. This was worked up largely in response to the

"Education and Modernization in Japan and England" by Marius B. Jansen and Lawrence Stone is reprinted by permission of Cambridge University Press from *Comparative Studies in Society and History*, IX (January 1967), 208–232.

Jansen and Stone are professors of history at Princeton University. Jansen's principal concern has been with the process of modernization in Japan, and he is the author of *The Japanese and Sun Yat-sen* (1954) and *Sakamoto Ryoma and the Meiji Restoration* (1961); and editor and co-author of *Changing Japanese Attitudes Toward Modernization* (1965). Professor Stone's range of interests are reflected in the titles of his books: *Sculpture in Britain: The Middle Ages* (1955), *An Elizabethan: Sir Horatio Palavicino* (1956), *The Crisis of the Aristocracy, 1558–1641* (1965), and *The Causes of the English Revolution, 1529–1642* (1972).

Part I is by Marius B. Jansen and parts II and III by Lawrence Stone. Each has had the benefit of the advise and criticism of the other.

stress foreign observers have placed on the importance of education in Japan's economic growth, and its introductory discussion called attention to three major areas of speculation: that Japan's growth since World War II was attributable to her reservoir of educated skills; that Japan, together with other countries with high growth rates (Canada, West Germany, Israel, the USSR, and the USA) had been particularly careful about the level of technological as well as of general education; and that in the nineteenth century only Japan and Denmark, among countries that faced modernization with handicaps of backwardness, over-population and poor resource bases, had laid sufficient emphasis on education, particularly of the rural sectors which bulked so large in their population.[1] With the titles under review we have for the first time careful accounts on which to base judgements as to the last proposition as it affects Japan. Except for long-dated accounts which were often little more than summaries of official histories, nothing like this has been available in Western languages before, while the Japanese accounts have been more specialized, less inclusive and less incisive.

The books are very different. Dore provides a careful account of the Tokugawa base line of the modern educational system, and Passin's essay is a thoughtful discussion of the way in which that system changed with and contributed to Japan's modernization. Dore's represents a project of over fifteen years' duration. His painstaking working of materials of many kinds provides a richly documented, though perhaps somewhat static, cross section of Tokugawa education. Passin's, an expansion of essays prepared in other contexts, is done with more sweeping strokes, to emphasize the dynamics of change; he is less concerned with detail than with direction, far more inclusive, and summary. Dore often writes for specialists [cf. p. 195; "Ogyū Sorai (if he really is the author of *Kenen danyo*) . . .], Passin for the generalist reader, for whom he also includes 146 pages—half the book—to reproduction of documents illustrating educational theory and social thought in Japan. Both have anticipated many of their conclusions and some of their language in previous publications,[2] and both have the versatility and breadth to enable them to place their subject matter within a larger framework.[3]

Both discussions of the Tokugawa period (1600–1868), to which Dore

---

[1] The English translation appeared in 1963 (Tokyo, Ministry of Education). For comment and summary see R. P. Dore, "Education in Japan's Growth," *Pacific Affairs*, XXXVII, 1 (Spring, 1964), pp. 66–79.

[2] For Dore: "Talent and the Social Order in Tokugawa Japan," *Past and Present*, No. 21, 1962; "Education," pp. 176–204 in R. E. Ward and D. A. Rustow, *Political Modernization in Japan and Turkey* (Princeton, 1964), "The Legacy of Tokugawa Education," in M. B. Jansen (ed.), *Changing Japanese Attitudes Toward Modernization* (Princeton, 1965), pp. 99–132. For Passin: "Education and Political Development in Japan," in J. S. Coleman, *Education and Political Development* (Princeton, 1965), "Writer and Journalist in the Transitional Society," in L. W. Pye, *Communications and Political Development* (Princeton, 1963).

[3] Passin in, especially, J. W. Bennett, H. Passin, R. K. McKnight, *In Search of Identity: The Japanese Overseas Scholar in America and Japan* (University of Minnesota Press, 1958), and Dore in *City Life in Japan: Life in a Tokyo Ward* (London, Routledge and Kegan Paul, 1958). Again, Passin in A. F. Raper *et al.*, *The Japanese Village in Transition* (Tokyo, SCAP, 1950), and Dore's definitive *Land Reform in Japan* (London, Oxford University Press, 1959).

devotes his entire volume and Passin some fifty pages, base many of their conclusions on one of the statistical efforts of the Meiji modernizers. The *Nihon
kyōiku-shi shiryō* (9 vols., 1890–1892) was compiled from replies submitted by
local authorities to surveys set by the Ministry of Education in 1883. Both
authors grant that it is full of problems for the historian. Reporting was neither
uniform nor complete. But on the whole later collections show that the
tendency was toward underestimation, both for schools and for attendance. It
is also possible to project the figures for that date back against total population
and age group estimates, and by doing so both Dore and Passin come to
virtually identical estimates of literacy at the beginning of the modernization
period. Passin feels male literacy of between forty and fifty percent is a "not
unreasonable estimate" (p. 47), and Dore, on the basis of far more elaborate
calculations, suggests that perhaps 43 percent of boys and 10 percent of girls
received "some kind of schooling" at the end of the Tokugawa period (p. 321).
Both authors also make good use of a compilation assembled by Ototake
Iwazō between 1915 and 1917 through interviews with oldsters who had
experienced commoners' education (*Nihon shomin kyōiku-shi*, 3 vols., 1928).
Taken together with the flood of prefectural histories that have been appearing
ever since, these sources do not seem unreliable. They can make little allowance, of course, for degrees of literacy, a vexing problem in any society and
nowhere more so than in one afflicted with the Sino-Japanese writing system.

Dore's chapters provide superb descriptions of the nature of Tokugawa
schooling and what it was the educated were given to read. He begins with
the fief schools. The samurai entered the Tokugawa period a largely illiterate
fighting caste; two and a half centuries of peace saw them separated from their
lands and, to a degree, their weapons, and transformed into a bureaucratic elite
from which the 300-odd fiefs selected their officials. No agency was more important in this change than the official, fief school. Begun in the seventeenth
century, its numbers grew rapidly in the eighteenth and early nineteenth
centuries. The *hankō* trained samurai in moral attitudes that were considered
a vocational necessity for a hereditary ruling class. The object of learning was
not intellectual pleasure or discovery so much as it was discipline and preparation for service, and to this end the Confucian classics, with their emphasis
upon status and authority, were approached with a reverential attitude. The
fief schools carried a heavy burden of ceremonial and bureaucratic regulation,
and their curriculum, which in the early eighteenth century could specialize in
one or another school of Confucian interpretation, gradually became restricted
to the orthodoxy of the Sung masters. "It was not," Dore grants, "an education
which intrinsically stimulated and held individual interest, nor did it appear to
contemporary [nineteenth century] samurai as a useful and desirable means to
the attainment of personal or group goals. It was quite plainly dull and in
addition almost meaningless" (p. 152).

The official schools did supplement their Confucian fare with other things.
Dore describes, and Passin emphasizes, the change of emphasis as the Shintō
revival of the "national scholars" brought Japanese studies into the curriculum
at the end of the eighteenth century. By late Tokugawa the loyalist historian

Rai Sanyo was almost as widely read in the schools as were the Chinese texts on which he modeled his (Chinese language) account of Japan's past. And in many areas and virtually all the important domains Western studies, chiefly of armament and war, also entered the curriculum. These trends constituted important changes in the rather torpid regimen of classical Chinese. They should be taken in conjunction with the useful reminder of John Hall several years ago that the civil arts were at best only one component of the fief schools, and that much time was spent on the military component of samurai education, an area in which instructors tended to be of higher rank.[4]

However dreary the Confucian curriculum he describes, Dore thinks more highly of the samurai education than did the "contemporary samurai" who found it "dull" and "meaningless." At the very least, he notes, it "trained in being trained." Samurai minds were trained and stretched in useful ways, they were prepared by even Confucian categories for other, more modern concepts. They were also trained for dedicated service and duty to the political community—first to the regional, and ultimately to the national, service. And yet, it may be suggested, virtually the same Confucian texts employed in Chinese academies did not, on balance, produce "ministers of modernization" in the same way. It has to be granted that contrasting factors in China—scholar-gentry involvement in the rural basis of society, the mystique of the universal state, and the examination system with its challenge and reward for ideological faithfulness—were too numerous to make the comparison very good. But to say this may mean admitting that it is difficult to say more than that Tokugawa Confucian education, *per se*, did not rule out modernization.

What of the commoners? Both Dore and Passin are careful to stress, and Dore to detail, the fact of commoner education in (Passin's happy term) "parish schools," the *terakoya*. Here again comparison with Manchu China would bring out further differences, for despite imperial encouragement of village schools official indifference and rural poverty seem to have combined to limit their number and importance. In Japan, Dore points out, a rapid expansion began around the end of the eighteenth century with children receiving training from teachers who were village employees.

The educational content of these schools was again Confucian, tinged with Buddhism. The *Jitsugo-kyō* reduced to stark simplicity the generalized exhortations of more sophisticated texts and stressed the same reverence for authority and filiality. "Your father and your mother are like heaven and earth; your teacher and your lord are like the sun and the moon. All other relations may be likened to useless stones." (Dore, p. 279). And the connection with educational attainment was immediate; "If a man does not study, he will have no knowledge. A man without knowledge is a fool." (Passin, p. 206, quoting Fukuzawa's citation of the same work.) Commoner moralists like Ishida Baigan could identify the way of learning with ethical attitudes and actions; "firstly behave prudently, serve your lord with righteousness and serve your parents with love, treat your friends with faithfulness, love men at large and

---

[4] "The Confucian Teacher in Tokugawa Japan," in *Confucianism in Action*, ed. D. S. Nivison and A. F. Wright (Stanford, 1959), pp. 296–7.

have pity on poor people . . . Do not neglect the family business, and as for wealth, measure what comes in and be aware of what goes out. Obey the laws and govern the family. The way of *gakumon* (learning) is roughly thus." [5] It is of some importance that, as Dore points out, authorities seldom had any fear of the spread of such education, since, in a society that accepted status and took it for granted, it equipped both ruler and ruled to perform their roles.

Both the authors agree that the spread of commoners' education had important elements making for modernity. For all groups, it meant a "training in being trained." Millions of families, Passin notes, had assimilated the routines that public education requires into their mode of life; extra-family sources of respect, prestige, and instruction, were part of the daily life of most villages in Japan. And when, in the nineteenth century, new challenges and orders meant a stream of government directives reaching into all parts of the island country, the literacy that had been attained made it vastly easier for the government to get its point across to its people.

There were, however, other notes than Confucian tones of harmony and status that distinguished Tokugawa and modern Japanese education. Dore shows how concepts of rewarding talent, testing it, and associating it with administrative responsibility developed as logical consequences of a more or less impersonal school system. The result was an even greater stress on achievement for those born within the special ranks, if only because their number was always larger than the supply of posts available. Indeed words like "achievement" and "ambition" hardly do justice to the frantic rush to excel that seems to have pervaded the schools in the times of crisis at the end of the Tokugawa period. Dore provides a striking example from a memoir: "We really went all out that month. If one of us got a page ahead the others would turn pale. We hardly took time off to chew our food properly, and we drank as little water as possible in order that the others should not get ahead in the time wasted going to the lavatory—so keen were we to get a line or two ahead of the others." [6] The Tokugawa social order, despite its nominal adherence to standards of ascription, was hardly static if it harbored such intense determination for achievement and self-realization. The ethic of achievement, enforced with the threat of shame and underscored by the duty of returning superiors' favors, extended to commoners, as Dore's selection of *terakoya* precepts makes plain: "Illiteracy . . . brings shame on your teacher, shame on your parents and shame on yourself. The heart of a child of three stays with him till he is a hundred as the proverb stays. Determine to succeed, study with all your might, never for-

---

[5] Passin, p. 40, quoting R. Bellah, *Tokugawa Religion* (N.Y., Free Press, 1957), p. 149. Ishida Baigan's teachings were directed at merchants, primarily, but similar sentiments could be culled from the writings of rural reconstructionists like Ninomiya Sontoku.

[6] P. 211. The quotation is from the memoir published in an inspirational magazine years later. That this sort of intensity is not dead can be seen from a remote "Spartan Academy" visited by Nagai Michio a century later, a school whose students display a kamikaze intellectualism directed toward success in the university entrance examinations and recite each morning in unison, "What someone else reads once, I will read three times; what someone else reads three times, I will read five times. Taking examinations is the student's battle. From this day forth I vow that I will study with the intensity of a madman or like a lunatic in order to achieve my goal." *Shūkan Asahi*, January 1, 1961.

getting the shame of failure" (p. 323). And the schools, of all kinds, helped, as Dore says, to stimulate such aspirations by offering a chance to realize them. Nor does it come as a surprise to find Education Minister Mori promising his normal school auditors (in 1885) that education will give their country "the leading position among all countries of the world" (Passin, p. 68).

It seems reasonable to conclude, as both authors do, that in the Tokugawa context the Confucian ideology of the schools affected this striving by helping to keep it channeled in directions conducive to the interests of the larger collectivity. The merchant's concern was to be his firm, the farmer's his community, and the samurai's his fief. Dore would, on balance, identify the commitment to political and national goals as one of the most significant benefits of Tokugawa education.

One must be careful here, and some cautions seem appropriate. The first is that it was the Japanese and particularly the samurai value structure through which the ideology was refracted that made it work the way it did. The self-consciously elitist, dedicated sense of responsibility which the samurai claimed meant that any texts in which they were schooled would affect them thus. It was not education that created this so much as an education that diffused it, first to the warriors and more importantly, in the nineteenth century, to the countrymen for whom they had become the ideal ethical type. We may, no doubt, be victims of the modern leaders and educators (most of them, in Meiji Japan, ex-samurai) but it is hard to remain unimpressed by their unanimity that something of the samurai ideal—the sense of social commitment, the courage and seriousness of individual responsibility—should be kept alive for future generations. Whatever there was to this spirit was affected, probably reinforced by Tokugawa education, but one wonders whether its roots were to be found in the schoolmasters or their work.

One misses also in Mr. Dore's discussion of the relation between Tokugawa education and Japan's modernization some exposition of the broader currents of intellectual life in Tokugawa Japan. His references show his familiarity with the sources and writers of the period, but his text might lead the reader to suppose that Tokugawa intellectuals stayed as close to pedantic orthodoxy as the schoolmasters whose work he describes. But in fact recent scholarship increasingly stresses the vitality and importance of the several strains of Confucian, nationalist, and Western traditions in Tokugawa Japan. We read of the way the rigorous philological scholarship of the Confucianists affected the Shintoists' explorations of the Japanese past, and learn of the important, if incongruous, alliance between scholars of Western and Shintō learning. The center of this tradition was to be found neither in samurai nor commoner schools, but in private academies whose founders often maintained a striking independence of political authority. Although the official fief schools turned to follow shogunal instructions in the last half century, feudal decentralization tended to permit considerable regional intellectual experimentation. Great Confucian political theorists like Ogyū Sorai (1666–1728), with their need to apply the general principles of ancient China to the problems of contemporary Japan, developed a strongly individual and voluntarist approach that emphasized doing as the sages would have done and not simply imitating what they did. All of this was of the greatest importance for the cultivation of a "practical learning" (*jitsugaku*) that later, when still more rational and practical models came to hand, could bridge the transition to modern ends with traditional values.[7]

Passin's discussion of the Tokugawa scene is in all respects congruent with Dore's, though more sketchy. He is more intent to stress the ferment of the nineteenth century before Meiji. For him the significant things about Tokugawa education are to be found in the way upper class education created a "common universe of discourse" among Japanese of all areas, and the consciousness of membership in more than a kind of local group. True nationhood, he suggests, was in effect already attained before the Meiji changes.

In his rapid sketch of educational changes thereafter Passin is full of thoughtful qualifications of the happy assurance of the Education Ministry's white paper about the relation of education to Japan's growth. For one thing, he reminds us that it was actually a long and difficult process. School enrollment moved up sharply only twenty years after the Meiji Restoration. Technical and vocational education did not precede, but grew apace with the industrialization that finally began to take shape after the 1890's were well underway. It will not do to credit vocational education with industrialization—they came together—nor will it suffice to relate, as the Education Ministry seeks to do, the "morals" textbooks with their (traditional) emphasis on frugality and self-denial to the high savings propensity of modern Japanese society. These are areas in which *post hoc, propter hoc* logicians can derive useful caution from the recollection that twenty years ago educational theorists like Robert Hall were attributing much of Japan's disastrous course to the deficiencies of the modern education system.[8]

These reflections serve to remind us that while we now search the Japanese experience to account for the success of modernization, a few decades ago the hunt was for evidence of inadequacies, and explanations for chauvinism, regimentation, and aggression. The Confucian-Shintō ideology of the modern educators, which seemed so menacing a generation ago, is now sketched in softer tones. For E. H. Norman the feudal background of Japanese politics explained what was wrong with it, while more recent theorists of modernization stress the benefits of the multi-centered, competitive setting of Tokugawa institutional developments. Now the doctrines of the Confucian educators share in this reappraisal.

In this discussion it is important to keep distinctions of period and purpose in mind. The most essential of these is the difference between modern "Confucianism" that served in a consciously codified code of values adopted as

---

[7] See on Ogyū, J. R. McEwan, *The Political Writings of Ogyū Sorai* (Cambridge University Press, 1962), and for a brilliant discussion of Ogyū's contribution to the modernization of political Confucianism, Maruyama Masao, *Nihon seiji shisō shi kenkyū* [Studies in the History of Japanese Political Thought] (Tokyo, 1952, and nine subsequent impressions).

[8] See, for instance, R. K. Hall, *Education for a New Japan* (New Haven, Yale University Press, 1949).

subject matter for indoctrination of the young by government leaders who feared the rise of an individualistic ethic, and the "Confucianism" of Tokugawa times. The latter was a way of looking at the world through certain categories, and a tradition that could encompass most others; the former was a narrow preserve jealously guarded against moral subversion. Most of the Tokugawa-Meiji leaders could display a largeness of mind and understanding because they were securely rooted in a tradition still vital and full of meaning, even when they criticized it as somehow inappropriate to the modern world. The second generation, however, invoked its grandfathers' ideology and values in order to intimidate the third. And as the "Confucianism" that resulted seemed smaller and more narrow, so did the men who praised it.

The time has come to take these matters up again. Passin's thoughtful comments, and Dore's masterful description of the Tokugawa scene, provide the materials for such a discussion, and move our consideration of Japan's education and modernization to a firm level for analysis.

II. Education in Tudor England

In the last decade the amount, quality and purposes of Tudor education have been the subject of vigorous and intensive research, and there have recently appeared two full-length books and one synoptic article which survey the field as a whole. One school of thought, headed by Professor Curtis, sees the period 1550–1660 as the true Age of Enlightenment, the time when the state, the intellectuals, the gentry and the merchants were agreed on the basic importance of serious education in creating a great society, and were determined to do something about it. This zeal was the product of many forces: the liberation of administrative and intellectual life from the straight-jacket of clerical monopoly; the stress placed by Humanists such as Colet, Erasmus and Vives on training in the Latin and Greek classics and in the Bible as essential prerequisites for the moral improvement of a ruling elite; the demand by Protestant Reformers for mass literacy to give access to the vernacular Bible and for increased secondary and higher education to mould the religious ideas of the new generation; and lastly the desire of social conservatives to prop up the hierarchical structure of society by training the hereditary elite to fill the key posts in the new secular state, and so keep social mobility to a minimum.

Everyone is now agreed that the old legend of the damage done to education by the Dissolution of Monasteries and Chantries is nonsense, and that in fact educational facilities at all levels increased at a tremendous pace during this period. It has been estimated that by 1660 up to 30 percent of all adult males were literate; that there was a school for every 4,400 persons (which may be compared to the 1870 figure of one for every 23,700); and that the proportion of the male population undergoing higher education was larger than at any time before the Second World War.

What is in dispute, however, is the quality of the education received, and its relationship to the character of the society. Access to grammar school and university was closed to bright children of the labouring poor, but it seems clear that the educational ladder was open to the sons of artisans, freeholders, yeomen and above. Controversy continues to rage over the functional utility of classical grammar as taught in the schools, over the degree to which the Universities adjusted to the new scientific, linguistic and historical disciplines, and how far both they and the Inns of Court were providing useful training for the gentry. Professor Curtis believes that although the formal curriculum remained virtually unaltered, the creation of Professorships in history, astronomy, anatomy, etc. provided public instruction in new subjects, that the output of the printing presses offered wholly new opportunities for private study and self-education, and that the system of the private tutor operating within a disciplined collegiate life superceded the old, admittedly decayed, organization of university teaching. If this is so, then instruction in subjects of practical interest to aspiring administrators, statesmen and justices was in fact provided within the interstices of the archaic framework of the universities.

If I understand her aright, Mrs. Simon takes a less optimistic view, although on many issues she seems a little uncertain of her final stance; it is often difficult to see the wood for the mass of trees she has planted. This is a pity, since her book is undoubtedly the most scholarly and comprehensive survey of the field which we possess. She has made a major contribution to our understanding of the relationship of the forces of humanism and religious reformation at work in the early Tudor period, but she seems less sure of herself as she moves into the Elizabethan age. Mr. Charlton's book is more superficial in its scholarship than that of Mrs. Simon, but he develops themes left unexplored by Mrs. Simon, such as the role of the private tutor and the Grand Tour, and he makes it crystal clear just where he stands, which is at the opposite pole from Professor Curtis. He argues that the curriculum in the grammar schools was a system of monotonous repetitive rote-learning which did little to open the mind and much to ruin the style. Milton contemptuously called the process "gerund-grinding," and among its more fantastic literary consequences were the works of Sir Thomas Browne (who once translated *festina lente* as "celerity contempered with cunctation"). As for the universities, he notes that they were still obsessed with Aristotelianism and had little officially to offer in the way of science, history or modern languages. Moreover even as centers of research they were lagging behind Europe: little serious Biblical or classical scholarship emerged from Tudor Oxford or Cambridge, and most dons seem to have been absorbed in the polemical sterilities of theological disputation, and in looking after their lucrative upper class pupils. If the landed classes succeeded in escaping most of the deleterious effects of this education, Mr. Charlton suggests that it was because they did not take it seriously, and had a good time instead. He thinks equally little of the education offered by the Inns of Court, where the aristocracy and gentry idled away their time rather than studied the Common law. The only type of Tudor education that he regards as having served a valuable purpose was that conducted by the private tutor in the home, followed by the Grand Tour abroad. It was, he argues, the advent

Education and Modernization in Japan and England   223

of the printing press, the mass translation of the classics, and the production of
a host of technical handbooks in English which allowed these naturally rather
lazy young men to pick up useful facts and ideas. And it was their travels in
Europe which broadened their minds and gave them a sense of perspective
within which to judge the institutions of their own country.

In conclusion, therefore, Mr. Charlton argues—and Mrs. Simon tends to
support him—that the seeds of modern education were laid in the sixteenth
century, but that they were mostly sterile. Such progress as was achieved was
the result of the initiative of isolated individuals, not of changes in organized
institutional practice. A modernization of English education had to wait for
the reforms of the late nineteenth century, with the introduction into the
universities of the Honours Schools we know today—and even then little
encouragement was given to science and none at all to technology.

As will be seen later, the charge that education in the sixteenth to nineteenth century period failed to adapt to a more modern, practical, and
scientific curriculum is true enough. Mr. Charlton's book is a valuable corrective to the somewhat uncritical respect with which Renaissance educational
ideas and practice are often regarded. There is reason to believe, however, that
the wholesale condemnation of the results of institutional education in the
sixteenth century is somewhat overdrawn. It is evident that some men *did*
survive the grammar school experience with a genuine love and appreciation of
classical literature, to judge by the contents of their libraries, and by their fond
familiarity with the classics, which they display by cramming their writing with
erudite quotations. Some did go up to the universities with serious intent and
learnt some logic, rhetoric and philosophy, as shown in their correspondence
with their parents, and in the accounts and letters of their tutors. Many did
pick up a good deal of knowledge of the Common Law, presumably at the
Inns of Court, to judge from their libraries, their speeches in Parliament, and
their correspondence about their interminable lawsuits. Moreover, although
the formal curriculum at the University was as sterile and old-fashioned as Mr.
Charlton described it, there are signs that here and there progressive dons were
teaching more modern subjects to their gentlemanly pupils, who were not
constrained by the need to pass an examination. In any case, what Mr.
Charlton has missed in his critical study of the quality of education, is the
extraordinary increase in quantity at every level, a change of such dimensions
as to create an entirely new intellectual environment. And finally the cultural
achievements of the age of Bacon, Ralegh, Ben Jonson and Donne are extraordinary by any standards, and cannot be entirely unrelated to the formal
educational background from which they emerged.[9]

There is very general agreement that the upper classes had reached a very
high level of intellectual attainment in the middle of the seventeenth century
—a fact attested by both English and foreign commentators and supported by

[9] See L. Stone, *The Crisis of the Aristocracy, 1558–1641* (Oxford, 1965), ch. XII; M. H.
Curtis. *Oxford and Cambridge in Transition, 1558–1642* (Oxford, 1959); H. F. Fletcher,
The Intellectual Development of John Milton (Urbana, 1956–61). L. Stone, "The Educa-
tional Revolution in England, 1560–1640," *Past and Present*, 28 (1964), pp. 41–80.

the evident knowledge of history, law, literature, architecture, music and the arts displayed by so many of the nobility and gentry of the day. Since only the nobility and higher gentry and a sprinkling of the lesser could afford the luxury of the private tutor and the Grand Tour, it must be assumed that the formal educational system, whatever its admitted deficiencies, was to no small degree responsible for this remarkable cultural efflorescence.

But whether one takes the optimistic or the pessimistic view of the practical value of this Renaissance education, the problem remains of explaining the single-minded fanaticism with which contemporaries pursued the mastery, in all its pristine purity, of a wholly dead language. Useful though the writings of the ancients are as repositories of knowledge and good sense on most moral and political issues, the fact remains that these lessons can just as well be imparted in the vernacular, through translation. Nor was it until several centuries later that the defenders of intensive study in Latin grammar fell back on the argument that this is the ideal device for training the mind, regardless of its practical utility, or lack of it.

There is, however, one possible explanation of the irrational passion with which the teaching of Latin was advocated in the Renaissance, (and has been defended ever since). It has recently been pointed out that the peculiar features of puberty rites among primitive tribes, as described in anthropological literature, provide an extraordinarily close parallel to western education in Latin grammar.[10] The function of the puberty rite is to act as a ceremonial introduction to manhood, and to full access to the privileges of the tribe. It takes the form of abrupt withdrawal from the family home; sexual and peer-group segregation in a compound, in association exclusively with other males of the same age; the pursuance of a course of life and study quite alien to the normal habits of both child and adult; submission to deliberately inflicted cruelties, especially flogging, as tests of courage and endurance; conformity to a series of severe and incomprehensible taboos; and instruction by bachelors in the mysteries of the tribe and the wisdom of the ancestors, all expressed in a secret language which has to be mastered.

Now the Renaissance saw a sharp rise of education at school and away from the home, and in the role that flogging played in the educational system, especially in England, where notorious floggers like Dr. Busby of Westminster were treated with extreme respect and veneration; that the language taught was now entirely divorced from normal life, as medieval Latin had not been; and that educators like Elyot deliberately stressed the association between learning Latin, which was accomplished between the ages of 7 and 15, and training in courage and fortitude. Thus Latin grammar was the Renaissance substitute for the medieval chivalric code, and performed the same function of detaching an elite of youths from its home environment and giving it a training which toughened it for adventure in the adult world, and taught it an esoteric wisdom which distinguished it from the rest of the population. It thus strongly reinforced the division between gentlemen and the rest, the rulers

[10] W. J. Ong, "Latin Language Study as a Renaissance Puberty Rite," *Studies in Philology*, LVI (ii), pp. 103–24.

and the ruled, producing a sharply differentiated elite with strong sado-masochistic tendencies (was this when the tradition of *le vice anglais* began?). Thus the functional result of teaching Latin grammar at schools was to reinforce the hierarchical structure of Tudor society by serving as a prolonged puberty rite for the selected few.

III. Japan and England: A Comparative Study

Two of the most striking success stories in the history of economic develop-ment have occurred in two islands lying just off the continents of Europe and Asia respectively. England evolved slowly, and early, and by processes internal to itself; Japan entered into the modern world rapidly and late by selective adoption of concepts and skills developed by others. A comparison of the social structure, educational program, and economic growth of Japan with those of England from the mid-sixteenth century to the early twentieth may neverthe-less reveal something of significance. There are three comparisons which can profitably be made here: between late Tudor England and Tokugawa Japan in its prime in the eighteenth century; between mid-seventeenth century En-gland and mid-nineteenth century Japan, both on the eve of revolution; and between nineteenth century England and late nineteenth and early twentieth century Japan.

The closest comparison in terms of social structures and educational systems is obviously the first. Both Elizabethan England and Tokugawa Japan were ruled by about 250 noble families (daimyo) and a very much larger number of gentry (samurai), the remainder of the population being taxed and governed in the interests of this two-stage elite. Both were headed by new authoritarian dynasties, Tudors and Tokugawas, who had recently established themselves by force of arms, had restored order to the countryside, and had secured their power and that of their followers by the confiscation and redistribution of church property, monastic land by the Tudors and, on a lesser scale, Buddhist temple lands by the first three shoguns. Both adapted and developed religious ideologies and institutions for political and dynastic purposes: the Anglican creed and church in England, Chu Hsi Confucianism in Japan. Richard Hooker and Hayashi Razan played a similar role in developing and justifying their respective conformist and deferential creeds by the use of moral and philosophical arguments to prove that the existing social order is ordained by God and Nature.[11] Both ruling families erected elaborate and expensive temples for the worship of the founder of the dynasty: Henry VII's chapel at West-minster, and the great shrine to Ieyasu at Nikkō. The English nobility crammed the parish churches with the ostentatious memorials of their ancestors; the daimyo enshrined their founding ancestors and held yearly services to exalt the prestige of their families. Up to the late seventeenth century in England,

[11] J. W. Hall, "The Confucian Scholar in Tokugawa Japan" in *Confucianism in Action*, ed. D. S. Nivison and A. F. Wright (Stanford, 1959), pp. 270–7.

and the early nineteenth in Japan, both economies were driven primarily by the demands of the elite for conspicuous consumption. Both developed an exalted sense of national destiny, buttressed by the Anglican religion for the one (it was a Tudor Bishop who opined that God is English), and by Shinto religion, much more gradually and locally, for the other. Both societies were based on the principle of hereditary ascribed status, supported by the legal institution of primogeniture and by strict rules of etiquette. Both societies depended for political and psychological unity in considerable measure on the attractive power of a sophisticated and expensive court life around the Prince in the capital city, Edo or London. Finally it is a remarkable fact that the merchant communities in Tudor England and Tokugawa Japan were both of them extremely traditional and conservative in outlook. In both societies such entrepreneurial initiative and such risk capital as there was seems to have come mostly from the upper landed classes.[12]

There were also, of course, some striking dissimilarities. Though both were ruled by the landed classes, the pattern of relationships was already contractual in the one, still feudal in the other. The encouragement of foreign trade was a prime motive of state policy for the one, the prevention of foreign trade a prime motive for the other. The bourgeoisie played at all times a far greater role in pre-industrial England than it ever did in Tokugawa Japan. Assimilation of a successful bourgeois family into the landed classes was fairly easy in the one (if only in the second generation), fairly difficult until towards the end in the other. In terms both of individual freedom and economic well-being, the condition of the tenantry and rural labourers was far better in the one than in the other, where personal servitude, ascription to the soil, and a crushing burden of taxation were the norm. Both official ideologies served as buttresses of the existing social order, but the English, unlike the Japanese, was under severe and continuous challenge from a potentially subversive variant, Puritanism and Dissent. Part cause and part consequence was that deference and hierarchy were moderately observed in the one, immoderately in the other, and that upper class radicalism was an endemic feature of the one, and very rare in the other until near the end.

At a fairly early stage both societies freed education from the monopoly of priests, England in the sixteenth century, Japan in the seventeenth. Both developed schools for their elite in which the children could be taught firstly—and most importantly—the virtue of obedience to superiors in order to preserve social stability; secondly, the art of war, which was the original justification of their privileged status; thirdly, the techniques and skills which would equip them for administrative chores in an increasingly bureaucratic society; fourthly, scholarly appreciation of the classics, in which all wisdom was believed to reside; and fifthly, the manners, skills, and aesthetic interests that distinguished them from the rest of society.[13] Three advanced thinkers of sixteenth century

---

[12] For England, see L. Stone, *The Crisis of the Aristocracy, 1558–1641*, ch. VII; for Japan, see J. Hirschmeier, *The Origins of Entrepreneurship in Meiji Japan* (Cambridge, Mass., 1964), chs. I, VII.

[13] Cf. Hall, *op. cit.*, p. 297, with Stone, *op. cit.*, p. 680.

England, Thomas Starkey, Nicholas Bacon, and Humphrey Gilbert, lobbied unsuccessfully for a state-supported school for the aristocracy; in late eighteenth century Japan the Bakufu set an example by endowing, supporting and operating a school for samurai, the Shōheikō. Mr. Dore's summary of the educational system of Tokugawa Japan reads almost exactly like an account of that of Jacobean England derived from the writings of Tudor educational theorists such as Roger Ascham, Richard Mulcaster, and Henry Peacham:

> . . . The means of education were provided by Chinese writings, especially the Confucian classics; its purpose was primarily to develop moral character, both as an absolute human duty and also in order the better to fulfill the samurai's function in society; a secondary purpose was to gain from the classics that knowledge of men and affairs and of the principles of government which was also necessary for the proper performance of the samurai's duties. Certain other technical vocational skills were necessary which could not be gained from classical Chinese study. Also, classical Chinese study itself brought certain legitimate fringe benefits in the form of life-enhancing aesthetic pleasures.[14]

Thus both societies adopted as the basis for their elite education a close, repetitive study of works written long ago in a foreign language—classical Latin in England, classical Chinese in Japan. Both concentrated on the mastery of a limited number of basic texts, which were thought to embody the summum of human wisdom and experience: Cicero, Virgil, Aristotle, Plutarch and the rest in England, the Four Books and the Five Classics in Japan. Just as Machiavelli drew his examples of statecraft from antiquity, so did the Japanese go back to the Chinese classics to learn about military tactics. Both regarded education as a form of physical and mental discipline, a disagreeable penance conspicuously and almost deliberately devoid of nearly all pleasure or intellectual stimulation. The attention of the children was kept focussed on the niceties of grammar and syntax by sadistic brutality in England, and by more subtle psychological pressures in Japan. Neither regarded scholarship as a desirable attribute for gentlemen, and the avid pursuit of learning was left to those of lower social status who were seeking a professional career. The purpose of schooling in both societies was rather the creation of an elite sufficiently well-trained to be of service to the state. Intellectual amateurism was the hallmark of both societies—as it is of all aristocracies. There was one striking difference however: military training continued to bulk large in Japan and martial values continued to be exalted far into the nineteenth century, whereas in England the military component of aristocratic education was already vestigial by the early seventeenth century.

Both systems handled the problem of merit versus rank by giving special privileges to the latter. In Oxford and Cambridge, as in the Japanese fief schools, the sons of high-ranking nobles sat apart, wore distinctive dress and were attended by their personal servants. Since the gentry and nobility rarely took degrees in England, they were hardly ever exposed to direct intellectual competition from their social inferiors. In both systems promotion by merit

[14] Dore, p. 59.

took second place after ascribed status, and was admitted only so far as was necessary to maintain the efficiency of the administrative system. When they reached manhood, many of the nobles patronized learned scholars and kept them in their entourage for the advice they could offer, for the teaching they could give their children, and for the prestige that such patronage could confer. The function of the *jusha* on a seventeenth-century Japanese fief exactly parallels that of Thomas Hobbes in the service of the Cavendishes, Earls of Devonshire, at Chatsworth. Hobbes' ideas about the need for authority, both in political order and in choice of ideologies, were very similar indeed to those of his contemporary Hayashi Razan, the *jusha* to the Shogun Ieyasu. The activities of the *jusha* in providing a systematic rationalization of the hierarchic social order are precisely those of the religious intellectuals of Tudor England, also working under state or aristocratic patronage.[15]

Below this upper class educational structure there also grew up in late sixteenth- and early seventeenth-century England and in early nineteenth-century Japan an educational system for commoners, financed by fees and private charity, which provided some technical and bookkeeping training for the middle classes. Below this again there developed in both countries a remarkable spread of elementary education which confined itself mainly to basic literacy and moral precepts—particularly, of course, the need for obedience to superiors.

It is worth noting that it was just at this period that England took the technological lead over Europe, not so much by its fertility of invention as by taking over the inventions of others (like Japan under the Meiji). This was a period in which the English showed an intense curiosity about the outside world, traveling far and wide over Europe and America and reporting back what they saw. England copied, and then developed, mining from the Germans, cannon-founding from the French, new textiles from the Dutch, ships and sails from the Portuguese and Spanish. Like the Japanese, most of these advances were the result of government planning rather than private investment, the motive being national security rather than economic growth for its own sake. But this government activity, plus lower-class technological education, in the end stimulated domestic enterprise and by 1626 a Venetian was remarking that "English people, to say the truth, are judicious people, and of great intelligence . . . and are very ingenious in their inventions."[16]

This curiosity about the outside world and this desire to absorb and develop the ideas of others stems from the fact that Elizabethans had little national pride in the English cultural heritage (only towards the end of the sixteenth century did reactive nationalism begin to take hold in Court circles). Compare this with the attitude of the Chinese when first faced with western superiority in military technology and astronomy in the early seventeenth century. Here the intense cultural pride of the classically trained Chinese mandarin class prevented any assimilation. "Military defeat was the technical reason why

15 Hall, *op. cit., passim.*
16 Quoted by C. M. Cipolla, *Guns and Sails* (London, 1965), pp. 41, 87 n. 2.

Western knowledge should be acquired, but it was also the psychological reason why it should not be." The Chinese preferred admitting military defeat to the psychological shock of facing up to the inferiority of their national literary culture when challenged by western science and engineering.[17]

The second comparison is between England and Japan on the eve of their revolutions, respectively in the mid-seventeenth and the mid-nineteenth centuries. The interest groups and the ideas behind the two revolutions have interesting similarities. Both were in part revolts of dissatisfied gentry, whose education had taught them that they had a duty to rule and how to do so, but whose aspirations for power and responsibility were blocked by a corrupt, inefficient and restricted court elite. Moreover both revolutions occurred at a time when the rate of literacy was somewhere about one third for adult males.[18] Both occurred after a generation of intellectual questioning and debate and after the appearance of many signs of weakening of the old hierarchic social relationships. Both revolutions were the prelude to far-reaching schemes for educational reform, based on the best foreign examples. One of the early steps taken by the Long Parliament was to invite the celebrated educationalist Comenius to pay a visit to England and offer his advice; during the Interregnum Oxford was filled with scientists, and schemes were drawn up for universal elementary education and a third university. Even after the Restoration of Charles II, the largely ineffectual efforts of the Royal Society in its early years to encourage military and industrial technological innovation are very similar in concept to the more thorough and far more successful steps taken in Japan just before and especially after the Meiji Restoration. It was in 1855 that the Shogun established the Yōgakusho, a school of western learning which within a few years was teaching western mathematics and science as well as western languages. Baconian projects for similar scientific institutions in seventeenth-century England remained still-born.

In Japan revolution was the necessary prelude to a great modernizing drive which a generation later set off a wave of technological innovation and economic growth. The seventeenth-century English revolution, however, had no such dramatic economic and scientific consequences. The reason for the difference lies less in differing aspirations than in differing success. In Japan the revolutionary leaders retained control and imposed their will on their fellow samurai and the population at large. In England the revolutionary experiment failed, and was followed in 1660 by a restoration of the old order. In any case the road to reform was far less clear to Oliver Cromwell than it was to the Meiji leaders. The former had no model on which to base himself, the latter knew just what a modern society looked like, and how to get to it. And finally the powers of government were very much feebler in the case of Cromwell, despite his military dictatorship; the Meiji reformers had at their disposal a much more sophisticated and efficient bureaucracy. And so in England the drive for educational, social and legal reforms was defeated,

[17] Cipolla, *op. cit.*, pp. 120–1.
[18] For England, see Stone, *op. cit.*, *Past and Present*.

technological advance seems to have been halted, and the country went back to the traditional rule by a conservative landed elite trained in the classics. Not only were the numbers passing through the educational system cut back, but the Ancients defeated the Moderns and the curriculum in grammar schools and universities was preserved unaltered into the nineteenth century. There was a reaction in terms both of quantity and quality.

The third comparison is between the two societies in the nineteenth century. Up to the First World War England continued to be ruled mainly by the landed classes, and up to the Second mastery of the classics, with the emphasis on form rather than content, remained the basis of upper-class education. Deliberately revived by the Victorian public schools as a device for teaching the children of the *nouveau riches* the values and culture of the old landed classes, and for training them in self-discipline and public service, this education was perfectly designed to equip an elite with the stern moral qualities needed for the efficient and paternalist administration of a tropical empire. It also provided the instruction which made possible the introduction of a competitive examination system for the rationalized bureaucracy created by the Northcote-Trevelyan reforms of 1855–70, as well as for the scholarship examinations in reformed Oxford and Cambridge. The purpose, and the results, of these arrangements was to perpetuate the rule of the upper classes into the new era, as England's greatest historian, F. W. Maitland, realized only too well. When in 1905 he fought (and of course lost) a battle to remove compulsory Greek as a requirement for entry into Cambridge, he remarked that "at bottom this is a social question. . . . Having learnt—or what is precisely the same thing—pretended to learn, Greek has become a class distinction which is not to be obliterated." [19]

This combination of restriction to a wealthy elite of access to the higher educational process, of a classical, formalistic, literary, moralistic curriculum, and of competitive entry into the bureaucracy by examination in familiarity with this body of literature, provides a very close parallel indeed to the institutional arrangements of Imperial China.[20] Both were perfect examples of what has been described as "sponsored mobility." [21] The social structure and elite standards are preserved intact by a process of deliberate selection by the existing elite of a small minority of children from the lower classes at an early age, for socialization in elite values and training in elite culture. By this means, competition is restricted and hierarchy preserved, while allowing some selective upward mobility to occur so as to replenish elite losses in numbers and talents.

Though the pressures for reform in England were indigenous and based on a wish to preserve the power of the elite and yet provide an efficient administration to run the urbanized society at home and a distant empire overseas, the precise devices adopted to secure this end appear to have been based in no small

---

[19] Quoted by W. H. Dunham, from *The Letters of F. W. Maitland*, ed. C. S. H. Fifoot, in *The Yale Law Journal*, 75 (1965), p. 178.

[20] R. Wilkinson, *Gentlemanly Power* (Oxford, 1964).

[21] Ralph H. Turner, "Sponsored and Contest Mobility and the School System," *Am. Soc. Rev.*, XXV (1960), pp. 855–67.

degree on the Chinese precedents. These were adopted first in India, where the examination system had been in operation as early as 1833 and where Trevelyan had seen it at work.[22] Valuable though the system was in creating better and more honest administration, its functional utility to either England or China in meeting the technological needs of a modern industrial society seems to have been virtually nil.

If we turn from nineteenth-century England to nineteenth-century Japan, some very striking differences become apparent. Between 1750 and 1870 England developed into the first industrialized society in the world, but retained its aristocratic social structure and its dysfunctional elite educational system. Japan began the same process a hundred years later, with other models to choose from. It retained much of its aristocratic power structure, but destroyed the elite education, many elite social privileges, and much of the elite anti-bourgeois ideology, in order to break through into the modern world. A ruthlessly modernising section of the elite seized power in a highly authoritarian society, and deliberately discarded everything which did not contribute to strengthening the resources of the state. Thus both countries retained the traditional pattern of authority throughout the industrializing phase—a fact of some interest to theorists of economic growth. Mr. Dore is probably right to argue, with Veblen, that it was the superimposition of rapid industrialization and mobility on a hierarchic and highly deferential social structure ruled by a militarist caste which created the atmosphere and the tensions which provoked the nationalist/imperialist outbreaks of 1890–1914 in England and the 1930's and 1940's in Japan. But late nineteenth-century Japan rejected the Chinese model of education and administrative recruitment, largely because of its proven military weakness in the face of the western nations, just at the moment when England adopted some of the model's most essential features. Victorian England was devising an improved version of the past in the education of its elite, both in the clear class divisions that were preserved (and still persist), and in the classics-oriented curriculum, while Japan was proceeding in precisely the opposite direction.

In 1869 there was founded Tokyo University, whose teachings were specifically designed to combine Confucian morality with western technology, and a decade or so later to foster Japanese nationalism. A year earlier the great educator Fukuzawa Yūkichi founded the first private university, the Keiō Gijuku, with its watchwords of independence and practicality. By his extremely popular writings (he had sold ten million copies by 1897) and by his teaching at the school, he did much to effect the fundamental shift of attitudes which turned the Japanese business man from an object of social contempt to a highly respected and valuable member of the community. The creation among the samurai of this new mentality, and the stress on the need for higher education for business activity, contrasts sharply with the gentlemanly contempt for business prevalent among the classically-trained elite of Edwardian England,

---

[22] Ssu-Yu Teng, "Chinese Influence on the Western Examination System," *Harvard Journal of Asiatic Studies*, 7 (1943); Y. Z. Chang, "China and the English Civil Service Reform," *Am. Hist. Rev.*, XLVII (1942).

and with that scarcity of graduates in English business which persist to this day.[23] Finally, in 1872 there was decreed the abandonment in Japan of the two-class educational system, and the introduction, based on a model partly French and partly American, of a unified and universal school system for all. This is a step which England has not yet taken one hundred years later, although compulsory elementary education was introduced in both countries at the same time in 1870.

Why, then, did the Japanese samurai accept this radical transformation of the educational system and the consequent reduction of their prestige and privileges, whereas their Victorian counterparts in England devised new and ingenious ways to retain their position and to defy the values of the economic system upon which the power of their country was based? Mr. Dore argues that acquiescence in the changes by the samurai was due firstly to the belief in the efficacy of the educational process in inculcating obedience (they had not been taught, as the English upper classes had learned the hard way in the seventeenth century, to associate widespread lower class education with political and social radicalism); secondly, to the absence of that class war which was so marked a feature of nineteenth-century England (the 1,200 odd peasant revolts over the two and a half centuries of Tokugawa rule might seem to cast some doubt on this idyllic picture, but Mr. Dore dismisses them as the "sporadic tantrums of irresponsible children not symptoms of a growing systematic malaise"); thirdly, to their intense desire for national power, which could only be achieved by modernization and all that goes with it; and lastly to a Confucian sense of paternal responsibility. The most compelling reason was surely the third, the realization that mass education was a necessary basis for national power and wealth. The questions put to prominent American educational experts in 1872 by the Japanese Chargé d'Affaires in Washington, and the replies he received, show beyond doubt that it was the overwhelming desire for economic and military predominance which was the driving force behind the educational reforms of the time.[24] That the reforms succeeded in their task is strikingly suggested by the subsequent history of Japan.

If these are the facts of educational policy, and the reasons for them, what effect did they have upon modernization? No one has yet tried to argue that the classical and literary education provided by the eighteenth-century English grammar school, or the conservative and slothful atmosphere of eighteenth-century Oxbridge, had anything to do with England's economic takeoff. He would have a hard time if he did, for so many other, more convincing, factors can be adduced to explain it: long experience of technological innovation going back to the late sixteenth century; remarkable scientific progress in the seventeenth century (which took place largely, although not entirely, outside the conventional educational system); ample natural resources of iron and coal in close juxtaposition to good water communications; capital accumulation from colonial trade; and so on, and so on. Education was certainly a factor, but the

[23] Hirschmeier, op. cit., ch. V.
[24] Passin, pp. 212–25.

significant elements here were not the classical curriculum of the landed elite. Firstly, there was a high rate of literacy among the population at large, which may have been up to 50 percent among young rural males by 1770.[25] Secondly, a more rational and pragmatic educational system flourished in one provincial area—Scotland—whence a steady brain drain supplied eighteenth- and nineteenth-century England with so many of the professional and engineering cadres which she needed. Hardly any of the great Victorian industrial entrepreneurs had been exposed to the classical, gentlemanly English educational process.

If we turn to Japan, the first question is how Tokugawa education made possible the Meiji reforms and so prepared the way for the astonishing economic growth a generation later. The very high rate of literacy in the mid-nineteenth century clearly put Japan in a class by itself compared with any other non-Western country, and this must be a factor of the greatest importance. Mr. Dore rightly argues that it had four effects. It ensured "a positive attitude towards the process of deliberately acquiring new knowledge"; it is evidence of growing mobility aspirations, that could finally be realized after the crust of social conservatism was broken by the Meiji Restoration: the idea of progress had already been implanted in Japanese minds; it widened the net of potential talent whence the future leaders of modernizing Japan could be drawn, as is shown by the fact that about a quarter of the leading entrepreneurs of the early Meiji era came from the peasantry;[26] lastly it accustomed the population to being governed by the written word.

But what of the training of the elite, the samurai? As we have seen, their education, like that of their counterparts in England, was ethical in objective, repetitive and unquestioning in method, and classical in content. According to Mr. Dore, however, this backward-looking education also played its part.[27] The most persuasive arguments depend on the quantity of education rather than the quality, in that the mere fact of being given some kind of mental training, whatever its content, accustoms men to the idea that education is normal and desirable in itself. It is more difficult, however, to explain the beneficial effects of this particular type of education. Mr. Dore's first argument is based on a Darwinian—or Toynbeean—theory of the survival of the fittest, namely that *some* survived the system with their intellectual curiosity not only unimpaired but positively stimulated by the challenge (just as *some* survived, and survive, a classical education at an English public school). Secondly, Mr. Jansen has emphasized that a very strong competitive instinct developed in these schools—much stronger than in their English counterparts, where competition was largely confined to the playing fields—and this was an important factor in creating the atmosphere of an "Achieving Society." The world view of Confucianism was basically rational, and therefore well adapted, in Weberian

[25] J. D. Chambers, "Three Essays on the Population and Economy of the Midlands," in D. V. Glass and D. E. C. Eversley, *Population in History* (London, 1965), p. 330, n. 13.
[26] Hirschmeier, *op. cit.*, p. 249.
[27] Mr. Dore's arguments are more clearly developed in his article in M. B. Jansen, ed., *Changing Japanese Attitudes toward Modernization.*

terms, for the modern world. There were, as Mr. Albert Craig has recently shown, few theological obstacles in neo-Confucianism to the reception of modern science, and the type of religious opposition which Galileo or Darwin encountered in Christian Europe did not occur in Confucian Japan.[28]

This argument makes very good sense, although it is an observed fact that modernization is not dependent on a *uniformly* rational view-point. In Japan the modernizing process was accompanied by a rapid growth in Shintoism deliberately fostered as an ideal tool for developing a national consciousness and national unity. Although its functional utility is beyond question, the fact remains that Emperor-worship was essentially irrational and primitive in outlook and played an important part in the outburst of nationalist excess and reckless military aggression of the early twentieth century. What needs explaining, moreover, is why Confucianism aided assimilation of western ideas in Japan, but in China acted as a mental block.

If nationalism, the lust for imperial military greatness, was the driving force for educational change, a further question is what it was that induced the samurai to study and to imitate western technology with such astonishing assiduity and lack of xenophobic jealousy. Twelve percent of the first educational budget of the Meiji era, and 2 percent of the total budget, was spent on sending Japanese students abroad to pick the brains of the West. Another 10 percent of the Ministry of Education's budget went on salaries to foreign teachers of languages, medicine, science and even philosophy and the law. Thus when the Ministry of Public Works set up a technical training department in 1871, it was entirely staffed by Englishmen and it was not until the 1880's that the number of foreign educators in Japan began to decline. One suggestion is that it was the very subservience and humility induced by the practice of unquestioning rote-learning in the educational process which made it psychologically easy for the Japanese to copy so enthusiastically the ideas and inventions of others. Just as it was the Tokugawa "training to be trained" which prepared the way for educational expansion, so it was the respect for knowledge, whatever its sources, which was responsible for the inclusion among the five articles of the Meiji Charter Oath of the objective of seeking knowledge throughout the world as a means of strengthening the Imperial throne.

If we turn to Victorian England we find that it had a ruling class with similar national aspirations, encouraged by a very similar educational process, but one which lacked the zeal for technological education and the willingness to learn by the experience of other nations which characterized the Japanese leaders. Even the introduction of examinations for the home civil service was resisted for fifteen years on the simple grounds that "the plan is Chinese," an objection which would have been utterly incomprehensible to the Japanese.[29] This resistance to alien ideas derived from the self-evident fact that mid-Victorian England had indeed very little to learn from foreigners about

---

[28] A. Craig, "Science and Confucianism in Tokugawa Japan," in Jansen, ed., *op. cit.*
[29] Ssu-Yu Teng, *op. cit.*, p. 304.

anything, from constitutions to locomotives. The memory of this remarkable era of intellectual, political and technical supremacy survived in the minds of Englishmen long after the reality had fled, whereas the Japanese had no such period of undoubted superiority to look back to, and were prepared to go to any lengths to maintain and strengthen their national independence and strength. Furthermore this English memory of past supremacy was strongly reinforced by the self-conscious amateurism and insular nationalism induced by a public school classical education, to which every successful late Victorian entrepreneur inevitably subjected the heirs to his fortune and his business. It was just at the peak of England's imperial expansion, at the end of the nineteenth century, that English industrial growth began to lag, that conservatism and inertia began to be the hallmark of the English entrepreneurial class. Whereas the reforming Japanese samurai launched a massive drive for university expansion and technological education copied from the various nations of the West, the English public school-trained leaders retained the elitist view of higher education as a preserve of the few, and their traditional snobbish contempt for base mechanic arts (now reinforced by the anti-materialist ideas of Matthew Arnold). By 1900 English university education was quantitatively beginning to fall behind those of America, France, and Germany and it was turning out far fewer chemists and engineers than its main economic rivals. Such was the cult of the amateur and the domination of classical studies in English universities that even in the humane field of history the lead had passed to Germany, where the professional training of the Ph.D. was now in full swing. As a result, entrepreneurship still existed in late Victorian England, but it took the form of organizational innovations in mass production and distribution, introduced by lower middle class men like Lipton, Guinness, Boot or Courtauld, men who had not been stamped in the classical public school and Oxbridge mould. It was the older businesses which stagnated, as the children of their creators absorbed the upper class ethic and turned their energies to social climbing, philanthropy and politics.[30]

A final question is why the Japanese samurai found it relatively easy to shed their classical educational system, whereas the English upper classes have clung to it with such extraordinary persistence. Here one can do little more than speculate, but it may be that it was the sheer arcaneness of classical Chinese scholarship, its utter remoteness from Japanese past history and contemporary experience which created that extraordinary compartmentalization which is such a feature of the modern Japanese mind. This habit of keeping different areas of knowledge and ideas quite distinct from one another may have helped samurai trained in the traditional way to grasp for the technology of the West, however alien it might be to them, and to copy without shame or embarrassment the inventions and institutions of other cultures as a means to the end of their own rampant nationalism.

The two other societies with a classical educational tradition were far less

---

[30] D. H. Aldcroft, "The Entrepreneur and the British Economy, 1870–1914," *Econ. Hist. Rev.*, 2nd Ser., XVII (1) (1964); C. H. Wilson, "Economy and Society in Late Victorian England," *loc. cit.*, XVIII (1) (1965).

conscious of the arcaneness of their studies, and so were under less pressure to compartmentalize. To the Chinese, the classics were a vital and living part of their own historical tradition, and for centuries cultural pride prevented them from assimilating western ideas. To the English the classics were in fact foreign, but they contrived to identify themselves with the classical world by various devices. In the sixteenth century, when the curriculum was first introduced, they did it (or some of them did) by developing the twelfth-century legend of the descent of the royal dynasty from Brutus, a Trojan fleeing from the doomed city after the Homeric siege. The Arthurian legend was dragged in to provide a Romano-British link, and in no time at all Queen Elizabeth found herself supplied with a coat of arms displaying her distinguished classical ancestry—including a quartering with the letters S.P.Q.R. [*Senatus Populusque Romanus*] on a diagonal bar.[31]

At the end of the nineteenth century the late Victorians and Edwardians could, and did, identify their society with that of Periclean Athens in its ideals and its constitutional arrangements, and with Augustan Rome in its sense of imperial mission. Both political parties found what they wanted in the classics. Fifth-century Greece appealed particularly to young Liberals like Richard Livingstone and Alfred Zimmern, the former going so far as to declare: "Trust in the people, tempered by caution, was Mr. Gladstone's definition of Liberalism. Leave out the three last words and you have the principles of Pericles." The role of slavery in Greek society was explained away by the assertion that "the difference between our industrial classes and the Greek slave is spiritual rather than material." Imperial Rome was naturally more attractive to Tories, and both scholars and pro-consuls—Lords Bryce and Cromer and Sir Charles Lucas—busied themselves with reinterpreting the Roman Empire in the light of the problems and aspirations of the British nearly 2000 years later. Moreover both groups could appreciate the sense of natural superiority over other peoples that runs through the Periclean funeral oration, and much of Roman literature. Thus the Edwardian ruling class responded immediately to the ideas which they thought they could extract from a reading of the classics: the cult of the amateur, the contempt for bourgeois activities, values and persons, the sense of national superiority and imperial responsibility, the idealization of such wholly masculine communities as the public school, the university and the army. Although even the defenders of the system were critical of the emphasis in the curriculum on form rather than content, a defect which if anything got worse as the twentieth century wore on, they were nevertheless firmly convinced that there was no incompatibility between a classical education and a modern, competitive, scientific, and industrial nation.[32]

---

[31] T. D. Kendrick, *British Antiquity* (London, 1950), pl. XI b.

[32] R. W. Livingstone, *The Greek Genius and its Meaning to Us* (London, 1912), p. 68 (see also pp. 239–50); *A Defence of Classical Education* (London, 1916), p. 187; A. E. Zimmern, *The Greek Commonwealth* (Oxford, 1911); P. A. Brunt, "Reflections on British and Roman Imperialism," *Comparative Studies in Society and History*, VII (1965), p. 227. The remark by Livingstone should be compared with the line taken by aristocratic apologists for the Southern Way of Life in the United States over the last hundred years (e.g., George Fitzhugh, *Sociology for the South, or the Failure of Free Society*, Richmond, 1854).

Apart from this highly speculative hypothesis, it is difficult to see, on the basis of the evidence supplied by Mr. Dore, that the character of traditional samurai education can have had any effect in creating this far-reaching difference of attitudes of English and Japanese elites towards industry and technology. And so it looks very much as if, in Japan as in England, technical innovation and entrepreneurial initiative occurred in spite of rather than because of the elite educational system, and under the leadership either of men trained outside the system altogether, as in England, or partly of outsiders and partly of men in open rebellion against their background and education, as in post-1868 Japan. Indeed other writers have pointed not to the survival but to the breakdown of the old educational system in the mid-nineteenth century and to the introduction of Japanese and western studies as key factors in the new situation. This certainly seems a more reasonable hypothesis and one which conforms more closely with the observed facts.[33] Mr. Dore himself concludes his more recent article with these apologetic words about the training of the elite: "It was a type of education which had to go in a modernizing country, but at least it had the honor to carry the seeds of its own destruction." It was England's misfortune that the seeds of destruction of a similar type of education, if seeds there were, should have fallen upon such stony ground.

[33] Hall, *op. cit.*; Hirschmeier, *op. cit.*, chs. V, VII.

Medicine, Modernization, and Cultural Crisis in China and India

Ralph C. Croizier

Early writers on modernization used to draw sharp distinctions between "traditional" and "modern" values and institutions, but this approach soon gave way to the realization that the interaction between the old and the new is a continuing one. Indeed, the very capacity of a society to undertake transformation depends on the ability of its leaders to maintain confidence in their policies, and to do this they must appeal to loyalties that often have deep roots in premodern values and institutions. The fact that in China and India indigenous premodern medicine has not only survived but receives strong official support is an interesting example of the continuing struggle of old and new.

Students of modernization commonly assume that, whatever else from the West may be rejected or modified to fit particular cultural and political preferences, science and technology are essential for any conscious effort to transform a traditional society. Indeed, despite the Western origins of modern science, would-be modernizers in Asia and Africa can reasonably claim that science is now universal. The degree to which it is possessed and practiced in various countries may differ, but in principle the spirit, methodology, and fruits of modern science are cosmopolitan, not bound to any particular culture. They are the legitimate property of all men aspiring to be modern. And from Tokyo to Nairobi all such men have passionately sought to possess them.

It is also commonly assumed that the dramatic advance of medical knowledge in the last century is one of the foremost achievements of modern science. Moreover, it is an achievement especially relevant to the massive health problems of the underdeveloped world and to the responsibilities of

"Medicine, Modernization, and Cultural Crisis in China and India" by Ralph C. Croizier is reprinted by permission of Cambridge University Press from *Comparative Studies in Society and History*, XII (July 1970), 275–296.

Croizier is professor of history at the University of Rochester, author of *Traditional Medicine and Modern China: Science, Nationalism, and the Tension of Cultural Change* (1968), and editor of *China's Cultural Legacy and Communism* (1969).

the new national governments there. Thus, both for its close association with science in general and for its special relevance to humanistic and national-istic goals, medicine would appear to be a vital part of modern science and technology. Of course, one might expect some resistance to modern medicine at the popular level when traditional habits and beliefs inhibit rapid ac-ceptance of new practices. Numerous anthropological field studies have shown that the close connection of health and illness concepts with cultural beliefs makes medical acculturation one of the less easily introduced technological changes in a traditional society.[1] Yet, at the level of the modernizing political and intellectual elite, one expects complete and unambivalent support for modern medicine.

However, the modern history of the two largest nations in Asia some-what belies such expectations. In China and India a substantial portion of the intelligentsia continues to defend the indigenous pre-scientific medical systems against replacement by modern medicine, and modernizing govern-ments give legal, financial, and institutional support to traditional medicine. The paradox lies not in how so much of the traditional medical beliefs and practices survives alongside newly introduced modern medicine (this is com-mon enough in the most modernized industrial societies), but in how traditional pre-scientific systems of medicine can continue to find strong sup-port among a pro-scientific modernizing elite. This has not happened, in any meaningful way, in either the modern West or in most of Asia and Africa.[2] But it is an unmistakable feature of recent Chinese and Indian history. The obvious question is, why?

First, we should note that it was only in traditional China and India that, independent of Europe, there developed well-integrated medical systems with a sophisticated theoretical basis preserved in a formal literary tradition. This cannot be said of the third great system of traditional medicine in Asia, Arabic, for it shares common Greek roots with European medicine. As for the rest of Asia, pre-modern medicine was largely derivative from one or more of these great traditions. Thus, only in India and in China has traditional medicine been a purely indigenous product contending against a foreign intruder on its own soil.

But this is only part of the total picture in these two countries, for the medical confrontation has taken place in the context of a much more general

[1] For China and India two interesting studies are Francis L. K. Hsu, *Magic and Science in Western Yunnan* (New York, 1943) and McKim Marriott, 'Western Medicine in a Village of Northern India,' in Benjamin Paul, ed., *Health, Culture and Community* (New York, 1955), pp. 239–68.

[2] Medical subcultures such as homeopathy, nature cures, or faith healing in the West, present a qualitatively different phenomenon. They do not enjoy 'respectable' support in their societies, and adherence to them by socially and intellectually respectable figures is dismissed as personal eccentricity. As for the persistence of selective use of primitive medicine by modern leaders in most Asian and African countries, this too is mainly at the private, personal level and not part of their public image and public policy. Cambridge or Sorbonne trained Prime Ministers in Africa may still half believe in certain witch doctor remedies, but they do not support schools and institutes to preserve the witch-doctors' medical 'system.'

crisis. In both these proud and ancient centers of Asian civilization (historically much more accustomed to the role of culture givers than receivers) the shock of massive cultural borrowing necessitated by Western material and technical superiority has been profound. At the heart of the cultural crisis so engendered has been the dilemma of how to take so much of Western institutions, techniques, and values and still remain faithful to one's own cultural identity—in a semantic formula popular since World War II, how to modernize without Westernizing, or more accurately, how to maintain the stamp of a distinctive national identity on the new culture one is building.

This has been a common problem throughout the non-Western world. As modern currents dissolve the traditional culture a new sense of nationalism has arisen which, in the name of national self-respect, makes elements of that traditional culture all the more precious, or even sacrosanct, as hallmarks of national identity. But in China and India this compulsion has, perhaps, been stronger than elsewhere. In any event, it is only there that it has strongly manifested itself in the medical field.

Before examining how this has occurred in modern China and India, it may be helpful to take a brief look at their respective medical traditions. Above all, neither of these medical systems should be confused with the 'primitive medicine' of traditional peasant society. Several features distinguish them from such simpler forms of medicine. First, there is a complex and predominantly rational theoretical basis. Second, it is contained in a large corpus of medical 'classics' of great antiquity. Third, the theoretical principles are intimately related to the dominant cosmological concepts of the society and its cultural values. Fourth, there exists a class of secular medical practitioners who are guardians of the classic medical tradition. This class of physicians stands apart from the common folk medicine practitioners of the society whose practices are often distorted reflections of the high medical tradition. Moreover, in his command of a literary tradition, the physician has pretensions to scholarly standing but suffers from the artisan, or tradesman, associations of practicing medicine as a profession. All of this makes the great pre-modern medical systems—Galenic in Medieval Europe, Arabic in the Middle East, Indian and Chinese in further Asia—as different from primitive or folk medicine as they are from modern scientific medicine.

In both China and India such well developed systems are very old. The Chinese attributed the origins of their medical tradition to the legendary culture heroes *Shen Nung* and *Huang-ti* of the third millennium B.C. In India the name of traditional Hindu medicine, Ayurveda (The Veda of Life), reveals its origins in the shadowy Vedic period of Indian history before 1000 B.C. during which Hindu religion and culture took form. Both emerge into the light of history as definite medical systems considerably later with the appearance of great physician-authors and the medical classics upon which subsequent generations of secular physicians based their practice. In China, the main period of this codification is the Han dynasty (206 B.C.–A.D. 220);

in India, the three greatest Ayurvedic classics appeared during the first six centuries of the Christian era.[3]

As for their theoretical principles, both may be said to have basically a homeostatic concept of health and disease. Health consists of maintaining a harmony or equilibrium within the human organism and disease is the result of physical or psychic (this allows for moral factors) disturbance of such equilibrium. Chinese medical theory discusses this in terms of the constant interaction of the dual forces in the universe, *yin* and *yang*, plus the flow through the body of that vital life force, *ch'i* (perhaps best translated as pneuma). This *ch'i* circulates in accordance with the mutual production order of the five elements (wood, fire, earth, metal, and water) out of which the universe—including the human microcosm of it—is composed. In Ayurveda homeostatic concept also lies behind a humoural physiology and pathology based on the three body fluids of air, bile, and phlegm. Apparently of early Buddhistic origins this theory of the three humours (*tridosha*) out-dates comparable Greek concepts.[4] On the basis of such theories (in both countries closely connected with prevailing cosmological ideas) elaborate physiological constructs were built with a subsequent neglect of practical anatomical investigation which led to an uncritical acceptance of past authority unparalleled even in the heyday of Galenic anatomy in Medieval Europe. In both societies religious taboos against dissection were contributing factors, but even more so the neglect of empirical anatomy reflects a general cultural conservatism and scholasticism.

Medical practice was highly deductive from the theoretical concepts. Thus, the frequent assertions by modern apologists that these are empirical systems of medicine need serious qualifying. This does not mean that both have not incorporated a great deal of empirical experiences within their respective deductive and speculative theoretical frameworks. For instance, in diagnostics both have highly developed the art of observing symptoms. But there is also a strong tendency to systematize and force these into the prevailing theoretical framework. Similarly Chinese and Indian medical tradition each has accumulated an enormous materia medica including many indisputably effective drugs which are administered either as specifics or more typically used in polypharmacy. Again, however, it should be remembered that the principles behind their prescription for recognized symptoms are far from empirical. There are also many other useful techniques for maintaining and restoring health, such as massage, yoga, exercises, and dietetics which

---

[3] Most supposedly universal medical histories still reveal a strong Western provincialism by giving very cursory treatment to classical Asian medical systems. The most distinguished work on Indian medicine is J. Filliozat, *The Classical Doctrine of Indian Medicine: Its Origins and Greek Parallels* (Delhi, 1964). Also useful is Henry Zimmer, *Hindu Medicine* (Baltimore, 1948). Available Western language works on China medicine are quite unsatisfactory. Perhaps still the best survey is Wong Chi-min and Wu Lien-te, *A History of Chinese Medicine* (Tientsin, 1932). Much more comprehensive and reliable is Ch'en Pang-hsien, *Chung-Kuo I-hsueh Shih* (*A History of Medicine in China*) (Shanghai, 1937).

[4] Filliozat.

have, at least partially, established their value in modern medical eyes. But probably the most fascinating therapeutic technique of Chinese medicine, acupuncture, has yet to prove its effectiveness by scientific criteria.

In sum, then, although the traditional medical systems of China and India are far from simple folk medicines, they are also obviously unscientific (or perhaps better, pre-scientific) in basis, no matter how many of their specific practices may be of real medical value. They are also almost entirely deficient in surgery. And, more serious for modern national health concerns, they lack any effective means for combating epidemics because of their lack of a germ theory of disease. That these two traditional medical systems should show considerable survival power in popular acceptance is to be expected; that they should offer a great deal of interest to medical historians and scientists alike is not at all surprising. But the kind of attention given to traditional medicine in both modern China and India is quite remarkable—and also significant for the recent cultural and intellectual history of both countries.

There has been a broadly similar pattern in the development of the movements for Chinese medicine and for Ayurveda. First, traditional practitioners took the decidedly untraditional step of organizing into professional associations to combat the threat of government support for modern medicine. Next, defense of 'national medicine' was taken up, as part of the modern nationalist movement, by political and intellectual figures far removed from the medical world. This, in turn, provoked a long, sometimes bitter, and generally indecisive debate between supporters and opponents of the traditional medical system.

In India, pro-Ayurveda agitation had the advantage of a foreign political power which could be charged with trampling Indian medicine along with Indian culture in general. Ever since the early nineteenth-century triumph of the Anglicists over the Orientalists in determining educational policy in India the British *raj* had exclusively supported modern medicine. Except for the small new urban elite, Hindu Ayurveda and Moslem Unani (a variety of Arabic medicine) persisted in common practice, but the official course was clearly set for eventual replacement of the old by the new, the native by the foreign. This long-range threat to their existence led the indigenous practitioners (*vaidyas*) to form the All-India Ayurvedic Congress in 1907. From 1920 on the most powerful nationalist body, the Indian National Congress, at least formally took up the cause of Indian medicine by annually passing resolutions calling for government support of 'Native Indian Medicine'.[5]

---

[5] The first chapter of the Udupa Committee report gives a cursory history of the Ayurvedic movement. Government of India, Ministry of Health, *Report of the Committee to Assess and Evaluate the Present Status of the Ayurvedic System of Medicine* (Delhi, 1959?). A more comprehensive and analytical account is given in Paul Brass, 'The Politics of Ayurvedic Education: A Case Study of Revivalism and Modernization in India,' essay prepared for forthcoming volume on *Education and Politics* edited by Lloyd and Susanne Rudolph. There is also the work of Charles Leslie including 'The Professionalization of Ayurvedic and Unani Medicine,' *Transactions of the New York Academy of Sciences*, Ser. II, Vol. 30, No. 4 (February, 1968), pp. 559–72 and 'The Rhetoric of the Ayurvedic Revival in Modern

Likewise in China it was the old-style physicians who first set up the cry to save native medicine from the hostile intentions of political authorities. After the Minister of Education in the new Republican Government had declared that replacement of traditional with modern medicine would be official policy, alarmed practitioners formed a political lobby, 'The Chinese Doctor's Committee to Save Medicine', in 1915. Partly because of the chaotic political situation, this and subsequent traditional associations of physicians lacked the organizational continuity of the All-India Ayurvedic Congress, but in purpose and composition they closely resembled the Indian organization. Chinese medicine also quickly attracted much broader support from a wide variety of cultural nationalists. They included such diverse figures as the warlord governor of Shansi province, Yen Hsi-shan, and the veteran Nationalist revolutionary, Chang Ping-lin. Only after the founding of the Nationalist Government in 1927, however, was this generalized support able to find a politically effective organizational focus in the Kuo I Kuan (Institute for National Medicine), with the right-wing Kuomintang politician Chiao I-t'ang as its President and both the Ch'en brothers, Ch'en Kuo-fu and Ch'en Li-fu, on its board of directors.[6]

Thus by the 1920s traditional medicine had found a home within the leading political party of each country's nationalist movement. Moreover, the goals, arguments, and rhetoric of its supporters were remarkably similar. While in both countries there were traditionalists who defied science and modernity, this was distinctly a minority viewpoint, especially in China. Much more common was a willingness, even eagerness, to criticize serious shortcomings in the present state of traditional medicine and stress the need for drastic reforms. Frequently this took the form of indirect praise through direct criticism. Present-day practice of Chinese medicine, or Ayurveda, was condemned: there were many ignorant quacks, practitioners jealously guarded trade secrets instead of altruistically serving humanity, much of the wisdom of the past had been lost or distorted by later corruptions. But all these defects were signs of decadence for which, in part, foreign rulers (Moslems and British in India, less plausibly Manchus in China) could conveniently be blamed. The present task was to recover the precious essence of the traditional medical wisdom from the dross that had accumulated around it. Real traditionalists stopped there with the classical revivalist formula, Hindu and Confucian, for returning to a lost excellence of antiquity.

But more common, and more influential in the twentieth century, was a new type of nationalistic conservative whose main concern was not the pristine purity of tradition, but rather the preservation of a national cultural

---

India,' Royal Anthropological Institute, *Proceedings*, No. 82 (May, 1963), pp. 72–3. I am grateful to Professor Leslie for first calling my attention to the Ayurvedic movement and its parallels with developments in China.

[6] The developments of support for Chinese medicine is discussed in detail in my study, *Traditional Medicine in Modern China: Science, Nationalism, and the Tensions of Cultural Change* (Cambridge, Mass., 1968), especially in Part Two, 'Medicine as a Cultural and Intellectual Issue,' pp. 59–150.

identity in a period of far-reaching foreign inspired change. He too might frequently talk about decay and the need for cultural renaissance, but he also felt the need to come to terms with things like science, progress, and modernity. This meant that he was receptive to very substantial changes so long as they did not seem to entail repudiation of the national tradition. In medicine it meant that he was receptive to adopting all the institutional apparatus of modern medicine—hospitals, clinics, legal standards, professional organizations—to serve the improvement and hence preservation of the national medicine. Even more important it meant that he was anxious to somehow incorporate modern science into the traditional medical system. This was no mean feat since there was the danger that once one started modernizing, or 'scientificizing', Ayurveda or Chung I, modern science would completely absorb the traditional medicine leaving nothing of a distinctive national tradition except a few specific drugs and remedies. There were plenty of modernists, especially those with a Western scientific education, who wanted just that, but it was not what medical nationalists had in mind. When they spoke of an integrated Ayurveda or a synthesis of Chinese and Western medicine they wanted a true synthesis that would take the best of Western medicine and modern science without completely eclipsing the essential elements of the unique national tradition.

For example, one of the earliest and most articulate exponents of integrated Ayurveda, Srinisava Murti, was convinced that the Indian system was basically scientific in spirit, that its apparently mystical and non-scientific theory really referred to natural physiological processes not yet completely understood in Western medicine.[7] Hence a purified Ayurveda, stripped of superstitious accretions, was eminently compatible with modern science—was in fact scientific—and could be combined in a common medical curriculum with Western medicine. The Government School of Indian Medicine, opened in Madras in 1925, was an attempt to implement and prove this view. Until very recently it was to remain the dominant one in the modern Ayurveda movement.

It has also been the prevailing view among defenders of Chinese medicine ever since the 1920s, especially in organizations like the Kuo I Kuan. The numerous writings on the subject by Ch'en Kuo-fu provide an excellent illustration of the attempts to reconcile the conflicting claims of modernity and cultural tradition.[8] Ch'en was convinced that it could be done in Chinese medicine where the proposed synthesis would produce a new and better medical system, scientific but still recognizably Chinese. This would be proof of the national genius in a sphere where modernists had found China's tradition sadly deficient. Moreover, as a contribution to world medical science it would help redress the balance of scientific and technological borrowing

[7] See his 'Memorandum on the Synthesis of Indian and Western Medicine,' in Government of India, Ministry of Health, Report of the Committee on Indigenous Systems of Medicine (Delhi, 1948), Vol. 2, pp. 256–77.

[8] Most of these appear in Ch'en Kuo-fu Hsien-Sheng Ch'üan-chi (Complete Works of Mr. Ch'en Kuo-fu) (Hong Kong, 1952), Vol. 6.

from the West. Although at times medical particularism would obscure this argument (Chinese, or Indian, medicine is best for us; Western medicine is best for Westerners) the satisfaction of showing the West that Asians too could find something of scientific value in their own national tradition made this theme very popular among nationalists in China and India alike.

In fact, the ring of nationalistic pride is unmistakable in the rhetoric on behalf of both Chinese medicine and Ayurveda. It can be seen even in the semantic controversy over what to call the foreign and indigenous medical systems. The very term 'Chinese medicine', (*Chung I*) is a neologism of nineteenth-century origins invented to distinguish the old from the new medicine introduced by medical missionaries and called *Hsi I*, 'Western medicine'. The self-conscious attachment to a particular tradition implicit in this recognition of 'Chinese' and 'Western' is in itself indicative of a fundamental shift in Chinese perspectives; the far more blatant association of medicine with nationalism in the term *Kuo I*, 'National medicine', carried this a step further by the end of the 1920s. In India the presence of Moslem culture in general and Unani medicine in particular gave Hindus a much earlier awareness of cultural differences. Nevertheless, there too the last century has seen a semantic battle with the Ayurvedists insisting on the term allopathy for standard Western medicine despite modern doctors' claims that 'scientific, or 'modern', medicine is more accurate.[9]

The similarity between the Indian and Chinese native medical movements in the decades prior to World War II extends beyond common arguments and patterns of support to the concrete demands made on the political authorities for supporting the respective systems of national medicine. In Nationalist China, The Institute for National Medicine (by far the most influential lobby for Chinese medicine) continually pressured the Government and ruling party on the two key issues of legal recognition and governmental financial support. On the first issue it was successful in securing virtually full legal equality for traditional practitioners with their modern counterparts. On the second, despite getting favorable resolutions passed at several Kuomintang Party Congresses, the supporters of Chinese medicine got less satisfaction. The key Ministries of the central government, Health and Education, were controlled by Western-educated modernists with little sympathy for the claims of traditional medicine. In fact, broad sections of the progressive intelligentsia and of the left-wing of the Kuomintang were strongly opposed to any concessions at all to what they saw as conservative obstruction of the growth of science in China. Eventually political pressure forced the granting of limited support for a semi-public, semi-private hospital and research center of 'National medicine' in Nanking, but the outbreak of war in August 1917 shelved all such plans.

[9] The use of the term allopathy also dates from the nineteenth century when it was used to distinguish regular Western medicine from homeopathy which has enjoyed considerable popularity in India. The retention of 'allopathy' in the Ayurvedists' terminology reflects their concern lest Western physicians appropriate the word 'scientific' solely for their own. This, in itself, is a significant indication of value changes in modern India.

Ayurvedic supporters in India ran into the same type of opposition, not just from British administrators but also from adherents of modern medicine within the Indian Nationalist movement. This split among modern Indian Nationalists over the Ayurvedic revival (symptomatic of the broader split over traditional culture) came into the open with partial Indian control over many provincial governmental matters under the dyarchy of the 1920s. To the dismay and chagrin of Ayurvedists they found many Indian political leaders no more sympathetic to the claims of Indian national medicine than the British had been. The sense of cultural betrayal is evident in charges against Westernized figures like Nehru, denounced as 'an idolized political demagog' who did not understand that 'political emancipation divorced of cultural freedom is not actual liberty of a nation'.[10] Similar charges echo these sentiments in China. For example, the militantly modern educator Fu Ssu-nien was characterized as a Chinese who 'except for the yellow color of his face, which for all his foreign clothes cannot be changed, has in thought, life and habits become completely Americanized'.[11]

The split between traditionalists and modernizers (or, more accurately, between those who thought traditional medicine could be modernized and those who did not) meant that most of the 'Ayurvedic revival' in India remained in private hands—establishing medical societies, journals, private schools, clinics, and hospitals—just as similar modernizing reforms of Chinese medicine had to depend on non-official organizations like the Institute for National Medicine. However, the federal structure of Indian politics permitted more regional variation. In a few provinces, Madras for example, Indian-run provincial governments gave recognition and financial aid to Ayurvedic institutions. But even there modern Western medicine had first call on government support.

Independence brought to a head the issue of what an Indian Government should do for native Indian medicine.[12] There has ensued a prolonged and indecisive struggle not unlike that waged in Nationalist China after 1927 between supporters and opponents of Chinese medicine.[13] The alignment of forces is indeed familiar: on the one side the scientifically oriented professional staff of the Government's Health Ministry and the more Westernized or cosmopolitan wing of the Congress Party, on the other side organized native physicians and their political allies. The political patrons of Ayurveda, however, are a much more heterogeneous group ideologically than were the right-wing Kuomintang adherents of Chinese medicine. This diversity is perhaps symbolized by the two most powerful patrons within Congress,

10 'Ayurveda and Congress President,' *Journal of Ayurveda*, Vol. 14, No. 8 (February, 1938), pp. 281–2.

11 'Hua-pei Kuo-i Lun-chan Shu-chi' ('A Record of the National Medicine Debate in North China'); *Ming-jih I-yao (Tomorrow's Medicine)*, Vol. 1, No. 1 (1935), p. 5.

12 After partition, this has meant almost entirely Ayurveda. Unani continues to exist in India but it obviously has no appeal to Indian nationalism.

13 There are faint echoes of this controversy in Taiwan since 1949, but the Government has generally given unequivocal support to modern medicine. See Croizier, *Traditional Medicine in Modern China*, Ch. X.

Deputy Prime Minister Morarji Desai on the far right and former Home Minister Gulzarilal Nanda on the socialist left. Outside of Congress, Ayurveda has drawn support from the conservative Hindu *Jan Sangh* party but also from individual socialists and even some Communists.[14] Actually the division between supporters and opponents of the Ayurvedic movement seems to be far less political than cultural. The former are generally much more traditional, or nativist, in their cultural orientation; the latter frequently are educated abroad and in any case firmly cosmopolitan and scientific in outlook.

These conflicting attitudes towards native medicine have produced a series of five major Government of India investigating committees during the period 1948–63. Their recommendations have varied widely from gradual replacement of native physicians while scientifically studying traditional drugs to support for the integrated Ayurveda approach, or even to a separate but equal status for Ayurveda in the total Indian health plan. At the national level not very much concrete action has come out of all this. In 1953 there was a Central Institute of Research in Indigenous Systems of Medicine established, and Ayurveda enjoys some recognition in the Ministry of Health, but it still occupies a very second-class status relative to modern medicine both in prestige and financial support.[15] More substantial governmental support for Ayurveda has come at the provincial level where, under the Indian constitution, a great deal of the actual power for developing and regulating medicine resides. Several important states including Uttar Pradesh, Gujarat, Punjab, and Kerala have given considerable support to Ayurvedic institutions. In most states, however, the Ayurvedic *vaidyas* and their schools occupy a very secondary position to their modern counterparts.

In fact, most of the nearly 100 schools and over 5,000 hospitals and clinics which represent the fruits of over half a century's efforts to modernize Ayurveda are still basically private institutions, many of them of a very low quality.[16] Moreover, the results of this institutional modernization have been far from satisfactory for the grand objective of producing a revitalized Indian medicine capable of holding its own against imported competition. It has not given the new Ayurvedic college-trained doctors equal status or prestige with their Western medicine counterparts; it has not achieved anything approaching full integration between the principles of Ayurveda and Western medicine. Finally, most alarming of all to cultural nationalists, several of the integrated colleges have dropped most of the Ayurvedic courses from their curriculum in response to student agitation for more scientific medicine.[17] Naturally Ayurvedists blame this on continuing governmental discrimination against Ayurvedic college graduates in competition with modern doctors, but the fact remains that taught in combination with Western medicine Ayurveda tends to be displaced.

[14] Brass, 'The Politics of Ayurvedic Education,' p. 46.

[15] For example, the third five-year plan allots less than 3 percent of total health expenditures specifically for Ayurveda. India, Planning Commission, *Third Five-Year Plan*, p. 651.

[16] Brass, p. 11.

[17] Leslie, 'Rhetoric of the Ayurvedic Revival,' p. 73.

This danger to India's medical tradition, coupled with frustration over failure to get unequivocal governmental support for preserving Ayurveda, has turned a large segment of the Ayurvedic movement completely away from the goal of integration, though not from the goal of institutional modernization. This Shuddha (pure) Ayurveda movement formally began with a conference of disgruntled practitioners and sympathizers at Bombay in 1952. The ideals set forth were to purify Ayurveda from its harmful contact with Western medicine by reverting to old-style teaching methods (the revered teacher-disciple relationship) and eliminating all modern subjects from the curriculum. The desirability and possibility of synthesis, or integration, was explicitly denied. Yet, despite these reactionary goals, the Shuddha Ayurvedists have also tried to come to terms with the institutional and organizational aspects of modernity. They too have supported schools, hospitals, professional organizations, government-imposed standardization of practitioners (according to their standards of course)—all very untraditional measures for avowed traditionalists.

This rather atavistic movement has met with considerable success in the last seventeen years, partly because of the pragmatic adoption of modern techniques and partly as a focus for general cultural conservatism. By 1958, about one-third of the Ayurvedic schools were 'pure',[18] several of these receiving provincial government recognition. At the national level, Desai and Nanda have been instrumental in establishing a Shuddha dominated Panel on Ayurveda in the Planning Commission. These successes, however, have probably not strengthened the Ayurvedic cause as a whole. Instead, by splitting the movement into two groups each with its own version of what true Ayurveda should be, it has weakened claims for governmental recognition and sponsorship.

We thus have, up to the present, something of a standoff in the Indian medical situation with modern medicine continuing to hold a favored position against a native opposition divided against itself. The effects of these divisions, controversies, and bitter rivalries on India's medical development and health conditions are beyond our province, although they have obviously not been beneficial.[19] However, on another level, the whole Ayurvedic revival and the Shuddha movement in particular seem deeply significant of the tension between cultural tradition and modernity in modern India—a tension obviously not yet resolved in the medical or in many other fields as well.

Post-1949 China presents some intriguing contrasts to these developments in India. For in China we have the paradox of the most revolutionary and militantly 'scientific' regime in Asia giving traditional medicine almost everything that Indian medical conservatives have been clamoring for in vain. Public hospitals and clinics, equal status and pay in government health services, research centers using old doctors as well as new, special colleges

[18] *Report of the Committee to Assess . . . Ayurvedic System of Medicine*, 1959, p. 32.
[19] Paul Brass concludes: 'The costs to India's medical development have been the failure to provide effective medical relief to the rural areas.' pp. 53–4.

for traditional medicine and the incorporation of traditional medical subjects in the curriculum of modern medical schools—virtually the whole program of the Ayurvedic revival (but only its integrationist wing) has been adopted by a Communist government which has been ruthlessly anti-traditional in most areas.

The paradox is heightened if one looks back at the first generation of Chinese Communists and fellow travellers of the May 4th era after World War I. There we find such notables as Ch'en Tu-hsiu and Lu Hsün bitterly condemning and ridiculing traditional medicine as part of the noxious heritage of ancient superstition which must be rooted out in a new scientific age.[20] This early Marxist contempt for the old and unscientific mellowed somewhat during the Communist Party's long years in the wilderness where a more pragmatic attitude towards using native things gradually developed. In medicine it was reflected in the substitution of some elements of traditional medicine for unobtainable modern medical supplies, and the toleration of traditional physicians so long as modern ones were in such short supply. But, as Mao himself said in a subsequently much quoted and much distorted speech at Yenan in 1944, 'our task is to unite those old-style [doctors] that can be used and to assist, stimulate, and reform them'.[21] The implication clearly was that they were to be used on a stopgap basis and replaced when that became possible.

This position seems logical enough for a pragmatic revolutionary and it was the basis for Communist policy towards Chinese medicine during their first few years in power. It meant tolerance for the old doctors and old medicine for the present, just as other doomed classes and institutions might be temporarily tolerated, but gave no guarantees for the future. By around 1954, however, official attitudes and policy towards Chinese medicine started to undergo a striking change. More and more officially inspired articles appeared praising the old medicine, not just for specific remedies, but as an integral body of medical thought—a medical system expressing the accumulated wisdom of the Chinese people and containing valuable lessons for modern science. Fostering, or ordering, close cooperation between the two kinds of doctors was intensified, but now it was made clear that the desired synthesis of Chinese and Western medicine must fully respect the basic principles of *Chung I*. To effect this, large scale programs were launched for having modern doctors study Chinese medicine on a full or part-time basis.

Along with this dramatic reappraisal of Chinese medicine went a full-blown campaign of ideological criticism against modern-trained doctors for

[20] The development of Communist policy on Chinese medicine is detailed in *Traditional Medicine in Modern China*, Part Three. I also discuss this in 'Traditional Medicine in Communist China: Science, Communism and Cultural Nationalism,' *The China Quarterly* (July–September, 1965), pp. 1–27 and in my forthcoming anthology, *China's Cultural Legacy and Communism* (Frederick Praeger Publishers, N.Y., 1969) Ch. XI.

[21] *Mao Tse-tung Hsuan-chi (Selected Works of Mao Tse-tung)*; Vol. 3 (Peking, 1955), p. 1010.

their 'bourgeois prejudice' in despising the 'medical legacy of the motherland'. These attacks, extending to some of the highest figures in the Ministry of Health, made it clear that the campaign was to be seen as part of the more general struggle against pro-Western and bourgeois influences among the intellectuals. The main targets, Deputy Minister of Health Ho Ch'eng and Northeastern Health Minister Wang Pin were accused of many sins ranging from lack of patriotism to persecuting old-style physicians. But the most serious charge was 'refuting the ability of the Party in the supervision of scientific and technical work.' [22] In Communist China the scientific experts of the Ministry of Health were not to be allowed to obstruct the politicians' determination of medical policy. To enforce discipline, a shake-up occurred at the top of the Ministry and ordinary modern-style doctors were given a large dose of Chinese medicine to study along with Marxism and the writings of Mao Tse-tung.

This trend continued through the mid-fifties reaching its apogee in the 'Great Leap Forward' of 1958–59. The ideological fervor and populist depreciation of technical expertise during that period were well suited to putting down Western-style medical experts by stressing the value of the native medical tradition. The emphasis on home-grown methods over imported technology also expanded the role of Chinese medicine in the total health plan. In the emotional letdown after the economic failures of the Great Leap Forward, enthusiasm for Chinese medicine subsided somewhat, although institutionally it remained an important part of China's total medical picture. More recently, the Great Proletarian Cultural Revolution's assault on bourgeois and revisionist experts has led to a renewed emphasis on the more simple and folk aspects of traditional medicine.[23]

Assessing the motivations behind the about-face, or at least shift, in Party policy since 1954 is not easy. Many practical factors, including the real medical value of many elements of traditional practice and its psychological comfort function to the general population in a period of extreme social stress, could be noted. We have already seen its political-ideological role in combating bourgeois tendencies among modern medical experts. Here, it is perhaps most useful to point out how the larger process of social and cultural revolution in China has made it possible for her most radical revolutionaries to embrace something so traditional as Chinese medicine. This was only possible once the force of tradition as a viable entity had been smashed— once the 'feudal' half of the 'semi-feudal, semi-colonial' China Mao talked about in New Democracy (1940) seemed no longer nearly so fearful as the bourgeois, Western, and cosmopolitan influence implied in the 'semi-

22 Jen Hsiao-feng, 'Criticise Comrade Ho Ch'eng's Error in his Policy Towards Chinese Medicine,' translated in Union Research Service, Vol. 3, No. 20 (June 8, 1956), p. 298.

23 Unlike in the 1950s, recent praise for Chinese medicine has avoided praising 'medical experts'—modern-style or traditional. The accolades are for 'barefoot doctors' practicing acupuncture or prescribing simple herbals after little or no formal training. See, for example, 'Rely on the Thought of Mao Tse-tung to Uncover the Great Medical Treasures of the Motherland,' Jen-min Jih-pao, March 1, 1969 (translated in Survey of the China Mainland Press, No. 4375, pp. 6–11).

colonial' half. Then, these still militant revolutionaries might find some good elements in the national tradition, elements useful as an antidote to Western cosmopolitanism and an expression of nationalistic pride. This is what happened to Chinese medicine. It does not indicate any latent traditionalism or return to the past among Mao and associates. Rather it is a testimony to their confidence (how well founded is beside the point) that the past is destroyed or at least tamed to serve their new purposes. There may be a strong element of nationalism in this, but it need not imply any weakening of the revolutionary impulse.

Yet, if the Chinese Communists have been more successful in reconciling diverging psychological compulsions towards modernity and cultural identity as well as in imposing a prescribed medical policy without the checks of a democratic political system, they have no more solved the basic medical question than have the Ayurvedists in India. The desired kind of synthesis or integration in both countries must preserve a recognizable core of the native tradition while absorbing all the benefits of science. So far, at the theoretical level, the *Yin-yang* and five elements behind Chinese medicine have defined scientific analysis just as surely as the three humors of Ayurvedic medicine. After more than half a century East and West have met at the medical level, but have not joined.

To return to the comparative question, what does the furor over traditional medicine in twentieth-century China and India tell us about general problems of cultural change in modern Asia or about the specific characteristics of those two countries? Perhaps more of the latter than the former. For, although the strikingly similar issues and rhetoric in the Ayurveda and Chinese medicine movements suggests that the universal impact of modern Western science and technology on traditional societies produces a common type of cultural crisis, the Indian and Chinese cases are unique in manifesting this so clearly in the medical sphere. We suggested at the beginning some of the obvious reasons for this uniqueness. It does not mean that the cultural crisis and all the problems inherent in coming to terms with science and modernity have missed the rest of Asia. It is just that, with the exception of Ceylon, traditional medicine has not provided a focus for modern nationalism.

But in China and India it unquestionably has become such a focus. This suggests a common denominator in the modern history of these two countries going beyond the purely medical. The uniqueness and autonomy of their respective medical traditions should be seen as part of the larger historical autonomy of these two ancient cultural entities. It was that autonomy—expressed in unbroken philosophic, religious, and literary traditions of great antiquity—that gave both China and India identity, cohesion, and a deep sense of superiority to surrounding people. It was what made both civilizations essentially impervious to foreign conquest (China admittedly more so than India); it was what made the Brahmin and the mandarin each know in his own way that he and he alone was the highest expression of civilized mankind. This cultural assurance could not be felt elsewhere—certainly not in Japan which lived under the shadow of China's historic magnificence, nor in the cultures and empires of Southeast Asia exposed to and torn between Hindu and Chinese culture, not even really in the Islamic world whose close contacts with Europe on the one hand and later Hindu India on the other provided constant reminders that the outsiders might be infidels but they were not barbarians. However effective this cultural assurance and feeling of superiority was in sustaining traditional China and India, it has not been functionally useful for the task of modernization in recent times when so much cultural borrowing has become so essential. This is why the modern cultural crisis has perhaps cut deepest of all in those two societies, for it has eroded their traditional basis of identity. Of course, a new identity has had to be worked out, and this process has been at the heart of modern Asian nationalisms. However, the new identity has had to be built out of the old one thus creating a strong basis for cultural nationalisms.

It is my thesis that this sense of cultural crisis and cultural nationalism infuses the native medicine movements in both China and India. This does not mean that those movements have been basically traditional, anti-modernist, or anti-scientific. Rather, they have both not so much defied science as attempted to find it in their own respective tradition. Both have been very untraditional in their willingness to modernize forms and institutions and generally to make substantive changes in content so long as a distinctive Chinese or Indian tradition remains, so long as a national identity is preserved.

Yet, despite these and all the more specific similarities we have noted between traditional medical movements in China and India, the differences may be just as significant for the particular responses in each nation to its modern cultural crisis. Politically the most striking difference in sources of support for traditional medicine would seem to be between the varied, but generally culturally conservative, group in independent India and the revolutionary Communist rulers of China. However, closer scrutiny suggests that there may be something of a common pattern here too. In both countries it has been the most Westernized, cosmopolitan intellectuals who, on the grounds of deep respect for science, have been most opposed to native medicine. In pluralistic India they continue to frustrate the more ambitious hopes of Ayurvedic supporters; in Communist China these Western-tainted 'experts' are no longer in a position to thwart the wishes of the less cosmopolitan 'reds'. The point is that in both China and India cultural and political conservatives have supported traditional medicine, but support has also come from those political radicals who have not been deeply immersed in modern Western culture and who hold a strong political animus towards the West. In this, Indian socialists and Chinese Communists have something in common in their attitudes towards traditional medicine, just as do Indian and Chinese conservatives.

But there is a danger in pushing such parallels too far. One still has to account for the Shuddha phenomenon in recent India and its apparent rejection of science, a movement for which there is no real parallel in China of the last forty years. It is not easy to assess the significance of the Shuddha development. In one sense, it has been as modern as integrated Ayurveda in adopting new organizational and institutional devices including an effective political lobby. But there is also the basic denial of science—the visceral reaction that, if modern science cannot validate the eternal truths of Ayurveda, so much the worse for science; Indian medicine and Indian culture will remain. In this, and in the more specific arguments by many Ayurvedists (not all of them Shuddha) used to defend such elements of the traditional lore as astrology, there seems to be a greater resistance to science and modernity than in China, Communist or Nationalist. The whole Ayurvedic debate, especially since Independence, seems to point to a much deeper cleavage in India between a cosmopolitan modernizing elite and a powerful opposition more willing to defy essential elements of scientific modernity in defence of native tradition. Over fifty years ago Hu Shih remarked of China that 'there is not a single person who calls himself a modern man and yet dares openly to belittle science'.[24] The recent course of the Ayurvedic movement suggests that the same might not be true for India.

[24] Hu Shih introduction to *K'e-hsüeh yü Jen-sheng Kuan* (Science and Philosophy of Life) (Shanghai, 1923), p. 3.

PART **4**

ADVANCED
MODERNIZATION

The general configuration of highly modernized societies may be judged from the "high" column of the indicators of economic development and social mobilization set forth earlier (pp. 162–163), and in some respects these advanced societies may appear to have completed the process of change. When in some realms of activity—primary and secondary education, urbanization, expansion of industry and services—a point is reached where no further development seems possible, it may appear that a steady state has been achieved similar to the relative equilibrium of the premodern era. Yet knowledge continues to grow, and with it the problems and opportunities of highly modernized societies. While some trends may appear to terminate, others are still unfolding, and new ones are emerging that have as yet attracted little attention.

The priority societies in the process of rapid transformation assigned to growth was accompanied by their emphasis on savings for investment and by their postponement of the gratification of many needs until such time as they were more fully developed. In some, as much as a quarter or more of their GNP (from 25 and 40 percent in Japan, and 25 to 30 percent in the U.S.S.R. between 1950 and 1970) was allocated to investment, and even in the earlier modernizing societies that did not develop quite so fast the growth of the economy had a higher priority than distribution of income for welfare. The table on Levels of Social Mobilization (p. 163) shows that though there is an enormous difference between the low and high levels of urbanization, education, health, and communications, the distribution of income as expressed by the proportion of it received by the lowest fifth and the highest fifth is not more equal among the highly modernized. Indeed, the lowest fifth may receive twice as much proportionally in the less developed countries as in the most developed. If these proportions are related to GNP per capita, of course, it is apparent that at high levels of development the lowest fifth in advanced societies receives 4 percent of an income ten or twenty times higher than that of the poor countries in which the comparable group receives 8 percent. Nevertheless, it is characteristic of societal transformation that substantial growth can occur with little or no modifications in income distribution. Once societies become highly modernized this emphasis changes and distribution begins to take priority over development. Women and ethnic groups who suffered discrimination in earlier times, as well as lower income groups generally, now make claims to equal treatment, and distribution becomes a matter of priority.

As societies develop they also become more complex. When growth was the main objective, it was relatively simple to promote the construction of industries, transportation systems, and cities. With the proliferation of specialized institutions and functions, the mobilization and allocation of resources and the formulation of adequate responses to the demands of many hitherto neglected interest groups become increasingly difficult. As societies develop they also tend to specialize and become more dependent on the international environment for both markets and raw materials. International competition increases, and a society's capacity for technological innovation may become the most important single factor in its development.

As societies become more complex they also become increasingly vulnerable. Few anticipated a generation ago the growing scarcity of the land, water, and air that have been so freely exploited in the past. The need for all societies to limit population growth is already generally accepted, and whether or not the end of economic growth is in sight due to the depletion of raw materials depends on the continuing inventiveness of science and technology. The highly modernized societies (the West, Japan, U.S.S.R.), with about a fifth of the world's population, already produce some four-fifths of the world's GNP and consume probably an equivalent amount of its resources. Known resources are not adequate today to supply China and India at the per capita level of the advanced societies even if they possessed the skills and institutions to achieve such a level.

If there were once those who equated modernization with unrestricted progress, they have by now learned better. The growth of knowledge enhances the human capacity for both destruction and creation. It has made possible a greatly expanded production of goods and services, but it has also led to the population explosion. One may still have reason to believe that population can be brought sufficiently under control and that new sources of energy can yet be found that will make it possible for all humankind to share the well-being now enjoyed by a relatively small minority. But many question whether this challenge can be met, especially if values and institutions remain tied to competing national sovereignties.

Personality and Structural Dimensions in Comparative International Development

Irving Louis Horowitz

Whether a society is "advanced" is a relative matter, and the measurement of degrees or stages of modernization remains controversial. Reliance on a single indicator, such as the ever popular GNP per capita, does not do justice to the multidimensional complexity of society. The value of this essay by Horowitz is that it subjects a wide range of indicators to critical examination. He also distinguishes between economic, and social and psychological indicators, the latter as expressed in measurable attitudes. Horowitz notes that different aspects of a society change at different rates, and in effect cautions students to be discriminating in attempting to define which societies are "advanced."

The tension between human volition and social necessity is central to developmental analysis. In comparative international research, the critical task is identifying equivalent phenomena, or at least analyzing the relationships between them as if things and events were consistent across national boundaries.[1] Yet, although the character of the problem, and the importance of finding solutions to it are widely recognized, there have been surprisingly few systematic attempts to deal with it in comparative studies on development. It might nonetheless be useful to briefly catalogue what these systematic attempts have been until now, and where they have taken us.

Moore's attempt at the typology of comparative studies[2] underlines our

"Personality and Structural Dimensions in Comparative International Development" by Irving Louis Horowitz is reprinted by permission of the author and publisher from *Social Science Quarterly*, LI (December 1970), 494–513.

Horowitz is professor of sociology at Livingston College, Rutgers University. Prominent among his many interests are the study of development, as reflected in *Revolution in Brazil: Politics and Society in a Developing Nation* (1964) and *Three Worlds of Development: The Theory and Practice of International Stratification* (1966); and the sociology of knowledge, to which he has contributed *The New Sociology* (1964), *Professing Sociology* (1968), and, as editor, *The Use and Abuse of Social Science* (1971).

[1] Adam Przeworski and Henry Teune, "Equivalence in Cross-National Research," *Public Opinion Quarterly*, 30 (Winter, 1966–67), pp. 551–568.

[2] Wilbert Moore, "Social Change and Comparative Studies," *Order and Change: Essays in Comparative Sociology* (New York: John Wiley, 1967), pp. 21–32.

present dilemma: The decision to conceptualize the developmental process in terms of one model rather than the other is often made on the basis of strategy rather than on the basis of scientific warrant. What is optimal for the researcher or convenient for the scholar may be a far cry from the requirements of the field situation itself. In some sense perceptions of development in terms of dyads, models, systems and stages take place simultaneously. Even though researchers select from a number of research strategies—which suggest that the developmental goal is already defined and evaluated and that research tasks are basically descriptive—"development" is a value still being defined rather than a goal whose means of attainment are clearly understood. The real problem confronting social scientists is still that of determining in general and in specific times and places, what developmental goals, values, and processes are.

The problems of comparative international research do not arise from anything unique to developmental studies, but from inherent dilemmas of applying the methodological research techniques developed in relation to other areas of social investigation, such as class stratification. Basic problems of social science methodology are not bypassed by doing work at a more or less macroscopic level; the magnitude of a research task is only one factor determining a methodological choice. Nevertheless, there are methodological and systematic formulations that seem particularly significant for solving problems in the field of comparative international development, and we will concentrate on these.

There can be no precise distinction between "attitude data" and "structural data" but, as heuristic devices they deserve consideration. Smith and Inkeles have written that "the term [modernity] may refer to two quite different objects. As used to describe a *society*, 'modern' generally refers to such structural factors as a national state characterized by a complex of traits including intensive mechanization, high rates of social mobility, and the like. When applied to individuals, 'modern' refers to a set of attitudes, values and ways of feeling and acting, *presumably of the sort either generated by or required* for effective participation in a modern society." [3] Smith and Inkeles appreciate the distinction between structural and attitudinal data, but choose to link both in the rubric of modernity. The difficulty with their resolution is that measures of modernization, as I shall seek to show, have been much more readily linked to changes in individual development than in the social structure. Specifically, the following will be emphasized.

1. The different attitudinal patterns associated with modernity involve two different but related problems: (a) the problem of consistency and (b) the problem of sequence.
2. The nature of the relationship between attitudinal data and structural data also involves two different considerations: (a) the problem of congruence, which basically defines the adequacy and equivalence of attitu-

[3] David Smith and Alex Inkeles, "The OM Scale: A Comparative Socio-Psychological Measure of Individual Modernity," *Sociometry*, 29 (Dec., 1966), pp. 353–377.

dinal data and structural data; and (b) the nature of the explanatory relationship. Assuming that we could obtain attitudinal data that cross-culturally would typify the degree of correspondence with the structural data what could we infer about the order of causality?

3. The qualitative aspects of the disjunction between modernization and industrialization, personal attitudes and social structures involve dual considerations: (a) the problem of decision-making and planning; and (b) the problems of national goals in an internationally fixed environment.

The Measurement of Attitudes and Values

There is an obvious correlation between individual attributes and the social structure in which they are positioned, and sociology is concerned with just this relationship. The symbolic interactionist school in particular provides insight into the social character of man, while both exchange theorists and psychoanalytic-oriented social scientists add weight to the argument that individual and structural variables are linked by the process of socialization. But beyond these established shibboleths, the two types of data stubbornly resist synthesis. The reasons for lack of correspondence between individual and structural information may be (1) the variables are incorrectly conceptualized; (2) indicators used are inappropriate for explanatory purposes; (3) there is a measurement or sampling error; (4) or finally, there is a significant time lag between accumulation of data and application to problems of the future. Since the last two possible errors are easily accounted for, we will concentrate upon the first two possibilities of error.

PROBLEMS OF CONSISTENCY

As the material bases of society change, human values and attitudes alter. But the question is, which attitudes change? In what direction, with what intensity, and at what rate? Will the process of industrialization of societies elicit a concomitant process of cultural homogeneity? Will world-wide processes of urbanization and industrialization homogenize the diverse cultures of the world and produce an "industrial man"? How will the population of diverse societies respond and adapt to demands of industrialization and urbanization?

An answer to these questions requires that we measure changes in the attitudes of peoples undergoing modernization.

Toward this end Inkeles describes modern man according to nine different themes.[4] He characterizes modern man by (1) receptivity to experiences and

---

[4] Alex Inkeles, "The Modernization of Man," in Myron Weiner, ed., *Modernization: The Dynamics of Growth* (New York: Basic Books, Inc., 1966), pp. 138–152.

openness to innovation and change; (2) a disposition to form or hold opinions over a large number of problems and issues that arise not only in his immediate environment but also outside it; (3) orientation to the present or future, rather than to the past; (4) planning and organizing beliefs as a way of handling life: (5) mastery of the environment in order to advance individual purposes and goals, rather than being dominated entirely by environmental needs; (6) confidence that the world is calculable and that other people and institutions can be relied upon to fulfill or meet obligations and responsibilities; (7) awareness of the dignity of others and a disposition to show respect for them; (8) faith in science and technology; (9) belief in distributive justice, in rewards based upon social contribution and not according to either whim or special properties of the person not related to such a contribution.

The traditional man is said to hold opposite views on these nine different themes; the difficulty is that this "overall modernity" rarely can be found in one person. Furthermore, while the scale of 119 items is said to "cohere psychologically" in the countries tested, this does not guarantee that the "structural mechanisms" are the same (even though the countries may reveal comparable levels of social development).

Smith and Inkeles show that they are aware of the dilemmas by their qualification: "Although we have stressed certain themes that cut across numerous concrete realms of behavior, some students of the problem prefer to emphasize attitudes and behavior relating mainly to certain important institutional realms, such as birth control or religion. Their position is certainly reasonable. . . . We have therefore included questions on such themes as restriction of family size, treatment of older people and obligations to one's parents and relatives, the importance of social change; the role of women; how to bring up children, attitudes towards religion, attitudes toward the consumption of material and physical goods, social and political problems of the community, the nation and the international realm, education and social mobility; and contact with media of mass communication. For each of these realms, one can define a position that can be considered more modern and an attitude one can define as more traditional, although at times the process of definition becomes very complex." [5]

If modern man is to be defined by such an attitude scale, it behooves us to question *how consistent* the attitudes of "modern men" really are along these different attitudinal dimensions. If a man is modern in one aspect (assuming that all the different attitudinal dimensions are indicative of modernity), can he also be expected to be modern in other aspects? Smith and Inkeles never explain why they use the term "modern." All living men, whether by choice or necessity, live in a contemporary world. Modernism and traditionalism may coexist in the same person, whatever the level of development of his society—since they signify approaches to the future, not approaches to real structural parameters.

[5] Smith and Inkeles, "The OM Scale," pp. 355–356.

Kahl has "measured" modernity with a high degree of sophistication, by demonstrating how the multi-dimensionality of modernism can be directly examined.[6] Kahl begins by setting up two ideal types: traditional and modern. From these he specifies a set of profiles in which each attribute may vary independently of others. All sorts of combinations are possible. Instead of using all the theoretically possible combinations and permutations (Parsons' five pattern variables alone would yield 32 types, and Kluckhohn's three main relationships with five sub-divisions would yield 243 types), Kahl switches from either/or attributes to *continuous variables*, which can then be inter-correlated, making it possible to derive personal profiles from modal profiles. But what can be done with such correlations?

Kahl specifies 14 different components of modernity. Each was conceived of as a separate variable that ranged from the traditional pole to the modern pole, with a number of possible intermediate points. He chose these particular components of modernity because of their relation to work and career values, without pretending to exhaust the relevant dimensions of modernity, or to restrict the definition of modernism to all 14 variables. The 14 variables were constructed as independent unidimensional scales. Kahl found that the core syndrome which he calls modernism consists of seven scales which were closely interrelated; they are: (1) activism, (2) low integration with relatives, (3) preference for urban life, (4) individualism, (5) low urban sub-community stratification, (6) mass-media participation and (7) low stratification of life chances. There are additional values he associates with modernism but these are operative to a lesser degree: trust in people, an attitude in favor of manual work and a distaste for traditional institutions and agencies of coercion. Kahl also noted a propensity to take risks in one's career and an attitude in favor of modern roles within the nuclear family. Surprisingly, occupational placement and low secularization were not associated with modernism!

In a general way, Kahl's study supports Inkeles' basic hypothesis that a syndrome of values remains as obscure in the quantitative rendering as it was in earlier qualitative forms. Comparing Kahl's study to Inkeles' is made difficult by differences in definitions. Underlying this dilemma is the problem of construct validity. As the work of Kahl and Inkeles illustrates, basic constructs may be quite similar and not mutually exclusive, even though the constructs are identified by different concepts and the substantive content of the concepts is organized differently. Thus various substantive components of a particular concept for one author (for example, activism for Kahl) are embodied in a number of different concepts for the other (for example, political activism, change and perception valuation, planning valuation, and general efficacy for Inkeles).

Every attempt to define modernism in terms of an operational set of variables results in the introduction of new ideas which have relatively little

[6] Joseph A. Kahl, *The Measurement of Modernism: A Study of Values in Brazil and Mexico* (Austin, and London: Institute of Latin American Studies, University of Texas Press, 1968).

to do with the original concept. A standard definition of modernization, for example, usually includes at least the following: belief in the primacy of science, or at least in the products of applied engineering, belief in a secular way of conducting affairs, and belief in the need for continuing changes in society and economy. But beyond these formulations, it often means intensified destruction of local and regional cultures in the name of national identity. Thus, modernism may be a goal for some and a handicap for others.[7] The answer will depend on who benefits from modernization, not by any intrinsic merits it is said to have.

This distinction points out a crucial problem in construct validation. Which of Kahl's 14 scales and Inkeles' 30 themes are *substantively* and *empirically* related to modernism? Both men claim to have summarized only those values that have been associated with modernism in the literature. Unless we develop a more rigorous, theoretical and empirical justification for the inclusion or exclusion of particular value components in a definition of modernity, these values must be seen as another product of industrialization. In a world already parceled out among the big powers, they are neither a consequence nor a cause of the motivation to achieve.

As these studies and others begin empirically to isolate the crucial components of modernism, and as theory develops, greater construct validation may be expected. Then, descriptions of the different types and degrees of individual modernity will begin to resolve the problem of consistency of attitudinal dimensions. Kahl's study has already empirically demonstrated some overall degree of consistency. In his identification of seven scales of variables that form the core syndrome of urbanization, he has noted, "on the average, a man who is high on some will also be high on the others, although there is room for variation." The specification of the different variations is the crux of the problem of consistency.

When controlled for socioeconomic status, the studies tend to parcel out the differences in "objective conditions" or structural indicators among the three countries. This enabled each study to show the relatively high degree of frequency with which attitudes are held, as distinct from the congruence between these attitudes. But their attitude data refer only to particular groups; structural data generally refer to the whole nation. The Kahl studies lack indications of model distributions or the standard deviations of attitudinal modernity for the whole population of three countries. Furthermore, the Kahl study illustrates that as long as "modernity" is *operationally defined* as the pattern of attitudes of "modern" groups (urbanites, for example), then the question of congruence is resolved by operational definition. A measure is needed to derive "cultural development" (changes in the values and attitudes) independently from "structural conditions." Without it, we cannot resolve the relationship of attitudinal data and structural data, since the size of the

---

[7] Irving Louis Horowitz, *Three Worlds of Development: The Theory and Practice of International Stratification* (New York and London: Oxford University Press, 1966), pp. 306–307.

"modern" group is probably related more to the *level* of development than to the *rate* of development.

THE SEQUENTIAL PROBLEM

Modernization of attitudes denotes a growth of consciousness. There is movement from one position to another in time; from "traditional to modern." Because modernization is multidimensional, there is also the problem of consistency among the different components of the concept, and the problem of sequence.

When social scientists describe the attitudes characteristic of traditional and modern societies, they assume a progressive transformation in the attitudes of developing man. But is such an assumption warranted? Assuming *a priori* that we can identify a cluster of attitudes as "traditional" and a cluster as "modern," we would then have to specify whether in fact in the process of development the "traditional attitudes" are transformed into the modern cluster of attitudes. For this purpose, longitudinal studies are needed. We need to know whether a rural person who moves to the city does in fact modify his traditional attitudes and become a "modern man."

Feldman and Hurn have begun to question the assumption of a simple sequence in the attitudinal dimension of modernism.[8] As they observe, most modernism studies deal only with cross-sectional data. The usual approach is to take a sample of urbanites and call their attitudes "modern," an approach obviously limited and biased against the "rural population." More importantly, the method itself generates the consistency found among attitudinal components of modernity. This is because attitudinal modernity is defined purely as a derivative of the structural factors, such as geographical residence or socioeconomic status. Ruralism is equated to traditional attitudes and urbanism with modernity, but the extent of ruralism (indicated, for example, by the percentage engaged in agriculture) is really a function of the structural conditions prevailing in the country.

Feldman and Hurn point out in a followup study of their Puerto Rico sample, some 10 years later, that (1) The process of modernization (defined in terms of the experience of mobility) does not differentiate between those who remained peasants and those who changed their status in the *direction* of their attitude change; (2) The experience of mobility does differentiate them according to degree of attitude change. Those who were mobile (experienced modernization) tended to have higher aspirations, for instance; (3) But there were also some reversals. For example, modernism studies assume that moderns tend to value education. Feldman and Hurn found out that those who were mobile tended to de-emphasize the value of education after their experience of mobility. But Feldman and Hurn quickly point

[8] Arnold Feldman and Christopher Hurn, "The Experience of Modernization," *Sociometry*, 29 (Dec., 1966), p. 293.

out that an "anti-education" stance should in some cases be considered modern. More education may not imply greater economic rewards if the employment opportunity structure is not expanding. The concept of modernism tends to lose its explanatory power in such a situation. Contradictory attitudes become customary. They conclude by saying that the basic impact of modernism is increased cognitive awareness. "There must be dissonance observed between general economic growth in contrast to one's own comparative stagnation. There must be cognitive awareness of the gap between advancement at one end of the social scale—say, education—and stagnation at the level of economic opportunity." [9]

Attitude "Waves" and Structural "Particles"

The Problem of Congruence—Descriptive Relationships. Cross-national studies dealing with attitudinal data show an impressively high degree of attitude convergence, considering the diversity in structural characteristics. Inkeles, for example, posits that values tend to converge in industrializing countries. Kahl writes: "These results support the position of Alex Inkeles that societal structures tend toward convergence in industrial (or industrializing) countries, creating sets of cultural values that reflect status positions and the exigencies of life that are associated with them, regardless of previously different national tradition." [10] One gets the misleading impression from Kahl that Brazil, Mexico and the United States have similar value configurations, for the syndromes of modernizing attitudes in the three countries are similar. "Cross-national comparisons" are really comparisons across and within socioeconomic groups in different countries. It is not comparisons of objective national conditions, since it is precisely these conditions that differentiate countries. To put it differently, one cannot strictly speak of "cross-national" studies when the samples used to compare the different countries are not representative of the three countries concerned.

To make worthwhile comparisons of attitudes one would need representative samples of the countries that would permit measurement of the respondents' subjective world, and comparison of this measure with "objective" socioeconomic indicators. One such macroscopic study is Cantril's work on *The Patterns of Human Concerns.* Cantril devised what he called a "self-anchoring scale." It was basically a projective type of interview scale by which the respondent's subjective world was the frame of reference: "A person is asked to define on the basis of his own assumptions, perceptions, goals and values the two extremes or anchoring points of the spectrum on which some scale measurement is desired . . . it was utilized in this study as a means of discovering the spectrum of values a person is preoccupied or concerned with and by means of which he evaluates his own life. He describes as the top anchoring points his wishes and hopes as he personally conceives them

[9] Feldman and Hurn, "Experience of Modernization," p. 294.
[10] Kahl, *Measurement of Modernism,* p. 54.

and the realization of which would constitute for him the best possible life. At the other extreme, he describes the worries and fears, the preoccupations and frustrations, embodied in his conception of the worst possible life he could imagine." [11]

Cantril used the ladder scale to rank the respondent's perception of his own "personal world" and the respondent's perception of the "nation," with respect to past, present and future. He expresses the problem of congruence in these terms: "Curiosity naturally arises as to how the ratings people give themselves and their nations on the ladder are related to the indices used by economists to measure the stage of development people are in." [12]

To measure the degree of congruence, Cantril devised a composite index of socioeconomic development for the 13 nations in his study, using 11 "structural variables." The countries were ranked for each of the 11 indicators and their relative standings were then converted to a 1.0 to 0.00 scale. The socioeconomic index thus obtained was:

NATION	DEGREE OF MODERNIZATION
United States	1.00
West Germany	.71
Israel	.67
Japan	.60
Poland	.45
Cuba	.35
Panama	.31
Yugoslavia	.19
Philippines	.17
Dominican Republic	.16
Brazil	.16
Egypt	.14
Nigeria	.02
India	.00

Cantril then proceeded to obtain the rank order correlations of the socioeconomic index and the ladder ratings. The correlations are given below:

NATIONAL		PERSONAL	
present	.47 $(P < .05)$	present	.67 $(P < .01)$
past	.39	past	.56 $(P < .05)$
future	.15	future	.11

Cantril explains the ratings by noting: "As would be expected, the correlation of the present personal rating with the socioeconomic indices is highest of all—in other words, an individual's personal experience now. Next

---

[11] Hadley Cantril, *The Patterns of Human Concerns* (New Brunswick, N.J.: Rutgers University Press, 1965), p. 22.

[12] *Ibid.*, p. 192.

in order is the person's estimate of his own ladder rating in the past and then a significantly high correlation between the present rating of the nation and its socioeconomic index. When it comes to the future, both for the individual and the nation, any clear-cut relationships break down." [13]

Cantril's data yield an important point: there is an *inverse relationship* between the subjective rating and the objective ratings. People in four highly developed countries tended to give themselves low present ratings, to rate their nation presently low, to rate the future for their country low, relative to their favorable position as measured by objective indices. For people in less-developed countries, it is vice versa.

The cross-national comparisons established by Cantril and his associates show a remarkable variation in the socioeconomic index and remarkable similarities in the ladder ratings, that is, in the attitude measures. And since both types of data are presumably "standardized," the differences must be attributed to something other than sampling techniques. His findings substantially bear out that there are odd disparities between structural and attitudinal data. Clearly, levels of industrial skills are built-in features of advanced countries—features which are far more difficult to "export" (presuming indeed even the intent of export) than the attitudes which emerge as a consequence of industrialism. One might say that the *products* of industrialism are largely responsible for modernization, while the *processes* of industrialism are largely responsible for economic development.

Another central problem in comparative international studies is the apparent gap between attitude research and structural analysis. If we attempt to measure differences between Argentina, Peru and the United States, as Miller has intriguingly done, we find that distinctions between them on a scale of 15 items relating to norms, values and attitudes, and judged by persons intimate with each of these nations, tend to be rather small.[14] This is immediately apparent in the reputational table provided (Table 1).

Even if the comparisons are drawn on a rotation base among Peru, Argentina and the United States, the mean differences, while going up slightly, still remain indecisive. The differences of 59 percent and 35 percent, while important, are too insignificant to settle the issue either of the existence of a Latin American homogeneity or an Inter-American homogeneity. This table provides little comfort for those who argue the thesis that Latin America can only be understood in contrast to and in contradistinction with the United States, since it is clear that modernization carries with it a "demonstration effect." And in the case of the Latin American middle classes this means the emulation and incorporation of North American values of achievement.

As the tabular material shows, not only are there differences in the items taken as measures of value among the three nations, but on some very

[13] *Ibid.*, p. 195.
[14] Delbert C. Miller, "The Measurement of International Patterns and Norms: A Tool for Comparative Research," (*Southwestern*) *Social Science Quarterly*, 48 (March, 1968), pp. 531–547.

TABLE 1. Mean Ratings for United States, Peru, and Argentina and the Difference Between Means of Peru and Argentina, Peru and United States, and Argentina and the United States[a]

Scale Item	Mean Ratings of U.S. N = 21	Mean Ratings of Peru N = 21	Ratings of Argentina N = 15	Difference Between Means of Peru and Argentina	Difference Between Means of Peru and U.S.	Difference Between Means of Argentina and U.S.
1. Social Acceptance	1.66	4.48	3.18	1.30	2.82	2.02
2. Health	1.38	4.66	2.93	1.73	3.28	1.55
3. Trust	1.75	4.86	3.27	1.59	3.11	1.52
4. Security	2.33	4.95	3.50	1.45	2.62	1.17
5. Family	5.42	1.85	2.71	.86	3.57	2.71
6. Child	1.33	4.43	2.80	1.63	3.10	1.47
7. Moral Code	2.00	4.90	2.75	2.15	2.90	.75
8. Religion	4.57	2.05	3.66	1.61	2.52	.91
9. Class	5.00	1.38	3.07	1.69	3.62	1.93
10. Consensus	1.57	4.57	3.92	.55	3.00	2.35
11. Labor	5.33	3.10	2.69	.31	2.23	2.64
12. Democracy	1.42	3.66	2.81	1.85	2.24	1.39
13. Work	1.52	4.76	3.07	1.69	3.24	1.55
14. Civic Activity	1.19	4.81	3.58	1.23	3.62	2.39
15. Property	1.19	3.29	3.59	.29	2.10	2.39
Grand Mean Difference of all Ratings =				1.33	2.93	1.95

[a] From Delbert C. Miller, "The Measurement of International Patterns and Norms: A Tool for Comparative Research," (*Southwestern*) Social Science Quarterly, 48 (March, 1968), p. 545.

important items Argentina is more like the United States than like Peru. Miller does not adequately respond to his data; instead he calls into question the already slightly tarnished notion of a Latin American civilization. It might be argued that Miller's 15 items are incomplete, that the inclusion of a more sophisticated set of measures of how personal satisfaction relates to political attitudes would help remove the tautological aspects in his findings.[15] While this seems a valid defense against criticism, the problem would not be resolved by merely widening the number of factors sampled, since the explanatory power of each factor would remain unexamined. Whether or not attitude factors are relevant when considered in terms of structural param-eters may have more to do with the industrial organization of production and consumption than do the cultural attitudes of the producing individuals toward the consequences of industrialism.

Data gathered by Feinstein suggest that objective differences between Argentina and the United States are much more extensive than one would believe possible from attitude surveys.[16] For example, measuring inflationary spirals and rates of growth and using the year 1950 as the baseline of 100, the United States data show that by 1957 the cost of living index was up 17 points; for Argentina, the cost of living index in the same period of time was up 226 points. Furthermore, the United States exhibited an annual rate of economic growth at 3.5 percent during this period; for Argentina, the annual growth rate was 1.9 percent. One might add that GNP in Argentina has shown no marked propensity to "leap" forward during the recent years, despite the shifts in political power. Furthermore, in 1957 Argentinian in-come was $439 per capita, whereas the United States was $2,079. The ten years since 1957 have witnessed continued growth in the United States, and an even slower pattern in Argentina. Now, Argentina shows income per person to be $680 in comparison to $4,050 per person in the United States.

The United States and Argentina do have modernizing phenomena in common. For example, the degree of illiteracy is extremely small in both nations. The percentage of the urban population in relation to the total population is high for both. The distributions are very different, however: the United States has a wide distribution of urban areas while Argentina has only one really major city and a capital area which accounts for roughly 45 per cent of the total population of the nation. Measures such as unioniza-tion and secondary education also rank high in both nations.

The really significant differences are in private investment of United States firms in Latin America compared to Argentine investments in North America. The constant rate of growth of United States investment in Latin America is too well known to require detailed commentary. Similarly, the near absence of any large-scale export, and certainly of any large-scale Argentine control over United States industry, is beyond contest. Use of these and many other

[15] See in this connection Kahl, *Measurement of Modernism.*

[16] Otto Feinstein, "A Changing Latin American and U.S. Foreign Policy," in Otto Feinstein, ed., *Two Worlds of Change: Readings in Economic Development* (New York: Double-day-Anchor, 1964), pp. 375–420.

similar variables would enable one to avoid the indeterminate kinds of comparisons with the United States that attitude surveys yield. For example, gross investment as percentage of GNP remained disappointingly stable in most Latin American countries during the past decade: only El Salvador, Guatemala, Nicaragua, and Panama succeeded in raising it. Savings in Latin America rose from 16.3 percent to 16.9 percent between 1951–1964, while income increased over 50 percent. But during the last five years savings have either failed to increase or even fallen slightly in spite of higher incomes per person. The most important symptom of national effort, the marginal rate of savings, at best failed to increase and remained at a level of 15 percent, or 20–30 percent lower than in India or Pakistan which have but a fraction of Latin American income per capita. The marginal rate of savings must be increased by at least 50 percent if self-sustained high growth is to be attained. The rates of industrial growth should be almost twice as high and the level of agricultural growth 50–60 percent higher than at present if the goals of full employment and of sustained growth of 2.5 percent per capita per annum are to be reached.

Foreign exchange also failed to increase sufficiently in the past decade. Since the mobilization of domestic savings seems to depend on complementary foreign exchange—prospective investors may not save if they see no prospects of obtaining foreign exchange for imports or machinery—the scarcity of foreign exchange may in part explain the scarcity of savings.

Lack of monetary stability and inflation still prevails in a good three-quarters of Latin American nations. Because we have learned that stabilization should not proceed at the expense of growth, and since it normally takes several years to increase the production and supply of domestic foodstuffs, only a gradual stabilization is attempted. Yet the price in terms of growth seems to be high in some countries (Argentina, Brazil, Colombia) even though the reduction in inflation has not been as much as planned. Monetary instability may discourage savings as well as impede progress in Latin American economic integration.[17]

A series of measures that economists employ indicates that the United States and Argentina (and Latin America as a whole) stand at the opposite ends of the developmental ladder on several major dimensions. The United States exports much more than it imports; nations such as Argentina have a difficult time maintaining any sort of equilibrium between exports and imports.[18] The rates of earnings on United States direct private investments abroad in Latin America averaged during the post-World War Two period more than 14.0 percent per annum—which is considerably higher than the earnings to investments ratio achieved on purely domestic capitalization. The

---

[17] See Paul N. Rosenstein-Rodan, "The Alliance for Progress and Peaceful Revolution," in *Latin American Radicalism*, I. L. Horowitz, Josué de Castro, and John Gerassi, eds. (New York: Random House, 1969), pp. 53–60.

[18] This same structural imbalance between export and import also characterizes over-ripe societies such as England and France. It might be tentatively noted that a number of processes characteristic of underdevelopment are also found in the phenomena of over-development.

TABLE 2. Indicators of Economic Development and Indemnization in Five Groups of Countries at Different Stages of the Process (1950–55 approximately)

	Mass Consumption Stage		Industrial Revolution Stage			Pre-Industrial Societies In Transition			Traditional Societies		
	U.S.	England	Germany (West)	Italy	Argentina	Brazil	Mexico	Ecuador	Congo	Haiti	Ethiopia
1. Economic Development											
a. GNP per capita, U.S. $ 1955	2,243	998	762	442	374	262	187	204	98	80	75
b. Energy consumption	7,834	4,594	3,266	992	1,033	329	817	157	56	75	43
c. Percent of active population in agriculture	12	5	14	29	25	61	58	53	84	nd	83
2. Modernization											
d. Gross birth rate (per 1,000 inhab.)	24.9	15.8	15.6	10.0	23.7	45.0	47.3	47.1	nd	nd	nd
e. Gross death rate (per 1,000 inhab.)	9.5	11.7	10.7	9.5	10.0	20.0	15.0	20.0	nd	nd	nd
f. Life expectancy at birth (years)	71	71	67	65	64	45	50	45	nd	22	nd
g. Percent living in cities of 20,000 inhab.	52	67	44	30	48	20	24	18	8	2.5	5
h. Percent who are literate (15 years and over)	97.5	98.5	98.5	87.5	86.4	49.4	56.8	55.7	37.5	nd	10.5
i. Percent university stud. per 1,000 inhabs.	18.2	7.7	4.8	2.9	7.5	1.2	2	1.5	0.1	nd	0.3
j. Percent that votes among adult inhabitants	63.0	78	88	94	90.0	42	50	46	nd	nd	3
k. Percent in middle occupation strata with respect to total active population	47	34	40	29	40	17	17.0	11	nd	nd	5.4

SOURCES: (a), (c), (g), (h), (j), Yale Data Program, *Basic for Cross National Comparisons*, New Haven, 1960; United Nations, *Statistical Yearbook*, 1960; (d); (e), (f), United Nations, *Report on World Social Situation*, 1957; (k), Data based on the information contained in S. M. Miller, "Comparative Social Mobility," *Current Sociology*, 9 (1960); and G. Germani, *Política y sociedad en una época de transición* (Buenos Aires: Paidós, 1962).

rate of earnings on Argentine direct private investments abroad during the same period averaged less than half this percentage, or under 7.0 percent—which is considerably less than the earnings to investment ratio achieved on purely Argentine sources of investment, and much less than the annual inflationary rates. When we add to these factors the underdeveloped and satellitic relationships; the chronic balance of payments deficits; minimal investment funds from underdeveloped nations in the advanced nations; the manpower drain from underdeveloped to the advanced nations; and the flow of finished goods at high prices from developed to underdeveloped nations in contrast to the flow of agricultural and mineral wealth from the underdeveloped nations, one can hardly perceive that modernization is often achieved in backward areas at the cost of postponing industrialization.[19]

The case of Argentina and the United States represents a Heisenberg indeterminancy situation. Both countries exhibit similar indicators of modernization—of cultural identification, but there is little correlation between their respective indicators of industrialization and foreign trade. Germani[20] estimates that on a cultural scale of *modernism*, Argentina ranks alongside Germany, England and even the United States; whereas on a scale of *industrialism*, it ranks closer to Brazil, Mexico, and Ecuador, and even some African countries (see Table 2). This therefore strongly supports the view that an immense gap exists between economic development and sociocultural modernization.

One way of working out a systematic theory that would resolve this particular variety of the Heisenberg principle would be to show how attitudes affect structures and, contrariwise, how structures affect attitudes. One might say that Lipset has already attempted the former, namely, to show the movement from attitudes to a change in social structure;[21] while this writer has emphasized the latter, namely, how structures affect attitudes.[22] Still, neither approach quite resolves the issues since the causal sequence involves trend analyses that the data themselves are not refined enough to yield up thus far. That is to say, the choice between an idealistic frame of reference, stressing the need for change in people, and an orientation toward revolutionary behavior or mass responses to structural inequities, is ultimately still determined by some kind of animal faith. I venture to say that lurking behind idealistic formulations is the researcher's belief in individual initiative and gradual change, while naturalistic formations equally tend to reveal a contrasting cluster of beliefs in mass organization and revolutionary change.

[19] See Comisión Económica para América Latina, *Boletín Estadístico de América Latina*. Vol. III, No. 1, Feb., 1966 (New York: United Nations, 1966); and *The Economic Development of Latin America in the Post-War Period* (E/CN) (New York: United Nations, 1964).

[20] Gino Germani, *Política y sociedad en una época de transición: de la sociedad tradicional a la sociedad de masas* (Buenos Aires: Editorial Paidós, 1962).

[21] Seymour Martin Lipset, "Values, Education and Entrepreneurship," in *Elites in Latin America*, Lipset and Aldo Solari, eds. (New York: Oxford University Press, 1967), pp. 3–49.

[22] Irving Louis Horowitz, "The Mental Set of Developing Man," in *Three Worlds of Development* (New York: Oxford University Press, 1966), pp. 291–332.

As far as possible, the degree of attitudes in contrast to structures has to be measured in terms of real consequences. We must ask ourselves whether modernizing attitudes toward achievement lead to a revolution in social structure or provide even a greater measure of security, wealth, power or other indicators of development. For instance, we should examine those nations in this hemisphere that had substantial sociopolitical revolutions in the twentieth century, namely, Mexico and Cuba in the Western hemisphere, and contrast them with those nations adopting a more evolutionary posture toward the same developmental goals, such as Chile, Argentina and Venezuela.

A serious problem in attitude surveys lies in achieving true comparabilities which are not tautological. If the cultural values of South American and North American peoples are compared, and the total cross-national sample is drawn from highly urbanized sectors, the values expressed by the respondents may represent modernization attitudes rather than point up real national similitudes.[23] This is made forcefully clear in a recent survey of Argentine attitudes on the Vietnam War. The sample revealed a sharp class demarcation in attitudes unlike what comparable surveys have indicated for the United States. This principle of qualitative specificity in survey questions—more often observed in the breach than in the execution—is illustrated in this survey questionnaire. When asked the causes of American intervention, the Argentine middle and lower classes tended to attribute it to the nature of capitalism, colonialism, imperialism, militarism. Only 19 percent of the upper classes saw these as causative factors, but 50 percent of the middle class and 45 percent of the lower class gave this as the answer. On the other hand, the upper classes assigned the causes of the war to the need to defend democracy, liberty, and the West (43 percent) or the status answer: the prestige requirements of a great world power (36 percent). The lower classes credited the "defense of democracy" answer in only 18 percent of the cases, and the status response in only 3 percent of the cases. On the question of how the war could be solved, the lower classes and middle classes saw the resolution in self-determination and sovereignty of the Vietnamese to the extent of 65 percent and 62 percent respectively; while the upper classes, in 45 percent of the cases sampled, saw the solution in restraining the expansion of communism and the totalitarian system of government.[24] This demonstrates that class factors seem much more powerful in explaining attitudinal differences than might be surmised from the customary social mobility questionnaires.

THE NATURE OF THE EXPLANATORY RELATIONSHIP—THE ORDER OF CAUSATION

Some authors immediately assign to attitudes a causal role in the developmental process, without dealing with construct validation, consistency,

---

[23] This seems a particularly acute problem in accepting the findings given in Gabriel A. Almond and Sidney Verba, *The Civic Culture* (Boston and Toronto: Little, Brown & Co., 1965).

[24] "Encuesta: Qué piensan los argentinos sobre Vietnam," *Primera Plana*, (March 5, 1968), p. 28.

sequence, and congruence. McClelland's need-achievement theory, while interesting, is difficult to accept as a stimulus for development because of the problem of validation.[25] Hagen's withdrawal of status respect theory seems even more far-fetched.[26] It would take an entire generation before the withdrawal of status respect would have significant developmental implications. On the other hand, following McClelland, one would have to revise all the different children's books and fairy tales so that they would manifest high "n-ach." And even then we would have to wait a generation for confirmation of the theory.

The causal role of attitudes and values in development continues to haunt social science thinking. The logic that may account for the persistence of such a viewpoint is that because there are no social structures dismembered from the individuals who operate and maintain them, and there are no individuals without attitudes and values, attitudes must thus have causal roles. This syllogism is a caricature, and yet it underlies the attitudinal approach to development. Even economics, which tends to rely more on objective (structural) data, makes assumptions about the attitudinal aspects of man, such as the much debased "rationality" of economic man.

To pose the question of which comes first—values or structures—is really to pose a "chicken-or-egg" debate. Both can be shown to be interlinked. The root question for applied social science is *where* should one break into the circle of causality? Since attitudes and structures can be logically considered as either causes or consequences, we must postulate the conditions in which it is more expedient, parsimonious, and effective to consider one as either cause or effect. It should be pointed out, though, that a single attitude can lead to different kinds of behavior, just as different attitudes can lead to a single behavior; an individual's behavior might not be significant unless translated into a group action, which in turn might not be significant unless translated into institutionalized behavior. On the other hand, institutionalization of processes, while rendering greater predictive validity, does not guarantee uniform effects on different people.

The need, therefore, is for "contextual types" of analysis, which take both attitudes and structures into consideration. We also need to know whether the relationships between the two are multiplicative and/or additive. Furthermore, we need to know the appropriate time-lags involved between the two kinds of indicators of change. We need to investigate threshold conditions. Just as in economics Rostow's "pre-conditions" must be attained before one can reach self-sustained growth, before the take-off stage,[27] we would like to know what the threshold points for attitudes effective in social change might

---

[25] Even David C. McClelland, who first offered his need-achievement theory in *The Achieving Society* (Princeton, N.J.: Van Nostrand Co., 1961), has considerably modified his claims in more recent work. See in particular "Personality Changes After Training," in David C. McClelland and David G. Winter, *Motivating Economic Achievement* (New York: The Free Press, 1969), pp. 324–335.

[26] Everett E. Hagen, "How Economic Growth Begins: A Theory of Social Change," *Journal of Social Issues*, 19 (January, 1963), pp. 20–34.

[27] See Walt W. Rostow, "The Take-off into Self-Sustained Growth," *The Economic Journal*, 66 (March, 1956), pp. 25–48.

be. The most promising lines of investigation are those that deal with processes, rather than static equilibrium models which have characterized social science for all too long.

The researcher must not lose sight of the limitations involved in the nature of the data utilized. For instance, attitude approaches to change and development tend to emphasize the innovative role of the middle class, but managerialism is only useful insofar as it presupposes the existence of a capitalist system of economic exchange. Klausner,[28] in his study of total societies, writes: "The 'total society' involves linking concepts belonging to different theoretical networks. The simplest case is that of the bi-disciplinary statement. A 'good' bi-disciplinary statement will involve two terms, each referring to a distinct theoretical system—for example, one referring to the personality and the other to the social system; or to distinct subsystems—for example, one referring to the polity and the other to the economy. The statement will also cite a mechanism that mediates the events in these two systems. Usually the mechanism consists of an interactive process within a specified social structure. The function of the mechanism is to transform an event in one system into an event in another system. If no mechanism is cited, the causes of the asserted co-occurrence of events remains indeterminate. The mechanism may be antecedent to the independent event, or forged by the interaction of the independent and dependent events, or be in a third system or subsystem which shares a boundary with both the dependent and independent events. A special case is that of the loop in which the independent and dependent events are two states of the same system. A mechanism in another system may be called upon to explain the change of state."

Conclusions

The choice between an intrinsic standpoint and an extrinsic standpoint is, at rock bottom, a decision in favor of either a theory of values (modernism) or a theory of interests (structuralism). To argue the case for underdevelopment is to argue a set of value premises related to backwardness. Whereas, to argue the case for the extrinsic causes of stagnation is to argue the case for an interest theory; namely, that it is primarily in the interest of the advanced nations to exploit the less developed nations.

The literature demonstrates that this methodological dilemma creates an enormous ideological chasm between those who believe that the fully developed nations require underdevelopment and those who believe they do not require underdevelopment. The solution to such a problem cannot be made *a priori*; it is obviously clear that both external factors and internal factors are important in accounting for development. What is remarkable is how few theorists attempt any kind of fusion between external and internal factors;

[28] Samuel Klausner, *The Study of Total Societies* (New York: Anchor Books, Inc., 1967), pp. 3–29 ("Links and Missing Links Between the Sciences of Man," pp. 28–29).

how little effort there has been in this direction. In the Lipset and Solari collection on developing elites, the essays can be divided between those social scientists who assume that internal factors and value problems are the key, and those who assume that the external factors and interest problems are the key.[29] Those who assume the value standpoint are invariably those who take attitudes as a measuring device, while those who take the interest approach use structural variables to prove their points.

The problem has been compounded rather than resolved by newer forms of methodology. The introduction of multiple variables in present computer techniques of analysis simply adds factors not previously considered in attempting to explain variance. But those who manifest faith in the additive value of factors fail to provide a scale of factor intensity to explain the problems at hand. It is peculiar as well as unfortunate that factor analysis has still not yielded insight into problems such as whether the Catholic life cycle of most Latin American peoples is a greater factor in their state of underdevelopment than the capitalist economic system. Indeed, the relationship between religious factors and economic factors remains clouded in Weberian rhetoric. Developmentalists lack a basis comparable to the analysis of capitalism provided for Western Europe and the United States. Approaching such a fundamental issue is further complicated by the tendency to add to the quantity of variables employed in the analysis, rather than reducing the number by a process of statistical condensation.

It has been argued by Daland that in Brazil the notion of economic planning is basically a ploy used to mobilize the population on a national basis into the political system.[30] The main purpose of planning, then, is not economic growth, but political mobilization. Further verification of this comes from that exceptional "case"—Japan, a nation which tends to confound most analyses of underdeveloped states and/or stagnant societies. Japan has exhibited a remarkable degree of internal development under a basic capitalist framework, and a remarkable degree of penetration by foreign capitalist nations. Yet its growth has not taken place after the sort of revolution that one is led to expect is necessary. On the other hand, the structural framework too demands an explanation for this, and urges upon us an explanation of Japanese exceptionalism in terms of the feudal class structures in that nation. The structural problem is thus directly connected to the nation-building issue.

Whatever the weaknesses of nation-building analysis, and they are many, it has the singular virtue of compelling an examination of the exchange system involved in bilateral national dealings. It focuses upon the direct relationships between any given underdeveloped nation and any given fully developed nation, and how that relationship specifically leads to certain kinds of outcomes. Thus, an analysis of the relationship between the United States and Bolivia, or the Soviet Union and Poland, may be the key pivotal framework for the discussion of underdevelopment. International comparison is not

[29] Lipset and Solari, *Elites in Latin America.*
[30] Robert T. Daland, *Brazilian Planning: Developmental Politics and Administration* (Chapel Hill, N.C.: University of North Carolina Press, 1967).

simply a general appreciation of the connection between fully developed and underdeveloped nations, but of very specific bilateral relationships between large and small nations. And here, as Apter and Andrain indicate,[31] structuralists and game theorists join hands in displaying the important role of the bargaining situation in which underdeveloped nations oftentimes try to get themselves into for the precise purpose of realizing their own internal aims and ambitions.

The structural approach permits us to move beyond an internal organismic explanatory system into a comparative framework. It also enables us to distinguish internal problems of underdevelopment from imperial problems of economic stagnation. Finally, it enables the researcher to single out key interactional connections (usually bilateral relationships) that are maintained between fully developed and semi-developed states.

Soares and Hamblin[32] have suggested one solution to the problem of combining census and election data with survey data: for each unit, national, state or county, the survey attitudinal response should be averaged. This average attitudinal response then could be combined in an analysis with other demographic or structural characteristics of that same unit. Thus the percent of the survey respondents who strongly agree with the survey item measuring "favorableness to revolution" might be correlated with the percent of unemployed (a measure of class polarization); the percent divorced (a measure of anomie); the percent urban (living in communities of 10,000 or more).

One remaining methodological problem is the adequacy of the survey sample for generalizing about each sub-unit. This would probably render some existing sample unsuitable for this purpose, since the respondents are highly clustered. However, in theory it is a simple matter to design a sample that would adequately represent each sub-unit. While the method of analysis may be limited for presently available survey data, there is no reason why new studies could not be made that would fulfill all the methodological requirements. Such an analysis has many advantages over present macroscopic analyses, since by and large these do not include any attitudinal data. If values, attitudes, beliefs do have an effect at the macro level, then certainly they would control significant portions of the variance in such analyses.

Coleman's report on *Equality of Educational Opportunity* has followed a similar procedure.[33] His survey involves many school characteristics, and in one analysis he correlates these school characteristics with various attitudinal characteristics which are averages of the individual responses in the school. It turns out that these attitudinal characteristics do control significant portions of the variance independently of the school's structural characteristics. The

31 David E. Apter and Charles Andrain, "Comparative Government: Developing New Nations," in *Political Science—Advance of the Discipline*, Marian D. Irish, ed. (Englewood Cliffs, N.J.: Prentice-Hall, 1968), pp. 82–126.

32 See Glaucio Soares and Robert L. Hamblin. "Socio-Economic Variables and Voting for the Radical Left: Chile, 1952," *American Political Science Review*, 61 (Dec., 1967), pp. 1053–1065.

33 James S. Coleman, *et al., Equality of Educational Opportunity* (Washington, D.C.: Department of Health, Education and Welfare, Office of Education, 1966).

dependent variable in this case is academic achievement. Coleman has been criticized for this averaging process, primarily because it is possible that such a reductionism fails to properly weight the factors. Demographic and structural variables all turn out to be proportions which are averages. There is no reason why other kinds of measures, particularly attitudinal measures, cannot be averaged in the same way and thus included in the same analysis.

Whether attitudes can be viewed as simply one more variable on a structural scale of measurement remains in contention. And this might better be resolved by psychological measures that are in fact comparable with all other forms of structural measures. If much past effort seems epigrammatic, it is simply because the level of analysis in developmental studies thus far has rarely gotten beyond aggregative data. What is needed are more sophisticated measures than are thus far available. The important contribution of the structural framework to discussions on development, beyond a non-Rostovian look at stages of growth, is that its conceptual richness uniquely enables the researcher to match up strategies of social development with the history of societies.

The conclusions which follow from this analysis, while tentative, are nonetheless compelling. First, the process of development involves subunits of industrialization and modernization. Second, these two main subunits may or may not be spatially or temporarily parallel. Indeed, available data indicate that for the most part they are quite distinct and even antithetical in certain periods. Third, as in the Heisenberg wave-particle effect, it is best to analyze and generalize about discrete processes entailed in development, rather than make a monistic assumption about the nature of changes in society. However, this does not necessarily mean an assent to dualistic formulations. Within the dual processes of industrialization and modernization, it is quite possible to make decisive choices by conceptualizing attitudinal data as one critical cluster of factors. In this way we can better determine what factors are independent and interdependent in any given national decision concerning priorities for social change.

The Politics of Public Education, Health and Welfare in the USA and Western Europe: How Growth and Reform Potentials Have Differed

Arnold J. Heidenheimer

This essay contributes to an understanding of the problems of convergence and divergence of modernizing societies by showing how those generally accepted as being "advanced" differ in the ways in which they allocate resources to health, education, and welfare. The author draws in particular a distinction between Western European policies, which are generally similar, and those of the United States. His conclusions point to the continuing and pervasive influence exercised by a society's heritage of values throughout the course of modernization.

Comparativists interested in the political dynamics of policy development, and students of public policy desirous of studying national programs in cross-national contexts, face similar dilemmas at present. There is a literature focusing on decision-making processes which often pays little regard to policy substance. There are statistical analyses of expenditure levels, but these are difficult to relate to the ample literature bearing on how particular substantive problems have been handled in specific national and local situations. As a result, political scientists interested in the cross-national study of broad policy

"The Politics of Public Education, Health and Welfare in the USA and Western Europe: How Growth and Reform Potentials Have Differed" by Arnold J. Heidenheimer is reprinted by permission of Cambridge University Press from *British Journal of Political Science*, III (July 1973), 315–340.

Heidenheimer teaches political science at Washington University in St. Louis. He is co-author of *Business Associations and the Financing of Political Parties* (1968) and author of *The Governments of Germany* (3rd ed., 1971).

An earlier version of this paper was presented to the 1972 meeting of the American Political Science Association, and benefited from panel comments from Professors Thomas Anton, Theodore Marmor and William Safran. It is related to a larger study being pursued with Carolyn Adams, which has involved valuable assistance by students at Washington University. I am also indebted for critical comments to Professors James W. Fesler, Frederic L. Pryor, Harold Noah, Arnold C. Anderson, and Richard Rose.

areas—such as those studying social policy development in Western Europe and America—are now engaged in the creation of historically based frameworks which will permit more fruitful analysis of differences in the patterns of development.

Those who do manage to hurdle the conventional boundaries between different policy sectors soon discover that, just as varying citizenships bestow different benefits on individuals,[1] so the proponents of expanded public social programs have been faced with different opportunities and with different confining conditions on the two sides of the North Atlantic; indicators of the range and coverage of European and American public programs, such as those noted below, make evident that programs in such social policy areas as social insurance, health care and post-primary education have exhibited quite different growth configurations.

This article seeks to identify some of the most significant contrasts between the priorities and allocation patterns in twentieth century American and West European social policies and in so doing endeavors to help map a complex political geography. Europe for the purposes of the article is defined to include Britain, Sweden and Germany (West Germany since 1945). Such a limitation stands in contrast to the global approach to policy comparison whose utility Groth has been among the first to explore.[2] But the strategy of retaining contextual contact by restricting the systems whose policy outputs are analysed has also been employed by other social scientists, such as Reinhard Bendix, Gaston V. Rimlinger, Frederic L. Pryor and Anthony King, who have also made various mapping contributions from the perspectives of their different disciplines.[3]

To the extent that I go beyond mapping to explore the roles some political factors may have played in shaping the contours of the map, causal linkages are suggested in the spirit of hypothesis-generation. Broad questions may sometimes call for bold initial explanatory formulations. Why, for example, has American post-primary education growth been 'ahead' of European growth patterns just as strikingly as public US health programs have been 'behind' comparable European ones? My strategy is to scan how European legislative and administrative policy instruments—here labelled jurisdictions—differed from American ones entrusted with similar responsibilities, and to explore the apparent consequences. Why did some European social policy 'imports', such as social insurance, become successfully 'Americanized' while others did not? Why were American models of broadening educational opportunity much more rapidly adopted in some European systems than in others? The explanations explored seek to develop insights concerning how institutional differences

---

[1] T. H. Marshall, *Class, Citizenship and Social Development* (Garden City, N.Y.: Anchor, 1965), p. 131.

[2] Alexander L. Groth, *Comparative Politics: A Distributive Approach* (New York: Macmillan, 1971).

[3] One might also mention the forthcoming studies by Hugh Heclo, *From Relief to Income Maintenance: Modern Social Policy-Making in Britain and Sweden* (New Haven: Yale University Press, 1974) and Andrew Martin, *The Politics of Economic Policy in the United States from a Comparative Perspective* (Beverly Hills, Sage, 1972).

imposed varied opportunities and confining conditions on, particularly, the interest associations of service suppliers and benefit recipients, thus influencing policy goals and program implementation.

Public Goods

OVERVIEW OF US AND EUROPEAN DEVELOPMENT

The most important differences in the sequence of public social policy introduction, and in the subsequent rates of expansion of coverage, benefit expansion and public expenditure commitment, may be summarized in terms of the following propositions:

1. Public *social insurance* and some other kinds of income maintenance programs were introduced in the US with about a one-generation lag behind Europe, but then exhibited growth rates which tended to bring the scope of American programs closer to those of the European.
2. With regard to *public education,* the broadening of US post-primary school opportunities occurred a generation earlier than in Europe, and European systems have only in the past few decades allowed their secondary and tertiary systems to enter the takeoff stage.
3. With regard to *non-education public services and benefits in kind,* such as health services and public housing, where markets have been dominated by private suppliers, US programs have lagged behind European ones by as much as two generations. These programs long remained in the 'non-takeoff' category, exhibiting low growth rates compared to their European equivalents.

These generalizations are subject to refinement and elaboration. I will not attempt to cite the substantiating evidence here, though some of it will be referred to below. The above categories may be viewed as exemplary and somewhat open-ended. None of them covers the public assistance programs which are predominantly associated with 'welfare' in the narrow American sense; they obviously do not exhaust the variety of benefits offered within the broader meaning of 'social welfare' in Europe.

HOW SOCIAL INSURANCE CAME LATE, BUT THEN 'TOOK OFF'

To the student of political participation, the order in which initial pension and social insurance programs were introduced presents something of a puzzle. In most European countries—such as Germany (1888), Britain (1908–11) and Sweden (1913)—social insurance was introduced at about the time most working-class males were granted the franchise in national elections. In the

United States, by contrast, a full century elapsed between the extension of voting rights during the Jacksonian period and the initiation of social insurance in 1935. However, as a historically-oriented scholar observed in 1960, although 'the US entered rather late on the social security road typically chosen by industrialized countries, it is now continuing on it in a linear pattern.'[4] Indeed, during recent decades the average rate of increase in social security expenditures in relation to GNP has been higher in the US than in most European countries. So popular has the basic old-age social insurance program (OASDI) become in the US that successive social programs, such as health insurance, have been pyramided onto it in order to facilitate their adoption.[5]

The timing of the introduction of public pensions seems to have been determined by complex relationships between the growth of labor unions, the prevailing ideologies, and the strategies of social demand anticipation on the part of governments. Pryor, who has pioneered the statistical measurement of the correlates of public programs, found that union development was the only variable that correlated positively with the introduction of social insurance up to 1913.[6] But in Europe governments often did not wait for socialist unions or parties to articulate demands. Rather, they pursued a pre-emptive strategy —in the case of both Bismarck in Germany and Lloyd George in Britain—of presenting the workers with social benefits in the hope of limiting their support for socialist class-based parties. In Europe the upper classes, or at least portions of them, found programs of social protection for the workers ideologically more acceptable in the pre-1914 era than did the more individualist, laissez-faire oriented elites of America. The slow and irregular growth of workers' organizations, moreover, posed insufficient stimuli for the latter to resort to the pre-emptive strategy.

Greenstone perceives 'the superimposition of an industrial economic order on a deeply entrenched democratic, procapitalist and federal political regime'[7] as having conditioned the low capacity of American labor to convert collectivist working-class demands into political issues. The resulting 'greater variation in political behavior' of American unions was borne out with regard to social insurance. Thus, the dominant AFL leadership under Samuel Gompers opposed those labor leaders who supported social insurance as a step toward greater social equality, claiming that 'governmental regulation must tend to fix citizens of the country into classes, and a long-established insurance system would tend to make these classes rigid.'[8] Gompers saw most public welfare measures as potential competitors to goals that the unions might pursue in bargaining with employers. Consequently, 'even as Sidney and Beatrice Webb

---

[4] Detley Zollner, *Oeffentliche Sozialleistungen und wirtschaftliche Entwicklung* (Berlin: Duncker and Humblot, 1963), p. 54.

[5] Theodore R. Marmor, *The Politics of Medicare* (London: Routledge and Kegan Paul, 1970), Chap. 2.

[6] Frederic L. Pryor, *Public Expenditures in Communist and Capitalist Nations* (Homewood, Ill.: Irwin, 1968), p. 475.

[7] J. David Greenstone, *Labor in American Politics* (New York: Knopf, 1969), p. 365.

[8] Gaston V. Rimlinger, *Welfare Policy and Industrialization in Europe, America and Russia* (New York: John Wiley and Sons, 1971), p. 83.

were . . . discussing the method of legislation as one of [British] labor's primary devices, the leaders of the American labor movement were opposing all forms of action involving law and politics.'[9] A generation later the welfare policy goals of US unions were still 'less extensive than the welfare programs actually enacted in many European countries'.[10]

In countries where workers had reasonably developed feelings of class consciousness, and where the claim of the dominant union federation to articulate the interests of the working class was not seriously disputed, the latter generally advanced or supported proposals for social insurance programs as instruments for the reduction of social inequalities. This was the case in Sweden and in Britain. In Germany, rival unions and the authoritarian government itself competed with the socialist unions for control of the working-class clientele and, since Bismarck's social insurance program was an instrument in that struggle, the socialist unions and the Social Democratic Party opposed it. Indeed Rimlinger compares the American and German union leaders—although they took opposite views on the desirability of increasing class consciousness—insofar as both showed 'more concern for the welfare of their organizations than for the welfare of the working class'.[11]

The American unions' most important political characteristic, as McConnell notes, has been their narrow constituencies. This was demonstrated through their amazingly low level of involvement in the planning of social security programs, even when they shifted to supporting social insurance during the New Deal period. Subsequently, they diluted their support for expansion of the program because of their concern for the development of private pension and welfare programs that did more to enhance their institutional security. To the degree that trade unionism generally 'created a sort of secondary industrial citizenship, which naturally became imbued with the spirit appropriate to an institution of citizenship',[12] American unions nurtured a spirit congruent with the particularist concepts of citizenship fostered by the political culture.

Among the affluent industrialized democracies there has been a consistent pattern of growth in social insurance, and among Western countries the size of social security budgets has tended to be most closely associated with how long they have been in operation.[13] Still, in recent years the spending level on public social insurance programs has remained lower as a percentage of GNP in high-income non-European countries like the US and Australia than in the middle-income European countries.[14] Taira and Kilby found that spending levels on

---

[9] Grant McConnell, *Private Power and American Democracy* (New York: Knopf, 1966), p. 83.

[10] Greenstone, *Labor in American Politics*, p. 363.

[11] Rimlinger, *Welfare Policy*, p. 80.

[12] Marshall, *Class, Citizenship and Social Development*, p. 122.

[13] Henry Aaron, 'Social Security: International Comparisons,' in Otto Eckstein, ed., *Studies in the Economics of Income Maintenance* (Washington, D.C.: Brookings Institution, 1967), pp. 15–17.

[14] Felix Paukert, 'Social Security and Income Redistribution: a Comparative Study,' *International Labor Review*, 98 (November, 1968), 425–50.

social insurance are associated not only with the age of the program but also with 'proximity to continental Europe'. They argue that 'in developed Western countries, resources have not been constraints on the extent of social security . . . hence no tight correlation between . . . GNP and social security development should be expected', and conclude that 'the forces that push the demand for and the development of social security are largely political'.[15] The popularity of private pension programs is now waning somewhat in the US, and political pressure has built up for the adoption of expansionary techniques—such as the automatic coupling of benefit levels to the cost-of-living index—that political leaders in Europe have helped to adopt in the last two decades.

EDUCATION: ITS MORE FAVORABLE PRECONDITIONS FOR 'TAKEOFF'

Elementary education was dispensed earlier as a free public good in the US than in Europe, but the distributive effect of this long remained conditioned by the fact that its provision remained uneven and consumption often effectively voluntary. After the Civil War the US approached the creation of a general system of compulsory primary education, which Prussia had established a century earlier. At this time the scope and recruitment of secondary education was as limited in the US as in Europe. 'Only a small minority of the community's children even began high school . . . The working class frequently viewed it as an upper-class institution, irrelevant to their aspirations and impossible for them to utilize since adolescent earnings were important to the family.'[16] Then, from the 1890s, the scope and functions of public secondary schools expanded to a degree that had no contemporaneous European equivalent.

In the 'takeoff' era of American secondary education, during which a new high school was established each day, the percentage of American 14-to-17 year olds attending full-time secondary schools quintupled from 6.7 per cent in 1890 to 32.3 per cent in 1920; and of course it has continued its upward trajectory since then. This growth coincided with the relative decline of the private school sector (to 1940) and by the 1920s caused the high school to be 'looked upon as an integral part of the school system, to be attended by children with little reference to social, economic or intellectual status'.[17] By 1928 the proportion of the age group which was attending general or academic secondary schools full-time was five times higher in the US than in Europe.[18] Successive quantitative thresholds were crossed in the US at least a generation before Europe. In terms of age cohort proportions enrolled in secondary

[15] Koji Taira and Peter Kilby, 'Differences in Social Security Development in Selected Countries,' *International Social Security Review*, xxii (1969), 139–53, pp. 145–6.
[16] Michael B. Katz, 'Secondary Education to 1870,' *Encyclopedia of Education*, viii (New York: Macmillan, 1971), pp. 163–4.
[17] Isaac Leon Kandel, ed., *Twenty-Five Years of American Education* (New York: Macmillan, 1924), p. 267.
[18] The percentages of 14–18 year olds attending school full time in 1928–30 were 33 per-

schools, the US passed the 10–12 percent mark about 1910, Europe generally not till after 1945; the 30 percent mark was passed by the US in the early 1920s, in Europe not until the 1960s.[19]

This unique American 'takeoff' of post-primary public education is difficult to explain purely in terms of political or economic variables. An explanation in terms of values and beliefs is probably pertinent in connection with a phenomenon fed from such deep socio-cultural taproots. Perhaps their essence is caught by Berthoff's suggestion that 'as keeper and official inculcator of the amalgam of economic and idealistic values later identified as the American Way of Life, the public school was the closest approximation to an American established church.' Taken in conjunction with the generally applicable laissez-faire taboos against government enterprise, these factors may help to explain why the turn-of-the-century public school was the 'only established American institution in which social reformers and the state could effectively join forces'.[20] In Europe, class privileges and antagonisms, and the unresolved jurisdictional conflicts between states and churches, prevented such a joining of interests.

Secondary education performed many functions useful to Progressive-era elites, among them the socialization of the stream of non-North European immigrants, the inculcation with values and skills approved of by future employers, and so on—aspects well covered in the recent literature. But it must also, during the crucial 'takeoff' decades, have appealed to the Yankee sense of a good bargain. Expenditures rose, of course, but they were kept down by practices which would not have been—and later were not—feasible in European settings, where secondary schools were high-standard and high-status institutions. In the 1890s some 90 percent of high schools were housed together with primary schools, and in 1903 the average teacher salary appears to have been only six-tenths as high as the hardly munificent average for other

cent in the US, 14 percent in Sweden, 16 percent in Germany, and 16 percent in England. In the US four-fifths of secondary pupils were in general secondary schools; in Europe two-thirds or more were attending vocational-type schools. N. Hans, 'Comparative Educational Statistics,' *The Yearbook of Education: 1934* (London: Evans, 1935), pp. 172–3, 180–3.

19 The enrolment in all secondary schools per 10,000 of population was, according to the sources utilized by Banks, as follows:

	US	Germany	Sweden	England
1890	32	74	42	
1900	68	89	42	
1910	99	99	57	
1920	247	117	61	83
1930	388	119	65	115
1946	581	205 ('50)	267	283
1960	571	231	278	673

Arthur S. Banks, ed., *Cross-Polity Times-Series Data* (Cambridge: MIT Press, 1971), Segment Six.

20 Rowland T. Berthoff, *An Unsettled People* (New York: Harper and Row, 1971), pp. 438, 440.

public employees.[21] Even in the more affluent 1920s, US per capita expenditures were only twice as high for secondary as for primary education, while in Europe the comparable ratios varied between 2.5:1 and 5:1.[22]

The individual mobility goals which provided the American high school with pupils also came to provide it with cheap labor, through the high utilization of female, and later increasingly working-class female, teachers, many of whose families may well have subsidized the public system.[23] Thus, at the same time that the post-Flexner 'elitization' of medicine headed the US towards its status as a high-income territory for predominantly male doctors, the 'democratization' of education reinforced the US position as a jurisdiction offering comparatively low incomes and status to a predominantly female teaching force.[24]

The social-levelling thrust helps explain why American labor unions were active supporters of post-primary education, whereas their European counterparts generally did not become interested until the 1930s, at first tepidly, and then more warmly in the 1960s. For the Europeans academic secondary education remained a bastion of middle-class values; for the Americans it had ceased to be so. Few European union leaders could have echoed the Cigarmakers' statement of 1890 that viewed schools and trade unions as 'complementary agencies of general social improvement'.[25]

The most pervasive tendency among all American interest groups of the period, however, was the extent to which, in Welter's words, they pursued the fundamental strategy of *substituting* education for other techniques of social action in attempts to cope with social problems.[26] Thus, Gompers rejected child labor legislation but supported higher standards of compulsory education. A housing reformer like Veiller rejected attempts to duplicate European models in public housing and instead recommended regulatory legislation backed up by formal education not only of landlords but also of janitors. The latter were to care for the tenements of New York, Boston and Chicago after attending training schools where they could 'learn both the theory and practice of their work'.[27] An admiring British visitor noted that American education had set itself the 'ideal of saving the country from the pauperizing curse of public charity'.[28] By 1935 education was still described as 'the only fully developed social service'.[29]

[21] Solomon Fabricant, *The Trend of Government Activity in the United States Since 1900* (New York: National Bureau of Economic Research, 1952), pp. 39, 60. Salary data calculated by author on the basis of data in above source.

[22] Hans, 'Comparative Educational Statistics,' p. 171. The US, in increasing its secondary teaching force tenfold between 1890 and the 1920s, added more teachers at this level than Germany had teaching at all levels in 1895. US education's share of all public social welfare expenditures climbed steadily to a peak of 56.8 percent in 1929. Its share of GNP first climbed slowly (1913–1.3 percent), more quickly in the 1920s (1929–2.4 percent), and then quickly again from 1947 (1966–4.7 percent).

[23] A possibly suggestive interview was with a Chicago teamster in 1900, 'who had encouraged his daughter's ambitions to become a school teacher only to find his own self-respect jeopardized: he was forced first to rent a new flat and buy new furniture; he was then expected to entertain his daughter's status-conscious, white-collar friends; what is more, as a result of his added expenses, the father was forced to send out his younger children to supplement his now inadequate wages; finally, his teacher-daughter threatened, at every

SOCIAL SERVICES AND IN-KIND BENEFITS: HOW SOME NEVER GOT TO THE TAKEOFF STAGE

European public social service programs, apart from education, often started out modestly, passed through a 'takeoff' period, and grew to claim substantial proportions of the GNP. Comparable American programs were often initiated a generation or two after Europe's, but, unlike American income maintenance programs like social insurance, they typically did not grow much. Regarding the dynamics of social security expansion, Rimlinger has noted that 'it can be observed that the expansion of the system is easier than its initial creation, because of the weaker ideological position of the opponents.' [30] This generalization would seem to hold true, too, for European social service programs, but not for many American ones.

After the initiation of state and federal health programs toward the close of the nineteenth century, American public expenditures for civilian health programs did not grow significantly in relation to GNP for half a century, and the ideological position of its opponents grew stronger rather than weaker. A national Board of Health was stillborn in 1883, and the Public Health Service remained an administrative ward of the Treasury Department until 1953. American public housing never reached 'takeoff' and has remained a stagnant and token program. Public child welfare services have expanded and contracted in irregular patterns, rather than exhibiting a consistent growth rate.[31]

Public health expenditures in the US constituted 0.4 per cent of GNP

sign of opposition from her father, to leave her home for more congenial surroundings.' Dana F. White, 'Education in the Turn-of-the-Century City: the Search for Control,' *Urban Education*, iv (1969), p. 178; Robert J. Havighurst and Bernice L. Neugarten, *Society and Education* (Boston: Allyn and Bacon, 1957), pp. 358–60.

24 Pryor, *Public Expenditures*, pp. 424, 428. Utilizing data from the 1950s, Pryor classifies the US as 'high,' or more than 3½ times average industrial wages for physicians' incomes, whereas countries like West Germany and Soviet Russia, are classified as 'low,' less than 2½ times industrial wages. For teachers, ratios of wages to average industrial wages for 1958 were 105 per cent for the US, 188 percent for West Germany, 185 percent for Austria, etc. See also Constantina Satilios-Rotschild, 'A Cross-Cultural Examination of Women's Marital, Educational and Occupational Options,' *Acta Sociologica*, xiv (1971), 96–113.

25 I. L. Kandel acknowledged that Europe would be slow to follow the American movement for universal secondary education because it was based more on equality than educational principles: 'Education,' *Encyclopedia of the Social Sciences*, v (New York: Macmillan, 1935), p. 421.

26 Rush Welter, *Popular Education and Democratic Thought in America* (New York: Columbia University Press, 1962), pp. 189, 241.

27 Lawrence Veiller, *Housing Reform* (New York: Sage Foundation, 1910), p. 189.

28 Reports of the Mosely Commission to the United States of America (London: Co-operative Printing Society, 1904), p. 398.

29 Alzada Comstock, 'Expenditures, Public,' *Encyclopedia of the Social Sciences*, vi, p. 7.

30 Rimlinger, *Welfare Policy*, p. 232.

31 Ida C. Merriam and Alfred M. Skolnik, *Social Welfare Expenditures under Public Programs in the United States, 1929–1966* (Washington: US Social Security Administration, 1968), p. 253.

in 1913, before the initial defeat of proposals to establish public health insurance. In 1932 they still accounted for only 0.7 percent of GNP. By 1964 they reached the 1 percent figure according to official statistics; but, if one deducts either or both of defense-connected and research expenditures, the proportion of GNP either remained static or actually declined.[32] Between 1950 and the early 1960s, the share of what the International Labor Office classifies as social security expenditures accounted for by public health service programs declined from about 10 percent to 6.6 percent in the US, while it increased from 18 percent to 23 percent in Sweden.[33] Expenditure statistics provide even more substantiation for the 'non-takeoff' thesis in the case of public housing.[34] Public housing and low-income housing subsidies constituted 0.05 per cent of GNP in 1936 and the same in 1965. Whereas US social insurance benefit payouts increased from $3.15 per capita in 1935 to $59 in 1955 to $121 in 1961, public housing expenditures per capita increased from ten cents to fifty-three cents to $1.06 over the same period.[35]

Factors associated with the initiation and takeoff of these public services have been less systematically examined than in the cases of social security and education. But, as will be shown below in the case of health, it is evident that the defensive strength of competing private suppliers of services was immensely greater in the American setting. This strength seems to have been associated, not only with the greater resonance which 'anti-socialist' appeals have always enjoyed in America, but also with the timing of successive implementation efforts. The period between about 1890 and the end of World War I saw immense strides in the professionalization, and corresponding interest group organization, of the skill groups involved in many socially relevant services. This occurred on both sides of the Atlantic, but most conspicuously during the Progressive period in the US.[36]

In Europe, public health insurance programs were introduced either before physicians were well organized, as in Germany,[37] or before they were cohesively organized, as in Britain in 1911. Similar attempts in the US a short while later ran into a determined opposition of a profession which had immensely strengthened its professional identity and organization in the preceding decades, and which succeeded in exercising its veto power within the pluralist American political structure.[38] In America more than in Europe, those pro-

---

[32] Merriam and Skolnik, *Social Welfare Expenditures*, pp. 192, 214.

[33] International Labor Office, *The Cost of Social Security: Sixth International Inquiry* (Geneva: International Labor Office, 1967), p. 322.

[34] Even the official document (Merriam and Skolnik, *Social Welfare Expenditures*, p. 161) ascertains that 'the amounts expended remained relatively modest.'

[35] Merriam and Skolnik, *Social Welfare Expenditures*, p. 193.

[36] Corinne Gilb, *Hidden Hierarchies: the Professions and the Government* (New York: Harper and Row, 1966), pp. 34–40; Rosemary Stevens, *American Medicine and the Public Interest* (New Haven: Yale University Press, 1971), Chap. 3; David Truman, *The Governmental Process* (New York: Knopf, 1951); Berthoff, *Unsettled People*, p. 450.

[37] Frider Naschold, *Kassenärzte und Krankenversicherungsreform* (Freiburg: Rombach, 1967), p. 152.

[38] Stevens, *American Medicine*, Chap. 7; Theodore F. Schlabach, *Edwin E. Witte, Cautious Reformer* (Madison: Wisconsin State Historical Society, 1969), pp. 112–15.

fessions employed in the public services developed a 'built-in aversion' toward the politicians whose influence was perceived as retarding their professional autonomy. Mosher has pointed out that socialization in many such professions involves a treatment of government as an 'outside agency', except for those particular areas in which the profession has dominant control.[39]

The successful resistance to public housing by real estate interests was obviously due more to greater business, rather than professional, opposition.[40] But professions like social work, which might have become active in favor of public housing, hardly did so. The historian of their conferences notes that 'no speaker before 1930 proposed a public subsidy for housing' and expressed his surprise that the profession gave 'such scant space on its programs to the way in which to secure suitable housing for families known so well to its members'.[41] The weakness of the proponents of public housing in the initial American legislative struggle of 1937 forced them to accept compromises which 'lastingly impaired public housing viability', and, according to Charles Abrams in 1969, would 'ultimately contribute to its demise'[42]—a prediction which has since come closer to realization.

Jurisdictions

PUBLIC JURISDICTIONS, PRIVATE MARKETS AND THE DEMAND FOR PUBLIC GOODS

In his survey of the development of social insurance in six countries, Rimlinger notes that 'the most democratic countries were slower to introduce social protection than the authoritarian and totalitarian ones.'[43] Demand articulation did not bear earlier policy fruits in the democracies partly because nineteenth century Britain and the United States were dominated by liberal elites subscribing to ideologies more hostile to protectionist programs, including social protection schemes, than were the ideologies of the elites in the more traditionalist authoritarian systems. In Prussia, not only bureaucrats but even industrialists favored the introduction of social insurance on paternalistic principles.[44]

In Prussia and Austria, governmental agencies had, since the absolutist era, continuously played a more active role in supplying social services. Their

39 Frederick Mosher, *Democracy and the Public Service* (New York: Oxford University Press, 1968), p. 109.

40 Lawrence Friedman, *Government and Slum Housing: a Century of Frustration* (Chicago: Rand McNally, 1968), pp. 105, 109.

41 Frank J. Bruno, *Trends in Social Work 1874–1956* (New York: Columbia University Press, 1957), pp. 227, 351.

42 Charles Abrams, 'Housing Policy—1937 to 1967,' in B. Frieden and William Nash, eds., *Shaping an Urban Future* (Cambridge: MIT Press, 1969), p. 36.

43 Rimlinger, *Welfare Policy*, p. 232.

44 Reinhard Bendix, *Nation-Building and Citizenship: Studies of our Changing Social Order* (New York: Wiley, 1964), pp. 81–3.

officials enjoyed much higher status than in Britain and the US and, because their public officialdoms had been reformed along bureaucratic lines at an earlier point in time, higher reputations for efficiency and incorruptibility.[45] In countries like Britain and the US, many official positions were in the nineteenth century still largely distributed on a patronage basis, and citizens' regard for both the probity and the efficiency of their incumbents was correspondingly lower.[46]

How, in this context, do we explain the sequence by which Britain and the US overcame their inhibitions and adopted versions of the previously distasteful continental programs? Why was Lloyd George more successful in introducing public pensions and health insurance than were Theodore Roosevelt or Woodrow Wilson? Most accounts have stressed ideological change and the emergence of the British Labour Party, but comparative explanations may be enhanced when one matches the dates of initial social insurance legislation with the dates of the introduction of civil service reform. The British Northcote-Trevelyan reform initiation in the 1850s preceded the initiation of American federal reforms through the Pendleton Act (1883) by a generation.[47] By the time Lloyd George came forward with his far-reaching public welfare proposals, the British public had had two generations in which to erase the image of corrupt and bumbling public servants inspired by earlier experience and by authors like Trollope. They could assume a high level of efficiency and impartiality on the part of both national and local civil servants. In the US, the corresponding transformation took place later and more incrementally, even on the federal level. However, by 1930 about 80 percent of federal appointive office holders were under civil service, so that Franklin Roosevelt could assume that the American public had developed at least a minimal trust in the administrative capacity of the national bureaucracy.

During earlier periods of American reform discussion, particularly during the Progressive era, mistrust of the probity and efficiency of public officialdom greatly strengthened the position of those who were opposed to public sector expansion on ideological and private-interest grounds. More than that, it deterred reformers from even proposing to endow public jurisdictions with more than regulatory powers. Examples can be found for most public service sectors:

> *Social Insurance, 1904:* John Graham Brooks, a leading specialist on social insurance gave the inefficient and wasteful conduct of most public administration as the major reason, together with its questionable consti-

[45] Eugene N. and Pauline Anderson, 'Bureaucratic Institutionalization in Nineteenth Century Europe,' in Arnold J. Heidenheimer, ed., *Political Corruption: Readings in Comparative Analysis* (New York: Holt, Rinehart and Winston, 1970), pp. 91–105.

[46] Samuel E. Finer, 'Patronage and the Public Service: Jeffersonian Democracy and the Public Service,' in Heidenheimer, ed., *Political Corruption*, pp. 106–28.

[47] The judgement of Robert Moses in *English Civil Service Reform* (New York: Columbia, 1903) that 'the conditions in the services of England and the United States at the beginning of reform were astonishingly similar' may be too strong. See also, Paul W. Van Riper, 'Adapting a British Political Convention to American Needs,' *Public Administration*, xxxi (1953), 317–30; Keith Callard, 'On the Ethics of Civil Servants in Great Britain and North America,' *Public Policy*, vii (1959), 134–56.

tutionality, for why it would be unwise for the US to embark on a social insurance program: 'The German success, such as it is, has been owing to a strictly competent and independent administration. With an administration like that which has controlled our [Civil War] army pensions, what would become of social insurance?' [48]

Housing, 1910: Lawrence Veiller, the leading advocate of slum housing reform, deprecated the idea that a 'higher standard of administration in the management of tenement houses' may be expected from city governments than from private owners. The politicians would be out for patronage and the civil service did not attract competent people:

> How are our city officers performing the functions with which they are now charged? Are our streets being properly cleaned? Is our police force being wisely administered? . . . Do public officers sell privileges to practice iniquity? . . . It would seem that we can widely postpone so important an experiment until we have achieved better municipal administration of those functions of government which now engage the attention of the authorities.[49]

Welfare Administration, pre-1929: E. C. Lindeman remarked that because of the assumptions of citizenship in a country like the US one might have supposed that 'the social services which the term public welfare ordinarily embraces would be thoroughly integrated . . . in the governmental machinery . . . Until recently, however, the contrary has been true.' He attributed the slow growth of centralized public welfare services to the high degree of local autonomy and to 'the early suspicious attitudes of social workers towards governmental relief and particularly outdoor relief, a position traceable in large part to the corruption of American politics and to the lack of opportunity for trained social workers to participate and direct the government services'.[50]

Such testimony supports the suggestion of Rakoff and Schaefer that 'the scope of *existing* governmental activity' vitally influences 'which social needs become translated into political demands and issues.' [51] The reformers of the Progressive period, unlike their European contemporaries, did not view existing governmental agencies, even at the national but especially at the local levels, as capable of assuming new administrative responsibilities. Later, state and local governments varied greatly with regard to even the formal provision for merit systems, and it was only the Social Security Act which forced merit systems on the states, as a condition for administering grant-aided public assistance programs. This and subsequent steps have only marginally improved the reputation of state and local bureaucracies, many of which are still frequently associated with corruption and scandal. In most American jurisdictions, the advantages of translating a social need into a political demand

[48] Bruno, *Trends in Social Work,* p. 259.
[49] Veiller, *Housing Reform,* pp. 79–83.
[50] E. C. Lindeman, 'Public Welfare,' *Encyclopedia of the Social Sciences,* xi, p. 688.
[51] Stuart H. Rakoff and Guenther F. Schaefer, 'Politics, Policy and Political Science: Theoretical Alternatives,' *Politics and Society,* i (1970), 51–77, p. 66.

have, in the view of many potential reformers, been counter-balanced by varieties of disadvantages that have weighed less heavily in the debates in Europe.

LOCAL JURISDICTIONS AND PUBLIC SERVICE DELIVERY

Most social welfare policies require, by their very nature, administrative activity at the local level and usually a sharing of competences with local government organs. Most European nations have at various times legislated fundamental reorganization of local government jurisdictions, often to increase their viability as instruments of welfare service delivery. This has seldom occurred in the US. Whereas income maintenance programs may centralize administration, most programs involving services and benefits-in-kind require significant involvement of local government agencies. Here it is important to note differences between US and European practices. American local government, in adjusting to new responsibilities, has rather spawned many additional service-specific local jurisdictions, such as school districts, water districts, sewage districts, etc. which may overlap with local government boundaries. These have been less frequently employed in Europe.[52] Also, insofar as local government officials in Europe are elected (and the appointive mode is more frequent at this level), they have gradually come to be more subject to the influence of nationally-integrated parties which provide guidelines for communal policy issues.

As regards educational jurisdictions, it is highly significant that the US and Britain, both of which had strong nineteenth-century local self-government traditions, shifted their institutional structures at the turn of the century in diametrically opposed directions. The British, who had been functioning with assortments of autonomous school boards, abolished 2,568 of these at one stroke through the Balfour Act of 1902, and transferred their powers to the general local authorities: the county and borough councils, which had earlier been amalgamated into larger and more viable units. In the US 'American political traditions of local independence make it nearly impossible to do this.'[53] One equivalent attempt, a 1917 New York State act which sought to require rural school boards to hand their powers over to local governments, had to be repealed because the school boards simply refused to abide by it.[54]

In the US, especially since the Progressive period, educators have been more successful than other service suppliers in detaching educational policy-making organs from the more politicized general local government jurisdictions. Because of the immense regional variations in local government structure and

[52] Samuel Humes and Eileen Martin, *The Structure of Local Government* (The Hague: International Union of Local Authorities, 1969), p. 75.

[53] Duane Lockard, 'Local Government,' *International Encyclopedia of Social Science*, IX (New York: Collier and Macmillan, 1968), p. 453.

[54] Harold Herman, *New York State and the Metropolitan Problem* (Philadelphia: University of Pennsylvania Press, 1963), p. 118.

nomenclature, the dimensions of the movement can be suggested most succinctly by means of expenditure data. By this measure, city corporations and
counties were expending 60 percent of local education expenditures in 1903;
the other 40 percent was shared by school districts, townships and other
types of units. By 1942 the school districts, etc. were expending 75 percent
of educational funds, cities and counties only one-quarter.[55] The school boards
were predominantly elected in non-partisan elections and had their own tax
resources. This institutional separation tended to give educators and related
interests greater autonomy, and probably a decided advantage over other
interests not provided with such special recognition and access.[56]

In the burgeoning world of American interest group pluralism, educators'
and parents' associations made the most of this opportunity and thus no doubt
contributed to the widening gap in public service allocation patterns between
Europe and the US in the first half of the twentieth century. In Britain or
Sweden, a city councillor might question whether an expensive high school
swimming pool ought to be given prioirty over a recreation center for the
elderly or a park for the unaffluent middle-aged. In the US he would not only
have been swimming against the priorities of a youth-centered culture, he
would have been open to the charge of sticking his nose outside of his proper
jurisdiction.

Coons, after reviewing the great inequalities produced by localist education
control at the turn of the century, reflect that 'a revolution might have been
expected, aimed at forcing education to become a centralized state function.' [57]
On the contrary, the state share of educational funding actually declined from
about 32 per cent in 1890 to 17 per cent in 1920. Later, state aid was increased
through minimum foundation programs, but because of political constraints
in state legislatures redistribution remained limited. The local tax revenues
persisted as the decisive variable, and consequently the variations in financial
resources available to schools of similar classification waxed immensely greater
in the US than in Europe, where the trend toward centralized financing and
administration was proceeding apace. In Europe, resource and financial
allocation in favor of the elite secondary schools was overt, and children in rural
areas with no post-primary schools did not have the chance to go on to even a
low-quality secondary school.[58] But even the least attractive European primary
school in a working-class district had to meet certain higher-level inspection
standards. In the US, local domination of public schools, so Kandel averred
in 1930, had led 'the richest nation on the earth to herd many of its children
into dismal and unsanitary hovels, under the tutelage of wretchedly underpaid
and proportionately ignorant, untrained and negative teachers.' [59]

[55] Fabricant, Government Activity in the U.S., p. 252.
[56] Robert H. Salisbury, 'Schools and Politics in the Big City,' Harvard Education Review,
xxxvii (1967), 408–24, p. 424.
[57] John E. Coons et al., Private Wealth and Public Education (Cambridge, Mass: Belknap
Press, 1970), p. 45.
[58] In the 1960s one-third of Hesse's small communes had not produced a single Gymnasium
graduate in the preceding decade. John H. Van de Graaff, 'West Germany's Abitur
Quota and School Reform,' Comparative Education Review, xi (1967), 75–86, p. 81.
[59] Kandel, Twenty-five Years of American Education, p. 214.

The extremes in school finance and teacher salary disparities that developed under the American local school board system are not conceivable within the framework of locally-administered welfare services in Europe—even where the services are administratively distinct from local government. German local sickness funds, which are analogous to US school boards in that they are obliged to provide medical services for fund members in their area, just as the latter are obliged to provide school facilities, could not conceivably pay doctors twice or even five times as much in a rich locality as in a poor one. The German sickness funds make collective agreements on fees with the regional doctors' associations, and determine the amount of dues and disbursement patterns. But, compared with American school boards, their decisions are much more limited by criteria set up by state and federal sickness funds' associations and by the federal legislature and the Ministry of Labor. All of the interests involved, doctors and fund officials, unions and employers, are aware that the funds have to adhere closely to basic guide-lines laid down by the federal legislation and to executive interpretations thereof.[60]

By contrast, there were in the US in the mid-1960s more than 3,000 independent school districts which maintained no schools at all and which existed primarily 'to avoid or minimize school taxation'. 'Education', concluded a business study group in 1966, 'presents the most puzzling problems to those who want to create rational, visible and competent jurisdictions of local self government.' It concluded that 'American preoccupation with public schools has tended to divert attention from other vital functions of local government' and that separatism had 'often led to strong and sometimes bitter competition between supporters of public schools and those who would strengthen other governmental functions'. More generally its authors stressed that the tremendous growth in special governmental districts of all kinds had 'resulted in unprecedented overlapping among local governments' and emphasized pointedly that 'the vigor and imagination that Americans devote to mechanization and new construction is in striking contrast to their hesitation to renovate institutions of local government'.[61]

THE COMPLEXITIES OF FEDERALISM

One of the most pervasive shortcomings of the American federal system emerges from the unwillingness and/or inability of higher-level and intermediary governmental authorities to monitor adequately the performance of social services wholly or jointly financed from federal and state revenues. In British education, where the financial relationship between local education authorities and the national government is analogous to that of US school districts to state governments, national inspectors check the adequacy of administration and instruction and have been credited with improving the quality

[60] William Safran, *Veto Group-Politics: the Case of Health Insurance Reform in West Germany* (San Francisco: Chandler, 1967), pp. 128, 145.
[61] Committee for Economic Development, *Modernizing Local Government* (New York: CED, 1966), pp. 32–3, 37–8.

and uniformity of instructional levels. By contrast, US state education officials view the enforcement of regulations as 'incompatible with their view of public education'. They express 'the same reluctance to interfere with local prerogatives that federal officials express about interfering with state prerogatives'.[62] In Germany *Land* governments often voluntarily adopt federal administrative guidelines, in order to further uniformity. In the US, state governments often fail to follow the guidelines even when they are legally required to do so; thus, of thirty-eight state programs audited by federal officials after they made use of federal education (ESEA-Title I) funds, no less than twenty-five were criticized for maladministration.[63]

By comparison with a federal system such as West Germany's, the spatial redistribution of public revenues is much lower in the U.S.[64] Students of comparative local politics have noted that, whereas in many countries local self-government is not 'an end in itself' but an 'instrument to energize human resources for social development,' in the United States 'nothing of this broad national purposefulness infuses the functioning of local government'.[65] Whereas in Germany about 80–90 percent of local government activity is carried on in pursuance of obligatory State programs,[66] in the US localities have had to be induced by federal grants to initiate many programs in the areas of housing, welfare and education, whose adoption remains voluntary. As Elazar points out: 'Though both national and state governments permit local governments to bend any given grant program in the direction desired locally, . . . if local initiative is not present, the opportunities remain unrealized'.[67]

Michel Crozier sees some advantages associated with the 'tremendous complexity of relationships' of American local government—such as the openness of the system, its ability to encourage diverse kinds of initiatives, and its accommodation to citizen participation at all levels—which partly compensate for the 'numerous jurisdictional problems'. But he also emphasizes that 'the feeble are not so well protected against the strong', and that the detours imposed by the complexity of jurisdictions constitute the 'focal point of American administrative dysfunctions'.[68] Comparing US federal grant programs to foreign governments with those extended to American states, Montgomery believes that it is 'even harder to eliminate waste in the use of aid resources, mainly through unintended benefits to those already privileged, in American states than in foreign countries'.[69]

[62] Jerome T. Murphy, 'Title I of ESEA: The Politics of Implementing Federal Education Reform,' *Harvard Education Review*, XLI (1971), 52–63, p. 53.

[63] National Advisory Council on the Education of Disadvantaged Children, *Title 1 ESEA: 1971 Annual Report* (Washington, D.C.: 1971), p. 6.

[64] Pryor, *Public Expenditures*, p. 489.

[65] International Studies of Values in Politics, *Values and the Active Community* (New York: Free Press, 1971), p. 208.

[66] Juergen Bertram, *Staatspolitik und Kommunalpolitik* (Stuttgart: Kohlhammer, 1967), p. 53.

[67] Daniel J. Elazar, *American Federalism: A View from the States* (New York: Crowell, 1966), p. 195.

[68] Michel Crozier, *The Bureaucratic Phenomenon* (Chicago: University of Chicago Press, 1964), p. 236.

[69] John D. Montgomery, 'Programs and Poverty: Federal Aid in the Domestic and Inter-

Social Service Extension

THE GOVERNMENTAL FRAMEWORK AND PROFESSIONAL CONTROL

The United States and Germany have both displayed a tendency to extend their public social benefits more selectively and in less consistent progression than have Britain and Sweden. Thus, among income-maintenance programs, family assistance programs followed old-age pensions in the two unitary systems with no more than a one-generation lag; but this sequence was not met in the US and Germany.[70] In the social service area, professionals such as physicians and teachers seem to have had greater influence in the two federal systems. Neither the US nor Germany has in the post-1945 period legislated restructuring reforms of the scope or dimension of the British National Health Service Act of 1948 or the Swedish educational comprehensivization reforms of 1950–1964. In those US and German service sectors where public social benefits were below those of other countries, the post-1945 decades saw a widening of the gap. Thus German secondary education capacity remained comparatively static,[71] while US public health benefits were held down, at least until 1965.

Especially since the Progressive era, the prevailing American technique of circumventing inept or corrupt state and local administrative agencies has consisted of creating specialist jurisdictions through which organized professional bodies exercise a mixture of *de jure* and *de facto* control over vital policies affecting their sectors. When professional registers were legally established in Britain, professional associations played a role in maintaining them, but the government retained 'the ultimate authority', reinforced by power to nominate a large proportion of the membership of the various professional councils. The Webbs emphasized 'the reluctance of Parliament to confer upon any profession complete powers of self-government.' [72] Comparable American state laws often 'remove the distinction between the private and the public' by making credentialing and other policies the 'prerogative of expert insiders who need hardly worry about opposition from untrained outsiders'.[73] Thus,

---

national Systems,' *Public Policy*, XVIII (1970), 517–38.

[70] Pension and family allowance initiation dates are: Sweden—1913, 1947; Britain—1908, 1945; Germany—1889, 1954; US—1935, none.

[71] According to OECD data Germany and Austria were the only countries in which secondary school enrolment increased by less than 50 per cent in the 1955–65 period. Growth indices for 1955–65 were Germany—1 percent, France 107 percent, Sweden 34 percent, UK 48 percent. *Development in Secondary Education* (Paris: OECD, 1969), pp. 26–30.

[72] Beatrice and Sidney Webb, 'Special Supplement on Professional Associations' *New Statesman*, IX (28 April 1917), p. 47.

[73] Henry S. Kariel, *The Decline of American Pluralism* (Stanford: Stanford University Press, 1961), p. 104.

the Alabama legislature simply legislated that 'the Medical Association of the State of Alabama is the State Board of Health', while in Connecticut the State Board of Medical Examiners consists of the Medical Society's Board of Censors. In 1952 three-quarters of state medical licensing boards were exclusively composed of physicians, who also held majorities on the remaining boards. By contrast the majority of equivalent education credentialing agencies had no teacher members at all, and only one was exclusively composed of teachers.[74]

The relative prestige of professions, which has been an important factor in determining how far their service delivery preferences have been accommodated, came to be related in quite different ways in the US and Germany to closeness of identification with the public sector. Thus, in the US, professions whose members were predominantly employed in the public sector, like teaching, have enjoyed significantly lower prestige than those predominantly self- or privately-employed. In Germany, something like the reverse has been the case: civil servants have ranked higher; professors are at the top of prestige scales; and gymnasium teachers possess 'exceedingly high socio-economic status', possibly equal to that of lawyers; physicians, by contrast, have felt acute status anxiety.[75] In the US physicians have occupied the top of prestige scales even while the great majority of them 'disdained public medical positions'. From their status at the 'pinnacle of the achievement and reward system', physicians in the 1950s still expounded 'the lofty and hostile attitude toward the political realm which was fashionable in the muckraking era'.[76] While American physicians established uniform professional standards without much guidance (as distinct from reinforcement) from public legislation, American teachers found the vastly varying state regulations and levels of support patterns a great handicap in their attempt to establish nationwide standards, credentials and accompanying prestige.[77]

In both countries the constitutional infeasibility of a national jurisdiction for these service areas coincided with the emergence of *status quo*-oriented associational leaderships. In American medicine after 1920, the more cosmopolitan university physicians 'abdicated voluntarily' from competition for AMA leadership, with the result that control of national, state and local medical societies 'fell to a mundane minority preoccupied with the business of medicine and blind resistance to change'.[78] In Germany after 1945 *Philo-*

---

[74] Myron Lieberman, *Education as a Profession* (Englewood Cliffs, N.J.: Prentice-Hall, 1958), pp. 93–4.

[75] Wolf Fuhrig, 'West Germany' in Albert Blum, ed., *Teachers Unions and Associations* (Urbana: University of Illinois Press, 1969), p. 113; Naschold, *Kassenärzte*, pp. 120 ff.

[76] William A. Glaser, 'Doctors and Politics,' *American Journal of Sociology*, LXVI (1960), 230–45, p. 237. Thus the editor of a leading medical journal wrote in 1951: 'The doctor's dilemma today emerges from the fact that politics is a dirty-hands business, and medicine has always been a clean-hands profession. Healing and heeling don't go together.'

[77] Thus compulsory school attendance laws were introduced in Massachusetts in 1854, but not until 1920 in Mississippi.

[78] John G. Freymann, 'A Doctor Prescribes for the AMA,' *Harper's*, 231 (1965), 76–80, p. 78.

logenverband leaders were jealously on guard against structural changes.[79] In both the US and Germany associational leaders were able to maintain a high degree of professional cohesion and membership coverage rates of 70 percent or more. Especially for the period 1920–50, the AMA had unusually high membership coverage by American standards, whereas the BMA's coverage was low by British standards.[80] American medicine disaccentuated distinctions between general practitioners and specialists,[81] the root of much divisiveness in European medical professions, and in the BMA's case the fundamental cause of fatal 'lack of control over its own membership in a crisis situation'.[82]

While doing a thorough job of educating the rank and file, the AMA was able to enforce its verdicts in good part because 'its dominant faction has effectively blended with the state'.[83] An analysis in the early 1940s of state professional licensing boards showed that in one-sixth of the cases the governor or other appointing official had to select all his nominees from a slate submitted by the professional society. In most cases the law required him to give 'due consideration' to their recommendations. James W. Fesler concluded that 'professional licensing boards are virtually the creatures of the professional societies' and recommended as 'essential' a reduction of their traditional independence.[84] For lack of such reforms, an AMA president could describe the health boards as 'adding the weight of government to the side of medicine'. Lowi generalized the process succinctly: 'Drainage has tended toward "support group constituencies", and with a special consequence. Parcelling out policy making power to the most interested parties destroys political responsibility.' [85] The statement by the New Deal social welfare planner Edwin E. Witte, made after the AMA would not compromise its opposition to health insurance— 'As long as the medical profession is opposed, we will not have health insurance. . . . I am willing to let the profession decide' [86]—exemplified the attitude. McConnell notes the implication: 'The structuring of much of the political system about the array of private associations and other small political units has selected from the values which Americans cherish and has emphasized

---

[79] Fuhrig, 'West Germany,' p. 106.

[80] Eckstein, *Pressure Group Politics* (Stanford: Stanford University Press, 1960), p. 29.

[81] Between 1929 and 1959 the incomes of US specialists and GPs became less disparate. Incomes of the former increased by about two and a half, those of the latter five-fold. The American specialist colleges operated 'largely without the strong social and regulatory overtones of the British models,' and the GP-specialist relationship has been marked by no 'clear demarcation of function.' Stevens, *American Medicine*, pp. 95, 185. In the US about 75 percent of physicians engage in some specialty practice, but in the more demarcated British profession only 22 percent, and in Germany 43 percent, do so. Romuald K. Schicke, *Arzt und Gesundheitsversorgung im gesellschaftlichen Sicherungssystem* (Freiburg: Rombach, 1971), pp. 88, 164.

[82] Eckstein, *Pressure Group Politics*, pp. 68, 107; Bentley B. Gilbert, *The Evolution of National Insurance in Great Britain* (London: Michael Joseph, 1966), pp. 413 ff.

[83] Kariel, *Decline of American Pluralism*, pp. 110–11.

[84] James W. Fesler, *The Independence of State Regulatory Agencies* (Chicago: Public Administration Service, 1942), pp. 49, 60, 70.

[85] Theodore J. Lowi, *The End of Liberalism* (New York: Norton, 1969), p. 86.

[86] Edwin E. Witte, *Social Security Perspectives* (Madison: University of Wisconsin Press, 1962), p. 317.

and given particular effect to narrow and material values. The cost is larger than we normally confess . . . in limitations on liberty, equality and numerous other public values.' [87]

In European education the status distinctions between primary teachers who lack, and secondary teachers who possess, university credentials have continued to be infinitely greater than those between GPs and specialists in either the US or Europe. The *Philologenverband* united most German academic secondary teachers in defense of status differentials, and, as its historic but curious name suggests, the maintenance of humanistic educational ideals. Some progressive secondary teachers joined with a majority of elementary teachers in the *Gewerkschaft Erziehung und Wissenschaft*, affiliated to the German Trade Union Federation, but this may in turn have led the GEW on several occasions to 'withdraw support from measures proposing innovations when questions of salary and status were at stake.' [88] Most gymnasium teachers and administrators tended 'to reject on ideological grounds the measures which they feel [might] dilute the high intellectual standards of the gymnasium' and were even accused of preventing an increase in the *Abiturienten* rate by raising the rate of failure where necessary.[89]

THE PROFESSIONS AND PUBLIC SERVICE EXPANSION

Although the one group is predominantly active in the private and the other in the public sector, American physicians and German gymnasium teachers have both in recent decades helped to keep the proportion of recipients of their State-financed services to minorities of some 10–20 percent of the potential clientele. Recipients of US public health benefits, especially before the adoption of Medicare in 1965, were predominantly the indigent, causing public health to have 'a distinctly lower-income clientele for all but its sanitary environmental activities'.[90] The able minority of German adolescents who were admitted to gymnasia were, by contrast, recruited predominantly from the top strata of society. In part, the lack of service expansion can be attributed to lack of the right mix of demand and participation inputs. Researchers have remarked on the low proportion of Germans, compared to Americans, who chose 'to change their way of life by increasing the length of their schooling',[91] while in the US the demand for an increased public

[87] Grant McConnell, 'The Public Values of the Private Association,' in J. Roland Pennock and John W. Chapman, ed., *Voluntary Associations* (New York: Atherton Press, 1969), p. 160.

[88] Saul B. Robinsohn and J. C. Kuhlmann. 'Two Decades of Non-Reform in West German Education,' *Comparative Education Review*, xi (1967), 311–30, p. 326.

[89] Van de Graaff, 'West Germany's *Abitur* Quota,' p. 81.

[90] Odin W. Anderson, *Health Care: Can There be Equity? The United States, Sweden and England* (New York: Wiley, 1972), p. 114.

[91] George Katona, Burkhard Strumpel and Ernest Zahn, *Aspirations and Affluence* (New York: McGraw-Hill, 1971), p. 162.

health role was concentrated among the less politically participant members of lower social strata.[92]

In the British and Swedish cases, political leaders could convincingly rationalize service extension in terms of broad social goals because nationally integrated parties and mass organizations provided effective links between legislative jurisdictions at the national level and administrative jurisdictions at the local. In the American case, politicans might have considered launching an initiative calling for a change in the pattern under which US infant mortality rates were higher than in most other Western countries,[93] but considerations of what it would have required to implement an effective program through the maze of state and local jurisdictions, interacting with voluntary planning agencies and private hospitals, contributed to this remaining a 'non-decision'.[94] Although the German educational system was more public and less fractionated than the American health system, in Germany, too, parties and mass organizations were inhibited until the mid-1960s from making secondary comprehensivization a highly visible social goal. The unions, including those representing the elementary teachers, were split by status and regional jealousies. Even in the SPD-led *Länder* school legislation of the 1950–65 period aimed essentially at the 'organizational consolidation of the traditional school system'.[95] while the SPD at this time never tried to organize public pressure on educational matters as did pressure groups on the opposing side.

In both settings the professional interest groups inhibited the political leadership from effectively tying service extension to broad social goals which could have mobilized a higher level of demand. In the pluralist American system, where local political jurisdictions compete through resource or tax favor inducements to attract the economically powerful, scarce high-prestige professionals are more easily able to transpose economic into political power than are even fairly well-organized skilled workers' groups. This holds less true for the West German system, where lower-echelon bodies like local governments and sickness funds have less financial autonomy. The economic power of physicians, whose scarcity value was increased by conscious AMA policy,[96] constitutes 'an overriding political resource',[97] especially in the US setting. By

[92] Sidney Verba and Norman Nie, *Participation in America* (New York: Harper and Row, 1972), pp. 280–4.

[93] Infant mortality rates per 1,000 live births in 1960 were: US, 26; England, 21.8; Sweden, 16.6. Decline in infant morality rates was slower throughout the 1960s in the US. Anderson, *Health Care*, pp. 148, 243.

[94] Anderson, describing another subsidy program that Congress set up in an attempt to affect disease incidence, noted that 'it must appear frightfully messy to British and Swedish observers . . . but given the federal system and the private ownership of the means of delivering health services, there was little alternative.' *Health Care*, p. 177.

[95] Peter Nixdorff, 'The Pace of West German Educational Reform as Affected by Land Politics' (unpublished Ph.D. dissertation, University of Florida, 1970), p. 135.

[96] Between 1906 and 1930 the number of medical schools was reduced from 162 to 76, and the doctor ratio from 157 to 126 per 100,000 population. The number of medical graduates was smaller in 1950 than it had been in 1904.

[97] Theodore R. Marmor and D. Thomas, 'The Politics of Paying Physicians,' *International Journal of Health Sciences*, i (1972), 71–8, p. 74.

contrast, industrial workers' unions, which might serve to articulate the demands of health care recipients, are characterized by disadvantageous economic positions, because of 'their lack of a monopoly of economic skills in their job markets' and their 'vulnerability to economic fluctuations and competition in a national market from low-wage, anti-union areas'.[98]

To the extent that the European countries are, in fairly clearly discernible rank order, much less tolerant of low-wage non-union sectors, unions are freer to define their political constituencies to encompass generalized welfare goals. In Sweden, where the unionized workers come closest to the maintenance of monopoly positions, they and their allied mass organizations were activated more highly and earlier on behalf of school comprehensivization than in Germany. Thus, the Swedish Co-operatives in 1949 published a book whose author presented the school struggle as the 'New Front in the labor movement's battle against institutionalized privilege' and called for a 'united effort' to overcome the 'secondary school's protracted resistance to fundamental change'.[99]

In order to relieve political pressures and to maximize administrative rationality, reformers in the unitary countries either completely reorganized the local government systems or by-passed them as instruments for service delivery. In conjunction with its education reforms, Sweden pursued the former alternative and in consequence reduced the number of communes from 2,500 to 275 in the course of a twenty-five-year period ending in 1975. The resulting consolidated units, with minimum populations of 8–10,000, were designed with educational service delivery as a key criterion, just as earlier the county units had been adapted to emphasize their roles as instruments of health service delivery.[100] In Britain, NHS planners—as part of what strikes Anderson as an 'anomaly among British ways of doing things'—by-passed local government, with the result that local administrators claimed that the NHS Act constituted 'an instrument for the greatest curtailment of local government functions which has taken place in 150 years'.[101]

In both Germany and the US public jurisdictions were poorly prepared to assume the responsibilities which the proposed educational and health expansions of the late 1960s were about to thrust upon them. Only a few German *Länder* have initiated local government amalgamations, and even these have not used potential comprehensive school catchment areas as a capability criterion.[102] In the US the task of administering and controlling Medicare and Medicaid programs could not be delegated to counties and cities, nor to non-existent equivalents of the German sickness funds, but was essentially entrusted to intermediary organizations like Blue Cross which had evolved under

[98] Greenstone, *Labor in American Politics*, p. 369.

[99] Rolland G. Paulston, *Educational Change in Sweden* (New York: Teachers College Press, 1968), p. 122.

[100] M. Donald Hancock, *Sweden: The Politics of Postindustrial Change* (Hinsdale, Illinois: Dryden, 1972), Chap. 4.

[101] T. H. Marshall, *Social Policy*, 3rd ed. (London: Hutchinson University Library, 1970), p. 116; Anderson, *Health Care*, p. 93.

[102] Joachim Lohmann, 'Entwicklung und Stand der Gesamtschulplanung in der Bundesrepublik Deutschland,' *International Review of Education*, xvii (1971), 50–7, p. 55.

medical-profession, rather than public, tutelage. No wonder that after five years of soaring federal outlays for the two programs, responsible Washington officials were still asking themselves: 'If the federal government has got that much of the market, how the hell do you get some leverage on it?' [103]

PROFESSIONAL ASSOCIATIONS AND DEFENSIVE ALLIANCES

Numerous analyses of the struggles surrounding the introduction of British health programs in 1911 and 1947–8 have stressed how intra-professional cleavages weakened the defensive position of the BMA. Eckstein and Gilbert have pointed out how fundamental divisions between GPs and specialists undermined the leadership's strategies and self-assurance,[104] while Forsythe even posits that it was this division of interest which made the NHS possible —'just as its absence in the United States has frustrated for so long the mildest form of socialized medicine'.[105] However, the contrast with the US health, as well as with Swedish and German educational struggles examined here, suggests that it is particularly in systems with fractionated and overlapping jurisdictions that cohesive associations of high-prestige professionals may achieve something close to medium-term veto powers over reform proposals affecting their service areas.

Probably the key to the AMA's success in developing its unique political clout is that, in sustaining a synchronized network of high-prestige local influentials, it has had command over just the sort of resources that American political parties typically lacked, except during occasional campaign periods. Swedish gymnasium teachers were prestigious in the 1940s, but cohesion equal to that of the AMA—in 1948 all but three of 234 secondary school faculties opposed initial steps toward integration of the primary and secondary sectors[106]—availed them much less. In part this seems to have been because their lower-prestige adversaries had the organizational means to rise to the challenge, but most importantly because the cohesive party and bureaucratic elites had other resources through which they could wear down the defenders of the *status quo* in a sustained, step-by-step struggle. Swedish and German secondary teachers were able to maintain their economic power so long as appointments were tied to university credentials and so long as limited university enrollments maintained a sellers' market for degree holders.[107] This position enabled them to maintain high salary levels compared to their equivalents in other countries until the Swedish labor market situation was reversed

[103] John K. Iglehart, 'Health Report,' *National Journal*, 10 July 1971, pp. 1444–5, 1449.

[104] Harry Eckstein, *The English Health Service* (Cambridge, Mass.: Harvard University Press, 1958), p. 113; Gilbert, *Evolution of National Insurance in Great Britain.*

[105] Gordon Forsythe, *Doctors and State Medicine* (Philadelphia: J. B. Lippicott, 1966), p. 4.

[106] Torsten Husen, 'Responsiveness and Resistance in the Educational System to Changing Needs of Society,' *International Review of Education*, xv (1969), 476–85.

[107] Ilse Gahlings, *Die Volksschullehrer und Ihre Berufsverbaende* (Neuwied: Luchterhand, 1967); Boyd Hight, "Teachers, Bargaining and Strikes: Perspectives from the Swedish Experience,' *UCLA Law Review*, xv (1968), 842–76.

in 1970. But in neither country does this appear to have been a decisive factor affecting their success in fending off impending school structure reforms. By contrast, the political success of the AMA can be attributed not only to its members' income levels and their sources,[108] but also to its ability to develop alliances based on similarity of economic interests. AMA members controlled resources beyond the reach of their European peers, for it was only in the US that the service providers were 'strong enough and with an entrepreneurial attitude characteristic of the economy in general to mount hospital and physician insurance plans under their own auspices and control'.[109] The resultant physician-hospital-insurance company alliance commanded resources that enabled it to approach on an equal footing the business associations for reciprocal support commitments.

The alliances that helped to hold the line against dilution of the German elitist secondary school systems were, by contrast, built essentially around culturally-based interests whose economic basis lay predominantly within the public sector. In Germany the *Philologenverband*'s allies were strata shaped by, or identified with, the cultural traditions of 'Gymnasium, University and Church,' which Kuhlmann sees as playing mutually reinforcing roles in preserving the identity of the post-1945 West German elites.[110] German *Land* legislators showed great empathy toward the German teachers' pressure to reverse some of the Occupation-imposed school reforms which would have opened wider the gates to academic secondary education. More than their Swedish equivalents, they were impressed by arguments that the gymnasia, as instruments of reviving German culture after the Nazi disaster, needed to be able to concentrate resources on the education of a new elite generation, and not be forced to dilute their resources. In Sweden simultaneous victories were being won by reform adherents who argued that some lower performance levels on the part of the more gifted needed to be risked, because 'the differentiation of aptitudes and the possibility of assessing them' were subsidiary to the goal of 'creating social and cultural unity'.[111]

More than in America, where education policies are largely set locally while religion is outside State jurisdiction, the cultural policies which constitute a mainstay of *Land* powers are of predominant interest to middle-class clienteles. Although they have relied almost exclusively on public financing, German gymnasia, universities and churches have provided few services for the working class, except in the case of working-class Catholic communicants.

---

108 In a 1956 survey of medical students only 4 percent said they would be 'very interested' in work with the Public Health Service or Veteran's Administration, 60 percent said they were 'not at all interested'; Glaser, 'Doctors and Politics,' p. 239. The proportion of doctors' incomes deriving from public and private health insurance sources in 1963 was about 38 percent in the US, some 63–80 percent in West Germany and 90 percent in Britain; Schicke, *Arzt*, p. 166.

109 Anderson, *Health Care*, p. 66.

110 Casper Kuhlmann, 'Schulreform und Gesellschaft in der Bundesrepublik Deutschland: 1946–1966,' in S. B. Robinsohn, ed., *Schulreform im gesellschaftlichen Prozess*, (Stuttgart: Klett, 1970), p. 170.

111 Torsten Husen, *Problems of Differentiation in Swedish Compulsory Schooling* (Stockholm; Scandinavian University Books, 1962), p. 54.

Even parents' associations have mostly been recruited from middle-class parents and tightly organized at state rather than local level.[112] Had these institutions been either predominantly subject to decisions made at the local level, as in the case of American schools, or at the national level, as in the case of British health services, they might have had greater difficulty in maintaining the class biases implicit in their gate-keeping practices. But as long as they were not strongly articulated, lower-class needs probably received least empathy at the *Land* level where the strongly entrenched ministerial bureaucracy to a large extent held 'alumnus' or overlapping memberships in one or another of the institutions committed to defense of the educational *status quo*. Kuhlmann holds that lack of agreement on a reform counter-model enabled the bureaucrats to play off divergent interest groups against one another—unions against the Catholic church, parent groups against researchers, secondary teachers against the SPD—thus neutralizing their impact.[113] As a consequence the secondary teachers succeeded in safeguarding 'all the advantages which they traditionally enjoyed over the elementary teachers'.[114] Prior to the full-scale joining of issues, it might have been possible for a 'progressive' American state like California to enact public health insurance in 1917, or for a 'progressive' *Land* like Hessen to enact comprehensivization in 1948. But, once nation-wide publics had been mobilized, the questions of whether large social goals could override the definition of educational or health care goals enunciated by a reasonably cohesive profession could only be settled in the national legislature.

Explications of the Politics of Policy

Several over-arching research hypotheses seem to be emerging from the recent work of scholars who have examined the correlates of public policy among various samples of political units. Thus, one respected group of researchers has concluded that 'political' variables often explain very little of the variance in allocation patterns, and that ecological and socio-economic variables are much more significant. Such findings have emerged particularly from cross-sectional studies of expenditure patterns among American states. Another line of interpretation, represented by Anthony King, argues that political factors matter, but that one factor, that based on beliefs and values, is probably more powerful than the others.[115] His analysis, like mine, is based on the contrast between the public policy patterns of North America and Western Europe.

My discussion has also focused on macro-analysis, but only within one

[112] Nixdorff, 'The Pace of West German Educational Reform,' p. 154.
[113] Kuhlmann, 'Schulreform,' p. 185.
[114] Fuhrig, 'West Germany,' p. 106.
[115] Anthony King, 'Ideas, Institutions and the Policies of Governments: a Comparative Analysis: Part III,' *British Journal of Political Science* (forthcoming).

broad sector of public activity, that of social policy. I have sought to marshall evidence and arguments which suggest that several kinds of political variables have probably been quite powerful influences on the divergent allocation patterns. I have particularly sought to explore, through the illustrative use of instances of policy development, whether and how political institutions and interest group structures have affected long term policy patterns. Since counter-hypotheses have been put forward by others, I have attempted a strong, well-founded presentation of the positive case.

Subsequent discussion will have to evaluate to what degree the differences that distinguish American political institutions form European, at the local as much as at the state and national levels, are causally linked to the notable variations in program sequence and allocation priority patterns. If the positive case is accepted, then the plausibility of my corollary argument—that differences in interest group power were at times, as in the case of health policy, large enough to account for delays in American public benefit provision—may be more evident. It may be observed that political parties and national political institutions have been referred to only marginally here. That is because I have been concerned with exploring the infrastructures on which these rest. I hope to explore more fully the role of political parties as agents of social policy reform in subsequent work.

The Changing Status of Women in Developed Countries

Judith Blake

In discussing individual modernity in the essay that follows this one, Inkeles notes the changes in men's attitudes toward women that accompany modernization; in this essay this theme is developed in some detail by Judith Blake. She describes the weakening of the legal and customary barriers to women's equality under advanced modernization, and notes that this process had been under way for some time before the contemporary movement for women's liberation gained prominence in the 1960's. By the 1970's some 40 to 50 percent of adult women had joined the paid nonfarm work force in the highly developed countries. This change was accompanied by a marked enhancement of personal independence, although in a majority of cases such employment remained secondary to work as housewives. Blake also examines the considerable variations among advanced societies in the professions employing women and in attitudes toward their employment.

The status of women has aroused widespread interest among students of population only recently. Investigators in the fields of economics, general sociology and political science have traditionally concentrated their attention on the status of men: on how men are ranked differently in society, on their economic opportunities in life, on the deference they can command and on the power they attempt to wield. The great works on class, status and power rarely mention women. The reason for this neglect of women's social position is instructive: the status of women is derived. From the standpoint of their ranked position in Western societies women are expected to participate throughout their life cycle in terms of kinship attachments to men: early in life to a father and later to a husband.

"The Changing Status of Women in Developed Countries" by Judith Blake is reprinted by permission of the publisher from *Scientific American*, ccxxxi (September 1974), 136–147.
Blake is professor of public policy at the University of California, Berkeley, and is co-author of *Family Structure in Jamaica* (1962) and *Western European Censuses, 1960* (1971).

Paradoxically, it is the derived nature of women's status that goes far toward explaining the demographer's special interest. The nature of women's position and the variations in its articulation with the status of men influence important variables with which students of population are concerned, in particular reproductive behavior and the size and quality of the labor force. For example, demographers have found that women, because of the linkage between their own lifetime position and the status of wife and mother, are typically well motivated to conform to social expectations regarding reproduction, such as the pressure to bear children until there are the desired number of living sons. Whether or not women participate in a secondary fashion in economic production in industrial societies—that is, whether or not they constitute "womanpower" on which a society can rely in addition to manpower—is closely connected to their primary status in the family. Thus in countries that have been chronically short of workers in recent years, such as France and Sweden, there is a lively interest in those aspects of women's position that impede their more extensive participation in the labor force.

Changes in certain demographic variables also have consequences for women's status. These too cannot fail to intrigue the demographer, who is as concerned with the impact of demographic trends on society as he is with the effects of social and economic structure on demographic behavior. The changes in migration, mortality and fertility that accompanied the Industrial Revolution appear to have profoundly disrupted the symmetry of the status of men and women. As a result, since the middle of the 19th century serious questions have been raised concerning the realism, as well as the legitimacy, of a continuing attempt in highly developed countries to prescribe one kind of position—a derived one—as being the primary status for *all* women.

Women's movements have appeared and reappeared in developed countries, each time focusing ever more closely on the central issue of women's derived status. As William L. O'Neill of Rutgers University has emphasized, "experience has demonstrated that the formal barriers to women's emancipation—votelessness, educational and occupational discriminations and the like—are less serious and more susceptible to change than the domestic, institutional and social customs that keep women in the home." Such movements advance the claim that all women should be afforded the opportunity to have their own nonderived, independent status without sacrificing a family life any more than men are required to do. Counterarguments that, whatever a woman may do on a secondary level, her primary place is as a wife and mother are, however, far from being silenced.

Against the background of these two polarized expectations, what is the position of women in highly developed countries today? Has it been changing significantly since World War II in the direction of an independent nonderived status? Or are alterations in many of women's activities merely superficial fluctuations superimposed on an underlying constant?

The highly developed countries to which I shall refer are the most economically advanced of those in Western Europe: Austria, Belgium, Denmark, England and Wales, Finland, France, the Netherlands, Norway, Sweden,

Switzerland and West Germany. I shall also take up the New World countries of Australia, Canada, New Zealand and the U.S. Although the inclusion of Japan and the developed Communist countries would have added fascinating points of comparison, such a task would have been handicapped by major cultural disparities as well as by the unavailability of comparable statistics. Even as it is analysis of the countries considered here has been impeded because all the detailed tabulations from the 1970 censuses have not yet been published.

What happened during the industrializing process that gave rise to the strains over women's status that are as vital today as they were when the "woman's movement" first found expression in the 1830's? Put very schematically, the answer is as follows: Men became increasingly independent of the economic contributions of the family as a unit at the same time that women and children became more economically dependent on the extrafamilial occupations of husbands and fathers. This major change in the economic relationships of family members was associated with the migration of industrializing peoples out of rural settings into the urban factories and bureaucracies of modernizing societies. This migration progressively removed work from the family milieu and put men in jobs away from home—jobs whose demands did not include participation by wives or offspring and whose criteria of performance emphasized each man's individual achievement. Conversely, the constraints of the household and the family made it extremely difficult for women to follow work into the outside world as it disappeared from the family unit, and their children could not readily participate in the highly rationalized and impersonal relationships of the adult world of work as it evolved. Thus, whereas in the rural ambience of family farms and enterprises husbands, wives and offspring had shared an economic dependence, gradually both wives and children became economic liabilities to the men. Although the families of poor, sick or deceased men worked in factories, in mines and in domestic service, such employment was associated with all the degradation of poverty. Except under the stress of dire necessity few married women would have left their families to work long hours at the onerous, exhausting jobs that characterized the industrializing process. Hence a significant share of the social reforms of the 19th century and the early 20th consisted in the amelioration of economic conditions so that wives could remain at home to care for the family and older children could go to school. Step by step women's sphere shrank to the household only and men emerged (at least ideally) as the sole participators in economic life. The status of women was no longer simply derived; it became cumulatively skewed and diminished.

Not surprisingly, by the full bloom of the Victorian era industrializing societies capitalized into a virtue what appeared to be a necessity. They elaborated all kinds of rationalizations and legitimations for the wrenching change in the position of women that was accompanying the Industrial Revolution and the demographic transition. In particular they tried to justify it by asserting that women's personalities and behavior actually conformed by nature to the restrictions of their new way of life. Exit the sturdy partner, the practical helpmate who carried her share of the family's earning and living. Enter the romantic, inhibited, swooning Victorian whose fragility required cosseting (and corseting).

Historians of "the woman's place" such as William O'Neill, Robert Smuts and William H. Chafe have made clear, however, that the domestic internment of women aroused protest even as it was taking place. Not only did at least some women balk at being removed from the flow of adult life and at having their derived status reduced to a total dependency; they also objected to the resulting inequities suffered by the many women who could not find or retain husbands. It was all very well for women to derive their status from men as long as those who could not marry, or who were widowed or deserted, could be absorbed into the kinship structure and attached to fathers, brothers, uncles or other male relatives. As family enterprises disappeared, however, such women had no economic role to play within the kinship group except perhaps as family servants—on sufferance simply for lack of a husband. Furthermore, as families migrated hither and yon in response to economic opportunity, family ties became attenuated and community opinion could no longer function to enforce kinship obligations. Unattached women—whether single, deserted or widowed—thus had to seek nonfamilial employment in a work world for which they were systematically unprepared and which, in turn, assumed that they were an anomaly. The "normal" course of events was for a woman to have a man to fend for her.

Yet in actual fact the proportion of women without husbands was very substantial during a good share of the industrializing period in many countries. For example, during the middle and late 19th century, at the very time when women were becoming acutely dependent on finding mates, the age at which women married and the proportion of those remaining unmarried were rising. John Hajnal has calculated that around 1900 in Belgium, Britain, Denmark, Finland, the Netherlands, Norway, Sweden and Switzerland between 40 and 50 percent of the women aged 25 to 29 were single and between 13 and 19 percent of those aged 45 to 49 were still so. Obviously as women became more dependent and their children became economically less useful, men had to be more circumspect before taking on such "hostages to fortune."

Moreover, even among those intrepid men who did marry many died early, well before their children had grown, leaving widows to fend for the family in a modern setting that had not yet come to terms with the still high probability of a husband's premature death. For the U.S. research by Peter R. Uhlenberg of the University of North Carolina has shown that among 1,000 white women born between 1890 and 1894 who survived to age 50, 100 never married, 225 were childless, 165 had fertile marriages that broke up (owing to death or intentional dissolution) and only 510—slightly more than half—experienced the "normal" pattern for a woman of having a fertile marriage that had not dissolved by the time she was middle-aged. In recent years the probability of the joint survival of a husband and a wife has increased in industrial societies, and spinsterhood and childlessness have declined, but the instability caused by death has been replaced by the personal instability of the marital relationship itself. Hence at no time so far during the modernizing process has it been realistic for all women to assume that they could rely on being wives and mothers as a lifetime status.

Even among those women who managed to catch and keep husbands the expectation that all wives would blithely submit to domestic encapsulation might have been more realistic if such domesticity had been congruent with the emerging constraints on family size. Paradoxically, however, even as women's status was being denuded of economic functions, many of the same forces were motivating couples to want fewer births, and the decline in infant and childhood mortality reinforced that motivation. For example, in the prototype case of England and Wales, E. A. Wrigley of the University of Cambridge has shown that live births declined from an average of 6.16 per woman to 3.30 among couples marrying in the decades 1860–1869 and 1900–1909 respectively. Among couples marrying in the period 1935–1939 there were on the average only 2.04 births per woman. With variations in timing and magnitude, this pattern of fertility reduction characterized all the highly industrialized countries of the West. Thus women's entire lifetime status was being geared ideologically to a function—reproduction—whose demands were diminishing in scope. Such a situation could not help but be unstable since, as far as the content of women's social position was concerned, they were rapidly becoming net losers.

Finally, the erosion of traditional acquired statuses among men in modernizing countries engendered a growing sense of illegitimacy about women's derived status. As the power of hereditary elites was vitiated and impersonal, achievement criteria rather than family position were employed for according men differential status and rewards, the derived nature of women's status became more anomalous with respect to that of men. Whereas in traditional European society men had been comparatively fixed in their status by their social position at birth, modernization and economic and political liberalism had begun to give men at least a fighting chance to achieve according to their talents. Women, however, were left to achieve by finding men to succeed in their behalf.

Given this host of incongruities between women's prescribed status and the realities of the modernizing world, it is hardly surprising that the "woman problem" has erupted periodically in at least some industrial countries. Such recurrences have even followed periods such as that of the 1950's, when feminine discontent seemed to be in a state of total remission. By the middle and late 1960's a number of countries—most notably the U.S. and Denmark, Finland and Sweden—began experiencing an upwelling of protest concerning women's status, although some, such as West Germany and the Netherlands, seemed fairly secure in the notion that women "normally" belong in the home. In assessing what women's current status actually appears to be with respect to the polar norms of independence of men on the one hand and dependence on them on the other, I shall concentrate on women's participation in the occupational world since World War II.

In making such an assessment one is interested in women's participation apart from both agricultural and unpaid family work. Therefore my calculations eliminate farming and family labor. In 1950 the fraction of women working as a percentage of the total number of women in the nonagricultural population of the New World countries clustered around the one-third mark. The fraction of working European women varied widely from slightly more than one-fourth for the Belgians and the Dutch to one-half or more for the Danes and the Finns. Nonetheless, on the average 41 percent of European nonfarm women were economically active in contrast to an average of 34 percent for nonfarm women in the New World. Thus the Europeans had proportionately more women working at mid-century than was the case in the New World countries.

It is frequently assumed that the percentage of women working has risen strikingly in the postwar period. This assumption is not borne out by the censuses. Instead, although a consistent and substantial gain in women's economic activity in the New World countries had by 1970 put them more on a par with their European counterparts, the work rates of women in the Old World countries averaged only a 1 percent gain between 1950 and 1960 and a modest increase of 10 percent between 1960 and 1970. Hence by 1970, 45 percent of the nonfarm women in the highly developed European countries for which we have information and 43 percent of nonfarm women in the New World were in the labor force. These averages, of course, conceal some striking increases in specific countries such as Australia, Canada, the U.S., Belgium and Sweden. On the basis of these data, however, it would be hard to assert that since World War II there has been a revolution in the propensity of women to work.

The overall work rates for all the countries since World War II reflect two important countervailing tendencies in women's behavior. The first trend is that between 1950 and 1970 women married at increasingly youthful ages in all the countries except Australia, Canada and the U.S. They also married in higher proportions in every one of the countries. As of 1970 more women had married by the prime adult ages of 25 to 34 than was the case in 1950. Since at any point in time married women work less than unmarried ones, the marrying behavior of these women over the 20-year period operated to depress the work rates. At the same time, however, there was a second trend for more of the married women to work. Indeed, if over the years married women had not decided to work in higher proportions than they had in 1950, overall work rates in all the countries would have declined, and in some of the countries they would have declined appreciably more than they actually did. The reason female rates of participation in the work force actually rose in almost all countries between 1950 and 1970 is that the increased tendency of married women to work more than offset the greater proclivity of all women to marry.

One can thus see that the status of women in highly developed countries has taken a novel turn in the 20-year period from 1950 to 1970. More young women have married (indeed, very few remain unmarried), but increased work activity has broadened the character of the derived status for at least a share of married women. In most of the countries included in my analysis it is no longer true that only a small minority of married women are active in modern sectors of the economy. Yet it still remains true that, no matter whether one looks at the proportion of married women working, the pattern of women's participation in the labor force with respect to age, the types of occupations in which women are engaged, the relative earnings of women or feminine attitudes toward the primacy of work, one finds that women typically participate in economic activity only as a secondary supplement to their primary status inside the home. It is true that the augmented work behavior of married women is bringing their derived status back into balance, the balance it had lost in the industrializing process. Nevertheless, this labor-force activity does not indicate, at least so far, that many women have achieved an independent occupational status.

To document the variation in the work rates of women according to age and decade for the countries considered here I plotted female work rates against age for each of the countries in 1950, 1960 and 1970 and then grouped the curves that were similar into five average types. (Austria, Finland, France and Norway were excluded because of the large role played in them by agriculture.) The five types took account of the magnitude of the peak in work rates during youth, the amount of the subsequent decline and the shape and level of the remainder of the work/age curve.

The results show that even at the highest levels of participation women's engagement in work differs dramatically over the course of their life cycle from the work rates of men. Furthermore, even at the most active ages female work rates do not approximate those of men until the men approach retirement. Thus not only do women show a sharp tendency to drop out of the labor force while they engage in family responsibilities but also at every stage of their life cycle women's work rates are at substantially lower levels than men's. The data from two countries in the 1970 period, however, exhibit a smaller decline in women's work rates after age 25 and a rapid recovery rate in the early thirties to levels approximating those of youth. This more continuous work rate is a new pattern for women in highly developed countries. It reflects a rising participation in the labor force by youthful married women, in some cases married women with young children.

Women's work experience differs from men's qualitatively as well as quantitatively, an important point in evaluating whether or not women have made significant changes in achieving an independent, nonderived status. For example, the International Labor Office estimates that part-time employment is widespread in Australia, Britain, Canada, West Germany, the Netherlands, the Scandinavian countries and the U.S. In Canada in 1961 nearly a fifth of the female labor force worked fewer than 35 hours per week. In Britain the figure was almost a sixth and in the U.S. in 1973 it was a fourth.

Women also concentrate markedly in particular occupational categories such as clerical, sales and service, and are excluded from management as well as those parts of the industrial and service sectors where highly skilled blue-collar jobs are found. This skewed occupational distribution is further evidence that most women have not yet come close to achieving a nonderived status.

The relatively high proportion of women in the professional and technical category is misleading. Women cluster in the low-level professions, the majority of professional women being schoolteachers, nurses, librarians and social workers. For example, in 1970 teaching and nursing accounted for 80 percent of the professional women in New Zealand and 63 percent of those in the U.S. (The figure for the U.S. has dropped significantly from 71 percent in 1960.)

Valerie Kincade Oppenheimer of the University of California at Los Angeles has found that for the U.S. the large increase in the demand for women workers since World War II has been a joint product of the sex-typing of jobs (that is, the earmarking of certain kinds of jobs as "female" occupations) and the fact that these particular kinds of jobs are located in the expanding service sector of the economy. Oppenheimer's analysis of the sources of the U.S. demand for female labor is paralleled in all the countries considered here, among which Canada, Belgium, England and Wales, the Netherlands and Sweden have already become full-fledged service economies (having more than half of their labor force in the service sector).

Although among those countries the women's occupations are similar in broad outline, it is important to note in the context of this discussion that there is some variation at the most prestigious professional levels. Marjorie Galenson of Cornell University has shown that for highly industrial countries there is a substantial variation from one country to the next in the proportion of physicians who are women. In the mid-1960's the proportion ranged between 16 and 23 percent in Denmark, Finland, Sweden, West Germany and Britain, but it was only 7 percent in the U.S. The comparative proportions of women dentists for 1960 are even more striking: a little more than 1 percent of the dentists in the U.S. were women, whereas in Norway the figure was a fifth, in Denmark and Sweden it was a fourth and in Finland it was more than three-fourths. Apart from the health professions, however, women do not figure significantly in high-level occupations in the countries considered here.

Nonetheless, there have been some noteworthy changes in the U.S. between 1960 and 1970. I have calculated that among physicians the number of women increased by 62 percent, raising their representation in this category from 7 percent to 9 percent. Women gained 149 percent among lawyers, increasing their representation from 2.4 percent to 4.7 percent. They advanced between 159 and 200 percent in engineering, architecture and college and university teaching, and among life scientists and physical scientists they rose 106 percent. In these fields too the increases for women were substantially greater than they were for men, and women now have a somewhat larger share of each category. In some of these high-level categories, however, women are known to concentrate at the lower echelons. For example, although 28 percent of the college and university teachers are women, most of them are on low rungs of the academic ladder.

In the light of the typically modest occupational status of women in highly developed countries, it is to be expected that they earn less than men even when the comparison is confined to full-time, year-round employment. Studies suggest that the complex causes for the difference are related less to wage discrimination per se than to the concentration of women in low-paying occupations and to the secondary role of work in their lives; men normally have greater continuity of employment, work longer hours and get more job training. Even so, with the sex differential in hourly wages being as high as 40 percent in a country such as the U.S. (a differential much larger than that between blacks and whites) the ordinary working woman is clearly still some distance from having an independent primary status.

Is it likely that the primary status of proportionately more women in highly developed countries will expand to include a vocation? In attempting to answer this question one must consider factors affecting both the supply of women wanting to work and the demand for their services in the economy. With regard to the supply, more women may feel free to work, more may need to work and more may be attracted by work. Opposing forces, however, are also operating. Let us examine the situation in more detail.

More women may feel free to work because their families are remaining relatively small. Surveys in most of the countries considered here give no evidence that women want larger families than they are currently having; in fact, if anything, the evidence indicates that the trend is toward even fewer children. Furthermore, married women are no longer bucking strong disapproval when they enter the labor force. For example, in the U.S. at the end of World War II the Gallup organization asked: "Do you approve of a woman earning money in business or industry if she has a husband capable of supporting her?" In 1945 the survey found that only 18 percent of the population approved. Almost two-thirds actively disapproved and 16 percent offered qualifications, such as that they would approve if there were no children. During the past six years I have commissioned the same question on a number of Gallup surveys. The results have been striking. By October, 1973, 65 percent approved of a married woman's working; moreover, among those under age 30, 83 percent were in favor of it.

More women may need to work because of inflationary trends in the economy, high rates of divorce and the fact that their children leave school to support themselves at a later age than they did a generation ago. With rapid rates of economic inflation gripping the highly developed countries, there is great pressure on families to maintain their living levels by increasing the family income. This effort to forestall the erosion of consumption may push some women into the work force who would never have taken this step to simply augment the level of spending by their family.

Trends in divorce have similar effects. The divorce rate has risen rather sharply since at least the middle of the 1960's in almost all the countries considered here. Thus more women may need to work both because more are divorced and because more go through the early nest-building stage of two or more marriages instead of one.

In addition, as higher education increasingly becomes an expectation instead of a luxury and the age at which children leave school to support themselves continues to rise, more families are faced with the "life-cycle squeeze." Using census data for the U.S., Oppenheimer has demonstrated that only at relatively high occupational levels do the average earnings of men peak at the same time that the needs of their families are also peaking, that is, when the children are adolescent and of college age. In occupations where the pay is moderate or low the average earnings peak at youthful ages, with the consequence that men at an age when family costs are heaviest are earning little more on the average than younger men, and in some occupations they are actually earning less. Hence the families of such men risk a deterioration in their standard of living unless extra income is brought into the household. The life-cycle squeeze appears to be a powerful motive for many middle-aged women to enter or reenter the labor force.

More women may also be attracted to work because they are more educated than their predecessors, because hours are becoming more flexible and because job benefits are greater. In almost all the countries being considered the proportion of women receiving the equivalent of a baccalaureate degree has been increasing and better-educated women are drawn by the job market more than their less educated contemporaries. In addition, if the incipient trend toward flexible working hours accelerates, data from surveys indicate that a substantial reserve of women await part-time opportunities. There are efforts in many countries to eliminate discrimination in fringe benefits and promotions for women. For example, Belgium has instituted major social-security reforms allowing a married woman to receive unemployment insurance, cash sickness benefits and a waiver of the qualifying period for medical care in the event that she leaves her job to have a child and then is reemployed.

Such compelling positive incentives for women to work are offset by some powerful depressants. Perhaps the most important is the overall assumption by both men and women that the primary obligation of a woman is to her home and family. In the U.S., Karen Oppenheim Mason of the University of Michigan and Larry L. Bumpass of the University of Wisconsin analyzed the answers to questions on sex roles in the 1970 National Fertility Study that were asked of women under the age of 45 who were married or had been married. The attitudes toward the primary status of women they found are congruent with the results from European surveys and with women's observed secondary commitment to work. Almost 80 percent of the 6,740 women interviewed in this national sample agreed with the statement "It is much better for everyone involved if the man is the achiever outside the home and the woman takes care of the home and family." Fewer than half of the respondents agreed with the statement "A working mother can establish just as warm and secure a relationship with her children as a mother who does not work." And more than two-thirds agreed with the statement "A preschool child is likely to suffer if his mother works." No significant differences appeared with respect to the age of the women interviewed.

Since these surveys show that it is so clearly normative for women to give primacy to their derived status if they marry and have children, few highly developed societies attempt to offer much supplementary help to married women who work. Even in countries such as France and Sweden where child-care assistance to working mothers is accepted as a social responsibility, facilities are often inadequate in both quality and number. In all advanced Western countries moderately priced, well-cooked takeout meals are typically a rarity. Working married women are thus very dependent on husbandly help, which, surveys have shown, is more likely to be forthcoming if the wife is employed but is usually insufficient in amount. As a result working women with families tend to be very hard pressed.

In 1965 and 1966 Alexander Szalai and his colleagues conducted a monumental study of how people budget their time in urban areas of 10 Western and Eastern European countries as well as the U.S. and Peru. They demonstrated that, regardless of the country, employed married women work longer hours than either employed men or housewives. Moreover, on weekends (particularly on Sundays), when many housewives cut back on their household tasks, employed women typically double the amount of time they spend on housework in an evident effort to catch up. Szalai and his colleagues point out: "The plight of the employed woman pervades all of our time-budget records. . . . After her day's obligations are done, she finds herself with an hour or two less time than anyone else. . . . The cramped nature of her time is reflected by marked constrictions in all leisure activities, particularly those relatively passive and recuperative ones such as sitting down to pass time reading a newspaper."

The results of this research conform to independent work done previously in France, the U.S.S.R., Sweden, Finland and Denmark. Indeed, it is significant that the Scandinavian "sex role" movement that began in the early 1960's has emphasized the importance of augmenting the household and child-rearing obligations of men. This change is regarded as mandatory if women are to experience an increase in opportunity to work outside the home and if, in the words of Eva Moberg (a leader in the Swedish woman's movement), they are to have more than just "conditional emancipation." Surveys on both sides of the Atlantic, however, indicate that men are typically willing to accord women broad political, civil and economic "rights," but only if they fulfill their household and family obligations too. Women are thus faced with a rather inflexibly structured choice: too much work or too much leisure. It would not be surprising if many women did not elect to be overworked.

The possibilities for greatly expanded work opportunities for women seem even less rosy when we look at the demand for their services. Projections of expanded demand for female labor all assume that there will be high rates of economic growth—rates that may be quite problematic over the next 25 years. Furthermore, the higher educational levels of women may be a mixed blessing unless the better-educated move out of traditional feminine occupations. The supply of female labor is becoming overeducated for the jobs that have been typed as feminine. Compounding the problem is the fact that major recent declines in the birth rates of some countries suggest that demand is actually contracting in the most important "female" profession: schoolteaching. Just how much these negative factors will be offset by a continuing shift of advanced economies to the service sector, where the demand for women has been highest, has not yet been investigated.

All these negative factors imply that, all other things being equal, there may be an upper limit in the highly developed countries on the demand for women at occupational levels attractive to them. This upper limit may be a major reason why countries such as Switzerland have ended up importing large supplies of foreign labor. The immigrants have done the jobs spurned by Swiss of either sex. The same pattern has prevailed in France and other developed countries that have had a large influx of immigrants since World War II.

From the evidence up to this point it seems almost academic to consider whether or not large proportions of women are on the verge of achieving a non-derived lifetime status in the highly developed countries. Indeed, survey data relating specifically to this issue reinforce the improbability of such an outcome. Studies in most of the highly developed countries show that significant proportions of women who work do not want to; also, among those women who are not working typically half or more either do not want to be employed or want only part-time jobs. In fact, the strongest preference among women appears to be for a part-time job: in effect a work situation that does not interfere with their primary status.

Women also do not seem to evince a widespread rejection of their derived status. For example, in 1972 a Harris survey asked a national sample of American women how often they felt that "having a loving husband who is able to take care of me is much more important to me than making it on my own" and "bringing up children properly takes as much intelligence and drive as holding a top position in business or government." Even among women under the age of 30 half said they "frequently" felt that having a loving husband was more important than an independent status, and an additional fifth admitted to having this feeling "occasionally." Only a fourth said they "hardly ever" felt that way. Among older women the importance of a loving husband was even greater. Similarly, more than 60 percent of all the women, even the young ones, said they frequently felt that being a mother is as challenging as having a high occupational position. Finally, few women (only a little more than 20 percent) indicated that they frequently hoped that their daughters would have "more interesting careers outside the home" than they had had. Half "hardly ever" entertained such a feeling. Survey data in other highly developed countries show no vast discontent among women. When they are asked, they typically seem to be as satisfied with life as men. Consequently it seems unlikely that high proportions of women will be impelled to swim upstream in these societies as they are currently constituted.

What does seem probable is that for some years to come a small but rising proportion of women will attempt to achieve an independent status. Factors that may encourage these women are the increasing moral support provided by the women's movement, some modification of sex-typed socialization and schooling, greater educational and career opportunities for women and a blurring of the difference in the way of life between being married and being unmarried.

As for the women's movement, although most women claim to be satisfied with a derived status, a growing and influential minority in many highly developed countries are actively dissatisfied with the popular expectation that all women should occupy that position. If Western societies are so committed to assuring men equal opportunity to develop their different talents, why should the diverse capabilities of women be expected to conform tranquilly to one mold? The incongruity of such an expectation, in addition to the resulting waste of talent and drive, has fueled women's movements with a constantly renewable source of energy. To be sure, surveys find that most women in the developed countries are unsympathetic to the tactics of women's movements. Yet there is a widespread sympathy for many of the goals, particularly for those relating to fair educational and occupational practices. Support has mushroomed for such cadres as the National Organization for Women in the U.S., and such groups are becoming increasingly able to provide moral backing and lobbying for the interests of those women who do want to make it on their own.

Will the minority find recruits among younger women as new cohorts come along? Some social scientists, I among them, believe they will unless the highly developed countries continue with their rigidly sex-typed socialization practices. Evidence concerning the socialization of women from birth onward indicates that there are extremely powerful pressures from all sources to select personality traits and behavior patterns that are believed to be congruent with the status of wife and mother. Among those who have conducted investigations in this area are Mirra Komarovsky of Barnard College, Alice S. Rossi of the University of Massachusetts, Eleanor E. Maccoby of Stanford University, Lois W. Hoffman of the University of Michigan, Inge Broverman and her colleagues at Worcester State Hospital and Matina Horner, now president of Radcliffe College. Their general finding is that American women are socialized for defeat in those same goals and tasks where men are socialized for success. Indeed, the degree to which seemingly "emancipated" industrial societies engage in sex-differentiated practices of child-rearing and indoctrination is just beginning to be understood. Writing in 1972 of her research on young people, Horner said:

"It is clear in our data that the young men and women tested over the past seven years still tend to evaluate themselves and to behave in ways consistent with the dominant stereotype that says competition, independence, competence, intellectual achievement and leadership reflect positively on mental health and masculinity but are basically inconsistent or in conflict with femininity. Thus despite the fact that we have a culture and an educational system that ostensibly encourage and prepare men and women identically for careers, the data indicate that social and, even more importantly, internal psychological barriers rooted in this image really limit the opportunities to men."

None of this research makes one sanguine about the possibility of revolutionary changes in the socialization of young girls. As the "implicits" of a society become explicit, however, they are at least available for scrutiny. Parents may gradually have a more informed choice in the way they rear their offspring and can thus become more aware of the stimuli and environments they wish to select. For example, analyses of the content of children's books show biases that some parents, once they become conscious of them, may reject as inappropriate for their children. Lenore J. Weitzman and her colleagues at the University of California at Davis have done a content analysis of the books winning the Caldecott Medal (a leading prize for children's books) during the late 1960's and early 1970's. A principal characteristic of these volumes is the invisibility of female characters, even when animals are included. In the sample of 18 Caldecott winners Weitzman and her colleagues found 261 pictures of males as against 23 pictures of females. Featured in the titles was a ratio of eight males to three females. In close to one-third of the books there were no women at all, and when they did appear they were typically inconspicuous. Not one woman in these books had a job or a profession. In the few cases where they did have leadership roles they were fairies or other mythical characters. A similar content analysis of children's books conducted in Sweden by Rita Liljestrom showed boys in situations emphasizing knowledge, action and intrigue, whereas girls were characterized as being devoted to clothing and personal appearance.

Are the current patterns of socialization appropriate even for women who will be primarily wives and mothers? Or are many aspects of such patterns relics of Victorian fantasy and Freudian theorizing? Broverman and her colleagues asked a sample of psychologists, psychiatrists and social workers, all in clinical practice, to assign traits to a mature healthy man, a mature healthy woman and a mature healthy adult of unspecified sex. The traits assigned to the man and the sex-unspecified adult were quite similar, but there was a significant difference between the concepts of health for sex-unspecified adults and for women. Broverman concludes: "Clinicians are likely to suggest that healthy women [are] more submissive, less independent, less adventurous, more easily influenced, less aggressive, less competitive, more excitable in minor crises, [have] their feelings more easily hurt, [are] more emotional, more conceited about their appearance, less objective, and [dislike] math and science. This constellation seems a most unusual way of describing any mature, healthy individual."

If some changes in the patterns of socialization are accompanied by greater educational opportunities for women, as seems to be the case in almost all highly developed countries, more women may move into fields of study leading to remunerative and prestigious occupations. In fact, as we have seen, this seems to be happening on a small scale in the U.S. Furthermore, in many of the highly developed countries such as Scandinavia, England and Wales, and the U.S., career opportunities are increasingly open to women.

Will this minority of highly-selected women typically have to forgo marriage and children in order to achieve? Probably not: they will merely have to be willing to run the risk. And this risk may seem less awesome in a world where the lines between marriage and nonmarriage, having children and not having them are becoming more blurred than in the past. Less rigid confinement of sexual relations to marriage means less of a penalty for late marriage or nonmarriage. The high risk of divorce, even for women with no career, also blurs the line between the married and the unmarried. Small families, even for full-time housewives, make the career woman with one or two children less of an anomaly. Both kinds of women will spend most of their lives without children around.

Why then will not high proportions of women become "emancipated" in this fashion? Why assume, as I have done, that only a minority will respond to changing socialization and opportunity? The answer is that even if one could assume that such changes will be sweeping, there are still underlying constraints over and above the ones I have already discussed. We must not, for example, confuse equality of opportunity with equality of outcome. Given a range of choice, we must expect women's achievements to be variable, just as the achievements of men are variable. In addition, educational and occupational achievement will inevitably expose the achieving women to risks of non-marriage and childlessness. While her peers are pursuing husbands the achieving woman is losing time from this activity, even though the number of men that she might want or who might want her is likely to be more limited than it is for other women. Exacerbating this risk is the paucity of occupations so fulfilling as to lead many women to risk impairing their marital opportunities.

Perhaps the most compelling fact of all is that women's derived status stands to benefit greatly from the opening up of genuine alternatives. For the first time women who want to be primarily wives and mothers will be in relatively short supply, as others are drained off into new opportunities and an additional "swing vote" hovers on the brink of decision. Given such a market situation men will have to make concessions concerning important features of women's derived status, concessions that no amount of exhortation by presidential and royal commissions has been able to bring about. Whatever these may be, whether they are more sharing of household and child-rearing tasks, greater economic equality and security of tenure or the elimination of double standards of morality, they will make the status of wife and mother more varied and advantaged than it is currently. Upgrading women's derived status inevitably places the alternatives to that status at a relative disadvantage. It means that women probably will choose the alternatives primarily for positive reasons such as satisfying their best talents and drives, rather than for negative reasons such as not wanting to be "a mere housewife."

It is idle to speculate what the various levels of derived status and non-derived status might become in some kind of equilibrium state. The main point is that two significant changes will have occurred. First, in Western societies there will be an opportunity for women to respond in a variety of ways to the selection of a lifelong position. Second, women's derived status will have regained at the very least the balance it lost during the Industrial Revolution and the demographic transition.

A Model of the Modern Man: Theoretical and Methodological Issues

Alex Inkeles

The results of Inkeles's latest comparative study of modernity in Argentina, Chile, India, Israel, Nigeria, and Pakistan are summarized in this essay. In the process of studying these six modernizing societies, he has developed a conceptual model of individual modernity based on analytic, topical, and behavioral considerations that serves to define the type of personality that one would expect to predominate under conditions of advanced modernization.

The term "modern" has many associations and carries a heavy weight of connotations. It is applied not only to men, but to nations, to political systems, to economies, to cities, to institutions such as schools and hospitals, to housing, to clothes, and to manners. Taken literally, the term could mean anything current that has more or less recently replaced something that was, in the past, the accepted or standard. In this sense, the first sailing vessels to replace the galleys propelled by oars were once modern, as was the clipper ship before steam, and steam before atomic power. Approached in this way, the modern becomes a catalogue rather than an entity, a random list of things rather than a concept.

Numerous scholars have sought to give the idea a more distinctive and coherent form. One line of thought treats the modern as the concrete embodiment of certain ways of doing things, as in patterns of education,

"A Model of the Modern Man: Theoretical and Methodological Issues" by Alex Inkeles is reprinted by permission of the author and publisher from *Social Science and the New Societies: Problems in Cross-Cultural Research and Theory Building,* ed. Nancy Hammond (East Lansing: Social Science Research Bureau, Michigan State University, 1973), 59–92. Inkeles is professor of education and sociology at Stanford University, and has played a leading role in developing several fields of social psychology relevant to modernization. The results of an extensive survey of Soviet society based on interviews with displaced persons, are summarized in *Social Change in Soviet Russia* (1968). His research (with Daniel J. Levinson) on the personality characteristics common to specific societies is set forth in "National Character: The Study of Modal Personality and Sociocultural Systems," *Handbook of Social Psychology* (2nd ed., 1968), Vol. 4, 418–506. More recently, he has directed, with David H. Smith, a comparative study of individual modernity in Argentina, Chile, India, Israel, Nigeria, and Pakistan, published in *Becoming Modern: Individual Change in Six Developing Countries* (1974).

urbanization, industrialization, bureaucratization, rapid communications, and transportation. Of course, some of these manifestations, such as cities, go back in man's history to points long ante-dating anything we would ordinarily call modern, while other developments, such as industrialization, do not. In any event, when emphasis is placed on the more or less simultaneous development of a set, complex, or syndrome of these patterns of social organization, then there can be little doubt that they were observed as such a syndrome in no nation before the nineteenth century and became really widespread in the world only in the twentieth. The modern, then, can be conceived of as a style or form of civilization characteristic of our current historical epoch, much as feudalism or the classical empires were characteristic of earlier historical eras. This form of civilization is not manifest everywhere in the world, just as feudalism was not present in all the world in the eleventh to the fifteenth centuries. Similarly, modernity in any given part of the world where it does appear is not exactly the same everywhere. It varies in accord with local conditions, the history of a given culture, and the time at which it was introduced.

Within these limits, there exists a syndrome of characteristics readily recognized at both the national and sub-institutional levels. The exploration of that syndrome is the focus of the activities of numerous scholars. Thus, Robert Ward[1] provides ten characteristics defining *economic* modernization; these characteristics include the intense application of scientific technology and inanimate sources of energy, high specialization of labor and interdependence of impersonal markets, large-scale financing and concentration of economic decision making, and rising levels of material well-being. Samuel Huntington[2] offers a more compact list of three processes that define *political* modernization: the replacement of a large number of traditional, religious familial, and ethnic political authorities by a single, secular, national, political authority; the emergence of new political functions, legal, military, administrative, and scientific, which must be managed by new administrative hierarchies chosen on the basis of achievement rather than ascription; and increased participation in politics by social groups throughout the society along with the development of new institutions such as political parties and interest groups to organize this participation.

Whereas the first line of analysis in the study of modernization gives emphasis to patterns of social organization, there is a second line that more emphasizes the cultural and ideational. Whereas the first approach more stresses ways of *organizing* and *doing*, the second assigns primacy to ways of *thinking* and *feeling*. The one approach is concerned more with the *institution*, the other with the *individual*. The first is more narrowly sociological and political, the second more sociological and psychological.

The socio-psychological approach considers modernization mainly as a

[1] Robert Ward, *Political Modernization in Japan and Turkey* (Princeton: Princeton University Press, 1964).

[2] Samuel Huntington, "Political Modernization: America vs. Europe," *World Politics*, XVIII (April, 1966), pp. 378–415.

process of change in ways of perceiving, expressing, and valuing. The modern is defined as a mode of individual responding, a set of dispositions to act in certain ways. It is, in other words, an "ethos," or a "spirit," in the sense in which Max Weber spoke of "the spirit of capitalism." As Robert Bellah expressed it, the modern may be seen not "as a form of political or economic system, but as a spiritual phenomenon or a kind of mentality." [3] As such, it is much less tied to a particular time and place than is the definition of modernity in terms of institutional arrangements. If modernity is defined as a state of mind, the same state of mind might have existed in Elizabethan England or even in Periclean Greece.

Of the two main themes in modernization, the institutional has received far more attention than the individual. Indeed, a conservative estimate is that major studies of economic and political modernization at the institutional level outnumber those at the individual some twenty to one. Once fully aware of this fact, the group formed at Harvard's Center for International Affairs to study the social and cultural aspects of economic development decided to commit itself more or less exclusively to studying the impact of the modernization process on the individual. [4]

Our decision stemmed from two convictions: First, we wanted to examine the impact on men, the human costs, if you will, of their exposure to the complex of urbanism, industrialism, mobility, and mass communication. A widespread belief, almost a fundamental conviction, among many intellectuals is that the process of industrialization inevitably brings with it great, indeed excessive, social disorganization, the disruption of social ties, and the consequent disorientation of the individual. Although the assertions are many, the facts are few. We began with the conviction that many of these claims were exaggerated, others unsupported by evidence, still others simply wrong. We believed that work in industry not only could be, but in many parts of the world actually *was*, an educational and liberalizing influence on the men who experience it. We felt it had the capacity to increase their initiative, to widen their participation in society, even to increase their sense of personal worth and dignity.

Our second conviction was that the effective functioning of a modern society requires that citizens have certain qualities, attitudes, values, habits, and dispositions, which can be inculcated in men by their experience at work in factories. Modern society has been characterized as a "participant" society. It requires of its citizens a readiness for new experience and an acceptance of innovation, a concern with public issues at the community and national levels,

[3] Robert N. Bellah, "Meaning and Modernization," *Religious Studies*, 4 (1968), pp. 37–45.
[4] The group was headed by Alex Inkeles, a member of the senior Center faculty, and included as principal members Edward Ryan, Howard Schuman, and David Smith. Support for the research came principally from a grant from the Rockefeller Foundation. Field work in India, Pakistan, and Israel was supported by the Office of Educational and Cultural Affairs. Department of State, through a grant of local currencies under Public Law 480. The National Science Foundation underwrote several major phases of the project, and the Air Force Office of Scientific Research provided funds for technical studies of translation and for computer time.

a sense of efficacy that encourages and supports programs of social change and the ability to move freely from place to place and to integrate one's self with new co-workers and new neighbors in new living arrangements. A nation can, up to a point, develop industrially and undergo large-scale urbanization without experiencing fundamental changes in the psychology of its population. It will then be a country with a developed sector, but it will not be a truly developed *nation*, much less a modern *society*. If many countries are to avoid the terrible national schizophrenia that affects those nations with a small, modernized sector and a vast hinterland of traditionalism, they must find some way of incorporating and integrating all of their citizens into the modern sector of society. Numerous students have stressed that development is not an automatic process. History is full of dramatic cases of interrupted and arrested development.[5] We believe that this condition is most likely to be produced when the modernization of industry or administration is not accompanied by changes in the mentality, in the attitudes and habits, of the population, which must, after all, operate the new industry and bureaucracy, consume its products, deal with its demands, respond to its appeals, and relate to its style of functioning.

What we wanted, then, was a study of modernization that focussed on the common man—the peasant and the worker newly entering industry. The study should deal with the experience of these men in their encounter with the new institutions of the emerging modern order—the factory, the city, mass media, political parties, large-scale, government bureaucracy. Our study should be conducted in developing countries, in which the process of modernization is most evident and in which the need for modern men is most pressing. To avoid the danger of premature generalizations based on a single combination of special attributes that might be quite fortuitous, we wanted a study conducted not in one but in several, quite different countries. To permit us to disentangle the complex web of influences that have been claimed to generate modernity, we felt that our study should not deal with a single source of influence but should precisely control and measure a large set of variables. This type of analysis should be based on large samples purposefully drawn to permit us to give answers to the theoretical and descriptive questions to which our research is addressed. To avoid prejudging, we felt that our research should not be based on a single, simple, and narrow conception of the modern but on a complex, elaborate, and differentiated conception that would permit us to study separately the elements and components of modernity—which, indeed, would permit us to test empirically the very idea of whether or not there is such a thing as a "modern man."

With this set of specifications, we began a large-scale comparative research project in six developing countries—Argentina, Chile, India, Israel, Nigeria, and Pakistan. Of the numerous aspects of the Harvard Project on the Social and Cultural Aspects of Development, I have selected for discussion in this forum what is perhaps the most fundamental issue: How shall we conceive

[5] See, especially, S. N. Eisenstadt, "Breakdown of Modernization," *Economic Development and Culture Change*, 12 (July, 1964), pp. 345–367.

of and measure individual modernization?[6] The form that my answer takes is not so much a discussion of competing strategies as a detailed exposition of one effort to elaborate a complex and reasonably complete model of individual modernity. Even within the course of this single effort, however, three different strategies in fact did compete for our attention and allegiance, so that in discussing this one effort I have a passing opportunity to comment on a number of others. Beyond this, I will take this occasion to indicate some of the forces that we believe generate more modern attitudes and behavior in individuals and to suggest some of the vicissitudes that accompany this process.

Conceptual Model of Individual Modernity

The great danger in any definition of the "modern" is that some more powerful group may arbitrarily impose its own traditional *values* on a less powerful group as if it were bestowing the same benefit it confers when it offers a railroad network, a television station, a well-equipped field hospital, or any one of a dozen other so-called miracles of modern technology. Do we not do something peculiar and distorting if we make the American business-man's grey flannel suit more modern than the Indian civil servant's high-necked coat or for that matter his *dhoti*? Isn't it potentially misleading, as well as arbitrary, to treat monogamy as more modern than polygamy? Indeed, are we not presuming a great deal when we consider an Arab chieftain more modern merely because he replaces his camel with a Cadillac or even a small jet plane? The tendency to equate the modern with foreign technology does not prevail only in the West. In the state of Bihar, in India, a man is considered more modern if he believes that food cooked on charcoal tastes better than food cooked on dried cow dung cakes and insists that factory cloth feels better on the skin than homespun cloth. He might be right on both counts, but should we consider him more modern merely because he uses charcoal and factory-spun cloth?

The issues are subtle, complicated, and difficult, and they could occupy us a long time, but if I pursued them all I would never get on to telling how we attempted to resolve the problem in our research. Indeed, I could argue that the position one really takes on these issues is manifested most clearly, not in what one says about them, but rather in the precise way in which one designs his measures of modernity.

In our questionnaire-guided interview, we touched on some thirty different

[6] The main outlines of the study and the principal findings will be reported in a book to be titled, *Becoming Modern*. Preliminary published reports on some phases of the project may be found in: Alex Inkeles, "The Modernization of Man," in Myron Weiner (ed.), *Modernization* (New York: Basic Books, 1966); and David Smith and Alex Inkeles, "The OM Scale: A Comparative Socio-Psychological Measure of Individual Modernity," *Sociometry*, XXIX (December, 1966), pp. 353–377. Documents describing the sample design and reproducing the questionnaire may be obtained by ordering Document No. 9133, American Documentation Institute.

themes and explored each in greater or lesser depth. All of the major themes were examined and tested to assess their relevance for our general research objectives. Some of the themes to which we assigned distinctive status we now view more as merely sub-themes. Other themes, which we earlier did not distinguish with the stamp of a key phrase and code letters, emerged either in our field experience or in the course of our analysis as important and worthy of the status we had assigned to other subjects. We take some pride, however, in the fact that no theme was used in our study unless a substantial theory linked it to modernization, a theory either accepted by us or affirmed by authorities whose standing in the field made testing their ideas important. As I tell our story and present our findings, I believe that it will be apparent that most of our decisions were justified by the outcome of the research.

The thirty-odd themes we explored are not a random list. They have a definite inner structure, a structure derived from the main research objectives of our project. They reflect the interests and ideas of the staff members who joined in this co-operative venture and the theories advanced by leading students of the modernization process. Although each theme could reasonably be explored in its own right, we originally conceived of some of them as holding together in a syndrome, or complex, of attitudes and values that for us constituted the core concept of modernity and the central focus of our research. This sub-set or syndrome of themes constitutes our *analytical model* of individual modernity.

This model did not, however, touch on all the themes that students of modernization have pointed to as major concomitants or effects of the modernization process. Many of these popular ideas were supported by some evidence but warranted further testing, others were virtually untested by empirical field research, and still others we believed were wrong and we wanted to prove them so. This second set of themes was selected on a more eclectic basis. They were not viewed as tied together in a distinctive pattern or syndrome. Each might stand or fall alone without affecting the validity of any other. We refer to them as the *topical themes* on modernization.

Both the analytical model and the topical themes dealt mainly with attitudes and values. We are cognizant of the possibility that a man might think and speak in the modern vein but still *act* in a more traditional way. It could be argued that the ultimate test of the modernization process lies not in its ability to teach a man how to give "modern" answers on a questionnaire, but rather in its ability to produce men who in their everyday lives perform like modern men. We could not assume that the connection between *thinking* modern and *acting* modern was automatic and perfect. Indeed, we had good reason to suppose that it might be tenuous and uncertain. We resolved, therefore, to collect materials that would permit us to judge the modernity of men by their actions rather than their words. This test of individual modernity we called our *behavioral measures*.

Let us now turn to a brief exposition of the theory and the content of each of these three approaches to modernization—the analytic model, the topical themes, and the behavioral measures—as they were actually elaborated in our research.

The Analytic Model

We began with the desire to develop a conception of individual modernity that did not blindly and arbitrarily impose Western customs and Western standards of value on the citizens of developing countries. Attaining a value-free measure of modernity is quite difficult, however. With the exception of Japan—and Russia if you wish to include it with the East—all the major nations we can consider modernized have a European tradition. Thus, it is extremely difficult to disentangle those elements of their social and cultural systems that are distinctive to, and necessary for, the maintenance of a modern society from those that are really "traditional" for these European societies but that have incidentally become associated with, in a sense "dragged along" into, the contemporary era along with the more modern institutions. For example, everyone has noted how the Japanese, and indeed the elites in most of the underdeveloped world, have adopted the Western businessman's suit and his shoes, even though, in fact, this attire is in no way necessary for the running of a modern society.

Our solution to the problem was to avoid an abstract list of values and instead to develop a list of modern qualities that met the demands or requirements of running a factory. We will encounter little argument, we trust, when we propose that the factory is one of the distinctive institutions of modern society. Indeed, industrialization is a very large part of the modernization process. Many would claim that it is the most essential element. Industrialization, in turn, depends on the factory—the large-scale, productive enterprise, bringing together large numbers of men in one work place, systematically ordering their relationship with one another on rational considerations expressed in formal rules, relying on concentrations of inanimate power and the systematic application of technology, and guided by a hierarchy of authority resting largely on technical skill and administrative competence.

The factory as an institution has no nationality; it is not English or French or Dutch or, for that matter, European. It does not violate the important taboos of any religious group, major or minor. There are no proscriptions against entering such a place, or working in such a place, In Islam, Hinduism, or Buddhism, and believers from all these religions have found it easy to take up work in factories. Because almost everyone wants the benefits of industry, taking the factory as the key to modernization minimizes the seeming imposition of alien institutions and their associated customs and values. We proposed, then, to classify as modern those qualities that are likely to be inculcated by participation in large-scale, modern, productive enterprises such as the factory and, perhaps more critical, that may be *required* in the staff if the factory is to operate efficiently and effectively.

There are, of course, many ways of looking at the factory as an institution. We do not claim that our list of qualities and requirements of factory life is exhaustive or even definitive. But each of the themes is important as an attribute of factory life and is, simultaneously, a quality of men that has more general relevance for life in a modern society. We further narrowed the range of themes by focussing particularly on those features of factory organization that we assumed would be notable to and would most influence a naïve worker from the countryside. We justified this approach by our special interest in the factory as a learning setting, as a school in ways of arranging things, of thinking, and of feeling, which contrasts markedly with the traditional village. Men who enter the factory after growing up in an urban setting will, of course, notice much less contrast between the environment in which they grew up and the one they encounter on entering the factory. In either instance, of course, we were assuming that the themes we selected were the most notable and influential. Only our research experience can indicate how accurate our assumption was.

Just how we derived these qualities from a study of factory organization may or may not be readily apparent. Unfortunately, in this report, I must restrict myself to a brief exposition of the qualities we defined as modern within the framework of our analytic model. Since I do not, at this point, offer any particular justification for our choice of themes, let me for present purposes assert that we simply defined the modern man as having these qualities.

Readiness for new experience and *openness to innovation and change* constitute the first elements in our definition of the modern man. We believe that the traditional man is less disposed to accept new ideas, new ways of feeling and acting. We are speaking, therefore, of something that is itself a state of mind, a psychological disposition, an inner readiness, rather than of the specific techniques or skills a man or group may possess because of the level of technology it has attained. Thus, in our sense, a man may be more modern in spirit, even though he works with a wooden plough, than someone who already drives a tractor. The readiness for new experience and ways of doing things, furthermore, may take a variety of different forms and contexts —in the willingness to adopt a new drug or sanitation method, to accept a new seed or adopt a different fertilizer, to ride on a new means of transportation or turn to a new source of information, to approve a new form of wedding ceremony or new type of schooling for young people. Individuals and groups may, of course, show more readiness for the new in one area of life than another, but we can also conceive of the readiness to accept innovations as a pervasive, general characteristic that makes itself felt across a wide variety of human situations. And we consider those who have this readiness to be more modern. Representative of the questions intended to tap readiness for new experience is the following:

> Suppose you could get along well enough where you are now, earning enough to provide food and other necessities for yourself and your family. Would you be willing to move to another place far from here where the language and other customs are different if *there* you could live twice as well as here?

Our assumption, of course, was that people open to new experience might more readily respond to the opportunity we described. In this example, the readiness to move might, naturally, be tempered both by the amount of economic pinch the man felt and by the importance to him of improving his standard of living. No question, however, is entirely unambiguous or uni-dimensional, and some of the most interesting problems in analysis come from disentangling the diverse motivational forces that may come to bear on an individual's answer to any one question.

The realm of the *growth of opinion* represents the second in our complex of themes. This area is itself divisible into a number of subthemes or scale areas. We define a man as more modern if he has a *disposition to form or hold opinions* over a large number of the problems and issues that arise not only in his immediate environment but also outside it. Pioneering work on this dimension has been done by Daniel Lerner of the Massachusetts Institute of Technology and was reported in his book. *The Passing of Traditional Society.* Lerner showed that in the Middle East the individuals within any country, and the populations of different countries, varied greatly in their ability or readiness to imagine themselves as the prime minister or comparable government leader and thus to offer advice as to what should be done to resolve the problems facing the country. The more educated the individual and the more advanced the country, the greater was the readiness to offer opinions in response to this challenge. The more traditional man, we believe, takes an interest in fewer situations and events, mainly those that touch him immediately and intimately, and, even when he holds opinions on more distant matters, he is more circumspect in expressing such opinions.

We assessed the individual's readiness to hold opinions on a wide range of subjects and issues by a series of different measures. A crude indicator was the number of times he responded to our questions by saying, "I don't know," or "I never thought about that." More informative were our evaluations of the number and themes of his replies to questions about the most serious problems facing his nation, his local community, and his family.

We also consider a man to be more modern if his orientation to the opinion realm is more democratic. Here, we mean that he shows more *aware-ness of the diversity of attitude and opinion around him,* rather than closing himself off in the belief that everyone thinks alike and indeed just as he does. In our conception, a modern man is able to acknowledge differences of opinion: he has no need rigidly to deny differences out of the fear that they will upset his own view of the world. He is also less likely to approach opinion in a strictly autocratic or hierarchical way. He does not automatically accept the ideas of those above him in the power hierarchy or reject the opinions of those whose status is markedly lower than his. In other words, *he puts a positive value on variations in opinion.* We tested these values by asking people whether it is proper to think differently from the village head-man or other traditional leader and, also, by asking whether the opinions of a man's wife or young son merit serious consideration when important public issues are being discussed. These questions proved to be a sensitive indicator in helping us to distinguish one man from another and, we believe, will be an important element in the final syndrome of modernity we will delineate.

Intimately related to our study of opinion but conceived as a separate dimension were our measures of *information*. We consider that being modern means not merely having opinions but being more energetic in acquiring facts and information on which to base those opinions. It is one thing to opine that capitalists are bad when you are explicitly asked your opinion, another to know actually what and where are Moscow and Washington.

Time is a third theme our measures deal with at some length. We view a man as more modern if he is oriented to the present or the future rather than to the past. We consider him more modern if he accepts fixed hours, that is to say, schedules, as something sensible and appropriate, or possibly even desirable, as against the men who think that fixed rules are something either bad or perhaps a necessity but unfortunately also a pity. We also define a man as more modern if he is punctual, regular, and orderly in organizing his affairs.

The relationship of this orientation to time to measures of modernity is a complex issue and presents me with an opportunity to point out that it is a mistake to assume that our measures of modernity differentiate between traditional and non-traditional people as they would ordinarily be defined. For example, we believe that the Maya Indians had a better sense of time than their Spanish rulers, and they preserve it to this day. The qualities we define as modern can, in fact, be manifested in a people who seem to be relatively unmodern when you consider the level of technology or the amount of power they have. We are talking about properties of the person, which, in turn, may be a reflection of the properties of a culture that could emerge in any time or place. That these qualities may be more widely diffused in industrially advanced countries does not make them a monopoly of those national groups.

Efficacy is a fourth theme, one that is especially important in our conception of the modern man. The modern individual believes that, to a substantial degree, man can learn to dominate his environment in order to advance his own purposes and goals, rather than being dominated entirely by that environment. For example, a man who feels efficacious is more likely to respond positively to the question, "Do you believe that some day men will fully understand what causes such things as floods, droughts, and epidemics?" The more efficacious man, even though in fact he has never seen a dam, would, we believe, say, "Yes, I think that some day man will do that."

The sense of efficacy is, of course, not limited to feelings concerning man's potential mastery over nature. It includes, as well, the belief that one can effectively do something if officials are proposing what one considers to be a bad law, that care will help prevent accidents, that human nature can be changed, and that men can arrange their affairs so that even nations can live in peace. His sense of efficacy, then, expresses the modern man's confidence in his ability, alone and in concert with other men, to organize his life to master the challenges it presents at the personal, the interpersonal, the communal, the national, and the international levels.

Planning is a theme closely related to efficacy, but we initially conceived of it as important in its own right. We consider a man more modern if he is oriented toward planning and organizing affairs and believes in planning as an approach both to public affairs and to his own personal life. We asked such questions about public affairs as: "What does the country need most: hard work by the people, the help of God, or a good plan on the part of the government?" And to assess thoughts about the more private, personal realm, we asked: "Some say that a boy should be taught to handle things as they come up without bothering much about thinking ahead. Others say that a boy must be taught to plan and arrange things in advance. What do you think?"

Calculability (or *trust*). By our definition, the modern man is one who has confidence that his world is calculable, that other people and institutions around him can be relied upon to fulfill or meet their obligations and responsibilities. He is more prepared to trust a stranger than is the traditional man. He does not agree that everything is determined either by fate or by the whims and particular qualities and characters of men. In other words, he believes in a reasonably lawful world under human control. This, therefore, is a theme we might also expect to find closely related to the sense of efficacy.

Distributive justice, especially with regard to technical skill, provides the seventh theme in our set. One of the central principles of modern organization is that rewards should be proportionate to skill and measured contribution to the purposes of the organization.

Exceptions to this rule are, of course, ubiquitous in modern society, but even so the principle is much more emphasized and practiced in such settings than in most traditional orders where rewards are more determined by power, by special status, or haphazardly, by the pleasure of those who control the distribution of benefits. The beliefs that rewards should be according to rule rather than whim and that the structure of rewards should, insofar as possible, be in accord with skill and relative contribution are what we call the sense of distributive justice. As thus formulated, the principle has its most obvious application to work in organizations such as factories or office bureaucracies. When applied to other roles such as that of a customer dealing with a merchant or a citizen dealing with an official the principle is often referred to as the principle of *universalistic*, as against *particularistic*, treatment.

Our chief measure of the sense of distributive justice is derived from a set of questions in which we first set the ordinary worker's pay as a standard (say, of 100 rupees per month) and then asked what should be the *relative* pay of a foreman, an engineer, a factory manager, and several professional workers such as a doctor and a school teacher. To assess attitudes about particularism we also added, in some countries, a few questions on special treatment; we asked, for example, whether our respondents thought it good or bad that people having business at a public office would first seek out a friend or acquaintance with connections before going to transact that business.

Aspirations, education, and the new learning. Each culture has a traditional wisdom, which is most widely diffused among and most strongly believed in by the peasantry and others who make up the common folk. In these settings, what formal schooling exists is often used for purposes of religious education and is devoted to inculcating and preserving traditional values. The secular school and the new learning, which we in the more developed countries take so much for granted, are radical innovations in many of the developing countries. The subjects taught and the values disseminated often compete with, may indeed challenge and contradict, the traditional wisdom. We defined the more modern man as having an interest in and placing higher value on formal education and schooling in skills such as reading and writing and arithmetic. He feels that modern learning and even science are not intrusions into a sacred realm, which should be left a mystery or approached only through religion, but rather that science and technology will benefit mankind by providing solutions to pressing human problems. We measured attitudes in this realm by asking how much schooling a man should try to get for his son if costs were no obstacle, whether schools should more teach morality and religion or the practical skills, and what the father prefers for his son's future occupation.

Awareness of, and respect for, the *dignity* of others is a quality many people feel has been lost in the modern world. If we wanted to make a judgment as to whether this quality was, in fact, more deeply instilled and more widely distributed in traditional societies, a great deal would clearly depend on which traditional society we used as a standard of comparison. Many intellectuals are firmly convinced that *all* men enjoyed greater personal dignity, even if they consumed fewer goods, when they lived in the pre-industrial, pre-urban age. We are not persuaded that this dictum is true. Indeed, in our study, we adopted the rather radical position that the factory may be a training ground that inculcates a greater sense of awareness of the dignity of subordinates and restraint in one's dealings with them. We feel that the manager in a factory is more obliged to respect the dignity of a worker than is the owner, boss, chief, or patron in his relationship to the peasant in the most traditional villages. Indeed, we expect that the modern man not only will be more protective of the dignity of weaker and subordinate persons in the work settings, but will extend the principle to other relationships and thus will manifest such behavior in his treatment of all those inferior in status and power, such as women and children. Thus, we asked: "Which of the following is more correct, regarding a boy's dignity: Is it less important than a man's, as important, or more important?"

THE ANALYTIC MODEL AND THE MODERN MAN

Taken together, this set of ten to a dozen themes constitutes our analytic model of the modern man. In contrast to the common man of traditional society, a modern man accepts innovation and change, is open to new experience for himself and those around him. He expresses this openness, in part, by valuing formal schooling and believing in the potential benefit of scientific and technological experimentation and exploration. He also expresses his openness by taking an interest in external affairs, seeking new sources of information about all manner of things including public events that do not necessarily touch his immediate life. His involvement and participation in the wider world is reflected in his holding opinions over a wide range of issues, in his awareness of the diversity of opinion of those in his environment, in his tolerance for differing opinions, and in his respect for the right to an opinion by those weaker and less prestigious than he is. The more modern man has a greater sense of efficacy. He feels less dominated by fate and is more convinced that man, by his own efforts and by combining his efforts with others', can organize to master nature and arrange social affairs to assure mankind a reasonable degree of security from calamity, conflict, disease, and hunger. This sense of efficacy rests, in part, on a feeling of confidence or trust in his associates, a sense of the calculability of organizations, superiors, co-workers, and subordinates, and of the reasonable certainty that they will fulfill their obligations to him. The feeling assures him of the support he requires for performing his share of the common task. Planning is for him a highly valued way of attaining both his personal goals and the collective tasks in which he participates. Intimately associated with this value is a strict sense of time and an insistence on the importance of the careful scheduling of events. The modern man expects to receive rewards in accord with his skill and his relative contribution to the common effort. For his part, he acknowledges the value of education and technical skill and its prepared to see them rewarded proportionately. But he feels that these rewards should be part of a formal system, governed by rules universally applied and not restricted to particular individuals and special circumstances according to accident or the whims of the powerful. Correspondingly, in his treatment of others, especially those weaker or less important than he, he is aware of, and avoids diminishing, the sense of dignity and personal worth of those under his care or control.

Any such list of characteristics conceived to represent a social type raises a host of issues. In certain ways the whole of our research effort is meant to deal with those issues. But a few matters must perhaps be dealt with individually.

To begin, let me acknowledge that our formulation of the dimensions of modernity, in fact, the very dimensions we have selected, is, necessarily, somewhat arbitrary. Thus, we are quite ready to acknowledge that the theme of calculability might better be expressed as trust; indeed, the items by which we measure calculability suggest as much. Furthermore, the logical and empirical distinctiveness of some of the dimensions we have defined separately is certainly open to question. It is not at all obvious, for example, that openness to new experience and the ready acceptance of change should be treated as separate dimensions. Equally, it might be argued that the sense of efficacy and the belief in planning both are facets of one more general underlying dimension. To a certain extent we ourselves held this belief from the beginning, but it seemed wiser initially not to prejudge such questions. To an important degree our research is intended to test the extent to which these, and others, *are* really distinctive dimensions. To maintain them apart initially in no way impaired our ability to join them later. In making such combinations, wholly different themes might well be introduced. Ever since Weber wrote *The Protestant Ethic*, "rationality" has been popular in discussions of modernization, and some of our items might be approached in terms of this concept. Similarly, many of them could be re-combined under the general rubric of "changed orientations to authority," which Bellah sees as one of the key elements in attitudinal modernization. But one must begin somewhere, with some distinctions, with some selection of the elements one conceives as making up modernity. No harm is done so long as we all recognize that this is a definitional statement, an analytic model to be tested, and not a dogmatic assertion that the elements we have designated are absolute, exact, and the only elements that could reasonably enter into a definition of modernity of attitude.

However clear and appropriate our *conception* of any dimension of modernity, our effort to *measure* it may be inadequate. Thus, it may be quite sound to consider the readiness for new experience characteristic of modern men. But asking a man if he would move to a strange land may not be much of a test of his openness to new experience. Although we were quite confident that, for the example of new experience, we had found the key to effective question wording, in other instances, such as time orientation and dignity, we were much less confident. Unfortunately, if a given dimension proves unrelated to modernity, we have no absolute test to tell us whether it is really so, despite our assumption to the contrary, or whether the apparent lack of association is derived from the awkwardness or inappropriateness of the questions we asked. Where we fail to find an association we can only try as honestly as possible to assess the adequacy of our questions, as such, area by area.

Although we may be correct in our assumptions about some of the dimensions we have selected for study, we may still be wrong in our most fundamental assumption that all the dimensions relate to each other as a syndrome of characteristics we can sensibly label *"modern man."* The sense of efficacy may indeed be something that distinguishes one person from another, and we may have succeeded in measuring it with a fine degree of precision. The same may be true of openness to new experience and respect for the dignity of subordinates. But it does not automatically follow that men who have a high sense of efficacy also are ready for new experience, or, even if they are, that they also are careful not to humiliate those weaker than they are. One of the fundamental assumptions of our research is that these qualities do indeed cohere, that they are a syndrome, that people who have one trait will also manifest others. In other words, we believe that we may speak not only of men who have one or another modern *characteristic*, but of men who may meaningfully be described in their wholeness as *modern men*. But we must acknowledge that the existence of this type of man is only an assumption, to be tested against the evidence. Moreover, to follow our study with interest, one need not necessarily accept either the general idea of a composite "modern man," nor each element in our list of dimensions without exception. Even if there is no effective syndrome, it may be important to discover who are the men with higher educational aspirations or a stricter sense of time and to learn what are the forces that gave them *these* more limited characteristics.

Alternatively, one may quite properly accept the idea that there is indeed a syndrome of attitudes that holds together but reject the assumption that some particular dimension is really a distinctive part of it. We have, for example, already mentioned the widespread belief—not unshared among the staff of our project—that modern man has less rather than more sensitivity to and respect for the dignity of others than did the traditional villager. Similar doubts might be held about the sense of time and the interest in planning. After all, to run a family farm takes a rigorous sense of time, and the farmer who doesn't plan ahead is likely to find himself far behind at harvest time. By contrast, the factory worker is paced more by the factory whistle and the rhythm of the machine or assembly line, and he can leave most of the planning of his work to the foreman and the engineer. It might then be that openness to new experience and a sense of efficacy go together and are found more among urban industrial workers, whereas a strong sense of time and high value on planning also go together but are more commonly values strongly held by peasants.

Finally, we must consider the relationship of our analytic model of modernity to other conceptions. Of course we are proud of such originality as our conception may display, but many of the other models of modern man that have been proposed in the recent past seem to have many elements in common with ours. We have already noted Lerner's interest in the opinion realm, which he expressed in the concept of empathy, or the "ability to see oneself in the other fellow's situation." He also proposed that a mobile society "has to encourage rationality," and in it "people come to see the future as manipulable rather than ordained and their personal prospects in terms of achievement rather than heritage." [7] We can recognize here much the same emphasis as that contained in our concepts of efficacy and our theme of aspirations and technical skill. Further, Lerner speaks of the mobile person as "distinguished by a high capacity for identification with new aspects of his environment; he comes equipped with the mechanisms needed to incorporate new demands upon himself that arise outside of his habitual experience." [8] Again, the strong resemblance of this idea to our concept of openness to new experience and readiness for change is apparent.

Similar parallels can be observed between elements in our conception of modernity and those proposed by several others. Robert Ward, for example, in his *Political Modernization in Japan and Turkey*, presents a list of eight features of what he calls "intellectual modernization"; and among them are items very similar to our themes of aspirations for new learning, acceptance of change, dignity, and growth of opinion. Ithiel Pool also defines the modern not in terms of GNP nor the proportion of the labor force in industry, but "rather in terms of values and modes of behavior" shared by a population. Among the values and ways of acting he describes as modern are elements

[7] Daniel Lerner, *The Passing of Traditional Society* (Glencoe: The Free Press, 1958), p. 48.
[8] *Ibid.*, p. 49.

closely akin to our themes of efficacy, aspirations, and openness to new experience.[9] Wilbert Moore lists among the more "specific values and principles of conduct appropriate to modernization" rationality in problem solving, punctuality, recognition of individually limited but systematically linked interdependence, and achievement and mobility aspirations, each of which is easily translated into the language of our list of themes.[10] Indeed, we can find similar themes delineated in work as far afield and as far back as the classical economic writings of the late nineteenth century. Thus, Alfred Marshall asserted that there were qualities that make a great industrial people and are wanted not in any occupation, but in all, such as: "To have everything ready when wanted, to act promptly and show resource when anything goes wrong, [and] to accommodate oneself quickly to changes of detail in the work done. . . ." [11]

In the light of this evidence we can hardly argue that our analytic model of modernization is bizarre or even terribly unorthodox. Although derived by a different process and following its own path from an initial concern with the factory as an organization, our analytic model includes many elements in common with those of other students of modernization who began from other starting points and were guided by different theoretical concerns. Our list is certainly more ramified than most, and our research does, perhaps, give greater emphasis to certain themes, such as the sense of efficacy or the openness to new experience. Nevertheless, the lists are basically similar. We are perhaps somewhat different in our insistence that the elements of the model hold together as a coherent *syndrome* of modern attitudes, but this idea is also implicit in the approaches of many of the scholars who have thought extensively about individual modernization. The basic distinction, therefore, is that we have not been content only to define the qualities of modern man. We have gone beyond this idea to render our definition operational by converting it into a set of specific measures. And we have gone further still in subjecting our ideas to an empirical test in several different cultures simultaneously to ascertain how far men in nature do approximate our model of the modern man and to determine the forces that make men modern.

The Topical Model

The analytic model of the modern man was derived primarily from a theoretical consideration of the requirements of factory life. The components were selected because they were assumed to cohere as a psychological syndrome.

[9] Ithiel De Sola Pool, "The Role of Communication in the Process of Modernization and Technological Change," in Bert F. Hoselitz and W. E. Moore (eds.), *Industrialization and Society* (Paris: UNESCO, 1963), pp. 275–293.

[10] Wilbert E. Moore, "The Strategy of Fostering Performance and Responsibility," in Egbert de Vries and J. M. Echavarria (eds.), *Social Aspects of Economic Development in Latin America*, Vol. I (Medina: UNESCO, 1963).

[11] Alfred Marshall, *Principles of Economics*, 8th ed. (London: Macmillan & Co., 1946), pp. 206–207.

While not arbitrary, such a conception is clearly limited and highly selective. Scholars studying the modernization process as it involves the individual often point to quite a few other problems as central issues. Some of these factors are identified as pre-conditions of modernization; that is, the assumption is made that, unless these issues can be resolved, a society's successful attainment of modernization will remain highly problematic. Others are identified as the accompaniments of consequences of modernization, the price, in a sense, that people pay for obtaining the benefits, such as they are, of entering the modern world. Each problem has its own sponsors, as it were, men who have particularly devoted their energies to its explication and investigation. In some instances their argument rests on a good deal of evidence; in others it is merely an assertion of opinion, however plausible.

Some of these problems were of special interest to one or more members of our research team, and to satisfy their interest we undertook to study them. Others, less interesting to us, still seemed issues of recognized importance sufficient to impose on us an obligation to include them in our research. We would thus provide further information, from *new* settings, that could be brought to bear on the standard issues of modernization research. Some of these problems had previously been studied in relative isolation, whereas our research provided an opportunity to relate them one to the other. There was finally a third set of issues about which we felt that either popular thought or expert opinion was in error, and we took the opportunity to see if evidence would support or disprove the opinion.

Because each of these problems was treated by itself, and because the set as a whole was not derived from any common conception or unified theory, we called the set our "topical model" of modernization. This part of our study dealt with about ten major areas, several of which were further divided into major sub-themes.

With the possible exception of religion, no institution of society is more often depicted as either an obstacle to or a victim of modernization than is the extended structure of kinship. Wilbert Moore sums up the prevailing opinion when he says: "In general, the traditional kinship structure provides a barrier to industrial development, since it encourages reliance of the individual upon its security rather than upon his own devices." [12] The image of these family ties as a *victim* of the modernization process is well presented in M. B. Deshmukh's report on the migrant communities in Delhi, where Deshmukh observed, "The absence of social belonging, the pressure of poverty, and the evil effects of the urban environment made . . . the family bonds, regarded to be so sacred in the villages, . . . of absolutely no importance" in the migrant colonies. [13]

After reviewing the question we concluded that there was certainly some

[12] Wilbert E. Moore, *Industrialization and Labor* (Ithaca: Cornell University Press, 1951), p. 79.

[13] M. B. Deshmukh, "Delhi: A Study of a Floating Migration," in *The Social Implication of Industrialization and Urbanization* (Calcutta: UNESCO Research Center on the Social Implication of Industrialization in Southern Asia, 1956).

truth to the frequent assertion that increasing urbanism and industrialism did tend to diminish the vigor of extended kinship relations. Examples of societies that emphasize extended kinship ties would be those with a strong clan system, as in China, or those in which life is organized around a kin-based compound community or a multi-generation, extended family such as the famous Zadruga of Yugoslavia, in which all the brothers, their wives, and their children occupied a common household, worked common land, and shared more or less equally in the benefits of their cooperative economy. We had little reason to doubt that, when urbanism increased the physical distance between kin and industrial employment decreased their economic dependence, the strength of kinship ties as manifested in common residence, frequent visiting, and mutual help in work would decline. A series of our questions inquiring about residence, visiting patterns, mutual help, and the like was designed to test whether these assumptions were true.

While ready to follow popular assumptions up to a point, we also came to the rather radical conclusion that in some ways industrial employment might actually *strengthen* family ties.[14] We felt that many of the common assertions about the family and modernization were much too sweeping and general, that they combined the extended and the immediate family, and that they failed to discriminate between degrees and types of kinship related-ness. It could well be, for example, that, while the experience of modernization weakened *extended* family ties, it would strengthen those to a man's family of *procreation* and would lead him to cling less to his mother and cleave more to his wife.[15] Again, it might be that, while a man gave less attention to his more extended kinship ties after moving to the city, the increased stability and improved well-being that characterize his life as an industrial worker might lead him to accept more fully some of his kinship obligations, at least as compared with his less secure and more impoverished brother still earning his living as a peasant in the village. We tested these relationships with a set of questions on kinship obligations, such as:

> Suppose a young man works in a factory. He has barely managed to save a very small amount of money. Now his relative [selected appropriately for each coun-try, such as a distant cousin] comes to him and tells him he needs money badly since he has no work at all. How much obligation do you think the factory worker has to share his savings with this relative?

[14] The stability of the family, and even of more traditional family ties, under conditions of urbanization and industrialization has been noted, among others, by Lewis for Mexico. Lambert for India, and Husain for Pakistan. See Oscar Lewis, "Urbanization without Breakdown: A Case Study," *Scientific Monthly*, LXXV, No. 1 (July, 1952), pp. 31–42: Richard D. Lambert, *Workers, Factories, and Social Changes in India* (Princeton: Princeton University Press, 1963); and A. F. A. Husain, "Dacca, Human and Social Im-pact of Technological Change in East Pakistan," in *The Social Implications of Indus-trialization and Urbanization* (Calcutta: UNESCO, 1963).

[15] This idea is in line with the main conclusion of Goode's world-wide survey of changing family patterns. Goode notes that the ubiquitous accompaniment of industrialization appears to be the weakening of extended kinship ties, a dissolution of lineage patterns, and a strengthening of the nuclear family. See William J. Goode, *World Revolution and Family Patterns* (Glencoe: The Free Press, 1963).

WOMEN'S RIGHTS

Intimately related to the changing pattern of family relations, but broader than it, is the question of the status of women in society. Most of the traditional societies and communities of the world are, if not strictly patriarchal, at least vigorously male-dominated. The extreme example, perhaps, is found in the Islamic religion, in which a man each day says a prayer of thanks to God for not having made him a woman.

We predicted that the liberating influence of the forces making for modernization would act on men's attitudes and incline them to accord to women status and rights more nearly equal to those enjoyed by men. We tested the men's orientation through questions on a woman's right to work and to equal pay, to hold public office, and to freely choose her marriage partner.

BIRTH CONTROL

Few points about the contemporary world have been better documented than the fact that in many under-developed countries population is increasing so rapidly as to equal and sometimes exceed the rate at which the supply of food and other necessities increases. Despite an annual growth rate of some three percent per year in per capita gross national product, some of these countries are either standing still or even falling constantly behind in the standard of welfare they provide for the population and in the general development of their economy. One solution obvious to almost everyone is to reduce the number of children born to the average family. Although birth control depends in great measure on scientific technology and on particular practices guided by that technology, even the most spectacular advances in science, such as the new contraceptive pills, cannot have the desired effect except as they may be supported by the motive to use them and by patterns of interpersonal relations that make that motivation effective. To assess attitudes in this area, therefore, we inquired into our respondents' ideas of the ideal number of children and into their readiness to restrict that number under various conditions.

RELIGION

Religion ranks with the extended family as the institution most often identified as both an obstacle to economic development and a victim of the same process. The classic case of resistance is that of the Asian religions, and many studies going back to Max Weber's have noted that religion is a major obstacle to modernization because it is the bulwark of nationalism and a repository of beliefs and values incompatible with modern science, technology, and the idea of progress.[16]

Many students of the subject argue rather vigorously that the individual's adherence both to the fundamental doctrine of his traditional religion and to the religious ritual and practice it requires of him will be inevitably undermined by urban living, industrial experience, and scientific education. Thus, speaking about West Africa, Dr. Geoffrey Parrinder notes: "It is sometimes said that Africans are incurably religious. . . . But the ancient religious beliefs cannot stand the strain of modern urban and industrial life. . . . [They] have been attacked by what someone has called 'the acids of modernity'." [17]

Systematic evidence for this proposition is, however, much less ample than one might imagine. We thought it appropriate, therefore, to attempt to ascertain the facts by asking a series of questions designed to measure religiosity and secularism, and we inquired into such matters as the role of God in causing and curing sickness and accidents and the contribution of a holy man, as against a great industrialist, to the welfare of his people. We also took note of the regularity with which our subjects prayed or otherwise fulfilled the formal ritualistic prescriptions and proscriptions of their religion.

We were prepared to find that the influences assumed to make for attitudinal modernity in general would also lead to greater secularism, that is, rising education, urbanism, and industrial experience would all lead to greater secularism, more faith in science and other remedies, and less reliance on religion. Yet we also made the less conventional assumption that the fulfillment of religious obligations *in practice*, especially in ritual, might actually increase as peasants shifted from their life as farmers in the village to workers in urban industry. As with the fulfillment of kinship obligations, we reasoned that the poor, harassed peasant would often lack the funds to pay for special religious services and would have neither time nor energy to undertake many of his ritualistic obligations, especially as the lack of local facilities might increase the trouble to which he must go in order to do so. We concluded, therefore, that, in the city, with religious facilities often more numerous and easily accessible and income steadier and more substantial, the industrial worker might find it less a burden to pay for the services his religion might require.

THE AGED

The special role of the aged is intimately linked to the strength of the family and the vigor of religion in most traditional settings. The respect,

---

[16] Milton Singer, "The Modernization of Religious Beliefs," in Myron Weiner (ed.), *Modernization*, pp. 55–67.

[17] Geoffrey Parrinder, "Religion in Village and Town," in [*Proceedings of the*] *Annual Conference, Sociology Section* (Ibadan, Nigeria: West African Institute of Social and Economic Research, University College, 1953).

indeed the veneration, shown for the aged is often considered one of the most distinctive marks, as well as one of the outstanding virtues, of the traditional society. It is widely believed that two of the most common, indeed almost inevitable, concomitants of industrialization, urbanization, and modernization in general are an eroding of the respect for the aged and the fostering of a youth culture in which old age is viewed not as a venerable state to which one looks forward, but rather as a dreadful condition to be approached with reluctance, even horror.

On this issue of age, as on the family and religion issues, we were not inclined to follow automatically the dominant opinion. It seemed clear that the structural changes accompanying modernization must certainly undercut the special position of the aged. In an era of technological revolutions, for example, it would be hard for the village elder relying on his long personal experience to preserve his authority indefinitely in competition with the agricultural expert relying on the latest scientific advances. As young people come to earn their own living in factories and shops without dependence on their father's land or animals, it seems inevitable that the father's authority over them should be lessened. The mass media and other models of new and competing styles of life should, in turn, make it difficult for the elders authoritatively to enforce the old norms and ways of doing things.

Yet we also felt that many analysts had perhaps exaggerated the corrosive effects of industrialism on the treatment of the aged. Nothing in urban living *per se* requires a person to show disrespect for the aged, and nothing in industrial experience explicitly teaches a man to abandon the aged. Many an old man and woman in the villages have been abandoned by their children because the children lacked the means to support them. Steadier wages and generally more stable conditions of life for those gainfully employed in industry could well enable those who enjoyed these benefits to be more exacting in their fulfillment of obligations to old people. And they might well be as respectful of the aged as their more traditional counterparts farming in the villages.

POLITICS

Political modernization has been cited by many scholars as an indispensable condition of the modernization of economy and society.[18] To characterize the citizen of a modern polity the word "participant" is often used, as is the word "mobilized." There is an expectation that the citizen of a modern polity will take an active interest not only in those matters that touch his immediate life, but also in the larger issues facing his community. His allegiance is supposed to extend beyond his family and friends to the state and the nation and its leaders. He is expected to join political parties, to support candidates, and to vote in elections.

[18] Lucian W. Pye, "Introduction," in L. W. Pye and S. Verba (eds.), *Political Culture and Political Development* (Princeton: Princeton University Press, 1965).

Our study was not designed to answer the question of whether or not a society could modernize its economy and still manage with a traditional political system. Nor is it appropriate for testing how far modern political institutions can operate effectively unless the citizens are also "participant" and "mobilized." But we were in a position to say how far men who were otherwise modern in their attitudes and values would also be modern in their orientation to politics. And the design of our study gave us an unusual opportunity to understand the social forces that generate in men those qualities the sociological studies of politics have identified as necessary or desirable in the citizens of a modern polity. We therefore added a large number of questions, in some countries as many as fifty, that permitted us to assess the politically specific and politically related attitudes of the subjects of our research. We included questions on political participation, attitudes toward politicians and the political process, evaluations of the effectiveness of the government, and levels of political knowledge and information.

INFORMATION MEDIA

Just as the wearing of a watch is often the first dramatic sign of a man's commitment to the modern world, the acquisition of a radio may be the act that really incorporates him into that world. In his study of modernization in the Middle East, Daniel Lerner treats the way in which people accept the mass media as one of the key elements in his classification of them as traditional, transitional, or modern. Indeed, he holds that "no modern society functions efficiently without a developed system of mass communication." [19] The model of modernization, he claims:

> exhibits certain components and sequences whose relevance is global. Everywhere, rising literacy has tended to increase media exposure; increasing media exposure has "gone with" wider economic participation (per capita income) and political participation (voting)....That ... same basic model reappears in virtually all modernizing societies on all continents of the world....[20]

Because other students of modernization, such as Ithiel Pool and Karl Deutsch, give heavy emphasis to mass communications as one of the key issues in the modernization process, we felt obliged to include it as one of the themes in the topical model. Our working assumption was that a modern man would more often expose himself to the media of mass communication—newspaper, radio, movies, and, where available, television. We considered it much more problematic that he would thereby shun the more traditional sources of information and advice such as village elders, traditional political leaders, or religious functionaries. Experience in research on communications behavior suggested that those who were very active in establishing contact with some sources of information tended to be outstanding in the frequency

[19] Daniel Lerner, *The Passing of Traditional Society*, p. 55.
[20] *Ibid.*, p. 46.

of their contact with *all* sources, modern and traditional. We were quite strongly convinced, however, that, when it came to *evaluating* the different sources of information, the more modern men would have greater confidence in and rely most heavily on the newer mass media, whereas the less modern would rely more on the more traditional sources. Indeed, we expected that the most traditional would look on the new-fangled mass media, such as the movies, as possibly dangerous and harmful to the morals of the young.

CONSUMPTION

His role as a consumer is one of the most problematic aspects of the life of a citizen in a developing country. On the one hand, we hear repeatedly that economic development is impossible unless the great bulk of the population enters the money economy and begins to demand and buy modern items of mass consumption. Otherwise, the argument runs, the market for goods is too small to support national industries that can operate profitably, the circulation of money is too weak to satisfy the requirements of a modern monetary system, the base of the tax system is too narrow, and so on. On the other hand, we so often encounter, the phenomenon of an alleged run-away inflation, presumably created by an uncontrolled demand for consumer goods that far outstrips the capacity to produce and, much more serious, far exceeds the growth in wealth and productivity. The result is that national outlays exceed national income by excessive amounts. To the extent that these outlays are for consumption rather than for investment in future production, deficit financing and mounting inflation follow each other in a vicious circle, economic stability is undermined, further investment is hindered, and economic stagnation or even retrogression must follow.

Economists can perhaps suggest some ways of resolving the apparent contradiction between these two models of development. For our part, we found ourselves reluctant to decide whether we should consider as more modern the man who believes mainly in savings or the man who believes that one should spend his newly-acquired income in obtaining beds, sewing machines, radios, bicycles, or whatever are, for his country, the most desired and reasonably accessible of the new goods of modern mass production. In the end, we came down on the side of spending. We predicted that the less modern man would be guided by his tradition and encouraged by his circumstance to consider frugality a virtue and the chasing after goods a frivolous and perhaps even slightly immoral preoccupation. By contrast, we expected the stimulus of the city and work in industry to persuade men that there was a plenitude of goods in the world for all to have. We also anticipated that his firmer financial position plus, perhaps, easier access to credit would stimulate the urban worker to affirm the rightness of a consumption ethic. Through various questions we solicited information about the goods a man owned and would like to own, and we sought his views on frugality and liberal spending.

SOCIAL STRATIFICATION

Traditional societies are generally defined as having closed class systems, in the extreme, possessed of a rigid caste structure. Mobility is minimal, men are born into the positions in which they will die, and sons succeed their fathers generation after generation. Status and prestige are assigned mainly on the basis of long-established, hereditary, family connections. Authority is feared and respected, often held in awe, and treated with an elaborate show of submission and deference. In an open, modern society, all of these features of stratification are supposed to be quite different. Along with the changed social structure, attitudes and values about stratification are expected to change significantly. Prestige comes to be assigned more on the basis of education and technical skill, and the belief that mobility is possible for one's self and especially for one's children becomes widespread. The move to industrial labor or white collar work is perceived by most who experience it as an improvement of their social standing. They come to feel more a part of society, citizens on an equal footing with others in the national polity. To test how far such patterns of change were being experienced in the countries we studied and to assess the relationship of changed attitudes about stratification and social classes to modernizing influences and to modern attitudes in other areas, we asked a series of questions dealing with the attitudes and experiences relating to social class and to social mobility.

PSYCHIC ADJUSTMENT

No belief is more widespread among critics of industrialization than the conviction that industrialization disrupts basic social ties, breaks down social controls, and therefore produces a train of personal disorientation, confusion, and uncertainty, which ultimately leads to misery and even mental breakdown among those who are "uprooted" from the farm and "herded" into the great industrial cities. The anthropologist Slotkin has stated:

> No matter how compatible industrialism may seem to be, since industrialism is usually a fundamental innovation, it and its ramifications tend to produce cultural disorganization. . . . Is forced rapid industrialization worth the severe cultural disorganization it usually entails, and its attendant social and personal maladjustment? Or is it more important to maintain cultural organization, conserving social and personal adjustment?[21]

We could not accept the assumptions that underlie this statement. It was our impression that in many traditional villages the strains of making a living, indeed of merely staying alive, were often enormous, as they certainly are in many parts of India and Pakistan, and for the hired hands who do most

[21] J. S. Slotkin, *From Field to Factory* (Glencoe: The Free Press, 1960), p. 31.

of the agricultural work on the large and nearly feudal Chilean hacienda, or *fundo*, as they call it. A fresh reading of many field studies and literary accounts of village life revealed jealousies, betrayal, exploitation, conflict, and hatred, which we could hardly see as inevitably conducing to good adjustment and sound mental health. By contrast, we noted that the shift to industrial work often seemed to guarantee more income and greater security. Opportunities for self-expression and advancement, and increments of status and prestige, often accompanied the move to the cities, and we felt that they would actually conduce to greater mental health among industrial workers, even in the sometimes chaotic setting of developing countries. We gained confidence in this rather radical position from the evidence of numerous studies on the relationship of mental health to occupation and status in the more advanced countries. These studies rather consistently showed an inverse relationship between mental illness and status in society as well as status *within* industrial organizations. In other words, those higher in skill and income generally had better mental health.

There seemed good reason to evaluate the move from farm to city work, and the move from new worker to experienced worker, as improvements in status. It was reasonable, therefore, to assume that in developing countries the experienced worker well integrated into the industrial system might be *better* adjusted than one still on the farm. This proposition could be entertained without denying the possibility that those newly arrived in the city, having lost the security of the place they knew well but not yet having found a secure place in the industrial order, might indeed manifest a high degree of psychic malaise.

To test these ideas we needed measures of personal adjustment. We therefore asked several fairly simple questions, about satisfaction with one's job, social status, and opportunities, like those that had served well as indicators of adjustment in studies of industrial social-psychology. We relied mainly, however, on a simple test of psychic adjustment, known as the Psychosomatic Symptoms Test, which had proven itself remarkably useful in culturally diverse situations as a quick and simple diagnostic assessment of individual mental health. We also administered the Sentence Completion Test, which is used mainly as a measure of personality traits in interpersonal relations, but which sometimes throws light on psychic adjustment as well.

This completes the list of special topics we undertook to study as a supplement to our investigation of the analytic model of individual modernity. As I noted earlier, our initial approach to these topics was to treat them as an unrelated assemblage of individual themes. For each we made a different assessment of its relationship to modernization. Nevertheless, examination of the full array of topics leads one inevitably to the supposition that all, or at least some sub-set, of these different themes may reflect one common underlying dimension of modernity. Men more independent of the extended family might also be more interested in practicing birth control, more accepting of scientific rather than religious explanations of natural events, and more ready to expose themselves to the media of mass communication.

The Behavioral Model

Sociology is often charged with being too abstract, divorced from the concrete reality of social life. Even when he leaves his study to go into the field, the sociologist almost invariably puts an instrument—his questionnaire —between himself and the direct observation of people in social action. Insofar as the sociologist wishes to study large numbers of individuals he does not have many alternatives. And many people are too quick to dismiss as unimportant those changes in men that are limited to changes in attitude. We are not persuaded of the justice of this point. What men do is much influenced by the climate of opinion in which they find themselves. If a man, especially a young man, hears all around him an opinion conducive to modern behavior he is likely to act in accord with his impulses in that direction even if the elders are expressing only *opinion* and are not themselves personally acting in a modern way. Yet we were aware that a questionnaire need not restrict itself to questions concerning *attitudes*. The questionnaire may also be used to elicit information concerning the behavior of the man who answers it. We were acutely aware of the possibility that many of our subjects might espouse, might even have sincerely adopted, modern attitudes and opinions, while they still continued to act in their usual traditional way in the course of their daily human relations. We wished, therefore, to obtain as much information as we could about the actual behavior of our subjects. The materials we gathered for that purpose we called "behavioral measures," and, taken together, they constitute the third, or "behavioral," model of individual modernity.

The self-reported behavioral measures were those on which the subject rated himself, in effect, by stating that he did or did not do certain things. For example, he was asked to indicate whether he had voted, to report how many times a week he attended religious services, read a newspaper or listened to the radio, and whether and how often he talked with his wife about politics, his job, and raising the children. Such self-reported behavior is, of course, subject to many distortions. A man may not remember accurately, or he may remember very well but give you one or another answer according to the impression he wishes to create. The same risks are run in inquiring into opinions, however, and we could not, therefore, accept the possibility of distortion as sufficient to rule out self-reported behavior as evidence relevant to our judgment of a man's modernity.

Nevertheless, we were sufficiently impressed by the potential limitations of measures of self-reported behavior to supplement them with such *objectively* ascertained measures as we could reasonably mobilize. Some of these measures were built into our interview procedure, and this device permitted us to rate all of our subjects. For example, to test how far a man might accurately be reporting that he read the newspaper or listened to the radio every day, we asked everyone to name several newspapers and radio programs, and we also tested them on the extent of their knowledge of political leaders who figured prominently in the news. We must acknowledge that a man might well really listen to the radio and not be able to tell us the names of any programs, but quite apart from judging his truthfulness we learn something important about him when we make this discovery.

Finally, the objective measures of behavior obtained through our questionnaire were supplemented by information form outside sources, notably the subject's factory. The problems inherent in collecting such information obliged us to restrict the investigation to a sub-sample of the factory workers in each country. For this sub-sample, however, we collected as much information about each worker's performance as the work situation and the factory records permitted. Each worker in the sub-sample was rated by his foreman or other supervisor on a series of scales as high or low in dependability, ambition, flexibility, competence, carefulness, and consideration for others. In addition, we went to the factory records and noted whatever information they contained on the man's productivity, his attendance record and punctuality, his participation in training courses, and the path of his promotions. Thus, we sought to deal with what many would define as the most critical aspect of the modernization process—its outcome in harder, more regular, more skillful work, in short, in that increased productivity that presumably leads to the economic progress believed to be the essential foundation for political and social modernization.

Summary

The three models of individual modernization—the analytic, topical, and behavioral—guided our thinking as our research took shape, and their mark is therefore clearly visible in the content of our questions and the general design of our questionnaire. The distinctions emphasized by the three models were useful in assuring reasonable thoroughness in the selection of themes within each area, yet they prevented us from taking too narrow a view of the process of modernization. The distinctions among the models viewed as dependent variables permitted us to be much more precise in deciding which influences to study among those generally assumed to generate modernity. Taken together, the three models served, therefore, as a convenient organizing principle within which to encompass the considerable diversity of the various themes and areas we explored in our research. Indeed, this seems an appropriate point to draw together the various elements touched on in the preceding pages, and I therefore present in Table 1 the complete list of the major topics in our questionnaire, each identified by its code letters and grouped under the model to which it has greatest relevance.

Useful as the models might be in organizing our thinking, they do introduce some artificial, or at least arbitrary, divisions not necessarily found in nature. The models lead us to separate into three parts some realms that might perfectly well be seen as more coherently joined in one. For example, in approaching the realm of opinion, the three-model arrangement induces us to treat general attitudes relevant to that realm as part of the analytic model, attitudes towards the mass media as one theme in the topical model, and the frequency with which a man listens to the radio as a theme in the behavioral model. Obviously, someone might want to ignore our distinction and treat all the questions as different aspects of a more general study of mass media and opinion in developing countries.

What applies to any one realm can indeed apply to all the dimensions taken together. Although each model was justified in its own terms as theoretically and empirically distinct, all could be conceived of as manifestations of a more general, unified, underlying dimension of modernity that could encompass elements of all three of the measures. It might well be that a man strong in the qualities of the analytic model, such as efficacy and readiness for new experience, would also be interested in politics, be inclined

T A B L E 1 . **Main Themes and Areas of the Questionnaire, by Key Letter and Model**

ANALYTICAL MODEL	TOPICAL MODEL	BEHAVIORAL MODEL
Aspirations, occupational and educational (AS)	Active public participation (AC)	Political activity (AC)
Calculability (CA)	Citizenship (CI)	Family behavior (BD and WR)
Change orientation (CH)	Consumption attitudes (CO)	Consumption behavior (CO)
Dignity (DI)	Family size restrictions (FS)	Information test (IN)
Efficacy (EF)	Identification with nation (ID)	Media information test (MM)
Growth of opinion (GO)	Kinship obligations (KO)	Opposites word test (OT)
Information (IN)	Mass Media (MM)	Psychosomatic test (PT)
New Experience (NE)	Religion (RE)	Sentence completion test (ST)
Optimism (OP)	Psychosomatics and adjustment (PT)	Interviewer's ratings
Particularism (PA)	Work Commitment (WC)	Supervisor's ratings
Planning (PL)	Women's rights (WR)	Factory records
Time (TI)		
Technical skill and distributive justice (TS)		

to grant women more rights, and so on through various themes of the topical model. This same man might, on our behavioral measures, prove to be well informed about the content of the mass media and be shown by the factory records as rarely missing work, as most punctual, and as having a high production record. Clearly, then, our materials permitted us to develop still a fourth model of modernity, one much more general, in that it includes elements of the analytic, topical, and behavioral models. We designated this model by the letters OM, which stands for "over-all modernity" measure, but we felt the choice particularly apt because, in Hinduism, OM is a mantra representing the triple constitution of the universe. Of course, we should keep in mind that OM, like the analytic model, is a theoretical construct. Until we have empirically tested the facts, it remains as assumption, a hypothesis only, that the elements of the other three models might indeed combine to yield a relatively unified measure of modernity. In fact, empirical testing of these ideas by analysis of our data shows that the relations between the different elements that may be considered alternative measures of individual modernity are quite complex and by no means obvious.

PART 5

INTERNATIONAL INTEGRATION

Most of the changes associated with the process of modernization take place within a society, and most of the information about this process is collected with reference to national states. Yet a modern state, despite the strong hold that most of them have on the loyalty of their citizens, is not necessarily any more permanent than the smaller political units it replaced in the course of the past century or two. Just as the larger of the modern federal systems (American, British, German, Soviet, Indian) gradually mobilized the authority to govern that had earlier been distributed among many regional and local entities, so the common problems faced by the advanced societies as they have become more interdependent is prompting them to seek cooperative solutions.

The diversities of cultural heritage, levels of development, and special interests are much too great in the last quarter of the twentieth century to make world government a realistic prospect. Even so, a variety of trends are pointing toward greater international integration. The challenges of foreign societies have always strengthened the unity of individual nations; today, however, the peoples of the world are confronted with the common challenge represented by their capacity for global self-destruction, unlimited population growth, worldwide pollution, and the depletion of resources. The revolution in human affairs that has led to worldwide development also requires worldwide institutions.

Some of the trends toward international integration require no elaboration. The need for international cooperation in political, economic, and social affairs was recognized before the First World War, and was widely accepted by the end of the Second. Numerous intergovernmental organizations, grouped mainly under the United Nations, have made significant progress in formulating common policies on issues about which governments have had their differences in the past. There are some 270 intergovernmental organizations today, and at the rate they are increasing there may well be three or four times as many by the year 2000. The role of intergovernmental organizations is less a question of numbers, however, than of the scope of the problems they seek to handle. In the 1970's such matters as environmental deterioration, food, population, and exploitation of ocean resources are for the first time being made formal subjects of international conferences in which most of the countries of the world participate. That these initial efforts have not been immediately fruitful is less important than the recognition by these countries of common responsibility for global problems. The European Economic Community, a more closely-knit organization than the U.N. and indeed the first true example of international integration, points the way toward the institutionalization of interdependence among highly developed states with a long tradition of mutual hostility.

Two further trends not directly related to intergovernmental relations may have a more important impact on international integration in the long run than intergovernmental activity: international migration and international nongovernmental organizations. One of the most characteristic features of societal transformation, as noted previously, is the internal migration in the course of which some three-quarters of a population moves from smaller communities to cities of a hundred thousand or more. This profound change in patterns of settlement is accompanied by a transfer of loyalties—of values in support of which individuals are prepared to contribute some of their resources and in times of crisis to sacrifice their lives—from the local community to the larger society. A similar process is now taking place on a global scale.

Humans have migrated for many centuries, but international migration in the modern era consists not of whole peoples on the move but of individuals and groups leaving their own society to seek a better way of life in another that offers more opportunities. The countries of the New World were populated essentially in this way, a gigantic transplanting of brain and brawn from the Old World. Today, many of the best-educated people from the less developed countries are moving to the more developed because of the greater opportunities they offer for self-fulfillment. This contemporary movement of peoples is sometimes criticized as constituting a "drain" on the less developed countries, depriving them of needed talent. In the nineteenth century there were also those who mourned the "deserted villages" abandoned by those moving to the cities. Yet this continuing resettlement of peoples is in fact part of a global urbanization. For those who move, self-fulfillment is a higher value than parochial nationalism, and this migration of skills is accompanied by a transfer of loyalties to more cosmopolitan conceptions of global scope that is a necessary precondition for a new world order.

A similar role of Gulliverizing a divided world by binding it with many small bonds of transnational loyalties is played by international nongovernmental organizations. These organizations have increased in number from no more than a dozen a century ago to some three thousand today, and at their present rate of growth they may number ten to twenty thousand by the year

2000. They include the widest possible variety of religious, professional, and commercial groups that unite people with the kind of common interests that can only be fully developed on a global basis. Among them are some 300 multinational corporations that seem to be gathering into their hands much of the world's manufacturing and trade.

The growth of international non-governmental organizations, like international migration, is often seen as a threat to the old order. There is no adequate international law to regulate them the way activities are regulated within national states, and they are sometimes viewed as instruments employed by the strong to take advantage of the weak. In a larger sense, however, the growth of worldwide business and professional organizations is no more than an ineluctable extension of development within nations, and must in due course call forth institutions for their regulation within a new world order. Global interest groups are vigorous in pressing their claims, and the establishment of transnational political movements devoted to the creation of a global political framework may be anticipated. The creation of such international forces is not a matter of fantasy, but neither is it likely to occur in the twentieth century. Those taking a longer view should nevertheless see international integration in some form as an extension of the process of modernization beyond national frontiers. Those concerned with a future world order should seek to anticipate the problems that lie ahead by learning as much as possible from the experience of societies in their earlier stages of modernization.

The Problem of the Convergence of Industrial Societies: A Critical Look at the State of Theory

Ian Weinberg

One of the critical controversies in writing about modernization concerns convergence. Is modernization a universal solvent that dissolves the residues of premodern values and institutions, or do the latter persist alongside of such core universals as science and technology, industrialization, education, and urbanization? The extent of international integration depends in no small degree on the reduction of the differences that continue to divide societies.

Weinberg reviews the extended debate on convergence, and goes on to note that the evidence required to reach a satisfactory resolution of the problem is still lacking. He recommends that, in further comparative studies, scholars remain alert to evidence of both convergence and divergence.

Introduction

Are industrial societies becoming alike? This crucial question, unfortunately sometimes treated as an assumption, has been of central theoretical interest

"The Problem of the Convergence of Industrial Societies: A Critical Look at the State of a Theory" by Ian Weinberg is reprinted by permission of Cambridge University Press from *Comparative Studies in Society and History*, XI (January 1969), 1–15.

When Weinberg died in 1969 at the age of 30, he had already made a name for himself as a sociologist with a keen sense of history. His study of *The English Public School* (1967) was concerned with the development of educational policy in response to multifaceted social change; and in an essay on "Social Problems Which Are No More," *Handbook of Social Problems* (1969), he discussed the ways in which problems long regarded as insoluble had been resolved in the course of modernization.

As the author points out in the article's first footnote, "This paper is a revised version of one delivered at the 1967 meetings of the American Sociological Association in San Francisco. I am indebted to Marion J. Levy Jr., Charles Tilly and Gerald Rosenblum for comments, though naturally my criticisms and conclusions are my own responsibility. I am grateful to the Humanities and Social Science Research Fund of the University of Toronto for support, and to my research assistant, Samrendrah Singh."

[Editor's note: Footnotes in the original article were numbered by page. With the pagination different here, I have taken the liberty of renumbering the footnotes consecutively throughout.]

since the appearance of the social sciences. The *philosophes*, with their optimistic belief in progress, were theorists of convergence because they believed in the perfectibility not of particular groups in society, but of all 'mankind.' [1] It was a radical, anti-relativistic notion to believe that Man not Men was the basic unit of study, the premise for speculation. For if Man acted the same everywhere, then forms of social organization must share essential analytic properties and be proceeding toward an equivalence of structural arrangements. Morally, good was to be found everywhere. Samuel Johnson remarked that 'the King of Siam sent ambassadors to Louis XIV, but Louis XIV did not send ambassadors to the King of Siam.' But Johnson sent his literary imagination on a diplomatic mission to Abyssinia in *Rasselas*, presumably to clear his mind of such ethnocentric cant. The cult of the Noble Savage was not only an aspect of eighteenth-century Romanticism, but an indication that Europeans, even Frenchmen, had something to learn from the simple lives of their primitive contemporaries. Like the *philosophes* many thought that the state, in the form of the benevolent despot, assured continual improvement, and often saw middling groups of intellectuals as allied with or advisory to the king in this great enterprise. It did not seem improbable that societies would converge to a similar political structure—with a strong state, an intellectual elite, and a mature *opinion publique*, a phrase that originated in pre-revolutionary eighteenth-century France. This vision failed when Mirabeau failed to implement it during the Revolution, and pre-revolutionary optimism turned into the pessimism of Comte and De Maistre.[2] If the former tried to salvage some of the optimism of his predecessors, the latter, at least, seemed to retreat to Filmer in denying the validity of written constitutions and in extolling the importance of God in granting political legitimacy.[3]

Actually the *philosophes* were not as radical as they appeared, and they were much influenced by physiocratic and mercantilist notions. Their justification of the benevolent despot resulted in the popularization of two orientations which had a lasting influence on later theorists of modernization and of the convergence of industrial societies where this was an integral part of such theories. First, they utilized the myth of the decentralized fixity and the Gothic barbarity of the Middle Ages, which was a popular Romantic idea. This contrasted with the dynamic attitude toward progressive social change and the efficient centrality of the benevolent despot. Second, they avoided the empiricist tradition begun by Bacon, Hobbes and Locke, which asserted that there was a democratic base to political systems. The state and the members of a society were discrete elements which when joined in an equation formed a sovereign political system. In this perspective the weights assigned to each could

---

[1] John B. Bury, *The Idea of Progress* (New York: Dover, 1955); Carl Becker, *The Heavenly City of the Eighteenth Century Philosophers* (New Haven: Yale University Press, 1935); Kingsley Martin, *French Liberal Thought In the Eighteenth Century* (New York: Harper & Row, 1963).

[2] Leon Bramson, *The Political Context of Sociology* (Princeton, N.J.: Princeton University Press, 1961).

[3] See Joseph De Maistre, *On God and Society* (Chicago, Illinois: Henry Regnery, 1959). This work was written in 1808–1809.

theoretically be subject to mathematical formulation. The strengths of each could be measured, stability and efficiency could be interpreted in scientific terms and translated into a model of what a political system ought to be. Divinity, which had hedged the king, was discounted because His influence could presumably not be measured, a foretaste of the later position of linguistic philosophy.

The *philosophes* did think in terms of systems, and helped to introduce Newtonian mechanics into the study of society. The theoretical analogy of the natural sciences reinforced their view that states were societies in a systematic way, yet despite their interest in practical affairs they were essentially non-empiricist.

In the nineteenth century, evolutionary theory, stimulated by a revival of Aristotelianism and the impact of Darwin, persuaded Marx, Spencer and others that industrial societies had common destinations, despite their origins. As regards the rest of the world, it was assumed that there was an inextricable link between Western and world history, so that similar development could be expected.[4] Marx expected that all processes of production and social organization would in time be based on scientific principles.[5] The similarity of these principles implied, therefore, a convergence in the structure and functioning of societies. Marx, List, Hildebrand and Bücher produced stage theories of economic development, in which there was the shared methodological assumption that societies moved toward industrialization in a common, unilinear progression.[6] The success of industrialism reinforced the idea of progress— indeed, Fay states that it was accepted as axiomatic.[7] Cultural relativism was not dead. After all, it was Weber's singular contribution to sociological theory to explain the appearance of capitalism in the West by drawing attention to the Protestant Ethic, for which there were no counterparts in other religions. But explanations of the convergence of industrial societies hardly touched on cultural differences. This was perhaps because industrialization was still limited to Europe and North America. Cultural differences between the nations in this area were slight when compared to the divergences between them and nations in other parts of the world. Moreover economists had borrowed the notion of Man from their *philosophe* predecessors, accepted universal assumptions about human behavior as a consequence, and were not concerned in the least that these assumptions might be culture-bound. From one point of view they were quite right, as economic theory was able to outdistance the other social sciences in constructing theoretical models because it was not bothered by cultural relativism. However, it is significant that, whatever the progress of economic science in such areas as price theory, its neglect of culture, of dis-

---

[4] Gerhard Masur, 'Distinctive Traits of Western Civilization: Through the Eyes of Western Historians,' *American Historical Review*, 67, No. 3 (April 1962), 608.

[5] Bert F. Hoselitz, 'Karl Marx on Secular Economic and Social Development,' *Comparative Studies in Society and History*, 6 (1964), 162.

[6] Henry William Spiegel, 'Theories of Economic Development: History and Classification,' *Journal of the History of Ideas*, 16, No. 4 (October 1955), 520.

[7] Sidney B. Fay, 'The Idea of Progress,' *American Historical Review*, 52, No. 2 (January 1947), 232.

ciplines such as history, sociology and anthropology, meant that it never produced a theory of economic development and of industrialization. Naturally the theories set forth tended to have some explanatory power for Western development, because it was the historical and sociological factors in that process which were the premises for model building. It was only when these theories were applied outside of the Western nations that their premises became painfully obvious.[8]

This limited and necessarily incomplete incursion into *wissensoziologie* demonstrates that theories of convergence and modernization are rooted in over two centuries of social and political theory. It is our purpose to show that there are still elements of convergence in modernization theory, some of which look suspiciously familiar, that this has obscured the concept of convergence, and introduced alien and historically false or limited ideas into the study of modernization. There will be an attempt to salvage the concept of convergence as worthy of more attention.

Convergence: The State of a Theory

The empirical and theoretical work addressed specifically to the possibility of convergence amounts to very little. It has been mainly concerned with the appearance of an occupational structure adapted to the needs of an industrial society, the well-known theory of the Demographic Transition, the change from an extended to a nuclear family system, the common modes of organization, both voluntary and formal, of the labor force, the increase in *per capita* real income and the appearance of a consumer market, and the correlation between high levels of income and education with political democracy.[9] There are implicit criteria of convergence in many discussions of industrialism and social change, which are not necessarily connected with technical theories of modernization. It is often assumed that industrializing societies undergo net

---

[8] Criticizing current 'agro-fugal' models of economic development, Postan pointed out that 'most of the reasons which people advance in favor of the overwhelming emphasis on industry are economic, and most of the economic reasons are historical.' M. M. Postan, 'Agricultural Problems of Under-Developed Countries in the Light of European Agrarian History,' *Second International Conference of Economic History*, II (Aix-en-Provence, 1962), 11.

[9] Alex Inkeles and Peter Rossi, 'National Comparisons of Occupational Prestige,' *American Journal of Sociology*, 61 (January 1956), 329–39; Seymour Martin Lipset and Reinhard Bendix, *Social Mobility in Industrial Society* (Berkeley and Los Angeles: University of California Press, 1959); Kingsley Davis, 'The Demographic Transition,' in Amitai and Eva Etzioni, eds., *Social Change* (New York: Basic Books, 1964), pp. 187–94; M. K. Nimkoff, 'Is the Joint Family an Obstacle to Industrialization?,' *International Journal of Comparative Sociology*, I (1960), 109–18; Wilbert E. Moore and Arnold Feldman, *Labor Commitment and Social Change in Developing Areas* (New York: Social Science Research Council, 1960); Marion J. Levy Jr., 'Some Structural Problems of Modernization and "High Modernization": China and Japan,' in E. F. Szczepanik, ed., *Proceedings of the Symposium on the Economic and Social Problems of the Far East* (Hong Kong: University of Hong Kong Press, 1962), p. 10; Seymour Martin Lipset, 'Economic Development and Democracy,' in *Political Man* (Garden City, N.Y.: Doubleday Anchor, 1959), chapter 2, pp. 27–63.

changes in a common direction toward increasing differentiation, individualism, the mobilization of the tradition-bound into markets, bureaucracies and other institutions, an increase in the extensity of state power, a reliance on widely known principles of technology, and the development of similar integrative mechanisms.[10] Much of the actual evidence has come to light in the course of comparative studies, which often have limited and not macrosociological aims.[11] Indeed scholars interested in comparative studies, despite the implicit criteria of convergence which they may assume, often seem determined to stress minor divergences while ignoring major areas of convergence. The exception, perhaps, is the study of the Soviet Union, in which there seems to be some satisfaction in pointing out convergence between that country and the United States.[12]

It may be that the lack of empirical studies focused on the theoretical possibility of convergence, especially among advanced industrial societies, has influenced scholars toward taking a sceptical view of the concept.[13] For there has recently been a surge of criticism denying even the most limited forms of convergence. Feldman, following Inkeles and Bauer, has stressed the limited convergence between the United States and the Soviet Union.[14] Hodge, Siegel and Rossi found that the prestige rankings of occupations remained constant between 1925 and 1963 despite fundamental structural changes in the labor force and in the direction of American industrialization; and Hodge, Treiman and Rossi have demonstrated the similarity of occupational prestige rankings between industrial and non-industrial societies.[15] The link between industrialism and the nuclear family system has been questioned, both because of the

---

[10] See S. N. Eisenstadt, 'Modernization, Growth and Diversity,' *India Quarterly*, 20 (January–March 1964), 17–42; for an attempt to retain some of these criteria against contrary evidence see his 'Breakdowns of Modernization,' *Economic Development and Cultural Change*, 12, No. 4, (July 1964), 345–67; Cyril E. Black, *The Dynamics of Modernization* (New York: Harper & Row, 1966); Neil J. Smelser, 'Mechanisms of Change and Adjustment to Change,' in Bert F. Hoselitz and Wilbert E. Moore eds., *Industrialization and Society* (The Hague: Mouton, 1966), chapter 2, pp. 32–54; Karl W. Deutsch, 'Social Mobilization and Political Development,' *American Political Science Review*, 55, No. 3 (September 1961), 493–515.

[11] For arguments in favor of limited comparative studies, see Reinhard Bendix, 'Concepts and Generalizations in Comparative Sociological Studies,' *American Sociological Review*, 28 (1963), 533, in which he warns that 'many concepts are generalizations in disguise.'

[12] Pitirim A. Sorokin, 'Mutual Convergence of the United States and the U.S.S.R. to the Mixed Sociocultural Type,' *International Journal of Comparative Sociology*, I (1960), 143–76; Irving Louis Horowitz, 'Sociological and Ideological Conceptions of Industrial Development,' *American Journal of Economics and Sociology*, 23, No. 4 (October 1964), 363; Marshall E. Dimock, 'Management in the U.S.S.R.—Comparisons to the United States,' *Public Administration Review*, 20, No. 3 (Summer 1960), 139–47.

[13] For an attempt to use existing data, but specifically focusing on the convergence of advanced industrial societies, see Ian Weinberg, 'Modernization, Elites and Class,' in Ian Weinberg, ed., *English Society* (New York: Atherton, in press).

[14] Arnold S. Feldman, 'The Nature of Industrial Societies,' *World Politics*, 12 (July 1960), 618.

[15] Robert W. Hodge, Paul M. Siegel and Peter H. Rossi, 'Occupational Prestige in the United States, 1925–1963,' *American Journal of Sociology*, 70, No. 3 (November 1964), 286–303; Robert W. Hodge, Donald J. Treiman and Peter H. Rossi, 'A Comparative Study of Occupational Prestige,' in Reinhard Bendix and Seymour Martin Lipset, eds., *Class, Status and Power* (New York: Free Press, 1966), pp. 309–21.

diversity of family systems found in industrial societies and because in some societies the nuclear family system may have antedated industrialization.[16] Blumer, considering the effect of early industrialization on the labor force, and consciously refuting the idea of a relationship between industrialization and social disorganization states that the process of industrialization is 'entirely neutral' in its social effects.[17] Goldthorpe denies that the convergence of patterns of stratification is inherent in the development of an industrial society, with specific reference to the United States and the Soviet Union.[18] De Schweinitz questions the link between industrialization and democracy.[19] Studying managerial organization in advanced industrial societies, Crozier has emphasized the cultural derivation of significant bureaucratic patterns, and Haire *et al.*, despite the uniformities they found, were struck by the influence of culture on managerial role definitions.[20] Clark Kerr and his associates, in reviewing their exhaustive inter-university research project on industrialism, found little uniformity in process or destination, apart from the fading of ideological fervor, and the increasing importance of central government and of educational expansion. Industrial societies converged to confusion, which they called 'pluralistic industrialism,' but this was not a state of equilibrium. Logically this leaves open, though it evades, the possibility of convergence. But their methodological assumption that industrialization as a process is engineered by different elites assumed the convergence of pre-industrial societies, but naturally led to divergence.[21]

Feldman and Moore seem to suggest that convergence may only be limited to the 'core' elements of an industrial system, so that all industrial societies possess these *minima*:

> This core would include the factory system of production, a stratification system based on a complex and extensive division of labor and hierarchy of skills, an extensive commercialization of goods and services and their transfer through the market, and an educational system capable of filling the various niches in the occupational and stratification system.[22]

[16] William J. Goode, 'Industrialization and Family Change,' in Bert F. Hoselitz and Wilbert E. Moore, eds., *Industrialization and Society* (The Hague: Mouton, 1966), chapter 12, pp. 237–59; Peter Laslett, 'The History of Population and Social Structure,' *International Social Science Journal*, 17, No. 4 (1965), 582–94; *The World We Have Lost* (London: Methuen, 1965).

[17] Herbert Blumer, 'Early Industrialization and the Laboring Class,' *Sociological Quarterly*, 1, No. 1 (January 1960), 5–14.

[18] John H. Goldthorpe, 'Social Stratification in Industrial Society,' in Paul Halmos, ed., *The Development of Industrial Societies* (Keele: October 1964), pp. 97–123.

[19] Karl de Schweinitz Jr., *Industrialization and Democracy* (New York: Free Press, 1964).

[20] Michel Crozier, *The Bureaucratic Phenomenon* (Chicago: University of Chicago Press, 1964); Mason Haire, Edwin E. Ghiselli and Lyman W. Porter, 'Cultural Patterns in the Role of the Manager,' *Industrial Relations*, 2, No. 2 (February 1963), 95–117.

[21] In their typology, the elites are the middle class, dynastic elites, revolutionary intellectuals, colonial administrators and nationalist leaders. Clark Kerr, John T. Dunlop, Frederick Harbison and Charles A. Myers, *Industrialism and Industrial Man* (New York: Oxford University Press, 1964).

[22] Arnold S. Feldman and Wilbert E. Moore, 'Industrialization and Industrialism, Convergence and Differentiation,' *Transactions Fifth World Congress of Sociology* (Washington, D.C., 1962), p. 146.

But both authors emphasize the elements of divergence. Elsewhere Moore has laconically stated that 'we are not yet brothers.' [23] He, more than any of the contemporary theorists of industrialization is sensitive to the rapidity of social change and the difficulties of predicting structural similarities.[24]

The psychologists and the social psychologists seem to be the only confident theorists of convergence. In his exploratory study Inkeles takes the factory system and the occupational structure as given, and working from a stimulus-response model finds that men in different countries react in a similar fashion to industrialism despite cultural differences.[25] The disciples of David Mc-Clelland have been arguing that an achievement orientation is a result of economic growth and a high level of N Ach (Need Achievement) is a prerequisite to it.[26]

Among sociologists Levy is perhaps the only theorist who is prepared to concede the possibility of convergence. He says that as the level of modernization increases, 'the level of structural uniformity among relatively modernized societies continually increases regardless of how diverse the original basis from which change took place in these societies may have been.' [27] By way of illustration, he presents a graph of convergence between four industrial societies, the United States, the U.S.S.R., Great Britain and France, and shows them converging asymptotically 'toward some impossibly high level of modernization.' [28] Theodorson, who states his intellectual debt to Levy, argues for the similarities in disorganization and re-integration, and for emulation of the West in the economic development of non-Western societies.[29] Levy's argument is a very powerful one because he fully accepts differences in historical development—or similarities. But what he says is that either differences or similarities do not matter the further along the path of development societies travel. It is the future that should be looked at, and not the past. Moreover the future of developing and developed societies needs to be considered and not the par-

---

[23] Wilbert E. Moore, 'Creation of a Common Culture,' *Confluence*, 4 (July 1955), 238.

[24] See his *Social Change* (Englewood Cliffs, N.J.: Prentice-Hall, 1963).

[25] Alex Inkeles, 'Industrial Man: The Relation of Status to Experience, Perception, and Value,' *American Journal of Sociology*, 66, No. 1 (July 1960), 1–31; see also his 'The Modernization of Man,' in Myron Weiner, ed., *Modernization* (New York: Basic Books, 1966), chapter 10, pp. 138–50; and W. A. Weisskopf, 'Industrial Institutions and Personality Structure,' *Journal of Social Issues*, 7, No. 4 (1951), 1–6; for an attempt to 'psychologize' Weber and to find the psychic source of modernization in late sixteenth-century English Puritanism, see Zvedei Barbu, 'The Origins of English Character,' in *Problems of Historical Psychology* (New York: Grove Press, 1960), pp. 145–218.

[26] See e.g., David C. McClelland, *The Achieving Society* (Princeton, N.J.: Van Nostrand, 1961); Robert A. LeVine, *Dreams and Deeds* (Chicago: University of Chicago Press, 1966); Bernard Rosen, 'The Achievement Syndrome and Economic Growth in Brazil,' *Social Forces*, 42, No. 3 (March 1964), 341–51; Norman N. Bradburn and David E. Berlew, 'Need for Achievement and English Industrial Growth,' *Economic Development and Cultural Change*, 10, No. 1 (October 1961), 8–21.

[27] Marion J. Levy Jr., *Modernization and the Structure of Societies* (Princeton, N.J.: Princeton University Press, 1966), vol. 2, p. 709.

[28] *Ibid.*, p. 710.

[29] George A. Theodorson, 'Acceptance of Industrialization and Its Attendant Consequences for the Social Patterns of Non-Western Societies,' *American Sociological Review*, 18, No. 5 (October 1953), 477–84.

ticular circumstances of their beginnings. He thus performs the not inconsiderable act of ignoring history by accepting it. He stands in stark contrast to a theorist such as Gerschenkron, who emphasizes what he calls D (the degree of backwardness of a country at the inception of economic growth) as the independent variable. This shapes the process of industrialization, and the dependent variable is heterogeneity in industrial and social organization.[30]

Moreover Levy has greatly influenced the study of political development and the possibility of the convergence of political systems. Apter states plainly that economic variable is independent, and the political system a dependent variable for industrializing societies.[31] Thus, there are 'more or less inevitable consequences' to industrialization. The four crucial consequences are the need for information, the growth of a scientific elite, the formation of pluralist groups, and the leadership of the scientific elite over other modernizing groups.[32] Industrializing societies have important groups which are the 'carriers' of democratic values, so that the prospect of convergence to democracy is uncertain but not improbable.[33] This is the clearest renascence of the Saint-Simonian and Leninist precept of the rule of the intellectually gifted, which has always been a favorite notion of analysts and activists disillusioned with the stolidity or backwardness of the mass.[34]

Convergence: Modernization and Evolutionary Functionalism

The concept of convergence has become often inextricably connected with modernization theory which, in its turn, uses an evolutionary-functional model, associated with Parsons, Moore, Smelser, Levy and Eisenstadt.[35] Modernization is defined as the use of inanimate resources for the multiplication of human effort, with manifold consequences for structural arrangements in an

30 See Alexander Gerschenkron, 'Typology of Industrial Development as a Tool of Analysis,' *Second International Conference of Economic History*, 2 (Aix-en-Provence, 1962) 487–505. Gerschenkron does not deny the processual similarity of industrialization in Western Europe, but disagrees with the validity of the model for Eastern Europe, and, by implication, with contemporary underdeveloped areas where the level of D is obviously high. See his 'Economic Backwardness in Historical Perspective,' in Bert F. Hoselitz, ed., *The Progress of Underdeveloped Areas* (Chicago: University of Chicago Press, 1951), pp. 3–29.

31 David E. Apter, *The Politics of Modernization* (Chicago: University of Chicago Press, 1965), p. 460.

32 *Ibid.*, p. 447.

33 *Ibid.*, p. 459.

34 Saint-Simon wanted to create a 'Council of Newton' to run a world dislocated by the French Revolution. See his 'Letter from an Inhabitant of Geneva to His Contemporaries' (1803), in Felix M. H. Markham, tr. and ed., *Saint-Simon, Selected Writings* (Oxford: Blackwell, 1952), pp. 1–11. That such theories are influenced by economic cycles is argued by Lewis S. Feuer, 'What is Alienation? The Career of a Concept,' *New Politics*, 1 (Spring 1962), 116–34.

35 Wilbert E. Moore says that the functional equilibrium model 'is the actual mainstay for the impressive body of generalizations concerning the consequences of modernization,' in 'Social Change and Comparative Studies,' *International Social Science Journal*, 15, No. 4

interdependent social system.[36] Societies evolve from small-scale, traditional, kin-oriented and relatively undifferentiated units toward large-scale industrial societies with a high degree of differentiation of organizations and roles. Traditional systems of action, such as the family, contract their scope, and industrial systems, such as the market, extend theirs. The use of inanimate resources 'constrains,' in Moore's terminology, the interdependent elements of the social system to adapt to industrialism.[37] A common terminus is often denied, even though industrial societies are 'teleonomic" because deliberate change is a shared feature and because societies solve their perennial problems, whether related to industrialism or not, in different ways. The objections to this approach become objections to convergence as such, and they are:

1. There is often an uncritical acceptance of evolutionary theory as the answer to the persistent dilemma of functional analysis as equilibrium analysis. The answer is of problematic utility because sociological research is often obstinately tied to cross-sectional analysis, and neo-evolutionism may be only a theoretical and limited solution to a persistent methodological problem. The inherent notions in much of modernization theory of a monolithic and dominant scientific elite, of the inevitable and expanded role of the state, its benevolence for the process of economic growth, and the dichotomy between desirable modernity and the static barbarity of traditional society, repeat the non-empirical and ideologically motivated errors of the *philosophes*. This comes out clearly in the work of Clark Kerr and his associates, in which they develop a typology of industrializing elites.[38] In some of his work, even Shils, who is well aware of rivalries between competing elites, seems to over-emphasize the elite of intellectuals.[39] Seligman emphasizes that elites must be 'integrated' (into a monolithic stratum?) for the purposes of development.[40] The fundamental assumption is that development works to differentiate out the elite

---

(1963), 524; see also Talcott Parsons, *Societies—Evolutionary and Comparative Perspectives* (Englewood Cliffs, N.J.: Prentice-Hall, 1966); Neil J. Smelser, 'The Modernization of Social Relations,' in Myron Weiner, ed., *Modernization* (New York: Basic Books, 1966), chapter 8, pp. 110–21; Marion J. Levy Jr., *op. cit.*; S. N. Eisenstadt, *Essays on Sociological Aspects of Political and Economic Development* (The Hague: Mouton, 1961); 'Social Change, Differentiation,' *American Sociological Review*, 29, No. 3, (June 1964) 375–86; *Modernization, Protest and Change* (Englewood Cliffs, N.J.: Prentice-Hall, 1966); and the references to some of his other work in note 2 on p. 4; Arnold S. Feldman, 'Evolutionary Theory and Social Change,' in Herbert R. Barringer, George I. Blanksten and Raymond W. Mack, *Social Change in Developing Areas* (Boston: Schenkman, 1965), chapter 11, pp. 273–84; Kenneth E. Bock, 'Evolution, Function and Change,' *American Sociological Review*, 28, No. 2 (April 1963), 229–37; Robert M. Marsh, *Comparative Sociology* (New York: Harcourt, Brace & World, 1967), p. 29.

[36] Levy says, 'A society will be considered more or less modernized to the extent that its members use inanimate sources of power and/or use tools to multiply the effects of their efforts,' *op. cit.*, vol. 1, p. 11.

[37] Wilbert E. Moore, *The Impact of Industry* (Englewood Cliffs, N.J.: Prentice-Hall, 1965), p. 12.

[38] See note 21.

[39] See Edward Shils, 'The Intellectuals in the Political Development of the New States,' *World Politics*, 12 (April 1960), 329–68.

[40] Lester G. Seligman, 'Elite Recruitment and Political Development,' *Journal of Politics*, 26 (1964), 612–26.

from the mass. The elite are the modernizers *par excellence*, who wish to build a nation, legitimate their own position, and mobilize the mass. The ambivalence of elites toward modernity is too often dismissed as a residual anti-colonialism. The power of the elites is naturally interlocked with the extension of state power, emphasized so much in the work of Eisenstadt.

It is interesting that the emphasis on elites in industrialization and modernization occurs at a time when analysts of advanced societies have been noticing their existence in the West.[41] There are important *caveats* to the emphasis on elites, apart from the recrudescence of *philosophe* thought. If elites do appear in all advanced societies, their power may cancel each other out, or else too much of their time may be taken up with bargaining rather than with decision-making. High levels of education mean that elites cannot automatically claim expertise, so that a large part of their efforts may be devoted to keeping ahead of a critical and educated laity. Specialization means that each elite, whether political or technocratic, is internally fragmented. Scientific elites may be overly dependent on the exigencies of politics to construct a permanent power base. In developing societies, the elites are limited by international political and economic facts and by their limited grip on their underlings.[42] Their ambivalence toward modernity may be simply a reasonable cognitive dissonance between welcoming change but wishing to preserve the culture of their societies.

2. The interdependence of social systems is exaggerated, yet Feldman and Moore are alone in alluding to this.[43] As the definition of modernization is basically technological, the result of tight interdependence is often a kind of functional-technological-determinism. The result is a theory, not unlike the Marxist one, in which functional-technological-determinism is substituted for the driving force of the economic substructure. It is interesting that Cyril Black, the historian, has greatly emphasized the importance of technology. As a means of analyzing the early adaptation to industrialization, the emphasis has its merits, but like its Marxist analogue it is a poor predictor. It limits the multidirectionality of industrial societies by its premises, though it argues for differences in its conclusions. On the other hand, such theorists as Moore and Levy attribute considerable importance to diffusion, specifically the diffusion of technology, despite the plaints of their critics that structural-functionalism does not allow for this. But it is important to remember that the diffusion of technology, as with the diffusion of political models, passes through a cultural filter. Technology is not exempt because of its peculiar reliance on abstract scientific principles, so that its consequences for social organization are diverse.

3. The evolutionary assumption of the 'survival' of modernized facets of the social system, and the 'mutation' of that system toward industrialization

---

[41] See Suzanne Keller, *Beyond the Ruling Class: Strategic Elites in Modern Society* (New York: Random House, 1963); Jay M. Gould, *The Technical Elite* (New York: Augustus M. Kelley, 1966); for a dissenting view see Robert A. Dahl, 'A Critique of the Ruling Elite Model,' *American Political Science Review*, 52, No. 2 (June, 1958), 463–70.

[42] Felicia J. Deyrup, 'Limits of Government Activity in Underdeveloped Countries,' *Social Research*, 24, No. 2 (Summer, 1957), 197.

[43] Arnold S. Feldman and Wilbert E. Moore, *op. cit.*, p. 166.

and very high modernization can lead to the false notion of 'total transformation.' Negatively, the theory suggests that convergence will occur insofar as 'traditional' patterns of action are bound to disappear. Sometimes a theorist will take Parsons' pattern variables too seriously, and argue for a simple, linear progression from diffuseness to specificity or from particularism to universalism.[44] This kind of convergence seems to exclude the possibility of social change of any significance which is unconnected with industrialization and which is partial or sectoral.

'Total' and industrial social changes often entail the uncritical acceptance of scholars such as Polanyi and Rostow, who are essentially 'stage' theorists of societal development.[45] Zebot, for example, adopts Rostow's model, and, after an examination of the United States, the Soviet Union and the underdeveloped nations concludes that 'a basic convergence of the world's economies towards certain common characteristics may be reasonably expected.' [46] Under the technological definition of modernization, no societies can be exempt from the process, because all societies make some minimal use of inanimate resources.[47] Asymptotically, none can, in the long run, escape 'total transformation.' Stage theorists use models which are usually extrapolations of Western industrialization synthesized into a set of general principles. By definition industrializing societies converge toward the Western model. Hodgen has drawn attention to the fact that such theories are revivals of medieval hierarchical thinking, and that their antiquity still does not prevent their recurrence.[48] It is only slowly being realized that some aspects of Western industrialization, such as urbanization, which had a dynamic effect, simply do not stimulate development as a matter of course elsewhere.[49]

The convergence toward 'total transformation' implied by close functional interdependence thus results in the fallacy of 'recapitulation.' This means that societies which are modernizing are bound to 'recapitulate' the growth processes of advanced, modernized societies because they are totally transformed through the constraints of modernization working themselves out in an interdependent social system. The model assumes that advanced industrial societies

[44] Bert F. Hoselitz, *Sociological Aspects of Economic Growth* (Glencoe, Illinois: Free Press, 1960). Sociological theory has often been attracted by such easy dichotomies—particularly Tönnies' *Gemeinschaft* and *Gesellschaft* and Durkheim's mechanical and organic solidarity.

[45] Karl Polanyi, *The Great Transformation* (New York: Farrar & Rinehart, 1944); W. W. Rostow, *The Stages of Economic Growth: A Non-Communist Manifesto* (New York: Cambridge University Press, 1960).

[46] Cyril A. Zebot, *The Economics of Competitive Coexistence: Convergence Through Growth* (New York: Frederick A. Praeger, 1964), p. 146.

[47] Levy says, *op. cit.*, p. 31, that 'modernization is a general process; it touches us all.'

[48] Margaret T. Hodgen, *Early Anthropology in the Sixteenth and Seventeenth Centuries* (Philadelphia: University of Pennsylvania Press, 1964); it has been argued that the urban revolution rigidified and led to the stagnation of Egyptian civilization at its highest point, Christopher Hawkes, 'The Prehistoric Roots of European Culture and History,' in Jacquetta Hawkes, ed., *The World of the Past* (New York: Alfred Knopf, 1963), p. 491.

[49] For the adverse effects of urbanization in new nations, see Philip M. Hauser, 'Urbanization: An Overview,' in Philip M. Hauser and Leo F. Schnore, eds., *The Study of Urbanization* (New York: John Wiley, 1965), chapter 1, pp. 1–47.

are already convergent, that they have reached some kind of terminal point or equilibrium. This fallacy first occurred in nineteenth-century embryology, when Haeckel argued that physiologically man as he existed repeated the general development of all of mankind in his personal growth. 'Recapitulation' depends on the acceptance of the idea of the successful integration of functionally interdependent, differentiated institutional areas, as well as on the premise of cumulative growth. Eisenstadt more than any other theorist has used 'integration' and cumulative growth, sometimes as a hope, and sometimes, it seems, as a *deus ex machina*.

The diffusion of Western technology in developing nations is often confused with the necessary appearance of Western structures. Lerner, who views modernization primarily as a communications process, insists that institutions cannot simply be exported and fitted into the new environment, but that they have a transforming effect. He states that 'traditional societies are passing from the face of the earth because the people in them *no longer want to live by their rules.*' [50] There is the implication that non-Western structures are too rigid and hostile to industrialism and necessarily block economic growth. But Nash's study of the introduction of a factory into Cantel demonstrates that industrialization need not be disruptive of traditional patterns of action.[51] Whether industrialization is autochthonous or derived it need not logically result in the destruction of what existed before. It often helps the process. Too often it is forgotten that the first industrial nation, England, was conservative in structure in the nineteenth century, and was viewed by von Ranke as possessing more of the remaining institutions of medievalism than any other European country.[52]

4. The notions of inevitability, *philosophe* utopianism, 'total transformation,' close functional interdependence, and 'recapitulation' tend to make modernization theory a genetic and teleological one. Sometimes theorists are sophisticated enough to anticipate this criticism, and take refuge in a denial of convergence in order to avoid teleology. Levy avoids teleology by the correct use of 'structural requisites,' for if their existence is posited because they are requisites, then teleology is the result.[53] But often analysts have an almost cybernetic view of development, in which economic or political elements are inputs which change the system in an invariant way and set it on a pre-ordained course. To then veer away from convergence, as do Kerr *et al.*, is to take refuge in what is essentially a doctrine of tychism, or of pure chance, which denies both the possibility and the responsibility of prediction. Moreover, it is not sufficiently clear that convergence does not in fact develop as a result of chance variation, rather than as a result of pure chance. A teleological theory prevents

[50] Daniel Lerner, 'The Transformation of Institution,' in William B. Hamilton, ed., *The Transfer of Institutions* (Durham, N.C.: Duke University Press, 1964), chapter 1, p. 14.

[51] Manning Nash, *Primitive and Peasant Economic Systems* (San Francisco: Chandler, 1966), pp. 110–19. Although Cantel approximated to as perfect an experimental situation as could be found outside of a laboratory, even Nash seems surprised at his findings.

[52] George P. Gooch, *History and Historians in the Nineteenth Century* (New York: Longmans, Green, 1928), p. 93.

[53] See Marion J. Levy Jr., 'Structural-Functional Analysis,' in *International Encyclopedia of the Social Sciences* (New York: Macmillan, 1968).

accurate historical analysis by explaining phenomena in terms of a preselected number of variables. Too little thus explains too much.

5. The psychological and social-psychological postulates of similarities between personality structures in industrial societies, and the concept of Need Achievement and the like seem to be the modern equivalents of economic man. Instead we are presented with Industrial or Entrepreneurial Man possessing universal characteristics. This may be as much a cultural projection as was economic man in the nineteenth century.[54] Such analyses tend to ignore social structures, or to assume that they are so malleable that an input of N Ach will cause a startling chain reaction. The importance of entrepreneurialism in developing nations is not thereby meaningless, but, as Barrett has pointed out in studying the Igbos, may be an aspect of structure rather than an input.[55] Structural arrangements are theoretically only givens—but their particularities and similarities have to be empirically established. Theories of Entrepreneurial Man are usually elite theories, and suffer from their intrinsic difficulties, which we have mentioned above.

The Possibility of Convergence

So far it has been argued that (a) there has been a limited amount of empirical work specifically undertaken to demonstrate convergence; (b) the notion of convergence has suffered by association with evolutionary-functional theories of modernization and (c) theorists of modernization have often denied the convergence of industrial societies while the fallacies in evolutionary-functionalism would seem to lead inevitably to the idea of the convergence of modernized societies.

There are two important observations to be made. The very little empirical work which supports the notion of convergence can reasonably be extended. Moreover, some empirical evidence which seems to deny the notion, such as recent work on occupational prestige rankings, may support convergence if it is remembered that societies may converge with industrialization because they had a great deal in common before the process began. This may be especially true if groups of societies, with shared cultural backgrounds, are compared, and, therefore, if the concept of convergence is made more relative. The gap between advanced and underdeveloped societies, as well as the attempt to generalize about both, obscures the fact that large-scale industrialism is a very recent phenomenon even in the West. For this reason observed convergences at this early stage are remarkable. The recency of large-scale industrialism must surely negate stark dichotomies between modernity and traditionalism and yet

---

[54] Daniel Lerner, 'The Transformation of Institutions,' in William B. Hamilton, ed., *The* Development Theory,' *Canadian Review of Sociology and Anthropology*, 3, No. 1 (February 1966).

[55] Stanley R. Barrett, 'The Achievement Factor in Igbo Receptivity to Industrialization' *Canadian Review of Sociology and Anthropology* [V (May 1968), 68–83].

emphasize the relativity of convergence. One of the reasons why industrial societies are so complex and differentiated is that pre-industrial structures have by no means disappeared. The relativity of convergence must also be tied to an awareness of chronology. The pioneers of industrialization and the latecomers are often discussed, as if the only importance of the distinction was that the latecomers would have certain advantages in experiencing the same process. Yet the relative lack of disparity between the times at which the United Kingdom, the United States, France and Germany industrialized means that the direction of the process was bound to be similar, given the available technology and social structure. A group of nations trying to industrialize today may experience a totally different process, though the aim of industrialization may be shared with the pioneers. Such nations may have to mount a much more radical attack on tradition than occurred in the process of Western industrialization. For all we know, the structural arrangements common to the pioneer nations, such as the centralized factory, the industrial city and the labor force, which are the conditions assumed by Inkeles, may simply not be characteristic of some latecomer processes of industrialization.

Also, the deductive method of theory construction, which denies convergence and yet logically leads to it, neglects empirical evidence and makes it difficult to further theory by additional data. It should be emphasized that this is a criticism of the method of theory construction as such and not of functionalism. One of the pathologies of industrializing societies, as Belshaw points out, is the lack of interdependence among institutional areas essential to economic growth.[56] Functional analysis is the only way by which these failures to interlock can be demonstrated. But functional interdependence must be empirically derived, to allow for the necessity, time-span, and intensity of the interdependence of different institutional areas. The empirical derivation of interdependence can therefore lead to an empirical basis for convergence, if the interdependencies necessary to and consequent upon industrialism are compared in different societies. But to presume tight interlocking is dangerous, and due allowance must be made for a looseness of fit between different elements of the social system, as Moore is constantly emphasizing. Although interdependence constrains the social system toward convergence if the prime element of change is the industrial sector, the looseness of fit means that some elements will not be constrained to change, that others by their distance or relative lack of connection with the industrial sector may be insulated from change, so that divergences between societies are to be theoretically accepted. Such divergences limit, but do not delete, the possibility of convergence.

Conclusion

The concept of convergence can perhaps be salvaged as a very useful device for comparative analysis if mistakes inherent in the methods of evolutionary-

[56] Cyril S. Belshaw, 'Social Structures and Cultural Values as Related to Economic Growth, *International Social Science Journal*, 16, No. 2 (1964), 223.

functional theories of modernization are avoided. What is recommended here is somewhat similar to the defense of convergence as a theoretical and empirical possibility made by Goldenweiser to his fellow ethnologists in the earlier part of the century.[57] He saw a limitation in the extensity of development. He rejected genetic convergence and suggested 'dependent convergence,' which he described as 'those similarities that develop from different sources, but under the influence of a common cultural medium.' [58] The convergences of industrial and industrializing societies are perhaps similarities that develop from the limited possibilities of adapting to large-scale industrialism, even if the time the process took place or differences between processes of industrialization themselves are evident. Such similarities should be empirically derived, without the further implications of teleology or common, over-arching or substructural equivalence. Essential to this conception is that the limited possibilities of adaptation are contrasted to the multiplicity of origins. Divergence is to be expected as well, for change variation probably occurs though complete confusion does not. Hopefully comparative studies will be undertaken, which are alerted to convergence as well as to divergence, without any *a priori* theoretical dismissal of either possibility.

[57] A. A. Goldenweiser, 'The Principle of Limited Possibilities in the Development of Culture,' *Journal of American Folklore*, 26 (1913), 259–90.
[58] *Ibid.*, p. 269.

Interdependence: Myth or Reality?

Richard Rosecrance and Arthur Stein

To those living in an era of petroleum shortages and international inflation, it seems clear that the interdependence of nations is growing. Yet students of international trade and politics continue to debate the subject. This essay offers new data tending to show that some forms of economic interdependence have definitely been growing, and that this has had an important influence on political institutions over the past fifty years. Nationalism remains so powerful, however, that Rosecrance and Stein question whether nation-states have the capacity to face the challenge of cooperation. Though economic interdependence is growing, the economic institutions that are needed to regulate this activity for the common welfare continue to lag.

One of the uncertainties of modern international relations is the degree of interdependence among states. Some theorists have asserted that interdependence is high and/or growing, and others have maintained that it is low and/or declining. Essentially, the debate about interdependence has proceeded in three separate phases. (1) In the aftermath of World War II, technology was heralded as the stimulus to an interrelationship among states: The world was shrinking; technological, military, and economic factors would produce interdependence even among erstwhile enemies.[1] (2) Later this conventional wisdom was challenged by Karl Deutsch and his associates, who purported to show that various economic indicators of external reference were declining.[2] International transactions were lessening relative to intranational transactions. More

"Interdependence: Myth or Reality?" by Richard Rosecrance and Arthur Stein is reprinted from World Politics, XXVI (October 1973), 1–27. Reprinted by permission of Princeton University Press.

Rosecrance is professor of international and comparative politics and director of the Situational Analysis Project at Cornell University. His publications include International Relations: Peace or War? (1973). Stein is a research associate of the Situational Analysis Project.

The authors would like to acknowledge their indebtedness to Professors Richard N. Cooper, Simon Kuznets, Robert Lipsey, Thomas Willett, and Raymond Vernon, and to Mr. Brian Healy, for advice or data used in preparation of this paper. They absolve them entirely, however, from any responsibility for errors of fact or argument in what follows.

[1] See inter alia, Emery Reves, The Anatomy of Peace (New York 1946), 268.

[2] See particularly, Karl W. Deutsch, Lewis J. Edinger, Roy C. Macridis, and Richard L. Merritt, France, Germany and the Western Alliance (New York 1967), chap. 13.

and more, citizens were turning to the nation-state for the satisfaction of their needs, and national economies were taking precedence over the previous international economy of the nineteenth century. This theme has recently been powerfully reinforced by Kenneth Waltz.[3] (3) In reaction to the claims of the Deutsch group, which initially predicted stalemate in European unification efforts and a greater autarchy for industrial states, new presentations of the argument in favor of interdependence have been made.[4] According to this view, interdependence among states is certainly increasing. A symposium on the international corporation partly reinforces Deutsch's view, while one on transnational processes argues against it.[5] The resultant of these theoretical vectors remains uncertain. In this essay we hope to offer new data and to provide a modest reconciliation of the contending claims, drawing a trial balance between them.

One of the problems in unravelling disagreements about interdependence is the absence of an agreed definition of the term. At least three different notions have been employed. In its most general sense, interdependence suggests a relationship of interests such that if one nation's position changes, other states will be affected by that change.[6] A second meaning, derived from economics, suggests that interdependence is present when there is an increased national "sensitivity" to external economic developments.[7] This "sensitivity" presumably can either be perceived or unperceived.[8] The most stringent definition comes from Kenneth Waltz, who argues that interdependence entails a relationship that would be costly to break.[9] This definition is different from the others in two senses: (1) It presumes a positive relationship between the interdependent units, such that each will suffer if the relationship is harmed; (2) relationships in which one party is affected by what another does would not necessarily be interdependent by Waltz's definition, because the effect might not be "costly." Since observers use such different definitions of the central term, it is easy to understand why they draw different conclusions about the presence or absence of interdependence in the contemporary world.

[3] Kenneth N. Waltz, "The Myth of Interdependence," in Charles P. Kindleberger, ed., *The International Corporation* (Cambridge, Mass. 1970).

[4] See Edward L. Morse, "Transnational Economic Processes," in Robert O. Keohane and Joseph S. Nye, Jr., eds., *Transnational Relations and World Politics* (Cambridge, Mass. 1972); Morse, "The Politics of Interdependence," *International Organization*, XXIII (Spring 1969); Oran R. Young, "Interdependencies in World Politics," *International Journal*, XXIV (Autumn 1969); and Richard N. Cooper, *The Economics of Interdependence* (New York 1968).

[5] See Keohane and Nye (fn. 4); Kindleberger (fn. 3).

[6] This meaning is close to that suggested by Morse and Young. Morse writes: "Interdependent behavior may be understood in terms of the outcome of specified actions of two or more parties (individuals, governments, corporations, etc.) when such actions are mutually contingent." Morse, "Transnational Economic Processes" (fn. 4), 29. See also Young (fn. 4), 726.

[7] See Cooper (fn. 4), 59.

[8] See also Robert D. Tollison and Thomas D. Willett, "International Integration and the Interdependence of Economic Variables," *International Organization*, XXVII (Spring 1973), 255–71.

[9] See Waltz (fn. 3), 205–7.

At the same time, Waltz's conclusion that interdependence is low or declining can be disputed even on the basis of the stringent definition he employs. The Waltz contentions run approximately as follows: Interdependence exists where there is a division of labor or a specialization of functions. Unlike units perform different functions or offer specialized services; they become interdependent when they perform these services for each other and when units come to rely on such specialization. On the other hand, if units are alike, they cannot offer different commodities or services; interdependence declines. Waltz also asserts that interdependence is lowest where like units have unequal capacities: Then, powers either cannot or do not have to take each other into account. As juridically like units, therefore, states can have little interdependence at any time and place. Since differences in *de facto* capacities among states have grown since World War II, interdependence is now at a nadir. This is not dismaying, however, for it is contended to be a "mistaken conclusion" that "a growing closeness of interdependence would improve the chances of peace." [10] To summarize this argument, interdependence is high where there are (1) unlike units; and (2) where the units are relatively equal in capacity.

A number of comments can be offered in rejoinder. First, if interdependence is taken entirely in the positive sense (where interests of states vary directly, not inversely), it is difficult to understand how a high degree of interdependence could be a cause for conflict. If relationships really were costly to break on all sides, this would be a factor for general international cooperation. Second, while it is true that interdependence may be high where there are unlike units involved in the relationship, it is by no means clear that such differentiation is the *necessary condition* of high interdependence. A most important form of interdependence, that of military alliance, arises when states offer the same defense resources to each other. By pooling their resources, they gain a joint security that each could not attain in isolation, and yet there is no necessary division of labor. Clearly such defense ties might be very costly to break.[11]

If military allies have relationships that are positively interdependent, enemies or adversaries manifest a high degree of negative interdependence in their relationships. Their interests are crucially linked in that it is assumed that if one improves his position, the other suffers. Yet, where such a high degree of interdependence (albeit negative) exists, there is no necessary differentiation of functions or division of labor. Rather, the interdependence of antagonists arises in part because rivals are alike: they compete for the same goals, utilize similar techniques, and seek to win over the same allies or to acquire the same real estate. The very continuance of competition over time, moreover, is likely to make them even more alike. Eventually, rivals may even develop certain positively interdependent goals. If they reside at the top of a hierarchy of nations, it may be a common interest to prevent any inroads on their joint

10 *Ibid.*, 205.

11 Mancur Olson, J., and Richard Zeckhauser, "An Economic Theory of Alliances," in Bruce M. Russett, ed., *Economic Theories of International Politics* (Chicago 1968).

position by other states. If war is likely to result in widespread mutual devastation, they may have a common interest in mutual accommodation and coexistence.

It may also be argued that the greatest interdependency in contemporary world politics subsists among the most highly developed powers, powers whose economic systems bear the greatest similarity to each other. In military terms, these powers could hurt each other grievously; in economic terms, they have the capacity to help or harm each other. At this juncture, the error of following the comparative-advantage, product-specialization argument too far is clearly portrayed. The basis for international trade today is not only marked product differentiation, but also the capacity of the domestic market. Europeans, Americans, and Japanese sell the bulk of their goods in each other's markets. even though typical approaches to comparative advantage would have them import raw materials from and sell industrial goods to the less developed countries.[12] The products which major industrial countries offer are not highly differentiated in the Ricardian sense; they all offer automobiles, consumer electronics, and industrial equipment. Differences exist, however, in marketing, pricing, quality, and sophistication. As we shall see later, the exchange of manufactured goods for manufactured goods is becoming *more* typical in international trade, not less so. It therefore does not follow that interdependence is low today, even if Waltz's strict definition of the term is employed.

At the same time, Waltz correctly points to the fact that nationalism and national interests are not secondary or obsolete phenomena in the contemporary world. Indeed, nationalism is a far more prominent factor in economic and political arrangements today than it was in the halcyon days of the nineteenth century. Prior to 1914, economic internationalism was the order of the day. Passports were unnecessary. Tariffs had only been recently reintroduced. National secrecy in military plans and the demand for patriotic loyalty on the part of citizens were surely less stringent than they are now. Nationalism was in fact strengthened by the reformist orientation of modern politics: Franklin Roosevelt, a domestic reformer who tried to put the United States on the road to economic recovery after the Depression, did so at the expense of the international economic and, to some extent, political system. When governments are expected to regulate the economy to obtain maximum welfare for their citizens, they must often slight the interests of economic and political partners. Citizens may also reflect such attitudes. They do not look to the international system for economic and political benefits, but to their national government. Socialism, nationalization, and domestic economic planning interpose national criteria on international economic forces. By almost any definition of the terms, economic and political nationalism have grown since the last decades of the nineteenth century. What effect has this development had upon interdependence?

By all three definitions, nationalism might have been expected to reduce interdependence. It might be argued that, if nations seek only to achieve their

---

[12] This approach is that of the Heckscher-Ohlin theorem emphasizing factor proportions.

own goals without any reference to the rest of the system, the linkage between units must decline. If nationalistic goals depend on supportive actions by other members of the international community, however, nationalism cannot be achieved in isolation. Not only does interdependence not decline in such circumstances, aggressive nationalism may lead to higher negative interdependence. The greater nationalism of the twentieth century therefore need not entail a reduction of interdependence. We still do not know whether interdependence will rise or fall, whether it will be positive or negative. The rest of this paper will be devoted to an answer to these questions in economic and political terms, considering data and developments of the past century.[13]

The Trade Sector

If we are to gain a greater understanding of present-day interdependence, the trade sector is critical. One of the long-standing contentions of those who assert that interdependence is low or declining is that national industrialization, at least in its later stages, involves a decreasing reliance upon foreign trade. As manufacturing economies develop, states rely more upon themselves for necessary goods and less upon imports from other countries. Karl Deutsch and Alexander Eckstein, in a pioneering study, tried to measure this phenomenon by the ratio of foreign trade to GNP over time.[14] They concluded that the ratio of foreign trade to GNP increased during the early stages of economic development, but decreased in the later stages of national industrialization.

It is not certain, however, that Deutsch's and Eckstein's data support their conclusions. Ratios for the 1950's, as given by the two investigators, are sometimes quite close to the highest of the series for several countries.[15] Moreover, the Deutsch-Eckstein study is based on current dollar figures.[16] Over the last century, domestic rates of inflation have tended to inflate GNP figures while,

[13] Interdependence may also increase due to scientific and technological developments. See Eugene B. Skolnikoff, The International Imperatives of Technology (Berkeley, Institute of International Studies, No. 16, 1972); see also his "The International Functional Implications of Future Technology," prepared for delivery at the 66th Annual Meeting, American Political Science Association, Los Angeles, September 8–12, 1970; John Gerard Ruggie, "Collective Goods and Future International Collaboration," American Political Science Review, LXVI (September 1972), 874–93; John H. Dunning, "Technology, United States Investment, and European Economic Growth," in Kindleberger (fn. 3).

[14] Karl W. Deutsch and Alexander Eckstein, "National Industrialization and the Declining Share of the International Economic Sector, 1890–1959," World Politics, XIII (January 1961), 267–99.

[15] See also Robert E. Lipsey, Price and Quantity Trends in the Foreign Trade of the United States (Princeton 1963), 39–44.

[16] There are no criteria by which to decide which ratio of foreign trade to GNP is more valid, the one based on current dollars or the one based on constant dollars. In its limiting case, the ratio based on current dollars would go to zero, and it would be irrelevant to point out that in constant dollars there was still some foreign trade of consequence. (We are indebted to Richard N. Cooper for this point.) However, in the Deutsch-Eckstein case, where even in current dollars the ratio for the 1950's was relatively high, it is more illuminating to look at ratios based on constant dollars.

due to revolutionary advances in transportation, export and import prices have not risen as sharply.[17] Robert E. Lipsey, therefore, recalculated the ratio of American exports to GNP in constant 1913 dollars. As Table 1 shows, there is no secular trend of a decline in foreign-trade ratios.

Calculations on other bases support the same conclusion. Table 2 shows that data to 1970 may even portray a slight increase in the ratio of American exports to GNP.

TABLE 1. Ratio of Exports to GNP Averaged by Decades, in Constant 1913 Dollars[18]

	RATIO OF EXPORTS TO GNP
1880–89	6.25
1890–99	7.24
1900–09	6.64
1910–19	7.69
1920–29	6.35
1930–39	5.06
1940–49	7.93
1950–59	6.65

TABLE 2. Ratio of Exports to GNP Averaged by Decades, in Constant 1958 Dollars[19]

	RATIO OF EXPORTS TO GNP
1930–39	4.91
1940–49	4.34
1950–59	4.93
1960–69	6.06

[17] The following table gives an indication of this phenomenon for the last decade:

Export, Import, and Consumer Prices for Selected Countries, 1970 (expressed in U.S. dollars; 1963 = 100)

	EXPORT	IMPORT	CONSUMER
Japan	110	106	149.5
West Germany	114	110	120.4
France	112	107	130.9
United Kingdom	112	110	139.3
United States	121	120	128.9

SOURCE: *International Financial Statistics* XXIV (December 1971), 32, 33, 35.

[18] See Lipsey (fn. 15), 430–31. This table is constructed using Kuznets' estimate of the U.S. Gross National Product. Because the Kuznets estimates deflate GNP, official statistics cannot be used to extend the Kuznets series.

[19] Source: United States Government, *Economic Report of the President* (1972). The lower ratios in this table are due to the use of official (undeflated) GNP indices.

The conclusion that ratios have not fallen and may even recently have increased is strengthened by the knowledge that the ratio for the nineteenth century is inflated because of the downward bias in GNP calculations. Deutsch and Eckstein admit that their national-product estimates "tend to understate the subsistence sector of the economy." [20] They accurately point out that much of the growth in GNP in industrialized states is due to the growth of the service sector, and that that very sector was substantially underestimated in GNP calculations for the previous century. It is therefore very difficult to square the available data with the conclusion that foreign trade as a share of GNP has declined as a consequence of higher industrialization.

Changes in the structure of trade, however, may lead to lower interdependence even though the foreign stake of many developed countries is high or increasing. If interdependence existed only when the relationship would be costly to break, it might be contended that trade at the turn of the century was more truly interdependent than it is today. Before World War I, a typical trade transaction probably involved an exchange of manufactured goods for raw materials; today, much of world trade consists of the exchange of manufactured goods among developed countries. Since these countries could theoretically adopt programs of import replacement, it is contended that interdependence has decreased.[21]

It is indeed true that trade in manufactured goods has greatly increased with time. Table 3 shows the trend in world exports of primary products, petroleum, and manufactured goods since 1950. While primary exports have almost doubled and petroleum exports nearly trebled, manufacturing exports have grown by a factor of seven.

These trends are reinforced by Table 4, which shows that raw materials have dropped and manufactured goods have risen as a percentage of imports and

TABLE 3. Trend in World Exports of Manufactures, Petroleum, and Primary Commodities, 1950–1969 (in billions of dollars)[22]

	PRIMARY COMMODITIES	PETROLEUM	MANUFACTURES
1950	30.28	—	22.97
1955	31.13	8.59	33.77
1960	36.71	10.63	57.74
1965	46.02	15.05	92.45
1969	56.02	21.54	149.73

[20] Deutsch and Eckstein (fn. 14), 271.

[21] See Waltz (fn. 3), 210.

[22] Source: International Bank for Reconstruction and Development, *Trends in Developing Countries* (Washington, D.C. 1971). Beginning in 1955, petroleum is included as Section 3 of the Standard International Trade Categories. Data exclude trade among Communist countries. It is interesting to compare these results with those offered by Albert O. Hirschman, *National Power and the Structure of Foreign Trade* (Berkeley 1945), 141–45: He found either no percentage increase in manufacturing trade as a proportion of the total, or a slight decline for major powers from 1913 to 1937. Longer-term figures, however, point to secular increases since 1954.

exports among developed countries since 1954. The increasing trade in manufactured goods, not surprisingly, is linked with an increase in the trade among developed countries. Table 5 shows that trade among industrial states has increased most dramatically in the last three decades.

These trends are consistent with the conclusion that interdependence has not increased, however; industrial countries, with flexible economies, should be able to reduce their dependence upon each other without great cost. But this argument must take account of yet another point. Not only do developed countries trade with one another mainly in manufactured goods: There is also, in trade among developed nations, an increasing dependence upon particular

TABLE 4. Raw Material and Manufactured Imports and Exports as a Percentage of Total Trade for Selected Industrial Countries[23]

		IMPORTS		EXPORTS	
		RAW/ TOTAL	MANU./ TOTAL	RAW/ TOTAL	MANU./ TOTAL
Germany	1954	71	27	15	84
	1968	43	53	9	90
Japan	1954	86	14	14	85
	1968	72	27	5	94
France	1954	70	24	28	65
	1968	39	60	22	74
Italy	1954	65	34	40	58
	1968	54	45	16	82
United Kingdom	1954	76	20	13	81
	1968	48	48	8	85
United States	1954	63	32	28	68
	1968	32	62	26	70

TABLE 5. Value Index of Direction of Exports, Developing Countries and Developed Countries ($1950 = 100$)[24]

	FROM DEVELOPED TO DEVELOPED	FROM DEVELOPED TO DEVELOPING	FROM DEVELOPING TO DEVELOPED	FROM DEVELOPING TO DEVELOPING
1938	42.1	31.0	31.3	28.3
1948	95.5	100.0	85.8	108.7
1950	100.0	100.0	100.0	100.0
1954	143.7	134.5	119.4	117.4
1959	213.8	176.1	140.3	126.1
1964	352.2	223.9	185.8	158.7
1969	598.7	331.6	271.7	223.3

[23] United Nations, *Yearbook of International Trade Statistics 1954 and 1968* (New York 1955 and 1970).

[24] Source: *Trends in Developing Countries* (fn. 22).

countries and particular commodities. Albert Hirschman has used an index running from 100 (when a country's exports go solely to one trading partner) to very low numbers (when a country's trade is evenly divided among a large number of countries).[25] This measure is known as the Gini coefficient, which is the square root of the sum of the squares of the fractions of trade with each country, multiplied by 100. Its upper limit is 100; the lower limit, assuming trade is evenly divided among 100 countries, would be 10. In 1945 Hirschman used it to calculate the dependence of one nation upon the trade of another. Thirteen years later, Michael Michaely furnished an estimate of the dependence of countries on trade in particular commodities.[26] We have updated these estimates with figures for 1961 and 1968. The evidence is incontrovertible: the recent growth of trade in manufactures among developed societies has not freed economies from the thrall of a few suppliers, nor has it reduced their dependence on imports of particular commodities. Perhaps surprisingly, industrial countries have become more dependent on particular countries for their trade, and are generally more dependent on the supply of particular commodities. Less developed countries may have increased their independence within the system. Table 6 shows the change in Gini coefficients for selected industrial and developing countries in dependence upon trade with particular states. Separate indices are given for imports and exports, indicating the degree to which trade has become geographically dependent.

It is noteworthy that among developed countries (with the exception of imports to Japan) the changes are all in a positive direction, indicating that trade has become more geographically concentrated among suppliers and markets with time. For the developing countries shown, with the exception of

TABLE 6.   Change in Gini Coefficients in the Geographic Concentration of Trade for Selected Developed and Developing Countries (change from 1954 to 1968)[27]

	EXPORTS	IMPORTS
Germany	3.5	4.2
Japan	9.9	−7.3
France	4.4	8.8
Italy	6.2	2.2
United Kingdom	1.9	1.0
United States	.5	4.9
Brazil	−4.7	−1.2
Mexico	−15.1	−17.1
Ghana	−10.8	−19.4
Turkey	−1.6	+3.2

[25] See Hirschman (fn. 22), 98–100.

[26] Michael Michaely, "Concentration of Exports and Imports," *Economic Journal* LXVIII (December 1958), 722–36.

[27] 1954 data based on Michaely, *ibid.*; 1968 data computed using D.o.T. totals from International Monetary Fund and International Bank for Reconstruction and Development, *The Direction of Trade Annual 1966–70* (Washington 1971).

TABLE 7. Change in Gini Coefficients in the Commodity Concentration of Trade for Selected Developed and Developing Countries (change from 1961 to 1968)[28]

	EXPORTS	IMPORTS
Germany	1.21	.53
Japan	2.98	.93
France	1.18	−.95
Italy	.03	3.27
United Kingdom	.04	−.81
United States	2.86	3.86
Brazil	−.19	−1.49
Mexico	−21.14	−2.92
Ghana	−1.38	−3.68
Turkey	+8.98	−6.77

Turkey, trade has become less concentrated geographically, and therefore it reflects a smaller degree of dependence. Table 7 gives similar evidence of the dependence on trade in particular commodities.

With the exception of changes in imports for France and the United Kingdom, commodity concentration for the major developed countries has increased in the past decade: Developed countries are now more dependent upon the import and export of particular commodities than they were previously. Developing countries show no such pattern, and Mexico's reduction of dependence on particular commodity imports and exports is striking. These findings modify conclusions about a reduction in interdependence among industrial countries. The concentration in trade among developed countries is growing. Diversification of suppliers and markets is harder to accomplish. To this degree, dependence and a mutual interdependence of all industrial countries has increased.[29]

There is a further point. The most satisfactory measure of interdependence is not the cost of breaking the relationship, but the degree to which economic interests are direct functions of one another. If the economic position of state A changes, will state B be affected? In the nineteenth century, there was a *de*

---

[28] Source: *Yearbook of International Trade Statistics 1961* and *1968* (fn. 23).

[29] On balance, the foreign-trade sector does not appear to be quite as useful for the measurement of relative interdependence as previous analysts have maintained. Although foreign trade is increasing relatively and absolutely among developed countries, that trade represents an exchange of manufactured goods. As a number of economists have pointed out, if governments can find substitutes for import or export markets among a few industrial countries, the growing effects of concentration do not necessarily increase interdependence. But even if substitutability exists economically, the problems of the political costs of switching from one market to the other and of the circumscription of political latitude involved in the process remain. For the latest review of the literature on trade as a measure of integration, and an excellent bibliography, see Cal Clark and Susan Welch, "Western European Trade as a Measure of Integration: Untangling the Interpretations," *Journal of Conflict Resolution*, xvi (September 1972), 363–82. Integration theorists might find it useful to examine other transnational economic sectors as well as trade, including those discussed below. One such attempt is outlined in Tollison and Willett (fn. 8).

facto interdependence of economic units, but political governors did not act in such a way as to maximize the economic interests of their unit. They therefore neglected external economic changes that had a great effect upon the domestic economic system. During the past half-century, political changes within society have made it impossible for political leaders to ignore the domestic impact of external economic forces. Today, therefore, they respond vigorously to external economic changes. Economic effects are now fully comprehended within the political realm. Thus, politically significant interdependence is much higher today than it was during the nineteenth century.

The Investment Sector

The investment sector reveals similar patterns. Those who argue that interdependence is decreasing can point to the change in the pattern of overseas investment over the past century.[30] Those who assert that it is rising can center their attention on the tremendous recent growth in foreign investment and on changing patterns of investment.[31] Much of the growth in foreign investment since World War II has been in direct investment (investment which results in an important share of ownership or control of a foreign corporation). By contrast, the leading authority on capital flows in the late nineteenth century observes that "portfolio investment was a far more important component of long-term capital movements before 1914 than direct investment; and it consisted much more of transactions in bonds and other debt instruments than in equities." [32] What direct investment there was in the nineteenth century tended to proceed from capital-abundant to capital-deficient areas.[33] While one-third of British long-term investments were in Europe, much of this was in capital-deficient areas such as Russia. Even when direct investment in other developed countries increased after World War I, investment in capital-deficient areas remained a large fraction of the total. In this period, American direct investment abroad typically flowed to Latin America.

The recent growth in overseas long-term investment has not only taken the form of direct investment, it has also increasingly gone to other developed countries. Tables B and C of the Appendix demonstrate this change. In 1936 and 1950, American investments were evenly divided between developed and less developed countries; in 1968, two-thirds of the book value of direct American investments were in developed countries. American direct investments in manufacturing has risen from 25.6 percent of the total in 1936 to 40.6 percent in 1968. These changes are revealed even more dramatically by an analysis of

---

[30] Kenneth Waltz notes, for example, that "in 1910, the value of total British investment abroad was 1½ times larger than her national income"; for the United States today, however, it is a meager 18 percent. Waltz (fn. 3), 215.

[31] See Cooper (fn. 4), chaps. 3, 4, and 5; Morse, "Transnational Economic Processes" (fn. 4), 36–37.

[32] Arthur Bloomfield, *Patterns of Fluctuation in International Investment before 1914* (Princeton Studies in International Finance, No. 21 1968), 3–4.

[33] *Ibid.*, 2–3.

capital flows. In 1957, 55.5 percent of the net capital flows from the United States went to less developed countries, with 46.9 percent going to Latin America. In 1968, 58.4 percent of American capital flowed to developed countries, with 31.2 percent going to Europe—an increase of 11.6 percent since 1957.[34]

With these changes, American investments have become more concentrated geographically and in terms of specific industries. Table 8 indicates this concentration.

TABLE 8. Geographic Concentration of U.S. Investment, 1929–1959[35]

	1929	1936	1943	1950	1959
Gini Coefficient	33.02	34.41	34.20	34.68	37.60

The conclusion to be drawn from these trends is that the stake of the developed countries, and particularly of the United States, in the international economic system has risen as it has become more concentrated.[36] Direct investments imply a higher stake in a foreign country than portfolio investments. Investments in manufacturing enterprises and in other developed countries have narrowed the focus of American investor activity and concern. More is at stake in specific markets, and in specific kinds of enterprises; there is more to lose than there was formerly.

The absolute increase in American direct foreign investment is matched by its relative growth as compared to other GNP indicators. Measured against domestic GNP, in current or constant dollars, the foreign-investment sector has grown rapidly. Table 9 makes this clear.

TABLE 9. Index of Growth of Foreign Direct Investment and U.S. GNP, 1968[37] (1959 = 100)

GNP in current dollars	179
GNP in constant dollars	148
Direct foreign investment	219

[34] See Tables D and E of the Appendix.

[35] Source: U.S. Department of Commerce, *U.S. Business Investments in Foreign Countries* (Washington, D.C. 1960), 92. Figures since 1959 would probably indicate an even higher degree of concentration, but Department of Commerce statistics no longer give country-by-country breakdowns of investment figures.

[36] It could of course be argued that a reduction in the number of suppliers or buyers does not necessarily raise the costs of such transactions to the United States. A few sources may be cheaper than many sources. But the circumscription does diminish U.S. political initiative; it narrows America's political latitude and thus links her interests more closely with the remaining sources of supply or markets.

[37] Sources: *U.S. Business Investments in Foreign Countries* (fn. 35), 92; *Survey of Current Business*, L (October 1970), 28; *Economic Report of the President*, 1972 (fn. 19), 195–96.

TABLE 10. Index of Growth of Foreign Direct Investment and U.S. GNP, 1968[38] (1950 = 100)

GNP in current dollars	303
GNP in constant dollars	199
Direct foreign investment	551

These comparative growth rates are even more remarkable if 1950 is taken as the base year.

This tremendous growth in the book value of American direct investment has been paralleled by a growth in the volume of operations of foreign affiliates compared with U.S. domestic concerns.[39] Domestic sales did not double between 1957 and 1968; however, the sales of foreign manufacturing affiliates rose by more than a factor of three. In 1968, the volume of sales abroad in manufacturing amounted to 10 percent of domestic sales in manufacturing.

Foreign earnings on direct investments of American corporations have also increased more rapidly than domestic earnings. Since 1950, domestic profits of corporations have risen by about 50 percent. But earnings on direct foreign investments have increased by more than 450 percent.[40] By 1969, foreign earnings on direct investments had risen to 28 percent of domestic earnings.[41]

This increased preoccupation with the foreign economic sector, moreover, was not confined to the United States. The growth of the multinational corporation has been so spectacular that today, "of the 50 largest economic entities (in the world), 37 are countries and 13 are corporations. Of the top 100, 51 are corporations." [42] It has been estimated that about one-quarter of the gross national product of the non-Communist world is earned by the business of such enterprises outside their home countries.[43]

It is of course true that foreign investment as a percentage of national income has decreased since 1913, but the type of investment which has occurred is such as to give its owner a substantial stake in the foreign sector. In contrast to the experience of the nineteenth century, current foreign investment is not simply credit, it is partial ownership. Control of productive facilities is involved. Today, transfers of technology are an exceedingly important part of direct investment. Since they are so important, it would be foolhardy for host countries to threaten them. But if the cost of breaking the relationship is so high, interdependence must also be high.

The political significance of interdependence is low when its salience is low. In 1913, economic interdependence had very low political salience; govern-

---

[38] *Ibid.*

[39] See Table F of the Appendix.

[40] See Table G of the Appendix.

[41] This figure of 28 percent would be higher if income from other (non-direct) foreign private assets had been included.

[42] Lester R. Brown, "The Nation State, the Multi-National Corporation and the Changing World Order," mimeo (U.S. Department of Agriculture, 1968), quoted in John McHale, *The Transnational World* (Austin 1969), 8.

[43] Raymond Vernon, *Sovereignty at Bay* (New York 1971), 383.

ments were not supposed to be responsive to or control external economic influences. Thus, the absolute high value of investment in 1913 had little political significance. Today the rate of increase of the foreign-investment sector and the increasing political responsiveness of governments have given high salience and significance to foreign investment.

The Financial Sector

The financial operation of the international economic system has changed greatly since World War I. Under the gold standard of 1880–1913, short-term capital movements were neither as extensive nor as disruptive as they have been in recent years.[44] The amount of funds available for "hot money" flows has now reached an all-time high. Table H of the Appendix shows that $71 billion is available in various currencies (mainly dollars) for short-term transactions. This huge pool of assets, sloshing from country to country, can easily undermine domestic monetary policy and strength. In 1968, an inflow of foreign funds into West Germany amounted to as much as 8.9 percent of the domestic money supply, greatly circumscribing attempts at an anti-inflationary policy. In the same year, France suffered an outflow of 22 percent of her international reserves, forcing her central bank to put a brake on expansionist policies.[45] In July 1972, speculation against the dollar was so intense that in just one day European central banks bought $1.5 billion to prevent the dollar from going beneath the level fixed by the Smithsonian Agreement of December 18, 1971.[46] Less than 14 months later, speculation forced a further 10 percent devaluation of the dollar, and in one day Germany took in $2.7 billion in exchange for marks. The Smithsonian Agreement, which once appeared to be a long-term solution, has now been abandoned.

If the sudden speculative movements of this vast pool of currencies are not to undermine domestic monetary stability and economic progress, and perhaps to cause a collapse of the whole Western trading system, governments will have to concert their countermeasures. Increasing recognition of the problem in the past fifteen years has led to the General Agreement to Borrow (GAB), various currency-swap arrangements, an enlargement of IMF quotas, and the creation of Special Drawing Rights (SDR's). Yet it is by no means certain that these and various pending arrangements will fully control the short-term flow of funds among Western and developed nations. The interdependence of the financial structure of trade is growing, but still higher cooperation among governments is necessary to ensure that it will not become a negative interdependence.[47]

---

[44] See Bloomfield (fn. 32), 87.

[45] See Lawrence Krause, "Private International Finance," in Keohane and Nye (fn. 4), 181–83.

[46] *New York Times*, July 19, 1972.

[47] See Susan Strange, "The Dollar Crisis: 1971," *International Affairs*, XLVIII (April 1972), 194.

Other changes have transformed the system since World War I. The old gold standard was based (not surprisingly) on gold as a medium of exchange. Minimum use was made of foreign currencies as reserves. At the end of 1913, the nations of the world held only $963 million in foreign-exchange reserves, and over half of these were possessed by Russia, India, and Japan.[48] Official gold holdings, in contrast, were more than five times as much.[49] With the move to a gold-exchange standard the percentage of national reserves accounted for by foreign-exchange holdings has gone up dramatically. Table I of the Appendix makes it clear that in 1945 gold accounted for 70 percent of international reserves, while foreign exchange totaled 30 percent. By the end of 1971, on the other hand, gold amounted to only 30 percent of world reserves, while foreign exchange represented 60 percent, and a new category of international reserves (SDR's and gold *tranche*) represented 10 percent.

These figures are even more instructive when analyzed in conjunction with the growth of world trade in the same years. In 1945, world exports in the non-Communist world totaled $34.2 billion. By the end of 1971, world exports were estimated at $334 billion, 977 percent of the previous figure. This means that since 1945, the value of world exports has more than doubled every eight years. This growth is more than double the growth rate of foreign-exchange holdings, more than four times that of total international reserves, and almost eight times the growth rate of gold holdings. In 1945, total international reserves were 39 percent greater than the value of world exports; by the end of 1971, total international reserves were only 40 percent of the total value of exports in one year. Thus, while the holdings of international reserves have not kept pace with the growth in trade, the degree to which they have kept up is due to vast increases in the holdings of foreign exchange.

This change also represents an increase in international interdependence. Gold was an undifferentiated asset; it could be earned from any sector, and spent in any sector. A nation had to discipline its trade overall, but not with specific countries. Today, bilateral trading relationships are far more important, and among those trading countries interdependence has increased. What is more important, while the countries whose currencies are media of exchange have some responsibility for disciplining their own financial policies, other countries also have a direct financial stake in their solvency. These other countries have an interest in not allowing reserve currencies to sink too low on international exchanges. Hence the rescue operations for the British pound and the U.S. dollar. Now that Swiss francs, German marks, and Japanese yen are being held as reserves, other nations also have a stake in maintaining the value of such reserves. These currencies may be able to benefit from rescue operations

---

[48] See Bloomfield (fn. 32), 7.

[49] *Ibid.*, 7. Peter Lindert disputes the traditional wisdom (and Arthur Bloomfield) by claiming that foreign currencies were used fairly extensively. However, even Lindert's data for 1913 show that only $1132 million were held in foreign-exchange reserves, which is 15.9 percent of the total world reserves. He also concurs that more than half of these official foreign balances were held in Russia, India, and Japan. See Peter H. Lindert, *Key Currencies and Gold, 1900–1913* (Princeton Studies in International Finance, No. 24, 1969), 12, 13, 76, 77.

at a later stage. Gold holdings in the nineteenth century did not produce this same stake, this same interdependence. Governments, recognizing this dependence upon currencies, have now gone so far as to create a new reserve unit, the SDR, the use and further extension of which will be entirely dependent upon international agreement. The interdependence of the financial system has now become formal.

The Political Sector

The development of political relations among states since 1913 has witnessed two major trends. Between 1919 and 1939, an essentially autarchic trend held sway, with nations striving to reduce their dependence upon others, first in political and later in economic terms. Because of the role of prewar alliances, World War I strengthened the tendency for nations to rely on themselves. The peacetime alignments which emerged in the thirties had little significance in time of crisis or war. Indeed, the only major powers which stood by their alliance commitments were Germany and Japan. The Soviet Union, France, Britain, and Italy all vacillated, and the United States remained out of the bargaining.

After World War II, however, nations came to believe that they could not ensure their own defense without help. National self-sufficiency would no longer provide security. In the wake of Hiroshima, many nations also concluded that major wars would be so horrendous that they could not be tolerated at all. Henceforth, minimal cooperation would be necessary even among adversaries. Arrangements were made for crisis communication and management.

In recent years, however, intergovernmental cooperation and interdependence have grown apart from military stimuli. It can even be argued that the alienation of publics from their governors has strengthened such trends. Contemporary government depends upon such a wealth of information and specialized expertise that the man in the street cannot keep up with what is happening, to say nothing of being able to make informed judgments. Under these circumstances, elections have come to be symbolic processes, largely devoid of intellectual content. Since people do not fully understand their governments, they tend to distrust them and to become resentful toward those in authority. But distrust of those in power nationally does not lead to any new foci of international loyalty and support. If national bureaucracies are immobile, international or supranational institutions are either weak or unresponsive to popular demands. Even in Europe there has been no marked substitution of international for national loyalties.

The difficulties of domestic governance have, paradoxically, forced governmental elites together. Although the masses cannot fully communicate with elites, and elites cannot talk to the masses except in the simplest terms, elites *can* talk to each other. National leaders are coming to recognize that, with individual variations, they are all in the same boat. Among developed societies at least, they face similar problems: the problem of remaining in power as the electorate becomes sullen and resentful; the problems of economic progress and of making their way in international politics while avoiding major war. Leader-to-leader diplomacy has been a way of learning from each other.

The failure of ideology to cope with real governmental problems has also brought leaders together. The barrage of information and the communications revolution have today either destroyed or rendered irrelevant most ideological systems of belief.[50] Rigid doctrinal approaches are discredited by new information. Rulership requires so much expertise and detailed adjustment that ideological systems offer few guidelines. Elites learn from each other, perhaps more than they do from their own publics; in one sense they help each other solve the problem of domestic governance.

Increased communication among leaders has not, however, put an end to nationalism. It is true, as Kenneth Waltz argues, that "the progress of internal integration and the increased intervention of governments in their domestic economies means that for most states the internal sector now looms larger than it once did." [51] While elites are looking outward, publics are turning to their national governments for the solution of social and economic problems. What Karl Kaiser calls "vertical interaction" (between government and society) has grown greatly in recent decades. Kaiser argues that "a high degree of horizontal interaction [between units of world politics] . . . does not lead to transnational politics unless there is vertical interaction." He goes on: "The higher the degree of interventionism on the part of national governments, the more vulnerable governmental policies become to processes on the level of transnational society which might thwart these policies. A democratic structure intensifies this relationship since it forces governments to be more responsive to disturbances." [52] He then concludes that a nation-state's participation in transnational politics is a function of the product of horizontal and vertical interaction:

$$tp = hi \cdot vi \ [53]$$

This equation suggests that, if vertical interaction increased and horizontal interaction remained the same, transnational politics would increase. But if transnational politics is any measure of the amount of interdependence among states, this conclusion can scarcely be accepted. If vertical integration and interaction were to increase greatly, as for example with the establishment of a totalitarian state, transnational politics would almost certainly decline rather than increase. Such an increase in vertical interaction would probably stimulate a decline in horizontal interaction with other states and societies, again preventing any increase in transnationalism. It is also not an accident that states convulsed by revolutionary impulses have been the least amenable to horizontal interaction with other states and societies. The domestic preoccupation of the vertical revolutionary process tends to cut links with other units. It

[50] See Zbigniew Brzezinski, *Between Two Ages* (New York 1970), Parts II-III.

[51] Waltz (fn. 3), 208.

[52] Karl Kaiser, "Transnational Politics: Toward a Theory of Multinational Politics," *International Organization*, xxv (Autumn 1971), 812.

[53] *Ibid.*

is also not surprising that the Communist countries, with the highest degree of vertical integration, where "the permanent intervention of governmental institutions in the social and economic life of society" has gone farthest, evince the fewest horizontal ties with other states and societies. There can be no conclusion, therefore, that vertical interaction *always* increases transnational politics and interdependence.

Conclusion

The earth is today poised between a world of nationalism and a world of transnationalism. The vertical interaction of nationalist processes has moved to a new peak. The horizontal interaction of transnational processes is higher than at any point since World War I. Moreover, it is growing rapidly. As both Kaiser and Morse have pointed out,[54] vertical interaction has made horizontal interaction relevant for political and governmental purposes. If vertical interaction were not so great, the world would be witnessing a return to the *apolitical* interdependence of 1913. However, a rapid further increase in domestic social change and vertical interaction, far from increasing transnational politics, could put an end to them.

Domestic governments lie at the nexus of vertical and horizontal interaction. They are impelled in one direction by the desire to satisfy the electorate and to build domestic support. They are impelled in another by the high degree of horizontal integration of the system. If they are to cope with the great transnational phenomena of the current age—the multinational corporation, the unrivaled impact of private financial transfers, and continuing trade problems—they must cooperate with one another. In some measure the two influences are complementary: If governments are to satisfy the demands of the electorate in economic and financial policies, they may have to cooperate more fully with other nations. Under the stimulus of economic nationalism, however, nations may also occasionally act *against* the multilateral cooperative framework.

Intergovernmental cooperation has slowly increased since World War II to provide for a steadily increasing level of international trade and financial stability. The gold pool, GAB, and swap arrangements were the achievements of the early sixties. SDR's and last-minute rescue operations for the dollar or the pound are the remedies of today. Yet, given the huge pool of Eurodollars and other currencies which can spill in or out of the domestic economic reservoirs of Western states, it is by no means assured that intergovernmental cooperation will be great enough to meet the need. Devaluation has often been the practical recourse, even though it represents national action against an agreed set of currency values.

American economic nationalism stimulated the U.S. moves of August 15, 1971 and February 12, 1973. The first eventually led to the Smithsonian Agreement of December 1971, but that agreement could not be maintained under

[54] *Ibid.*, 811–12; Morse, "Transnational Economic Processes" (fn. 4), 44–45.

the continued pressure of monetary speculation. A further 10 percent devaluation of the dollar, on February 12, 1973, led to the float of European and Japanese currencies. Even after the second American devaluation, however, the dollar and a number of other currencies remained vulnerable to speculative assault. After each autarchic move, the damage to the Western trading mechanism has been patched or repaired. But it is not certain that intergovernmental cooperation will be great enough to meet all crises in the future. It is, for example, uncertain that the Common Market countries will be able to keep their currencies in fixed alignment under current pressures. Neither is it certain that the Europeans will be able to avoid import surcharges if their currencies float too high for domestic political acceptability. In this sense, the American precedent of August 1971 may now be employed by European states. The problem of speculative flows of hot money has by no means been solved.[55]

Today, therefore, whether interdependence will emerge as positive or negative will depend largely on old-fashioned cooperation among governments. Governments can heed nationalistic, autarchic, or reformist demands of the citizenry. Even if they do not do so, however, the onrush of economic transnationalism is so rapid that it is not certain that governments can keep abreast of it. When antiquated forms of cooperation fail, nationalistic alternatives may be substituted.

In the international system today there is a phenomenon akin to Ernst Haas's "spill-over" in the Common Market. Nations that strive to carry out existing functions required by the exigencies of transnational flows and domestic demands must move to a higher level of cooperation. Horizontal interaction is increasing so rapidly, however, that the past apparatus of intergovernmental institutions and policy is no longer adequate. Haas presumed that, within an already partially integrated structure, this would lead to further integration of policies and institutions. Whatever the mandates of functional cooperation within customs unions, however, the international system as a whole does not prescribe such results. The failure to meet the challenge of higher necessary cooperation could mean a higher possibility of conflict. The objectives at stake are much greater than heretofore, but it is not certain that the current structure of interdependence will permit them to be achieved.

---

[55] See Susan Strange (fn. 47), 215; Edward L. Morse, "Crisis Diplomacy, Interdependence, and the Politics of International Economic Relations," World Politics, xxiv (Spring 1972 Supplement), 123–50. As many have noted, one response to the failure of agreed currency values could be to move to freely floating exchange rates. So far, however, there is little evidence that nations would not try to extract the maximum national leverage from such a situation. After August 15, 1971 and after the failure of the Smithsonian Agreement, many nations engaged in "dirty floating," supporting the dollar and preventing their own currencies from rising to market level.

Appendix

TABLE A.* Percentage Distribution of Trade for Selected Developed and Less Developed Countries in Accordance with the Various Types of Interchange: 1954 and 1968

		Raw-Raw	Man-Man	Inv	Raw-Man	Total
West Germany	1954	16	25	8	51	100
	1968	9	47	14	30	100
Japan	1954	12	16	20	53	100
	1968	5	27	1	67	100
France	1954	28	24	7	41	100
	1968	21	63	7	9	100
Italy	1954	32	41	20	7	100
	1968	16	45	2	37	100
United Kingdom	1954	11	22	16	50	100
	1968	7	54	17	22	100
United States	1954	34	26	23	17	100
	1968	26	61	7	6	100
Brazil	1954	37	1	13	49	100
	1968	37	8	7	48	100
Mexico	1954	2	28	27	44	100
	1968	16	22	22	40	100
Nigeria	1954	15	1	15	70	100
	1968	17	8	6	69	100
Panama	1954	38	1	65	−3	100
	1968	45	1	48	6	100

Raw-Raw: Exchange of foodstuffs and raw materials against foodstuffs and raw materials.
Man-Man: Exchange of manufactures against manufactures.
Inv: Exchange of commodities against "invisible items."
Raw-Man: Exchange of manufactures against foodstuffs and raw materials.

* Computed using Albert O. Hirschman's method, *National Power and the Structure of Foreign Trade* (Berkeley 1945), chap. VII. Data from *Yearbook of International Trade Statistics, 1954 and 1968* (fn. 23).

TABLE B.* Percentage of U.S. Book Value of Direct Investment by Geographic Area: 1936, 1950, 1959, and 1968

	1936	1950	1959	1968
Developed Countries	51.2	48.3	56.5	66.9
Canada	29.2	30.4	34.2	30.1
Western Europe	18.8	14.7	17.8	29.9
Less Developed Countries	48.4	48.6	39.1	28.8
Latin America	41.9	37.7	27.6	20.2

* The percentage not accounted for is due to a category called international, unallocated.

TABLE C. Percentage of U.S. Book Value of Direct Investment by Category: 1936, 1950, 1959, and 1968

	1936	1950	1959	1968
Mining and Smelting	15.4	9.6	9.6	8.4
Petroleum	16.1	28.8	35.1	29.1
Manufacturing	25.6	32.5	32.6	40.6
Public Utilities	24.5	12.1	8.1	4.1
Trade	5.8	6.5	6.9	8.1
Agriculture	7.2	5.0	2.2	—*
Other	5.4	5.6	5.5	9.7

* No separate category.

SOURCES for Tables B and C: *Survey of Current Business* (October 1970), 28; U.S. Department of Commerce, *U.S. Business Investment in Foreign Countries* (Washington, D.C. 1960), 92–93.

TABLE D. Percentage of U.S. Net Capital Flows by Area: 1957 and 1968

	1957	1968
Developed Countries	40.1	58.4
Less Developed Countries	55.5	35.7
Canada	28.9	19.5
Western Europe	11.6	31.2
Latin America	46.9	21.1

TABLE E. Percentage of U.S. Net Capital Flows by Category: 1957 and 1968

	1957	1968 (Preliminary)
Mining and Smelting	8.0	1.7
Petroleum	56.7	33.3
Manufacturing	17.4	36.5
Public Utilities	7.7	*
Trade	1.7	*
Finance and Insurance	7.8	*
Miscellaneous	.6	28.4

* No separate category.

Sources for Tables D and E: *Survey of Current Business* (October 1970), 29; U.S. Department of Commerce, *U.S. Business Investments in Foreign Countries* (Washington, D.C. 1960), 137.

TABLE F. Index of U.S. Foreign and Domestic Sector in Manufacturing in 1968 (1957 = 100)

Manufacturing Exports	189	
Sales by Direct Manuf. Affiliates	326	
Total Foreign Sales		262
U.S. Value Added by Manuf.	193	
U.S. Manuf. Sales	175	

Sources:
Domestic Sales: United States Government, *Economic Report of the President* (1972), 244;
Value Added: 1957: U.S. Bureau of the Census, *Annual Survey of Manufactures 1966* (Washington, D.C. 1969), ii; 1968: *Annual Survey of Manufactures 1968* (Washington, D.C. 1971), *Press Release* #M68 (AS-6), 1 & 2;
Manuf. Exports: *U.S. Statistical Abstract* (1970), 480; *U.S. Statistical Abstract* (1963), 875;
Sales by Affiliates: *Survey of Current Business* (October 1970); U.S. Department of Commerce, *U.S. Business Investments in Foreign Countries* (Washington, D.C. 1960), 110.

TABLE G. Earnings on District Foreign Investments and Foreign Earnings as Percentage of Domestic Corporate Profits

| | Earnings on Direct Foreign Investments* | | Foreign Earnings as Percentage of Domestic Profits |
	Million $	Index (1950 = 100)	
1950	1,892	100	9
1951	2,365	125	13
1952	2,457	130	15
1953	2,386	126	15
1954	2,534	134	16
1955	3,036	160	14
1956	3,527	186	16
1957	3,799	201	18
1958	3,260	172	19
1959	3,589	190	16
1960	3,969	210	19
1961	4,278	226	21
1962	4,815	254	20
1963	5,247	277	20
1964	5,827	308	19
1965	6,384	337	17
1966	6,732	356	16
1967	7,170	379	19
1968	8,268	437	22
1969	9,497	502	28

* Earnings category was obtained by adding (1) earnings of U.S. direct investment abroad, and (2) direct investment receipts of royalties and fees. Income from other (non-direct) private assets has *not* been included.

Sources:
Profits: 1950–1962: *Survey of Current Business*, September 1965, 53; 1962–1963: *ibid.*, July 1966, 5; 1964: *ibid.*, July 1968, 24; 1965–1966: *ibid.*, July 1969, 22; 1967–1970: *ibid.*, July 1971, 18.
Royalties and fees: *ibid.*, June 1970, 34–35.
Earnings of U.S. direct investments abroad: 1950–1959: *Balance of Payments Statistical Supplement*, rev. ed. (Washington, D.C.: U.S. Department of Commerce, Office of Business Economics, 1963), 184; 1960: *Survey of Current Business*, August 1962, 22–23; 1961: *ibid.*, August 1963, 18–19; 1962: *ibid.*, August 1964, 10–11; 1963–1970: *ibid.*, October 1971, 28–29.

TABLE H. Net* Estimated Size of Eurocurrency Market (in billions of dollars)

	Eurodollar Market	All Eurocurrencies
1964	9.0	**
1965	11.5	**
1966	14.5	**
1967	17.5	**
1968	25.0	**
1969	37.5	44.0
1970	46.0	57.0
1971	54.0	71.0

* Net of interbank deposits within Europe. However, net includes banks' assets and liabilities vis-à-vis their own countries (foreign currency position vis-à-vis residents).

** Not estimated by B.I.S.

Source: *Bank for International Settlements.*
1964–68 Eurodollar: *Thirty-Ninth Annual Report* (Basle 1969), 149;
1969–70 Eurodollar: *Forty-First Annual Report* (Basle 1971), 164;
1969–71 Eurocurrency: *Forty-Second Annual Report* (Basle 1972), 155;
1971 Eurodollar: *Forty-Second Annual Report* (Basle 1972), 148.

TABLE I. International Reserves (billions of dollars, end of year)

	1945	1955	1965	1971
Gold	33.3	35.8	41.4	39.2
of which: U.S.	(20.1)	(21.8)	(14.1)	(11.1)
Foreign Exchange	14.3	17.0	23.0	79.5
of which: U.S. $	(4.2)	(8.3)	(15.9)	(51.1)
£ Sterling	(10.1)	(7.6)	(6.7)	(7.8)
Gold *Tranche* position at the IMF	—	1.9	5.4	6.9
SDR's	—	—	—	6.4
Total	47.6	54.7	69.8	132.0
Addendum: World Exports	34.2	84.0	165.4	334.0*

* Estimated quarterly data expressed as annual rate.

Sources: For 1945, 1955, and 1965, Richard N. Cooper, *The Economics of Interdependence* (New York 1968), 51; for 1971, *International Financial Statistics* (September 1972).

The International Functional Implications of Future Technology

Eugene B. Skolnikoff

Most students of modernization see technology in some form as the underlying source of change in the modern era. The greater per capita productivity resulting from the replacement of muscles by machines has led to specialization, interdependence, and integration. Affecting local communities initially, these processes have transformed the structural framework of human activity. Administrative structures smaller than the national state no longer wield a great deal of authority, and many foresee the time when the nation-state itself may give way to structures with larger jurisdictions.

In this essay Skolnikoff explores the directions that technology is likely to take in the years ahead, and the pressures this development is likely to exert in calling for closer cooperation among states in their mutual interest.

Technological advance and the increasing application of technology have had profound effects on the international issues confronting nations, effects often quite different from those originally anticipated on common sense grounds. Technology, instead of minimizing consciousness of national sovereignty, *seems* to have exaggerated it; instead of discouraging the emergence of weak, small states, has made proliferation of states possible; instead of bringing about sharp changes in the attitudes and assumptions of governments toward foreign affairs, has allowed continuation of "traditional" approaches to the workings of the international system.

This essay will outline some of the future international implications of continued rapid developments in technology, with emphasis on the impact of technology on international intergovernmental machinery. Likely technological developments, in a time frame of 10-20 years, are going to generate

"The International Functional Implications of Future Technology" by Eugene B. Skolnikoff is reprinted from the *Journal of International Affairs*, XXV No. 2 (1971), pp. 266–286. Copyright by the trustees of Columbia University in the City of New York. Permission to reprint the article is gratefully acknowledged to the editors of the *Journal*.

Skolnikoff is professor of political science at the Massachusetts Institute of Technology and author of *Science, Technology, and American Foreign Policy* (1967) and *The International Imperatives of Technology: Technological Development and the International Political System* (1972). He served on the staff of the President's Special Assistant for Science and Technology from 1958 to 1963.

important performance demands on the international system going well beyond, in scale and intensity, the requirements placed on the system today. These demands will result from the increasing constraints on independent national action coupled with much more intensive requirements for international activities carried out by international machinery. Moreover, because of the diffusion of decision-making with regard to many technologies, these demands have a certain "inevitability" which means they cannot be prevented or ignored by governments. The conclusions drawn will raise important questions about the viability of the prevailing model of the international system: sovereign states vying for security and advantage, with the primary locus of decision-making within the states. They will also raise questions about the ability of the existing international machinery and the existing attitudes of governments to cope with the changed situation. The actual technical situation justifies a position somewhere between the apocalyptic and the complacent. There are in a variety of areas, particularly pollution, the seeds of unparalleled disaster. More information could show that the world now faces irreversible environmental changes that require drastic and urgent international political action, though available information does not support such a conclusion.[1]

The specific functions of international organizations can be represented in the following typology:

A. *Service*
   1. Information exchange
   2. Data-gathering, analysis, and monitoring of physical phenomena
   3. Consultation and advice
   4. Facilitation of national and international programs
   5. Coordination of programs
   6. Joint planning
   7. Small-scale funding
B. *Norm Creation and Allocation*
   1. Data-gathering and analysis for establishment of norms
   2. Establishment of standards and regulations
   3. Allocation of costs and benefits
C. *Rule Observance and Settlement of Disputes*
   1. Monitoring adherence to standards and regulations
   2. Enforcement of standards and regulations
   3. Mediation, conciliation, and arbitration
   4. Appeal of standards and regulations
   5. Adjudication
D. *Operation*
   1. Resource and technology operation and exploitation
   2. Technical assistance
   3. Conduct of research, analysis, and development
   4. Financing of projects

[1] *Man's Impact on the Global Environment*, Report of The Study of Critical Environmental Problems (SCEP) (Cambridge, Mass.: M.I.T. Press, 1970).

Environmental Alteration

This is perhaps the newest major technological subject to receive critical public and political attention. Suddenly, governments find themselves under growing pressure to protect the "environment." Every international organization is also directly involved in some way; for a few, it is becoming a significant part of their activities. Developments of technology for deliberate manipulation of the weather, already extant or likely, can be thought of conveniently in three categories: micro-modification, modification of storms, and large-scale climatic modification. The inadvertent modification of weather or climate is also possible.

The evidence associated with cloud-seeding experiments in micro-modification suggests that rainfall can be increased locally from 5 to 20%. T. F. Malone anticipates that by 1980 "naturally occurring rainfall can be either augmented or diminished locally by proven techniques" and that by the end of the 1980's "the probability is high that rainfall several hundred miles downwind from the site of the operations can be increased or decreased at will." [2] Problems are sure to arise within countries and between nearby countries with regard to water distribution. Second, a need for international cooperation in operational matters is likely also to emerge, for at times the actual seeding may have to be done over foreign territory or international waters. Eventually, a different kind of international issue will emerge: how to allocate what is, in effect, the finite resource of atmosphere-borne fresh water. Clearly, a major problem of international resource allocation will exist.

The prospect of being able to divert or suppress hurricanes is now with us. Experiments in the U.S. (August 1969) using silver iodide appear to have been successful in reducing the maximum velocity of Hurricane Debbie by 31 and 15% on alternate days. [3] If modification activities could deflect the course of a hurricane, the possibility of claims for damage or water deprivation could result. Operational activities with regard to hurricane modification must necessarily be carried out in an international environment, even at times over several different national territories. Also on the technological horizon are bold schemes for melting the Arctic ice cap by means of chemicals (carbon black), a dam across the Bering Straits (often proposed by Russian scientists), dispersing the Arctic cloud cover, or pumping warm Atlantic water into the Arctic basin. [4] The purpose would be to alter radically the climate of the

---

[2] T. F. Malone, "Current Developments in the Atmospheric Sciences and Some of Their Implications for Foreign Policy," in *The Potential Impact of Science and Technology on Future U.S. Foreign Policy*, Papers presented at a Joint Meeting of the Policy Planning Council, Department of State, and a Special Panel of the Committee on Science and Public Policy, National Academy of Sciences, June 16–17, 1968, at Washington, D.C., pp. 82–97.

[3] "Advances in the Eye of a Storm," *New Scientist*, December 25, 1969, Vol. 44, No. 681, p. 630.

[4] P. M. Borisov, "Can We Control the Arctic Climate," *Bulletin of the Atomic Scientists*, March 1969, Vol. XXV, No. 3, pp. 43–48.

Northern Hemisphere, in particular to warm and provide increased moisture for the vast Siberian region. The probable effects of removing the Arctic ice cover vary from forecasts of entirely benign and beneficial effects (more temperate climate with increased rainfall in Siberia, Europe, and as far south as the Sahara), to predictions of the onset of a new ice age and substantial increases in the ocean level as the Greenland ice cap melts. Obviously much more information of the likely effects is required before any such project can be allowed to proceed. But, it must be realized that the resources required for such a project may *not* be beyond the capabilities of a single large state (a Bering Straits dam is entirely feasible at costs comparable to large continental dams). Moreover, if the economic payoff is as fantastic as warming Siberia, the incentive to proceed would be enormous. What international machinery does the world have to govern such a project?

Weather modification technology can also lead to strategic or tactical military capabilities, thereby affecting the balance of power. It can be used as a weapon in economic warfare, diverting water needed for agriculture or hydroelectric power. Conversely, it can be used as a tool for enhancing economic development and welfare. Such uses of this technology may depend critically on the international means developed for controlling it, for allocating its benefits, and preventing its misuse.

This technology depends directly on increased scientific understanding of the atmosphere. The underlying research and data-gathering is being carried out partially under national auspices, but the major components are two international programs associated with the World Meteorological Organization (WMO) and the International Council of Scientific Unions (ICSU). One is called GARP—the Global Atmospheric Research Program—and the other the World Weather Watch (WWW).[5] These two related programs may themselves create important requirements for new or revised international machinery to operate the programs when they are farther along. The potential implications of the knowledge gained through the international programs also establish a requirement for, in some sense, "controlling" the application of the knowledge in accordance with internationally agreed purposes.

Inadvertent modification of weather and climate is occurring as a natural concomitant of this century's accelerating application of technology, the growth of the world's population, and the urbanization being experienced in all countries. The world *could* be heading for a major catastrophe. From 1880 to 1940, the average temperature of the earth increased by 0.4°C, while in the last 25 years, the temperature has decreased by 0.2°C.[6] Are these climatic fluctuations of the last 80 years natural variations, or a result of man's activities? There are a number of ways in which man's activities could disturb the atmospheric heat balance.

One is the accretion of carbon dioxide in the atmosphere, as would be

[5] Malone, *op. cit.*, p. 87.
[6] Gordon J. F. MacDonald, "The Modification of Planet Earth by Man," *Technology Review*, October-November 1969, Vol. 72, No. 1, pp. 27–35. The information that follows is drawn from this article, except where noted.

expected from an increased consumption of fossil fuel. The result of a CO_2 "blanket" is to trap solar energy reflected from the earth's surface, creating a hothouse effect. The accretion of CO_2 would correlate with the increase in the earth's temperature until 1940, but not with the subsequent decrease. A possible explanation of this phenomenon is that the CO_2 concentration is being overwhelmed by atmospheric particle pollution. That is, dust from urban, industrial, or agricultural activities can affect the thermal balance primarily in the opposite direction to the CO_2. The dust forms a barrier to solar radiation, thus reducing the energy reaching the earth. In addition, the dust forms nuclei for low-level cloud formation which serve to reflect some additional solar radiation back to space. "At present, on the average, about 31% of the earth's surface is covered by low cloud; increasing this to 36% would drop the temperature about 4° C, a drop close to that required for a return to an ice age." [7]

There are also other possibilities of considerable concern. The earth's albedo (the percentage of incoming solar radiation directly reflected outward) is being changed by man-made alteration of the earth's surface. Dense urban areas and highways reflect more radiation than forest or agricultural land. These changes could also lower the surface temperature. Additionally, there are unknown factors such as rocket exhausts in the upper atmosphere which may affect the transfer of radiation, or water vapor exhaust from jets and SST's which spread ice crystals at very high altitudes producing a haze and cloud cover with undetermined, but potentially significant, consequences.[8] The list of possible calamities could be considerably extended. But the simple point is that there is a good probability that the changes in the atmosphere brought about by "multiplying man's" multiplying use of technology are leading the planet to significant climatic changes. This danger may arise in critical form within the next twenty years.

The world has already seen several dramatic illustrations of premeditated large-scale actions with potentially substantial global environmental effects. The fallout from atmospheric atomic tests is one example. Others have included high-altitude U.S. and Soviet nuclear tests and the orbiting by the U.S. of a belt of copper filaments for a military communications experiment. The latter two illustrate the interesting kinds of problems these capabilities raise.[9]

In the case of both the U.S. 1962 high-altitude nuclear shots—called Project Starfish—and the copper filament experiment—Project Westford —, advance notice of the experiments was given by the U.S. Government. In both cases, extensive analysis was made within the U.S. of the predicted

[7] Reid A. Bryson and Wayne M. Wendland, "Climatic Effects of Atmospheric Pollution," presented at the American Association for the Advancement of Science National Meeting, December 27, 1968 (mimeo) quote some of this evidence.

[8] Bryson and Wendland, *ibid.*

[9] See Eugene B. Skolnikoff, *Science, Technology and American Foreign Policy* (Cambridge: The M.I.T. Press, 1967), pp. 84–92, for an extended discussion of the communications experiment.

long- and short-term effects of the experiments. In the Westford case, in fact, the government made impressive efforts to publicize the analysis in advance, and to encourage scientists in other countries to make their own analyses. This did not prevent a substantial negative reaction from the world scientific community. The Westford experiment followed the predictions exactly: the filaments have fallen out of orbit as expected.[10] The same cannot be said for Project Starfish. Rather, there were substantial effects that did *not* accord with the predictions: some of the released electrons became trapped in the earth's magnetic field, with some long-lasting effects on scientific experimentation.[11]

Two points must be noted in these examples. One is that the scientific analysis prior to the experiments was not infallible. The other is that the U.S. Government, even though it demonstrated substantial responsibility in allowing prior publication and analysis of security-related experiments, was still prepared to proceed unilaterally in the face of doubts raised by the world-wide scientific community, and in the face of the knowledge that miscalculations would affect the entire globe, not just the U.S.

Several lessons for the future requirements for international machinery emerge from this listing of only a few phenomena associated with man's large-scale tampering with the environment. It is essential that we know more about the processes of the environment to plan for the full range of effects that will follow specific large-scale actions. Machinery to control technology could take many forms, varying from independent national capabilities to some kind of "impartial" international body. Machinery with a genuine international capability would necessitate development of ancillary mechanisms for appeal, adjudication, monitoring, enforcement, and assessment of damages and claims.

It may be necessary to contemplate international responsibility for, or even international operation of, some large-scale technology as a way of guaranteeing equitable distribution of benefits and genuine concern for possible harmful side-effects. The high cost of some projects may also force them into the international arena.

With a rapidlly growing population and with rapid increases in industrialization and urbanization, both the needs and the wastes of society grow at exponential rates. A world population expected to grow to nearly 5.0 billion by 1985 from a little over 3.5 billion in 1970 would lead to more than a 40% increase in requirements for food, energy, and natural resources just to maintain the present unsatisfactory economic levels.[12] These requirements will, in fact, be substantially increased by the economic growth levels in all countries and the corresponding increase in industrialization. But to meet these requirements it will be necessary to use massive quantities of fertilizer and insecticide,

---

10 I. I. Shapiro, "Last of the Westford Dipoles," *Science*, December 16, 1966, Vol. 154, No. 3755, pp. 1445–1448.

11 Bernard Lovell, "The Pollution of Space," *Bulletin of the Atomic Scientists*, December 1968, Vol. XXIV, No. 10, pp. 42–45.

12 United Nations Economic and Social Council, "World Population Situation," Note by the Secretary-General, doc. E/CN.9/231, September 23, 1969 (Population Commission, 15th Session, November 3–14, 1969).

transport and burn growing quantities of fuel, dispose of more agricultural and industrial waste, transform more agricultural land into houses and highways, cut down more forests, find more fresh water supplies, etc. All this will substantially alter our present environment and add substantially to the environmental pollution problem. It is not a single problem, but an enormously complicated interrelationship. The implications of a change in one aspect cannot be approached adequately without consideration of the total system.

The use of DDT and related organochlorine compounds to control insect pests has been a major factor in making it possible to feed and improve the health of the present world population. But now we realize that the accumulation of these persistent pesticides in the food chain is toxic to some forms of animal life. Many animal species have been endangered, and the background concentration for man has in some cases exceeded presently accepted limits. Perhaps the most disturbing recent development is a report that DDT interferes with photosynthesis of marine phytoplankton, a phenomenon that could have catastrophic effects on the living resources of the sea.[13] Several countries have now banned, or severely curtailed, the use of DDT-related compounds; the U.S. acted in mid-October, 1969. There is controversy as to whether effective substitutes for DDT are available. When they are, the costs are likely to rise. Thus, we quickly come to hard choices between starvation or disease on one hand, and gradual accretion of DDT levels on the other, between economic growth and stagnation. Who is to make these choices? Are there alternatives? Ultimately, who pays? It is instructive that in present debates in the U.N. and other international bodies, the developing countries are understandably much less concerned with pollution problems than the developed countries.

The industrial sulphur effluents of one country are claimed to come down as sulphuric acid in another.[14] The problem can be solved most easily by using sulphur-free fuels, but that would cut off the market for oil from the Middle East and Venezuela. Oil pollution at sea, with attendant serious effects on bird and marine life and on recreation, becomes a grave menace as the size of tankers increases in order to satisfy growing energy-demands of civilization. A single accident can become a disaster; and the exploitation of seabed oil resources, with the likelihood of occasional accidents, is sure to increase sharply in the near future. Whatever measures are taken to reduce these risks, they will, at the least, raise the price of oil—with political consequences.

The general problem of solid waste disposal has astonishing dimensions. In the U.S. alone, the magnitude of solid wastes today is estimated to be 140 million tons of smoke and noxious fumes, 7 million automobiles, 20 million tons of paper, 48,000 million cans, 26,000 millions bottles and jars, 3,000 million tons of waste rock and mill tailings, and 50 trillion gallons of

[13] Paul R. and Anne H. Ehrlich, "The Food-From-The-Sea Myth," *Saturday Review*, April 4, 1970, pp. 53–65.

[14] Kenneth Mellanby, "Can Britain Afford to be Clean?," *New Scientist*, September 25, 1969, Vol. 43, No. 668, pp. 648–650.

hot water along with a variety of other waste products.[15] The waste problem is aggravated by the conscious development of plastic and other containers that are not degradable in the environment.

The expected growth in the use of nuclear power as a major source of energy will greatly aggravate the problem of safe disposal of atomic waste, which in turn may change the economics of the nuclear power industry. Even the relatively low-level release of radioactivity from "normally" operating nuclear power plants may be a severe problem.[16]

IMPLICATIONS OF ENVIRONMENTAL ALTERATION FOR INTERNATIONAL FUNCTIONS

Research, analysis, and information about the changing environment are needed rather desperately. The goals are several:

A. Simply to know on a continuing basis what, in fact, is going on;
B. To determine the likely effects of present trends, and to establish tolerances;
C. To develop alternatives to, or modification of, current practices when necessary; and
D. To establish hard data on the costs and benefits of alternative courses of action for political decision.

This is clearly the most immediate set of requirements, and one that has been recognized now by many international organizations.[17] Developing the information is the (politically) easy part of the job. The implications of the information for further action will prove more difficult.

The primary need is for establishing international norms for effluents, for solid waste disposal, for tanker routing, for actions in the event of ship accidents, etc. Free flow of trade, in fact, will also require uniform standards among nations. Where pollution has more subtle effects, and requires for its amelioration unaccustomed domestic limitations in certain fields, the political problems will be more serious. For example, if limitations are required on the amount of grassland covered over each year (as regarding the earth's albedo), or if limitations must be put on the total use made of specific technologies each year, then we will be seriously affecting areas never before

[15] United Nations Economic and Social Council, 47th Session, "Problems of the Human Environment," Report of the Secretary-General, doc. E/4667, May 26, 1969, p. 5.

[16] Barry Commoner, "Attitudes Toward the Environment: A Nearly Fatal Illusion," address for presentation at Unanticipated Environmental Hazards Resulting from Technological Intrusions Symposium, Annual Meeting of the AAAS, Dallas, Texas, December 28, 1968, (mimeo.).

[17] "Problems of the Human Environment," Report of the Secretary-General, *op. cit.*, which lays out the general objectives of the U.N. Conference on the Human Environment to be held in Sweden in 1972.

subject to any form of international regulation (or in many countries even national regulation). Limitations on research and development itself may even become a serious political issue if a judgment can be made that the direction new technology may take would seriously exacerbate environmental problems. The prospective technologies of peaceful use of nuclear explosions and weather modification, and the actual technologies of supersonic aircraft might be limited.

Creation of norms implies other functions as well, especially the question of allocation. The costs of testing standards, or of banning the use of certain technologies, will not be evenly distributed. The costs of giving up or replacing some pesticides and herbicides will not only be measured in dollar terms, but also in terms of human life and health. Similarly, the costs of controlling industrial waste will fall unequally on certain nations because of their particular geographical positions, their dependence on certain resources, or their emphasis on certain industrial processes. Who should pay—the producer, the consumer, or the nations most offended by the particular pollutant? How is this to be determined? Moreover, a nation's competitive position in international trade may be substantially affected by the measures it must take. Regulations must, therefore, be international simply to maintain fair competition; universally-applied regulations may damage the competitive position of some countries, thereby raising issues of equity.

The allocation function requires an appeals and adjudicative mechanism. A means of developing technical analyses which are recognized as fair and impartial will be essential. A damage assessment and claim procedure will be necessary to settle violation of the international standards. Finally, a monitoring and enforcement procedure is implied to insure compliance. This could continue to be "passive," as is generally the case now, in the sense that nations tend to conform voluntarily to standards on the basis of a calculation of their own best interests. A more "active" means of enforcement may be necessary if the present pattern is not adequate.

The Oceans

The oceans have been the focus of some of man's earliest technological developments, and also his first attempts at codifying international law. Today, they are the scene of application of the latest technology, and as a result the cause of much re-thinking and re-shaping of international law. Rapidly advancing technology for underwater extraction of organic and mineral resources; improving knowledge of the likely extent of the resources, especially seabed oil; and continued exponential growth in energy demand—all combine to make the political and legal questions associated with ocean resources controversial. Technological developments, spurred by the promise of high return on investment, will make it possible to operate in deeper and deeper underwater environments. With the expectation that the "world's greatest supplies of fossil fuels" lie on the continental rise, one can quickly see both the motivation and potential payoff of technological developments.[18] Other resources of the seabottom are also of potential interest, particularly manganese, nickel, copper, sulphur, and the "detrital" minerals.

The major international questions, of course, have to do with who owns the resources on or under the seabed; thus, who has rights beyond the continental shelf to their exploitation and to their benefits? Whatever institutional arrangement is established for regulation of the seabed, it would not only have to have a means for deciding who has access to the seabed, but also a procedure for distributing publicly whatever benefits accrue. In addition, a means for monitoring and enforcing decisions, regulations, and standards could well become necessary, whether it was carried out by an international mechanism, or by agreement among national entities.

There are several important aspects to the international issues surrounding living resources of the sea. One is the trend in present fishing practices and technology related to maximizing yields. It is a controversial issue, but some scientists estimate the potential harvest of the sea to be not very much greater than present annual harvests (about 60 million metric tons). The Food and Agriculture Organization (FAO) estimates less than twice the present catch size as the likely maximum that can be expected.[19] In fact, with improved technology and greater fishing effort, *depletion* of fish resources would result unless effective control methods are undertaken. A second aspect is the increasing knowledge of the migratory patterns of fish. This knowledge can create difficulties if it allows a nation to take fish that have been traditionally harvested by other nations at a different stage of the migratory cycle, or if the fish are taken at a stage of the cycle before they breed. A third aspect is the possibility of aquaculture, that is, artificially improving the nutritive value of the sea, and "raising" fish.

There are several other oceanic activities of great economic or political importance which will also be the focus of extensive technological development in the near future. Transportation will go in the direction of larger and faster vessels and probably true submersibles. Military applications will tend toward larger and quieter nuclear missile submarines for the deterrent force, more devices for submarine detection, and probably also more anti-submarine forces. With the increasing vulnerability of land weapons, the undersea missile launchers will steadily take on more importance, possibly replacing land-launched missiles entirely. The undersea environment will inevitably be a primary focus for arms control measures, as it already has.

In view of these increased uses, the problem of congestion of the ocean environment arises. Many applications are pertinent to the same areas of the ocean, potentially congregating ships for fishing and transport, submarines, unmanned buoys, and permanent drilling platforms in the same vicinity. Entirely new regulations and rules of the road may have to be developed.

---

[18] P. M. Fye, A. E. Maxwell, K. O. Emery and B. O. Ketchum, "Ocean Science and Marine Resources," in Edmund A. Gullion, ed., *Uses of the Seas*, The American Assembly, Columbia University, (Englewood Cliffs, N.J.: Prentice-Hall, 1968), pp. 17–68.

[19] Food and Agriculture Organization, Committee on Fisheries, Fifth Session, Rome, April 9–15, 1970, "Fishery Aspects of the Indicative World Plan and Proposed Follow-up," doc. COF1/70/3, January 26, 1970.

IMPLICATIONS FOR INTERNATIONAL FUNCTIONS

Whatever regime is established for the deep seabed, it will have to be concerned with the exploitation of resources beyond the limits of national jurisdiction. Presumably, licensing authority would be involved, which means establishing criteria and making choices. If that regime is given genuine management responsibility for the seabed, or ownership of the resources, then the whole ramification of functions from licensing through norm creation, rule observance, appeal, adjudication, and operation all follow.

For fisheries regulation, one sees the same basic functions: denying benefits and rights to one country in favor of another; the existence of machinery for appeal, monitoring, and enforcement of decisions; and an ability to develop or obtain independent technical information. Similar steps will be necessary to prevent the serious depletion of protein-supplying species endangered by overfishing. With rather less impact, the need to handle the growing congestion resulting from uses of the seas will also require international machinery.

Outer Space

The space-launching powers will undoubtedly continue space activities, though with less political urgency.[20] The interest in receiving economic returns from space, and in minimizing the costs by sharing, will undoubtedly grow. Satellite applications that can assist in the planning and management of forestry and agriculture activities are almost certain developments during the time period of interest. Based on the ability to scan large areas with a variety of sensor devices, satellite systems will provide invaluable information for allocating water use, anticipating crop size, and many other land management activities. Such services are likely to become essential once they are adopted as a regular input to a nation's economic system.

Another exciting application of satellites is in the search for mineral and organic resources. It is quite likely that satellites can be used to prospect for minerals, or at least to identify promising locations for ground exploration. Such information may have considerable economic and strategic interest, raising troublesome questions about information control and access, control of the application of this technology, and international operation.

The number of satellites serving as relay communications systems will increase substantially in order to meet the expanding demand for communications channels. The systems themselves are likely to be increasingly

[20] The information for this section comes from many sources, but in particular the report of the U.S. National Academy of Sciences, National Research Council, "Useful Applications of Earth-Oriented Satellites," Washington, D.C., 1969 and "Selected Space Goals and Objectives and Their Relation to National Goals," Battelle Memorial Institute Report No. EMI-NLVP-TR-69-2 to NASA, July 15, 1969.

sophisticated, with much larger channel capacity, well-defined beam (geographical) coverage, increased power, and other specialized capabilities. Whether there will be a single global system or multiple national systems is not clear at this time. The demand for frequencies will add enormously to the problems of allocation of the frequency spectrum. Direct broadcasting from satellites to augment home or community antennas is under development today. The U.N. Working Group on Direct Broadcast Satellites estimates that direct broadcast into community or augmented home receivers will be technically feasible by 1975.[21] However, the actual development of direct broadcast systems will depend on complex economic, political, and technical criteria.

The increased interest in observing the planet and its environment for research, exploration, exploitation, monitoring, and enforcement purposes will lead to the development of satellite-centered data-gathering and dissemination systems. These will be sophisticated satellites, with their own sensors, and tied to sensors and read-out stations throughout the globe. Such systems will also add to the pressure for frequency and orbital space allocations, and will raise questions of international versus national management, economic efficiency, security of information, joint planning, etc.

Expansion in air transportation, as well as introduction of high-speed marine transport, will require greatly improved navigation airs, a need very much in evidence today in transatlantic air routes. Satellite navigation systems are likely to offer the most attractive answer to such needs. Adequate allocations for frequency and orbital requirements, as well as the question of management, will again be central.

FUNCTIONAL IMPLICATIONS OF SPACE

These stand out quite clearly, and, in fact, have already resulted in the creation of several new international institutions, most notably INTELSAT, the consortium for communications satellites, and the European cooperative space research and launcher development organizations (ESRO and ELDO). The first functional international requirement will be operating mechanisms for many of the systems mentioned above. In most cases, national ownership and operation will not be adequate as a permanent arrangement for political reasons. Some of the information generated by the space capabilities will have serious economic and even strategic consequences, most notably information on likely new resources, on fish movements, and on weather, Important questions about the ownership of the information and its availability to national or commercial interests will have to be dealt with by international means.

Whole fields of human activity will come to depend on some of the systems once they are in operation—for example, weather forecasting, navigation and

---

[21] United Nations, Committee on the Peaceful Uses of Outer Space, Report of the Working Group on Direct Broadcast Satellites, doc. A/AC.105/51, February 26, 1969.

air-traffic control, and crop-planning. For reasons of equity and political feasibility, therefore, there will be strong pressure that these be internationally-run systems. Many of the systems may involve differential application costs as well as differential benefits to some portions of the globe. Questions of allocation of benefits and costs, and of pricing policy will, therefore, have to be dealt with by international machinery. Some communication systems may have a profit potential, or at least seriously affect the profit potential of existing land-based systems in the same fields. Complex problems of equity will have to be settled through international action. The procurement of equipment will also raise questions of economic equity. Which countries will receive development and procurement contracts? INTELSAT is plagued with this problem now. The desire to share in the economic and technological benefits of development and production of communications satellites is clearly one of the motivations behind competing proposals.

Interest in spreading the costs of space development and exploration is likely to encourage more cooperative space efforts than are envisioned today, possibly involving international machinery in the process. Direct broadcast satellites will raise thorny problems of technical standards for the satellites themselves, television standards, regulation of broadcast coverage and inter-ference (including jamming), and, or course, frequency and orbit allocation. Some form of international control of broadcast content cannot be excluded. Greatly increased activity in the near-earth environment will, in turn, require a space regime capable of establishing norms and making allocations for various contemplated uses. The existing and potential military uses of space (essentially surveillance, communications, and tracking) will greatly compli-cate that task.

Natural Resources

The availability of natural resources—mineral, organic, and hydrological —is a perennial source of concern. Whatever the short-term situation, the world has a finite supply of mineral and fossil fuel resources. The world's demand for metals has been growing at a rate of more than 6% per annum for nearly a decade.[22] The entire metal production of the globe before World War II was about equal to what has been consumed since. Some materials are, or soon will be, in short supply: helium, mercury, tin, silver, manganese, chromium, titanium, tantalum, and tungsten.[23] Of these, helium and mercury have unique properties and no satisfactory substitutes are presently known. The nuclear-energy minerals have the same character. Thus, mineral con-servation measures may be required and would have to be of international

[22] T. S. Lovering, "Mineral Resources from the Emerged Lands," in *Potential Impact, op. cit.*, p. 43.

[23] Preston E. Cloud, Jr., "Approach to Assessment of the World's Mineral Resources," in *Potential Impact, op. cit.*, p. 30.

scope to be meaningful. The present situation seems to be that not as much is known as should be about the actual global resource situation.

The assumption that the market mechanism can be relied on to call forth new supplies from lower-grade ores is not valid for those metals in which sharp discontinuities of concentration occur. Lead, zinc, and mercury show this characteristic, as do some of the more common metals outside of their basic ore deposits.[24] The assumption that cheaper energy can make extremely low-grade ores profitable ignores the fact that low-grade ores would require enormous costs in the handling and processing of rock.[25] A persistent and vexing problem is the efficient use of existing resources in the light of future needs rather than of present technology and economics.

FUNCTIONAL IMPLICATIONS OF RESOURCE SCARCITY

The most immediate necessity is international development of a geochemical census of the earth's crust in order to determine the real resource situation. The uneven distribution of the world's resources, and the uncertain extent of those resources, may together create increasing pressure for an international approach to their management and efficient use. The U.S. and other developed countries are, by far, the largest consumers of raw materials today, and may be preempting the possibility of other countries using those resources for their own future development. This could become a serious political issue producing pressures for machinery to manage, allocate, and regulate the use of resources. In addition, the growing use of resources has a direct relationship to the pollution problem. Regulations growing out of the need for pollution control may well be realized as limitations on national consumption of various kinds of raw materials.

Food

The Green Revolution of the late 1960's, which appears at least to have postponed a threatened worldwide famine, is a coincidental product of several factors: timely development of new technology in the form of new seed strains, good weather in critical areas, and the willingness of farmers to plant the new varieties. But this development is only a temporary reprieve, not a long-term solution, as long as population pressures continue to increase. The FAO's "Indicative World Plan for Agricultural Development" (IWP) designed to highlight food-related issues and requirements until 1985, points out that agricultural production on the average must show an annual average increase of between 3.2 and 3.8% as compared to the average 1962 figure of

[24] Lovering, *op. cit.*, p. 39.
[25] *Ibid.*

2.8%, a substantial long-term change in the average.[26] Moreover, this assumes no change in already inadequate levels of food quality and caloric intake. If some increased demand is also postulated, the annual increase required for developing countries will be 3.9%.[27] In short, the danger of a catastrophic worldwide famine is likely to be with us for a long time.

FUNCTIONAL IMPLICATIONS OF FOOD PROBLEMS

The international implications largely depend on one's point of view, a different situation from some of the other topics discussed here. It is conceivable that the situation will remain roughly as it is: concern and limited attempts to help, some international machinery devoted wholly to the problem, but in the main a national approach. It is also possible that the food and larger development problems will receive increasing attention from the world community as a whole, and lead to substantially new or expanded functions on the international scene including management and allocation of resources—money, fertilizer, pesticides, water, machinery, etc.—to bring about adequate food production, distribution, and quality. The particular kind of event that could bring about such functional developments most rapidly would be the onset of a major crisis, whether it be widespread famine or some environmental crisis.

Population

Population control is without question the single most serious environmental problem the world will have to face in the next 50 years. From the economic, the cultural, and the sociological points of view, it appears essential that population growth be brought under control. But that clear imperative encompasses many problems. One is simply: how? Others involve judgments about optimum sizes of populations, distributions among races and nations, motivations, and other issues of considerable subtlety and sensitivity. It is clear that the finite resources of the earth, including open space, cannot support a continuously expanding population indefinitely. And whatever the optimum size of population may be, the preservation of at least some present Western values would be jeopardized by populations very much larger than those postulated by 1985 or 2000 (in excess of 6 billion). Of course, values may change along with population growth and new technology, as they have today in comparison with the past.

A time may come when enforced birth control is unavoidable. This social control may well be based on international, at least as much as national,

---

[26] G. Cheld, "Famine or Sanity," New Scientist, October 23, 1969, Vol. 44, No. 672, pp. 178–181.

[27] Ibid.

considerations. In the immediate future, direct intervention in birth control will probably remain an individual, or at most a national, matter. But the international consequences of unchecked birth rates are likely to create substantial political pressure for restrictions which will have to be universally applied, or at least universally agreed upon. This, in turn, implies some kind of international negotiation and international machinery to help carry out the agreement. There remains the question of how birth rates can be controlled even if there is the personal or political will to do so. Many legal, sociological, technical, and psychological birth control techniques are now in use, most centered around the idea of family planning. The family planning approach is sound, but the decision is left in the hands of the family itself. It is entirely possible that individual preferences may keep the birth rate up too high on the average, even in developed, long-lived societies.

At the same time, the prospects are not good for development of chemical agents that might be adequate to the task, due to legal and political problems at least as much as to technical ones. One definition of adequacy implies a chemical that has long-term effects so that only one dose is required. The most desirable goal would seem to be an agent that produces indefinite sterility, but is reversible on a temporary basis. If state control is ever required, such a technology would be the easiest to adapt. However, present practices for developing and testing new drugs make it most unlikely that any such drug could be developed.[28] The difficulties are that: 1) new drugs are tested by the FDA in the American environment, not the environment of other countries; 2) safety requirements are so stringent that development of new drugs are discouraged on cost grounds, and the prolonged test period impedes influencing the population problem soon enough; and 3) there exists no independent national or international scientific body of appeal to which FDA decisions can be presented and challenged on scientific grounds.[29] To the extent that the necessary technology for population control is yet to be developed—a controversial point since many believe that existing technology used in the family planning approach, coupled with health and development programs will do the job—some new international procedures will be required to change the ground rules for that development.

General Observations

Stanley Hoffmann has observed succinctly that "The vessel of sovereignty is leaking." The consciousness of independence and license for nations to do as they please, mentioned originally, is illusory. Many technological developments today make it a partial truth at best. Self-interest in the use of many technologies makes it mandatory for nations to reach agreements

---

[28] Carl Djerassi, "Prognosis for the Development of New Chemical Birth Control Agents," *Science*, Vol. 166, No. 3904, Oct. 24, 1969, pp. 468–473.

[29] *Ibid.*

that constrain their freedom of action, for to do otherwise would deny the use of the technology, or bring about various forms of retaliation. The constraints are usually freely entered into, and in that sense can be thought of as self-imposed, but they are nevertheless limitations on sovereignty. What is striking is how far this erosion of sovereignty has already gone. Essentially all of the functions which will be necessary by the 1980's in fact have their counterparts today. Some are rudimentary and *de facto*. But others, even in the politically difficult regulatory area, are surprisingly extensive and effective. The status of today's functionalism is critical in evaluation of the capability of the existing international system to evolve into what will be required in the 1980's. However, even if the entire complex of intergovernmental organizations were performing well today, the increase in the tasks and responsibilities of the system that will be called for in a very few years will not be realized unless conscious steps are taken now to prepare for that time. Moreover, the general performance of international machinery today, notwithstanding its effectiveness in some areas, leads to considerable skepticism that it provides an adequate base for expansion and increase in responsibility without substantial modification.

The growing constraints on freedom of national action, and the increased responsibility flowing to international organizations, will mean that the locus of decision-making will increasingly be forced from the national to the international arena. Nations will not necessarily lose their voice in the control of specific issues, but an increasing number of issues will have to be settled in an international environment. It seems quite likely that there will be a tendency for interest groups within nations to look increasingly to the international organizations in their area of concern, accentuating the expansion of international decision-making.

A countervailing trend, however, will be the growth in political and economic saliency of the technological subjects discussed here. Of relatively marginal interest to governments in the past, their implications will force them closer to the center of the political stage. Inevitably, that will also imply greater national sensitivity to any loss of control, and thus increased resistance to any delegation of responsibility to international bodies over which governments exercise only limited control. That could also mean that these subjects will begin to look more like the "high politics" issues of national security and power relationships of today, and become more central concerns of governments.

But these issues are so pervasive in society, and cut across so many of the direct concerns of individuals and interest groups, that governments will never be able to speak with a single voice in these matters. In fact, the problem of integration of policy at the national level, often raised with regard to the effective operation of international organizations, will become even more difficult. It may be that we must look to the international level to provide the necessary integration, rather than primarily to the national level. If so, it is another example of the way in which the focus of decision-making is likely to move toward the international scene.

The nature of the issues emerging from advancing technology and its side-effects emphasizes the connectedness of things. Increasingly, issues can not be neatly divided into boxes labelled "oceans," "agriculture," "health," and so forth; rather, they interact with each other. This is no less true domestically than internationally and will be a major problem in the future, making current questions of jurisdiction and coordination of international organizations pale into simplicity. Additionally, the complexity and size of modern technological and organizational systems make the task of innovation exceedingly difficult.

We can point to what may be the hopeful beginning of increased public interest in some countries in the substantive issues that have been raised in this analysis, particularly environmental control and pollution. It will surely take such public interest, expressed in political activity, to bring about the kind of controls on man and his works, whether national or international, that will be required for survival. Accompanying this increased public interest in protection of man's environment there seems to be a growing recognition that governments do not have the right to act unilaterally in technological areas when the effects may spread beyond national borders. It remains to be seen how this recognition will develop, but it will be a prerequisite for substantial movement in the direction of international decision-making.

There is also, at least in the U.S., a disturbing reaction to technology itself, a reaction which could take on dangerous "Luddite" aspects. To the extent that the solutions to technology-caused problems may lie in technology itself, this anti-technology reaction could seriously inhibit progress toward protecting the future. It may manifest itself first in pressure to keep budgets for science and technology to a minimum and to exercise tight control in those very areas that are essential for understanding and ameliorating the physical and social problems the world faces.

The political environment in which international organizations will have to function will also change. Developments in the nuclear arms race and political tension in general will substantially affect the possibility of meeting the issues raised here. Political developments between the superpowers will obviously have a profound influence on the evolution of international machinery. China must be a part of the resolution of these technology-related issues. One can anticipate major conflicts of interest becoming serious sources of tension between North and South.

Whatever the political developments of the next two decades, "inevitable" technological developments will pose major new demands on the international system. Determination of the optimum course of system evolution must depend, in part, on an evaluation of existing international machinery in terms of requirements for the next 20 years. Whether "evolution" will be enough, or whether we will need a "revolution" in the existing international order, is a controversial judgment. Will governments and organizations recognize the extent of the problem in time, even if moderate change in the system would be adequate? Clearly the need for understanding the issues involved is urgent.

Transgovernmental Relations
and International Organizations

Robert O. Keohane and Joseph S. Nye

*Political development has been characterized by the gradually expanding
jurisdiction of administrative authorities. In Western Europe the
evolution from the* regna *of the early Middle Ages (see Strayer's essay in Part 2)
to the nation-states of the nineteenth century and to the European
Economic Community today reflects a consistent pattern even though one
that has been immensely costly in human lives and agonizingly slow.
Although the nation-state may be only a stage in political development, it
is a structure that has proved unusually able to hold the loyalties of its
members and to resist the cession of sovereignty to larger entities.*

*This essay by Keohane and Nye recognizes that nations have not been
very successful in cooperating through the United Nations and other
intergovernmental organizations, and that transnational nongovernmental
organizations have as yet had little influence on governments. They
argue, however, that transnational organizations create an understanding
of the common interests of peoples that are likely in the long run to
affect governmental organizations as well. In presenting their argument, they
also review alternative positions and discuss the problems of definition
that are critical to a creative dialogue in this field.*

"Realist" analyses of world politics have generally assumed that states are
the only significant actors; that they act as units; and that their military security

"Transgovernmental Relations and International Organizations" by Robert O. Keohane and
Joseph S. Nye is reprinted from *World Politics*, XXVII (October 1974), 39–62. Reprinted
by permission of Princeton University Press.

Keohane and Nye are professors of political science at Stanford University and Harvard
University, respectively, and are co-editors of *Transnational Relations and World Politics*
(1972). Nye is also author of *Peace in Parts: Integration and Conflict in Regional Organization* (1971).

In their first footnote to the article, Keohane and Nye state: "We have profited from discussions of the subject with Hayward Alker, Graham Allison, Robert Dickerman, Samuel
Huntington, Alex Inkeles, Peter J. Katzenstein, Stephen Krasner, John Ruggie, Robert
Russell, Harrison Wagner, and other members of the Transnational Relations Study Group
at the Harvard Center for International Affairs. Support for this research was provided by
the Ford Foundation."

objectives dominate their other goals.[1] On the basis of these assumptions it is easy to conclude that international organizations—defined as intergovernmental organizations—are merely instruments of governments, and therefore unimportant in their own right. Compared with the hopes and dreams of world federalists, the Realist position reflects reality: international organizations in the contemporary world are not powerful independent actors, and relatively universal organizations such as the United Nations find it extraordinarily difficult to reach agreement on significant issues. It is therefore not surprising that students of world politics have paid relatively slight attention to these entities, particularly after hopes for a major United Nations peacekeeping role were dashed in the early 1960's.

The Realist model on which the above conclusions about international organizations are based is now being called into question. Faced with a growing complexity of actors and issues, a number of analysts have begun to pay more attention to transnational relations. In this article we will contend that if critiques of Realist models of world politics are taken seriously, they not only call into question state-centric conceptions of "the international system," but also throw doubt upon prevailing notions about international organizations. If one relaxes the Realist assumptions, one can visualize more significant roles for international organizations in world politics.

In an important recent contribution to the literature on transnational relations, Samuel P. Huntington argues explicitly that international organizations are relatively insignificant in contemporary world politics:

... internationalism involves agreement among nation-states.

... every international organization at some points finds itself limited by the very principle which gives it being.

The international organization requires *accord* among nations; the transnational organization requires *access* to nations. . . . International organizations embody the principle of nationality; transnational organizations try to ignore it.

While national representatives and delegations engage in endless debate at UN conferences and councils, however, the agents of the transnational organizations are busily deployed across the contents, spinning the webs that link the world together.

Internationalism is a dead end.[2]

Like Huntington, we begin with the proposition that transnational relations are increasingly significant in world politics. But we reach very different conclusions about the roles of international organizations.

Before making the arguments systematically in the remainder of this paper,

[1] For a general discussion, see Robert O. Keohane and Joseph S. Nye, Jr., eds., *Transnational Relations and World Politics* (Cambridge, Mass. 1972). For documentation of the point based on a survey of the literature, see John R. Handelman, John A. Vasquez, Michael K. O'Leary, and William D. Coplin, "Color it Morgenthau: A Data-Based Assessment of Quantitative International Relations Research," paper delivered to the International Studies Association, March 1973.

[2] Samuel P. Huntington, "Transnational Organizations in World Politics," *World Politics,* xxv (April 1973), 333–68; quotations from pp. 338, 339, and 368 respectively.

we must briefly deal with the issue of how transnational relations should be defined. Huntington defines "transnational organizations" as organizations sharing three characteristics: they are large bureaucracies; they perform specialized functions; and they do so across international boundaries. He explicitly includes governmental entities, such as the United States Agency for International Development (AID) or the Central Intelligence Agency (CIA) and intergovernmental entities such as the World Bank, along with nongovernmental organizations such as multinational enterprises, the Ford Foundation, and the Roman Catholic Church. Although this definition has virtue of pointing out similarities between governmental and nongovernmental bureaucracies operating across national boundaries, it obscures the differences. Some of Huntington's observations are clearly meant to apply only to nongovernmental organizations. He argues, for instance, that "The operations of transnational organizations . . . usually do not have political motivations in the sense of being designed to affect the balance of power within the local society." [3] But this hardly applies to the Agency for International Development or the Central Intelligence Agency, both of which he designates as "transnational." He contends, on the basis of literature about multinational enterprises, that personnel arrangements of transnational organizations move toward dispersed nationality patterns, in which country subdivisions are primarily managed by local personnel; yet no evidence is presented that this is true for AID or the CIA, much less for the Strategic Air Command—another "transnational" organization by Huntington's definition. Furthermore, the trends over time seem to diverge, and when Huntington discusses these trends, he finds himself distinguishing between "U.S. Government-controlled transnational organizations" and private groups.[4]

The anomalies into which Huntington is led convince us that for most purposes it is useful to retain the governmental-nongovernmental distinction, thus facilitating the task of examining both the differences between patterns of governmental and nongovernmental activity and the effects of each on the other. Only if one were to use organization theory in a sustained way to explain behavior of large bureaucracies that operate across international boundaries would it seem wise to adopt Huntington's definition.

The argument leads us also to reconsider some of our own past usage. In this article we will restrict the term "transnational" to nongovernmental actors, and the term "transgovernmental" to refer to sub-units of governments on those occasions when they act relatively autonomously from higher authority in international politics.[5] In other words, "transnational" applies when we

---

[3] *Ibid.*, 358.

[4] *Ibid.*, 348–49.

[5] This is a slight modification of our usage in the volume cited above. We used the term "transnational interactions" to refer to "interactions in which one actor was nongovernmental," and the term "transnational relations" as a generic category that included both "transnational and transgovernmental interactions." We have become convinced that this was unnecessarily confusing. For a stimulating critique of our language as well as our ideas, see R. Harrison Wagner, "Dissolving the State: Three Recent Perspectives on International Relations," *International Organization*, xxviii (Spring 1974).

relax the assumption that states are the only actors, and "transgovernmental" applies when we relax the assumption that states act as units.

Our choice of definition is not a matter of semantics but is related directly to the argument of this paper. Transnational activity makes societies more sensitive to one another, which may lead governments to increase their efforts to control this nongovernmental behavior. Such efforts, if pursued by more than one government, make governmental policies sensitive to one another: since one government may deliberately or inadvertently thwart the other's purposes, governments must design their own policies with the policies of others in mind. The result of this may well be attempts at policy coordination, which will increase direct bureaucratic contacts among governmental sub-units, and which may, particularly in a multilateral context, create opportunities for international organizations to play significant roles in world politics.

In the argument that follows we will first elaborate our concept of transgovernmental relations. In succeeding sections we will discuss the role of international organizations in facilitating or promoting various types of transgovernmental relations and the utility of international organizations as points of policy intervention in transnational systems. In our conclusions we will return to the question of the complexity of the connection among transnational relations, transgovernmental relations, and international organizations over time.

I. Transgovernmental Relations

During the last century, governments have become increasingly involved in attempting to regulate the economic and social lives of the societies they govern. As a result, they have become more sensitive to external disturbances that may affect developments within their own societies. For instance, integration of money markets internationally, in the context of governmental responsibility for national economies, has made government policy sensitive both to changes in interest rates by other governments and central banks, and to movements of funds by nongovernmental speculators. These sensitivities are heightened further by the expanding decision domains of transnational organizations such as multinational business firms and banks, reinforced by decreases in the cost of transnational communications.

As the agenda broadens, bureaucracies find that to cope effectively at acceptable cost with many of the problems that arise, they must deal with each other directly rather than indirectly through foreign offices.[6] Communications among governments increase. International conferences and organizations facilitate direct contacts among officials of what were once considered

---

[6] Karl Kaiser has been a pioneer in developing arguments about what he calls "multi-bureaucratic politics." See in particular his "Transnational Politics: Toward a Theory of Multinational Politics," *International Organization*, xxv (Autumn 1971), and "Transnational Relations as a Threat to the Democratic Process," in Keohane and Nye (fn. 1).

primarily domestic government agencies. In the words of a former White House official, "it is a central fact of foreign relations that business is carried on by the separate departments with their counterpart bureaucracies abroad, through a variety of informal as well as formal connections. (That is especially true in alliance politics. But to a point, it also applies elsewhere.)" [7] There have always been such contacts. What seems to be new is the order of magnitude of transgovernmental relations, as bureaucracies become more complex and communications and travel costs decrease.[8]

We define transgovernmental relations as sets of direct interactions among sub-units of different governments that are not controlled or closely guided by the policies of the cabinets or chief executives of those governments. Thus we take the policies of top leaders as our benchmarks of "official government policy." Lack of control of sub-unit behavior by top leadership is obviously a matter of degree, and in practice by no means free of ambiguity. The policy of the central executive is often unclear, particularly on details, and policy means different things at different organizational levels. "One man's policy is another man's tactics." [9] As one observer has put it, "Central policy is always waffled; actors latch on to the waffled parts and form coalitions to shift policy at their level." [10] Nonetheless, to treat all actors as equal and to ignore the existence of a political hierarchy charged with "course-setting" and maintaining some hierarchy of goals is to misrepresent both constitutional and political reality.[11] It is precisely because this central policy task has become more difficult in the face of greater complexity that both the opportunities and the importance of transgovernmental interactions may be expected to have increased.

It is quite conceivable that executives entrusted with responsibility for central foreign policy, such as presidents and prime ministers, will themselves attempt to collaborate with one another in ways that conflict with the behavior of their respective bureaucracies. Yet we will regard only the relatively autonomous activities of the lower-level bureaucracies, as opposed to those of top leadership, as being transgovernmental. Otherwise, we would find ourselves in the anomalous position of regarding a head-of-state meeting, at which new initiatives that deviate from established policy are taken, as an example of "transgovernmental politics" when indeed it is almost the paradigm case for the state-centric model whose inadequacies we are criticizing. The point of our terminology is to focus attention on bureaucratic contacts that take place

---

[7] Testimony of Francis Bator before the Subcommittee on Foreign Economic Policy, Committee on Foreign Affairs, House of Representatives, July 25, 1972. *U.S. Foreign Economic Policy: Implications for the Organization of the Executive Branch*, 110–11.

[8] See John F. Campbell, *The Foreign Affairs Fudge Factory* (New York 1971), 204 ff., for figures on the United States. On Britain, see Anthony Sampson, "The Institutions of British Foreign Policy," in Karl Kaiser and Roger Morgan, eds., *Britain and West Germany: Changing Societies and the Future of Foreign Policy* (London 1971).

[9] Raymond Bauer, "The Study of Policy Formation," in Raymond Bauer and Kenneth Gergen, eds., *The Study of Policy Formation* (New York 1968), 2.

[10] M. S. Hochmuth, comments at Transnational Relations Study Group Seminar, Center for International Affairs, Harvard University, February 8, 1972.

[11] Stephen Krasner, "Are Bureaucracies Important?" *Foreign Policy*, VII (Summer 1972).

below the apex of the organizational hierarchy—rather than merely to apply a new label to behavior that is easily subsumed by traditional models.

In view of our interest in the opportunities that transgovernmental relations may create for international organizations, we will concentrate in this essay on *cooperative* behavior among governmental sub-units. It should be recognized, however, that conflict is not excluded from transgovernmental relations any more than from other aspects of world politics. Occasionally, direct contacts among sub-units may themselves be conflictual. A case in point is "close surveillance" of each other's activities by the American and Soviet navies in the 1960's, which higher-level officials sought with some difficulty to control. Our emphasis on cooperative direct contacts does not, therefore, exclude the possibility of transgovernmental clashes of interests.

We will distinguish two major types of essentially cooperative transgovernmental behavior. Transgovernmental *policy coordination* refers to activity designed to facilitate smooth implementation or adjustment of policy, in the absence of detailed higher policy directives. Another process, *transgovernmental coalition building*, takes place when sub-units build coalitions with like-minded agencies from other governments against elements of their own administrative structures. At that point, the unity of the state as a foreign policy actor breaks down. Although transgovernmental policy coordination and transgovernmental coalition building are analytically distinct processes, they merge into one another at the margin. While bearing in mind that the distinction is in some sense an artificial convenience, we will look at the two processes in turn.

TRANSGOVERNMENTAL POLICY COORDINATION

The most basic and diffuse form of transgovernmental policy coordination is simply informal communication among working-level officials of different bureaucracies. Such communication does not necessarily contradict the conventional conceptualization of states as coherent coalitions vis-à-vis the outside world, although it may have side effects that influence policy. Face-to-face communications often convey more information (intended or unintended) than indirect communications, and this additional information can affect policy expectations and preferences. It is well known that international organizations frequently provide suitable contexts for such transgovernmental communication. As one official said of INTERPOL, "What's really important here are the meetings on a social level—the official agenda is only for show." [12]

Where patterns of policy coordination are regularized, it becomes misleading to think of governments as closed decision-making units. It has been argued, for example, that in the 1960's Canadian officials in Washington were "often able to inject their views into the decision-making process at various stages, almost as if they were American, and to actually participate, particularly

[12] *New York Times*, October 1, 1972.

in the economic sector, in the formulation of American policy." [13] In the Sky-
bolt affair of 1962, British complacency about American planning, before can-
cellation was announced, was reinforced by "a steady stream of reassurances
[that] flowed back and forth between the Air Forces. The USAF saw a staunch
ally in Her Majesty's Government, and *vice versa*." [14]

From regularized coordination over a period of time, changes in attitudes
may result. When the same officials meet recurrently, they sometimes develop
a sense of collegiality, which may be reinforced by their membership in a
common profession, such as economics, physics, or meteorology. Individual
officials may even define their roles partly in relation to their transnational
reference group rather than in purely national terms. Thus, in discussing trade
discrimination in the 1950's, Gardner Patterson argued that "an important
cost of discrimination was the necessity of reporting on it and defending it
periodically in semi-public forums. . . . It was costly not just in terms of time
and effort, but perhaps more important, in terms of the embarrassment of
having many members of the 'club'—professional colleagues—charge that
another member was not living up to some of its international commitments. . . ." [15]

Regularized patterns of policy coordination can therefore create attitudes
and relationships that will at least marginally change policy or affect its implementation. This has been evident particularly in relations among close allies
or associates, for instance between the United States and Canada[16] or among
countries of the British Commonwealth. Even in relations among countries
that are politically more distant from one another, policy coordination between
bureaucracies with similar interests may occasionally take place. According to
press reports, at any rate, United States and Soviet space officials who were
engaged in technical talks on space cooperation in 1971 went considerably
further than the National Security Council had authorized at that time.[17]

Patterns of regularized policy coordination have a significance that is not
limited to the examples we have cited. As such practices become widespread,
transgovernmental elite networks are created, linking officials in various governments to one another by ties of common interest, professional orientation, and
personal friendship.[18] Even where attitudes are not fundamentally affected and
no major deviations from central policy positions occur, the existence of a sense
of collegiality may permit the development of flexible bargaining behavior in
which concessions need not be requited issue by issue or during each period.

[13] Dale Thompson, Testimony before Standing Committee on External Affairs and National
   Defense, House of Commons (Canada), *Minutes of Proceedings and Evidence*, April 28,
   1970.

[14] Richard E. Neustadt, *Alliance Politics* (New York 1970), 37.

[15] Gardner Patterson, *Discrimination in International Trade: The Policy Issues* (Princeton
   1966), 36.

[16] See K. J. Holsti, "The United States and Canada," in Steven Spiegel and Kenneth Waltz,
   eds., *Conflict in World Politics* (Cambridge, Mass. 1971).

[17] *New York Times*, December 4, 6, and 16, 1971.

[18] Our thinking on the subject of elite networks was stimulated by our friend and valued
   colleague, the late Ivan Vallier, who was undertaking systematic research on elite networks
   in Latin America until his death in January 1974.

James Coleman has suggested that the development of "political bank accounts," where a mental reckoning of political credits and debits relaxes the need for all payoffs to be immediate, is dependent on the existence of small-group collegiality.[19] When such behavior—once the prerogative of monarchs and diplomats—spreads throughout governments, the policy structure becomes more complex and decentralized. Some of the clearest examples of such behavior have been reported by students of the political processes of common markets, such as the European Community or the Central American Common Market, where the development of a sense of collegiality enabled officials and ministers in many instances to press policy coordination beyond what would otherwise have been the case.[20]

TRANSGOVERNMENTAL COALITION BUILDING

Transgovernmental policy coordination shades over into transgovernmental coalition building when sub-units of different governments (and/or inter-governmental institutions) jointly use resources to influence governmental decisions.[21] To improve their chances of success, governmental sub-units attempt to bring actors from other governments into their own decision-making processes as allies. When such coalitions are successful, the outcomes are different than they would be if each coalition partner were limited to his own nationality. The politics of such situations are more subtle and the rules less clear than in the classical coalition theorists' cases of electoral coalitions where resources are directly transferable into influence through a set of generally accepted rules, or national bureaucratic coalitions in which players hold formal positions that legitimize their rights to participate.

Transgovernmental coalitions may be employed by sub-units of powerful states such as the United States as means by which to penetrate weaker governments. U.S. aid agencies in the 1950's and 1960's frequently played a large role in writing requests for aid from the U.S. on behalf of potential recipients, and on occasion even served a liaison function among several ministries of a foreign government.[22] In Turkey, where the Planning Office and the Finance Ministry had equal authority but contradictory views on a U.S. aid project to bring local officials together, a *de facto* coalition developed between AID officials and Finance Ministry officials.[23] The Chilean military under Allende was willing to

[19] James Coleman, "Political Money," *American Political Science Review*, LXIV (December 1970), 1074–87.

[20] See Leon Lindberg and Stuart Scheingold, *Europe's Would-Be Polity* (Englewood Cliffs, N.J. 1970); Lawrence Sheinman, "Some Preliminary Notes on Bureaucratic Relationships in the EEC," *International Organization*, XX (Autumn 1966); and Joseph S. Nye, Jr., "Central American Regional Integration," *International Conciliation*, No. 562 (March 1967).

[21] This definition is based on the article by William A. Gamson on "Coalitions," in the *International Encyclopedia of Social Science*.

[22] Theodore Geiger and Roger Hansen, "The Role of Information in Decision Making on Foreign Aid," in Bauer and Gergen (fn. 9).

[23] Based on conversations with a participant (1973).

bear possible domestic opprobrium in order to receive American military aid. To some observers, the American strategy appeared to be an attempt to use transgovernmental politics to keep the Chilean Government divided.[24]

Transgovernmental coalitions, however, can also help agencies of other governments penetrate the U.S. bureaucracy. In 1961, when the U.S. Weather Bureau disagreed with the State Department's position at the United Nations on the control of the World Weather Watch, the Director of the U.S. Weather Bureau telephoned his Canadian counterpart and they discussed the common interests of their respective weather bureaus. The position of the two weather bureaus became the official Canadian position, which led in turn to defeat of the State Department's proposals.[25] In the late 1960's, a U.S. Defense Department official, worried that delay in returning Okinawa to Japanese control might harm United States-Japanese relations, worked out with a Japanese counterpart how to phrase Japanese messages to ensure that they would enter the right channels and trigger the desired response in the U.S. bureaucracy.[26] In 1968, an Air Force general, to whom the responsibility for negotiating with Spain about military bases had been delegated, conferred secretly with his Spanish counterparts without informing civilian officials of the progress of his negotiations, and agreed to a negotiating paper that proved to be unacceptable to the Department of State. As this last case indicates, transgovernmental coalitions are not always successful: the agreement reached, which would have been favorable to the Spanish Government, was disowned by the United States, and a negative reaction against Spain took place in the Senate.[27]

It is obviously a necessary condition for explicit transgovernmental coalitions that sub-units of government have broad and intensive contacts with one another. In some sense, a degree of transgovernmental policy coordination is probably a precondition for such explicit transnational coalitions. A second set of necessary conditions has to do with conflict of interest among sub-units and the degree of central control by top executive leaders. For a transgovernmental coalition to take place, a sub-unit of one government must perceive a greater common interest with another government, or sub-units of another government, than with at least one pertinent agency in its own country; and central executive control must be loose enough to permit this perception to be translated into direct contacts with the foreign governments or agencies in

[24] *New York Times*, December 9, 1972.

[25] Edward Miles, "Transnationalism in Space: Inner and Outer," in Keohane and Nye (fn. 1).

[26] Based on conversations with a participant (1972).

[27] In the cases of the weather bureau and the Spanish bases, the United States Government was divided while the smaller state apparently had a relatively unified policy. In terms of coherence, these relationships were asymmetrical in favor of Canada and Spain, respectively. Spain, Nationalist China, Israel, and Canada are among the countries that have taken advantage of the size and diversity of the United States Government to create asymmetries of coherence in their favor to counter asymmetries of power in favor of the United States. See Robert O. Keohane, "The Big Influence of Small Allies," *Foreign Policy*, II (Spring 1971). For Canadian cases, see Roger Swanson, "The United States Canadian Constellation I: Washington, D.C.," *International Journal*, XXVII (Spring 1972), 185–218; Holsti (fn. 18); and J. S. Nye, "Transnational Relations and Interstate Conflict: An Empirical Analysis," *International Organization*, XXVIII (Autumn 1974).

question. Figure 1 illustrates four types of political situations based on these two dimensions.

F I G U R E 1 . Conflict of Interest and Executive Power in Foreign Policy: Four Types

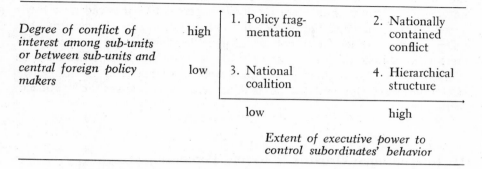

Degree of conflict of interest among sub-units or between sub-units and central foreign policy makers	high	1. Policy fragmentation	2. Nationally contained conflict
	low	3. National coalition	4. Hierarchical structure
		low	high

Extent of executive power to control subordinates' behavior

Sub-units in a governmental system of Type 1 are most likely to seek, or be amenable to, transgovernmental coalitions. High conflict of interest among sub-units of the government suggests that there may be sub-units of other governments with which advantageous coalitions can be made; low executive power indicates that the central officials' ability to deter such coalitions is relatively small. In the other three types, by contrast, the conventional assumption of unitary actors is more likely to be valid for external affairs, although for different reasons. In Type 2 conflict is contained by a strong executive; sub-units may perceive potentially advantageous transgovernmental coalitions, but they do not dare attempt to consummate them directly. In Type 3, low conflict of interest among domestic governmental sub-units ensures that the option of national coalition generally seems more attractive than the transgovernmental alternative, even in the absence of strong central control. Type 4, of course, exemplifies the traditional situation: national coalition reinforced by effective hierarchy.

Relatively frequent contacts among governmental sub-units, looseness of governmental hierarchies (low executive control), and relatively high conflict of interest within governments are all necessary conditions for the development of explicit transgovernmental coalitions. But they are not in themselves sufficient. In the first place, for coalitions to be feasible, actors with common interests must be able to combine their resources effectively. That means that political resources (such as funds, prestige, information, and consent—where required, for instance, by the rules of an international organization) of actors outside a government must be valuable to at least some actors within it. This requires a political context that is relatively open and free of xenophobia, since in a xenophobic society foreign resources are heavily devalued, or regarded negatively, by virtue of their origin. Even in democratic societies, the borderline between legitimate transgovernmental behavior and treason may be unclear.

The need for resources that can be aggregated suggests that transgovernmental behavior may be particularly important in issue areas in which functionally defined international organizations operate. The procedures of the organization itself, for reaching agreement among its members, insure that the resources of one actor—at least its votes—may be useful to another; insofar as the organization has a specialized, functional orientation, the activities of national representatives may not be closely supervised by top leaders or their agents. More generally, the greater the natural sensitivity of governmental policies and the wider the acceptance of joint decision making on issues that cross national lines, the greater the legitimacy of transgovernmental bargaining is likely to be. An international organization, by symbolizing governments' beliefs in the need for joint decision making, tends to strengthen the legitimacy of this activity.

II. International Organizations and Potential Coalitions

Recurrent international conferences and other activities of international organizations help to increase transgovernmental contacts and thus create opportunities for the development of transgovernmental coalitions. The number of intergovernmental organizations more than tripled between 1945 and 1965. Nongovernmental organizations have grown even more rapidly.[28] In Europe, the Commission of the European Communities has played a major role in the growth of such contacts, with the result that "there is a steady flow of national economic and administrative elites to the seat of Community decision-making." [29] These elites are drawn from many sectors of national bureaucracies, by no means entirely from foreign offices. The pattern is not confined to Europe: In 1962, of some 2,786 people who represented the United States at international conferences, more came from other departments of the government than from the State Department.[30]

Governments must organize themselves to cope with the fact that the flow of business, including such conferences, is often transacted under the auspices of international organizations. The organizations' definitions of which issues cluster together and which should be considered separately may help to determine the nature of interdepartmental committees and other arrangements within governments. In the long run, therefore, international organizations will affect how government officials define "issue areas." The existence of the International Monetary Fund and the General Agreement on Tariffs and Trade, for example, helps to focus governmental activity in the monetary and trade fields,

---

[28] J. David Singer and Michael Wallace, "Intergovernmental Organization in the Global System, 1815–1964," *International Organization*, xxiv (Spring 1970); Robert C. Angell, *Peace on the March: Transnational Participation* (New York 1969).

[29] Lindberg and Scheingold (fn. 20), 80.

[30] Arnold Beichman, *The "Other" State Department* (New York 1967), 92.

in contrast to the area of private direct investment, in which no comparable international organization exists.

The fact that international organizations bring officials together should alert us to their effect in activating *potential* coalitions in world politics. Many sub-units of governments, which do not as a matter of course come into contact with each other, may have common or complementary interests. Indeed, we may speak of some potential coalitions as *de facto* "tacit coalitions" if the independent actions of one member seem to serve the interests of others and vice versa. One of the important but seldom-noted roles of international organizations in world politics is to provide the arena for sub-units of governments to turn potential or tacit coalitions into explicit coalitions characterized by direct communication among the partners. In this particular bit of political alchemy, the organization provides physical proximity, an agenda of issues on which interaction is to take place, and an aura of legitimacy. Informal discussions occur naturally in meetings of international organizations, and it is difficult, given the milieu, for other sub-units of one's own government to object to these contacts.

It is intriguing to ask specifically why some potential coalitions become active while others remain merely potential. It is easy to see why the parallel interests of the American and Soviet armed forces (in large military budgets) are not reflected in transgovernmental coalitions between military officers in the superpowers; but it may be more difficult to determine whether the common interests of central bankers in a stable currency system have been implemented as fully by transgovernmental contacts as they might have been. To take another example, the natural allies of the American farmer—and therefore of the Department of Agriculture—in seeking access to European markets are the European urban dwellers and European finance- and consumer-oriented ministers, rather than the European farmers and agriculture ministers. However, this kind of potential coalition between agriculture officials in the United States and non-agriculture officials in Europe is difficult to organize, since regular contacts have not been established. The contrast between the difficulty involved here and the close ties existing among European agriculture ministries is instructive. Where analogous agencies with close patterns of working relationships have common interests and participate in the same international organizations, it is likely to be much easier to create coalitions on the basis of those common interests than where the potential coalitions include a variety of actors that are not used to working closely with one another.

Even without an active secretariat, therefore, international organizations are of considerable relevance in many issue areas of world politics because they help to transform potential or tacit coalitions into explicit ones. When issues are linked or dealt with in institutional arenas with broad mandates, heterogeneous coalitions can be formed. Narrow institutional mandates discriminate against such coalitions. Thus, by defining the issues to be considered together, and by excluding others, international organizations may significantly affect political processes and outcomes in world politics, quite apart from active lobbying by their secretariats.

The second important role for international organizations, however, is the active one. Most intergovernmental organizations have secretariats, and like all bureaucracies they have their own interests and goals that are defined through an interplay of staff and clientele. International secretariats can be viewed both as catalysts and as potential members of coalitions; their distinctive resources tend to be information and an aura of international legitimacy. As Robert Cox has put it, "the executive head needs to fortify his position by alliance with domestic pressure groups. He must not limit himself to 'foreign' politics but know how to make domestic politics work in favor of his policies." [31] To the extent that the conditions enumerated in Part I of this article permit sub-units of governments to engage in transgovernmental coalitions, we would expect international secretariats or components of secretariats to form explicit or implicit coalitions with sub-units of governments as well as with nongovernmental organizations having similar interests .

Examples of alliances between parts of secretariats and governments are not hard to find. Many organizations have divisions that are regarded as fiefdoms of particular governments.[32] In a number of cases, lower-level officials of a secretariat have lobbied with governments in efforts to thwart the declared policy of their secretaries-general.[33] Representatives of UN specialized agencies in developing countries often strengthen old-line ministries against their rivals in central planning offices.[34] Chilean conservatives have used IMF missions to bolster their political positions.[35] With reference to the World Health Organization (WHO), Harold Jacobson argues that "many government representatives to WHO almost can be viewed as the director-general's agents or lobbyists within country sub-systems." [36] In some cases, international organizations initiate the formation of transgovernmental coalitions; in others, they or their own sub-units are recruited to the coalitions by sub-units of governments.

It must be recognized, however, that this activist, coalition-building role of international organizations is usually closely circumscribed. By no means is it a sure recipe for success. Yet the alternatives of passivity or of frontally challeng-

---

[31] Robert W. Cox, "The Executive Head," *International Organization*, xxiii (Spring 1969), 225.

[32] See, for example, J. S. Nye, "UNCTAD: Poor Nations' Pressure Group," in Robert W. Cox and Harold K. Jacobson, eds., *The Anatomy of Influence: Decision Making in International Organization* (New Haven 1973).

[33] James Magee discusses a situation in which FAO bureaucrats conspired with African governments to thwart the director's decision to relocate two offices. "ECA and the Paradox of African Cooperation," *International Conciliation*, No. 580 (November 1970).

[34] See Leon Gordenker, "Multilateral Aid and Influence on Government Policies," in Robert W. Cox, ed., *International Organization: World Politics* (London 1969). A related example is provided by the Jackson Report, which indicated that its investigations "revealed example after example where Departmental Ministers have advocated policies in the governing bodies of the particular agency which concerned them (e.g., a Minister of Agriculture in FAO, or a Minister of Education in UNESCO) which were in direct conflict with his government's policies toward the UN system as a whole." United Nations, *A Study of the Capacity of the United Nations Development System*, Vol. I (Geneva 1969), v.

[35] See Albert Hirschman, *Journeys Toward Progress* (New York 1965), 291 ff.

[36] Harold K. Jacobson, "WHO: Medicine, Regionalism, and Managed Politics," in Cox and Jacobson (fn. 32), 214.

ing traditional notions of national sovereignty are usually less attractive. Secretariat officials often find the only feasible alternative to be to help governments, or sectors of governments, to perceive problems differently and to use their own resources in innovative ways. For example, as Ruggie points out, the World Weather Watch is not a supra-national operation but a set of national activities that the World Meteorological Organization (perceived as an ally by most weather bureaus) helps to coordinate, and the distribution of whose results it encourages.[37] Similarly, Maurice Strong has defined the role of the UN Environmental Office as one of stimulating the creation of new environmental units in member states, serving as an ally providing information and prestige for them, and thus encouraging a redefinition of "national interests."[38]

Coalition building shades down into transgovernmental policy coordination in this example, as is frequently the case. On a long-term and somewhat diffuse basis, the communications that take place as a result of policy coordination and conferences may be as important as the coalitions that form on particular issues. As we have seen earlier, international organizations facilitate face-to-face meetings among officials in "domestic" agencies of different governments who would have little to do with each other in traditional interstate politics. Strategically-minded secretariats of international organizations could very well plan meetings with a view toward this transgovernmental communications function. Recurrent interactions can change officials' perceptions of their activities and interests. As Bauer, Pool, and Dexter have pointed out in their discussion of the United States politics of foreign trade, concentrating only on pressures of various interests for decisions leads to an overly mechanistic view of a continuous process and neglects the important role of communications in slowly changing perceptions of "self-interest."[39]

CONDITIONS FOR THE INVOLVEMENT OF INTERNATIONAL ORGANIZATIONS

To the extent that transgovernmental relations are common in a given issue area, under what conditions should we expect international organizations, in the sense of intergovernmental organizations, to be involved in them? One set of cases is obvious: where the international organization itself has created the network of elites. Thus, both the International Labor Organization (ILO) and the World Health Organization (WHO), as described by Cox and Jacobson, are characterized by extensive "participant subsystems" that link national trade unions, employers, and government officials to the ILO secretariat, and health-care professionals to WHO's bureaucracy.[40]

[37] John G. Ruggie, "The World Weather Watch," unpub., 1972.
[38] Based on conversations with Strong during 1972.
[39] Raymond Bauer, Ithiel de Sola Pool, and Lewis Dexter, *American Business and Foreign Policy* (New York 1963), chap. 35, esp. pp. 472–75.
[40] See Harold K. Jacobson, "WHO: Medicine, Regionalism, and Managed Politics," pp. 194–205; and Robert W. Cox, "ILO: Limited Monarchy," pp. 114–27, in Cox and Jacobson (fn. 32).

More generally, however, we would expect international organizations to become involved in transgovernmental politics on issues requiring some central point or agency for coordination. This implies that international organizations are likely to be most extensively involved on complex, multilateral issues in which major actors perceive a need for information and for communication with other actors, in addition to the traditional functions, as listed by Skolnikoff, of "1) provision of services, 2) norm creation and allocation, 3) rule observance and settlement of disputes, and 4) operation." [41] Insofar as patterns of politics follow the transgovernmental mode, increasing the number of actors will tend to create greater demands for communication with other actors (often of different types), as well as for information about both technical and political conditions. International secretariats staffed with knowledgeable individuals, even without traditional sources of power, have the opportunity to place themselves at the center of crucial communications networks, and thereby acquire influence as brokers, facilitators, and suggestors of new approaches. They will continue to be dependent on governments for funds and legal powers; but the relevant agencies of governments may be dependent on them for information and for the policy coordination, by a legitimate system-wide actor, which is required to achieve their own objectives.

III. International Organizations and Intervention in Transnational Systems

Thus far we have discussed two ways in which international organizations are relevant in world politics—as arenas and as members of transgovernmental coalitions. They may also be important as points of potential governmental intervention in predominantly nongovernmental transactional systems.

Analysts of world politics have begun to talk less about *the* international system, and to realize that there are significant variations among systems in different issue areas.[42] There are differences in degree of interdependence of units, in hierarchy among units, and in clarity of the demarcation of the systems' boundaries.[43] There are also differences in degree of governmental participation. In many issue systems, nongovernmental actors account for a major portion of activities that cross national boundaries. To the extent that this is the case, we can refer to the issue system as a transnational one. The more transnational a system, the more likely it is that nongovernmental actors constitute the basic initiating and compelling forces in it. That does not imply

---

[41] Eugene B. Skolnikoff, "Science and Technology: The Implications for International Institutions," *International Organization*, xxv (Autumn 1971), 772.

[42] James N. Rosenau, "Pre-Theories and Theories of Foreign Policy," in R. Barry Farrell, ed., *Approaches to Comparative and International Politics* (Evanston, Ill. 1966), 73–74. For another suggestive discussion of world politics in terms of networks of systems, see John Burton, *Systems, States, Diplomacy and Rules* (Cambridge 1968), esp. pp. 6–10.

[43] For a discussion of the conditions of existence for a system, see the article by Anatol Rapoport on "Systems," in the *International Encyclopedia of the Social Sciences*, p. 452.

that governments are absent from these systems. On the contrary, they may be very important actors. But their actions will be largely focused on regulation and control of transnational activities.

Governments frequently attempt to use international organizations to achieve this regulation. Secretariats of international organizations may themselves perceive problems in the operation of these systems, as well as opportunities for their organizations to act effectively. The same is true of nongovernmental actors or sub-units of governments that may have interests at stake. Thus, the control of important transnational systems is and will remain a significant political focus for the activity of international organizations.

Analysis of this struggle for control, and the implications it has for international organizations, may be facilitated by thinking of transnational systems as having five key points of policy intervention insofar as any two states are concerned, with correspondingly more as additional states are included:

1. internal measures in country A;
2. border measures by country A;
3. international or transnational organizational measures;
4. border measures by country B;
5. internal measures in country B.

As a simple example, consider the following hypothetical incident in a transnational system based on a free market for skilled labor. Filipino doctors leave their native country to work in American hospitals for much higher salaries, with the consequence that a Filipino peasant dies from a simple disease because his village has no doctor, while there is a relative abundance of Filipino doctors in some American hospitals.

Figure 2 illustrates the five points at which policy can affect this transnational system: two (1 and 5) are generally considered purely "domestic"; two (2 and 4) are "border controls" where the interdependence of states is recognized but jurisdiction lies with only one state; and one (3) is an operating intergovernmental bureaucracy. Similar diagrams could be drawn for other transnational systems, including those involving monetary relations, trade, environmental pollution, and international investment. In all these cases, movements of people, funds, goods, or pollutants across national boundaries can be affected at any of these five points of intervention, insofar as two countries are concerned. As the two examples labeled "counter" in Figure 2 indicate, state policies may tend to thwart as well as to complement one another.[44]

In principle, domestic measures, border controls, and international organizations can complement, countervail, or substitute for each other. From a system-wide point of view, therefore, the policy problem in the abstract is merely one of finding the most efficient point or combination of points of intervention. For the monetary system, an economist may ask which combination of fiscal and monetary policy changes, exchange controls and/or trade barriers, and changes in IMF or GATT rules will produce the desired equilibrium. In

---

[44] Where a larger number of countries is involved, problems of effectiveness become much more complex, and interdependence is likely to be more intricate.

FIGURE 2. A Transnational System of "Brain Drain"

	1 Village in Philippines *Phil. Internal*	2 Manila (Port of Exit) *Phil. Border*	3 *I.O.*	4 Boston (Port of Entry) *U.S. Border*	5 U.S. Hospital Staffed by Foreigners *U.S. Internal*
Points of Policy Intervention, with possible Strategies to Reduce "Brain Drain" or Counter-strategies Tending to facilitate it:	(persuade doctors to stay through financial or other incentives)	(deny exit visas or impose exit levies)	(WHO sends doctors to Philippines)	(restrict entry visas)	(discriminate against foreign doctors)
				(*counter:* encourage entry of skilled personnel)	(*counter:* recruit foreign doctors)

practice, however, different groups generally have different interests and different degrees of influence at various points of policy intervention. Although there may be more or less common interest in system management, there are also likely to be conflicts. The holders of certain sets of interests may prefer that only certain potential points of policy intervention be used, and only in particular ways. Others may be opposed to all controls on transnational systems from which they benefit. Thus the choice of points of intervention is itself an important policy decision that imposes constraints on subsequent action. Insofar as control over an international organization confers influence over a transnational system, or a means to discourage intervention at some other policy point in the system, the organization can be an important stake in political conflict.

ACTORS' STRATEGIES AND THE USES OF INTERNATIONAL ORGANIZATIONS

If transnational relations are important in a set of issues, an explanation of outcomes made simply in terms of "sovereignty" and "national interests" will be insufficient. There is also, however, a distributional question. Some actors may believe that they are adversely affected by transnational activities and will seek strategies to cope with these perceived problems.

The most obvious response by disadvantaged groups is to use the weapons of sovereignty against the transnational adversary. Insofar as national regulation can be effective, groups with national political strength can redress the balance. In the field of international trade, tariff and non-tariff barriers are familiar strategies. To curb direct investment, nationally oriented groups may resort to expropriation, strict regulation, or bans on the flow of capital or technology. For example, the AFL-CIO in the United States supported the restrictive Burke-Hartke bill as a means of legislating relief from problems of "runaway plants" and the "export of jobs."

The chief difficulty with national solutions in the context of interdependence is that they may not only be ineffective, but may lead to policy conflicts among states, as governments attempt to counter the adverse effects of other governments' actions. This is the familiar "beggar-thy-neighbor" problem, applicable to a wide variety of issues in which interdependence is high. National actions to reduce the adverse effects of *societal* interdependence may have the paradoxical effect of increasing *policy* interdependence: that is, such measures may increase the extent to which governments depend on the actions of other governments for the achievement of their own goals.

In such a situation of policy interdependence, sub-units of governments are likely to resort to transgovernmental policy coordination or transgovernmental coalition building, as discussed above, making use of existing international organizations to facilitate these relationships. Yet in the context of intense transnational activity by nongovernmental actors, this may lead not merely to transgovernmental coalitions but to mixed coalitions including nongovernmental as well as governmental agents. According to one description of a preparatory session for the Conference on the Law of the Sea, for instance, officials of the United States Department of the Interior and representatives of certain multinational enterprises (both of which favored a definition of a wide continental shelf) lobbied with representatives of foreign governments against the declared U.S. policy (preferred by the Departments of State and Defense) of a narrow shelf.[45]

Such a strategy is inappropriate for actors whose political resources are predominantly domestic. Having perceived that national self-encapsulation is a futile strategy, or having tried such a strategy unsuccessfully, actors may seek to politicize (i.e., increase the controversy over) an issue. By increasing controversy, they would hope to raise the level in the government at which the issue is considered—in order to reduce the scope for transgovernmental and transnational political strategies. Central political officials—responsible directly to the public in one way or another—would then negotiate internationally in the interests of nationally based groups. This could be called a national-assertion strategy (represented by the Nixon-Connally policies of 1971), as distinguished from a national protection strategy (illustrated by the Burke-Hartke bill). Thus, as Robert Russell has shown, transgovernmental coalitions among central bankers and working-level officials were increasingly constrained even before the events of 1971, as monetary issues became more controversial.[46] Such a strategy may well lead to the decline of international organizations which were established on different premises. In some cases, however, issues may be politicized partly by using international organizations to bring them to the attention of higher-level officials. The point is illustrated by the examples of UNCTAD in the trade field, and by UN investigations into operations of multinational firms.

Issues are unlikely, in general, to remain indefinitely at the top level of governmental attention. Politicization may facilitate the resolution of issues, or at least the establishment of new structures and new assumptions within which particular questions can be settled at lower levels of the governmental hierarchy. International organizations may also be important at this "de-politicization" stage, in once again facilitating transgovernmental coalitions. But the important point here is that if substantial restructuring has taken place, the coalitions that form will be different than they were before. Potential coalitions that could not be actualized in earlier periods may become possible now, and different groups may benefit. Thus, an international monetary organization set up to monitor floating exchange rates would look quite different from the IMF of the 1960's which was premised on fixed but adjustable rates. An international organization established to keep non-tariff barriers within stated limits might give more leeway to coalitions of protectionist groups than GATT, with its prohibition on quantitative restrictions.

---

[45] This situation was described to us by two government officials. See also Ann Hollick, "Seabeds Make Strange Politics," *Foreign Policy*, ix (Winter 1972–73).

[46] Robert W. Russell, "Transgovernmental Intersection in the International Monetary System, 1960–1972," *International Organization*, xxvii (Autumn 1973).

It is therefore too simple to contend, as is often done, that the basic strategic choice is between national encapsulation and internationalism. Internationalism has many dimensions, with very different implications for group interests as well as for normative values. International strategies by interested groups, as we have indicated, may take any of three forms: (1) exploitation of transgovernmental or mixed transnational-transgovernmental coalitions within an established framework of policy, and through established international organizations; (2) politicization of issues to remove them from transgovernmental bargaining, reemphasizing the role of responsible top officials of governments; and (3) restructuring of issues, as a result of a period of politicization, so that new transgovernmental and mixed coalitions can become effective, perhaps under the aegis of new or substantially altered international organizations. The second and third strategies, in particular, are not mutually exclusive but may reflect different phases in a cycle. When internationalization as a strategy for dealing with transnational issues is considered, distinctions such as these should be made.

IV. Conclusions

It should be clear from the examples we have chosen that we do not regard the involvement of international organizations in transnational and transgovernmental coalitions as necessarily contributing to global welfare or equity. Like other political institutions, international organizations reflect the interests as well as the attitudes of actors that are powerful in them. Opportunities for impact by international organizations by no means assure their autonomy or their dedication to the commonweal. Increased opportunities for certain international organizations may in some cases lead to the fragmentation of an international effort, which Sir Robert Jackson criticized, or to the pursuit of the interests of well-placed groups at the expense of the interests of less fortunate but larger sectors of the population. The effects of transgovernmental politics on the efficacy of democratic control may be very serious.[47] In some circumstances, an expansion of the influence of international organizations in ways such as we have suggested here may be undesirable. There is no magic wand that makes it unnecessary to undertake detailed, case-by-case normative analyses of the actions of international organizations.

With respect to empirical projections, our prognosis differs from that of the international functionalists and others who see transnational systems and societal interdependence as making national governments obsolete.[48] While there are some valid elements in the functionalist scenario, we suggest the following alternative view as somewhat more plausible.

The development of transgovernmental relations, as well as the involve-

---

[47] See Kaiser in Keohane and Nye (fn. 6).

[48] See, for example, Angell (fn. 28); and David Mitrany, *A Working Peace System* (Chicago 1966).

ment of international organizations in them, is generally stimulated by the activities of elites trying to cope with increased *societal* interdependence. Dynamic nongovernmental forces frequently provoke increased governmental efforts at control. However, as a side effect of increasing interchange among elites, transgovernmental politics and the activities of international organizations are likely to increase *policy* interdependence. That is, the policies of relevant actors—central foreign policy organs of governments, other governmental agencies, transnational actors, or secretariats of international organizations—will increasingly depend for their success on actions and reactions of other actors. Succumbing to one form of interdependence may be the price one pays for avoiding another. Efforts to cope with policy interdependence will in turn further broaden the scope of interstate agendas, involve more bureaucracies (national, international, and transnational), and thus provide more occasions for transgovernmental relations. For top leaders this leads to the further problem of losing effective control of their own sprawling and transgovernmentally active bureaucracies. A continuing struggle between groups favoring transgovernmental policy patterns and those supporting a return to strategies of national assertion or national protection is likely to ensue. Figure 3 provides a highly simplified sketch of some of the causal relations that may contribute to political struggles of this type.

This is not an argument for the superiority of international or transnational as opposed to national solutions, nor does it suggest a general view of the merits of international institutions. We have simply sought to establish the political significance of international organizations in certain issue areas—as arenas and members of transgovernmental coalitions, and as potential points of intervention in transnational systems. International organizations are not necessarily weak "because they are inherently the arenas for national actors," or because they require "*accord* among nations." [49] Which bureaucracies represent the nation? Who defines the "national interest," and how does it change over time? Is there transgovernmental coordination? Are there mixed coalitions of transgovernmental, transnational, and international actors? Viewed from the perspective of these questions, it is not always—or only—the transnational organizations that are "busily deployed across the continents spinning the webs that link the world together." [50]

FIGURE 3.   Hypothetical Causal Relations Involving Transnational Systems and Transgovernmental Relations

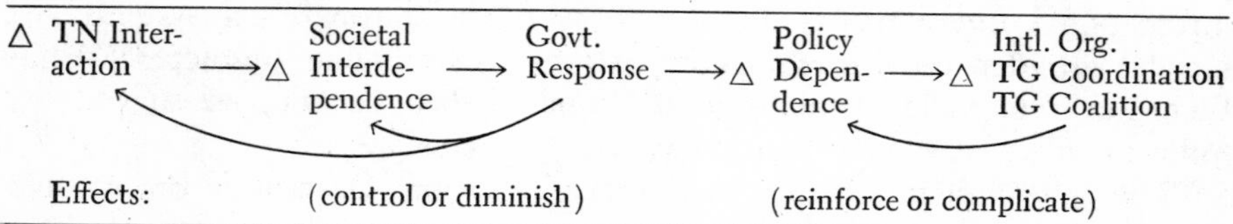

49 Huntington (fn. 2), 338.
50 *Ibid.,* 339.

A major policy task for those who create and manage international institutions is to ask themselves whether there are areas of activity in which international organizations could make an impact by aligning their activities with sub-units of governments. As Ruggie points out, traditional images of interstate politics and international organizations as entities "above" states unduly constrain institutional imagination.[51] Understanding the transnational and transgovernmental politics of an issue as well as the technical, economic, or military nature of the problem may permit a wider choice of organizational strategy and structure, and in some cases more constructive outcomes.

International organizations are rarely optimally efficient, and they are frequently quite unsatisfactory. Some improvements are possible, but many government officials will always find them hard to live with. For the foreseeable future, however, it seems that they will be impossible to live without. And if that is true, their political role and impact on various issues in world politics deserve both more and a new type of attention.

---

[51] John G. Ruggie, "The Structure of International Organization: Contingency, Complexity, and Post-Modern Form," *Peace Research Society*, Papers, xviii, 1971, 73–91.

Index

Abortion, 207, 211
Abrams, Charles, 288
Absolute monarchy, 170, 172, 178, 180
Acupuncture, 242
Aged, role of, 339–340
Agriculture, 6, 15, 29, 173, 174, 181, 208, 209
Alembert, Jean Le Rond, 122, 127, 128
Alker, Hayward, 49
Almond, Gabriel A., 39, 40–42, 44, 46, 52, 57–59, 117, 130
American Federation of Labor (AFL), 281
American Indians, 20
American Medical Association (AMA), 296, 297, 301–302
American Revolution, 170
Analytic model of individual modernity, 325–335, 346–348
Analytico-causal and inventive approach, 17–18
Anderson, Odin W., 300
Andrain, Charles, 276
Anthropology, 1, 5
Apter, David E., 46, 47, 65, 91, 96, 117, 119, 122, 126, 127, 128, 276
Arabic medical system, 239, 240
Arendt, Hannah, 32
Argentina, 134
    attitudes and values, 266–269, 272
    economic growth, 268–270
Aristocracy, 175–177, 184, 185
Aristotle, 26, 111
Arnold, Matthew, 235
Asian Drama (Myrdal), 90, 103
Attitudes and values, 149, 159–160, 164, 166, 175, 258–277
    explanatory relationship, 272–274
    problem of congruence, 264–266
    problems of consistency, 259–263
    sequential problems, 263–272
    see also Individual modernity, model of
Australian bushmen, 20
Austria, 288
Authority, rationalization of, 170, 172

Bacon, Francis, 91, 127, 354
Balfour Act of 1902, 291
Banking, 152, 153, 183
Barrett, Stanley R, 365

Bauer, Raymond, 357, 423
Beaumarchais, Pierre Augustin Caron de, 125
Beccaria, Cesare, 120, 125
Behavioral model of individual modernity, 325, 345–348
Bellah, Robert, 322, 333
Belshaw, Cyril S., 366
Bendix, Reinhard, 30, 34, 38, 51, 69, 70, 74, 76, 77, 78, 79, 82, 91, 96, 103, 279
Berthoff, Rowland T., 284
Biggerstaff, Knight, 146–160
Binder, Leonard, 46, 47
Birth control: see Contraception
Birth rates, 204, 205, 208, 210–213, 309, 315
Bismarck, Otto von, 281, 282
Black, Cyril E., 28, 51, 65, 67, 79, 89, 91, 118, 126, 128, 167–169, 362
Blake, Judith, 305–319
Blumer, Herbert, 358
Bock, Kenneth E., 64
Bodin, Jean, 177
Boisguillebert, Pierre Le Pesant, 121
Bolshevik Revolution, 59
Boniface VIII, Pope, 113
Borrowing, 23, 105, 106, 107
Bourgeoisie, 174, 175–176, 177, 182, 226
Breakdown of modernization, 96, 98, 103, 134–135
Brewer, Garry D., 59–60
British Medical Association (BMA), 297, 301
Brooks, John Graham, 289
Broverman, Inge, 317, 318
Brown, Bernard E., 165–185
Browne, Sir Thomas, 222
Brunner, Ronald D., 59–60
Bücher, Karl, 355
Buffon, Georges Louis Leclerc de, 122
Bultmann, Rudolf, 19
Bumpass, Larry L., 314
Bureaucracies, 21, 82, 141, 171, 413–414
Burma, 134

Calculability, 330, 332
Cantril, Hadley, 264–266
Capetian dynasty, 177, 178
Capitalism, 1, 9, 27, 99–103, 275